Look Your Best with Ami Pro™

Susan Plumley

que

Screen reproductions in this book were created with Collage Plus from Inner Media, Inc., Hollis, NH.

Look Your Best with Ami Pro is based on Lotus Ami Pro Versions 2.0 and 3.0.

Publisher: Lloyd J. Short

Associate Publisher: Rick Ranucci

Product Development Manager: Thomas H. Bennett

Book Designer: Scott Cook

Production Analyst: Mary Beth Wakefield

Graphic Imaging Specialist: Dennis Sheehan

Production Team: Jeff Baker, Claudia Bell, Jodie Cantwell, Paula Carroll, Brad Chinn, Michelle Cleary, Jerry Ellis, Bob LaRoche, Laurie Lee, Jay Lesandrini, Caroline Roop, Linda Seifert, Tina Trettin, Sue VandeWalle, Johnna Van Hoose, Lisa Wilson, Phil Worthington

Dedication

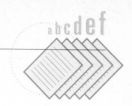

To my husband, Carlos, and to my family, Marie, Geneva, Carlos, Bessie, and Bobby, for their support and understanding.

Credits

Product Director
Charles O. Stewart III

Production Editor
Diane L. Steele

Editors
Gregory Robertson
Elsa M. Bell
Cindy Morrow
J. Christopher Nelson
Sara Allaei
Gail Dutton
Vickie West

Acquisitions Editor
Tim Ryan

Technical Editor
Nancy Haney

Composed in 1 Stone Serif and MCPdigital by Que Corporation.

About the Author

Susan Plumley owns and operates Humble Opinions, an independent consulting firm that offers training and seminars in most popular software programs. Her B.A. is in Art and English from Marshall University. She worked as a teacher, a typesetter, a graphic artist, a proofreader and purchaser, and as a supervisor in a commercial print shop before starting her own business in southern West Virginia. Susan is also the author of *Look Your Best with Word for Windows* and a contributing author to *Using Ami Pro 3*, Special Edition.

Trademark Acknowledgments

Que Corporation has made every effort to supply trademark information about company names, products, and services mentioned in this book. Trademarks indicated below were derived from various sources. Que Corporation cannot attest to the accuracy of this information.

1-2-3, 1-2-3 for Windows, DIF, Freelance for Windows, Samna Word, and Symphony are registered trademarks and Lotus Manuscript, SmartPics, and Allways are trademarks of Lotus Development Corporation; Adobe Type Manager is a trademark and PostScript is a registered trademark of Adobe Systems Inc; Ami Pro is a trademark of Samna Corporation, a wholly-owned subsidiary of Lotus Development Corporation; Bitstream, Charter, and Fontware are registered trademarks of Bitstream Inc; CorelDRAW! is a trademark of Corel Systems Corporation; dBASE and MultiMate are registered trademarks and MultiMate Advantage is a trademark of Ashton-Tate Corporation; DCA is a registered trademark of Digital Communications Association, Inc; IBM is a registered trademark and DisplayWrite is a trademark of International Business Machines Corporation; Enable is a trademark of The Software Group; GEM Paint is a trademark of Digital Research Inc; Harvard Graphics is a registered trademark of Software Publishing Corporation; Hewlett-Packard and LaserJet are registered trademarks of Hewlett-Packard Company; LaserWriter is a registered trademark of Apple Computer, Inc; Linotronic is a trademark and Helvetica, Times, Times Roman, Garamond, Palatino, and Linoscript are registered trademarks of Lynotype-Hell Company; MacPaint is a registered trademark of Claris Corporation; Paradox is a registered trademark of Borland International, Inc; PC Paintbrush is a registered trademark of Z-Soft Corporation; PeachText is a registered trademark of PeachTree Software, Inc; PowerPoint, Microsoft Excel, Microsoft Windows, Microsoft Windows Write, Microsoft Word, MS-DOS, and Word for Windows are registered trademarks of Microsoft Corporation; SmartWare is a registered trademark of Informix Software, Inc; SuperCalc is a registered trademark of Computer Associates International, Inc; SuperPaint is a trademark of Silicon Beach Software, Inc; Ventura Publisher is a registered trademark of Ventura Software, Inc; WordPerfect and DrawPerfect are registered trademarks of WordPerfect Corporation; WordStar and WordStar 2000 are registered trademarks of MicroPro International Corporation.

Trademarks of other products mentioned in this book are held by the companies producing them.

Acknowledgments

I want to thank the many people who contributed to the completion of this project. Foremost, I'm grateful to Que for assembling an excellent team to work on this book. Thanks to Chris Katsaropoulos and Tim Ryan in Acquisitions for having faith in me. Thanks, too, to Diane Steele and her editing team for their organizational skills and attention to detail. And a special thanks to Chuck Stewart, not only for his energy and expertise in developing this project, but for his unwavering support and patience.

I also express my sincere appreciation to my family for understanding what a time-intensive project writing a book can be; and to my husband, Carlos, for his love and encouragement. Finally, thanks to Lotus for a superior product; Ami Pro is indeed an Amiable Professional!

S.P.

Table of Contents

II Creating Business Documents

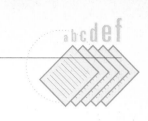

III Creating Business Forms

Introduction

If you are one of the many Ami Pro users, you probably purchased this book to learn more about working with design, using type, formatting documents, improving the look of your word processing documents, and enhancing your proficiency with Ami Pro. You already know that Ami Pro is a remarkable program with the capability to produce distinguished documents, and you are ready to learn how to produce such documents. The first step is to learn more about the benefits of this superb program.

Advantages of Ami Pro for Document Design

Ami Pro offers you many advantages for designing your own documents. As a powerful page-formatting program, Ami Pro indexes, footnotes, sets headers and footers, draws rules and borders, imports graphics, and makes document design easy. As an equally powerful word processing program, Ami Pro checks spelling; performs mail merge; and formats tabs, indents, margins, columns, and text. Working with Ami Pro, you discover that the following features are the major benefits of the program:

Feature	Benefit
Time Saver	When you typeset your own documents, you save time writing copy, making corrections and alterations, and by gaining quick turn-around. Ami Pro's special features make spell-checking, revising, replacing, and changing copy and layout quick and easy.
Document Control	By typesetting your own work, you have complete control over the final document. If you don't like the way it looks, you can change the design. You also can make last-minute copy changes.
Software Integration	One of Ami Pro's most important benefits is its compatibility with other Windows and non-Windows software applications. You can convert other word processing programs to Ami Pro and import spreadsheets, graphics, and databases. Ami Pro comes with a draw program, charting program, and 100 clip-art files.
Money Saver	Formatting your own documents in Ami Pro saves typesetting costs by reducing errors; you shorten turnaround and publication time, which saves overall costs.

Who Should Read This Book

Look Your Best with Ami Pro is a book for business people, graphic artists, and casual users. Ami Pro is for anyone who wants to learn how to design professional-looking documents. If you need to produce a creative letterhead design, form, brochure, company newsletter, elaborate business report, or even a book, *Look Your Best with Ami Pro* is for you.

Although this book assumes that you have some previous knowledge and use of Ami Pro, the directions are clear and easy to follow. After reading *Look Your Best with Ami Pro* and practicing with some of the exercises, you can produce a professional-looking document.

If you have worked with Ami Pro but lack practical experience in design and page layout, *Look Your Best with Ami Pro* teaches you the rules, terms, and proper application of the design elements. The document chapters offer itemized instructions.

If you're new to Ami Pro and to page formatting, the design and typography chapters in this book teach you how to plan and produce an attractive, well-designed document. *Look Your Best with Ami Pro* also gives you detailed, step-by-step instructions for producing actual letterheads, forms, brochures, and newsletters. As an extra bonus for new users, Appendix A offers the basic screen, keyboard, and mouse uses with both Versions 2.0 and 3.0 of Ami Pro.

If you're a graphic artist experienced in design but unfamiliar with desktop publishing, you will benefit from the design and typography chapters. The document chapters also demonstrate creative arrangements of text and graphics on which you can build your own designs.

Finally, for anyone who has ever worked with a print shop, or plans to, this book provides detailed information about planning and purchasing printing. From special design considerations to ink and paper choices, you can plan your next project with confidence and a new understanding of how print shops work.

How To Use This Book

Look Your Best with Ami Pro is divided into sections for easier use. Part I covers design and typography and Parts II through VI explain how to format actual documents.

Part I is a tutorial in design. Beginning with Chapter 1, "Learning Design Strategies," you develop a better understanding of how to produce a professional document. Part I is also a reference section that provides guidance in the use of type and other design elements.

Look Your Best with Ami Pro offers ideas and techniques to improve the look of your documents as well as a basic understanding of why some printed pieces look good and others do not. You learn about the design elements that attract readers and the elements that maintain their interest.

Parts II through VI concentrate on specific projects you can produce with Ami Pro. Each lesson and document chapter becomes progressively more difficult. If you do each lesson in order, by the time you complete this book, you will be quite proficient with Ami Pro.

On the other hand, if you just want to use particular designs or documents, *Look Your Best with Ami Pro* suits your purpose as well. Each lesson explains the steps required to produce a particular document.

Study the beginning of the book well to learn all you can about purpose, planning, design, typography, and dealing with a print shop. With these basics under your belt, follow the directions in the document chapters to apply your knowledge to actual business, sales, and promotion pieces. You soon will be able to create your own quality material.

What Is in This Book

Today's market generates an abundance of brochures, flyers, pamphlets, newsletters, notices, and advertisements—all in competition with your material. The materials you notice, read, and keep are well designed and creative. *Look Your Best with Ami Pro* shows you how to produce the high-quality work that will stand out from the competition.

Part I, "Understanding Design and Typography," explains the design and typographical elements of documents produced by desktop publishing. From planning your document to having it printed, this section covers every aspect of page design.

Chapter 1, "Learning Design Strategies," shows you how to prioritize and organize your copy and how to choose a format. This chapter includes suggestions on targeting your audience, developing design consistency, and adding emphasis to your document.

Chapter 2, "Using Elements of Design," shows you how to plan the size, shape, and type of your document. This chapter tells you how to balance text and graphics on the page, create margins and columns, add graphics for emphasis, and produce style sheets. Chapter 2 includes strategies for

enhancing readability, adding white space and contrast, planning successfully, and avoiding design pitfalls.

Chapter 3, "Defining and Explaining Typography," expands on Chapter 2 by defining and explaining how to use type, fonts, spacing, alignment, text arrangement on the page; and how to produce style sheets in desktop publishing. Chapter 3 defines and illustrates the terms that Ami Pro users and typesetters employ. You learn how to size heads and body text; emphasize type with elements such as bullets and callouts; and produce logos.

Chapter 4, "Planning and Purchasing Printing," is an overview of printing terms and services. This chapter suggests the types of print shops to use for certain jobs, describes the different kinds of paper and ink available, and identifies finishing options such as folds and fastening techniques.

Part II, "Creating Business Documents," gives you step-by-step instructions for producing specific documents. Each chapter illustrates designs ranging from fundamental type solutions to more intricate type and graphic designs. This section also gives instructions and keystrokes for several designs and offers extra design alternatives with critiques of each example.

Chapter 5, "Producing a Letterhead," offers designs you can produce in Ami Pro. You learn about bullets, line spacing, and storing your letterhead in a glossary data file for later use.

Chapter 6, "Producing Letters," shows you how to produce different letter layouts. This chapter also includes pointers on using the spell-checker and adding boxes and borders. From the formal business letter to a creative advertising letter, this chapter presents several design options.

Chapter 7, "Producing Envelopes," explains how to create separate envelope designs, set up your printer, match your letterhead design, and work with mailing regulations.

Chapter 8, "Producing a Resume," offers resume design strategies that include the traditional text only, text and graphic blend, and innovative styles.

Chapter 9, "Producing a Program," gives printer tips, layout suggestions, and design completion instructions.

Chapter 10, "Producing a Memo," discusses how to save a style sheet for later use. The Document Information box helps you track your memos. This chapter also offers the keystrokes for several designs.

Part III, "Creating Business Forms," gives you instructions for producing specific business forms, such as purchase orders and expense reports.

Chapter 11, "Producing a Fax Cover Sheet," shows you how to produce distinct layouts and advises you about page and text elements that fax well and how to attract attention with your fax.

Chapter 12, "Producing a Purchase Order," discusses form strategies, including setting a form to typewriter spacing, saving in a glossary data file, and using Ami Pro's table feature.

Chapter 13, "Producing an Expense or Travel Report," shows you how to set up the basic form and apply several design alternatives.

Chapter 14, "Producing an Order Form," shows you how to create several forms and discusses additional design alternatives.

Part IV, "Creating Sales Documents," covers the printed matter you give to customers. With the design strategies included in each chapter, this part of the book may be the one you use the most.

Chapter 15, "Producing an Advertisement," covers designs for use in a newspaper ad, an insert, or a mailing—including ways to grab the customer's attention and overwhelm your competition.

Chapter 16, "Producing a Flyer," presents individual designs that you can use in any business.

Chapter 17, "Producing a Brochure," details distinct ideas for creating and typesetting a brochure for your business. This chapter includes directions for incorporating tables and drawing charts in Ami Pro as well as using graphics, such as rules and borders.

Part V, "Creating Newsletters," explains the basic techniques of producing simple and complex newsletters for customers or employees.

Chapter 18, "Producing a Basic Newsletter," includes information on style sheets, consistency between issues, headers and footers, and nameplates. This chapter also offers several design choices.

Chapter 19, "Producing a Complex Newsletter," takes the design and layout processes a step further. This chapter incorporates creating a masthead, using logos, and adding tables and charts.

Part VI, "Creating Long Documents," introduces you to Ami Pro's special features, such as page numbering and floating headers and footers, and the directions for applying them. This section shows you how Ami Pro makes it easy to produce long documents.

Chapter 20, "Producing a Business Report," offers ideas and solutions for designing business reports, including updating with Ami Pro's data exchange features.

Chapter 21, "Producing a Book," explains specific formulas for how to use or create chapter and master documents, revision marking, footnotes, table of contents, index, and page numbering.

Look Your Best with Ami Pro also includes five appendixes.

Appendix A, "Getting to Know Ami Pro 2.0 and 3.0," explains the basics of Ami Pro to the new user. This appendix includes illustrations of the screen, keyboard, and mouse, and summaries of the Ami Pro draw, charting, and table features. Appendix A also lists several shortcut keys.

Appendix B, "Using Other Programs With Ami Pro," encompasses the use of Windows and non-Windows applications. This appendix covers using the Clipboard, converting text, importing graphics, and applying data exchange methods.

Appendix C, "Using Printers and Output," tells you about the kinds of printers you can use with Ami Pro and includes output samples, definitions, and applications. Appendix C discusses the advantages and disadvantages of dot-matrix, inkjet, and laser printers, as well as image setters.

Appendix D, "Adobe Type Manager Fonts," contains a list of Wingding and Symbol fonts available in Ami Pro. This appendix also includes samples of other ATM fonts, such as Arial, DomCasual, and Shelley Allegro Script.

Appendix E, "Glossary of Desktop Publishing Terms," provides you with the most recent language associated with desktop publishing.

Conventions Used in This Book

The document chapters (5 through 21) give specific instructions that contain mouse movement, combination keys, and entering text.

If you're not familiar with mouse terms, such as click, double-click, and drag, refer to Appendix A. For more detailed explanations of keyboard directions, refer to Appendix A.

Ami Pro uses many combination keys to carry out commands. When you see a plus sign (+) between two keys—as in Ctrl+B—you hold down the first key and press the second key.

Ami Pro underlines one letter in each menu and dialog box command to signify a keyboard option. By pressing the Alt key plus the underlined letter key, you can access that particular menu or function with the keyboard. In this book, the underlined letter is in **bold**.

Any typing you are asked to do, whether it be text or in a dialog box, appears in **bold**. Representation of on-screen messages or text appears in a `special typeface`, and *italic* type indicates emphasis or introduces new terms.

Understanding Design
and Typography

OPENING NIGHT!

Manhattan Players Present

BEYOND
ENMITY

A PLAY BY S. J. BENDER

featuring

Erin Linkous
Brandon McIntyre

Hattan Theatre
111 W. 24th Street

Includes

1. Learning Design Strategies

2. Using Elements of Design

3. Defining and Explaining Typography

4. Planning and Purchasing Printing

1

Learning Design Strategies

Creating a successful design—the arrangement of text and graphics in a document—involves many steps. The first step is the most important: planning and preparing your design for a specific purpose. The main purpose of printed material, for example, is to convey a message to the reader. Likewise, the main purpose of design is to convey a message that attracts your readers' attention and persuades them to pick up the printed material and read it, creating readers rather than browsers.

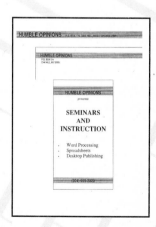

For detailed information on how to create a document like this see page 20.

Many print shops require a seven-year apprenticeship for typesetters.

A common mistake in page layout and design is to crowd the page with text and graphics, affording no rest for the reader's eye.

With so many printed documents competing for attention, a design must be exceptional to win a reader's attention. Creating a good design is an art. Typesetters in print shops work for years to develop proficiency in layout and design. A thorough knowledge of the elements of good design and a good deal of practice are important parts of developing this proficiency. This book gives you the tools and hands-on practice you need to produce attractive, professional-looking designs and develop design proficiency quickly.

Elements of design, such as balance, white space, integration of graphic elements and images, and typography are discussed in detail in Chapters 2 and 3.

Desktop publishing (page formatting on a computer) has changed the way the public perceives the typeset page. Before the appearance of the personal computer and desktop publishing programs, professional typesetters produced high-quality pages that attracted the attention and respect of the public. The popularity and affordability of the PC with desktop publishing capabilities, however, has made it easy for anyone to create documents.

Many "new" desktop publishers are not trained in design and typography and, therefore, produce unattractive, unprofessional material. The declining quality of printed documents has desensitized the public to the point that only masterful designs grab attention. To get your message noticed in this kind of environment, you must create professional, high-quality designs that convert browsers into readers.

The elements of design are the building blocks you use to convey your message. In this chapter, you learn how to identify five critical components: the purpose of your document, your intended audience, the message you want to convey, the life of your document, and the steps you take to plan the successful design of your project. After you accomplish these tasks, you begin organizing the elements of type and graphics to create your design. This preparation and planning is essential to the success of any document.

Determining the Purpose of Your Document

Before you plan a document for publication, you need to know the specific *purpose* for the document. What do you want the document to accomplish? Consider, first, the end result you desire. Then decide how to accomplish that end.

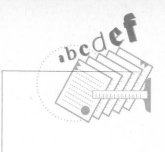

Do you want to sell a product? If so, what makes this product advantageous to the customer? What are the benefits in price, service, availability, warranty? How much does it cost, and are there any special discounts? Why is your product better than its competition?

Suppose that you want to explain new safety regulations to fellow workers. Which employees do the regulations affect the most? How do the regulations affect them, and what do they think about the changes? Can you explain each regulation? Can you provide a different slant on the explanations, such as cost effectiveness, time constraints, or efficiency? Are there any graphic images, such as cartoons, photographs, or illustrations available to emphasize the new regulations?

Do you have more than one goal or purpose for your document? Suppose that you want to introduce a new line of hair care products. Furthermore, you have an old product line of skin cream you want to sell out, and then discontinue. Can you effectively relate these goals; or should they remain separate? Can you announce that the sale of the skin cream, for example, is to make room for the new product line? Could you, instead, offer discounted skin cream for anyone who purchases a bottle of the new shampoo?

Choosing your purpose is an all-important first step to planning any document. You can then aim everything in your document—text, graphics, and design elements—to promoting your purpose and achieving the desired results. Directly related to deciding the purpose of your document, is targeting your audience.

Understanding Your Audience

To plan the specific design of your document, you also need to know your intended audience. Who are you trying to reach with your document? Will the audience be your customers, prospective customers, fellow employees, your boss, a group of professionals, the general public? Use terms and phrasing familiar to your audience. You address customers in one way, employees in another; you write to a group of computer users differently than to a group of shoppers. You cannot successfully communicate with readers unless you know who they are.

After you know who your audience is, you need to learn more about them. Because each audience has its own communication needs, the more you know about your readers, the more easily you can plan and prepare the appropriate design for your document. Are your readers male, female, young, old, employers, employees? Research your audience by reading competitors' pieces, visiting the library, or doing a telephone survey.

You can use jargon in a document to attract a specific audience.

Plan the document to address the readers directly, focusing on their interests. The better you custom-design each document for your readers, the more successful you will be in getting your message across.

> *Desktop publishing makes it easy for you to create a basic letter, for example, and tailor it for many different audiences.*

Knowing What You Want to Communicate

After you determine the specific purpose of your document and identify the audience, the next step is to determine what you want to communicate so that you can design your document accordingly. Suppose that the purpose of your document is to sell a product. The essential information you must communicate to your readers is the product's price, the product's features, and the specific benefits the product offers your prospective customers.

If you are running for political office, you want to tell your audience why you are the best candidate, what you can offer them, and how your views relate to your constituents.

> *In your document design, emphasize the one major point that you want to communicate quickly to your audience.*

You must design your document to present the elements of your specific message to the reader in the best possible way. To enhance the piece, you can choose to emphasize a single feature, such as the price, by using bold or italic type, rules, screens, and so on.

Determining the Life of Your Document

The intended "shelf life" of your document, the length of time your material is relevant, depends on the content of the piece and the medium you use to get your message to the reader. Consider, for example, the following differences between a newspaper ad that sells a product and a brochure that describes the upcoming semester's classes:

- The purpose of the newspaper ad is to interest readers sufficiently to get them into the store. The short life of the ad is defined by the length of its appearance, usually one day to one week; the competitive nature of newspaper ads on the same page that readers may scan too quickly or not at all; and the fact newspapers are almost always tossed after being read one time. A newspaper ad design, therefore, must have impact; it must grab attention at first glance.

- A brochure that describes a list of upcoming semester classes has a longer life because the customer may refer to and use the content of the brochure this week, next month, or three months from now, and the brochure is a stand-alone publication for which the main competition is other similar brochures. The design of this type of brochure, therefore, encourages relaxed and comfortable reading.

When you begin your document design, consider the "shelf life" you want your document to maintain and then plan your document accordingly.

Planning Your Document

After the preliminary work is done, you can begin to organize the content, select the format, determine the trim size, and choose the finish for your document. Again, the purpose of the document helps determine the size, shape, format, and appearance of the final product. In addition, as you plan your document, use consistency and emphasis as tools to attract readers and keep their interest. Through planning and organizing, you can create a well-designed, professional-looking document.

Organizing Your Document

Write your copy, keeping in mind the purpose of the document. Outline your main topics and subtopics first; then form them into well-written, interesting text. The outline helps you organize your material and write concise but descriptive sentences. Even the heads and subheads must persuade your audience to read the copy.

Don't be afraid to revise your copy to exactly the way you want it. As most successful writers attest, the best writing almost always comes from rewriting, and anything less than superbly written copy will not hold your readers' interest. Make sure that your message is clearly stated and easy to understand and that your terminology, spelling, and grammar are impeccable.

Gather tables, charts, art work, photos, or other graphic images that reinforce your message. Graphic images can get your message across many times faster and more efficiently than the text, because the first thing a reader sees is the graphic image.

Use the active voice and exciting, descriptive heads to attract the reader's attention.

Don't discard any elements you cut from the page. Keep these deletions, along with other information you may want to add, in case page formatting opens up unexpected holes in the copy.

Make sure that any graphic you use directly supports the message, however. If the image is trivial or doesn't contribute directly to the message, the reader may skip the entire document. Anything less than an effective graphic image is wasted space and may cost you your readership.

Selecting the Format

Part of your design strategy includes the *format* of your document— a flyer, brochure, letter, newsletter, or book. The format you choose depends on the purpose of the document, the size, the amount of copy, and the method of distribution. If you plan to distribute the piece by mail, for example, it must conform to postal regulations in size and shape.

A flyer is a good format for hard-sell, dated material. Usually printed on one side of an 8 1/2-by-11-inch sheet of low-grade paper, a flyer may contain short lists, brief descriptions, and factual information. *Hard-sell* employs high-pressure techniques that command the readers' attention. Using display type, bold type or bulleted lists, and words and phrases such as *Save*, *One Week Only*, and *Red Hot Specials* are hard-sell techniques.

A brochure, on the other hand, is appropriate for soft-sell, reference material. You usually print brochures in two or more colors on both sides of high-quality paper, folded into two, three, or four panels. *Soft-sell* assumes the reader's initial interest in the product or service. In a brochure, you use detailed descriptions in small but readable type, restrict the amount of very large type, and perhaps refer to the benefits the customer receives in a bulleted list or screened box.

Determining the Size

The size of the document depends on the amount of copy, format, size, quantity printed, and method of distribution. Consider, too, how the customer will store or carry your document and how the size of your document compares with what your competition is printing. When you determine the document size, you must consider the impact of each of these factors.

Depending on the amount of copy and the format, you can use any size document from smaller than a flyer to larger than a newsletter, as the document requires. A newsletter, for example, is usually 11 by 17 inches folded to 8 1/2 by 11 inches.

To determine the size of the document, you must consider the quantity—the number of final copies to be printed. Do you want 50 on a laser printer, 500 on a photocopier, or 10,000 at a print shop?

Your determination of the document size also depends on the method of distribution you choose. A newsletter to be picked up from a countertop can be any size. Some documents designed for distribution through the U.S. postal system, however, are subject to size restrictions. A document distributed as a postcard, for example, must conform to specific postal regulations.

When determining the size, you also should consider what happens after readers receive the document. Can they store it easily? Can they slide it into a pocket or insert it into a standard three-ring binder?

Finally, ask yourself if the size of the document helps it stand out among your competitors' documents? An unusual size can attract special attention to a document surrounded by a sea of advertisements. Carefully consider all these factors before determining the size of your documents.

The document size has a direct effect on the cost and time involved in reproducing a document. Chapter 4 provides further discussion of quantity considerations.

Choosing the Finish

Part of planning your document is choosing the finishing techniques that apply. Traditionally, certain formats correspond with specific finishing techniques. Finishing techniques include folding, fastening, padding, and numbering.

Folding is a common technique used in such documents as letters, brochures, newsletters, invitations, and books. Depending on the size and format of your document, you may use a parallel, French, or accordion fold. A letter normally uses a parallel fold, for example; an invitation commonly requires a French fold; and a road map is an example of an accordion fold.

The accordion fold is the most expensive fold for a print shop to perform; choose another fold for your document if at all possible.

You also can choose one of many fastening techniques. As with folding, the method of fastening matches the size and format of the document. Stapling, plastic spiral binding, and padding are three common fastening methods. Reports, magazines, and some books usually require stapling; however, these document formats may use plastic spiral binding if pages are frequently added or removed from the document. Padding is a temporary fastening technique used for notepads, calendars, and forms.

Consider the finishing techniques of your document in the planning stages to avoid mistakes near the end. Chapter 4, "Planning and Purchasing Printing," explains these techniques.

Maintaining Consistency

First impressions of a printed document are critical. A document that doesn't impress the reader at first glance probably will be ignored. *Consistency* can help you create a positive first impression with a clear, simple, well-organized page; consistency in design and typography is vital to the success of any document.

Design elements such as balance, margins, columns, rules, and screens promote consistency. *Balancing* the distribution of the type and design elements on the page creates a pleasing document. Keeping individual pages balanced throughout the document by using the same number of columns and the same margin widths enhances consistency. Repetition throughout the document of such elements as rules and screens ties the document together to create consistency. Chapter 2, "Using Elements of Design," explains these design elements in detail.

Typography, typeface, type size, spacing, and alignment also can contribute to consistency. If the text on the page is consistently easy to read throughout the document, the reader is more likely to read the entire message. Chapter 3, "Defining and Explaining Typography," further defines typography and its related components.

Organization is a key to consistency. By arranging your text and graphics on the page in a pleasing and logical manner, you add a sense of consistency. You can design this arrangement by putting the most important part of your text first, the second most important part next, and so on, giving the reader a sense of order and structure.

Repetition also enhances consistency. You can repeat important words or facts in your copy, such as *Save* in a sales ad or *Now Due* on an invoice, to help achieve consistency. You can achieve consistency by repeating design and type elements, as well. You can use two-point rules above all heads, end each section with the company logo, use the same size and style for heads throughout the document, use equal spacing in all body text, or use the same size bullets on all pages.

Figure 1.1 illustrates the concept of consistency within an advertisement. Notice the typeface, type size, margins, and graphics. The majority of the text in the ad is in the Times Roman typeface—in only three sizes. The graphics also promote consistency because all the bullets are the same and the rules are the same width and length.

Figure 1.2 shows the same ad with much less consistency. Three typefaces and too many attributes fight each other for attention. In addition, the graphic elements create a busy look for the ad.

B e consistent with the wording or phrasing of heads and subheads in your documents.

GRAND OPENING
humble opinions

OFFERING INSTRUCTION
- Desktop Publishing
- Word Processing

June 3
9:00 a.m. - 5:00 p.m.
117 E. Main Street • (304) 555-2323

Fig. 1.1   Consistency in a newspaper advertisement.

Grand

Opening

humble opinions

OFFERING INSTRUCTION
- Desktop Publishing
* Word Processing

June 3
9:00 A.M. - 5:00 P.M.
117 E. MAIN STREET
(304) 555-2323

Fig. 1.2   Inconsistency in the same advertisement.

Consistency is just as important in company documents as in stand-alone special flyers and brochures. Company letterheads, newsletters, and business reports can use similar elements to bind them together. All these documents need not be formatted in the same way, but you can use one logo, a particular typeface, or a color to tie the documents together. Customers respond well to such consistency; seeing a familiar logo over and over or recognizing the same typeface or graphic elements may make readers feel more comfortable and more willing to read a document.

Figure 1.3 demonstrates consistency among a letterhead, envelope, and brochure for the same company. Subsequent chapters refer frequently to consistency among company documents.

Adding Emphasis

Another tool that can help you create a good first impression is *emphasis*. You can emphasize a subject in a variety of ways, by using a graphic element to frame a photograph, white space to offset a story, a pie chart to track profits, or column rules to lead the reader's eye to an important item. Two additional vehicles for adding emphasis are typography and color.

C hapter 3 offers examples of using emphasis with type.

With typography, for example, you can use 72-point type to emphasize the word *Sale* and headline type to make the names of products stand out. You also can use bullets, callouts, jumplines, boldface, and italics.

You can emphasize an important topic with a splash of color around it, use a four-color chart or photograph, or use an effective contrasting color for a large headline. Of course, to apply this option, you need a color printer or a print shop.

Knowing when not to use emphasis is equally as important as knowing when to use it. Too much emphasis in a document creates disorder and clutter. With too much emphasis, the reader cannot understand the truly important information because everything competes for attention. Figure 1.4 shows a flyer with an appropriate amount of emphasis. Figure 1.5 demonstrates the abuse of emphasis in the same flyer. Remember to add emphasis to only one idea or topic per document. Chapters 2 and 3 discuss additional techniques for adding emphasis.

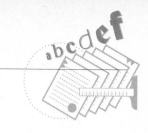

HUMBLE OPINIONS P.O. BOX 174 OAK HILL, WEST VIRGINIA 25901

HUMBLE OPINIONS
P.O. BOX 174
OAK HILL, WV 25901

HUMBLE OPINIONS

presents

SEMINARS
AND
INSTRUCTION

- • Word Processing
- • Spreadsheets
- • Desktop Publishing

(304) 555-2323

Fig. 1.3 Three documents from one company that use similar elements for consistency.

OPENING NIGHT!

Manhattan Players Present

BEYOND ENMITY

A PLAY BY S. J. BENDER

featuring
Erin Linkous
Brandon McIntyre

Hattan Theatre
111 W. 24th Street

Fig. 1.4   A flyer with emphasis applied properly.

OPENING NIGHT

MANHATTAN PLAYERS
PRESENT

BEYOND ENMITY

A PLAY BY S.J. BENDER

FEATURING
ERIN LINKOUS
BRANDON
MCINTYRE

HATTAN THEATRE
111 W. 24TH STREET

Fig. 1.5   A flyer with overuse of emphasis.

No single design solution is appropriate to all documents. The design elements you choose for a document should depend on the specific purpose of the document, the audience, the copy, and your personal preferences. The following chapters of this book offer guidelines to help you make these decisions, with suggestions that enable your creativity to shine through.

Recapping

This chapter covers information that you need to remember as you work your way through this book. The following steps to planning and organizing your document provide a recap of this information to refresh your memory and give you a quick reference guide:

1. Decide the purpose of your document, understand your audience, and know what you want to say.

2. Write the copy and gather supporting graphic images.

3. Organize the copy by ranking the important items.

4. Decide format, size, quantity, distribution method, and finishing techniques. Remember the intended shelf life.

5. Create consistency throughout the document.

6. Select one important topic or point to emphasize.

2

Using Elements of Design

After you determine the specific purpose of a document, your next step is to choose the document design, including elements such as size, shape, format, and layout. These elements make a document attractive, effective, and practical. Effective use of basic design elements can help you communicate your message to your readers—the primary purpose of any document.

For detailed information on how to create a form like this see page 29.

You can learn about design by looking at documents. Keeping in mind that the mission of good design is to entice readers to pick up a document, try to determine what attracts you to a particular document. Is it graphics, headlines, color, white space, or a combination of these elements?

Studying a variety of documents and identifying the design elements that interest you can give you a base on which to build your own designs. Follow the rules of the design elements presented in this chapter to learn how to organize and complement your message. By following time-tested typesetting rules, you can produce attractive, professional-looking documents that attract readers and communicate your message. This chapter and Chapter 3, "Defining and Explaining Typography," cover these typesetting rules and conventions.

Most word processing and desktop publishing programs use traditional typesetting terms.

The language of design and typography you will learn in these chapters has its roots in the past—retaining some identifying names and discarding other labels that no longer apply. Modern typesetters still keep the rules and language from the early newspaper days of handset type: leading (LED-ing), galleys, parallel columns, picas, uppercase and lowercase, and so on. Most of the leftovers from the days of the typewriter, however, are no longer suitable for today's documents, including double-spacing, narrow margins, caps for emphasis, five-space indents at the beginning of paragraphs, and two spaces between sentences.

With so much competition in today's market, only the most attractive and professional-looking documents succeed. This chapter presents design alternatives that have a positive influence on the reader. In addition, you learn, step-by-step, the most effective way to design your document to communicate your message. Read Chapters 2 and 3 completely before doing any planning, sketching, or designing in Ami Pro so that you understand how the elements of design interrelate.

Planning with Thumbnail Sketches

As discussed in Chapter 1, "Learning Design Strategies," the first step in creating a successful design is to plan your design for a specific purpose. If the purpose of the document is to sell a product, for example, plan your design to promote that product. Knowing the purpose is the easy part, however. The hard part is to move your design from initial concept to finished product. A helpful tool many designers use to go from rough idea to finished design is a *thumbnail sketch*, a rough sketch or layout of the document page (see fig. 2.1).

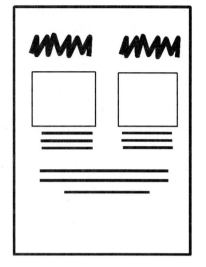

Fig. 2.1   Thumbnail sketches for a flyer design.

In these rough sketches, draw in all heads, columns, rules, and boxes for graphics. Use no detail or actual text; concentrate instead on design elements such as balance, white space, and facing pages—elements explained in detail later in this chapter. Combine these elements until the result is pleasing to the eye. After you complete your sketches, create a rough draft of one or two pages.

Creating a Rough Draft

A *rough draft* is a detailed expansion of the thumbnail sketch, in the same size as the final document, that specifies the design elements to be used. The term is often shortened to *rough*. Plan the number of columns and their placement, considering the width of the page. Determine how much copy you have and how you will format it. Do you, for example, have copy that can form narrow columns, such as lists or short sentences, or do you have copy and graphics that need wider columns? Make sure that you plan for sufficient *gutter* or *alley* space (the space between columns).

Determine the location of text and images, placing related articles or captions near art or photos. Consider clustering similar photos or art work. Clustering five photographs of new products on one page, for example, instead of spreading them over three pages, attracts readers and persuades them to look more carefully at all the photos. Also make sure that you keep all related items within the document close together. Items that relate, such as an article about the rising cost of housing, a line graph comparing housing costs from 1985 to 1990, and

Organize your material by the priorities you set for the document.

photographs of a $45,000 home and a $100,000 home have more impact on the reader when placed close together.

Plan the type sizes to use. After you write the body of your message, prioritize it. Choose important words and phrases as heads and sub-heads. These heads should stand out for immediate recognition. Chapter 3, "Defining and Explaining Typography," covers in detail ways to emphasize heads and subheads.

You can make a grid of horizontal and vertical lines that cross periodically on the page to form guidelines for text and graphic placement (see fig. 2.2). In the figure, the grid on the left plans for two columns with gutter space. The horizontal rules divide areas for heads, subheads, graphics and body type, as shown on the right. Using a grid is especially helpful at this stage of planning your document.

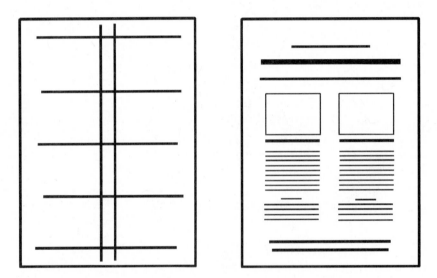

Fig. 2.2 A sample grid and a layout designed by using the grid.

If you haven't already done so, you need to decide whether you will fold, mail, perforate, or fasten your document. Each process affects the layout. A photograph placed on a fold will crease, for example, making it less attractive and less effective; a mailing piece must have sufficient space for address labels and postage; and any perforated ticket or card requires space for the perforation, which should be placed on at least two edges for easier removal of the perforated section. For more information about these procedures, refer to Chapter 4, "Planning and Purchasing Printing."

A rough isn't necessarily the final design (see fig. 2.3). Before you're finished, you may have to change the layout because of copy length, additional graphics, design constraints, or other unforeseen circumstances.

Fig. 2.3   A sample rough for a flyer.

As you prepare the thumbnails and roughs, apply the design elements outlined in this book. Remember that you can use emphasis to set off the more important ideas, but no one design element should overwhelm the others. Rather, the elements should work together to create the effect of *oneness*. This unity enables the reader to concentrate on the message. A design should do nothing but invite the reader to read.

Choosing Page Orientation

A basic design element is the page orientation of the document: *portrait* (vertical) or *landscape* (horizontal). Each orientation has specific uses and employs the design elements in particular ways. The orientation you choose depends on four conditions that affect your document: purpose, copy, dimensions, and quantity.

- *Purpose.* Traditionally, the purpose of a piece dictates its shape. Therefore, the printing trade assigns orientations to particular documents. If a document is designed for a standard three-ring binder or to be slipped easily into a pocket (vertical formats), the orientation is portrait. On the other hand, travel logs and many other business forms (traditionally horizontal formats) are more

Use design consistency, even when planning with thumbnail sketches and rough drafts.

efficient in landscape orientation. Any document designed for mailing must be finished to landscape orientation to conform to postal regulations.

- *Copy.* Determine how much copy you have and how the information flows on the pages. Is the copy in short lists that you can include in narrow columns, or in long paragraphs of text that require wide columns? Do you have many headlines or subheads? Can you separate these heads with rules or boxes? Is the art horizontal or vertical? Can the text also fit the same orientation as the artwork? If so, mirror this orientation with the page orientation.

- *Dimensions.* The finished size of the document is determined mainly by the amount or type of copy. If you list sections of text by priority, you can include only the text necessary to get the message across, and you ensure that you delete the lower priority text when you need to cut text. Tables, charts, and graphics take up more room than text and frequently require an increase in document size. The method of distribution also may affect document size. Documents you hand out on the street will be considerably smaller than those documents you display in store windows.

- *Quantity.* Reproduction costs weigh heavily in determining the ultimate size of your document. The cost of printing 1,000 small flyers, for example, is considerably less than the cost of printing 1,000 window displays. Additional factors to consider include paper and postage—the lighter the paper stock, the less expensive it is to mail.

Portrait Orientation

Orientation dimensions are given in width by height; thus, standard letterhead with *portrait*, or vertical, orientation is 8 1/2 by 11 inches. Portrait orientation is appropriate for lists of words or short sentences, graphics or photos more tall than wide, shorter headlines, and using many subheads. You can fit large amounts of text in this mode if you use two or three columns per page.

Letters, newsletters, resumes, and business reports are usually in portrait orientation (see fig. 2.4). Some types of flyers and books also can be in portrait mode.

In printing, measurements for portrait or landscape orientation are expressed in width, then height.

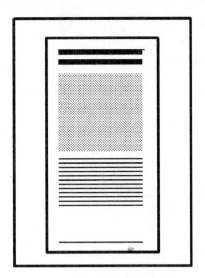

Fig. 2.4 A sample flyer in portrait orientation.

Landscape Orientation

Landscape, or wide, orientation (see fig. 2.5) is measured by height first, then width (11 inches by 8 1/2 inches). Use this orientation for long headlines, wide graphics or photos, and more pictures than text. This mode is also well-suited for spreadsheets, tables, charts, flyers, brochures, envelopes, programs, some forms, and many books.

I n Ami Pro, you can change orientation within a document by inserting a new page layout.

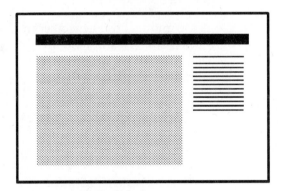

Fig. 2.5 A sample layout of a flyer in landscape orientation.

Planning the Size of the Document

Document size depends on many factors. Consider the purpose and the traditional sizes that fit this purpose. A book with many pages, for example, should be a small trim size that the reader can easily hold; a form with little fill-in may be small; and a newsletter for persons with impaired vision may use a large format to accommodate the large type required. Before you can communicate your message successfully, the reader must be comfortable with the document (it must be easy to read, use, and store). Choosing the proper size for your document purpose helps you accomplish this task.

The following factors govern the size of the document:

- Amount of copy

- Number of images (photos, art, spreadsheets, tables, or charts)

- Kind of document: brochure, newsletter, flyer, program, book, or magazine

- Means of distribution

- Paper size limitations of your printer

- Budget constraints

- The kind and size of paper

As you consider the preceding information, remember that some document sizes have proved efficient and advantageous over the years. Print shops use these sizes over and over again, mostly because of paper sizes that reflect press run sizes and other automated shop equipment. Print shops purchase paper in large sheets and cut them to standard sizes, keeping waste to a minimum. Even if you aren't taking your finished document to a print shop for printing, you still can take advantage of the following common cut sizes:

Paper Size	Kinds of Use
8 1/2 by 11 inches	Folded to 5 1/2 by 8 1/2 inches or to 3 2/3 by 8 1/2 inches, as in a brochure
11 by 17 inches	Folded to 8 1/2 by 11 inches for a four-page newsletter or presentation folder
3 5/8 by 8 1/2 inches	For a rack card
6 by 9 inches	For a book or magazine

Paper Size	Kinds of Use
6 by 10 inches	For a book cover or presentation document

Depending on the laser printer you use, you may be limited to 8 1/2-by-11-inch paper or smaller. Some laser printers also accept 8 1/2-by-14-inch paper, but if these sizes do not meet your needs, the problem is not insurmountable. If, for example, you want to produce an 11-by-17-inch newsletter that folds to 8 1/2 by 11 inches, you can format the four 8 1/2-by-11-inch pages on the computer and use a copy or print shop to produce an 11-by-17-inch finished document.

Balancing Design Elements

Text and graphics must *balance* on the page so that one does not dominate the other. A balanced page design attracts readers and leads them through the document in logical steps, helping them mentally organize and retain the information after just one reading. Page layout uses three major kinds of balance: *symmetrical*, *asymmetrical*, and *modular*. To keep from confusing the reader, use only one kind of balance throughout a document.

Symmetrical Balance

Symmetrical balance is the distribution of the text, graphics, and white space so that all elements correspond on opposite sides of a point (usually the center). Thus, what you see on one side of the center guide is produced exactly on the opposite side. Symmetrical balance is a formal, sophisticated, even balance that usually guarantees consistency within the document.

Figure 2.6 shows two examples of symmetrical balance; the center guide on both samples is the gutter space between columns.

Because the text and graphics are not exactly the same, you must measure the *visual weight* of each page by the elements. Consider text as the gray of the page (a page of nothing but type gives the impression of being gray). Graphics, art, photos, and illustrations are gray if they are light, but black if they are very dark or heavy. Measure the white of the page in the margins, gutter space, area around headlines and graphics, and even within the text (left- or right-aligned text has more white space than justified text). By balancing the grays, blacks, and whites on a page, you balance the actual text, graphics, and white space.

When you use your printed document as camera-ready copy for a print shop, you should use a laser or inkjet printer; see Chapter 4.

You can symmetrically balance a page from left to right, top to bottom, or both.

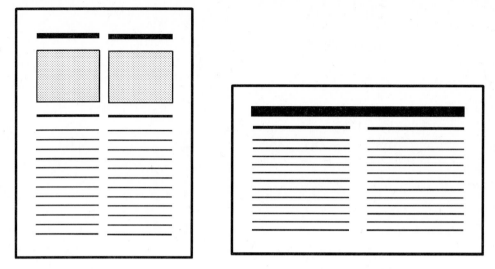

Fig. 2.6 Symmetrical balance in portrait and landscape orientations.

When judging asymmetrically balanced documents, squint your eyes; any part of the page that stands out is not balanced.

Asymmetrical Balance

With *asymmetrical* balance, the elements on either side of the center guide do not exactly correspond, but the overall weight of the elements remains about the same (see fig. 2.7). In this mode, you balance large areas of gray with large areas of white, or small black areas with larger gray areas. Asymmetrical balance results in a more free-form, informal, and more interesting document than does symmetrical balance, but can be more difficult to use properly and consistently.

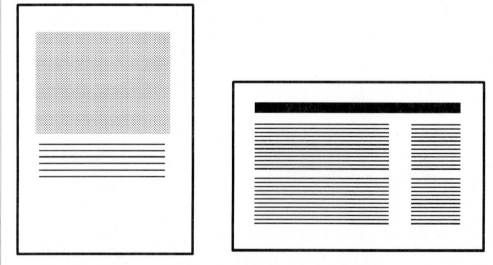

Fig. 2.7 Asymmetrical balance in portrait and landscape orientations

Modular Balance

Modular balance uses intersecting guidelines to form boxes across the page, placing text and graphics in the boxes to form an ordered, systematic layout. You can begin forming the *grid*, or *modules*, by dividing the page into two or three sections. Then divide these sections into two or three more sections (see fig. 2.8).

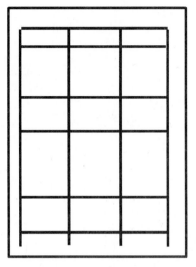
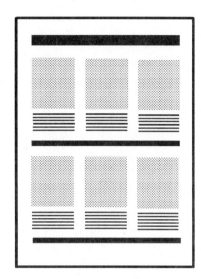

Fig. 2.8   The modules on the left converted to a page using symmetrical balance.

The modular layout can be symmetrical or asymmetrical. You achieve symmetrical balance by dividing the page in half, vertically or horizontally, and placing the text and graphics within the guidelines. You accomplish asymmetrical balance with the grid by varying placement or by combining several boxes to construct various size areas for text. Figure 2.9 shows the preceding sample grid with asymmetrical balancing of text and graphics.

The balance you choose should be consistent throughout the document. Slight variations, such as white space within asymmetrically balanced pages, can add emphasis and interest.

Using White Space for Contrast

Use *white space* within a document to provide contrast, emphasis, and a rest for the reader's eyes. Headlines, text, and graphics have far more impact when surrounded by white space. As a rule, balance white space throughout the page with text and graphics (gray space) on a 50-50

White space emphasizes text and graphics.

ratio. Although this amount of white space may seem excessive, you can use white space in many ways.

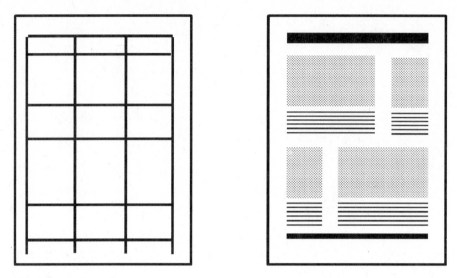

Fig. 2.9 The modules converted to an asymmetrically balanced layout.

Margins are perhaps the most effective way of implementing white space. If you have a small amount of copy, you can make the margins one inch, two inches, or even wider. The margins need not be even on all sides; a design is often more effective with a large margin on one side and smaller, equal margins on the other three sides (see fig. 2.10).

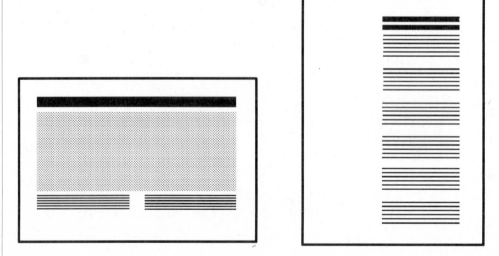

Fig. 2.10 Use of white space to create effective uneven margins.

When designing your page, squeeze white space to the outside of the page. Sometimes this practice can result in odd-shaped margins, but uneven margins are preferable to large pockets of white space trapped inside the page. Trapped pockets of white space prevent you from achieving balance, waste valuable space, and create obstacles to the eye.

Establishing Margins

Margins—the areas surrounding text blocks and graphics—are important to any document. This space serves as white space and as breathing room in contrast to the gray areas of text and graphics. Although gray space is often referred to as the *active* or *live* part of the page, don't consider the white space as dead. White space serves an important function, especially in margins; its impact provides ease of reading and emphasizes the message.

Margins also help provide consistency from page to page throughout a document. After you choose a formula for the margins of a particular document, stay with that formula. Don't change margins just for the sake of design (unless you mirror margins for facing pages), and don't change the margins to squeeze in an extra bit of text. Chapter 3, "Defining and Explaining Typography," suggests alternative methods for these problems.

The size of the margins depends on the amount of copy you're working with. The more copy and fewer pages you have, the smaller you need to make the margins. Always leave a margin of at least 3/8 inch on all sides of a document unless the document *bleeds* (discussed later in this chapter). You must maintain this minimum margin for the following reasons:

- All printers set an invisible margin around the edge of the paper that does not print. Yours may be 3/8 or 1/2 inch. You can easily test the printer by creating a 1-inch ruled box around the edges of an 8 1/2-by-11-inch page and then printing the page. Measure the portion of the rule the printer did not print and use the result as a guideline for the smallest possible margin.

- No ink or printing can be present on the gripper. *Gripper* is a term used by the press operator that refers to the point where the press grabs the paper to pass it through the press. Depending on the type of press used, the gripper may be at the top, bottom, or side of the page. To be safe, always leave at least a 3/8-inch margin all the way around the document.

ripper also refers to the mechanism on the press that grabs the paper to pull it through.

A far better alternative, however, is to leave more margin (recall the 50-50 white space rule). If you want contrast, emphasis, and a fighting chance to get the reader's attention, use more margin. Readers looking at a gray page of text and crowded graphics may take their attention elsewhere. Margins of 1/2 inch, one inch, or larger are not merely acceptable, but preferable.

Keep the top margin fixed throughout the document; text and graphics should line up evenly along the top. If the top margins are kept intact, the document will have a sense of unity and continuity. The bottom margin is more flexible. Years ago, printers thought that even, flush bottom lines of text were the only way to set type. Now, however, the only flush lines of text necessary are the lines at the top. Columns that you deliberately leave uneven at the bottom can create valuable white space. Leave out everything that isn't important to the overall message and let the white space speak for itself.

As a rule, use less margin on top and more on the bottom. The side margins (unless you're producing a book) should measure the same as the top margin. You can set up a flyer, for example, with a bottom margin of 1 1/2 inches; top, left, and right margins of 3/4 inches; or a bottom margin of 2 inches and top and sides of 1 inch each. If the document demands order and evenly balanced pages—as in a legal brief, company report, or formal letter—follow these traditional typesetting guidelines.

If you can apply wider margins with a wealth of white space, don't hesitate to do so. Consider the copy, the kind of document you're preparing, and the design elements you apply to it. Unequal margins are unusual in today's market; most typeset pieces employ the traditional rules of measurement because they are easy and safe. Because uneven margins are so distinct and demand attention in any document, however, using this technique ensures that your message is communicated. Figure 2.11 shows common margins for a newsletter and a brochure; figure 2.12 shows more creative use of margins and white space.

Occasionally you may need to make minor exceptions to these guidelines on margin usage, as the following sections describe.

Margins with Headers and Footers

An important function of margins is to provide room in the document for headers and footers. To incorporate these elements, margins must be wide enough for the added text when you produce a newsletter, book, paper, or other document with page numbers. When planning a

As with the fixed top margin, keep left and right margins consistent throughout a document.

Slightly wider bottom margins give a document more weight on the bottom, making the document appear more stable.

If you cannot afford extra room in your document for a header or footer, don't use the header or footer.

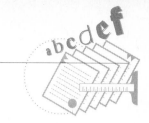

document of this nature, you need to plan for a wider margin at the top if you use a header or at the bottom if you use a footer. Allow at least an extra 1/4 to 3/8 inch.

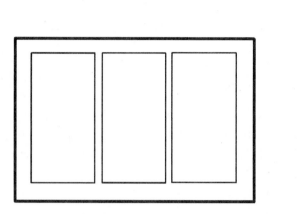

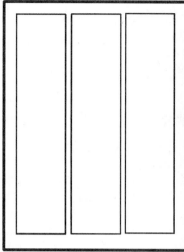

Fig. 2.11 Layouts with traditionally spaced margins and gutters.

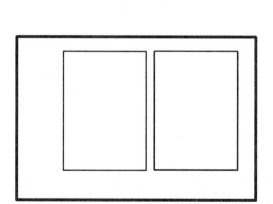

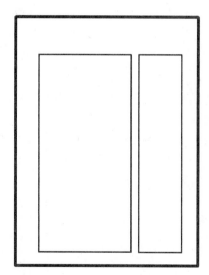

Fig. 2.12 Layouts using white space for interesting margins.

A *header* or *footer* consists of text or graphics that describe the body of the document in some way—for example, company name, logo, page number, author's name, chapter or document title, date, or subject matter contained on the particular page. You can place headers or footers on odd- or even-numbered pages only, or on facing pages. Never place a header or footer on the first page of a document or the first page of a chapter.

You can format a header or footer in a variety of ways. Usually the type is bold or italic and the point size is smaller than the body text. Headers and footers also frequently incorporate a horizontal rule—from margin edge to margin edge—that separates them from the body of the document.

Margins with Bleed

Bleed describes the effect when any element on the page—except white space—goes through the margin and *runs* off the edge of the paper. Although bleeds offer a nice effect, they can be difficult to design. When you use this element, never bleed only off the bottom of the page—the reader's eye is led off the page and away from the document. An element that bleeds top and bottom, or side and bottom, works well, however. You also can bleed off the top or sides, or off both at the same time so that the reader's eye drops into the page. Side bleeds can give a nice effect with graphic lines, screens, or boxes. Another option is a three- or four-sided bleed. Figure 2.13 shows a bleed on three sides in landscape orientation and a bleed off one side in portrait orientation.

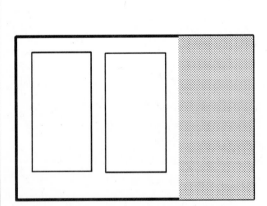

Fig. 2.13 Examples of bleed.

Laser printers cannot execute a bleed. As discussed earlier, all printers have a margin around the paper edge that doesn't print. If you want a bleed in a document, you must take it to a print shop. Printers charge extra for bleeds because they require oversized paper that must be trimmed to the final size (remember the gripper needed for the press). A bleed on four sides is more expensive than a bleed on one, two, or three sides.

Binding Margins

When you format a book, the margin rules differ from most other publications. A book, paper, or report that is side-stitched (stapled on the left) or punched with holes for use with a binder, must have a wider margin on the binding side. Without the extra margin space, the text near the middle of the book becomes unreadable because the binding covers it.

A binding margin is never less than 1/2 inch. The margin usually is 3/4 to 1 inch, or even larger if the book is exceptionally thick. If you print on both sides of a page, the binding margins shift for left and right pages. The right-hand pages have a larger margin on the left, and the left-hand pages have the binding margin on the right (see fig. 2.14).

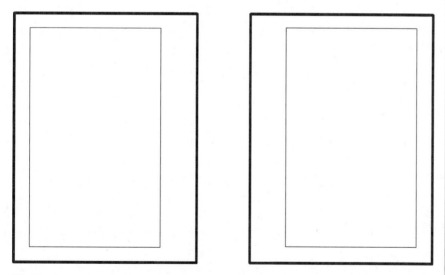

Fig. 2.14 The binding margins of a book with pages printed on both sides.

Planning Columns

Columns that use the flow of text from the bottom of column one to the top of column two, and so on, are called *snaking* or *newspaper* columns.

If text is difficult to read because the lines of text are too short or require excessive hyphenation, your columns are too narrow.

Some documents may require a division of copy by *columns* to help you organize the placement of text and graphics. Nonprinting vertical guides create boundaries by which you lay out the columns on the page. The first point to remember when designing columns is that English is read from left to right. Therefore, text should flow from the left-hand column to the right. Because the main purpose of the document is to present information to the reader in a format that is easy to understand and follow, don't be so creative with the columns that you confuse the reader. The flow of text must be logical.

When using portrait orientation, you should have no more than four columns per page; with landscape orientation, use no more than six columns per page. Too many columns can create a cluttered appearance and become hard to follow. Lines of text also must be short to fit in narrow columns, and graphics may be too small to be effective. Figure 2.15 shows a page layout in landscape orientation that uses six columns.

Fig. 2.15   Six columns for a brochure design.

For design purposes, columns need not be of equal width (see fig. 2.16); you can combine wide and narrow columns to create interest. Beginning with a grid, experiment with different column widths as you sketch the rough draft. Lay out one wide column and three narrow ones, or two wide and one narrow. When you're satisfied with the layout, fit your copy into the columns according to content. Include a brief, bulleted list or a tall, thin graphic in a narrow column, for example, and place a wide photograph or lengthy story in a wide column. When experimenting in this manner, make sure that your copy fits the column layout throughout the entire document and be consistent with the width and placement of the columns.

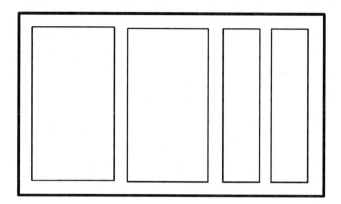

Fig. 2.16   A brochure using landscape orientation and uneven columns.

Establishing Line Length

When you plan column width, consider the *line length* of the type. The width of the column determines line length, which influences readability. Lines that are too long or short can be hard to read. Newspapers follow the general rule that the optimum line length is 1 1/2 times the width of the lowercase alphabet. Another line-length rule to follow concerns the type size: the smaller the type size, the shorter the line. Likewise, the larger the type size, the longer the line. Figure 2.17 shows two examples of line length.

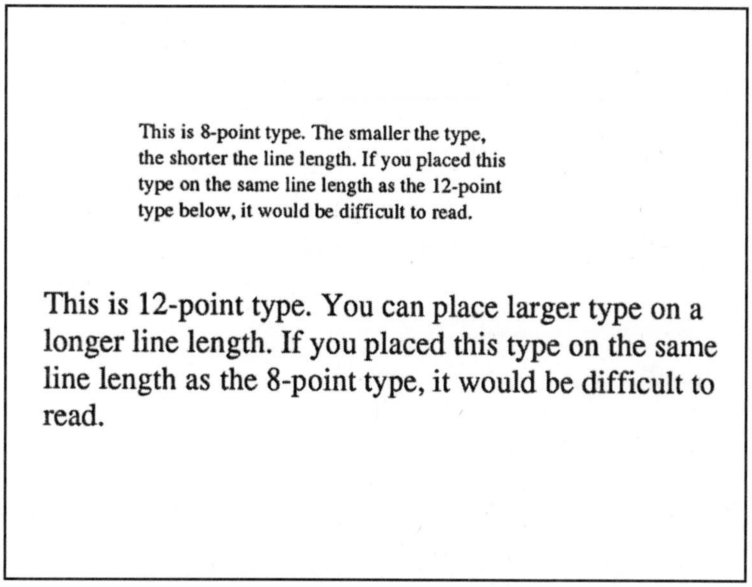

This is 8-point type. The smaller the type, the shorter the line length. If you placed this type on the same line length as the 12-point type below, it would be difficult to read.

This is 12-point type. You can place larger type on a longer line length. If you placed this type on the same line length as the 8-point type, it would be difficult to read.

Fig. 2.17   8-point and 12-point type line lengths.

Another way to measure line length is by characters per line (cpl). The optimum number is 35 to 40 cpl (1 1/2 lowercase alphabets in 10-point type is 39 characters). When following this system, make sure that you count letters, spaces, and punctuation marks. The minimum line length is 20 cpl, and the maximum is 60 cpl. If you must use wide columns, such as 60 characters per line, choose a typeface with a wide font. You may use 60 cpl, for example, in a letter to the elderly, with 12-point type in one column to make it easier to read. However, because the majority of readers find 35 to 40 characters per line the most comfortable, try to limit your line length to these recommendations. New Century Schoolbook and Goudy are examples of wide typefaces.

Including Gutters

Consider the gutter, or alley, as a margin or breathing room between two columns. Leaving sufficient space between columns is important (refer to fig. 2.15); narrow gutters can make the text in columns hard to read or force a reader's eye to jump to the column to the left or to the right when following a sentence. Very wide gutters, however, tend to separate ideas or a continued story. Limiting gutters to 1/4 to 1/2 inch is a good compromise. Remember to keep the gutters consistent throughout the document.

Producing Columns in Ami Pro

Rule is the typesetter's term for line.

Ami Pro offers two ways to produce columns in a document: using the Column Layout option in the Page menu, which enables you to set up the columns with gutter space and optional vertical rules, and using *frames*. Within frames, you can set up columns with gutter space and optimal rules; the settings and options are the same as for columns in page layout. Ami Pro also enables you to set up columns with the Table feature, although you should reserve this option for columns that require simple layout.

Using Page Layout

By choosing the **Page** menu and choosing **Modify Page Layout** (with the mouse, click **Page** and then click **Modify Page Layout**; with the keyboard, press Alt+P,M), you can *snake*, or flow, text from one column to the next quickly and easily so that the text continues to fill columns without prompting. As you continue typing at the end of the first column, Ami Pro automatically moves the cursor to the top of the

second column. Ami Pro also enables you to balance these columns as equal lengths or, if you choose, to break the columns. Because broken column bottoms are usually uneven, be sure that the column tops are flush.

Ami Pro enables you to edit the text in layout view, while in column format. Several chapters in this book describe this procedure in detail, including Chapter 9, "Producing a Program," Chapter 17, "Producing a Brochure," and Chapter 18, "Producing a Basic Newsletter."

Producing columns with frames works similarly. The only difference between the **P**age and **F**rame menus is that the **P**age menu contains the **M**odify Page Layout option, and you choose **M**odify Frame Layout from the **F**rame menu. Procedures for setting the number of columns, gutter width, and so on are the same.

Using the Table Feature

Another way to create columns in Ami Pro is to use the Table feature. A *table* consists of columns and rows of cells that contain text, graphics, or both. By choosing Tools Tables (with the mouse, click Tools, then Tables; with the keyboard, press Alt+L,B) and typing the number of rows and columns you want to appear, you can format text in tabular or side-by-side columns. Again, Ami Pro enables you to edit within the table columns. You also can add vertical or horizontal rules. Chapter 14, "Producing an Order Form," covers this procedure.

Creating Facing Pages

Documents are often only one or two pages long. You can prepare one-sided pages or arrange all the copy on the front and back of one sheet. If the document has four or more pages, however, you must arrange pages as *facing* (or double-sided) pages.

Figure 2.18 illustrates a four-page newsletter, in which page one is a right-hand page, page two is a left-hand page facing page three, and page four is a left-hand page. Right-hand pages are always odd-numbered (1, 3, 5, and so on); left-hand pages are always even-numbered (2, 4, 6, and so on).

This page-numbering system works the same whether you're producing a 4-, 8-, or 64-page publication. You can apply facing pages to portrait or landscape orientation.

A mi Pro's powerful frame feature enables you to modify columns in frames just as you would in page layout.

C hapter 19 illustrates using a table for newsletter columns.

BACK (left) Pg. 4	FRONT (right) Pg. 1		INSIDE (left) Pg. 2	INSIDE (right) Pg. 3

Fig. 2.18   Facing pages of a four-page newsletter.

Y ou generally format the last page of a newsletter somewhat differently from its facing page to accommodate mailing panels, calendars, and so on.

Designing facing pages so that they look good together is important. Be consistent with columns, margins, gutters, graphics, rules, headlines, and body text. The design of a page may work on its own, but when viewed with its facing page, the elements may clash. Be sure that all elements and design choices complement each other. If the design elements are distracting, inconsistent, or cluttered, the result distracts and therefore prevents the reader from concentrating on the message. Figure 2.19 shows a common layout for a four-page newsletter that demonstrates consistency in the facing pages.

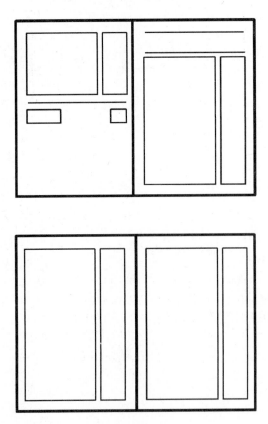

Fig. 2.19   Layout for a four-page newsletter.

You can add contrast to facing pages by *mirroring* the design so that the columns, balance, and white space on one page are reflected on the facing page. This method of organization has an attractive appearance, is consistent throughout, and adds some variation (see fig. 2.20).

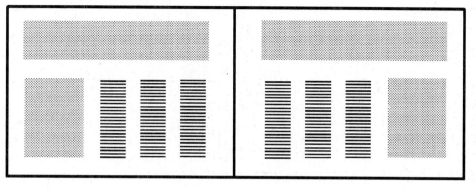

Fig. 2.20 Landscape orientation using a mirrored balance.

Because consistency is important in typeset documents, use tools that help achieve this goal whenever possible. One such tool, a *style sheet*, is a list of descriptions frequently used in a document. These descriptions may include margins and columns; type size, style, and face; line and paragraph spacing; tabs and indents; and text alignment.

After creating a style sheet, use it repeatedly to create consistency between documents. When producing a monthly newsletter, for example, build the document on the same style sheet each time. In this way, regular readers immediately recognize the style and format and feel comfortable before they even open the newsletter.

In Ami Pro, a style sheet also can contain extra features—text, graphics, glossary data files, and macros—to help you with the design. Ami Pro also supplies many document style sheets, or you can create your own custom style sheets. Table 2.1 explains the contents of a style sheet. For more information, consult the Ami Pro Reference Manual.

Table 2.1   Contents of a Template

Contents	Definition and Function
With Contents	Any text that may be the same in every document, such as the return address in a letter or *To, From,* and *Comments* in a memo

continues

Table 2.1   Continued

Contents	Definition and Function
Styles	Determines character and paragraph formatting, such as font, type size, spacing, alignment, tabs, and indents.
Glossary data files	All text and/or graphics used in several documents, such as letterhead, logo design, and masthead
Macros	Mini-programs that perform specific functions in Ami Pro, such as searching and replacing, and finding bookmarks

Enhancing the Page with Graphics

Besides the design elements already mentioned, *graphics*—including horizontal rules, borders, boxes, screens, vertical rules, and images—are essential components of good design. Using graphic elements on the page adds interest and diversity. Too many elements can create chaos, however. Graphics should enhance, not ornament, the text; excessive decoration distracts the reader from your message. This section covers the guidelines that govern the judicious use of graphics.

Using Rules

Rules are any lines included on the page. A rule can extend from margin to margin or from gutter to gutter (to border a column); a rule can add emphasis to a word, phrase, or headline by extending the width of the type. Rules are usually measured in points and can be of varying widths.

In Ami Pro, you choose rules by selecting a line pattern or sample. Ami Pro does not label the widths of the rules. When you use a new rule width in the document chapters, however, the width of that rule appears in parentheses. Appendix A lists the widths of all rules used in Ami Pro.

Use a rule to direct the eye. As figure 2.21 illustrates, a wide rule above a major head and smaller rules above the subheads can help tie together the main points of the document. Notice that the rules are above the heads. This practice has evolved from the days of the typewriter, when text was underlined for emphasis because bold and italics were not

Graphic elements include rules, screens, borders; graphic images include illustrations, line art, photographs.

Notice that the rules in figure 2.21 are proportional. Rules above the main head are wider than rules above the subhead.

available. Bold and italics are more attractive than underlining, so typesetters now steer as far away from underlining as possible, even when using a rule.

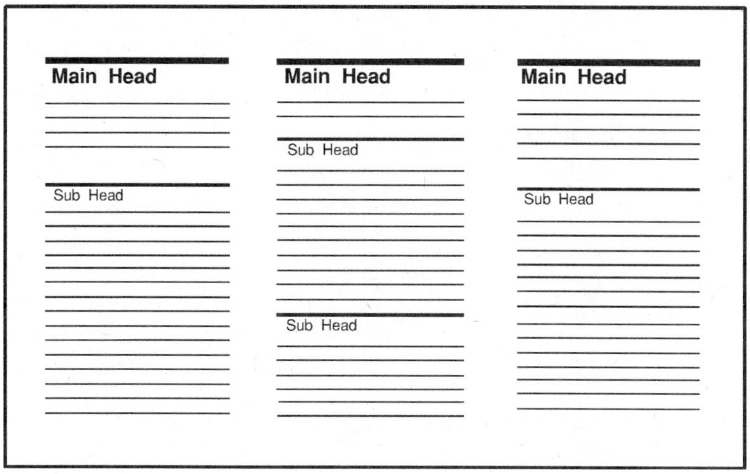

Fig. 2.21   Incorporating rules to tie together main topics and the subheads.

Rules can effectively tie together certain elements, such as columns or pages, within a document. Adding a margin-to-margin rule to a header or footer establishes continuity between pages. Rules placed above or below columns also connect these elements with each other and with columns on other pages. A rule can establish a stopping point for the eye; a thick rule at the bottom of the page, for example, is a signal for the reader to stop. Be careful, however: use a *stopping rule* only when you really want the reader to stop.

Vertical rules, available in the same widths as horizontal rules, are also useful in document design. Use vertical rules to separate columns of left-aligned text; a thin rule between columns keeps the reader's eye from jumping to the adjacent column. Add the rule to the gutter space; don't use a rule *instead* of gutter space.

In some instances, you should not use vertical rules. The gutters of a brochure, for example, leave space for folds. If you place a rule in the gutter, you defeat the purpose of the fold (to divide the columns), and you complicate matters for the person who must fold the brochures exactly on the rule. A rule in the fold is not attractive and may cost you more money. Keep in mind, also, that the page is already gray enough; you need white gutter space more than a rule. With left-aligned text, however, the line endings naturally create white space, and a rule becomes a desirable element.

Don't use vertical rules in place of gutter space, in place of a fold, or with justified text.

You can use rules to divide lists, graphics, and numbers. To divide items in a table, for example, use single rules. Use thick or double rules to divide the heads from the table items. *Callouts*—text taken from the body and set in another type size to attract reader interest in the story or to add information to a graphic image—often use rules to good advantage above and below the text.

You have many opportunities to use rules in almost every document. As always, be consistent. Don't vary thicknesses, length, and direction too much without a plan to promote the message of the text. Every element you use on the page should in some way promote your message.

Using Borders

A *border*, or box, is another graphic element that directs attention to specific items. Because rules make up a box or border, the measurements of border widths are similar. The addition of the *shadow box* creates a pleasing three-dimensional effect. Ami Pro enables you to adjust the width and the position of the shadow.

Ami Pro enables you to set inside and outside margins for frames in Modify Frame Layout.

Include white space with all boxes. Never draw a box past the column guides into the gutters, and always leave room around the box so that the outside of a box doesn't butt against other type. Elements within the box, whether graphics or text, also must have space around them. Without the white space, the box just clutters the document.

You can use a box to isolate certain messages from the rest of the copy, but make sure that the information in the box is related to the other information on the page. In a newsletter on design, for example, an article about margins and columns may take two of the three columns on a page. The third column may contain a box with a short article about the importance of white space.

Draw attention to an announcement by placing it in a box to isolate it from other text. A double or thick rule around an announcement can help reinforce the importance of the announcement. To further enhance the box, you can add a screened background, as shown in figure 2.22. The figure combines a box, a screen, and text to draw attention to the message. Notice, too, that the box has sufficient margin space between the text and the borders of the box.

A box can encompass the entire page, include part or all of a column, divide cells and rows in a table, and contain text or graphic images. Only your imagination limits the uses of boxes—just follow the suggested guidelines for using graphic elements in documents.

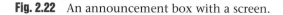

Announcing
GRAND OPENING
humble opinions
JANUARY 9-12
9:00 a.m. - 5:00 p.m

Fig. 2.22 An announcement box with a screen.

Adding Screens

Screens can add emphasis to your boxes. Add a screen to an announcement or story, placing a border around the screen. Because screens are transparent, the text shows through. Be careful, however, that you keep the screen light enough to read the text. Printing text over a 10- to 40-percent screen makes reading easier. When the screen is darker than 40 percent, the text tends to blend in with the background.

Observe the margin rules when using screens. When the screen has no border, avoid running the text to the very edge. Making the screen exceed the line of type by one or two characters results in a more attractive document.

Using Graphic Images

A graphic image can originate from any number of sources, including Ami Pro paint or draw programs; scanners; or any graphic program that can save images in TIFF, EPS, HPGL, PIC, WMF, WPG. Appendix B provides a complete list and explanations of each file extension. Ami Pro enables you to scale, crop, add borders, and frame images. The borders available for framing a picture are the same as for rules and boxes.

As with a box that contains text, make sure that you surround a graphic image by enough white space to let the image *breathe*. *Scaling*—adjusting the size of your graphic—or *cropping*—cutting part of the image out of the picture—gives you control over white space within a framed graphic. You can use Ami Pro's drawing feature to scale and crop graphic images.

Ami Pro does not label the screens in terms of percentages. The lightest screen is approximately 10%, increasing incrementally by 10%.

Ami Pro offers image processing options to adjust contrast, lightness, and darkness of scanned halftones.

The space outside the graphic is also important. Place a margin on all sides of the frame between the graphic and the text, as shown in figure 2.23.

GRAPHIC IMAGES

Import graphic images such as paint and draw programs, scanned images, spreadsheets, and clip art to Ami Pro for Windows. Ami Pro makes it easy with frames. Refer to Appendix B for more information.

Included with your Ami Pro package is a drawing program. You can use it to crop or alter any of your graphic images.

Graphic images must have white space. To effectively use white space, include it both inside the frame and outside.

Left-aligned text in columns, such as this example, affords plenty of white space for any graphic you might add. The graphic to the left has a border with white space inside, and outside. Allow graphic images to breathe. They have more impact on the reader if they are surrounded by sufficient space.

Fig. 2.23   A scanned graphic in a framed box with appropriate white space.

Consider *clustering* images such as photos, illustrations, clip art, and scanned art rather than spreading these elements out. A grouping of images is more appealing to the eye. Also consider *resizing* images so that a dominant picture takes precedence over others. The largest photo (or image) attracts the reader's eye; the smaller images in the cluster then guide the reader's eye through the remainder of the page.

Remember that the purpose of any graphic image in the document is to help the reader comprehend the message. Effective use of graphics enhance rather than minimize the message.

Understanding Types of Documents

U se a graphic image to illustrate your purpose, not to fill space.

Nearly as many document types—brochures, newsletters, books, forms, magazines, programs—exist as there are people to read them; the variety is endless. The following sections describe some of the more common types of documents and include sample layouts.

Flyers

A *flyer* is a quick-sell advertisement designed to announce, introduce, or remind. A flyer can quickly describe sales, grand openings, new items, or products.

Use a flyer to attract immediate attention and get your point across quickly. When you design the flyer, use a short, hard-sell technique that includes a list of products, items, or services, or a short list of dates, times, and places with no unnecessary explanations. Use descriptive adjectives and a minimum of text.

You can print a flyer on one side of a sheet of paper, with one column or two, using large type and bullets. Common flyer sizes, in portrait or landscape orientation, include 5 1/2 by 8 1/2 inches, 8 1/2 by 11 inches, or 8 1/2 by 14 inches. The orientation and placement of text and graphics depend on the copy.

Flyers have no shelf life; they are throwaways because of dated information or the distribution method. Figure 2.24 shows a sample rough of a flyer. Chapter 16, "Producing a Flyer," guides you through the process of producing a flyer.

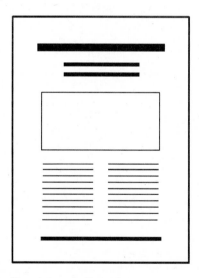

Fig. 2.24 Layout of a flyer in portrait mode.

Brochures

A brochure explains, instructs, details, or informs; therefore, design your brochures for a longer shelf life—to be kept by the customer for future reference. A brochure may include a list and description of products, a detailed explanation of services, or a price list.

Design the cover (page 1 or the front panel that is appropriate for the document) for soft-sell, gently inviting the reader to open and read the contents. Inside, describe the details of the service or product, perhaps with art, logos, or pictures. Titles, headlines, subheads, and captions accompany body text in a brochure. The back panel contains summary points in a bulleted or numbered list, a return address, logo, and often a mailing panel. A logical development of ideas leads the eye through the brochure, starting with the front panel or cover, continuing through the inside, and finishing with the back panel.

Figure 2.25 shows a sample rough for the outside three panels of a six-panel brochure. Panel 1 (the right panel) uses a graphic image with several large headlines. The middle panel (panel 6) contains the required mailing information, and panel 5 (to the far left) is a summary of points and the address of the company.

B e sure that your brochure includes information on what your company or product can do for the customer.

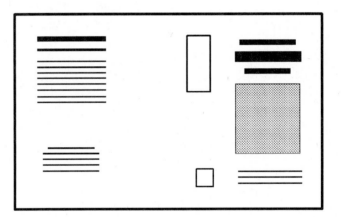

Fig. 2.25   The outside three panels of a six-panel brochure.

N otice the wide margins and gutters in figure 2.26 that provide generous white space.

Figure 2.26 shows the inside of the same brochure, with panels 2, 3, and 4, from left to right. A rule above the text ties the three columns together. The text, with one graphic image, is set up in a simple three-column format.

Brochures usually are printed in the landscape mode—11 inches by 8 1/2 inches for three columns or 14 inches by 8 1/2 inches for four columns. A brochure also can be in the portrait mode—11 by 17 inches, folded to 8 1/2 by 11 inches; 8 1/2 by 11 inches, folded to 5 1/2 inches by 8 1/2 inches; or 8 1/2-by-11-inch single sheets, fastened together. Chapter 17, "Producing a Brochure," describes the details of producing a brochure.

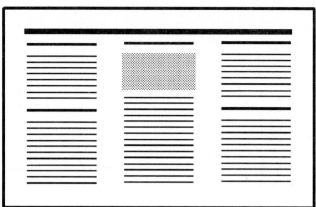

Fig. 2.26   The inside three panels of a six-panel brochure.

When you design a brochure as a permanent reference, make sure that the information, such as prices that may change, is current for the intended shelf life of the document.

Newsletters

You can find newsletters in many sizes, shapes, and designs. A newsletter generally has from 1 to 16 pages, with 1 to 4 columns per page, in portrait or landscape mode. Depending on the purpose, a newsletter can be a throwaway or have a longer life.

Newsletters serve many functions: explain, instruct, detail, inform, announce, introduce, repeat. Companies use newsletters to inform clients or employees or to sell products and services. Some companies even make a business of selling informational newsletters.

Newsletters usually have a *logo* on the front panel. This logo, an easily recognized symbol with decorative type and catchy words or phrases, appears on every issue for consistency. A *dateline*, or *folio*, may appear under the logo. Sometimes centered, sometimes on left and right tabs, the dateline includes the date and, if appropriate, the volume and number of the document.

Headers or footers provide additional consistency. Although some printers consider these elements unnecessary in a four-page document, a header or footer always adds a professional touch. Never place a header or footer on the first page, however. A header includes the page number; it also may give the publication's name, date, volume, or issue number.

Although not absolutely necessary, a table of contents is a good idea in a newsletter that is more than four pages long. By placing a small boxed

Chapters 3 and 5 describe sample logos.

table of contents the front page that showcases four or five items of interest in the publication, you can help draw the reader into the newsletter.

Always include a *masthead*, usually on page two, that contains the editor's name and address, circulation, contact persons, reporters, deadlines for copy, volume number, date, fees, and credits.

If you plan to mail the newsletter, provide each copy with a return address, postage permit, and a place for the mailing labels. Be sure that the postage permit matches the regulations of the postal service for the exact placement, wording, and punctuation in a postage permit box.

The most important design point for a newsletter is consistency between issues. Although individual page layouts differ from issue to issue, the masthead, dateline, publication information, and design elements (column number and width, balance, gutter space, and white space) should remain nearly the same each time. Type styles, spacing, and graphic elements should be consistent.

A newsletter should reflect the design of other publications produced by the same company, tying them together so that they are quickly recognizable. You can accomplish this consistency by using the company's logo in a particular position or by using the same color ink or paper.

Popular sizes for newsletters are 8 1/2 by 11 inches, printed on both sides; 11 by 17 inches, folded to 8 1/2 by 11 inches or smaller for mailing; or 22 by 17 inches, both sides, folded to 11 by 17 inches and then to 8 1/2 by 11 inches (see fig. 2.27).

Forms

Create a style sheet to use with forms for easy design and layout.

So many different forms are used in business each day that identifying all varieties is impossible. A form usually contains text, lines, and boxes. Most forms leave spaces for information such as name, address, phone number, and perhaps descriptions of items, quantities, total costs, and sales tax. You can create fill-in formats for any forms you need to design.

If you design a form to be filled in by a typewriter, placing the rules for typewriter spacing is important. When setting paragraph spacing (*leading*) for the body text, 12-point leading equals single line typewriter spacing, 18-point leading equals 1 1/2 line typewriter spacing, and 24-point leading equals double spacing. Ami Pro makes this task easy by describing leading in terms of line spacing or points.

Be sure that you measure from the top of the form using the same spacing when you place heads, subheads, and so on. Place the company name, address, logo, and name of the form on single-, 1-1/2-, or double-spacing so you don't throw the first typewritten line off. If you change the type size in the middle of the form, recheck the spacing. With Ami Pro, you can produce forms easily with the Table format features described in Chapter 12, "Producing a Purchase Order."

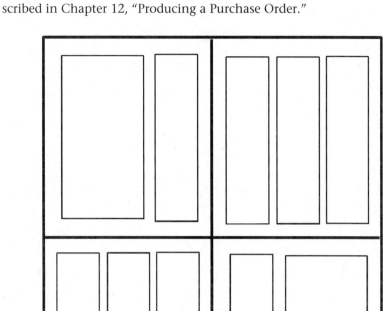

Fig. 2.27 One side of a 22-inch-by-17-inch newsletter with the mirrored balance of columns.

Books

With books of 8 to 12 pages or more, use headers and footers, page numbers, a table of contents, and an index. Chapter 21, "Producing a Book," discusses more detailed information.

When publishing a book with many chapters and miscellaneous elements, organizing the directories or floppy disks properly is important. Organize all information—text files, graphics, spreadsheets, and formatting—according to individual chapters. Save all related data in the same directory or on the same disk.

Create or load a style sheet from Ami Pro to apply to each chapter. A style sheet defines page orientation, margins and columns, headlines, body text, headers, footers, page numbers, macros, and glossaries. The style sheet can also help you achieve consistency throughout the book.

Traditionally, book margin designs provide for easy reading. The bottom margins are usually the largest, inside margins the next largest (to accommodate a binding), and the top and outside margins are the same. Remember that books have facing pages, which your design must accommodate.

Finally, plan the length of the book in sets of four or eight pages because of the way a commercial print shop prints a book. All documents with four or more pages print in a *signature*, or *imposition*, that is folded to form the proper page order. Depending on the trim size of the book, signatures can run on a press in 4-, 8-, or 16-page sets. Figure 2.28 shows a sample of a 4-page signature (meaning four pages up). Don't be concerned with setting up the signature on the computer, but try to plan the document in groups of four. You don't want to pay for three blank pages at the end of the book.

To see where page numbers fall in a four-page signature, take a sheet of typing paper and hold it in the portrait mode. Fold the top edge down to align with the bottom edge. Then fold the left edge to align with the right edge. Now number each page (front and back) consecutively from 1 to 8. Unfold the sheet, and your page numbers should match the numbers shown in figure 2.28.

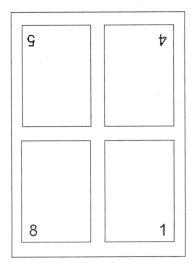 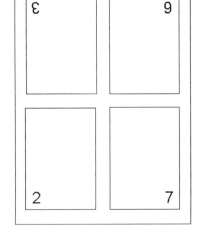

Fig. 2.28   A four-page signature.

Recognizing Design Flaws

When designing page formats, certain rules apply that you should never break. The reasons for these rules vary, but most important is readability. The following list is a summary of things *not* to do:

- Don't overwork the design by including too many graphics, rules, boxes, screens, heads, subheads, or too much bold or italics. Be consistent, and add some contrast. Figure 2.29 is an example of an overworked design.

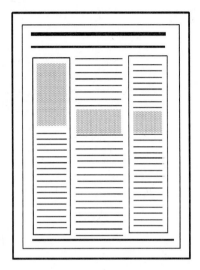

Fig. 2.29   A design with too many boxes and rules.

- Don't start working at the computer without first forming a plan. Gather all text and graphics and prepare a rough before you format.

- Don't change the balance in the middle of a document (see fig. 2.30). Be consistent.

- Don't forget the 50-50 white space rule. Figure 2.31 shows a page with too much gray; this kind of design flaw can make the reader give up even before beginning to read.

Fig. 2.30   A distracting change of balance from page to page.

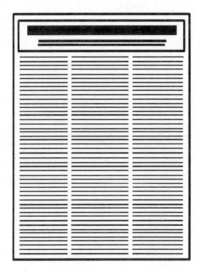

Fig. 2.31   A crowded, overly gray page.

- Don't work with margins under 3/8 inch. Remember that with margins, more is better.

- Don't stray from the margin or column guides.

- Don't change column sizes from page to page to fit copy. Plan ahead.

- Don't use a line length that is too long or too short. Both can distract the reader.

- Don't take space away from gutters to fit in more text. See Chapter 3 for alternative ways to add text effectively.

- Don't design facing pages that clash (see fig. 2.32). Consistent balance and graphic elements can help hold a design together.

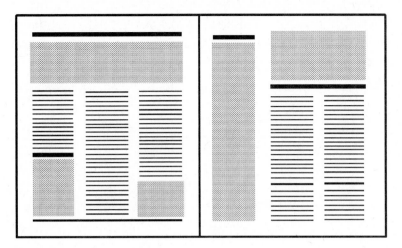

Fig. 2.32   Facing pages that clash.

- Don't use too many graphic rules, borders, or boxes (see fig. 2.29). The general rule is to use no more than one boxed element per page.

- Don't forget the white space (*breathing room*) on the outside and inside of a box or frame.

Recapping

The following steps provide a recap to help refresh your memory and give you a quick reference guide for designing your own documents:

1. Prepare a disk or directory on which to save the document and all its components.

2. Prepare the copy. Enter the handwritten and typewritten material into a word processor.

3. Prepare the graphics.

4. Make thumbnail sketches of the proposed layout.

5. Make a rough draft of two or three pages.

6. Create a style sheet or use one of Ami Pro's.

7. Set page size, orientation, margins, and columns.

8. Begin to format in Ami Pro.

3

Defining and Explaining Typography

Typography, one of the most important elements of design, refers to the style, arrangement, or appearance of typeset elements and the general appearance of the printed page. This chapter presents information about typography as it applies to desktop publishing and to Ami Pro.

For detailed information on how to create a form like this see page 71.

Typography is not just about the font, the style, or the size of the type you choose. It's also about your message, the design of your document, aesthetics, readability, and your reader. A reader judges the type you choose for your document and the way you present it. When looking at a printed page, the reader decides whether to pick up the document and read it and whether to keep the document or throw it away. The reader's decision is often primarily influenced by the strength of your design.

Remember that the purpose of any printed document is to convert a browser into a reader by attracting and maintaining a reader's attention. With careful planning and consideration, you can produce documents that attract and keep a reader's attention.

Understanding Typography Terms

The terms and uses of type date back to the days of handset type. *Roman*, *kerning*, *serif*, x-height, *leading*, and *fonts* are a few familiar terms. These terms are still used today by *typesetters* who compose the typeset page, printers, and word processing and desktop publishing program users.

Type essentially refers to printed characters. In the days of handset type, type referred to the actual blocks the typesetter printed. The term has many derivatives: *typeface*, *type style*, *font*, and *type family*. These traditional terms have changed in meaning with the development of desktop publishing. The following sections provide a brief description of the terms, their traditional meanings, and their significance today.

Typeface

A *typeface* is a specific style or design of the actual letters of type. Helvetica and Times Roman are the two most popular typefaces today. All typefaces rest on a common baseline and have the following characteristics:

- The *x-height* is the height of a font's lowercase letters (such as *a*, *c*, and *x*) that do not have ascenders or descenders.

- An *ascender* is the portion of the lowercase letters *b*, *d*, *f*, *h*, *k*, *l*, and *t* that rises above the x-height of the typeface.

- A *descender* is the portion of the lowercase letters *g*, *j*, *p*, *q*, and *y* that falls below the baseline.

The *baseline* is the invisible line on which all characters rest, as shown in figure 3.1.

The art of setting type is called *typography*.

Because many fonts have unusually long or short ascenders and descenders, the x-height is a better measurement of the actual size of a font than the type size measured in points.

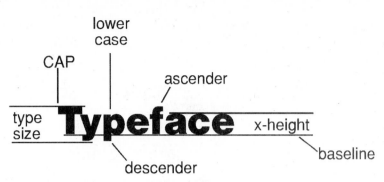

Fig. 3.1   The common elements of all typefaces.

Stroke describes the thickness or weight of the lines that form the letter. *Serifs* are the fine cross strokes across the ends of the main strokes of a character. A serif may be rounded, curved, or stressed. *Stress* refers to the distribution of weight in an individual letter. Helvetica has an even stress; Times Roman is *weighted* to the left. Stress also can refer to slant, as in italic or script types.

In a typeface, each character has components similar to the other characters in the typeface (see fig. 3.2). All Helvetica letters, for example, are *sans serif* with a uniform stroke and *vertical emphasis*. Vertical emphasis refers to the upright stress of the stroke. All Times Roman letters are of varied stroke and have *serifs* that soften the vertical emphasis.

The two-font rule limits the number of typefaces in a particular document to no more than two different typefaces; more than two typefaces can be distracting to the reader. Use one typeface consistently throughout the document for headlines, bylines, and captions; use the other for body text. Helvetica and Avant Garde, for example, are good headline typefaces. For contrast, use Times Roman or Bookman as body text.

U se a serif typeface for the body text and a sans serif typeface for heads and subheads.

Helvetica

Times Roman

Fig. 3.2   Helvetica and Times Roman typefaces.

Type Families

A *type family* includes many typefaces. The common elements of stroke, stress, and serifs identify a particular typeface and the type family to which it belongs. Most desktop publishing programs and font packages use five major families of type, each distinctive in its look and mood: Roman, Sans Serif, Miscellaneous, Text, and Script. Figure 3.3 illustrates these families.

Roman

Sans Serif

MISCELLANEOUS

Text

Script

Fig. 3.3   The five major type families.

Roman

Roman type is a serif type with a varied stroke; it is dignified, classical, and legible, making it an excellent choice for body text. Times Roman, the most popular Roman type, is very common. Newspapers, books, and magazines use Times Roman almost exclusively because it is so easy to read. The serif adds a horizontal flow to the type, making the letters easily recognizable and particularly suitable for body text. Bookman, Garamond, and New Century Schoolbook are additional examples of Roman type. Another traditional category of serif type is the Square Serif. The onset of desktop publishing has combined Roman and Square into one type family.

A Square Serif type has a blunt, blocked serif that projects a forceful, somewhat disjointed appearance. Although excellent for display type or headlines, Square Serif type is not appropriate for body text because the shape of the serifs makes the type hard to read. The Square Serif family includes Palatino and Bodoni.

Sans Serif

Sans serif type has no serifs; the characters are straight, with little or no curved shapes or adornment. A sans serif type usually has a uniform stroke and vertical stress that results in a modern, contemporary, efficient appearance. Although sometimes hard to read in very large amounts of text, you can use sans serif type successfully in captions, headlines, forms, and contracts. Helvetica is the most popular sans serif type. Other sans serif typefaces include Futura and Avant Garde. Avoid using Avant Garde for body text, however, because its rounded letters are exceptionally hard to read.

Sans serif type families usually include a condensed version of the typeface as well as a black or heavy version. Either of these versions is excellent for display type. *Display type* is any showy and/or 48-point or larger type that attracts attention to a document.

Miscellaneous

The Miscellaneous type family has become especially popular with the advent of desktop publishing and drawing programs. Miscellaneous includes any type that is shadowed, outlined, mirrored, or extremely ornate. Use this type for very short display heads (preferably only one per document) and never as body text.

The Miscellaneous category also can include *symbol* and *dingbat* fonts. In these fonts, the letters are symbols, such as pi, accent gravé, arrows, pointing hands, scissors, bullets, and numbers with circles around them. You can find these fonts useful in many documents, but don't overuse them.

Text

Text is a stately, noble, decorative type family that is appropriate only for small amounts of text in formal pieces, invitations, and diplomas. Text typeface is very difficult to read and illegible in all uppercase text. Old English is the most popular Text font in use today.

Uppercase Square Serif type is excellent headline type.

For effective and easy reading, use the Miscellaneous type family in a 36-point or larger size.

Because Text type faces are generally smaller than most other typefaces, don't use Text in smaller than 18-point size.

Script

Script is a decorative, cursive type family that simulates handwriting with its graceful, fluent type. Chancery, Brush, and Linoscript are popular scripts. Reserve the script family for use in invitations, diplomas, or announcements; never use it as body text or in all uppercase letters. Script is hard enough to read without adding the extra burden of uppercase letters.

Fonts

The original meaning of the word *font* was a collection of all characters of one size and typeface: 10-point italic Times, for example. With the advent of desktop publishing, however, it has become a catch-all term that encompasses all sizes and styles of a particular typeface. Now, for example, 6-point to 96-point bold italic Times is considered a font.

Styles

Styles, or *attributes*, denote the characteristics of a typeface, such as bold, italic, light, condensed type that appears to be crowded and thin, extra bold, or any combination of these attributes. Most typefaces include at least bold and italic; many typefaces also include condensed and extra bold. Never use any of these styles as body text.

Measuring Type

Type size is the size of a font, measured in *points* from the top of the tallest ascender to the bottom of the lowest descender. One point equals 1/72 inch; 12 points equal a *pica*; 6 picas equal an inch (thus, 72 points to the inch). Picas are standard measures in printing and typesetting. With 6 picas per inch, close measurements of gutter, spaces, and type are easier than with 1/16, 1/8, 1/4 inch, and so on. Most desktop publishing programs offer the choice of measuring in picas or inches. The measurement you use is a matter of personal preference. Figure 3.4 shows common sizes and uses of type.

Body Text

The main portion of any document is the body text. Common sizes for body text are 9, 10, 11, and 12 points. Type smaller than 9 points is too small to read comfortably, and body text larger than 12-point type is also difficult to read unless it is geared for visually impaired readers.

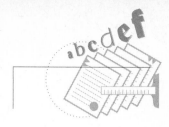

Body Text
9-point type
10-point type
11-point type
12-point type

Subheads
12-POINT BOLD
14-Point Italics

Heads or Headlines
18-Point Bold Italics
24-POINT BOLD
36-Point Bold Italics
48-POINT BOLD

Display Type

60-Pt. Narrow

72-Pt. Bold

Fig. 3.4 Common type sizes.

Headings

In major headings, 18-, 24-, 36-, or 48-point type are the better choices. Heads can be bold, bold italic, or, if short (two to four words), all upper-case. Notice that the common sizes do not include 19, 23, 37, or 44. Although most programs offer you the choice of these odd sizes, avoid using them. The common sizes have been time-tested as the most effective sizes for most situations. An 18-point head, for example, fits 10-point body text well and is comfortable to read. A 19-point head may not be that different in size, but it looks different on the printed page. Your screen also may not show the proper size if you choose an odd point size, and your printer may not be capable of printing it. For more information about screen and printer fonts, see Appendix C.

Subheads

Use subheads to categorize main topics. The subhead is more significant than the body text, yet less important than the heads. Usually bold, italic, or all uppercase, a subhead can be 12- or 14-point type, depending on the size of the document. The larger the page, the larger the point size.

Display Type

Display type is large, sometimes ornamental type that you can use sparingly in documents to grab attention. The size of the display type depends on the size of the document, the length of the word or phrase, and the space the rest of the copy uses. Display type can be 48-, 60-, 72-point size or even larger. At this time, the largest available type in a desktop publishing program is 256 points. Some programs enable you to create a 125-point font and then scale it to 400 percent when printing. The size of the type you use depends on the program and the fonts installed in your printer. Bit-mapped fonts are seldom larger than 72 point; PostScript fonts provide the largest sizes. For more information about bit-mapped and PostScript fonts, see Appendix C.

Type Sizes

Different typefaces of the same size may not measure the same. Further-more, each manufacturer of type has its own version of each face. Script and Text fonts, for example, are almost always smaller than serif or sans serif fonts. Type in 18-point Chancery looks more like 14-point type when printed. Similarly, 28-point Old English type looks more like 18-point type when printed. Any font made by ITC is larger than other manufacturers' type of the same size. Helvetica and Avant Garde are generally larger than Times Roman or Palatino (see fig. 3.5).

Chancery
Helvetica
Times Roman

Fig. 3.5 18-point Chancery, Helvetica, and Times Roman.

Although desktop publishing programs offer many type sizes for use in documents, limit the number of sizes you use in one document to avoid distracting your readers. Use no more than four different sizes in a one-page document, and no more than eight in a longer document. Figure 3.6 shows proper sizing for types in an 8 1/2-by-11-inch sales flyer. Notice the use of display type, heads, and subheads. Display type, in this case, is Times Roman set in extremely large type size.

When you choose type sizes, determine the most important ideas in your copy. Arrange your copy from the most important ideas to the least important. Decide what information will most attract the reader and make the headline the largest type on the page. Keep proportion in mind as well. A flyer with 60-point display type and 10-point body text is not proportional. Strive for balance in your visual presentation.

Using Attributes To Improve Your Document

Attributes, or styles, emphasize a word or group of words. Examples of attributes include bold, italic, bold italic, all uppercase letters in short headings or subheads, and condensed or expanded type. Applying an attribute to a small amount of text is more emphatic than applying it to large blocks of text. Avoid using too many different attributes in a document; a little bold and italic is fine; but using bold, italic, all upper-case, and condensed type in one document is too much. Figure 3.7 illustrates the appropriate use of attributes in a document.

Never use an attribute, such as bold, italic, or uppercase, as body text; the text is impossible to read.

SAVE ON ❶

OFFICE ❷
SUPPLIES

- Chairs
- File Cabinets

- Calculators
- Electric Typewriters ❸

- Computer Paper
- Legal Pads

2 DAYS ONLY-JUNE 12 & 13 ❹
9:00 a.m. to 5:00 p.m. ❸

Davis Office Supplies ❹
112 East Street ❸

❶ 36-point bold Helvetica

❷ 60-point bold Times Roman

❸ 28-point lightface Helvetica

❹ 28-point bold Times

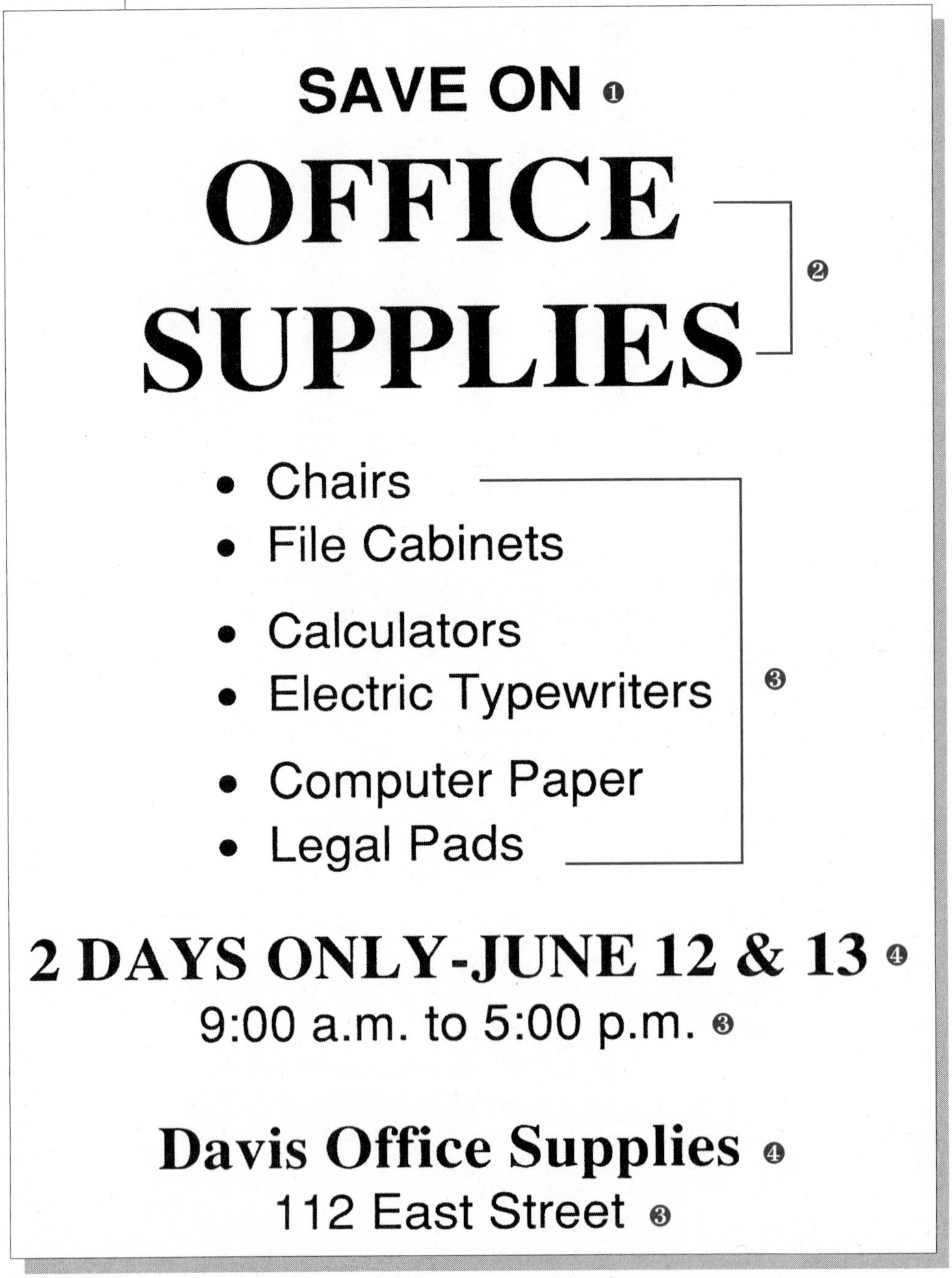

Fig. 3.6 A sample flyer with three type sizes, two type styles, and two typefaces.

You can easily misuse attributes. You should use underlining, for example, only with a column of numbers. Too much underlining makes a document more difficult to read and creates an unprofessional look. Reserve double underlining for the total of a column of numbers.

Using bold, italic, and all uppercase letters in the same document, particularly on the same page, works against readability, as figure 3.8 illustrates. If the reader must strain to read your document, the document will probably not be read.

You can use uppercase letters at the beginning of each word in a headline or subhead or with the first word only. Sometimes all uppercase letters may be appropriate for a short head. All uppercase letters for body text is never appropriate, however, just as all lowercase letters are never used for a heading.

Using Spacing

Your document must include white space for the sake of design and readability. Crowded text and too much gray on the page fatigues a reader's eyes. To include white space in a document, you can use wider margins (as discussed in Chapter 2, "Using Elements of Design"). You also can increase white space by controlling the spacing within the text.

When reading, the eye does not look closely at each word. Instead, the reader uses the shape of words—the presence of ascenders and descenders in relation to the body of the word—to recognize words. This process explains why all uppercase is hard to read. You can use the spacing of letters, words, lines, and paragraphs to help your reader get through your material quickly and easily.

You use four main categories of spacing in typesetting documents: letter, word, line, and paragraph spacing. When you apply spacing, be consistent to keep the reader on track and help prevent diversions.

Letter Spacing

The spacing between letters can make a word easier or harder to read. Certain letters fit together to form instantly recognizable pairs, such as *th*, *er*, *sp*, and *ly*. When too much space occurs between letters, however, recognizing letters as pairs is more difficult. This problem is the main reason typesetters rarely use monospaced fonts, such as Courier, for documents. In a *monospaced* font, each letter takes up exactly the same amount of space, whether the letter is an *i* or an *m*. Figure 3.9 compares Courier and Helvetica. Notice how the difference in the letter spacing makes Helvetica much easier to read.

Letter spacing is one reason condensed type is never used as body text; the letters are too close together for comfortable reading of more than one or two words at a time.

HUMBLE OPINIONS

Software Packages

Do you want to learn more about your software programs, spreadsheets, databases, word processing and desktop publishing programs? **Humble Opinions** offers training and instruction in many of the popular software packages for the personal computer.

Purchasing Printing

How well do you communicate with your print shop? Is your printing right? If not, you may need help with your projects. Learn terms your printer uses, and how they apply to you and your print job. **Humble Opinions** can help you get that job done, precisely and on time.

Planning The Future

What are your software needs? Which program can help you organize your daily chores? A growing business must have the proper tools to expand. **Humble Opinions** can help you choose effective software programs that help you plan your future.

Fig. 3.7   Attributes used for emphasis in a document.

HUMBLE OPINIONS

Software Packages

Do you want to learn more about your **software programs,** *spreadsheets, databases, word processing* and *desktop publishing programs?* **Humble Opinions** offers *training and instruction* in many of the popular **software packages** for the personal computer.

Purchasing Printing

How well do you communicate with your *print shop?* Is your job always *printed right?* If not, you may need help with your projects. Learn *terms* your printer uses, and how they apply to you and your print job. **Humble Opinions** can help you get that job done, precisely and on time.

Planning Your Future

What are your **software needs?** Which program can help you organize your daily chores? A growing business needs *proper tools* to expand. **Humble Opinions** can help you evaluate and choose *effective* **software programs** that help you plan your future.

Fig. 3.8   Overuse of attributes in a document.

Courier is a monospaced font. Each letter and
punctuation mark occupies exactly the same
amount of space. For this reason, Courier is
difficult to read.

Helvetica is a proportionally spaced font. Each letter is only
as wide as it needs to be. Helvetica is much easier to read
than Courier.

Fig. 3.9   Letter spacing in Courier and Helvetica.

Kerning is a technique that brings letters closer together so that their
spacing looks correct. Most desktop or word processing programs space
letters properly without requiring adjustment. Some letter pairs, however, may need manual adjustment—for example, *AV*, or *WA* (see
fig. 3.10).

AVANT   AVANT

Fig. 3.10   Letter pairs before (left) and after (right) kerning.

Ami Pro automatically spaces letters. When using larger type for heads,
however, you may need to kern letter pairs. You can manually kern
letter pairs in Ami Pro only if your printer is PostScript. Choose the Tools
menu, then User Setup. In the Setup dialog box, choose Options, and
when the Options dialog box appears, choose Pair Kerning, along with
Flow in Background, in the Options box. *Pair kerning* requires more time
and memory for Ami Pro to perform than if you didn't turn on kerning;
if the Flow option is selected, the document displays and prints faster.

Word Spacing

Correct spacing between words is critical to ease of reading. Words too
close together create a dense gray page that is uninviting to a reader. On
the other hand, words spaced too far apart create "holes," or large areas
of white space between words apparent in the overall gray of the page.
Too much or too little spacing makes the reader work too hard to get the
message (see fig. 3.11).

Words can be spaced too close together. If word spacing
is too tight, the gray of the page is too dense, causing the
reader to search for each individual word. Justified text
can be the root of the problem, combined with a column
that is too narrow.

Word spacing is important to readability. Too much
space between words can create "rivers" of white space
that flow through the page. Text that is justified
tends to create wide word spacing if hyphenation is
turned off.

Fig. 3.11   Words spaced too close together (top) and too far apart (bottom).

Fully justified text, which is aligned flush left and flush right, often causes problems with spacing by creating large gaps between words or letters. To avoid this problem, you can use *discretionary hyphens*, created by pressing Ctrl+- (hyphen). Ami Pro uses the discretionary hyphen only when necessary to better space the line of type. Be aware that a discretionary hyphen is different from a plain hyphen. A discretionary hyphen appears only when needed, whereas a plain hyphen is a permanent part of the word. If you insert a plain hyphen by pressing the hyphen key only and then later insert or delete text, causing the text to move, the hyphen still appears in the middle of the word.

One more note about word spacing: never use two spaces after a period. This method is a leftover from the days of typewriters and monospaced fonts. Using two spaces at the end of a sentence creates holes in the text. If you have difficulty remembering not to press the space bar twice, you can enter text in your usual manner and then perform a search and replace to delete the double spaces.

Line Spacing

You can adjust the line spacing to add a small amount of extra text to a page.

Line spacing, interline spacing, and *leading* (*LED-ing*) all refer to the amount of space between two lines of text. You are probably familiar with the single-, one-and-a-half-, and double-spacing of typewriters; Ami Pro uses the same terms for line spacing. In Ami Pro, you also can measure line spacing in points (by choosing the measurement box in any dialog box). If you prefer, Ami Pro automatically spaces lines for you, increasing the space in proportion to the size of the type. With most documents, you probably don't need to adjust the spacing.

The tallest character in a particular typeface and size is the guideline for measuring line spacing. Uppercase letters, ascenders, and descenders all must have enough space to prevent them from overlapping letters above or below them. The typical line spacing equals 20 percent of the size of the font, although many word processors and desktop publishing programs use 30 percent.

Because type sizes are measured in points, you may want to learn the measurements for leading in points as well. For example, 10-point type uses 12-point leading (called *10 on 12* and written as *10/12*). 14-point type uses 16-point leading, and 18-point type uses 20- or 22-point leading.

If you need to adjust the leading for a layout, remember that the larger the x-height of a typeface, the more leading you need. Sans serif type, because of its vertical emphasis, also requires extra leading to improve readability. Headlines may require less leading for effortless reading, and body text may require more for the same purpose. You can enlarge the spacing to meet the needs of your document; however, you can reduce the leading only to the size of the body type, to 10-point type on 10-point leading, for example. This spacing is close but workable. Figure 3.12 shows three examples of leading with the same size body type.

This is 10-point Times Roman on 12-point spacing. This spacing works well for body text. It is comfortable to read because there is enough space between the lines.

This is 10-point Times Roman on 14-point spacing (auto). This spacing is still comfortable for the reader, and it allows you to spread out your copy to fill extra space.

This is 10-point Times Roman on 16-point spacing. You may want to use this spacing if your line length is longer than usual for 10-point type or to fit copy.

Fig. 3.12 Different leading used with the same size body type.

As a general rule, add more space above the head and less space below the head.

Line spacing is also a good way to achieve extra white space. A headline or subhead always needs space above and below it to set it apart from the page. Typesetters handle this problem by creating a *space*, a paragraph style (usually 4-point or 6-point type on 6-point leading) that provides a set amount of extra space. When needed, the space is applied above or below the head or subhead to give it more breathing room. Only a paragraph return appears on the line. You can accomplish the same effect by adding extra line spacing.

Paragraph Spacing

Add no more than two lines of space between body text paragraphs. The preferred spacing is 1 to 1 1/2 lines.

After the letters, words, and lines of your document have the proper amount of space, you may want to add extra space between paragraphs. Remember this simple rule: if you indent the first line of the paragraph, don't add an extra line of space between paragraphs; if you don't indent the first sentence, add at least one line of space between each paragraph. If readers can easily find the first sentence of a paragraph, they can understand the division of topics in the document more easily. Figure 3.13 shows examples of paragraph spacing and indentation.

Indent the first line when you are not adding extra space between paragraphs. Formatting your body text in this manner allows you to fit more copy on the page.

The indent of the first line indicates the beginning of the paragraph and adds valuable white space to a very gray page. Indenting the first line looks better when your type is justified.

If you left-align your text, consider using extra spacing between the paragraphs instead of indenting the first line. The ragged right adds white space and an indented first line on the left would serve to confuse the reader.

Of course, applying left-aligned text with extra paragraph spacing means you will not fit as much copy on the page. Perhaps you can add more pages.

Fig. 3.13 Examples of paragraph spacing with and without indentation.

Using Text Alignment

Alignment is a method of organizing text. Body text, headlines, tabs, and all text must have an alignment (left- or right-aligned, centered, or fully justified). With any text alignment you choose, make sure that the alignment remains consistent throughout the entire document. Changes in alignment from page to page can be disconcerting to the reader. Figure 3.14 illustrates each of the four text alignments.

Left-Aligned Subhead

Left-aligned heads, subheads and body text provide consistency of design. The reader always knows where the next line begins. In addition, the ragged right line endings create white space.

Right-Aligned Subhead

Text that is right-aligned
should be short and
very interesting.

Center-Aligned Subhead

Any centered text should be short
and be well-arranged. Also make sure
that the line length is pleasing to the eye.

Justified Text

Never justify a subhead or head. Because the type is larger, it will space unequally to fit. It would not look good. Therefore, this justified text has a left-aligned head. Again, justified text allows you to fit more copy on the page.

Fig. 3.14 Examples of text alignment

Left Alignment

Left-aligned text has a flush left margin and ragged right margin. Using left-aligned text for body text has many advantages. The ragged right margin adds valuable white space to break up the page. Of course, if the right margin is too ragged, the white space can be distracting. Left-aligned text generally has very little or no hyphenation, and should never have more than two hyphens in succession. You can use discretionary hyphens, however, to keep the ragged right line endings more even. If the right margin is too ragged and has too many hyphens, you need to adjust the column width.

Another advantage of left-aligned text is that equal word spacing occurs naturally, providing an even texture to the gray of the page. Left-aligned text works well in narrow columns because it directs the reader's eye to the beginning of a line quickly and easily. Similarly, left-aligned headlines and subheads enable readers to find the next topic easily and add additional white space. When left-aligning text, place a vertical rule in the gutters to help divide the columns and add a professional touch to the page.

One disadvantage to left-aligned text is that you cannot fit in as much copy on a page as with fully justified text. If you have a large amount of copy and few pages on which to set it, left-aligned text may take up too much space.

Right Alignment

Right-aligned text, with its flush right margin and ragged left margin, is rarely used for body text. Right alignment is reserved for a headline or subhead to attract attention. If you use right-aligned heads, be sure to mix upper- and lowercase; never use all uppercase. Also make sure that the heads are very short and that the overall design of the piece reflects and reinforces the use of right-aligned text.

Avoid using right-aligned text for heads or subheads of more than three or four short lines or for captions and callouts. Right-aligned text is also not appropriate for body text because it is very difficult to read.

Center Alignment

Centered text, used most often for headlines, subheads, and datelines, has ragged left and right margins. Center alignment provides even word spacing, visual interest, and an air of dignity to the document. Centered heads work well with fully justified body text.

Don't use too much line spacing with left-aligned text; too much space can make the text hard to read.

Always use justified body text with right-aligned heads to emphasize the flush right alignment.

You can use centered text for figure or photograph captions to create a balanced effect.

Although rarely used for body text, you can center certain items: lists of names or dates, invitations or announcements, and very short lines of text in a flyer. Centered body text is hard to read because the reader's eyes must search for the beginning and end of each line.

Full Justification

Fully justified text has flush left and right margins. It is perfect for long materials such as books, articles, or reports. The page appears organized, quiet, and comfortable for the reader.

Fully justified alignment enables you to fit more copy on the page, because, unlike left-aligned text, justified text uses all the space on the line. Avoid any temptation to reduce gutters with justified text; because of the even gray appearance of the page, you need the white space of the gutters. Add extra space to the gutter if possible.

Watch for uneven word spacing with fully justified text. Justification sometimes forces long words to the next line or squeezes short words to the current line. When using fully justified text, always make sure that automatic hyphenation is turned on. Manual manipulation of the line, including editing the text or adjusting letter spacing in a line, is sometimes necessary. Discretionary hyphens often are helpful for correcting uneven word spacing.

Never use fully justified text for headlines. A headline, or subhead, in larger type than the body text, is too hard to justify without getting unequal and unsightly word spacing.

Using Indentation

An *indentation* (indent) is the distance from the left margin to the beginning of the text or from the right margin to the end of the text. Indents control the width of the paragraph. You can apply an indent to the first sentence of a paragraph or to the left and/or right of an entire paragraph so that it stands out from the rest of the text.

A positive measurement indents the text toward the center of a page or column. A 2-inch indent from the left, for example, indents the paragraph two inches. A negative number used as an indent, such as –1 inch, produces an *outdent*, or *hanging indent*. Used for bullets, numbered lists, or subtitles, a hanging indent is a useful tool for text formatting (see fig. 3.15).

OUTDENT	An outdent is where a subtitle, a bullet, a number, and so on, hangs to the left while the rest of the paragraph indents.

Fig. 3.15   A hanging indent used for a subtitle.

Using Tabs

A *tab* is an organizational tool that enables you to line up lists of items across a line. You can align names, numbers, and prices, with tabs. A tab stop enables you to move to a specific point quickly and efficiently by pressing the Tab key.

A tab aligns to the left, right, center, or decimal point. These alignments are similar to text alignments. Left tabs are flush left and ragged right.

Right tabs are flush right; they work well with a left tab and *leaders*— periods, hyphens, or solid lines between the items on the left and the items on the right that *lead* the eye to the end of the line (see fig. 3.16). If you use a leader with a right tab, be sure to press Tab and the space bar before typing the item to be aligned on the right tab. This space separates the leader from the item, making it easier to read.

Humble Opinions ------------------------------	C. O. Plumley
Computer Supplies ---------------------------	S. U. Blackwell
Software Unlimited--------------------------------	T. O. Angle
Modems R Us ------------------------------------	R. I. Barrett

Fig. 3.16   Leaders used with a right tab.

Use a center tab for names, places, or other special items. Make sure that you allow enough space from the margin for the longest line; otherwise, the tab will not work.

A decimal tab is especially useful for lists of numbers, percentages, or currency. The tab stop is on the decimal point; any numbers containing a decimal point automatically align on the decimal point. Figure 3.17 shows examples of center and decimal tabs.

```
Dell Industries --------------------------------------- $12,702.00
HO Consultants --------------------------------------- 1250.00
Bender Products, Inc. --------------------------------- 34.99
```

Fig. 3.17   Examples of center and decimal tabs.

Organizing Text on a Page

Now that you understand the basic terms of typesetting and the characteristics of type, you can begin organizing your text on the page. Chapter 2, "Using Elements of Design," discusses ways of organizing the page. Producing thumbnails and roughs is an excellent way to begin; using columns and grids also can help you place your text.

After composing the body of your document, create heads and subheads that describe the text in an interesting and stimulating way. Use active verbs in the heads whenever possible to attract the reader to the text, and set the heads in a type that separates them from the body of the document. The definitions presented in the following sections can help you choose type sizes for heads, subheads, and body text.

Display Heads

A *display head* is a heading in a 48-point or larger size and, sometimes, in an ornate font. A display head attracts attention with its content. Words such as *Sale, Announcement,* and *Grand Opening* are all candidates for a display head. Avoid creating display heads of more than three or four words and use only one display head per document. Of course, you don't have to use any display heads at all; many documents look better with regular headlines. Refer to figure 3.4 for examples.

Display type can be 48, 60, or 125 point. The size of the display type depends on the size of the rest of the type in the document.

Heads

Heads, or *headlines,* are short, concise phrases that attract attention and organize the page. You can use a different type style from the body text or the same type style in a larger size and bold. Heads can be left-aligned, right-aligned, or centered; they can be bold, bold italic, or all uppercase (if short). Typical sample headlines are *Refrigerators Half Price, Designer Scarves Are Here,* and *Newsletter Wins Award.* Refer to figure 3.4 for examples.

Heads can be in 18-, 24-, 36-, or 48-point type, depending on the size of the other type in the document.

Subheads

Subheads further divide a topic under a heading. Smaller than the head but larger than the body text, a subhead should be bold or italic to be noticeable. Subheads help break up the copy for easier reading; they also supply visual contrast to a gray page and identify the contents of specific paragraphs. Subheads can be in a contrasting typeface, bold, italic, or indented and left-aligned, right-aligned, or centered.

Subheads can be 12- or 14-point type.

Be consistent throughout each document, limiting your use of typefaces (remember the two-font rule). If, for example, your body text is Times Roman and your heads are bold Helvetica, your subheads may be bold Times or bold italic Helvetica. Sample subheads to follow the preceding heads are *All Brands of Refrigerators are in Stock, Choosing Your Scarf to Match Your Shoes,* or *Company Newsletter Editor is Proud.* Refer to figure 3.4 for examples.

Captions

A *caption* is text that briefly explains illustrations, artwork, photos, or figures. A reader often looks at a caption before reading the body text of a document. Captions are important tools for getting the message to the reader.

Place captions next to, above, or below the illustration or photo. Traditionally, captions are placed beneath the photo or illustration. Changing the tradition by offsetting the photo and placing the caption to the left or right creates an exciting change in design, attracting more attention. Placing a caption above a photo or illustration produces a mini-head effect that also can pull the reader into the document.

Align the caption with the body text, making it the width of the illustration if possible. You can center short captions to match your headlines, but make sure that they are consistent throughout your document. Because captions usually are 8- or 9-point italic type with close leading, a typeface such as Helvetica or another sans serif font is easy to read.

Body Text

Body text makes up the bulk of your copy. Set body text in paragraph form, left-aligned or fully justified, and choose a typeface that is easy to read, such as Times Roman. Most people who browse through printed material read the heads, subheads, and captions before the body text. Keep this in mind when designing and writing your heads and subheads.

When a document contains photos—especially striking, interesting photos—the reader's eye almost always moves to the photo before the caption. If these items keep the reader's interest and the items accompany a story or article, the eyes move next to the article.

Text for Emphasis

In addition to the methods already described, you also can attract attention to topics in a document using jumplines, callouts, large first characters, bullets, numbered lists, and logos. The following sections discuss the techniques for using these items.

Jumplines

A *jumpline* continues a story or article on another page. Sometimes a jumpline also can be a method of leading the reader into the document. You can place the beginning of a story or article on the first page of a newsletter, for example, and use a jumpline to direct the reader to page 3 to continue the story or article. The reader must open the newsletter to complete the story and, you hope, find something else of interest. Newspapers use jumplines in this way—they begin several important articles on the front page and continue them elsewhere in the paper.

Remember that whenever you use jumplines, some readers will not make the jump. Instead, they read other articles, meaning that the remainder of the jumped article probably will be ignored. A good use of jumplines, provided that the main head is strong enough to attract the reader's initial interest, is to direct the reader to the following page.

A jumpline is usually written in all lowercase italics and placed in parentheses at the end of the column. The type may be a point or two smaller than the body text. The alignment can be centered, or left- or right-aligned. All that is necessary is a statement such as the following:

(continued on page 3)

Break the story at the end of a paragraph or sentence. To continue the story, place a small, abbreviated head at the break, telling readers where they can find the rest of the story. On the *jump page*, repeat the abbreviated *jump head*, and tell readers the page number from which the story was jumped.

Callouts

A *callout* is a short, pithy statement or phrase taken from the body text to entice the reader into reading the entire piece. It is usually set in

U se design considerations to direct the reader's eye on the page.

A rticles continued with jumplines in a newspaper usually include the most important information on the first page.

12- or 14-point bold or italic text, centered or left-aligned high on the page (ideally, in the center column of a three-column page). The callout is always the same width as the column, with plenty of white space around it. A box or rules above and below the callout text provides a nice touch. Figure 3.18 shows a callout in a column of text from a newsletter.

Use a callout to attract the attention of the reader to the page. As he skims through your newsletter, or article, he sees an interesting phrase in the callout that makes him want to read more!

A callout says read me first!

A callout should never break into the middle of a sentence or paragraph. Always place it at a natural break, high up on the page, and remember to balance it with the rest of the text and graphics on the page. Don't do more than one callout per page.

Rules, borders, or shadow boxes are excellent ways to separate the callout from the rest of the text and give it some emphasis. Make sure you allow for plenty of white space! Choose 12- or 14-point light face, bold, italics or bold italics type for a callout.

Fig. 3.18 A callout drawing attention to the story.

Large First Characters

When designing longer documents, such as newsletters, magazines, or books, you may use a large first character, or *drop cap*, for emphasis at the beginning of each section (see fig. 3.19). A large first character is usually just the first letter of the first sentence in a section or chapter. You can break up large amounts of text in this manner, instead of using subheads. A good rule of thumb is to use no more than one drop cap per page. However, for gray pages, one drop cap at the top of the page and one at the bottom is also acceptable. More than two drop caps make your document look cluttered. A similar but infrequently used technique is to raise the uppercase letter so that it extends well above the first line of type.

L arge first characters, sometimes called drop caps, are a decorative effect with no other real value. Although they are nice, use them sparingly at the beginning of a chapter, or a section. Under no circumstances use them at the beginning of every paragraph.

Fig. 3.19   A drop cap used for emphasis.

When using 12-point body text, a large first character can be 28 to 36 points and bold. (The drop cap in figure 3.19 is 36 points.) A drop cap also can be a different typeface or enclosed in a shadow frame for more emphasis. Be consistent with large first characters: if you choose 36-point bold to use with 12-point body text, use the same ratio throughout the document.

Bullets

A *bullet* is a dot, asterisk, or other symbol that organizes and attracts attention to a list of items (see fig. 3.20). Beginning each list item on a new line and placing a bullet in front of it makes the list easier to read. Bullets should be consistent throughout the document in size, indentation, and amount of space following the bullet. Bullets imply that no one item on a list is more important than the other items. If a bulleted item has more than one line, make sure that the bullet is on a hanging indent so that it doesn't get lost in the text.

A mi Pro 3.0 offers a wide variety of bullet choices, including arrows, diamonds, and squares.

> Use bullets to emphasize a list:
> - Always indent the bullet and text.
> - If a line wraps, be sure it is at the same indent of the previous line.
> - Avoid using different bullet symbols within one document.

Fig. 3.20 Bullets used to make a list easy to read.

Numbered Lists

In contrast to bulleted lists, numbered lists signify an order of importance to the items they contain. Numbers also specify how many items the list contains. Use a hanging indent for numbered lists so that the reader can move easily from one item to the next.

Logos

A *logo* is another tool that provides emphasis. A symbol of identity, a logo projects a particular image for a company or product. You can design a logo out of text by stretching, condensing, reversing, or rotating the type. You can place the logo type on a curve, in an envelope to stretch it, or in perspective. You also can place text in a frame, position a rule above or below the text, or reduce the leading so that two words touch.

Ami Pro offers many possibilities for designing logos. Figure 3.21 shows four logos designed in Ami Pro. When designing logos, you can ignore most type rules. As long as the logo is easily recognizable, fairly small, and used consistently, it is open to all your creativity.

Producing Style Sheets

A *style sheet* refers to the formatted page and text, the overall design of the columns, margins, tabs, and so on. A style sheet also lists assignments for typeface, type size and style, spacing, alignment, and indents. You use a particular style sheet for a particular type of document. A newsletter style sheet, for example, is different from a form style sheet. You can, of course, format each individual paragraph of body text, each head, and each tab. A style sheet, however, enables you to format the element once, save it as a paragraph style, and then use it over and over again throughout the document and later in other, similar documents.

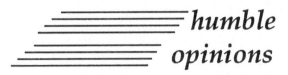

Fig. 3.21 Sample logos designed with Ami Pro.

A style sheet ensures consistency within and between documents. Suppose that in the first issue of a newsletter, all major headings are set 18 point, bold, and centered. Every head in the document conforms to this description. When you produce the second issue of the newsletter, you can use the style sheet you created for the first newsletter to set all major settings in the second issue in 18 point, bold, and centered. The style sheet ensures that the two issues look alike and saves you much time setting up the paragraph styles.

As mentioned in Chapter 2, "Using Elements of Design," Ami Pro has built-in style sheets. You also can create your own style sheets. For consistency and efficiency, use a style sheet with any document you frequently produce.

Understanding Design Flaws

Readability is among the primary reasons for making good design and type choices. If your work is not easy to read or the design is distracting, you are wasting your time producing the document. The most important thing to remember is the comfort and interest of the reader. The following list describes the choices to avoid when setting type:

- Don't use too many typefaces in one document; remember the two-font rule.

- Don't use all uppercase with Script and Text fonts.

- Don't use bold or italic as body text.

- Don't use all uppercase for more than three or four words.

- Don't place two spaces after a period.

- Don't use too many type styles or sizes in a document. Too much variation confuses and distracts the reader.

- Don't use type larger than 12 points or smaller than 9 points for body text.

- Don't use more than two hyphens in a row. Watch the letter and word spacing. If you have too many hyphens, try adjusting the column width.

- Don't use plain hyphens; use discretionary hyphens.

- Don't use inconsistent line and paragraph spacing. The reader should be able to scan effortlessly across the page.

- Don't apply more than one alignment to body text in a document. Match the alignments of body, heads, and subheads.

- Don't make captions as large as body text, but don't make them too small to read. As a general rule, make the caption one or two points smaller than the body, in bold or italic.

- Don't indent a paragraph too much. Use the line length as a guide. A 2 1/2-inch line length, for example, requires no more than a 1/4-inch indent. A 4-inch line length, however, may use up to a 1/2-inch indent. Avoid using indents of less than 1/4-inch and more than 1/2-inch.

- Don't indent the first sentence more than 1/4 inch. Always use a tab to indent, never spaces.

- Don't use too many callouts, jumplines, bullets, bold, or italic.

- Don't use different styles of bullets in the same document.

- Don't work without a style sheet.

Recapping

Use the following steps as a quick reference guide:

1. Gather and organize all materials before beginning your project.

2. Put your copy in priority order. Place your most important facts at the top of the page with large headlines to match, then your next most important items with smaller heads, and so on.

3. Set up a style sheet for your document. Plan the typefaces (no more than two), type sizes, type styles, alignment, and spacing.

4. Plan any emphasis type, such as callouts, bullets, and logos.

5. Refer to "Recapping" in Chapter 2.

4

Planning and Purchasing Printing

When your document is complete, you need to reproduce it. You should decide on the method of reproduction during the document planning stages; designing your document around the possibilities and limitations of the reproduction process helps you avoid problems. If you need only a small number of copies, you can print the document on your laser printer. If you need a large number of copies, however, using your laser printer to produce the copies is not cost effective. Instead, you need the services of a commercial or quick print shop.

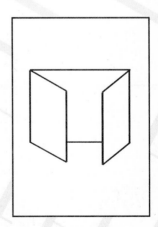

For detailed information on how to create a document like this see page 105.

The method of re-production you choose depends primarily on the number of copies you need. Special techniques, such as adding color or perforating, also may affect your choice.

This chapter covers printing services, price quotations, paper and ink choices, and a few finishing procedures, such as folding and fastening techniques. The information is presented only as an overview. If you have more detailed questions, consult your print shop.

Reviewing Design for Printing

Commercial printing is expensive; the more you prepare for a commercial printer's procedures, the less you pay. You can perform certain tasks during layout that make commercially printing your document easier and less expensive.

If you have a laser printer, you can use the output for commercial printing. Your document may need finishing touches, however, such as crop marks or halftones. You can paste up these elements yourself or have the print shop do it. If you want high-quality output, you can take your document to a service bureau or a print shop equipped with a high-resolution imagesetter.

Working with Paste-Up

Paste-up means bringing together all the pieces of your completed document in final form so that the page can be photographically reproduced. If your document requires crop marks, photographs, artwork, and illustrations, it needs paste-up work.

A page formatted so that it needs *no* changes, modifications, additions, or deletions, is *camera ready*. Camera-ready copy goes to the camera department, where a negative is made of the final document. The negative is used to make a *plate*, which then goes to the final step: the press.

Although with Ami Pro you can create camera-ready pages that require no paste-up, many of the documents you design to be printed commercially will require paste-up. The following sections describe the paste-up processes that you can use to make your print jobs more efficient.

Crop Marks

Crop marks are lines (drawn outside the actual document) that define the trim size (see fig. 4.1). If the *trim size*, or actual size of your document, is 8 1/2 by 11 inches, you draw crop marks to define that size. The person at the print shop who trims your completed document uses your crop

marks to measure the actual size of the document. Crop marks help define margins and the placement of the text and graphics within the margins. Ami Pro enables you to add crop marks to your document before printing to an output device.

To add crop marks in Ami Pro, choose the **P**rint menu; then choose **O**ptions. In the Options dialog box, choose Crop **m**arks. The crop marks print only if you are printing to paper that is large enough to include them. If you print a 7 1/2-by-9-inch document to an 8 1/2-by-11-inch sheet of paper, for example, the crop marks print on the paper. If you print an 8 1/2-by-11-inch document to an 8 1/2-by-11-inch sheet of paper, however, the crop marks do not print; you must add them yourself if you plan to take your job to a print shop. All documents printed in a commercial print shop must have crop marks.

I f you use Windows Version 3.1 and a PostScript printer, contact Microsoft for an updated printer driver to use crop marks with Ami Pro.

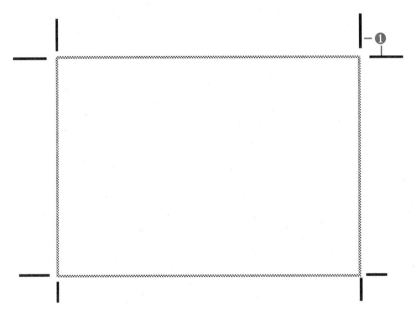

1 Crop marks

Fig. 4.1 Crop marks on the page to tell the printer the actual, or trim, size of the document.

PMTs and Halftones

You can paste up art work and illustrations in their original form if they are clear, clean (no smudges), and black or red. Other colors, such as blue and green, do not reproduce well. If your art is not satisfactory, the print shop makes a PMT. A *PMT* is a black-on-white reproduction of the art, reproduced on photographic paper—just like a photograph but without gray tones.

In order to print photographs, the photos must be reproduced in the camera department of a print shop. Any photograph you want to use in your document must first be made into a *halftone*. A halftone breaks up the image of a photograph into a series of dots. These dots vary in size, and they combine to trick the eye into seeing the grays of a photograph.

Halftones can either be PMT halftones (on photographic paper) or negative halftones (on negative film). Negative halftones are used primarily for very large, detailed photographs or in books that feature photographs. The quality is very high—and so is the price. PMT halftones are much less expensive and look fine in most cases.

If you plan to use photographs in your document and have it printed by a print shop, submit your photos to the print shop to have the halftones made while you format the document. You then can perform the paste-up yourself, or hire the print shop to do the paste-up as part of the print job.

Gripper and Bleed

As mentioned in Chapter 2, "Using Elements of Design," you must pay special attention to the margins of a document. Gripper and bleed are two factors that affect the margins of a document. *Gripper*, the area that the press uses to pass the sheet of paper through, is important. Always leave at least 3/8 inch on all sides of your document for gripper. If you don't, the print shop either reduces the overall size of your document or cuts the paper larger to provide the room the press needs. Either option costs more money than planning the gripper when you format your document.

You may decide to bleed one, two, three, or all four sides of your design, in which case you do not need the gripper. As you may recall from Chapter 2, a *bleed* is the effect when a graphic runs off the edge of the printed document. To create a rule or border bleed, the bleed must be pasted up—by you or by the print shop.

When a print shop cuts paper for a document that bleeds, the paper is cut larger than the trim size so that the ink doesn't run off the edge of the paper. Gripper is formed by the margins of the oversized paper. After printing, the document is trimmed to size. To bleed one side of your document is expensive; to bleed more sides is more expensive.

Mailing

If you want to mail your document, you may have to contend with additional paste-up considerations; make sure to create a mailing panel

R emember that a laser printer cannot print to the edges of a sheet of paper.

R emember to consider the weight of your printed document and the cost to mail it.

large enough to provide room for the mailing labels, the return address, and the mailing permit (which you or the print shop must add) or stamp.

Another important suggestion from the postal service is that no text other than the address be placed below the address line (see fig. 4.2). The post office uses OCR (Optical Character Recognition) scanners to read and sort addresses on mail. The OCR scanners read the address upward from the bottom. Nonaddress text printed along the bottom of an envelope or other mailed materials is rejected by the OCR and must be hand sorted. That rejection means that your document is delayed in reaching its destination.

More postal regulations are explained in Chapter 7, "Producing Envelopes." If you have further questions concerning mailing regulations, contact your postmaster.

Humble Opinions
P. O. Box 174
Oak Hill, WV 25901

Fig. 4.2 No nonaddress text below the address line.

One last point about mailing: if you have a bar code, you can print it directly onto the document. The post office can supply a slick (camera-ready PMT) of your bar code and *Facing Information Mark* (FIM) for you to use. An FIM is a type of bar code located along the top edge of the envelope or business reply card. An FIM assists the OCR scanner with identifying and separating certain business and courtesy reply mail.

Working with Output

Output is the page that comes from your printer—whether it's a laser, dot-matrix, inkjet, or high-resolution device. Depending on your printer, the resolution may be good enough for use at a print shop. *Resolution* refers to the concentration of dots per inch, or *dpi*. The higher the resolution of your output, the sharper and clearer your text and graphics.

Postal regulations state that both the bar code and FIM must be in specific positions. If you have any questions about placement, let your print shop place the bar code for you.

For more information about the types of printers to use with Ami Pro, see Appendix C.

A print shop that prints your document should out put it to a high resolution system at no charge to you.

Always ask for a quote for your job from several types of printers; a quick copy shop may or may not charge you more than a commercial print shop.

Some printers (dot-matrix and pin printers) produce output that works best for proofing purposes only. Most laser printers produce 300 dpi output. This resolution is satisfactory for photocopying and most offset printing. An option that may be available to you is an output service. Your print shop may have the facilities to output to a 1265 dpi or 2530 dpi, or higher resolution system.

When searching for a print shop, be sure to ask about high-resolution output. Also make sure that the shop has a computer, disk size, printer fonts, and version of Ami Pro compatible to yours. For more information about printers, output, and screen and printer fonts, see Appendix C, "Using Printers and Output."

By planning and designing your documents for commercial printing, you save time and money. In addition, you have more control over your design—and the final printed piece—if you follow the guidelines outlined in this section.

Choosing Printing Services

Before you choose a print shop, visit several in your area. Ask questions and ask to tour the shop. After you identify the two or three best shops, request quotations on your print job from each of them. Comparing quotations helps ensure that you get the best value for your money.

If your priorities are quick turnaround, inexpensive price, and fair quality, a quick copy shop may suffice. If, however, you want high-quality work and you're willing to pay for it, you may want to take your job to a commercial print shop. Both types of shops have advantages and disadvantages. Although several other types of shops are available, this section concentrates on the two most common print shops: quick copy printers and commercial printers.

Quick Copy Shop

A *quick copy shop* (quick print) is one that generally photocopies by using the xerographic process and can copy short- to medium-length jobs quickly. Standard page sizes for photocopying are 8 1/2 by 11 inches and 11 by 17 inches, although the quick print shops usually can copy almost anything smaller than these two standard sizes.

Some quick copy shops also have a small press and can produce some offset printing—usually using only black ink; those shops that can provide color often charge a great deal for the service. These shops often

subcontract large offset jobs, typesetting, bindery work, or camera work. If a quick copy shop "farms out" large jobs, such as calendars, booklets, or a document with many photographs, the price for the job may be higher than a commercial printer would charge.

The quality of quick copy shop work can range from poor to excellent. When you request a quotation, ask for some samples of the shop's work. Remember to ask whether the shop will complete your work in-house.

Commercial Printer

A *commercial print shop* can print almost anything in almost any size. Commercial print shops also run any number of ink colors—from one color to four colors. The selection of colors is wider and the color-printing process can be less expensive than at a quick copy shop. A commercial shop generally employs one or more people in the typesetting, paste-up, and camera departments, as well as pressmen and bindery workers. Most commercial printers do their work in-house; they may use a special-purpose printer from time to time.

Commercial shops usually produce high-quality work. Offset printing always looks better than copy work. The turnaround time averages from a week to a month, depending on your job. The price is almost always higher than at a quick copy shop. When you're considering a commercial printer, remember to ask for samples and a quotation.

Choosing Paper

Paper comes in many sizes, finishes, colors, and weights. Your printer can suggest the proper paper for your job. Request samples of paper from the shop before you get a price quotation. Because the cost of the paper can account for 30 to 50 percent of the cost of the entire job, your choice of paper is important. This section briefly discusses the characteristics of paper.

Size

Papers at a print shop usually come in large sizes that can be cut down for each job. Although many more sizes exist, two common sizes are 23 by 35 inches and 25 by 38 inches. Eight 8 1/2-by-11-inch pieces of paper can be cut from a 23-by-35-inch sheet with little waste. If you keep the trim size of your document within a common size range, the paper for your job can be cut more efficiently, which makes your job less expensive.

In the case of business cards, ask your print shop for the cost of using a special-purpose printer. This option may be less expensive than using your local printer.

The print shop you choose should suit the particular job. To spread out your work so that you don't have to depend on just one shop for every job, find two or three shops of each type.

For printing large quantities of your document, you may want to have the shop order a special size paper. Remember that the cost will be higher.

Weight

Paper *weight* is an important consideration when choosing the right paper for the right job. Weight is calculated by the ream (500 sheets). The weight of 500 sheets of 23-by-35-inch paper may be 50#, 60#, 70#, or 80#. The heavier the weight of the ream, the heavier each individual sheet.

Finish

The *finish* (the texture of the paper) affects how the printed text and images appear. The standard finishes include smooth, vellum, linen, and enamel. Enamel, smooth, or vellum are the best finishes for the rich, dark tones of photographs (halftones). Text looks good on just about any finish. The finish that you choose is primarily a personal preference; choose the finish according to price and how the paper looks. Linen, for example, looks classy and sophisticated. A smooth-finish paper is basic and simple. Ask for samples of finishes from your print shop.

Opacity

Opacity is important if you want to use both sides of a sheet of paper, as you would when printing a newsletter or brochure. The greater the opacity of a sheet of paper, the more opaque it is and the less you can see through it. If your document has large, heavy images to print, avoid a low-opacity paper. Weight also affects the opacity of paper; the heavier the paper, the more opaque it is.

Brightness

Brightness describes the capability of the paper to reflect light. Paper is rated from brightest to least bright as 1, 2, or 3. A very bright paper improves halftone reproduction. For the best results in a document that contains many photographs, use a paper with a brightness rating of 1.

Grain

Grain is the direction in which the majority of the paper fibers run. The grain affects the way the paper runs on the press and the way it folds.

You can use most paper weights from 20# to 80# with your laser printer.

For photographs and small type, avoid deeply "toothed" special finishes, such as rippled or laurentine.

Be especially careful when printing both sides of a lightweight enamel finish paper (50#); it usually is transparent.

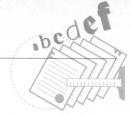

The grain should always run parallel to the spine fold of a newsletter, book, or magazine. Your printer should know how to use the grain of your paper with your particular document.

If your document is a rack card or uses heavy cover paper that folds, remember to make the printer aware of the grain requirements before the print job begins.

Color

Paper comes in many colors. Print shops usually stock the more common colors. White is always available, as is ivory. Pastel colors—pink, green, blue, canary—are common in most paper colors. Accent colors such as Apache red, prime yellow, or cobalt blue, also are usually stocked. These colors are a bit more expensive. Fluorescent and metallic colors are generally special order items and are expensive. Paper samples from the print shop can help you choose the color you want.

Types

There are as many paper types as there are colors. Common types of paper include book paper, bond paper, and letterhead paper. Each paper type has specific uses. You wouldn't, for example, use the same paper to print a flyer and a postcard.

Book Paper

Book paper is the most common paper used. Book paper comes in three types: offset, coated, and text. These types are interchangeable, but each has its own special properties.

- *Offset* is used for newsletters, booklets, and programs. Common finishes are smooth, vellum, linen, and laurentine. Many colors are available, and weights range from 50# to 80#. Offset book paper is fairly inexpensive.

- *Coated* is perfect for photographs. Coated book paper comes in glossy or matte finishes. The paper, which is usually white or ivory, is available in weights that range from 50# to 100#. Prices of coated papers vary, although this type should cost no more than an offset paper of the same weight.

Some print shops prefer to cut more pages out of a sheet rather than considering the grain, which may yield fewer pages per sheet.

Consider ink colors when choosing the paper color; for example, light blue ink on blue paper may not be readable.

Don't use 50# enamel paper. This weight is not opaque, it is difficult to print and fold, and it looks inexpensive.

T ext paper, because of the deep texture, is not suitable for 8- or 10-point type.

W hen ordering printed envelopes to match your letterhead, instruct the print shop to include 500-1000 extra plain, white, bond paper envelopes for every day use.

R ecycled paper is becoming more popular and less expensive. Ask your printer for samples.

- *Text* book paper is a heavier, more deeply finished paper. Reserve this paper for special projects, such as invitations, booklets, or programs. The weights available range from 60# to 80#. Many colors are available. The finish is rough and toothy, which makes text book paper unsuitable for photographs. Text paper has a classy look and is usually expensive.

Bond and Sulphite Paper

Very inexpensive papers, *bond* and *sulphite*, come in 16# and 20# weights. These papers are available in many colors and either smooth or vellum finishes. Bond and sulphite papers are less costly than most other papers and are ideal for flyers, scratch pads, and one-sided printing.

Letterhead Paper

Letterhead paper (with matching envelopes) is available in 20# or 24# weights and has a *watermark* (an embossed logo of the company that makes the paper). A good-quality paper in the letterhead family is rag paper. (*Rag* refers to the cotton content, such as 25 percent or 100 percent.) A variety of colors is available and finishes include smooth, laid, and linen. Considering the quality of the paper and the impression that nice letterhead paper creates, this paper is not too expensive.

Cover Paper

Cover paper is a heavier "board" grade used for business cards, rack cards, booklet covers, and tickets. Cover paper is available in coated and uncoated finishes. Uncoated cover paper matches letterhead and offset papers in finish and color so that you can use them in combination (for example, a letter and business card). Uncoated cover paper comes in 65# and 80# weights; many colors; and smooth (called *antique*), linen, or laurentine finishes. Uncoated cover paper is the least expensive of the cover papers.

Coated cover paper matches other coated papers. Coated cover paper is measured differently. The weights are 8-, 10-, and 12-point cover (8-point cover is equal to 100#). Coated cover paper is available in white or ivory, and can be coated on one side or two sides. Coated cover paper can range from inexpensive to very costly.

You can find many other paper types: carbonless for forms, label paper for bumper stickers, index and tag for inexpensive posters or postcards, and the list goes on. Check with your printer for suggestions on the paper type, finish, and color to suit your job.

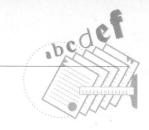

Working with Ink

When choosing your paper, consider the color(s) of ink you want to use. Any one color of ink, in combination with a colored paper, can create a two-color effect without the added expense of a two-color print job. Outlined letters, graphic rules, boxes, and especially screens, produce the effect of a two-color job. Remember, however, that black is a color to a printer. If you use black and red ink on a document, your document is a two-color job.

Black ink runs on presses every day; it's the most common color. Black is used extensively because it's very effective and the least expensive ink. Black ink on any color of paper looks good, and black ink used with any other color of ink looks good, as well.

Generally, if you're using two colors of ink, you should choose two contrasting colors, such as black and any color, red and blue, or red and green. Using two colors is more expensive, but the effect can be dramatic.

Avoid using white ink—it doesn't print very heavy and requires a dark paper, which can be hard to read. Don't use yellow ink for text; it is difficult to read. Save yellow for screens, lines, or graphic elements.

Using Standard Inks

Standard colors of ink are those that come premixed. Many standard colors are attractive and inexpensive. Common standard inks are black, Dutch fireball red, warm red, wedgewood blue, process blue, forest green, pantone purple, and process yellow. Ask your printer to show you a standard ink chart or some samples.

Using PMS and Special Inks

PMS stands for Pantone Matching System. The PMS Swatch Book contains 500 ink colors in various shades and tints. These ink colors are more expensive than standard inks. The pressman mixes the color when the job is ready to run. For that reason, if you order a second printing of your document at a later date, the PMS color may not match the color of the first print run exactly.

Special inks include thermographed, metallic, and fluorescent. These inks are expensive and difficult to run.

Black ink made with carbon is environment-friendly.

You may ask your printer whether any already-mixed PMS colors are available. If you find one you really like, you shouldn't be charged extra.

Thermographed ink is raised ink, and the printing process called *thermography* is difficult. A document is run through the press, printing the text in ink. Powder is then sprinkled on the text while the ink is wet, and the document is run through an oven to set the powder. Using thermographed ink is an expensive process, especially if the print shop does the work in-house. Ask your printer to use a special-purpose printer for thermographed business cards; the price is usually less expensive.

Metallic and fluorescent inks usually are thin and difficult to run on the press. For this reason, these inks are costly and may not look good. Always ask your printer for samples if you plan to use one of these inks.

Finishing Techniques

The finishing processes take place in the bindery of a print shop. Some printed pieces require more time in the bindery than others. *Finishing* includes trimming, folding, inserting, gathering, padding, perforating, die-cutting, punching, scoring, laminating, numbering, and fastening. This section offers an overview of the common procedures you may encounter.

Fastening and folding are probably the two most common finishing techniques you need to use for your documents. If, however, your document requires a different treatment, ask your printer for advice.

Folding

Many of the jobs for which you will plan printing require *folding*. A mechanical folder completes the majority of folding in a print shop. Some folds are easier, taking less time and costing less than other types of folds. Always check your final printed piece to be sure it has been folded evenly and looks good. You should be aware of are the following folding problems:

- Using more than five folds on one document is very difficult to do. You pay more for this service, and you may not be happy with the results.

- Folding sometimes cracks the spine of a book cover or heavy paper, because the paper is being folded against the grain without first being *scored*. Scoring is a process that uses a strip of hardened steel to crush the grain of the paper, thereby creating a straight line for folding. If the spine is cracked, the print shop is responsible, and the problem should be corrected at no charge.

- Enamel and cover papers are difficult to fold.

W hen using a metallic or fluorescent ink, ask your printer for quotes comparing the special ink to a standard ink color.

The following sections cover the most common folds—parallel, barrel, French, and accordion.

Parallel Fold

Brochures, letters, and flyers usually are folded twice, with a *parallel* fold. The most common fold, the parallel fold also is the easiest and least expensive. Figure 4.3 shows a brochure marked for two parallel folds (an accordion fold with only two folds).

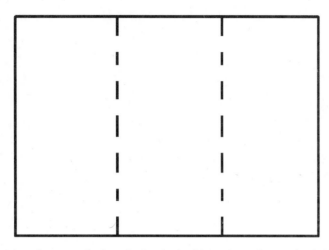

Fig. 4.3 A brochure marked with the dashed lines to indicate the folds.

Barrel Fold

A *barrel* fold is used, for example, with a six-page newsletter printed on 25 1/2-by-11-inch paper. After folding, the finished size is 8 1/2 by 11 inches (see fig. 4.4). A barrel fold is a bit more complicated than a parallel fold, because of the steps involved in setting up the mechanical folder.

French Fold

A *French* fold is commonly used for note cards and invitations and is a difficult fold to do well. The first fold is lengthwise and the second is at a right angle to the first fold (see fig. 4.5). The problem with a French fold is that one fold must go against the grain of the paper, causing it to crack and fold unevenly. Many times, a mechanical folder executes the first fold, and the second fold is made by hand, which, of course, makes the French fold expensive.

If you have a small number of pieces to French fold, consider folding them yourself to save money.

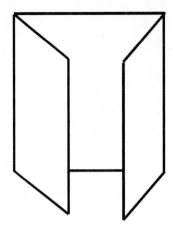

Fig. 4.4 The barrel fold.

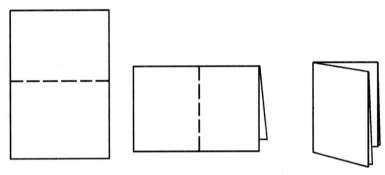

Fig. 4.5 The French fold.

Accordion Fold

Accordion folds resemble the folds in a road map. They are the most difficult type of fold. The setup of the folding machine changes many times during the process; therefore, the accordion fold is expensive. Figure 4.6 shows a common accordion fold with three folds. Accordion folds can include as many folds as necessary, although a folding job of more than five folds is difficult to execute.

Fastening the Final Product

The most common type of finishing is one of the *fastening* methods. Stapling is the customary method of fastening; padding and drilling also are possibilities. The binding of the document depends completely on its purpose and size.

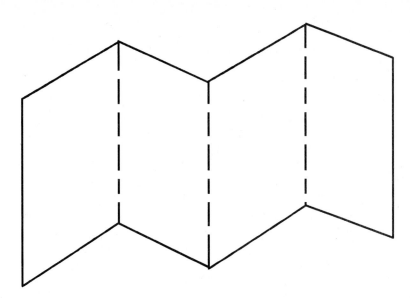

Fig. 4.6   An accordion fold.

Looseleaf

A very common method of fastening, called *looseleaf*, is to drill or punch holes on the left margin of single pages. These pages are gathered and inserted into a ring binder or plastic binding. Plastic binding is an efficient way of fastening. It looks somewhat like spiral binding but pages can be removed and replaced easily. Plastic binding is suitable for many types of documents, such as reports, programs, and catalogs.

Side Stitch

Side stitch, or side binding, is a method of fastening single sheets on the left side with staples. Side-stitched documents must have at least a 3/4-inch margin on the fastened side; pages in the middle of the document will not be readable if you don't allow a sufficient margin. Side stitching is a good method of fastening for jobs with 100 to 300 pages, and it is inexpensive.

Saddle Back

Saddle back, or saddle stitch, uses staples on the fold. A common and efficient method of fastening, saddle stitching often is used for newsletters and magazines. This method is inexpensive and works well with booklets up to 64 pages long.

Padding

Padding, applying glue to one edge of stacked pages, can be used for any document that requires temporary fastening, such as scratch pads, calendars, and forms.

Getting Price Quotations

Because prices vary greatly from shop to shop, you should get price quotations from several printers for every job before you print it. Make sure that the quote is in writing, and keep your copy in case any questions (from you and from the printer) arise later. Most quotes are good for 30 days, provided you don't make alterations after the document is in process.

The print shop's quotation includes the cost of materials and labor for your job: paste-up, camera, stripping, plate-making, paper, ink, and press and bindery time. The more information you give the print shop, the more accurate the quotation will be. Describe your document in detail and, if possible, add a *mock-up*, or scaled model, of your document.

You should include the following items when requesting a price quotation from a print shop:

- The date you request the quote, your name, and phone number.

- The date you need your document.

- The type of document—brochure, flyer, or newsletter, for example.

- The quantity—for example, 1,000, 2,500, and 5,000. A quote usually includes three quantities.

- The trim size and the finished size—for example, a four-page newsletter measuring 11 by 17 inches (the trim size) and folding to 8 1/2 by 11 inches (the finished size).

- The number of ink colors (remember that black is a color) and whether the ink is specially mixed or standard.

- Whether the document is printed on one side or two.

- The type of paper (such as 70#, white linen offset).

- Whether the document is camera ready (includes crops, PMTs, and so on) or typeset, requiring minimum paste-up.

- The number of halftones.

I f the print shop does not honor the price quotation your received, question the price, complain, or even refuse the job.

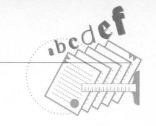

- The number and type of folds.

- Finishing techniques—padding or stapling, for example.

- Any special instructions, such as bleeds, negative halftones, numbering, and mailing.

Recapping

The following steps recap this chapter to help refresh your memory and to give you a quick reference guide whenever you need it:

1. Plan and lay out your document, keeping in mind gripper, bleed, and mailing requirements.

2. As you design your document, consider finishing techniques such as fastening and folding.

3. Prepare your document for the print shop by adding crop marks, PMTs, and halftones, or by transferring your files to a disk for high-resolution output.

4. Consider the quantity when you are choosing a reproduction process for your document.

5. Visit several print shops; request paper and ink samples.

6. Prepare a quotation request including all information and a mock-up of your document.

7. Get quotations from several printers before choosing the shop to do your job.

Creating Business Documents

II

---

humble opinions P. O. Box 174 · Oak Hill, West Virginia 25901

March 25, 1993

J. W. Jenkins
1455 West 48th Street
St. Albans, WV 25605

Dear Mrs. Jenkins:

We wish to express our gratitude for your business during the past year. Your company has been a pleasure to serve; your staff is always courteous, patient and friendly.

We are pleased to take this opportunity to offer you, our special customer, a chance to enter our free contest! There is no purchase necessary. All you have to do is fill out the enclosed post card and return it to us within 14 days. Our company is giving away a personal computer worth over $2,000 at the end of April. It is our way of saying thank you to special customers like you.

Please return the post card to us as soon as possible. We will contact you by May 3 to let you know if you won this valuable computer.

Again, thank you for your patronage. We hope to continue doing business with you for many years.

Sincerely,
D. J. Halsey, President
Humble Opinions

Includes

Producing a Letterhead

An attractive letterhead is one of the most important tools of a successful business. When customers receive an appealing document from your business, they are more likely to read it. An impressive letterhead sells a business as well as its products and services. The company's name, address, and phone number serve as a reminder of that business each time a customer receives a letter.

HUMBLE OPINIONS CORPORATION
COMPUTER AND SOFTWARE CONSULTANTS
POST OFFICE BOX 174   OAK HILL, WEST VIRGINIA 25901
(304) 465-5156   (800) 467-2823

For detailed information on how to create a form like this see page 131.

Include all company phone numbers in your letterhead: fax, local, toll-free, and so on.

Refer to Chapter 2 for information about balancing text and graphic elements on the page.

See Appendix B to learn which file formats Ami Pro accepts, how to import a scanned image, and how to display text from another program.

In addition to the name, address, and phone number of the company, you can add the president's name, a list of board members, office and home phone numbers, addresses of subsidiaries, graphics, or even a logo. Be careful not to clutter the letterhead with too much information; leave space for the actual letter.

The space a letterhead uses depends on the information included, its placement, and any graphics used. The letterhead should occupy no less than 1/2 inch, horizontally or vertically. The maximum space, including the margin at the top of the page, should be no more than 1 1/2 inches. If you plan to place text at the bottom of the letterhead (the address, a phrase, or a rule, for example), be sure to leave at least a 3/8-inch bottom margin. Pay close attention to the margins of your letterhead. The top and side margins can be anywhere from 1/2 to 1 inch. Any less than 1/2 inch looks crowded. Remember, the primary purpose of the letterhead is to identify the sender without overwhelming the contents of the letter.

If you want to include a logo in your letterhead design, you can create one with Ami Pro's Drawing feature, or you can use one of the 100 clip-art designs included with your Ami Pro package. On the other hand, your logo may consist only of text. This chapter includes several examples of logos designed in Ami Pro.

The following sections introduce four different letterhead designs, showing the keystrokes to produce them in Ami Pro. The first design is simple and uses the Ami Pro basics. The second, third, and fourth designs employ more of Ami Pro's features and become progressively more difficult to produce. At the end of the chapter are three designs, without specific keystrokes, that may inspire you in your letterhead design.

The instructions include steps for both mouse and keyboard users. If you aren't familiar with Ami Pro, refer to Appendix A for screen, mouse, and keyboard basics. If you use the keyboard, remember that you press the bold letters in the commands in combination with the Alt key (File is Alt+F, for example).

Use the default settings in these examples unless you are specifically instructed to change them.

You also can use a glossary data file as a newsletter nameplate, or as a heading for a fax cover sheet, memo, or form.

Finally, you learn to use the first design in this chapter to create a glossary. A glossary data file consists of text, graphics, or clip art that is used over and over again in various documents. All instructions for saving and retrieving a glossary data file are described in detail near the end of this chapter.

You can save any of the documents in this chapter as a glossary file. You can print any of these designs from your laser printer, photocopy them, or use them as camera-ready copy for a print shop.

Producing a Basic Letterhead

The first letterhead design is formal. To create the impression of importance and value, the company name is large (36 points), the typeface is Times Roman, and the letterhead stretches from margin to margin (see fig. 5.1). Use of large and small caps within the company name adds to this impression. Repetition of the use of caps in the address creates unity within the design, and changing the typeface to Helvetica for the address creates variety. This design introduces some basic features of Ami Pro that can acquaint you with the program, features such as center alignment, tabs, and small caps.

At the end of the chapter, you use this letterhead design to create a glossary data file. If you are familiar with Ami Pro, you may want to skip this first design; you also can use any of the other designs in this chapter for the glossary data file.

You use the default style sheet to begin most documents in this book. You can alter the style sheets in Ami Pro and then save them under either a new name or the old one. The ~DEFAULT.STY style sheet in Version 2.0 or the _DEFAULT.STY style sheet in Version 3.0 uses TimesNewRomanPS as its Body Text font. If your printer does not support this font, you can change it in just one document or change it in the style sheet for use over and over again, as follows:

- To change the font in one document, choose **S**tyle **M**odify Style. (If Ami Pro displays a dialog box stating that your printer does not support this font, choose OK or press Enter.) When the Modify Style dialog box appears, choose Tms Rmn in Face. Choose OK or press Enter.

- To change the style sheet permanently, choose **S**tyle Save As a Style Sheet after performing the style change. The Style Sheet dialog box appears, showing the default style sheet highlighted. You then choose OK or press Enter. When Ami Pro asks whether you want to overwrite the style sheet, choose Yes.

Consider substituting an ATM font, such as CaslonOpenFace, for the Times Roman heading.

HUMBLE OPINIONS CORPORATION

Post Office Box 174, Drawer P   Oak Hill, West Virginia 25901

(304) 469-6166

Fig. 5.1   A formal letterhead design created with large and small caps.

To create the style sheet and text for the first letterhead, follow these steps:

1. Choose File New.

2. In the New dialog box, choose Style Sheet for New Document. From the file list, choose the default style sheet by clicking it or by pressing the down arrow. Choose OK or press Enter.

3. Choose Page Modify Page Layout.

4. In the Modify dialog box, choose Margins.

5. Under Margins, choose Left. Type .5 for the left margin. The measurement should be in inches; if it isn't, you can change it by selecting the measurement box. Change the Top, Bottom, and Right margins to .5. Choose OK or press Enter.

6. At the insertion point, type the following:

   Humble Opinions Corporation(Enter)
   (Tab)**Post Office Box 174, Drawer P**(Tab)**Oak Hill, West Virginia 25901**(Enter)
   (304) 469-6166

To format the text, follow these steps:

1. Select `Humble Opinions Corporation` either by dragging the mouse cursor over the line of text, or by placing the cursor in front of the H, pressing and holding the Shift key, and pressing the right arrow until the line of text is selected.

2. From the SmartIcons, choose the icon to center align the text, or press Ctrl+C (Version 2.0) or Ctrl+E (Version 3.0).

3. With `Humble Opinions Corporation` still selected, choose Text Font. The Font dialog box appears, showing Tms Rmn as the default typeface.

4. In Size, choose 36 point. Choose OK or press Enter.

5. To make the first line of text bold, click the SmartIcon for bold or press Ctrl+B.

6. Deselect the text by clicking elsewhere on the page or by pressing the Esc key.

7. Select `umble`. Choose Text Caps.

8. A secondary command menu appears; choose Small Caps. Deselect the text.

You may want to substitute your company's information in these letterhead designs.

You cannot adjust the size of the small caps command; alternatively, however, you can use the Text Font menu to change type size.

9. Repeat steps 10 and 11 with `pinions` and `orporation`.

10. Select the second line of text, from `Post Office` through `25901`.

11. Choose Text Font. The Font dialog box appears.

12. In Face, choose Helv. In Size, choose 12 point. Choose OK or press Enter.

13. With the text still highlighted, choose Style Modify Style.

14. In the Styles box, choose Alignment.

15. Choose the Left Tab icon either by clicking it or by pressing the Tab key until the second button is selected.

16. Place the cursor on the upper half of the ruler in the dialog box; click at 1". Choose the right tab button and click at 6.5" on the ruler.

    Alternatively, on the keyboard, press Shift-Tab to move to the ruler. Then press the right-arrow key to move to 1". Press the space bar to add the tab. Choose the right tab icon. Press the right-arrow key to move to 6.5" on the ruler; press the space bar to add the tab.

17. Before exiting the dialog box, choose Use Style Tabs. Choose OK or press Enter. Deselect the text.

18. Select `ost` in `Post`. Choose Text Caps.

19. A secondary command menu appears. Choose Small Caps. Ami Pro returns to the document.

20. Repeat steps 18 and 19 with `ffice`, `rawer`, `ak`, `ill`, `est`, and `irginia` in the address line.

21. Select the phone number. Choose Text Font. Change the text to Helv 10 point. Center the text.

To save and print the letterhead, follow these steps:

1. Choose File Save As.

2. In the Save As dialog box, place the cursor in the File Name text box and type **Ltrhead1**. Choose OK or press Enter.

3. Choose File Print. Because the defaults for number of copies (1 copy) and pages (1 to 9999) are the correct settings, choose OK or press Enter.

Y ou must select Use Style Tabs so that Ami Pro recognizes tabs you set in this dialog box.

Producing a Letterhead with Graphic Rules

You may want to use the second design, depending on your business, for less formal correspondence. The ways in which you use attributes and place the text greatly affect the look and feel of your document. In figure 5.2, the italic lowercase type gives an informal look to the letterhead. That look, in combination with the right-aligned head and address, adds an active, almost dynamic, feeling to the letterhead. Graphic rules contribute to the effect, as does defining the boundaries on the top and bottom margins. Potential variations to this style include artwork or a photograph to the left of the company name, or moving the address to the bottom center of the page for a lighter effect.

In producing this letterhead, you learn some new techniques in Ami Pro. You align the text by using the menu commands, create bullets, and add borders to the page. To create the style sheet and text for the second letterhead, follow these steps:

1. Choose File New.

2. In the New dialog box, choose Style Sheet for New Document. From the file list, choose the default style sheet by clicking it or by pressing the down arrow. Choose OK or press Enter.

3. Choose Page Modify Page Layout.

4. In the Modify dialog box, choose Margins.

5. In Margins, choose Left. Type .5 for the left margin. The measurement should be in inches; if it isn't, you can change it by selecting the measurement box. Also change the Top, Bottom, and Right margins to .5. Choose OK or press Enter.

6. Type the following:

> **humble opinions**(Enter)
> **P. O. Box 174**(2 spaces, press Alt+0183, 2 spaces)**Oak Hill, WV 25901**(2 spaces, press Alt+0183, 2 spaces)**(304) 469-6166**

To format the graphic rules and the text, follow these steps:

1. Choose Page Modify Page Layout.

2. In the Modify dialog box, choose Lines.

3. In Around Page, choose Top and Bottom.

4. In Style, choose the third line from the top (a 2-point rule).

If you add a logo to this design, place it on the right.

Alt+0183 is the ANSI character for a bullet. Press and hold the Alt key while typing 0183 on the numeric keypad (with Num Lock turned on). Most printers can print the ANSI characters.

Users of Ami Pro 3.0 can use the ANSI character or insert a different bullet style by choosing Edit Insert Bullet. Then choose a bullet style and choose OK.

5. Select both lines of text by dragging the mouse cursor over the text.

6. Choose Text Alignment.

7. A secondary command list appears; choose **Right**. The text right-aligns. Deselect the type.

8. Select `humble opinions`. Choose Text Font. The Font dialog box appears.

9. In Face, choose Tms Rmn. In Size, choose 36 point. Choose OK or press Enter.

10. On the SmartIcon bar, click the icon for italic or press Ctrl+I. Select the bold icon or press Ctrl+B. Deselect the text.

11. Select the address line. Press Ctrl+I to italicize the text.

To save and print the letterhead, follow these steps:

1. Choose File Save As. In the File Name text box, type **Ltrhead2**. Choose OK or press Enter.

2. Choose File Print. Because the defaults are already set, choose OK or press Enter.

Producing a Traditional Letterhead

Helvetica and Times Roman is the most commonly used typeface combination in typesetting today.

You can use many layout options for a traditional, or formal, letterhead. The text should be easy to read and dignified. Depending on your company, you may include the names of the officers or board members, additional phone numbers and addresses, and so on. Figure 5.3 illustrates a traditional letterhead design. The design uses both Times Roman (for the company name and address) and Helvetica (for the officers' names and phone numbers). The rules separate the head to make it more significant.

Ami Pro features introduced in these instructions include adding a rule to a paragraph style and changing and applying the Styles box.

humble opinions

P. O. Box 174 · Oak Hill, WV 25901 · (304) 469-6166

Fig. 5.2　The second letterhead, designed to be energetic and dynamic.

Humble Opinions Corporation

P. O. Box 174 · Oak Hill, WV 25901

G. E. Worthington, President
(304) 468-6868

K. A. Vuranch, Vice President
(304) 468-5252

Fig. 5.3 A traditional letterhead design that lists two officers of the corporation.

To create the style sheet and text for the letterhead in figure 5.3, follow these steps:

1. Choose File New.

2. In the New dialog box, choose Style Sheet for New Document. From the file list, choose the default style sheet by clicking it or by pressing the down arrow. Choose OK or press Enter.

3. Choose Page Modify Page Layout.

4. In the Modify dialog box, choose Margins. Change all margins to .5. Be sure that the measurement is set to inches.

5. Type the following:

   Humble Opinions Corporation(Enter)
   P. O. Box 174(5 spaces, Alt+0183, 5 spaces)**Oak Hill, WV 25901**(Enter, twice)
   G. E. Worthington, President(Tab)**K. A. Vuranch, Vice President**(Enter)
   (304) 468-6868(Tab)**(304) 468-5252**

To add the rules and to format the text, follow these steps:

1. Choose Page Modify Page Layout.

2. In the Modify dialog box, choose Lines.

3. In Around Page, choose Top; in Style, select the second rule (a 1-point rule). Choose OK or press Enter.

4. Select the first two lines of text, from `Humble Opinions` through `WV 25901`.

5. Use the SmartIcon to center-align the text or press Ctrl+C (Version 2.0) or Ctrl+E (Version 3.0). Deselect the text.

6. Select `Humble Opinions Corporation`. Choose Text Font. In the Size text box, choose 36 point. Choose OK or press Enter.

7. With the text still selected, choose Text Spacing. In the Spacing selection box, choose 1 1/2. Choose OK or press Enter.

8. Use the SmartIcon to make the selected text bold or press Ctrl+B. Deselect the text.

9. In the second line of text, the address line, select just the bullet.

10. Choose Text Font. Change the Size to 14 point. Choose OK or press Enter.

11. Use the SmartIcon to make the bullet bold. Deselect the bullet.

Avoid using heavy rules, such as the fourth or fifth line styles in Ami Pro. Heavy rules unbalance the page and overwhelm the letterhead.

Ami Pro 3.0 users can select the bullet size from Edit Insert Bullet, skipping steps 10 and 11.

12. Select the entire address line. Choose Text **S**pacing. In the Spacing selection box, choose **C**ustom. Delete the contents of the custom spacing text box and type **.30**. The measurement should be in inches. Choose OK or press Enter.

Ami Pro does not enable you to add a rule above or below a line of text or a paragraph unless you create a new style or modify an old one. Ami Pro styles are named Body Text, Bullet, Number List, Subhead, Title, and so on. Each style sheet comes with styles of type already formatted for your use. The default style sheet you use in this document, for example, sets the title in the Arial MT font at 18 points, center-aligned. You can use or change any style assigned to a style sheet, as you did in the first set of instructions in this chapter. You also can add your own styles to the style sheet so that you can use them repeatedly.

To create a new style for the address line, follow these steps:

1. Select the address line, P. O. Box 174 through 25901. Choose **S**tyle Create Style.

2. In the New Styles text box, type **Address**. Choose Modify. The Modify Style dialog box appears.

3. In Modify, choose Lines.

4. Choose Line **B**elow and the second line pattern (a 1-point rule). Under Line **B**elow, in **S**pacing type **.10**. Choose OK or press Enter.

5. Choose Styles **S**elect a Style. The Styles box appears and remains on-screen until you close it.

   The Styles Box lists all styles attached to the style sheet you are using. The Styles box appears in the upper right corner of the screen, but you can move it by clicking the mouse in the title bar of the box and dragging the box elsewhere on the screen. To apply a style from the Styles box, either click the style's file name or press the function key listed beside the style you want. You also can press Ctrl+Y to move to the Styles box and use the arrow keys to scroll. Press the space bar or Enter to select the style and return to the document. To close the Styles box, click its control button in the upper left corner and choose Close, or double-click the control button. On the keyboard, press Ctrl+Y to move to the Styles box, then press Alt+space bar to access the control button. Then choose Close.

6. With the address line still highlighted, find Address in the Styles box and select it. The style applies to the address in the letterhead.

To format the officers' names and to set the tabs, follow these steps:

1. Select the last two lines of type, from G. E. Worthington through (304) 468-5252.

2. Choose Text Font. In Face, choose Helv; in Size, choose 10 point. Choose OK or press Enter.

3. Choose Style Modify Style. The Modify Style dialog box appears.

4. Choose Alignment. In Tabs, choose the right-hand tab.

5. On the ruler, click at 7.5".

   Alternatively, on the keyboard, press Shift-Tab to move to the ruler and press the right-arrow key to move to the 7.5" mark. Press the space bar to add the tab.

6. Be sure to choose Use Style Tabs. Choose OK or press Enter.

To save and print the letterhead, follow these steps:

1. Choose File Save As. In the File Name text box, type **ltrhead3**. Choose OK or press Enter.

2. Choose File Print. Choose OK or press Enter.

You can alter this letterhead design to include other information about the company. Figure 5.4 shows the same heading, but with officers and board members listed along the left side. In the listing, the phone numbers are excluded and the type is 8 point so that it does not take up too much space or overwhelm the contents of the letter. The list could be longer if necessary, as long as the text remains in one column and along the left edge of the page.

Producing an Innovative Letterhead

An innovative letterhead design may be appropriate for your business. A graphic arts or desktop publishing business, dance school, art gallery, museum, nature center, or child care facility are a few examples of businesses that can use a less formal, more inventive letterhead design.

You can be creative in many ways with Ami Pro. Ami Pro enables you to use frames in designing a document, and these frames let you divide information, reverse type, and add graphic images such as artwork, clip art, and logos.

The following chapters further explore the creative use of frames in your documents.

Humble Opinions Corporation

P. O. Box 174 · Oak Hill, WV 25901

OFFICERS
G. E. Worthington, President
K. A. Vuranch, Vice President
K. E. Richards, Treasurer
L. W. Williams, Secretary

BOARD MEMBERS
S. A. Parker
G. R. Cramer
P. A. Brice
D. E. Stasson
D. L. Linkus
J. O. Blackman
E. V. Curtis
S. E. Blackwell

Fig. 5.4 An alternate design for the traditional letterhead.

In the following letterhead, you use two frames. One contains the name of the company in reversed type (white type on a black background); the other frame contains the address and phone number (see fig. 5.5). To produce this design successfully, your printer must be capable of reversing type, and it must have enough memory to complete the printing. If you are unsure about your printer's capabilities, check your printer manual.

To set up the page for the letterhead design, follow these steps:

1. Choose File New.

2. In the New dialog box, choose Style Sheet for New Document. From the file list, choose the default style sheet. Choose OK or press Enter.

3. Choose Page Modify Page Layout.

4. In the Modify dialog box, choose Margins.

5. In Margins, choose Left. Type .5 for the left margin. The measurement should be in inches; if it isn't, you can change it by selecting the measurement box. Change Top, Bottom, and Right margins to .5. Choose OK or press Enter.

To create the first frame and reversed type, follow these steps:

1. In SmartIcons, choose the frame, or choose Frame Create Frame. Choose Manual.

   Alternatively, in the Create Frame dialog box, press the Tab key to choose Manual, and then press Enter.

2. The mouse cursor appears as a Frame icon. Draw the frame so that it looks similar to figure 5.5 (its size is 4.8" by .75"). Using the mouse, drag the cursor to create the frame. Using the keyboard, press space bar+arrow to draw the frame.

3. To place the cursor in the frame, double-click inside the frame.

   Using the keyboard, you first must select the frame. Choose Edit Go To or press Ctrl+G, and the Go To dialog box appears. Next, choose Next Item to go to the Next item selection box. Use the down arrow to select Frame, then press Enter; the frame is selected. Finally, press Enter again to access the cursor within the frame.

4. Type the following:

   HUMBLE OPINIONS

5. Select HUMBLE OPINIONS, then choose Text Font.

You can check the size of the frame by choosing Frame Modify Frame Layout. In the Frame selection box, choose Size & Position. The Width and Height appear in the Size box, and you can change these settings. Be sure that your frame is the right size.

6. In the Size selection box, choose 36 point; in color, choose white. Choose OK or press Enter.

7. Click outside the frame to deselect it. With the keyboard, press Esc twice.

8. Select the frame.

9. Choose Frame Modify Frame Layout.

10. In Frame, choose Type. In Display, choose Square Corners.

11. In Frame, choose Lines & Shadows. In Background, choose black.

12. In Frame, choose Size & Position. In Margins, change Bottom to 0. Choose OK or press Enter. The type appears white on a black background.

To create the second frame and its type, follow these steps:

1. Follow steps 1 and 2 in the preceding directions to create the second frame, positioning it similarly to the one in figure 5.5. The size is 2.5" by .75".

2. Select the frame; choose Frame Modify Frame Layout.

3. In Frame, choose Type. In Display, choose Square Corners.

4. In Frame, choose Size & Position. In Margins, change all to 0 in Version 2.0; select Clear Margins in Version 3.0. Choose OK or press Enter.

5. Place the cursor in the frame and type the following:

(space, space)**POST OFFICE BOX 174**(Enter)
(space, space)**OAK HILL, WEST VIRGINIA 25901**(Enter)
(space, space)**(304) 469-6166**

6. Select the text (the last line may not show in the frame until you change the type size). Choose Text Font.

7. In the Size selection box choose 10 point. Choose OK or press Enter.

8. Choose Text Spacing. In the dialog box, choose Custom. In the Custom text box, type **.16**. Choose OK or press Enter.

To save and print the document, choose File Save As. In the File Name text box, type **ltrhead4**, and then choose OK or press Enter. Choose File Print, and then choose OK or press Enter.

HUMBLE OPINIONS

POST OFFICE BOX 174
OAK HILL, WEST VIRGINIA 25901
(304) 469-6166

Fig. 5.5 The company name reversed in one frame of the letterhead with the address in normal type.

Creating a Glossary Data File

A glossary data file is a file in which frequently used text and graphics are stored for future use. Letterheads, form letters, greetings, mastheads, and logos can be stored as a glossary data file, then retrieved and placed into documents again and again. A glossary data file contains two fields and two delimiters.

Fields are directions that tell Ami Pro to perform a specific function, such as record, place a bookmark, insert index entries, and run a macro. A *delimiter* indicates the end of a field or the end of the data. A delimiter can be any symbol that is not used in the original data, such as the dollar sign, pound sign, percent sign, and even an ANSI or ASCII character.

In the next example, you use the tilde (~) and the pipe (|) because they are not commonly used symbols. The following instructions show you how to create a glossary data file and then how to retrieve it and place it into a new document.

To create the glossary data file, follow these steps:

1. Choose File **O**pen. In the list of Files, choose LTRHEAD1.SAM. Choose OK or press Enter.

2. The glossary record must be contained in a new Ami Pro document. Choose File **N**ew.

3. In the New dialog box, under **S**tyle Sheet for New Document, choose the default style sheet. Choose OK or press Enter. The new document window is small and cascades on top of the first document. You can work with the window in this mode, or you can enlarge the window.

4. Choose **P**age **M**odify Page Layout. In Margins, change all margins to **.5**. Choose OK or press Enter.

5. At the insertion point, type the two delimiters, ~|, and press Enter.

6. Version 2.0 Users: Type the field name and glossary data file, including the two delimiters, as shown:

   Record ID~Record Text|(Enter)

   Version 3.0 Users: skip step 6.

7. Type the ID name:

   Version 2.0 users: **ID~letterhd**(Enter)

   Version 3.0 users: **~letterhd**(Enter)

Y ou can have multiple glossary records in the same file.

A mi Pro 3.0 users, deselect **R**eplace Current File.

8. Switch windows by clicking the title bar of LTRHEAD1.SAM, or choose **Window** and choose LTRHEAD1.SAM.

9. Select the letterhead. Choose **Edit Copy**.

10. Switch windows to the second, untitled document.

11. Place the cursor on the last paragraph return on the page (the last time you pressed Enter). Choose **Edit Paste**.

12. Place the cursor at the end of the phone number and press Enter.

13. Press the pipe delimiter key (|).

14. Choose **File Save As**. In File **N**ame, type **letterhd**. Choose OK or press Enter.

15. Close both documents, LTRHEAD1.SAM and LETTERHD.SAM. Choose File, then choose Close twice.

To insert the glossary record into a new document, follow these steps:

1. Choose **File New**.

2. In the New dialog box, choose **Style Sheet for New Document**. From the file list, choose the default style sheet. Choose OK or press Enter.

3. Choose **Page Modify Page Layout**.

4. In the Modify dialog box, choose **Margins**.

5. Under Margins, change the **Left**, **Top**, **B**ottom, and **R**ight margins to **.5**. Choose OK or press Enter.

6. Choose **Edit Insert**. A secondary command list appears. Choose **Glossary Record**.

7. In the Insert Glossary Record selection box, choose **D**ata File.

8. In the **D**ata File text box, type **letterhd** and choose OK or press Enter. Ami Pro returns to the Insert Glossary Record selection box.

9. Select letterhd and click Insert.

    Alternatively, press Tab until the glossary is selected, then press Enter.

Looking at Design

You can set up a letterhead in Ami Pro in many ways. You may want to try the following three designs on your own (see figs. 5.6, 5.7, and 5.8). All three work well as glossary data files. You also can have the final design copied or printed at a print shop.

When you use this glossary in other documents, if your margins aren't set to 1/2 inch in the new documents, your letterhead may not look the same as the original.

You need only perform steps 7 through 9 once per glossary. The next time you want to use this glossary, set up the document margins and place the cursor. Type the name of the glossary and press Ctrl+K.

HUMBLE OPINIONS CORPORATION

POST OFFICE BOX 174 · OAK HILL, WEST VIRGINIA 25901
(304) 469-6166   (800) 467-2323

Fig. 5.6 A letterhead design created in Ami Pro by using the Frame and Drawing features.

HUMBLE OPINIONS, INC.
Computer and Software Consultants

P. O. Box 174   ·   Oak Hill, West Virginia 25901
(304) 469-6166   (800) 467-2323

Fig. 5.7   A letterhead design that uses clip art from AmiDraw.

HUMBLE OPINIONS CORPORATION
COMPUTER AND SOFTWARE CONSULTANTS
POST OFFICE BOX 174 · OAK HILL, WEST VIRGINIA 25901
(304) 469-6166 · (800) 467-2323

Fig. 5.8 A letterhead design with a grouping of graphic images as part of the logo.

You can create the first letterhead by using frames. Figure 5.6 illustrates a variation of the use of reversed type. The logo is white type in a frame with a black background, which is placed within another frame. The rule under the company name was created by choosing Tools Drawing.

AmiDraw, a collection of 100 clip-art files, is packaged with Ami Pro. AmiDraw files contain art you can use with your letterhead design. Figure 5.7 illustrates a design that incorporates an AmiDraw file in a round-cornered frame. Note that the shadow of the frame is on the left, to lead the eye into the letterhead. The name of the company is small because the computer is the attention-getter. The margins of the type form a boxed look to mirror the frame of the logo.

You can arrange artwork to create an interesting effect, as shown in figure 5.8. Four computer-related clip-art files from AmiDraw are grouped in four round-cornered frames. Repeating that frame for the text ties the letterhead together. The company name is in 24-point type, but uses a lightweight typeface instead of bold. This lighter weight typeface places more emphasis on the graphic images and makes the overall effect light and airy. Centering the text within the frame adds some variety as well.

You also can import other graphics files; see Appendix B for a list and instructions.

Recapping

In this chapter, you created several letterhead designs and learned about Ami Pro features, including how to add bullets and small caps and how to create reversed text.

Create an interesting logo by reversing display type in a frame.

6

Producing Letters

Letters are the foundation of today's business world. Letters inform, request, and confirm daily business transactions. Often, letters create the first (or last) impression on a customer for you. An attractive letter can make a positive first impression.

For detailed information on how to create a form like this see page 150.

All elements of the business letter contribute to the first impression. The letterhead is probably the first noticeable aspect of the letter; therefore, your letterhead should be one that positively represents and promotes your business. Because the message of the letter must be easy to read, the design should contribute to readability. Finally, good grammar, punctuation, and spelling also influence the initial impression.

In Chapter 5, "Producing a Letterhead," you created various letterheads and perhaps found a design that suits your purpose. In producing your letter, try to mirror the design elements used in the letterhead. Extra interparagraph spacing, for example, may repeat the light, airy feeling in the letterhead; justified text may reflect vertical rules on a page; or left-aligned text may emphasize a left-aligned letterhead design. Notice the mirrored, or repeated, elements of design in the letters you create in this chapter.

This chapter tells you how to produce three letter designs. The first design is a traditional business letter; you use the glossary record you created in Chapter 5 as the letterhead in this design. Less formal, the second letter includes graphic rules and a table. The third design is an example of an advertising letter. The three additional designs at the end of this chapter offer suggestions and inspiration for your own designs.

The Ami Pro features you use in this chapter include the Table feature, justified text and hyphenation, spell checking, and more extensive work with frames. Another Ami Pro feature you use in the first design is Document Information. Doc Info helps you identify your documents, which is particularly important with letters.

Printers and type-setters often refer to graphic lines as rules.

The instructions for creating Doc Info appear only in the first set of steps, but you may apply them to any document you produce in Ami Pro.

Designing a Traditional Business Letter

A traditional business letter is formal in design and direct in its message. The design in figure 6.1 uses the conventional letterhead you saved as a glossary data file in Chapter 5. Note the repeated design elements. The company name is open and diffused; the body text mirrors that element with interparagraph spacing and left-aligned text. Using Times Roman in both the company name and the body text creates additional unity.

HUMBLE OPINIONS CORPORATION

Post Office Box 174, Drawer P   Oak Hill, West Virginia 25901

(304) 469-6166

November 4, 1992

Mr. J. C. Gillenwater
Oak Hill *Post*
Drawer PO
Oak Hill, West Virginia 25901

Dear Sir:

Thank you for your recent purchase of software and training. I believe this package offers enormous advantages for your company. After we install the software, someone will schedule your employees for training at your convenience.

Please do not hesitate to call us if you have any problems, questions or comments. We look forward to working with you and your staff.

Sincerely,

D. J. Halsey

Fig. 6.1 A formal business letter.

To create the page layout and insert the glossary data file, follow these steps:

1. Choose File New. The New dialog box appears.

2. In Style Sheet for New Document, choose the default style sheet. Choose OK or press Enter.

3. Choose Page Modify Page Layout. The Modify dialog box appears.

4. In Margins, choose .5 for all margins. Choose OK or press Enter.

5. At the insertion point on the current document, type **letterhd**. Press Ctrl+K. Ami Pro inserts the glossary record.

   You can use this shortcut only if you specified the Glossary Data File in the Insert Glossary Record dialog box. See Chapter 5 for complete instructions.

To enter and format the text, follow these steps:

1. Press Enter three times and type the following:

   (Tab)**November 4, 1992**(Enter twice)
   Mr. J. C. Gillenwater(Enter)
   Oak Hill Post(Enter)
   Drawer PO(Enter)
   Oak Hill, WV 25901(Enter twice)
   Dear Sir:(Enter twice)
   Thank you for your recent purchase of software and training. I believe this package offers enormous advantages for your company. After we install the software, a member of our training staff will schedule your employees for training at your convenience.(Enter twice)
   Please do not hesitate to call us if you have any problems, questions, or comments. We look forward to working with you and your staff.(Enter twice)
   (Tab)**Sincerely,**(Enter three times)
   (Tab)**D. J. Halsey**

2. Select November 4, 1992. Choose Style Modify Style. The Modify dialog box appears.

3. In Style, choose Alignment. Choose the Left Tab button.

4. Place a tab at 4.75" on the ruler.

5. Choose Use Style Tabs. Choose OK or press Enter.

   Because you changed the tabs in the Body Text style, the two tabs at the end of the letter—and any tab in this document—automatically

position at 4.75". You did not change the style sheet permanently, however; your changes only apply to this one document. See Chapter 5 for instructions for changing a style sheet.

6. Select `Post` in the address. Choose italics, using the SmartIcons or pressing Ctrl+I. Because `Post` is the name of a newspaper, it needs to be in italics.

The 1/2-inch margins are necessary for the letterhead to fit the page. The letter margins should be somewhat indented, however, to make the letter look better. If you do not indent the body of the letter, it will extend 1/2 inch beyond either side of the letterhead, making the line length too long.

To indent the letter margins, follow these steps:

1. Select the text from `Mr. J. C. Gillenwater` to the end of the body of the letter, `with you and your staff`.

2. Choose **Text Indention**. The Indent dialog box appears.

3. Set **All** to .5; set From **Right** to .5. Choose OK or press Enter.

Now that you have your letter formatted attractively, you don't want to ruin the effect with misspelled words. Use Ami Pro's spelling checker to help you avoid embarrassing misspellings.

To check the spelling of your letter, follow these steps:

1. Place the cursor in front of the date. Choose **Tools Spell Check**. Choose OK or press Enter.

2. The Spell Check dialog box appears to question any misspelled words (such as `Gillenwater`). You can choose Skip All, Skip, Add to Dictionary, or Cancel. In this case, choose Skip. Ami Pro continues the spelling check until it reaches the end of the document.

> Ami Pro 3.0 users also may want to use the grammar checker.

To save and print your letter, follow these steps:

1. Choose **File Save As**. In the File **Name** text box, type **letter1**. Choose OK or press Enter.

2. Choose **File Print**. The default setting is one copy. Choose OK or press Enter.

The following instructions are steps for using Ami Pro's Document Information, or Doc Info. Using this feature, you can list a file name, directory, style sheet, a description of the document, and any other key words you want to add. Ami Pro lists statistics about the document, such as date created, date revised, number of pages, and

> Ami Pro automatically updates the data contained in the Doc Info fields, such as names of editors, writers, or clients.

Description in the Doc Info dialog box refers to the Save as a Style Sheet option. If you saved this style sheet as new, you list the changes in the Description text box to view when you begin a new document. This situation does not apply to this particular document.

number of words. Ami Pro does not automatically update the statistics data; you must select Update in the dialog box to update the information. Ami Pro does automatically update directory and file information, revision dates and times, and editing time. The Doc Info feature is a valuable tool for organizing and finding your Ami Pro documents—especially your letters. Use Doc Info before opening a file to view key words and descriptions.

To create Doc Info for the preceding letter design, follow these steps:

1. Choose File Doc Info. The Doc Info dialog box appears.

2. In Keywords, type the following:

Gillenwater, J. C.(down arrow)
Oak Hill Post(down arrow)
Software training

You can print the Doc Info with your document by choosing File Print. In the Print dialog box, choose Options. In the Print Options dialog box, choose With Doc Description. Choose OK and press Enter. Ami Pro returns to the Print dialog box. Choose OK and press Enter to print.

Designing a Letter with Text and Graphics

You can produce a business letter with the help of a glossary data file by feeding a printed or copied letterhead into your printer, or by designing the letterhead at the time of writing. Any of the designs in this and the preceding chapters work as glossary data files. In the following design, you create a simple letterhead at the same time you write the letter. Once again, you can save the letterhead, the entire letter, or any part of the letter as a glossary data file.

The table, saved in a glossary data file, can be used in other letters, forms, and brochures.

The informal letter design in figure 6.2 is a text-and-graphic combination. The typeface for the company name and the body of the letter is Times Roman. Only the company address is in Helvetica, which adds contrast and interest. The page rules at the top and bottom define the margins, and the table makes the information easy to read.

Humble Opinions Corporation

P. O. Box 174 · Oak Hill, WV 25901 · (304) 469-6166

December 6, 1992

Mr. J. L. Bender
212 Forest Drive
Huntington, WV 25701

Dear John:

Thank you for requesting information about our new courses. I have gathered some figures I am sure will interest you. The following table lists the facts you need to fill out the order form.

Code	Course Title	Course Description	Cost
CL-12	Desktop Publishing	Ami Pro Version 2.0	$240
WD-19	Word Processing	Ami Pro Version 2.0	$240
SP-24	Spreadsheet	Lotus 1-2-3 Versions 2.3 and 3.0	$225
DR-40	Planning Printing	Design, Paper, Ink, Finishing	$290

I would be happy to answer any further questions; feel free to call me. I hope to see you and your staff for training soon.

Sincerely,

Sue Plumley

Fig. 6.2 An informal business letter with a table to present specific information.

This table is a basic one; later chapters describe more complex tables. Ami Pro provides you with many options for creating tables: You can add varied rule thicknesses, vary the column widths and row heights, format the type within the table, and so on. With the flexibility of the Table feature, you easily can match the design of the letter within the table to create unity. In this case, the rules in the table reflect the rules of the page, and the typeface is the same.

To create the page, the letterhead, and the body text of the letter, follow these steps:

W hite space within the design makes the letter easy to read.

1. Choose File New. The New dialog box appears.

2. In Style Sheet for New Document, choose the default style sheet. Choose OK or press Enter.

3. Choose Page Modify Page Layout. The Modify dialog box appears. The default margins are acceptable at 1" for top, bottom, left, and right.

A rule thicker than 2 points is too heavy for the balance of the letter.

4. In the Modify dialog box, choose Lines. In Around Page, choose Top and Bottom. In Style, choose the third line style—a 2-point rule.

5. Press Enter and type the following:

   Humble Opinions Corporation(Enter)
   P. O. Box 174(2 spaces, Alt+0183, 2 spaces)**Oak Hill, WV 25901**
   (2 spaces, Alt+0183, 2 spaces)**(304) 469-6166**(Enter four times)
   (Tab)**December 6, 1992**(Enter twice)
   Mr. J. L. Bender(Enter)
   212 Forest Drive(Enter)
   Huntington, WV 25701(Enter twice)
   Dear John:(Enter twice)
   Thank you for requesting information about our new courses. I have gathered some figures I am sure will interest you. The following table lists the facts you need to fill out the order form.(Enter five times)
   I would be happy to answer any further questions; feel free to call me. I hope to see you and your staff for training soon.(Enter twice)
   (Tab)**Sincerely,**(Enter three times)
   (Tab)**Sue Plumley**

6. Select Humble Opinions Corporation. Using the SmartIcons, center and bold the type. Alternatively, press Ctrl+C (Version 2.0) or Ctrl+E (Version 3.0) to center, Ctrl+B to bold.

7. Choose Text Font. The default font is Times Roman. In Size, choose 24. Choose OK or press Enter.

8. Select the address line beginning with P. O. Box 174. Use the SmartIcon to center this line.

9. Choose Text Font. In Face, choose Helv; in Size, choose 10 point. Choose OK or press Enter.

10. Select December 6, 1992. Choose View Show Ruler. The ruler appears at the top of the text area.

11. To set the tab by the ruler, you must activate the ruler. Using the mouse, click the upper half of the ruler.

    Alternatively, choose Edit Go To. Choose Ruler in the Next Item dialog box and press tab to choose Go To ^H. Press Enter.

12. Choose the left tab button, either by clicking it or by pressing the Tab key until the left tab button is selected.

13. Place the cursor in the top part of the ruler and click at 5" on the ruler to set the tab. Alternatively, press Shift-Tab to move to the ruler, then press the right arrow to the 5" mark. Press the space bar to add the tab.

14. Select Sincerely, and Sue Plumley. Set the tabs on the ruler at 5".

To create the table in the letter, follow these steps:

1. Place the cursor at the third paragraph return after fill out the order form.

2. Choose Tools Tables. The Create Table dialog box appears.

3. In Number of Columns, type 4; in Number of Rows, type 5. Choose Layout. The Modify Table Layout dialog box appears.

4. In Default Columns, for Width type 1.00. In Gutter Size, type .16.

5. In Default Rows, Choose Automatic to turn it off.

6. In the Options selection box, turn on Center Table on Page. Choose OK or press Enter. Ami Pro returns to the Create Table dialog box. Choose OK or press Enter again. Ami Pro returns to the document; table gridlines appear at the cursor.

7. Place the cursor in the first column, first row of the table. Choose Table Column/Row Size. The Size dialog box appears.

8. In the Columns text box, for Width type .75. Choose OK or press Enter.

I f you need to clear default tabs on the ruler, drag the tab markers up or down off the ruler. Alternatively, with the cursor on the ruler, use the right-arrow key to move to an unwanted tab marker and press Del to remove it. Version 3.0 users, choose Clear Tabs.

A utomatic governs the height of the row in the table. When turned off, Ami Pro does not automatically increase the height of the row when text wraps.

9. Repeat steps 7 and 8 for each of the remaining columns. The widths of the remaining columns are as follows:

The second column is 1.65".

The third column is 2.68".

The fourth column is .68".

10. Place the cursor in the first column, first row of the table and type the following:

Code(Tab)**Course Title**(Tab)**Course Description**(Tab)**Cost**(Tab)

11. Select the table text you entered. Using the SmartIcons, choose bold and center.

12. Choose Text Font. The default font is Times Roman. Change the size to **10**. Choose OK or press Enter.

13. Type the text from figure 6.2 into the table. Press Tab to move from cell to cell.

14. Select the four rows in the column, `Code`, `CL-12` through `DR-40`. Choose Text Indention. In the Indent dialog box, for All type .03. Choose OK or press Enter.

15. Select the four rows under `Cost`, `$240` through `$290`. Choose Text Alignment Right.

To apply the lines to the table, follow these steps:

1. Select the first row of the table. Choose Table Lines/Shades.

2. In the Position selection box, choose Outline and Right. In Line Style, choose the second rule—a 1-point rule. Choose OK or press Enter.

3. Select the rest of the table. Choose Table Lines/Shades.

4. In the Position selection box, choose Outline and Right. In Line Style, choose the second rule. Choose OK or press Enter.

To save and print your document, follow these steps:

1. Choose File Save As. In the File Name text box, type **letter2**. Choose OK or press Enter.

2. Choose File Print. The default is set for one copy. Choose OK or press Enter.

Pressing the Tab key in a table moves the cursor to the next cell. Pressing Shift-Tab moves the cursor to the preceding cell. The direction arrows also move the cursor from cell to cell: up, down, left, or right. Pressing Enter in a cell adds another line to the row (only if Automatic is turned on.)

Designing an Advertising Letter

Many times a company sends a letter to its customers as a form of advertising. The letter may offer a special deal or coupons, or announce a grand opening or a contest. With the availability of computerized mailing lists and programs that sort and label mail, advertising letters are becoming more and more popular.

An attractive advertising letter is more likely to be read by the customer. As the designer, you can add graphic images, rules, or bullets to make the letter eye-catching. Because the letter must be easy to read, however, don't clutter it with too much formatting. Keep in mind, too, that an effective advertising letter is no longer than one page. Don't overwhelm your customer!

Figure 6.3 is an example of a brief yet tastefully designed advertising letter. The triple rule around the page is unusual and eye-catching. Note that the text is justified, mirroring the line of the rule. Bullets attract attention to the list of gifts, and the interparagraph spacing breaks up the page with white space. Ami Pro features introduced in these instructions include hyphenation, page rules, hanging indents, and altering a style in a style sheet.

To create the page and text in figure 6.3, follow these steps:

1. Choose File New. The New dialog box appears.

2. In Style Sheet for New Document, choose the default style sheet. Choose OK or press Enter.

3. Choose Page Modify Page Layout. The Modify dialog box appears. In Margins, change all settings to **1.5"**.

4. In Modify, choose Lines. In Around Page, choose All; in Style, choose the only triple rule pattern—a 1-point, 2-point, 1-point rule. In Position, choose Middle. Choose OK or press Enter.

5. Press Enter twice and type the following:

   Congratulations!(Enter)
   You have been selected for a special promotion! We are offering this deal to only 300 homes in your state and you live in one of those homes! Let me begin by telling you there is absolutely no obligation to buy. All we ask is that you allow us a few minutes of your time. For allowing us that, you win a FREE vacation to Florida!(Enter twice)
   Just look at what you can win:(Enter)
   (Tab)**Five days at a luxurious hotel**(Enter)

I n the Modify Lines dialog box, Position refers to the placement of the rule. Inside is closest to the text area, whereas Outside is in the margin, closest to the page edge. Middle, in this case, is .75" from the edge of the paper and .75" from the edge of the text area.

(Tab)**Three free meals**(Enter)
(Tab)**Limousine service**(Enter)
(Tab)**Free tickets to the sights and attractions in the area**(Enter twice)

6. At this point, continue entering the text from the letter shown in figure 6.3.

7. At the end of the last paragraph, type the following:

(Tab twice)**Sincerely,**(Enter)
(Tab twice)**Cheatem Resorts**(Enter four times)
P. S.(Tab)**You are welcome to invite as many as four family members or friends to accompany you on your FREE vacation.**

To format the text, follow these steps:

1. Place the cursor at the top of the page. Choose Tools Spell Check. Respond to any questions from the spelling checker.

2. Choose Style Modify Style. In the Style selection box, be sure that Body Text is selected.

3. In Modify, choose Alignment. Set the left tabs on the ruler at .5" and 3.75". Choose Use Style Tabs.

4. In the Alignment dialog box, choose Justify. Turn on Hyphenation by selecting it. Choose OK or press Enter.

5. Select Congratulations!. Choose Text Font. The default font is Times Roman. In Size, choose 18.

6. Use the SmartIcons to bold the text.

7. Choose Style Select a Style. The Styles box appears in the upper-right corner of the screen.

8. Select the text from Five days at a luxurious hotel through Free tickets to the sights and attractions in the area. In the Styles box, choose Bullet 1.

9. Choose Style Modify Style. The Modify dialog box appears.

10. In Style, be sure that Bullet 1 is selected. In the Modify dialog box, choose Spacing.

11. In Line Spacing, choose Custom. Type .26. Choose OK or press Enter.

12. Select P. S.. Choose bold. Choose View Show Ruler.

By adding extra leading to the bulleted list, you add to the design, readability, and overall effect of the advertising letter. These small typesetting tricks make a document look professional.

Congratulations!

You have been selected for a special promotion! We are offering this deal to only 300 homes in your state and you live in one of those homes! Let me begin by telling you there is absolutely no obligation to buy. All we ask is that you allow us a few minutes of your time. For allowing us that, you win a FREE vacation to Florida!

Just look at what you can win:
* Five days at a luxurious hotel
* Three free meals
* Limousine service
* Free tickets to the sights and attractions in the area

What more could you ask for? There is no obligation. No salesman will call at your home.

Remember, you are under no obligation to buy. A few minutes of your time is all we ask. We will be calling you in a few days to discuss this exciting vacation with you. We hope you will consider traveling to our palatial resort and touring our complex. We are located just seven hours from you! Once you have discussed your future with us, you will be awarded your FREE vacation to Florida!

We are looking forward to talking to you. Remember, we will call you in a few days to arrange for your FREE vacation!

Sincerely,
Cheatem Resorts

P. S. You are welcome to invite as many as four family members or friends to accompany you on your FREE vacation.

Fig. 6.3   An advertising letter with a triple page rule.

13. Activate the ruler by clicking it with a mouse. Alternatively, choose **Edit Go To**. Choose Ruler in the Next Item selection box; press Tab to choose Go to ^H, and press Enter.

14. On the ruler, move the lower indention triangle to 2" (so that it is even with the tab you set earlier). Drag the triangle with a mouse; alternatively, use the Tab key to move the triangle and press 2 to set the indention with the keyboard.

To save and print your document, follow these steps:

1. Choose **File Save As**. In the File **Name** text box, type **letter2**. Choose OK or press Enter.

2. Choose **File Print**. The default setting is one copy. Choose OK or press Enter.

Looking at Design

You can create a variety of business letter designs in Ami Pro by using frames, page rules, and graphic images. Often a simple letter design is the most effective. Figure 6.4 illustrates a simple design, created by using the Frame feature in Ami Pro. The round-corner frame complements the wide margins and the white space. The letterhead is unpretentious; the entire letter is informal. This design works well for sending a note about business to a friend.

When creating form letters in Ami Pro, use the merge feature to personalize each letter.

Using the frame function in Ami Pro affords you flexibility in your design. Figure 6.5 uses frames to create the rules at the top and bottom of the page. The frame height is no more than 1/8 inch. By turning on the top and bottom double rule in a frame and turning off the side rules, you create twice the rules.

Altering the margins of a letter can supply interesting white space. In figure 6.6, the left and top margins are only 1/2-inch wide, whereas the right and bottom margins are 2 inches. The vertical rule on the left emphasizes the narrow margin, as does the alignment of the company name and address. Justified body text helps to define the wide right margin.

Bender Printing and Associates
2114 East Main Street
Oak Hill, West Virginia 25901

November 12, 1992

Mr. B. N. Crowder
211 Reservoir Drive
Lexington, KY 32321

Dear Bob:

In response to your request, I have enclosed several paper samples. I believe the white offset linen, 70# may be the best one for your job. It matches other materials your company has printed, it fits the proposal, and the price is right.

Imagine the white linen with your shade of blue and the warm red of your logo. The logo, in particular, would be prominent on white. The texture of the linen would make the graphic rules stand out, as well.

If I can be of further help, don't hesitate to call me at 304-464-3131. I look forward to working with you on your newest project.

Sincerely,

Sue Bender

Fig. 6.4 An informal letter design.

humble opinions P. O. Box 174 · Oak Hill, West Virginia 25901

March 25, 1993

J. W. Jenkins
1455 West 48th Street
St. Albans, WV 25605

Dear Mrs. Jenkins:

We wish to express our gratitude for your business during the past year. Your company has been a pleasure to serve; your staff is always courteous, patient and friendly.

We are pleased to take this opportunity to offer you, our special customer, a chance to enter our free contest! There is no purchase necessary. All you have to do is fill out the enclosed post card and return it to us within 14 days. Our company is giving away a personal computer worth over $2,000 at the end of April. It is our way of saying thank you to special customers like you.

Please return the post card to us as soon as possible. We will contact you by May 3 to let you know if you won this valuable computer.

Again, thank you for your patronage. We hope to continue doing business with you for many years.

Sincerely,
D. J. Halsey, President
Humble Opinions

Fig. 6.5 Double rules created with the Frame feature of Ami Pro.

Bender Printing and Associates
2114 East Main Street
Oak Hill, West Virginia 25901

November 12, 1992

Mr. B. N. Crowder
211 Reservoir Drive
Lexington, KY 32321

Dear Bob:

In response to your request, I have enclosed several paper samples. I believe the white offset linen, 70# may be the best one for your job. It matches other materials your company has printed, it fits the proposal, and the price is right.

Imagine the white linen with your shade of blue and the warm red of your logo. The logo, in particular, would be prominent on white. The texture of the linen would make the graphic rules stand out, as well.

If I can be of further help, don't hesitate to call me at 304-464-3131. I look forward to working with you on your newest project.

Sincerely,

Sue Bender

Fig. 6.6 Wide margins with added design elements to emphasize the white space.

Recapping

In this chapter, you learned how to import a glossary data file, use Doc Info, and create various types of business letters. Working with the table and frame features enables you to divide and organize information in your letters and other documents.

7

Producing Envelopes

Producing envelopes is effortless in Ami Pro: changing page orientation is easy, adding logos or art is simple with frames, and using style sheets helps produce an envelope design over and over again quickly and smoothly. This chapter instructs you in setting up your own style sheets, two for a vertical feed printer and one for horizontal feed. If one of these style sheets doesn't work with your printer, try one of Ami Pro's. Ami Pro supplies several envelope style sheets, one of which probably suits your printer.

HUMBLE OPINIONS
P. O. Box 174
Oak Hill, WV 25901

For detailed information on how to create a form like this see page 162.

The envelope designs in this chapter correspond to many of the letterheads you created in Chapter 5, "Producing a Letterhead," so that you can see how an envelope and letterhead relate. Matching letterhead styles with the envelope styles is important for unity and consistency among company pieces.

New Ami Pro techniques you learn in this chapter include creating and saving style sheets, creating styles with paragraph rules, centering tabs, switching page orientation, and altering page size.

Planning Your Envelope Design

Planning your design is the important first step to producing your envelope. Consider the postal regulations first, then your printer capabilities. Finally, design your envelope to match your letterheads. The following sections describe, in detail, these three steps to planning your envelope design.

Postal Regulations and Guidelines

When planning your envelope design, you must consider postal regulations and guidelines. The United States Post Office recommends certain guidelines and requires that you observe definite regulations concerning mailed materials. The *guidelines* guarantee your mail speedy, efficient, and accurate processing and delivery. If your envelope does not conform to *regulations*, however, the post office cannot process your mail at all. Many of the following guidelines are not yet regulations, but the postal service plans to legislate them as such in the near future. Complete, detailed booklets such as *Postal Addressing Standards* and *A Guide to Business Mail Preparation* are available from your post office.

A primary reason the post office requires you to meet these regulations and recommends that you follow these guidelines is the *optical character recognition (OCR) scanner*. The OCR scanner, used by all major post offices, reads addresses, sorting and distributing mail at a rate of 36,000 pieces per hour—from adding the ZIP+4 to sorting directly to the letter carrier. If your mail qualifies for the OCR, delivery is much faster.

Size

Mailed material has minimum and maximum size requirements. The minimum height is 3 1/2 inches, the minimum length is 5 inches;

Be sure that your printer is capable of printing envelopes; check your printer reference manual.

The post office offers seminars and detailed information about business mailings. Contact your local postmaster for more information.

If the OCR scanner cannot read your address, it rejects the envelope. Rejected mail must be sorted by hand, which slows down delivery time.

anything smaller cannot be mailed. Be especially attentive to the size of any post cards or return reply cards you design; somehow it's easier to make them too small. These size limits are a regulation of the Postal Service.

The maximum sizes for mailed pieces are guidelines rather than regulations. A maximum height of 6 1/8 inches and length of 10 1/2 inches ensures that your piece can pass through the OCR scanner. Remember, any mail passing through the OCR scanner is processed and delivered faster.

Boundaries

The recommended placement of the mailing (delivery) address is a guideline, as is the placement of the return address. Most mailed pieces contain only the return and mailing addresses. The placement of bar codes and facing identification marks, however, are regulations. Bar codes and FIMs are used in business mailings, bulk mailings, and return replies.

A *bar code* is a system of encoding ZIP code information on letter mail; the bar code is located near the lower-right corner of a mailed piece. The bar code is read by a bar-code sorter to speed up the sorting process. A facing identification mark (*FIM*) is used in addition to a bar code and is located along the upper-right edge of the mailed piece. FIMs provide a means of sorting business and courtesy-reply mail, and also separate preprinted bar codes for processing. You can request that your post office assign you a bar code and FIM for your business mail.

Figure 7.1 illustrates a #10 envelope with the measurements for placement of address, bar code, and so on. A #10 envelope is standard business size (9 1/2 inches by 4 1/8 inches).

- *Return address.* The return address should be in the upper left corner. As long as the return address does not fall below the second line of the mailing address, no other restrictions apply to the return address.

- *Mailing address.* The mailing, or delivery, address should be indented from the left and right margins at least 1 inch. Also, the mailing address should end (city, state, and ZIP) at least 5/8 inch from the bottom. The first line of the delivery address should be no more than 2 3/4 inch from the bottom of the envelope.

- *Bar code.* As illustrated, the bar code can be placed in an area 5/8 inch by 4 1/2 inches in the lower right corner of the envelope. Another bar code placement option is after the city, state, and ZIP code of the mailing address.

Oversized pieces of mail are sorted by hand.

- *FIM.* The FIM must be within 1/8 inch of the top envelope edge, and placed between 1 3/4 and 3 inches from the right edge.

❶ Return address
❷ Mailing address
❸ FIM
❹ Bar code

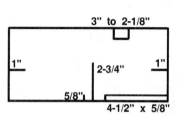
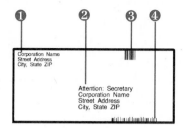

Fig. 7.1 Correct placement of mailing address, bar code, FIM, and return address (left); example of a properly addressed envelope (right).

Additional Copy

Any extraneous copy on an envelope, such as logos and advertising copy, should not print below the address. If additional copy is printed below this line, the OCR scanner rejects the mail and processing and delivery take longer. One exception applies: The OCR cannot read red ink.

Postal Permits

A *postal permit* is assigned to you by the post office to use in place of stamps on your mail. Normally, you pay a monthly fee adjusted to the type of permit you use. The most common permits are bulk rate, non-profit, and business reply, although many other types of permits are available.

The post office is very particular about the wording and placement of your permit. Remember the following general rules about permits:

- You must use readable type in the permit (9-point Helvetica, all caps, centered, for example).

- You must confine the permit in a graphic box.

- You cannot use any punctuation within the permit.

- You must use the specific wording assigned to you by the post office for your permit.

After you receive your permit, you can use it on any bulk mailings you do. If you plan to use a permit, see your postmaster for details.

Always consult your postmaster if you have any questions.

You can print additional copy in red ink anywhere on the envelope without fear of rejection by the OCR scanner.

Never use a postal permit to mail one or two pieces from a mailbox; your permit may be revoked.

Print Quality

Print quality refers to typeface; to letter, word, and line spacing; and to printer quality; in other words, print quality refers to readability. Observing a few guidelines ensures that your addresses are readable by the OCR scanner. The following guidelines refer to the mailing address only:

- Use an easily readable typeface. A sans serif type such as Futura, Helvetica, or Univers works best for the delivery address. If you prefer serif type, try New Century Schoolbook or Friz Quadrata; the letters are fully formed and easily recognizable.

- Left-align the type.

- Use no more than 20% screens.

- Avoid types that are bold, italic, expanded, or condensed.

- Be sure that letter and word spacing are in a normal, readable range.

- Use line spacing, or leading, at least two points over the type size.

Laser printers produce the best quality for mailed materials other than having them offset printed. An inkjet or dot-matrix printer also does fine as long as the type is not broken or fuzzy.

I f you use a color printer to print the mailing address, don't use red ink; the OCR scanner cannot read red ink.

Printer Capabilities

Each type of printer deals with envelopes in a different way—and some do not print them at all. Before you spend time designing and creating an envelope, be sure that your printer is capable of printing it. Check your printer manual first, where you should find valuable information about size, orientation, and feed.

Your printer may have a *platen feed*. If so, you feed envelopes into your printer one at a time. On the other hand, your printer may have a built-in *envelope feed*, which means that you can print many envelopes before refilling the feeder. Most laser printers have a *vertical feed*, which means that you feed by the narrow edge of the envelope. On a laser printer, you also need to set the printer menu to accommodate envelopes. Inkjet and dot-matrix printers usually have a *horizontal feed* (the long edge feeds). With a dot-matrix printer, you may need to remove the tractor-fed paper to insert an envelope.

The *style sheet* is an important part of planning your envelope design. After you set up a style sheet, you can produce envelopes with very little effort. A style sheet defines page size, margins, typefaces, sizes, and styles.

The instructions in this chapter give you the steps to set up a style sheet for both horizontal- and vertical-feed printers. Placement of the return and mailing addresses may need to be adjusted to fit your particular printer. If one of the style sheets in this chapter does not work, try one of Ami Pro's envelope style sheets.

Envelope and Letterhead

If you use a letterhead for your business, your envelope should match the design in logo, typeface, rules, graphic images, and so on. Naturally, you cannot put as much information on an envelope as you can on a letterhead, and you shouldn't. Only the company logo, name, and address should appear on an envelope. You can add the president's name or a short, catchy phrase as well. Leave off phone numbers, board members, and officer's names—you don't have enough room.

Notice that each of the envelope designs in this chapter matches a letterhead in Chapter 5. Matching envelopes and letterheads give your customer the impression that yours is an organized, proficient company.

Creating a Style Sheet for a Vertical-Feed Printer

This style sheet works with many printers that feed vertically, or short end first. Some laser printers and inkjet printers can use this style. Again, be sure to check your printer manual for information about envelope feed method, paper tray, and so on.

To create a style sheet for a vertical-feed printer, follow these steps:

1. Choose File New. The New dialog box appears.

2. Choose the default style sheet. Choose OK or press Enter.

3. Choose Page Modify Page Layout.

4. In the Modify box, choose **Page Settings**. In Page Size, choose Custom. In the Custom box, type **9.00 (width) x 4.12 (height)**. The measurement should be in inches.

5. In Orientation, choose Landscape.

6. In Modify, choose Margins & Columns. In Margins, set the Left to .35, the Right to .25, the Top to .35, and the Bottom to .50.

The return address design should be a miniature re-creation of your letterhead design.

7. In Tabs, set a left tab at 4.25" on the ruler. Choose OK or press Enter.

8. Choose **Style** Save as a Style Sheet.

9. In the Save as a Style Sheet dialog box, type **envelope**. Choose OK or press Enter.

This style sheet sets the page size and margins for a #10 envelope. You can begin typing and formatting your return address immediately. To position the cursor for the mailing address, go down six lines (by pressing Enter), then press the Tab key. Your cursor is positioned to type the mailing address.

Creating a Style Sheet for a Center Vertical-Feed Printer

Many laser printers include a center feed tray for envelopes. If yours is one of these printers, this style sheet should work for you. To create the style sheet for a center vertical-feed printer, do the following:

1. Choose **File New**. The New dialog box appears.

2. Choose the default style sheet. Choose OK or press Enter.

3. Choose **Page Modify** Page Layout.

4. In Modify, choose **Page Settings**.

5. In Orientation, choose **Landscape**.

6. In Modify, choose **Margins & Columns**.

7. Set the Left margin to **2.00**, the Right to **1.00**, the Top to **2.50**, and the Bottom to **3.25**. Choose OK or press Enter.

8. Choose **Style** Save as a Style Sheet.

9. In the Save as a Style Sheet dialog box, type **envelope**. Choose OK or press Enter.

This style sheet sets the page size and margins for a #10 envelope. You can begin typing and formatting your return address immediately. To position the cursor for the mailing address, go down six lines (by pressing Enter), then press the Tab key. Your cursor is positioned to type the mailing address.

Create the letter-head in your style sheet, and save **With** Contents in the **Save as a Style Sheet** dialog box. Anytime you use that style sheet, your return address automatically appears.

After finishing the design, save **With** Contents when you save your style sheet so that your return address remains a part of the style sheet.

Creating a Style Sheet for a Horizontal-Feed Printer

A horizontal feed is one in which the long edge of the envelope feeds into the printer. Most dot-matrix and inkjet printers feed this way. Some laser printers also may use horizontal feed. To create the style sheet for horizontal feed, do the following:

1. Choose File New. The New dialog box appears.

2. Choose the default style sheet. Choose OK or press Enter.

3. Choose Page Modify Page Layout.

4. In Modify, choose **Page Settings**.

5. In Page Size, choose **Custom**. In Custom, type **9.00 (width) x 4.12 (height)**.

6. Choose Margins & Columns. Set the **Left** margin to **.35**, the **Right** to **.50**, the Top to **.25**, and the Bottom to **.75**. Choose OK or press Enter.

7. Choose Style Save as a Style Sheet.

8. In the Save as a Style Sheet dialog box, type **envelope**. Choose OK or press Enter.

This style sheet sets the page size and margins for a #10 envelope. You can begin typing and formatting your return address immediately. To position the cursor for the mailing address, go down six lines (by pressing Enter), then press the Tab key. Your cursor is positioned to type the mailing address.

W hen you create your final design, save your stylesheet With Contents.

Creating a Traditional Envelope Design

The first design matches the letterhead design in figure 5.1 in Chapter 5. Using Times Roman for the head, the company name is in large caps and small caps (see fig. 7.2). The address uses the small caps also, but with Helvetica. This design is basic, yet formal and sophisticated.

To create the first envelope design, do the following:

1. Choose File New. The New dialog box appears.

2. In Style Sheet for New Document, choose the envelope style sheet you created for your printer. Choose OK or press Enter.

3. Type the following:

   Humble Opinions(Enter)
   P. O. Box 174(Enter)
   Oak Hill, WV 25901

4. Select `Humble Opinions`. Choose bold.

5. Choose Text Font. In Size, choose 18 point. Choose OK or press Enter. Deselect the type.

6. Select `umble`. Choose Text Caps. In the secondary command menu, choose Small Caps. Repeat with `pinions`.

7. Select the two address lines. Choose Text Font. In Face, choose Helv; in Size, choose 10 point. Choose OK or press Enter. Deselect the type.

8. Select the `ox` in Box. Choose Text Caps. In the secondary command menu, choose Small Caps. Repeat with `ak` in Oak and `ill` in Hill.

9. Choose File Save As. Type **env1**. Choose OK or press Enter.

10. Make sure that your printer is set up for envelope printing.

11. Choose File Print.

You can use your company name and address instead of the samples shown in this book.

Alternatively, you can save as a style sheet.

HUMBLE OPINIONS
P. O. BOX 174
OAK HILL, WV 25901

Fig. 7.2 A traditional design for the return address of a business envelope.

Creating a Text and Graphic Envelope Design

The second envelope design incorporates graphic rules above and below the return address. Using Ami Pro, you easily can customize the length of these rules. Figure 7.3 illustrates an envelope design that matches the letterhead in figure 5.3 of Chapter 5. The typeface is center aligned, Times Roman. As in the letterhead, the address is on one line and separated by a bullet. Because an envelope is smaller than a letterhead, the design elements are also smaller.

Humble Opinions Corporation
P. O. Box 174 · Oak Hill, WV 25901

Fig. 7.3   A professional-looking envelope design.

To create the envelope design, follow these steps:

1. Choose File New. The New dialog box appears.

2. In Style Sheet for New Document, choose the envelope style sheet you created for your printer. Choose OK or press Enter.

3. Type the following or enter your own information:

   (Tab)**Humble Opinions Corporation**(Enter)
   (Tab)**P. O. Box 174**(2 spaces, Alt-0183, 2 spaces)**Oak Hill, WV 25901**

4. Select Humble Opinions. Choose Style Create Style. The Create Style dialog box appears.

5. In the New Style text box, type **Env head**. The Modify Style dialog box appears.

6. In Modify, choose Font; in Face, choose Tms Rmn; in Size, choose 12; in Attributes, choose Bold.

7. In Modify, choose Alignment. In Tabs, select the center tab and position it at 1.5" on the ruler. Choose Use Style Tabs.

8. In Modify, choose Lines. In Lines, choose Line Above. Choose the first line pattern (a .75-point rule).

9. Directly under the line patterns, choose Spacing. Type .05.

10. In Length, choose Other. Type **3.10**. Choose OK or press Enter. Ami Pro returns you to the original document.

11. Choose Style Select a Style. The Styles box appears.

12. Select Humble Opinions Corporation. Choose env head from the Styles box.

I n Ami Pro 3.0, you can select various bullet styles by choosing Edit Insert Bullet.

T imes Roman is the default typeface.

T his spacing sets the type .05 inches from the line, for "breathing room."

To format the style for the address, follow these steps:

1. Select the address line of text. Choose **S**tyle Create Style. The Create Style dialog box appears.

2. In the New Style text box, type **env address**. Choose OK or press Enter. The Modify Style dialog box appears.

3. In Modify, choose Font. Set the type Size at 10 point.

4. In Modify, choose Ali**g**nment. In Tabs, choose the center tab marker and position it at 1.5" on the ruler. Choose **U**se Style Tabs.

5. In Modify, choose Lines. In Lines, choose Line **B**elow. In **S**pacing, type **.05**. The measurement should be in inches.

6. In Length, choose **O**ther. Type **3.10**. Choose OK or press Enter.

7. Select the address. In the Styles box, choose env address.

8. Choose File Save As. Type **env2**. Choose OK or press Enter.

9. Make sure that your printer is set up for envelope printing.

10. Choose File Print.

Creating an Innovative Envelope Design

The design for a return address of an envelope can include graphic rules or images, reversed type, or any other design element that makes it stand out. The next design employs a frame with reversed type for the company name (see fig. 7.4). The company name is all caps, just as the letterhead design it matches in Chapter 5 (see fig. 5.5). You can see a difference between the two designs. The letterhead has a ruled box surrounding it, but the envelope's address doesn't, because adding the ruled box to the envelope would crowd the small area. The typeface, reversed type, and alignment, however, do resemble the letterhead and work well for a matching set.

Refer to your specific style sheet instructions for information on positioning the cursor for the mailing (delivery) address.

Designs for an envelope need not match the letterhead exactly, but be sure that the typefaces and alignment are the same.

HUMBLE OPINIONS
POST OFFICE BOX 174
OAK HILL, WEST VIRGINIA 25901

Fig. 7.4   Envelope design with reversed type for the company name.

Alternatively, you can draw the frame by clicking the mouse pointer on the Create Frame SmartIcon.

The position of your frame depends on the margins of your style sheet. When Ami Pro returns to the document, reposition the frame to the top left corner of the text area.

In the Lines dialog box, an X in a check box means that the option is turned on; click or select the box to turn off the option.

By removing the paragraph spacing below the text, you can fit the large type in the box.

To create the envelope design, do the following:

1. Choose **F**ile **N**ew. The New dialog box appears.

2. In **S**tyle Sheet for New Document, choose the envelope style sheet you created for your printer. Choose OK or press Enter.

3. Choose **F**rame **C**reate Frame. The Create Frame dialog box appears.

4. In the Size dialog box, in **W**idth type **2.85**; in **H**eight, type **.45**. Choose OK or press Enter.

5. Choose **F**rame **M**odify Frame Layout.

6. In Frame, choose **T**ype. In Text Wrap Around, choose No Wrap Beside.

7. In Display, choose **S**quare Corner.

8. In Frame, choose **S**ize & Position. In Margins, choose Clear Margins.

9. In Frame, choose **L**ines & Shadows. In Lines, turn off all lines.

10. In Shadow, choose **N**one. In **B**ackground, choose Black. Choose OK or press Enter.

11. Place the cursor in the frame. Double-click or use the keyboard to choose **E**dit **G**o To. In the **N**ext item dialog box, choose Frame. Press Tab to move the cursor to Go To ^H. Ami Pro returns to the document; the frame is selected. Press Enter to place the cursor in the frame.

12. Type the following:

    (space)**HUMBLE OPINIONS**

13. Select the type. Choose **T**ext **F**ont. In **S**ize, choose 18 point. In the color bar, choose white. Choose OK or press Enter.

14. Choose **S**tyle **M**odify Style. In the Modify Style dialog box, choose **S**pacing.

15. In Paragraph Spacing **B**elow, delete the contents and type **0**. Choose OK or press Enter.

16. Select the frame and resize it to look like figure 7.4.

    Alternatively, you can choose **F**rame **M**odify Frame Layout. In **S**ize & Position, type **2.45** for the **W**idth; type **.29** for the **H**eight.

17. Place the cursor beneath the frame. Type the following:

    POST OFFICE BOX 174(Enter)
    OAK HILL, WEST VIRGINIA 25901

18. Select the two address lines. Choose **Text Font**. Change the **S**ize to 10 point. Choose OK or press Enter.

19. Choose **Text In**d**ention**. In the Indent dialog box, choose **A**ll. Type **.05**. Choose OK or press Enter.

20. Choose **File Save As**. Type **env3**. Choose OK or press Enter.

21. Make sure that your printer is set up for envelope printing.

22. Choose **File Print**.

Looking at Design

Following are a few more designs that match the letterhead designs from Chapters 5 and 6. After designing your letterhead, the envelope is easy. Figure 7.5 illustrates a design that matches figure 5.6 in Chapter 5. The reversed logo is in a frame. The text wrap around feature (**F**rame **M**odify Frame Layout) is set to **W**rap Around. This setting allows the company name and address to be placed beside the frame. Again, the typefaces match those of the letterhead, and the graphic rule separates the two lines of type.

HUMBLE OPINIONS CORPORATION
POST OFFICE BOX 174 · OAK HILL, WEST VIRGINIA 25901

Fig. 7.5   Envelope design with logo and graphic rule.

AmiDraw files and other clip art, scanned art, and paint and draw graphics are all possibilities for adding to letterhead and envelope design. Figure 7.6 illustrates a design that incorporates an AmiDraw file; figure 5.7 in Chapter 5 also uses this clip art in a letterhead design. The placement of the art and type in the envelope design reflect their use in the letterhead. The company name is all caps, light face, and centered on a center tab. The address and phrase center on a tab as well.

If your frame is not positioned so that its edges are exactly on the left and top margins, your cursor may not appear beneath the frame. To correct this situation, reposition the frame.

You can use a logo or line art from many other software applications; refer to Appendix B.

HUMBLE OPINIONS, INC.
Computer and Software Consultants
P. O. Box 174 · Oak Hill, WV 25901

Fig. 7.6   Envelope design with clip art from AmiDraw.

As an alternative, you can choose only one image to add to the envelope design.

Figure 7.7 represents a simpler envelope design to match figure 5.8 in Chapter 5. Figure 5.8 uses four computer clip-art images in frames to the left of the letterhead. To add four images to an envelope would clutter the small area. As an alternative, the round-corner frame and the type have been used for this design. The frame, typefaces, and spacing resemble the letterhead, and the envelope looks clean and uncluttered.

HUMBLE OPINIONS CORPORATION
POST OFFICE BOX 174 · OAK HILL, WEST VIRGINIA 25901

Fig. 7.7   A round-cornered frame enclosing the company name and address.

Figure 7.8 is another example of a matching envelope. Its mate is figure 6.2 in Chapter 6. You can use either the frame feature to produce the rule above the head or the paragraph style.

Humble Opinions Corporation
P. O. Box 174 · Oak Hill, WV 25901

Fig. 7.8   A basic envelope design.

Frames in Ami Pro make it easy to add a rule to any side of a design. Figure 7.9 shows a rule to the left of the return address. This design matches the letterhead in figure 6.6 of Chapter 6.

Bender Printing and Associates
2114 East Main Street
Oak Hill, West Virginia 25901

Fig. 7.9 A rule to the left of the address for added interest.

Figure 7.10 illustrates how the envelope design changes from the letterhead design. The matching letterhead is figure 6.5 in Chapter 6. Larger type and heavier doubled rules are used in the letterhead design. The envelope design uses thin double rules but repeats them above and below the return address. Remaining the same are the typeface and the alignment; the difference in the rules adds interest and contrast.

humble opinions
P. O. Box 174 · Oak Hill, West Virginia 25901

Fig. 7.10 An interesting variation of the letterhead design for the envelope.

Recapping

In this chapter, you learned how to create a style sheet for an envelope that works with your specific printer. In addition, you learned to match the envelope design to your letterhead for unity between company pieces.

I f you use the paragraph style to produce the line, be sure that you choose Style Create Style.

Producing a Resume

A resume is a tool you use to get a job. Naturally, it is important to have the education, experience, and references required for a particular job and to list all of your qualifications on a resume. It's also important that the resume looks good, and this chapter addresses that concern. Presenting your resume in a clear and concise manner makes it easier for an employer to read your qualifications—and it presents a positive impression of you.

For detailed information on how to create a form like this see page 173.

The following sections provide one approach to writing a resume; you may want to research resume writing further in your local library.

Planning Your Resume

Restrict the length of your resume to one page; second and third pages are seldom read. An employer who receives a flood of resumes for one position appreciates the short, concise summary. If you need to shorten your resume, list facts instead of writing paragraphs. List only the facts that apply to the particular job for which you are applying. Because you are formatting your resume yourself, you easily can customize it to each prospective job. In addition, you always can add a one-page cover letter to your resume to explain other pertinent information. A cover letter should be formatted in the same style as your resume.

The type of information you include in your resume is flexible. Your name, address, and phone number should appear at the top of the resume because the employer must be able to contact you. You don't have to include your age, sex, marital status, or even your health on your resume, although you may choose to include that information. Primarily, you should cover education, experience, and available references.

A career objective or brief statement about the job you seek is important; you can add the statement to the resume or include it in the cover letter. You should be able to describe in one sentence the type of position you seek; try not to limit that position to just one field, if possible. For example, if you're applying for a position in software sales, but you can also install and repair hardware, train new users in various software programs, and run an accounting program, mention all of the above in your career objective.

List education and experience separately; list the more impressive first. The information within each category should begin with the most recent. When listing your education, be sure to include the college or university name, the city, and state. You should list degrees and majors. If you have a college education, you don't need to list your high school. At any rate, do not list anything earlier than high school—never include your junior high, middle, or elementary school.

When accounting for job experience, be very careful with dates and names. Usually, list the dates first; month and year are sufficient. After listing the dates, the name of the company, the city, and state, you should list the duties you performed. The amount of detail you use depends on the particular requirements of the position you seek and how much room you have on the resume.

B ulleted lists make important facts stand out on a resume.

Y ou can add other pertinent information, such as seminars attended or personal experiences.

Y ou can list any pertinent classes that apply to the prospective job.

References may be listed on a resume. Most often, however, you simply state, "Submitted upon request." If you do list references, be sure to list full names, company names, addresses, and phone numbers. Also, be sure to check with your references before including their names. Three references are usually enough to include with a resume.

You can print your resume directly from your printer instead of taking it to a print shop or copy shop. For less than 100 printed pieces the price for offset could be outrageous, and resumes usually look fine when printed on your printer (especially an inkjet or laser printer). Another option is to have your printed resume copied onto letterhead paper at a copy shop.

You should always print your resume on letterhead-quality paper. Use paper with a watermark (see Chapter 4, "Planning and Purchasing Printing"). You can use rag paper such as Strathmore, a linen finish (Swan Linen), or a laid finish (Classic Laid). These papers are not expensive and make a good first impression. Also, consider that a colored paper stands out in a stack of resumes. Because most other applicants will use white and ivory paper, you should consider using light blue or green. But no matter what paper color or finish you use, black ink is the easiest to read on a resume.

The following sections introduce several designs for resumes, ranging from the traditional to the innovative. If you're a lawyer or accountant, you may want to use the basic, traditional resume. If you're an artist, a writer, or a salesperson, try one of the innovative designs in this chapter.

Among the new features of Ami Pro introduced in this chapter are using the Smartype macro, formatting an indent style, formatting two columns, and printing front and back.

To save time in re-creating the following documents, you only need to type the resume one time. You can save it to another file to use for each subsequent design. This way you can spend more time designing than typing! You may want to type your own resume instead of using the text in the example.

Designing a Traditional Resume

The design of the resume in figure 8.1 is simple and conservative. The name and address appear at the top center of the page. Each category of information stands out in the left margin. The facts are indented to balance the page. Indented and left-aligned type create white space on both the left and right margins of the page.

If you list references separately for submission upon request, be sure that you format them in the same style as your resume, for consistency.

To make a positive impression, be sure to use the same paper type and color for your resume, cover letter, references and envelope.

If you apply for a job requiring creativity, an artistic resume is the best way to show your talent.

If you need more space for factual information than the example provides, you can reduce the indentation.

Susan J. Bender

1128 Smith Street
Beckley, West Virginia 25801
(304) 251-1212

CAREER OBJECTIVE

Position typesetting with desktop publishing, graphic art design on computer.

EDUCATION

WV College of Graduate Studies, Beckley, WV
Graduate courses in education

Marshall University, Huntington, WV
Graduate courses in pottery, art history, education

Marshall University, Huntington, WV
BA in Art, English, graduated 1976

EXPERIENCE

5/91 - Present — Self-employed
Contract typesetting to various individuals, businesses, print shops in the area

4/90 - 5/91 — BJJ Printing Company, Beckley, WV
Purchaser, proofreader, typesetter, graphic artist

3/87 - 4/90 — BJJ Printing Company, Beckley, WV
Typesetter, paste-up, graphic artist

2/77 - 6/88 — Alcove Printing Company, Huntington, WV
Paste-up, graphic artist

8/76 - 2/77 — Alcove Printing Company, Huntington, WV
Paste-up

REFERENCES

Submitted upon request

Fig. 8.1 A traditional resume.

To create the first resume design, follow these steps:

1. Choose File New.

2. In the New dialog box, choose the default style sheet. Choose OK or press Enter.

3. Type the following, or enter your own information:

   Susan J. Bender(Enter)
   1128 Smith Street(Enter)
   Beckley, West Virginia 25901(Enter)
   (304) 251-1212(Enter four times)
   CAREER OBJECTIVE(Enter)
   Position typesetting with desktop publishing, graphic art(Shift+Enter)
   design on computer.(Enter twice)
   EDUCATION(Enter)
   WV College of Graduate Studies, Beckley, WV(Enter)
   Graduate courses in education(Enter twice)
   Marshall University, Huntington, WV(Enter)
   Graduate courses in pottery, art history, education(Enter twice)
   Marshall University, Huntington, WV(Enter)
   BA in Art, English, graduated 1976(Enter twice)
   EXPERIENCE(Enter)
   5/91 - Present — Self-employed(Enter)
   Contract typesetting to various individuals, businesses,(Shift+Enter)
   print shops in the area(Enter twice)
   4/90 - 5/91 — BJJ Printing Company, Beckley, WV(Enter)
   Purchaser, proofreader, typesetter, graphic artist(Enter twice)
   3/87 - 4/90 — BJJ Printing Company, Beckley, WV(Enter)
   Typesetter, paste-up, graphic artist(Enter twice)
   2/77 - 6/88 — Alcove Printing Company, Huntington, WV(Enter)
   Paste-up, graphic artist(Enter twice)
   8/76-2/77 — Alcove Painting Company, Huntington, WV(Enter)
   Paste-up(Enter twice)
   REFERENCES(Enter)
   Submitted upon request

4. Place the cursor at the top of the page. Choose Tools Spell Check. Choose OK or press Enter. Respond to any queries from the spell checker.

5. Choose Tools Macros. In the secondary command menu, choose Playback. The Play Macro dialog box appears.

The default margins of this style sheet are 1"; you do not need to specify the margins for this example.

6. From the list of **Macros**, choose Smartype. Choose OK or press Enter.

The Smartype macro changes all double hyphens to em dashes, all quote marks to typographical quote marks, and apostrophes to single typographical quotes. These details make your typeset piece look more professional, and the macro takes only a few seconds to run.

To see other macro descriptions, choose Macro Description and highlight a Macro name in the **Macro** list in version 2.0; Version 3.0 lists the macros descriptions automatically. If the **Macro** list is empty, you did not install the macros; consult your reference manual.

7. Choose File Save As. In the File **Name** text box, type **resume4**. Choose OK or press Enter.

8. Choose File Save As. In the File **Name** text box, type **resume3**. Choose OK or press Enter. Resume1 is the document you use for *this* design.

9. Repeat step 8, but Save **As resume2**. Repeat, again, and Save As **resume1**.

10. Select Susan J. Bender. Choose Text Font. In the Size box, choose 18 point. Choose OK or press Enter.

11. Use the SmartIcons to choose bold and center, or press Ctrl+B, Ctrl+C in version 2.0; Ctrl+E in version 3.0.

12. Select the next three lines: the two address and one telephone number lines. Click the center SmartIcon or press Ctrl+C (2.0); Ctrl+E (3.0).

13. Select CAREER OBJECTIVE and choose bold. Repeat for EDUCATION, EXPERIENCE, and REFERENCES.

14. Place the cursor in the word Position. .. Choose Style Create a Style. The Create Style box appears.

15. In New Style text box, type **Indent**. Choose Modify or press Enter. The Modify Style dialog box appears.

16. In Modify, choose Alignment. In All, type **1.75**. Choose OK or press Enter.

17. Choose Style Select a Style. The Styles box appears. With the cursor placed in the first paragraph, choose Indent.

18. Place the cursor in the words Graduate courses. Choose Indent in the Styles box. Repeat with the rest of the text that is indented in

figure 8.1. Then place the cursor anywhere in the line of text
`Graduate courses in education.`

19. Choose File Save. Choose OK or press Enter.

20. Choose File Print. Choose OK or press Enter.

Designing a Text and Graphic Resume

Graphic lines enhance any document, and Ami Pro enables you to add a variety of lines. This design incorporates two page lines and a paragraph style line to change the look of the resume (see fig. 8.2). Formatting changes include centering the heads and extending the indentations from the first document. This design combines the use of Times and Helvetica for contrast and adds a bullet character to divide the address.

To create the resume in figure 8.2, follow these steps:

1. Choose File Open. In the list of Files, choose RESUME2.SAM. Choose OK or press Enter.

2. Use the default 1" margins of this style sheet.

3. Choose Page Modify Page Layout.

4. In the Modify box, choose Line. In Around Page, choose Top and Bottom. In Style, choose the third rule (a 2-point rule). Choose OK or press Enter.

5. Place the cursor in front of `Susan J. Bender`. Press Enter to create a space after the rule. Choose `Susan J. Bender`. Choose center and bold.

6. Choose Text Caps. In the secondary command menu, choose Upper Case.

7. Choose Text Font. In Face, choose Helv; in Size, choose 18 point. Choose OK or press Enter.

8. Change the style name of this and the next two lines so that when you modify Body Text later, you do not affect these lines of text. To change the style name, highlight the text; choose Style Select a Style; and in the Styles box, choose Body Single.

9. To bring the entire address on one line, place the cursor after the last 1 in `1128 Smith Street`. In SmartIcons choose center, or press Ctrl+C (2.0), or Ctrl+E (3.0).

10. Enter 3 spaces, Alt+0164, 3 spaces. Press Del to remove the paragraph return.

If you use this design with a resume that contains more information, you can reduce the indention and shorten the tabs.

In Ami Pro, modifying a style using the Style menu affects overall formatting; modifying a style using the Text menu affects only the selected word, line, or paragraph. See step 25.

11. Select the bullet character. Choose Text Font. In Size, choose 10 point. Choose OK or press Enter.

12. Select the phone number, and choose center. Apply the Body Single style from the Styles box.

13. To create a paragraph line, place the cursor on the next line (the blank line). Choose **S**tyle Create Style.

14. In the New text box, type **Line**. Choose Modify or press Enter. The Modify dialog box appears.

15. In Modify, choose Lines. Choose Line Below, and choose the third line pattern (a 2-point rule). Choose OK or press Enter.

16. From the Styles box, choose Line to apply the Line style.

17. Place the cursor anywhere in CAREER OBJECTIVE. Choose **S**tyle Create Style.

18. In the New Style text box, type **Head**. Choose Modify, or press Enter.

19. In Modify, choose Font. In Face, choose Helv; in Size, choose 14 point, **B**old.

20. In Modify, choose Alignment. In the Alignment dialog box, choose Center.

21. In Modify, choose **S**pacing. In Paragraph Spacing, in the **B**elow text box, type **.05**. Choose OK or press Enter.

22. Highlight CAREER OBJECTIVE and apply the Head style from the Styles box. Repeat with EDUCATION, EXPERIENCE, and REFERENCES.

23. To indent the body text, choose **S**tyle **M**odify Style. In the Style selection box, choose Body Text.

24. In Modify, choose Alignment. In First, type **.85**.

25. In Tabs, select the left tab. Place the tab at 1.75" on the ruler. Choose **U**se Style Tabs. Choose OK or press Enter. Delete the soft paragraph return after graphic art under the career objective.

26. To apply the tabs to the second lines in each paragraph (such as Graduate course in education), place the cursor at the beginning of the line and press Tab. Follow figure 8.2 to identify the remaining lines that need tabs.

27. Select Submitted upon request. Press Ctrl+C (2.0) or Ctrl+E (3.0) to center and apply the Body Single style.

28. Choose File Save. Choose OK or press Enter.

29. Choose File Print. Choose OK or press Enter.

SUSAN J. BENDER

1128 Smith Street ¤ Beckley, West Virginia 25801
(304) 251-1212

CAREER OBJECTIVE

Position typesetting with desktop publishing, graphic art design on computer.

EDUCATION

WV College of Graduate Studies, Beckley, WV
Graduate course in education

Marshall University, Huntington, WV
Graduate courses in pottery, art history, education

Marshall University, Huntington, WV
BA in Art, English, graduated 1976

EXPERIENCE

5/91 - Present — **Self-employed**
Contract typesetting to various individuals, businesses,
print shops in the area

4/90 - 5/91 — **BJJ Printing Company**, Beckley, WV
Purchaser, proofreader, typesetter, graphic artist

3/87 - 4/90 — **BJJ Printing Company**, Beckley, WV
Typesetter, paste-up, graphic artist

2/77 - 6/88 — **Alcove Printing Company**, Huntington, WV
Paste-up, graphic artist

8/76 - 2/77 — **Alcove Printing Company**, Huntington, WV
Paste-up

REFERENCES

Submitted upon request

Fig. 8.2 A resume with text and graphic rules.

Designing a Short Resume

If your resume is not particularly long, it might look unsubstantial when typeset. Figure 8.3 demonstrates a design solution for this problem. The resume is still short; however, the wide right and bottom margins make it look like you designed it that way. A graphic rule on the left mirrors the left-aligned type. The indents and tabs on the left, along with the ragged right, create interesting use of white space. This is a very simple design to produce, and it's an attractive use of text and graphics.

To create the resume in figure 8.3, follow these steps:

1. Choose File Open. In the list of Files, choose RESUME3.SAM. Choose OK or press Enter.

2. Choose Page Modify Page Layout.

3. In Modify, choose Lines. In Around Page, choose Left. In Style, choose the third line pattern (a 2-point rule). In Position, choose Close to Inside.

4. In Modify, choose Margins. In Margins, select .5 for the Left; .75 for the Top; 2.75 for the Right; and 2.00 for the Bottom. Choose OK or press Enter.

5. Choose Style Modify Style. In the Styles box, choose Body Text.

6. In Modify, choose Alignment. In All, type .25.

7. In Tabs, set two left tabs: one at .75" on the ruler, the other at 1.25". Choose Use Style Tabs. Choose OK or press Enter.

8. Select Susan J. Bender. Choose Text Font. Choose 14 point bold. The default font is Tms Rmn. Choose OK or press Enter.

9. Place the cursor after the phone number. Press Enter.

10. Choose Style Modify Style.

11. In Style, choose Body Single. In Attributes, choose Bold. Remove two paragraph returns between the phone number and CAREER OBJECTIVE.

12. In Modify, choose Alignment. In All, type .25.

13. In Modify, choose Spacing. In the Paragraph Spacing box, choose Above and type .15. Choose Below and type .05. Choose OK or press Enter.

You can also use a screened line in place of a solid one for a different visual effect.

14. Select CAREER OBJECTIVE. In the Styles box, choose Body Single. Repeat with EDUCATION, EXPERIENCE, and REFERENCES.

15. Place the cursor in front of `Position typesetting with desktop publishing`. Press Tab. On the next line, beginning with `design`, press Tab.

16. Continue to break lines and enter tabs throughout the document, going by figure 8.3. Add one tab at the beginning of each first line and add 2 tabs at the beginning of each second line, as shown in the figure.

17. Choose File Save. Choose OK or press Enter.

18. Choose File Print. Choose OK or press Enter.

Designing an Innovative Resume

If you're applying for a position in which creativity is necessary, you may want to design an innovative resume. This design presents an unconventional approach to a resume design. With Ami Pro's drawing feature and clip-art files, you can choose from a variety of artwork to add to your document. One change that's exciting about this design is that it's landscape oriented. Using an 8 1/2-by-11-inch sheet of paper, the document prints on both sides, then folds in half to make a four-page booklet or program.

Figure 8.4 illustrates the inside of the booklet. The name, address, phone number, and a clip-art file are placed within a frame at the top of the page. The rest of the resume falls beneath this heading. You divide the page into two columns with a wide gutter space and wide outer margins.

Figure 8.5 illustrates the outside of the resume, which prints onto the back of the preceding sheet. The cover (right column) uses another clip-art file to attract attention. Use of the same graphic border creates unity, as does the repetition of the typefaces, Times Roman and Helvetica.

If you want to include samples of yourwork, such as photographs, illustrations, or short stories, consider making an eight- or twelve-page booklet.

Susan J. Bender
1128 Smith Street
Beckley, West Virginia 25801
(304) 251-1212

CAREER OBJECTIVE

Position typesetting with desktop publishing, graphic art
design on computer.

EDUCATION

WV College of Graduate Studies, Beckley, WV
Graduate course in education

Marshall University, Huntington, WV
Graduate courses in pottery, art history, education

Marshall University, Huntington, WV
BA in Art, English, graduated 1976

EXPERIENCE

5/91 - Present — Self-employed
Contract typesetting to various individuals, businesses,
print shops in the area

4/90 - 5/91 — BJJ Printing Company, Beckley, WV
Purchaser, proofreader, typesetter, graphic artist

3/87 - 4/90 — BJJ Printing Company, Beckley, WV
Typesetter, paste-up, graphic artist

2/77 - 6/88 — Alcove Printing Company, Huntington, WV
Paste-up, graphic artist

8/76 - 2/77 — Alcove Printing Company, Huntington, WV
Paste-up

REFERENCES

Submitted upon request

Fig. 8.3 A design solution for a short resume.

 Susan Bender 1128 Smith Street · Beckley, West Virginia 25801 · (304) 251-1212

CAREER OBJECTIVE

Position typesetting with desktop publishing, graphic art design on computer.

EDUCATION

WV College of Graduate Studies
Beckley, WV
Graduate course in education

Marshall University
Huntington, WV
Graduate courses in pottery, art history, education

Marshall University
Huntington, WV
BA in Art, English, graduated 1976

REFERENCES

Submitted upon request

EXPERIENCE

5/91 - Present — **Self-employed**
Contract typesetting to various individuals, businesses, print shops in the area.

4/90 - 5/91 — **BJJ Printing Company**
Beckley, WV
Purchaser, proofreader, typesetter, graphic artist.

3/87 - 4/90 — **BJJ Printing Company**
Beckley, WV
Typesetter, paste-up, graphic artist

2/77 - 6/88 — **Alcove Printing Company**
Huntington, WV
Paste-up, graphic artist

8/76 - 2/77 — **Alcove Printing Company**
Huntington, WV
Paste-up

Fig. 8.4 The inside of the "booklet" resume.

Fig. 8.5 The outside (cover) of the "booklet" resume.

To begin creating the inside pages of the innovative resume, follow these steps:

1. Choose File Open. In the list of Files, choose RESUME4.SAM. Choose OK or press Enter.

2. Choose Page Modify Page Layout. The Modify dialog box appears.

3. In Modify, choose Margins & Columns. In Number of Columns, choose 2. In Gutter Width, type 1.5.

4. In Margins, choose .75 for all four margins.

5. In Modify, choose Page Settings. In Orientation, choose Landscape. Choose OK or press Enter.

6. Choose View Full Page.

7. In SmartIcons, select the Frame icon and draw the frame from the left margin to the right. The size of the frame is 9.5 by 1.35 inches. You can verify the size in Modify Frame Layout.

    Alternatively, with the keyboard, choose Frame Create Frame. In Size, choose Width, and type 9.5; choose Height, and type 1.35. Choose OK or press Enter.

8. Position the frame by clicking it once and dragging it to the top margin of the document. To deselect the frame, click the page outside the frame.

    Alternatively, choose Edit Go To. In the Next item box, choose Frame, press Tab to Go To ^H, and use the arrows to position the frame. To deselect the frame, press Esc.

9. Choose View Working or Standard. With the frame still selected, choose Frame Modify Frame Layout.

10. In Modify, choose Lines & Shadows. In Style, choose All and the second line from the end of the list. This is a double rule: the outer rule is 3 point, the inner rule is 1 point.

11. In Shadow, choose None. Choose OK or press Enter.

12. Enter the text in the frame.

    Alternatively, cut and paste the first three lines from the original resume.

13. Select Susan Bender. Choose Text Font. Choose Helv, 18 point bold. Choose OK or press Enter.

The gutter width, in this example, separates the "pages" of the booklet.

In landscape orientation, you can more easily draw a frame across the entire page in full page view.

To import the clip art, you must create another frame. Follow these steps:

1. Choose **F**rame Create Frame, or click the Frame in SmartIcons. Draw a small frame (approximately 2 inches square) inside the first frame. Refer to the figure for placement of the clip art.

2. Choose **F**rame Modify Frame Layout.

3. In Frame, choose **L**ines. Turn off **A**ll lines. In Shadow, choose **N**one.

4. In Frame, choose **S**ize & Position. In Margins, choose **C**lear Margins. Choose OK or press Enter.

5. Choose File **I**mport Picture. The Import Picture dialog box appears.

6. In File **T**ype, choose AmiDraw. In **F**iles, choose ARTTOOLS.SDW. Choose OK or press Enter.

7. With the frame still selected, choose **F**rame Bring to Front.

8. Place the cursor in the larger, original frame in front of Susan Bender. Press Enter twice to lower the line of text to match the figure.

To format the text inside the resume, follow these steps:

1. Place the cursor before CAREER OBJECTIVE. Press Enter twice.

2. Choose **S**tyle Create Style.

3. In the New Style text box, type **Head**. Choose Modify or press Enter.

4. In the Modify dialog box, choose Font. Choose Helv, 12 point, and bold.

5. In the Modify box, choose **S**pacing. In Paragraph Spacing, choose **A**bove and type **.25**; choose **B**elow and type **.10**. Choose OK or press Enter.

6. Choose **S**tyle Select a Style. In the Styles box, assign the Head style to CAREER OBJECTIVE, EDUCATION, EXPERIENCE, and REFERENCES.

7. Choose **S**tyle Create Style. In the New Style text box, type **Body Indent**. In **B**ased on, choose Body Text. Choose Modify, or press Enter.

8. In the Modify box, choose Alignment. In All, select **.35**. Choose OK or press Enter.

If the clip art is not centered in the frame, use the mouse to choose Tools Drawing, and then use the Grabber Hand in the SmartIcons to drag the image anywhere in the frame.

Add the space above and below the headings to separate them from the other text—a detail that makes your document look professional. By applying the space to the style, you make it easier to format all the heads at one time.

9. Select the text under each heading and apply the Body Indent style from the Styles box.

10. Edit the text to match figure 8.4 by breaking lines and bolding company names and university names.

11. Select REFERENCES and Submitted upon request. Choose Edit Cut or press Shift+Del in 2.0 or Ctrl+X in 3.0. Reposition the cursor before EXPERIENCE. Press Enter and move the cursor up one line. Choose Edit Paste, or press Shift+Ins in 2.0 or Ctrl+V in 3.0.

12. Apply the Body Indent style from the Styles box to Submitted upon request.

13. Press Enter. Place the cursor on the blank line and change it to the Body Text style. Press Enter twice more to place EXPERIENCE at the top of the second column so that it is even with CAREER OBJECTIVE.

14. Choose File Save. Choose OK or press Enter.

To format the front cover, follow these steps:

1. Place the cursor at the end of the second column of the first page. Choose Page Breaks. In the Breaks dialog box, choose Insert Page Break. Choose OK or press Enter.

2. The cursor appears on page two, at the top of the first (left) column. Press Enter. Move the cursor up one line with the arrow key.

3. Choose Page Breaks. In the Breaks dialog box, choose Insert Column Break. Choose OK or press Enter.

4. To move the cursor to the second column, press the down arrow, or click the mouse in the second column.

5. To view the column markers, choose View Show Ruler.

6. To view the entire page so that you can draw a frame, choose View Full Page.

7. Use the Frame SmartIcon to draw a frame, or choose Frame Create Frame.

8. Choose Frame Modify Frame Layout.

9. In Frame, choose Size & Position. In Width, type 3.90; in Height, type 7.00.

10. In Frame, choose Lines & Shades. In Lines, choose All. In Style, choose the double rule (the second pattern from the bottom). In Shadow, choose None. Choose OK or press Enter.

A mi Pro picks up the style for the subsequent paragraph from the last paragraph return. In this example, Submitted upon request is Head style until you change it back.

P age and column breaks assure your text won't move to another column when you edit it.

11. Place the cursor in the frame. Press Enter twice and type the following:

RESUME(Enter twice)
OF(Enter twice)
SUSAN(Enter)
BENDER

12. Select all four lines of text. In the SmartIcons, choose bold and center.

13. Select RESUME. Choose Text Font. Choose Helv, 24 point. Choose OK or press Enter.

14. Select OF. Choose Text Font. Choose Helv, 18 point. Choose OK or press Enter.

15. Select SUSAN. Repeat with BENDER. Choose Text Font. The default font is Tms Rmn. Choose 36 point. Choose OK or press Enter.

To create the frame and import a clip-art file, follow these steps:

1. Use the SmartIcon or choose Frame Create Frame to draw a frame within the original frame. Place the frame so that it looks similar to the clip-art positioning in figure 8.5.

2. Choose Frame Modify Frame Layout.

3. In Frame, choose Lines & Shadows. In Lines, deselect All. In Shadow, choose None.

4. In Frame, choose Size & Position. In Margins, choose Clear Margins. Choose OK or press Enter.

5. Choose File Import Picture. AmiDraw should be the selected File Type. In the list of Files, choose DISKICON.SDW. Choose OK or press Enter.

6. Choose File Save. Choose OK or press Enter.

7. Choose File Print One Page at a Time. Choose OK or press Enter.

Looking at Design

You can explore many alternatives to formatting resumes. You can be as traditional or as creative as you choose. Figures 8.6 and 8.7 illustrate other creative ideas for a one-page resume. The frames in figure 8.6 divide the information in an easy-to-follow layout. The first frame is screened with a 10% background (Frame Modify Frame Layout Lines & Shadows) with a shadow to make it the most important feature of the page. The margins are wide, so there is plenty of white space; however, if you need room for more information, the margins can easily be reduced.

You should print on the back of the first sheet of this document.

To avoid over-emphasizing, do not add shadows and screens to all three boxes.

SUSAN J. BENDER
1128 Smith Street · Beckley, West Virginia 25801
(304) 251-1212

CAREER OBJECTIVE

Position typesetting with desktop publishing, graphic art design on computer.

EDUCATION

WV College of Graduate Studies, Beckley, WV
Graduate course in education.

Marshall University, Huntington, WV
Graduate courses in pottery, art history, education.

Marshall University, Huntington, WV
BA in Art, English, graduated 1976

EXPERIENCE

5/91 - Present — Self-employed
Contract typesetting to various individuals, businesses, print shops in the area

4/90 - 5/91 — BJJ Printing Company, Beckley, WV
Purchaser, proofreader, typesetter, graphic artist

3/87 - 4/90 — BJJ Printing Company, Beckley, WV
Typesetter, paste-up, graphic artist

2/77 - 6/88 — Alcove Printing Company, Huntington, WV
Paste-up, graphic artist

8/76 - 2/77 — Alcove Printing Company, Huntington, WV
Paste-up

REFERENCES

Submitted upon request

Fig. 8.6   A creative layout for a resume.

SUSAN J. BENDER

1128 Smith Street · Beckley, West Virginia 25801 · (304) 251-1212

CAREER OBJECTIVE

Supervisory position of typesetting, paste-up, and camera departments. Production scheduling, purchasing, proofreading, typesetting, and graphic arts.

EDUCATION

West Virginia University, Morgantown, WV	MA English, 1982
WV Institute of Technology, Montgomery, WV	BA Printing, 1977
WV College of Graduate Studies, Beckley, WV	Graduate courses in Printing Technology
Marshall University, Huntington, WV	Graduate courses in business management
Marshall University, Huntington, WV	BA in Art, English, graduated 1974

EXPERIENCE

5/91 - Present — **Humble Opinions**, Self-Employed
Contract typesetting to various individuals and print shops in area. Contract software instruction including word processing, desktop publishing, and spreadsheets. Present seminars on Planning and Purchasing Printing, Software Needs, and Desktop Publishing.

4/90 - 5/92 — **BJJ Printing Company**, Beckley, WV
Purchaser, production manager, job scheduler, supervisor of typesetting and paste-up, proofreader. Duties included ordering paper and bindery supplies, scheduling jobs for entire shop, customer service and sales, plate-checking, proofreading, designing customer art.

3/87 - 4/90 — **BJJ Printing Company**, Beckley, WV
Typesetter, paste-up, graphic artist, proofreader, purchaser. Duties included typesetting, page layout, logo design, customer art work, design, writing and production of company materials, proofreading, purchasing for camera, typesetting, and paste-up departments.

2/77 - 6/88 — **Alcove Printing Company**, Huntington, WV
Typesetter and graphic artist, purchaser. Duties included typesetting, page layout and design, logo design, purchasing paper and bindery supplies.

8/76 - 2/77 — **Jerrald Printing**, Montgomery, WV
Typesetter, paste-up artist. Duties included page make-up and design, paste-up, and purchasing typesetting and paste-up supplies.

REFERENCES

Submitted upon request.

Fig. 8.7 A resume design for fitting a lot of information on one page.

If you have a great deal of information to fit on one page of a resume, try to allow for readability and white space. Figure 8.7 illustrates one solution to this design problem. The Education listing uses tabs to organize the material, creating more space between lines. The Experience information is written in paragraph form to include more text on the page.

Recapping

In this chapter, you learned one approach to writing a resume and several approaches to designing a resume. In addition, you learned to use the Smartype macro, format a document in two columns, and create an indented body text style.

U se justified (and hyphenated) body text if you need more room for information. See Chapter 3 for more space-saving ideas.

9

Producing a Program

Businesses use programs for conventions, seminars, classes, and even special events, such as golf tournaments. The purpose of the program is to inform. When designing it, remember that the participants are already in attendance at the event—don't waste valuable space persuading them to attend. Instead, concentrate on the information the participants need once they arrive.

For detailed information on how to create a form like this see page 208.

Programs describe events, activities, speakers, demonstrations, and so on. Programs also list times, room numbers, and dates. You can include descriptions of events or biographies of speakers, if you have the space in the program. Often programs display advertisements as well.

The most common size of a program is 8 1/2 by 11 inches. Portrait-oriented programs are as popular as landscape-oriented programs. A landscape-oriented, 11-by-8 1/2-inch program may be printed on both sides and then folded to form four pages. Printed on one side or two, in a length of 2 pages to 16, the design of a program is flexible. The size you choose depends on your printer capabilities and the amount of copy you have.

If you plan to reproduce more than 50 or 100 programs, you should take the job to a copy shop or print shop. You can have the program reproduced on 60# or 70# offset, 70# or 80# enamel, or even 70# text. You can, of course, copy your programs onto lighter paper (20# or 50#), but only if you are working with a one-sided design. A variety of colors is available, and with one or even two colors of ink you can produce a high quality, professional-looking program.

To re-create the examples offered in this chapter, you type the original program only once; then save it under different file names so that your time is spent formatting the pages instead of typing. Also remember that if you plan to use one of the designs in this book you can save it as a style sheet once you produce the design. Remove the text from the document and keep the basic style for later use.

Some new Ami Pro features introduced through the examples in this chapter include screened frames, the vertical ruler, page tabs, and text wrap around the frame.

Designing a Basic Text Program

This program prints one side of an 8 1/2-by-11-inch page (see fig. 9.1). The program is divided into two columns and uses tabs to organize the information. This design employs frames to create the one-column heads. Note that the event times are all on a right tab. This method is the traditional form of setting times for easier reading. The information following the right tab is on a left tab to help the eye find the next item.

Don't crowd the text just to fit it into one or two pages. Adjust the length of your copy by cutting optional information or by adding pages; remember the importance of white space.

Ragged right and ragged left text make it hard for the reader to find the beginning of the line. Using a right tab and a left tab, in this case, helps direct the eye.

Desktop Publishers' Convention and Trade Show

PROGRAM

THURSDAY, DECEMBER 3
10:00 a.m. to 4:00 p.m.
Trade Show in Progress   Room 117

9:00 a.m.	Continental Breakfast	Rm. 212
9:30 a.m.	Welcoming Address Speaker: Jeff Barrett, DT Pub	Rm. 214
10:00 a.m.	Personal Computers Speaker: Jane Wilson, T & L	Rm. 215
11:00 a.m.	Round-Table Discussion The PC in Business Speakers: David Conners, T & L Sara Franks, Litcom Publishing Tom Patten, Satern Inc.	Rm. 216
12:00 noon	Lunch Break	
1:00 p.m.	Software Packages Speaker: Jeff Barrett, DT Pub	Rm. 223
2:00 p.m.	Round-Table Discussion Today's Software Market Speakers: Wyatt Franklin, L & M Cheryl Thomas, Level Best, Inc. Debra Dickerson, Ware Experts	Rm. 216
3:00 p.m.	Demonstrations PCs and Software Packages	Rm. 223

FRIDAY, DECEMBER 4
10:00 a.m. to 4:00 p.m.
Trade Show in Progress   Room 117

9:00 a.m.	Continental Breakfast	Rm. 211
10:00 a.m.	Dot Matrix Printers Speaker: Jim Sanders, LTOP	Rm. 212
11:00 a.m.	Inkjet Printers Speaker: Geneva L. Johnson, J Assoc.	Rm. 213
12:00 noon	Lunch Break	
1:00 p.m.	Laser Printers Speaker: O. D. Plumley, Plum Corp.	Rm 244
2:00 p.m.	High-Resolution Output Speaker: O. D. Plumley, Plum Corp.	Rm. 233
3:00 p.m.	Demonstrations PCs and Software Programs	Rm. 333
3:30 p.m.	Round-Table Discussion Service Bureaus Speakers: Jeff Barrett, DT Pub O. D. Plumley, Plum Corp. Jim Sanders, LTOP Geneva L. Johnson, J Assoc.	Rm. 216
4:30 p.m.	Closing Comments Speaker: Wyatt Franklin, L & M	Rm. 216

WHITE HAVEN INN AND RESORTS

DECEMBER 3 - 4, 1992

Fig. 9.1   A basic, two-column program that lists dates, events, and room numbers.

To create the basic file for all the program designs, follow these steps:

1. Select File New. In Style Sheet for New Document, choose the default style sheet. Select OK or press Enter.

2. Type the following:

Desktop Publishers' Convention(Enter)
and Trade Show(Enter twice)
PROGRAM(Enter twice)
THURSDAY, DECEMBER 3(Enter)
10:00 a.m. to 4:00 p.m.(Enter)
Trade Show in Progress(4 spaces)**Room 117**(Enter twice)
(Tab)**9:00 a.m.**(Tab)**Continental Breakfast**(Tab)**Rm. 212**(Enter twice)
(Tab)**9:30 a.m.**(Tab)**Welcoming Address**(Tab)**Rm. 214**(Enter)
(Tab twice)**Speaker: Jeff Barrett, DT Pub**(Enter twice)
(Tab)**10:00 a.m.**(Tab)**Personal Computers**(Tab)**Rm. 215**(Enter)
(Tab twice)**Speaker: Jane Wilson, T & L**(Enter twice)
(Tab)**11:00 a.m.**(Tab)**Round-Table Discussion**(Tab)
Rm. 216(Enter)
(Tab twice)**The PC in Business**(Enter)
(Tab twice)**Speakers: David Conners, T & L**(Enter)
(Tab twice)**Sara Franks, Litcom Publishing**(Enter)
(Tab twice)**Tom Patten, Satern Inc.**(Enter twice)
(Tab)**12:00 noon**(Tab)**Lunch Break**(Enter twice)
(Tab)**1:00 p.m.**(Tab)**Software Packages**(Tab)**Rm. 223**(Enter)
(Tab twice)**Speaker: Jeff Barrett, DT Pub**(Enter twice)
(Tab)**2:00 p.m.**(Tab)**Round-Table Discussion**(Tab)**Rm. 216**(Enter)
(Tab twice)**Today's Software Market**(Enter)
(Tab twice)**Speakers: Wyatt Franklin, L & M**(Enter)
(Tab twice)**Cheryl Thomas, Level Best, Inc.**(Enter)
(Tab twice)**Debra Dickerson, Ware Experts**(Enter twice)
(Tab)**3:00 p.m.**(Tab)**Demonstrations**(Tab)**Rm. 223**(Enter)
(Tab twice)**PCs and Software Packages**(Enter twice)
FRIDAY, DECEMBER 4(Enter)
10:00 a.m. to 4:00 p.m.(Enter)
Trade Show in Progress(4 spaces)**Room 117**(Enter twice)
(Tab)**9:00 a.m.**(Tab)**Continental Breakfast**(Tab)**Rm. 211**(Enter twice)
(Tab)**10:00 a.m.**(Tab)**Dot Matrix Printers**(Tab)**Rm. 212**(Enter)
(Tab twice)**Speaker: Jim Sanders, LTOP**(Enter twice)
(Tab)**11:00 a.m.**(Tab)**Inkjet Printers**(Tab)**Rm. 213** (Enter)
(Tab twice)**Speaker: Geneva L. Johnson, J Assoc.**(Enter twice)
(Tab)**12:00 noon**(Tab)**Lunch Break**(Enter twice)

(Tab)**1:00 p.m.**(Tab)**Laser Printers**(Tab)**Rm. 244**(Enter)
(Tab twice)**Speaker: O. D. Plumley, Plum Corp.**(Enter)
(Tab)**2:00 p.m.**(Tab)**High-Resolution Output**(Tab)**Rm. 233**(Enter)
(Tab twice)**Speaker: O. D. Plumley, Plum Corp.**(Enter twice)
(Tab)**3:00 p.m.**(Tab)**Demonstrations**(Tab)**Rm. 333**(Enter)
(Tab twice)**PCs and Software Programs**(Enter twice)
(Tab)**3:30 p.m.**(Tab)**Round-Table Discussion**(Tab)**Rm. 216**(Enter)
(Tab twice)**Service Bureaus**(Enter)
(Tab twice)**Speakers: Jeff Barrett, DT Pub**(Enter)
(Tab twice)**O. D. Plumley, Plum Corp.**(Enter)
(Tab twice)**Jim Sanders, LTOP**(Enter)
(Tab twice)**Geneva L. Johnson, J Assoc.**(Enter twice)
(Tab)**4:30 p.m.**(Tab)**Closing Comments**(Tab)**Rm. 216** (Enter)
(Tab twice)**Speaker: Wyatt Franklin, L & M**(Enter twice)
WHITE HAVEN INN AND RESORTS(Enter)
DECEMBER 3 - 4, 1992

3. Spell check your document by choosing Tools Spell Check.

4. Choose Tools Macros. Choose Playback.

5. In the list of Macros, select SMARTYPE.SMM. Choose OK or press Enter.

6. Choose File Save As. Save this document first as **Program4**. Save again as **Program3**, then **Program2**, and finally as **Program1**. Program1 is the document you use first.

To format the page and the text of the first program, follow these steps:

1. Choose Page Modify Page Layout.

2. In Modify, choose Margins & Columns. In Margins, choose .5" for all.

3. In Number of Columns, choose 2. For Gutter Width, type .5. Choose OK or press Enter.

4. Choose View Full Page.

5. Draw a frame along the top margin of the page, either by clicking the Frame icon, or by choosing Frame Create Frame.

6. Choose Frame Modify Frame Layout.

7. In Frame, choose Type. In Text Wrap Around, choose No Wrap Beside.

8. In Frame, choose Size & Position. In Margins, choose Clear Margins. The size of the frame is Width 7.5", and Height 2".

You can copy the frame to speed up your formatting.

You can enter a size in the Points text box, if your printer is capable of printing the size you type. If the Points option is gray, your printer cannot print any size font other than those listed in the Size dialog box.

Remember that the type sizes should remain proportional for overall balance to the page.

9. In Frame, choose Lines & Shadows. In Lines, deselect All. In Shadow, choose None. Choose OK or press Enter.

10. Choose Edit Copy (or press Ctrl+Ins in 2.0; Ctrl+C in 3.0) to copy the frame. Choose Edit Paste (or press Shift+Ins in 2.0; Ctrl+V in 3.0). Move the second frame to the bottom margin.

11. Choose View Working. Select the text from Desktop Publishers' through PROGRAM. Choose Edit Cut. Position the cursor in the frame and choose Edit Paste.

12. Select the text, Desktop Publishers' Convention and Trade Show. Choose bold and center.

13. Choose Text Font. Choose Tms Rmn, 32 point. If you do not have the option of 32-point type, choose 24 point. Choose OK or press Enter.

14. Select PROGRAM. Choose bold and center. Choose Text Font. Choose 24 point if you used 32 for the first head, or 18 point if you used 24 for the first.

15. Select the next three lines of text, from THURSDAY through Room 117. Choose center. Repeat this step with the text from FRIDAY through Room 117. Bold THURSDAY, DECEMBER 3 and FRIDAY, DECEMBER 4.

16. Choose Style Modify Style. The Modify Style dialog box appears. In Style, choose Body Text.

17. In Modify, choose Font. In Face, choose Tms Rmn. In Size, choose 10 point.

18. In Modify, choose Alignment. In Tabs, set the first tab as right-aligned at .75" on the ruler. Set the second tab as left at .95"; set the third tab as left at 2.75". Choose Use Style Tabs. Choose OK or press Enter.

19. At the bottom of the page, adjust the size of the bottom frame to force FRIDAY, DECEMBER 4 to the second column. Be sure that FRIDAY and THURSDAY are even along the tops of the columns.

20. Select the text from WHITE HAVEN to DECEMBER 3 - 4, 1992. Choose Edit Cut Edit Paste to place this text in the bottom frame.

21. Select WHITE HAVEN INN AND RESORTS. Choose center and bold. Choose Text Font. Choose Tms Rmn, 24 point. Choose OK or press Enter.

22. Select DECEMBER 3 - 4, 1992. Choose center and bold. Choose Text Font. Choose Tms Rmn, 18 point. Choose OK or press Enter.

23. Choose File Save.

24. Choose File Print.

Designing a Traditional Landscape-Oriented Program

Most programs are printed on both sides of a landscape-oriented 8 1/2-by-11-inch sheet and then folded in half to produce four 5 1/2-by-8 1/2-inch pages: the sheet prints in landscape orientation, folds, then reads in portrait orientation. The following traditional program uses this design. The first side consists of the back cover (the left column) and the front cover (the right column). Figure 9.2 illustrates the first side of the program design. A clip-art file from AmiDraw dresses up the front cover; a list of exhibitors adds to the back cover. Lines that border the top and bottom margins of each column tie the document together and define the smaller pages. These lines repeat on the inside of the program.

Figure 9.3 illustrates the inside of the program. The lines at the top and bottom of the columns, or pages, create unity and consistency. Near the bottom of each page is an example of an advertisement separated from the program activities with another rule. Again, the event times are on a right tab for easier reading.

Notice that an abundance of white space makes the program easier to read.

To produce the outside cover of the program, follow these steps:

1. Choose File Open. Select PROGRAM2.SAM. Choose OK or press Enter.

2. Select Page Modify Page Layout. The Modify dialog box appears.

3. In Modify, choose Page Settings. In Orientation, choose Landscape.

4. In Modify, choose Margins & Columns. In Margins, set all to .5".

5. In Number of Columns, choose 2. For Gutter Width, type 1. Choose OK or press Enter.

The one-inch gutter allows for extra margins when a piece is folded.

6. At the insertion point, press Enter three times. Move up to the first line.

7. Choose Style Create Style. In the New style text box, type Line Above. Choose Modify or press Enter.

8. In the Modify dialog box, choose Lines. Select Line Above and the third pattern (a 2-point rule). In Length, choose Margins. Choose OK or press Enter.

Desktop Publishers' Convention and Trade Show

PROGRAM

White Haven Inn, Washington, DC
December 3 - 4, 1992

TRADE SHOW EXHIBITS AND DEMONSTRATIONS
10:00 a.m. to 4:00 p.m.

TRADE SHOW EXHIBITORS

DT Publishers

T & L, Ltd.

Satern, Inc.

Litcom Publishing

L & M

Ware Experts

J Associates

Plum Corporation

Humble Opinions

Washington Chamber of Commerce

White Haven Inn and Resorts

December 3 - 4, 1992

Fig. 9.2   A traditional "booklet style" program.

THURSDAY, DECEMBER 3

9:00 a.m.	Continental Breakfast	Rm. 212
9:30 a.m.	Welcoming Address Speaker: Jeff Barrett, DT Pub	Rm. 214
10:00 a.m.	Personal Computers Speaker: Jane Wilson, T & L	Rm. 215
11:00 a.m.	Round-Table Discussion The PC in Business Speakers: David Conners, T & L Sara Franks, Litcom Publishing Tom Patten, Satern Inc.	Rm. 216
12:00 noon	Lunch Break	
1:00 p.m.	Software Packages Speaker: Jeff Barrett, DT Pub	Rm. 223
2:00 p.m.	Round-Table Discussion Today's Software Market Speakers: Wyatt Franklin, L & M Cheryl Thomas, Level Best, Inc. Debra Dickerson, Ware Experts	Rm. 216
3:00 p.m.	Demonstrations PCs and Software Packages	Rm. 223

During your stay, enjoy our luxurious:

Golf Courses	Spa	Restaurants
Tennis Courts	Pool	Night Club

WHITE HAVEN INN AND RESORTS

FRIDAY, DECEMBER 4

9:00 a.m.	Continental Breakfast	Rm. 211
10:00 a.m.	Dot Matrix Printers Speaker: Jim Sanders, LTOP	Rm. 212
11:00 a.m.	Inkjet Printers Speaker: Geneva L. Johnson, J Assoc.	Rm. 213
12:00 noon	Lunch Break	
1:00 p.m.	Laser Printers Speaker: O. D. Plumley, Plum Corp.	Rm. 244
2:00 p.m.	High-Resolution Output Speaker: O. D. Plumley, Plum Corp.	Rm. 233
3:00 p.m.	Demonstrations PCs and Software Programs	Rm. 333
3:30 p.m.	Round-Table Discussion Service Bureaus Speakers: Jeff Barrett, DT Pub O. D. Plumley, Plum Corp. Jim Sanders, LTOP Geneva L. Johnson, J Assoc.	Rm. 216
4:30 p.m.	Closing Comments Speaker: Wyatt Franklin, L & M	Rm. 216

WELCOME TO WASHINGTON, D.C.

Visit our booth at the Trade Show
for information about the Washington area!

Sponsored by the Washington Chamber of Commerce

Fig. 9.3 The inside of the program; page one in the left column, page two in the right column.

9. Choose Style Select a Style. The Styles box appears. Choose Line Above to apply to the first paragraph return on the page.

10. Move the cursor down one line, press Ctrl+C (2.0), Ctrl+E (3.0) to center the cursor, press Enter twice and type the following:

    TRADE SHOW EXHIBITS AND(Enter)
    DEMONSTRATIONS(Enter)
    10:00 a.m. to 4:00 p.m.(Enter twice)
    TRADE SHOW EXHIBITORS(Enter twice)
    DT Publishers(Enter twice)
    T & L, Ltd.(Enter twice)
    Satern, Inc.(Enter twice)
    Litcom Publishing(Enter twice)
    L & M(Enter twice)
    Ware Experts(Enter twice)
    J Associates(Enter twice)
    Plum Corporation(Enter twice)
    Humble Opinions(Enter twice)
    Washington Chamber of Commerce(Enter four times)
    White Haven Inn and Resorts(Enter twice)
    December 3 - 4, 1992(Enter five times)

11. Select and bold `TRADE SHOW EXHIBITS AND DEMONSTRATIONS`, `TRADE SHOW EXHIBITORS`, `White Haven Inn and Resorts`, and `December 3 -4, 1992`.

12. Choose Style Create a Style. In the New text box, type **Center**. Choose Modify or press Enter.

13. In Modify, choose Tms Rmn, 12 point. Choose OK or press Enter.

14. Select the text from `TRADE SHOW EXHIBITS AND` to `December 3 - 4, 1992`. In the Styles box, assign the style Center to the text.

15. Place the cursor at the bottom of the first column. Choose Style Create a Style. In the New text box, type **Line Below**. Choose Modify or press Enter.

16. In the Modify dialog box, be sure that the Style is Line Below. In Modify, choose Lines. Select Line Below and choose the third pattern line style. Use the default length, Columns. Choose OK or press Enter.

17. Assign Line Below from the Styles box to the last paragraph return in the first column.

18. Move the cursor to the top of the second column. Press Enter twice. Move up to the first paragraph return and assign Line Above to it. Be sure that both column lines are even.

19. Select `Desktop Publishers' Convention` and `Trade Show`. Center and bold the text.

20. Choose Text Font. Choose Tms Rmn, 32 point. Choose OK or press Enter.

21. Select `PROGRAM`. Choose center and bold. Choose Text Font. Choose Tms Rmn, 18 point. Choose OK or press Enter.

22. Press Enter again. Select Tms Rmn, 14 point, bold, and type the following:

    White Haven Inn, Washington, DC(Enter)
    December 3 - 4, 1992(Enter)

23. Position the cursor on the second paragraph return beneath `December 3 - 4, 1992`. Assign the style Line Below to that return.

24. Draw a frame between the text and `Trade Show` and `PROGRAM`. Adjust the size of the frame so that it reaches from the left margin of the column to the right margin of the column. Adjust the bottom of the frame so that the Line Below is even with the line at the bottom of the left column.

25. Choose Frame Modify Frame.

26. In Modify, choose Size & Position. In Margins, choose Clear Margins.

27. In Modify, choose Lines & Shadows. In Lines, deselect All. In Shadow, choose None. Choose OK or press Enter.

28. Choose File Import Picture.

29. The File Type should be AmiDraw. In Files, choose COMPUTER.SDW. Choose OK or press Enter.

30. If the clip art is not in the center of the frame, center it by using the Drawing feature.

You may need to reduce the size of the image while in Drawing.

31. Choose File Save.

32. Choose File Print.

To create the inside of the program, do the following:

1. Choose the Next Page icon (at the bottom right of the status bar). At the top of the first column, page two, press Enter. Move the cursor to the top of the page.

2. Apply the Line Above style to this paragraph return.

3. Select THURSDAY, DECEMBER 3. Choose bold. Delete the following two lines—the time and trade show text. Repeat this step with FRIDAY, DECEMBER 4.

4. Choose **Style Modify Style**. In **Style**, choose Body Text.

5. In **Modify**, choose **Font**. Choose Tms Rmn, 10 point.

6. In **Modify**, choose **Alignment**. In Tabs, set the first tab as right at .75" on the ruler; the second as left at 1"; and the third as left at 3.75". Choose **Use Style Tabs**. Choose **OK** or press Enter.

7. Choose **View Show Ruler** so that you can see the column boundaries on the ruler. At the bottom of the first column, draw a frame that goes from the left margin to the right margin of the column.

8. Choose **Frame Modify Frame Layout**.

9. In **Frame**, choose **Type**. In **Display**, choose **Square Corners**. In **Text Wrap Around**, choose **No Wrap Beside**.

10. In **Frame**, choose **Lines & Shadows**. In **Lines**, choose **Top and Bottom**. In **Style**, choose the third pattern. In **Shadow**, choose **None**. Choose **OK** or press Enter.

11. Choose **Edit Copy**, then **Edit Paste**. Position the second frame at the bottom of the second column.

12. Place the cursor in the first frame (first column, page two). Press Enter and type the following:

    During your stay, enjoy our luxurious:(Enter)
    (Tab)**Golf Courses**(Tab)**Spa**(Tab)**Restaurants**(Enter)
    (Tab)**Tennis Courts**(Tab)**Pool**(Tab)**Night Club**(Enter twice)
    WHITE HAVEN INN AND RESORTS

13. Select the first three lines of the preceding text. Choose **Text Font**. Choose Helv, 10 point.

14. Activate the ruler to set the tabs.

15. In the ruler, set the tabs as left at .25", 1.75", and 2.75". Deselect the ruler by clicking on the page, or by pressing Esc.

16. Select WHITE HAVEN INN AND RESORTS. Center and bold the text. Choose Text Font. Choose Helv, 14 point. Choose OK or press Enter.

17. In the second column, apply the Line Above style to the first paragraph return.

18. To be sure that the heads THURSDAY and FRIDAY are even, press Enter three times at the bottom of the column.

19. In the frame at the end of the second column, type the following:

    WELCOME TO WASHINGTON, D.C.(Enter twice)
    Visit our booth at the Trade Show(Enter)
    for information about the Washington area!(Enter twice)

20. To format the text, select WELCOME TO WASHINGTON, D.C. Choose Center and bold, Helv, 14 point.

21. Select the rest of the text in the frame. Choose Center, Helv, 10 point.

22. Choose File Save.

23. Choose File Print.

Designing a Text and Graphic Program

Graphic rules and boxes help divide information in a document. If, for example, you want to add descriptions of certain activities to your program, you can use a graphic box to outline that information. In addition to separating information from the rest of the program, the box adds interest and attracts attention.

The design in figure 9.4 uses graphic boxes in this way. The design is a simple one to produce, yet the program looks good and is brimming with information. A rule at the top of the page helps to balance the weight of the boxes. Furthermore, white space surrounds the schedule to help balance the gray of the boxed text.

Notice the interesting use of white space within the boxes and in the schedule.

Desktop Publishers' Convention and Trade Show

THURSDAY, DECEMBER 3

9:00 a.m.	Continental Breakfast	Rm. 212
9:30 a.m.	Welcoming Address Speaker: Jeff Barrett, DT Pub	Rm. 214
10:00 a.m.	Personal Computers Speaker: Jane Wilson, T & L	Rm. 215
11:00 a.m.	Round-Table Discussion The PC in Business	Rm. 216

ROUND-TABLE DISCUSSION — THE PC IN BUSINESS

Speakers: David Conners, T & L; Sara Franks, Litcom Publishing; Tom Patten, Satern Inc. What are the advantages of the Personal Computer in business today? These experts discuss programs such as word processing and desktop publishing, their applications to the business world, system requirements and costs, and the future of the Personal Computer.

12:00 noon	Lunch Break	
1:00 p.m.	Software Packages Speaker: Jeff Barrett, DT Pub	Rm. 223
2:00 p.m.	Round-Table Discussion Today's Software Market Speakers: Wyatt Franklin, L & M Cheryl Thomas, Level Best, Inc. Debra Dickerson, Ware Experts	Rm. 216
3:00 p.m.	Demonstrations PCs and Software Packages	Rm. 223

DEMONSTRATIONS — PCS AND SOFTWARE PACKAGES

Fifty-four personal computers, each set up with a different software package! Every conceivable type of personal computer including 286, 386, 486, and notebooks will be on display. In addition, we have a printer for every computer! Laser, inkjet, dot matrix, color inkjets, and image typesetters are available for you. Word processors, spreadsheets, databases, desktop publishing, accounting, and personal checkbook are just a few of the programs we have. Demonstrations will last as long as there is someone to watch.

Fig. 9.4 A text and graphic design for a program.

These instructions only lead you through the first page of the program; you design the second page in the same way. If you want to practice, you can do so by referring to figure 9.5 and formatting the second page. This is a good example of a program that is printed on both sides.

To produce page one of the program, follow these steps:

1. Choose File Open. Choose PROGRAM3.SAM. Choose OK or press Enter.

2. Choose the Page Modify Page Layout.

3. In Modify, choose Margins. In Tabs, clear tabs, set the first tab as right at 2.75" on the ruler; set the second as left at 3.25"; set the third as left at 5.75".

4. In Modify, choose Margins & Columns. In Margins, set all at .5".

5. In Modify, choose Lines, then Top. In Style, choose the second pattern. Choose OK or press Enter.

6. Place the cursor at the top of the page and press Enter.

7. Select and bold the first two lines of text, Desktop Publishers' Convention and Trade Show.

8. Choose Text Font. Choose Helv, 24 point. Choose OK or press Enter.

9. Select and delete Program.

10. Select and bold THURSDAY, DECEMBER 3. Choose Text Font. Choose Helv, 12 point. Choose OK or press Enter.

11. Delete the next two lines of text—the event times and the line beginning Trade Show in progress.

12. Choose Style Modify Style. In the Style selection box, select Body Text.

13. In Modify, choose Font. Choose Tms Rmn. The default is 12 point. Choose OK or press Enter.

14. Choose View Full Page.

15. Draw a frame between the text for the 11:00 a.m. Round-Table Discussion and the text for the 12:00 Lunch Break.

16. Turn the horizontal ruler on by choosing View Show Ruler. Turn the vertical ruler on by choosing View View Preferences; in the Preferences dialog box, select Vertical Ruler. Choose OK or press Enter.

Ami Pro provides SmartIcons that represent both rulers to make it faster and easier to turn them on and off; select Tools User Setup. The horizontal and vertical rulers display only in layout view.

17. Choose Frame Modify Frame Layout.

18. In Frame, choose Lines. In Style, choose the second pattern. In Shadow, choose None.

19. In Frame, choose Type. In Display, choose Square Corners.

20. In Frame, choose Size & Position. Set the Left and Right margins to .30". In Width, type **7.5"**; in Height, type **1.5"**. Choose OK or press Enter.

21. Select the frame and choose Edit Copy. Choose Edit Paste. Reposition the second frame at the bottom of the page.

22. Choose View Working. Place the cursor in the first frame, press Enter, and type the following:

ROUND-TABLE DISCUSSION(space, Alt+0151, space)**THE PC IN BUSINESS**(Enter)

23. Cut the names of the speakers from the original text and paste the text into the frame. Press Enter and type the following:

What are the advantages of the Personal Computer in business today? These experts discuss programs such as word processing and desktop publishing, their applications to the business world, system requirements and costs, and the future of the Personal Computer.

24. Select and center the first two lines of text in the frame. Select and bold ROUND-TABLE through BUSINESS. Choose Text Font. Choose Helv, 12 point. Choose OK or press Enter.

25. Place the cursor in the second frame and type the information from figure 9.4. Format the text as in step 22.

26. Choose File Save.

27. Choose File Print.

Designing an Innovative Program

You can design a creative program in many ways. You can use graphic images, boxes, screens, and so on. This program design in figure 9.6 uses a wealth of white space and graphic boxes with deep shadows for contrast. The program is shorter, offering only event times, activities, major speakers, and room numbers. The design includes no explanations or descriptions. However, this program uses only one page; if you want to add descriptions, you can print on the back of this design.

If you are creating page two, select both frames, copy them, and paste them to page two.

Don't be tempted to fill the white space with graphics or text; let the white space speak for itself.

FRIDAY, DECEMBER 4

9:00 a.m.	Continental Breakfast	Rm. 211
10:00 a.m.	Dot Matrix Printers Speaker: Jim Sanders, LTOP	Rm. 212
11:00 a.m.	Inkjet Printers Speaker: Geneva L. Johnson, J Assoc.	Rm. 213

INKJET PRINTERS

J Associates brough twenty-seven inkjet printers, ten of which are color, to demonstrate output. These printers are new and hot! If you have ever thought about buying an inkjet, don't miss this lecture and demonstration!!!

12:00 noon	Lunch Break	
1:00 p.m.	Laser Printers Speaker: O. D. Plumley, Plum Corp.	Rm 244
2:00 p.m.	High-Resolution Output Speaker: O. D. Plumley, Plum Corp.	Rm. 233
3:00 p.m.	Demonstrations PCs and Software Programs	Rm. 333
3:30 p.m.	Round-Table Discussion Service Bureaus	Rm. 216

ROUND-TABLE DISCUSSION — SERVICE BUREAUS

Speakers: Jeff Barrett, DT Pub; O. D. Plumley, Plum Corp.; Geneva L. Johnson, J Assoc. How do you start your own service bureau? What are initial expenses? What equipment do you need? These experts discuss the pros and cons of starting your own service bureau, as well as start-up and operating costs, hardware and software requirements, and the probabilities of success.

4:30 p.m.	Closing Comments Speaker: Wyatt Franklin, L & M	Rm. 216

WHITE HAVEN INN AND RESORTS
DECEMBER 3 - 4, 1992

Fig. 9.5   Page two of the program; the back of page one.

Desktop Publishers' Convention and Trade Show

THURSDAY, DECEMBER 3

9:00 a.m.	Continental Breakfast	Rm. 212
9:30 a.m.	Welcoming Address Speaker: Jeff Barrett, DT Pub	Rm. 214
10:00 a.m.	Personal Computers Speaker: Jane Wilson, T & L	Rm. 215
11:00 a.m.	Round-Table Discussion The PC in Business	Rm. 216
12:00 noon	Lunch Break	
1:00 p.m.	Software Packages Speaker: Jeff Barrett, DT Pub	Rm. 223
2:00 p.m.	Round-Table Discussion Today's Software Market	Rm. 216
3:00 p.m.	Demonstrations PCs and Software Packages	Rm. 223

FRIDAY, DECEMBER 4

9:00 a.m.	Continental Breakfast	Rm. 211
10:00 a.m.	Dot Matrix Printers Speaker: Jim Sanders, LTOP	Rm. 212
11:00 a.m.	Inkjet Printers Speaker: Geneva L. Johnson, J Assoc.	Rm. 213
12:00 noon	Lunch Break	
1:00 p.m.	Laser Printers Speaker: O. D. Plumley, Plum Corp.	Rm 244
2:00 p.m.	High-Resolution Output Speaker: O. D. Plumley, Plum Corp.	Rm. 233
3:00 p.m.	Demonstrations PCs and Software Programs	Rm. 333
3:30 p.m.	Round-Table Discussion	Rm. 216
4:30 p.m.	Closing Comments Speaker: Wyatt Franklin, L & M	Rm. 216

Fig. 9.6   Graphic boxes with deep shadows contrasting the white space of this program.

To create the innovative program in figure 9.6, do the following:

1. Choose File Open. Choose PROGRAM4.SAM. Choose OK or press Enter.

2. Choose Page Modify Page Layout.

3. In Modify, choose Margins & Columns. In Margins, set all to .5". Choose OK or press Enter.

4. Select Desktop Publishers' Convention and Trade Show. Choose Helv, 24 point, bold. Move Convention and Trade Show to the second line as in figure 9.6.

5. Select and delete PROGRAM. Select and delete the two lines that follow THURSDAY, December 3 and FRIDAY, December 4.

6. Choose View Full Page. Be sure that both the vertical and horizontal rulers are showing.

7. Draw a frame that is 4.25" wide by 4.45 " high, and position it similarly to the top frame in figure 9.6.

8. Choose Frame Modify Frame Layout.

9. In Frame, choose Type. In Display, choose Square Corners. In Text Wrap Around, choose No Wrap Beside.

10. In Frame, choose Size & Position. In Margins, set all to .25".

11. In Frame, choose Lines & Shadows. In Style, select All and the second line pattern. In Shadow, choose Deep and choose the bottom left arrow for placement of the shadow. Choose OK or press Enter.

12. Copy the frame, paste it, and reposition the second frame similarly to the second frame in figure 9.6.

13. Choose View Working.

14. Select all of Thursday's program, cut it, and paste it into the frame.

15. Select THURSDAY, DECEMBER 3. Choose Tms Rmn, 14 point, bold.

16. Choose Style Modify Style. In Style, choose Body Text.

17. In Modify, choose Font. Choose Tms Rmn, 10 point.

18. In Modify, choose Alignment. In Tabs, set the first tab as right at .75" on the ruler; the second as left at 1"; and the third as left at 3.25". Choose Use Style Tabs. Choose OK or press Enter.

19. Delete all speakers' names under Round-Table Discussions.

20. Select all of Friday's program text, cut it, and paste it into the second frame. Delete the speakers' names under Round-Table

For consistency, both frames should be formatted with the same line and shadow.

Discussion. Format FRIDAY, DECEMBER 4 as Tms Rmn, 14 point, bold.

21. Select and delete the location and the date.

22. Choose File Save.

23. Choose File Print.

To break up the white space in this design, you can add a light screen to the frames. A screen also makes the boxes stand out from the page and attracts even more attention (see fig. 9.7).

To add a screen to the frames, follow these steps:

1. Select the first frame. Choose Frame Modify Frame Layout.

2. In Frame, choose Lines & Shadows. Choose Background. A dialog box of color and screen choices appears. Choose the third row from the top, second square from the right. Choose OK or press Enter. Ami Pro applies the screen to your frame.

3. Repeat steps 1 and 2 for the second frame.

Looking at Design

You can format a program in many ways so that it is easy to read. As you've seen, white space, columns, frames, and even pages help to divide and organize information. Leader tabs also help in formatting. Figure 9.8 illustrates a program design that uses leader tabs to connect the activity and the speaker. Leader tabs that lead the eye across the page are especially useful for one wide column, as figure 9.8 illustrates. The other new design features introduced in figure 9.8 include the combination of initial caps and small caps in the heading gives a completely different look to the piece. A left-aligned heading, location, and date combined with right-aligned tabs for unusual white space and small graphic images identify the beginning of each day's program.

Figure 9.9 illustrates another design solution for the landscape orientation. The rule at the top defines the page, but everything else is right-aligned. The box, the leader tabs, and the head all repeat the alignment. The thicker rules add contrast to the white of the page. You can add a screen to the box for even more contrast. One day's program information appears on the first page; a second page (printed on the back of the first page) would be necessary for a second day's activities.

Depending on your printer set-up and fonts, you may need to adjust the size of the frames.

Version 3.0 users can change the background of both frames at the same time by selecting Frame Group.

Always type a space between a leader tab and the following text to avoid crowding the text.

When you use heavy lines or screens and print on both sides of the document, be sure to use a heavy paper, such as 70# or 80#, so that the graphic elements won't show through.

Desktop Publishers'
Convention and Trade Show

THURSDAY, DECEMBER 3

9:00 a.m.	Continental Breakfast	Rm. 212
9:30 a.m.	Welcoming Address Speaker: Jeff Barrett, DT Pub	Rm. 214
10:00 a.m.	Personal Computers Speaker: Jane Wilson, T & L	Rm. 215
11:00 a.m.	Round-Table Discussion The PC in Business	Rm. 216
12:00 noon	Lunch Break	
1:00 p.m.	Software Packages Speaker: Jeff Barrett, DT Pub	Rm. 223
2:00 p.m.	Round-Table Discussion Today's Software Market	Rm. 216
3:00 p.m.	Demonstrations PCs and Software Packages	Rm. 223

FRIDAY, DECEMBER 4

9:00 a.m.	Continental Breakfast	Rm. 211
10:00 a.m.	Dot Matrix Printers Speaker: Jim Sanders, LTOP	Rm. 212
11:00 a.m.	Inkjet Printers Speaker: Geneva L. Johnson, J Assoc.	Rm. 213
12:00 noon	Lunch Break	
1:00 p.m.	Laser Printers Speaker: O. D. Plumley, Plum Corp.	Rm 244
2:00 p.m.	High-Resolution Output Speaker: O. D. Plumley, Plum Corp.	Rm. 233
3:00 p.m.	Demonstrations PCs and Software Programs	Rm. 333
3:30 p.m.	Round-Table Discussion	Rm. 216
4:30 p.m.	Closing Comments Speaker: Wyatt Franklin, L & M	Rm. 216

Fig. 9.7   Added screens to contrast with white space.

Desktop Publishers' CONVENTION AND TRADE SHOW

White Haven Inn, Washington, DC
December 3 - 4, 1992

PROGRAM

THURSDAY, DECEMBER 3

9:00 a.m.	Continental Breakfast Rm. 212	
9:30 a.m.	Welcoming Address	Jeff Barrett, DT Pub
	Rm. 214	
10:00 a.m.	Personal Computers	Jane Wilson, T & L
	Rm. 215	
11:00 a.m.	Round-Table Discussion - The PC in Business	David Conners, T & L
	Rm. 216	Sara Franks, Litcom Publishing Tom Patten, Satern Inc.
12:00 noon	Lunch Break	
1:00 p.m.	Software Packages	Jeff Barrett, DT Pub
	Rm. 223	
2:00 p.m.	Round-Table Discussion - Today's Software Market	Wyatt Franklin, L & M
	Rm. 216	Cheryl Thomas, Level Best, Inc. Debra Dickerson, Ware Experts
3:00 p.m.	Demonstrations - PCs and Software Packages Rm. 223	

FRIDAY, DECEMBER 4

9:00 a.m.	Continental Breakfast Rm. 211	
10:00 a.m.	Dot Matrix Printers	Jim Sanders, LTOP
	Rm. 212	
11:00 a.m.	Inkjet Printers	Geneva L. Johnson, J Assoc.
	Rm. 213	
12:00 noon	Lunch Break	

Fig. 9.8   A creative program design using leader tabs and graphic images.

DESKTOP PUBLISHERS' CONVENTION AND TRADE SHOW

PROGRAM

THURSDAY, DECEMBER 3

9:00 a.m.	Continental Breakfast	Rm. 212
9:30 a.m.	Welcoming Address Jeff Barrett, DT Pub	Rm. 214
10:00 a.m.	Personal Computers Jane Wilson, T & L	Rm. 215
11:00 a.m.	Round-Table Discussion - The PC in Business David Conners, T & L Sara Franks, Litcom Publishing Tom Patten, Satern Inc.	Rm. 216
12:00 noon	Lunch Break	
1:00 p.m.	Software Packages Jeff Barrett, DT Pub	Rm. 223
2:00 p.m.	Round-Table Discussion - Today's Software Market Wyatt Franklin, L & M Cheryl Thomas, Level Best, Inc. Debra Dickerson, Ware Experts	Rm. 216
3:00 p.m.	Demonstrations - PCs and Software Packages	Rm. 223

Fig. 9.9 An innovative use of white space in a landscape design.

Recapping

In this chapter you learned to create both portrait- and landscape-oriented programs that organize information as well as present it in interesting ways. Some Ami Pro features, such as page tabs, text wrap-around, and screened boxes, can be used in other documents you create.

10

Producing a Memo

Almost everyone in business sends memos every day. Memos inform, remind, list, question, and confirm. Subjects for memos are wide and varied. Some memos may include information about a meeting, or deadline, or a list of requirements; others may request details, such as a spreadsheet, chart, or table, needed for a meeting; still others may be reminders of appointments or meetings. A memo can simply send a friendly hello.

HUMBLE OPINIONS
P. O. BOX 174 · OAK HILL, WV 25901 · (304) 255-5555

TO:

FROM:

DATE:

SUBJECT:

REPLY:

For detailed information on how to create a form like this see page 224.

Design the memo to fit the purpose: casual for fellow workers, formal for the CEO.

Adobe Type Manager (ATM) fonts add style to your memos.

If you create any of the following designs and save them as style sheets, you may want to enter your own information instead of using the example.

Memos can be sent in-house to presidents, secretaries, board members, supervisors, or any employees of a company. Memos also can be sent outside the company, perhaps to lawyers, accountants, bankers, and branch offices.

Generally, memos contain banner lines such as To, From, and Date. Memos may also include additional banner lines like Subject or Reply. The word Memo, or Memorandum, can be a heading. Another heading may be the company name, address, and logo; however, include this heading only if you send the memo out of the company. Another option uses the sender's name as a heading. For in-house memos, a simple, informal approach is best.

This chapter instructs you in the creation of several memo designs, some for in-house use and some for out-of-company use. This chapter also covers formal and informal memo designs, and traditional and innovative designs. You learn a variety of new Ami Pro features throughout these instructions, such as using the Adobe fonts included with Ami Pro, creating table styles, setting tabs within a table, and using the Send to Front/Back frame feature. Another feature in Ami Pro described here is the Document Information feature. Doc Info helps you organize your memos and lets you view descriptions of the memo before opening it.

Ami Pro's style sheets make producing memos effortless. First, Ami Pro comes with pre-designed memo style sheets you can easily use. Second, this chapter shows you how to set up your own style sheet so that you can customize it to your needs. By learning how to set up your own style sheet, you learn more about the features in Ami Pro and how to use them. After you set up your style sheet, you can use it over and over.

Producing a Basic Memo

The first design is a basic memo to be used in-house (see fig. 10.1). The word MEMO is large enough to attract attention. The banner lines include key information, although you can add other pertinent heads if you need them.

In the following instructions, you create the memo style sheet, produce a memo document using that style sheet, create a Document Information file, and then view the description of your memo in the Open dialog box. To create the memo style sheet, follow these steps:

1. Choose File New. The New dialog box appears.

2. In Style Sheet for New Document, choose the default style sheet. Choose OK or press Enter.

3. Type the following:

   MEMO(Enter three times)
   TO:(Tab, Enter twice)
   FROM:(Tab, Enter twice)
   DATE:(Tab, Enter twice)
   SUBJECT:(Tab, Enter)

4. Select MEMO. Choose bold and center.

5. Choose Text Font. Choose Helv, 72 point (or as large as your printer allows). Choose OK or press Enter.

6. Select the banner lines. Choose Tms Rmn, 12 point.

7. Choose Page Modify Page Layout. The Modify dialog box appears.

8. Choose Margins & Columns. In Tabs, set a left tab at 2.25" on the ruler. Choose OK or press Enter.

9. Choose Style Save as a Style Sheet.

10. In the Save as Style Sheet dialog box, type **Memo1**. Choose With Contents. Choose OK or press Enter.

11. Choose File Close. Ami Pro asks if you want to save the document. Choose No.

If your printer does not allow the display type sizes (60, 72, 96 point, and so on), consider using type created in a draw program and imported to Ami Pro.

You save the style sheet, but not the document. Ami Pro identifies the document as [Untitled]. You can begin your document without closing, at this point, and save it as a document. By closing and beginning a new document, however, you can see how the style sheet works. The memo you produce in this section is a basic one. Figure 10.2 illustrates the finished memo.

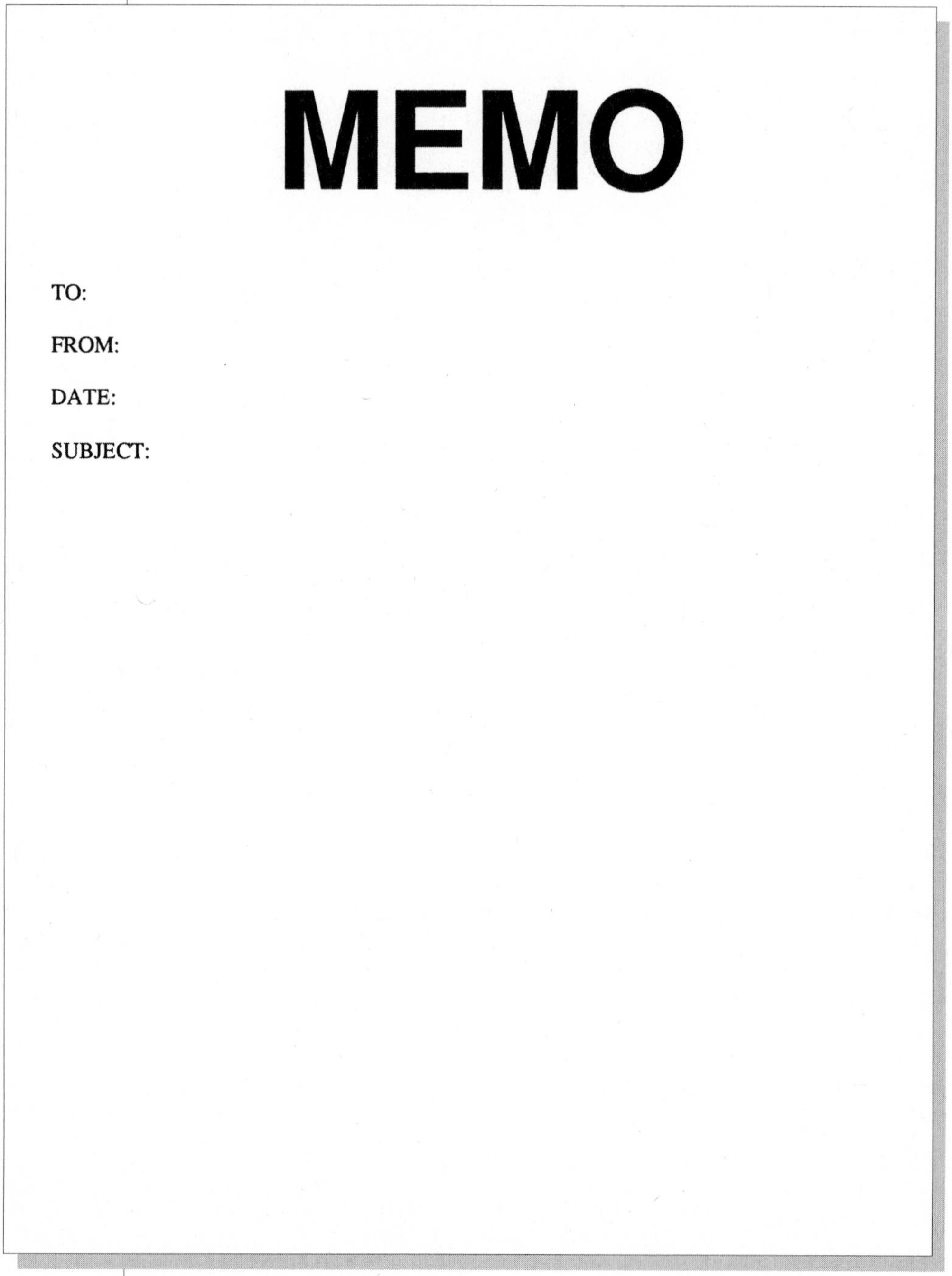

MEMO

TO:

FROM:

DATE:

SUBJECT:

Fig. 10.1 A basic memo format.

MEMO

TO: David Wyatt

FROM: S. J. Bender

DATE: October 12, 1992

SUBJECT: Word Processing Seminar

As mentioned in the staff meeting, our company is offering seminars during the first week in December for all employees. The word processing seminar is one I think will interest you. It takes place at the McGrath Hotel, December 4, from 8:00 a.m. to 4:00 p.m. Please let me know by this Friday if you will attend. Thank you.

Fig. 10.2   A memo document to use for the Doc Info file.

To create a document using your Memo1 style sheet, follow these steps:

1. Choose File New.

2. In Style Sheet for New Document, choose MEMO1.STY. Choose OK or press Enter. MEMO1.STY appears at the bottom of the list.

3. Place the cursor after the Tab in the line TO: and type the following:

   David Wyatt(press down arrow twice)
   S. J. Bender(press down arrow twice)
   October 12, 1992(press down arrow twice)
   Word Processing Seminar(Enter twice)
   As mentioned in the staff meeting, our company is offering seminars during the first week in December for all employees. The word processing seminar is one I think will interest you. It takes place at the McGrath Hotel, December 4, from 8:00 a.m. to 4:00 p.m. Please let me know by this Friday if you will attend. Thank you.

4. Choose File Save As. Save the file as **memo1**. Choose OK or press Enter.

To create a Document Information file for this memo, follow these steps:

1. Choose File Doc Info. The Doc Info dialog box appears. Figure 10.3 illustrates how the dialog box looks when you complete it.

2. In the Description text box, type the following:

   Word Processing Seminar December 4

3. In Keywords, type the following:

   Expect Reply from David by Friday, Oct. 16, 1992

4. Choose Update. Ami Pro updates the statistics. Choose OK or press Enter.

5. Choose File Save. Choose File Print. Choose File Close.

To view the description of your memo document, choose File Open, select MEMO1.SAM, and enable the Show Description option.

Figure 10.4 illustrates the Open Dialog box with the description of MEMO1.SAM.

File names that begin with a character appear in the list before those beginning with a letter. Ami Pro 2.0 uses the tilde (~) and Ami Pro 3.0 uses the underline (_) to begin the name of each Ami Pro style sheet. If you want your files to list before Ami Pro's files, begin your file names with an ampersand (&).

Note that Ami Pro completes the statistics such as File name, Directory, and Style Sheet in the dialog box, as well as the Date Created and Time Created.

By updating statistics, you can quickly view the file size, editing time, and so on.

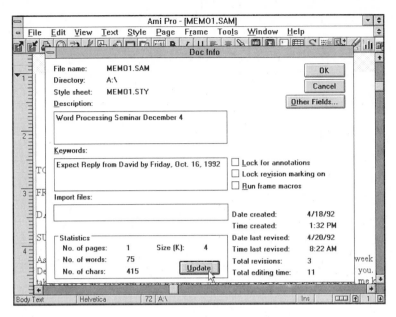

Fig. 10.3 The completed Document Information dialog box.

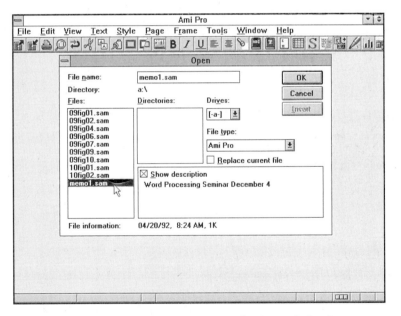

Fig. 10.4 The description of MEMO1.SAM in the Open dialog box.

You can use the Doc Info dialog box to help you identify your memos, letters, and documents. You can select each one and view the description without having to open the document first.

Producing a Text and Graphic Memo Design

Ami Pro's table feature makes tables easy to create, modify, and use in many types of documents.

Most memos use rules or boxes to divide and organize the information. Ami Pro offers you many ways to add these rules or boxes. You can add page graphics, paragraph rules, frame graphics, or you can use the Table feature. The next memo design uses the Table feature to add graphics and to organize the information.

Figure 10.5 illustrates the memo designed by using Ami Pro's Table feature. Wide margins create interesting white space surrounding the boxed information. The company's name and address span the width of the table to reinforce the left and right margins. The table is made up of five rows and one column. It's easy to add more space in any row by pressing Enter if you need more room for messages.

Again, you may want to type your own information in place of the example and use the Save as a Style Sheet option to save this design as a style sheet for later use. To produce the second memo design, follow these steps:

1. Choose File New. The New dialog box appears.

2. In Style Sheet for New Document, choose the default style sheet. Choose OK or press Enter.

3. Choose Page Modify Page Layout.

4. In Modify, choose **Margins & Columns**. Change the **L**eft, **R**ight, and **B**ottom margins to 1.75" and the **T**op to 1.25". Choose OK or press Enter.

5. Type the following:

   HUMBLE OPINIONS(Enter)
   P. O. BOX 174(2 spaces, Alt+0183, 2 spaces)**OAK HILL, WV 25901**(2 spaces, Alt+0183, 2 spaces)**(304) 255-5555**(Enter four times)

6. Select HUMBLE OPINIONS. Center and bold the text. Choose **T**ext **F**ont. Choose Tms Rmn, 36 point. Choose OK or press Enter.

7. Select the address line. Center the text. Choose **T**ext **F**ont. Choose Tms Rmn, 14 point. Choose OK or press Enter.

8. Place the cursor on the last paragraph return. Choose Too**l**s **T**able.

Version 3.0 users click the right mouse button.

Ami Pro 3.0 users can alternatively use Edit, Insert, Bullets to add a different bullet symbol.

9. In the Create Table dialog box, for Number of Columns, type **1**. In Number of **Rows**, type **5**. Choose **Layout**.

10. In the Layout dialog box, in Default Columns, choose **Width**. In the **Width** box, type **4.85**.

11. In Default Rows, turn on Automatic either by clicking the check box or by pressing **A**.

12. In Gutter Size, type **.11**.

13. In Options, choose **Center Table on Page**. Choose **OK** or press **Enter**.

14. Ami Pro returns to the Create Table dialog box. Choose **OK** or press **Enter**.

15. Select the table. Choose **Tables Lines/Shades**.

16. In the Lines/Shades box, in Position, choose **All Sides**. In Line Style, choose the third pattern. Choose **OK** or press **Enter**.

17. The cursor is placed by default in the table, first row. Type the following:

    (Enter) **TO:**(Enter, down arrow)
    (Enter) **FROM:**(Enter, down arrow)
    (Enter) **DATE:**(Enter, down arrow)
    (Enter) **SUBJECT:**(nine Enters, down arrow)
    (Enter) **REPLY:**(nine Enters)

18. Choose **Style Modify Style**. In Style, choose **Table Text**.

19. In Modify, choose **Font**. Choose **Helv**, **12** point.

20. In Modify, choose **Alignment**. In Indent, for All type **.25**. In the From Right box, type **.25**.

21. In Tabs, set a left tab at **1.25"** on the ruler. Choose **Use Style Tabs**. Choose **OK** or press **Enter**.

22. Place the cursor after `TO:`. Press **Ctrl+Shift+Tab** to insert a tab in the table. Repeat this step after `FROM:`, `DATE:`, `SUBJECT:`, and `REPLY:`.

23. Choose **File Save As** to save as a document. Choose **Style Save as a Style Sheet** to save as a style sheet. (Be sure to choose **With Contents** if you save as a style sheet.)

24. Choose **File Print**.

Note that Ami Pro adds the Table menu only after you insert a table.

If your table gridlines are not showing, turn them on by choosing View View Preferences, Table Gridlines, and OK.

Ami Pro 3.0 users can place the cursor in the table and press the right mouse button; the Modify Style dialog box appears.

HUMBLE OPINIONS

P. O. BOX 174 · OAK HILL, WV 25901 · (304) 255-5555

TO:
FROM:
DATE:
SUBJECT:
REPLY:

Fig. 10.5 A memo created with the Table feature.

Producing a Traditional Memo

The next design is a traditional design with two twists. Although the design seems relatively simple, the screened rule along the top margin and the unusual typeface of MEMO make it interesting (see fig. 10.6). These two new twists may be useful to you in another document as well.

You may want to type in your own information. To produce the traditional memo design, follow these steps:

1. Choose File New. The New dialog box appears.

2. In Style Sheet for New Document, choose the default style sheet. Choose OK or press Enter.

3. Choose Page Modify Page Layout.

4. In Modify, choose Margins & Columns. In Tabs, set a left tab at 2" on the ruler.

5. In Modify, choose Lines. In Around Page, choose Top. In Style, choose the seventh pattern (the thickest in the list is a 12-point rule).

6. Activate the color bar by clicking the down arrow, or pressing the down arrow on the keyboard. Choose the gray screen pattern in the right column, fourth square down. Choose OK or press Enter.

7. Press Enter and type the following:

   MEMO(Enter three times)
   DATE:(Tab, Enter twice)
   TO:(Tab, Enter twice)
   FROM:(Tab, Enter twice)
   SUBJECT:(Tab, Enter twice)

8. Select MEMO. Boldface the text. Choose Text Font. Choose CaslonOpenFace, 48 point. Choose OK or press Enter.

   CaslonOpenFace is an Adobe font included in your Ami Pro package. If you do not have ATM (Adobe Type Manager) installed, or it does not work with your printer, use Times Roman.

9. Choose File Save As to save as a document. Choose Style Save as a Style Sheet to save as a style sheet. (Be sure to choose With Contents if you save as a style sheet.)

10. Choose File Print.

When you set a Page tab, the measurement begins at the page edge; when you set a Style tab, the measurement begins at the margin edge. In this example, the page margin is 1", and the tab is 1" from the margin.

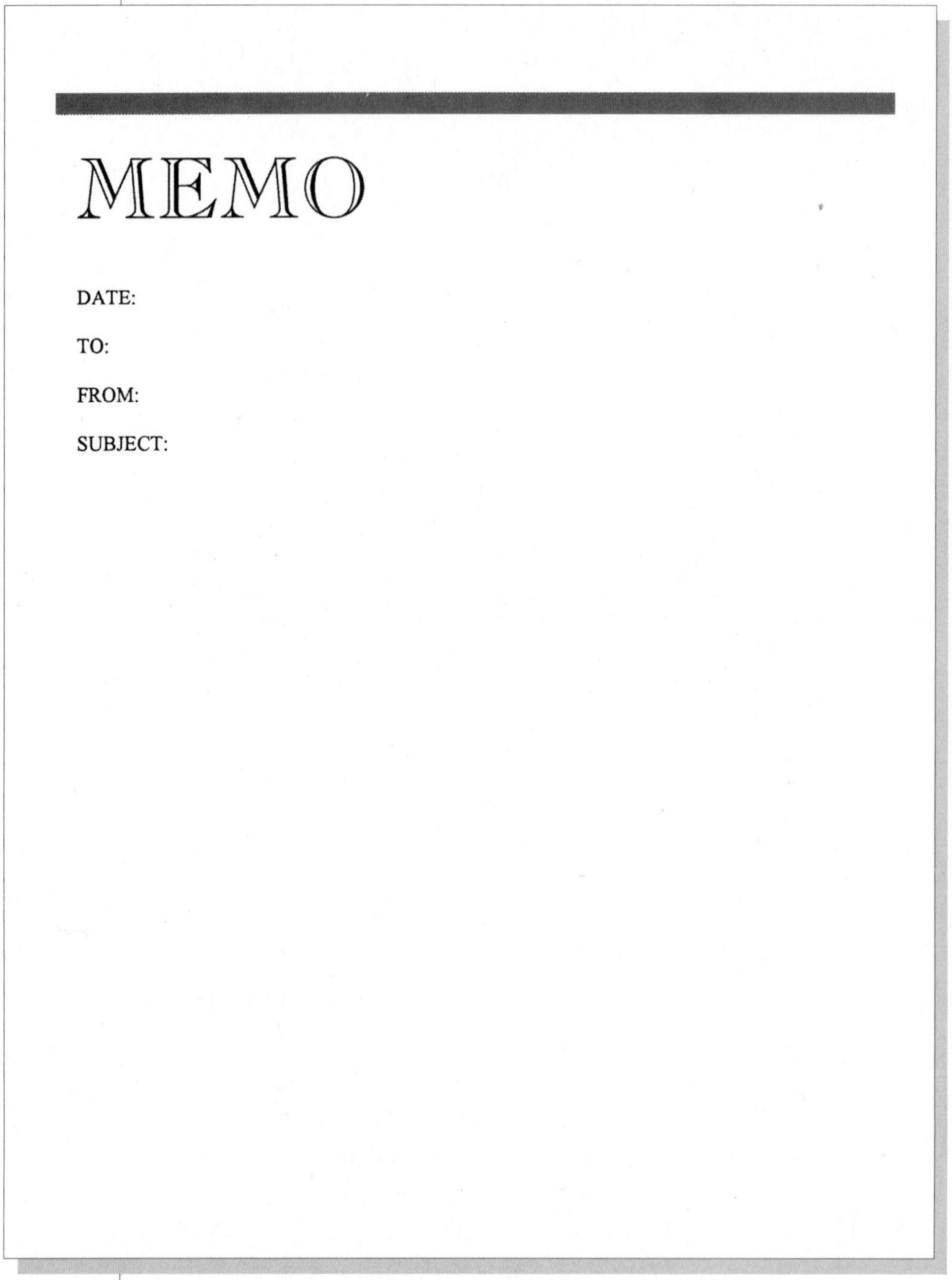

MEMO

DATE:

TO:

FROM:

SUBJECT:

Fig. 10.6 A traditional memo with added interest.

Producing an Innovative Memo

With Ami Pro, you can create many different varieties of memos. Thus far, you have used the Table feature and page rules to create graphics in your memos. The next design uses two frames to produce an entirely different effect.

Figure 10.7 illustrates the memo design that uses two frames. The first frame is lightly screened and contains the key information plus banner lines. The second frame is opaque white, placed on top of the first frame, and may contain any message or reply. The font used for the company name is another ATM font. If you do not use ATM, you can substitute Helvetica.

To produce the innovative memo, follow these steps:

1. Choose File New. The New dialog box appears.

2. In Style Sheet for New Document, choose the default style sheet. Choose OK or press Enter.

3. Draw a frame, either by clicking the Frame SmartIcon, or by choosing Frame Create Frame. You adjust the size of the frame in the following steps .

4. Choose Frame Modify Frame Layout.

5. In Frame, choose Type. In Display, choose Square Corners.

6. In Frame, choose Size & Position. In Size, for Width type 6.60. For Height, type 9.00. The measurement is in inches.

7. In Margins, set all to .30.

8. In Frame, choose Lines & Shadows. In Lines, choose All. In Style, choose the second pattern, In Shadow, choose None. In Background, choose the third gray screen down, second from the right.

9. In Frame, choose Columns & Tabs. In Tabs, set a left tab at 1.25". Choose OK or press Enter.

10. Place the cursor in the frame.

11. Type the following:

    HUMBLE OPINIONS(Enter)
    P. O. Box 174(4 spaces)**Oak Hill, West Virginia 25901**
    (4 spaces)**(304) 255-5555**(Enter 3 times)
    MEMORANDUM(Enter 3 times)
    To:(Enter twice)
    From:(Enter twice)
    Date:(Enter)

For examples of ATM fonts used with Ami Pro, see Appendix D.

12. Select HUMBLE OPINIONS. Bold and center the text. Choose Text Font. Choose FrankGothCd if you use ATM, or Helv if you don't use ATM. Choose 36 point.

13. Select the address and center it. The address font should be the default Tms Rmn, 12 point.

14. Select MEMORANDUM. Boldface and center the text. Choose Text Font, Tms Rmn, and 18 point.

15. Choose View Full Page to draw the second frame. Draw the second frame inside the first; again, you size the frame and position it in the next steps.

16. Choose Frame Modify Frame Layout.

17. In Frame, choose Type. Choose Square Corners. In Display, choose Opaque.

18. In Frame, choose Size & Position. In Size, for Width type **5.90**; for Height, type **4.95**.

19. In Position on Page, for Down from Top, type **4.65**. For In from Left, type **1.27**. In Margins, set all to **.25**.

20. In Frame, choose Lines & Shadows. In Lines, choose All. In Style, choose the second pattern. In Shadow, choose None. Choose OK or press Enter.

21. Choose File Save As to save as a document. Choose Style Save as a Style Sheet to save as a style sheet. (Be sure to choose With Contents if you save as a style sheet.)

22. Choose File Print.

Looking at Design

You have many options for working with frames, tables, and graphics in Ami Pro. The designs in figures 10.8, 10.9, and 10.10 may give you some ideas for your own memos.

A landscape orientation is useful for certain information such as spreadsheets, graphs, or tables. Ami Pro enables you to import spreadsheets from other programs, or you can create tables and charts in another Ami Pro document, and then bring them into your memo. See Appendix B, "Using Other Programs with Ami Pro," for more information on importing files, exchanging files, and so on.

Version 3.0 users can place the cursor over the frame and click the right mouse button.

When you have two or more frames in a document, you can overlap them. If the top frame is opaque, it hides part or all of the bottom frame. Choose Frame Modify Frame Layout; in Frame, choose Type; in Display, choose Opaque. You can also switch the frames from top to bottom. Choose Frame Send to Front or Frame Send to Back.

HUMBLE OPINIONS

P. O. Box 174   Oak Hill, West Virginia 25901   (304) 255-5555

MEMORANDUM

To:

From:

Date:

Fig. 10.7   An innovative use of frames in a memo design.

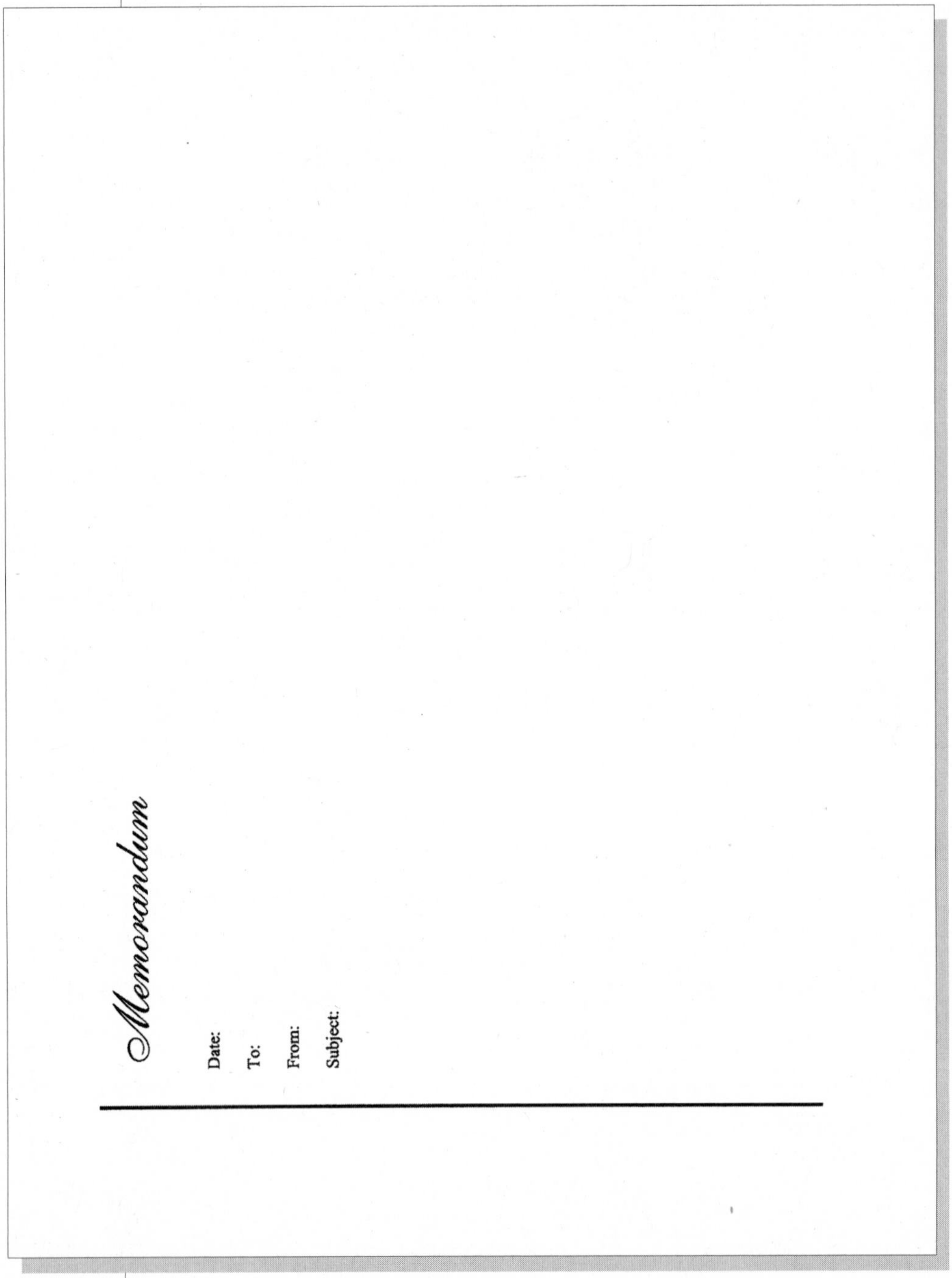

Memorandum

Date:

To:

From:

Subject:

Fig. 10.8   A landscape-oriented memo.

Fig. 10.9 An informal memo utilizing clip art.

MEMO

DATE:

TO:

FROM:

SUBJECT:

Fig. 10.10   A memo design using three frames to form the graphic rules.

Figure 10.8 illustrates a simple, landscape-oriented memo. The design provides ample room for a table, columns of numbers, a chart or two, or a spreadsheet. The heading is another ATM typeface, Shelley AllegroScript, but any italic type would look good. Notice, too, that the head is not boldfaced; the lightfaced type combined with the italic type gives a light feeling to the document. The rule on the left is a page rule that serves to confine the type.

There may be times you send informal memos for which you could use the design in figure 10.9—perhaps you can use it as a message on a bulletin board. This memo uses a landscape orientation. The art is an AmiDraw clip-art file called CARDHOLD.SDW.

You first draw a very large frame and remove all lines and shadows from the frame (choose Frame Modify, and in Frame, choose Lines & Shadows). Import the picture, and then either draw another frame within the clip art or open the Drawing feature to place the heading and banner lines (choose Tools Drawing). Note the word Memo in 36-point ATM Brush Script. This typeface complements the informal look of the memo.

Using frames in Ami Pro provides you with the versatility to add graphic lines in many different ways. Figure 10.10 shows a design in which you use only three frames, with only the top and bottom lines turned on. The first frame covers the entire text area; the second frame positions within 1/4 inch of the top of the first frame and extends to just below the word MEMO. The last frame begins below SUBJECT: and extends to within 1/4 inch of the bottom line of the first frame. This creates an interesting lined effect and divides the information. This use of frames divides and organizes the sections of the memo.

A dd a horizontal rule along the top margin to give the design a different look.

M ake the second frame transparent so that all clip art shows.

Recapping

In this chapter you not only learned how to create a memo, but how to apply several Ami Pro features to your documents. You can use tables, frames, clip art, ATM fonts, and graphic elements to enhance and organize other documents, as well.

Creating Business Forms

Starlight Productions

Post Office Box 174
Oak Hill, West Virginia 25901
(304) 255-5555

ORDER FORM

BILL TO:

SHIP TO:

PO NUMBER	CONFIRM?	DATE:
CASH?	BID NO.:	SHIP VIA:
CHARGE?	C.O.D.?	SHIP WHEN?

QTY.	PRODUCT #	DESCRIPTION	PRICE EACH	TOTAL PRICE
		Thank You!		

If you are tax exempt or use a Direct Pay Permit, please enclose a copy.

TERMS: NET; DUE ON RECEIPT

SUBTOTAL	
STATE TAX	
TOTAL	

Includes

11

Producing a Fax Cover Sheet

A fax, or facsimile transmission, is a transmission over telephone lines. Businesses send faxes to other businesses, customers, and branch offices. Faxes inform, confirm, question, order, purchase, and even sell. Fax advertising is a popular trend. Companies create faxes that advertise their services or products and send them in the evening when the phone rates are low. Most often, however, you use faxes to complete your business tasks quickly and conveniently.

For detailed information on how to create a form like this see page 252.

Faxes should always begin with a cover sheet. A *fax cover sheet* identifies you or your company, the date, who is sending the fax, and who should receive it. You can add other information such as the time the fax was sent, the number of pages following the cover sheet, or a message. You can simply type or write your fax cover each time you send a fax—but that doesn't look professional. In addition, typewritten or handwritten material isn't always legible when faxed. Using a fax cover sheet designed specifically for your company creates a better impression and assures that your message is readable after transmission.

Many factors affect the readability of fax transmissions. Most fax machines output to special fax paper, although some fax machines print to laser printers that produce good, clean copy. Traditional fax paper, however, has a very hard, slick surface. Often the output is fuzzy, and the text is broken and hard to read. Another problem with faxes is the "noise" on phone lines. Noise can interfere with the fax transmission, rendering your message unreadable. For these reasons, your fax cover and all faxed materials should be as clean and sharp as possible before transmission.

To ensure readability in your fax cover sheet, follow these simple guidelines.

- *Type.* Type should be no smaller than 10 point. Larger type, such as 12 and 14 point, faxes very well. After transmission, italic and condensed type is nearly impossible to read. Never use a script or text typeface on a fax—these typefaces are hard enough to read under normal conditions.

- *Margins.* The margin width is important to a fax cover because some fax machines don't pick up the original document all the way to the edge of the paper. To be safe, leave at least a 1/2-inch margin on all sides.

- *Graphics.* Graphics work well in a fax. They attract attention and divide information so that it is organized and easy to read. However, don't use lines narrower than 1 point. Thinner lines may not look good once they transmit, and they may not transmit at all.

- *Paper size.* The size of the cover sheet is limited by the fax machine. Most machines take an 8 1/2-inch wide sheet of paper. Fax paper, for the most part, comes in rolls. Therefore, any length of paper can work, but—for convenience to you and the receiver—an 8 1/2-by-11-inch sheet is your best choice. Shorter faxes may stick in the machine or get lost on the receiving end. Longer faxes, such as 8 1/2-by-14 inches or longer, are difficult to store. The designs in this chapter are all 8 1/2 by 11 inches.

*S*urveys are another popular use for faxes; consider surveying your customers about new products or services, customer service, suggestions for improved product lines, and so on.

*A*void light (5% to 20%) screens or screened lines in your fax cover; they do not transmit well.

- *Paper type.* Some companies use their letterhead as a fax cover sheet. This practice works well for keeping company pieces together; however, it is not wise to actually fax letterhead paper. Letterhead paper is expensive, and the receiver of the fax doesn't see the paper—only the design. Rather than wasting your expensive letterhead paper on faxes, copy the design onto 20# sulphite paper first and use the less expensive paper as fax cover sheets.

This chapter presents several traditional and creative fax cover designs. The following sections introduce some new Ami Pro features, including placing text vertically and adjusting line spacing with points. Once again, you may want to enter your own text and save one of these designs as a style sheet for use later.

You can use a glossary data file of your letterhead (see Chapter 5).

Designing a Basic Fax Cover Sheet

The first design, as shown in figure 11.1, looks clean and professional. The sharp, clear text faxes well, and all the identifiers are present. The banner lines used in this figure are in Helvetica typeface, providing a contrast with the company name in Times Roman. You might want to add a company logo for emphasis.

To produce the fax cover sheet shown in figure 11.1, follow these steps:

1. Choose File New. In the New dialog box, choose the default style sheet. Choose OK or press Enter.

2. Type the following:

    HUMBLE OPINIONS(Enter)
    P. O. BOX 174(2 spaces, Alt+0183, 2 spaces)**OAK HILL, WV 25901**(Enter)
    (304) 255-5555(2 spaces, Alt+0183, 2 spaces)**FAX (304) 251-1155**(Enter three times)
    FACSIMILE TRANSMISSION(Enter twice)
    FROM:(Enter twice)
    ATTENTION:(Enter twice)
    PAGES (Including Cover Sheet):(Enter twice)
    COMMENTS:

3. Center the first four lines of text, from HUMBLE through FACSIMILE TRANSMISSION.

4. Select HUMBLE OPINIONS. Choose bold. Choose Text Font. Choose Tms Rmn, 24 point. Choose OK or press Enter.

Always include your fax number in a fax cover sheet; 800 numbers are also a good addition.

Ami Pro 3.0 users can choose a different bullet by selecting Edit Insert Bullet.

5. Select the remaining text, from `P. O. BOX 174` through `COMMENTS`. Choose Text Font. Choose Helv. The default is 12 point. Choose OK or press Enter.

6. Select `FACSIMILE TRANSMISSION`. Choose bold. Choose Text Font. Choose Helv 14 point. Choose OK or press Enter.

7. Choose File Save As **fax1**. Choose File **Print**.

Designing a Text and Graphic Fax Cover Sheet

Chapter 2 explains more guidelines concerning the use of graphic lines in your documents.

The second fax cover design uses graphic lines to separate the company information from the fax information. Two lines in this design are page lines, and one is a paragraph lines. Lines are a good addition to any fax sheet. They organize the information for you and for the receiver, and they are attractive. Figure 11.2 illustrates the text and graphic design for a fax cover sheet. This design uses 2-point lines.

To create the second design, follow these steps:

1. Choose File **New**. In the New dialog box, choose the default style sheet. Choose OK or press Enter.

2. Choose Page **Modify Page Layout**.

3. In Modify, choose Lines. In Around Page, choose Top and Bottom. In Style, choose the third pattern. Choose OK or press Enter.

4. Press Enter and type the following:

   HUMBLE OPINIONS CORPORATION(Enter twice)
   P. O. BOX 174(Tab)**(304) 255-5555**(Enter)
   OAK HILL, WV 25901(Tab)**FAX (304) 251-1155**(Enter three times)
   DATE:(Enter twice)
   ATTENTION:(Enter twice)
   FROM:(Enter twice)
   PAGES (including cover):(Enter twice)
   COMMENTS:(Enter twice)

5. Select, bold, and center `HUMBLE OPINIONS CORPORATION`. Choose Text Font. Choose Tms Rmn, 24 point. Choose OK or press Enter.

6. Place the cursor on the paragraph return (the blank line) below HUMBLE OPINIONS CORPORATION. Choose Text Font. Choose 6 point to create a 6-point space.

7. Select the next two lines, from P. O. BOX 174 through the fax number. Choose **Style Modify Style**. The default style is Body Text.

8. In Modify, choose **Font**. Choose Helv, 10 point. Choose OK or press Enter.

9. In Modify, choose **Alignment**. In Tabs, set a right tab at 7 1/8" on the ruler. Choose **Use Style Tabs**. Choose OK or press Enter.

10. Select the text from the address through COMMENTS:.

11. Choose **View Show Ruler**. Activate the ruler.

12. Using the indent markers on the ruler, set the left margin to line up with the H in HUMBLE (approximately .35"). Set the right margin to line up with the N in CORPORATION (approximately 6.2"). Deselect the ruler.

13. Place the cursor on the paragraph return below OAK HILL, WV 25901. Choose **Style Create Style**. In the Create Style dialog box, type **Line** as the name of the new style. Choose Modify or press Enter.

14. The Modify Style dialog box appears. In Modify, choose **Lines**. Choose Line **Below** and the third line pattern. Choose OK or press Enter.

15. Choose **Style Select a Style**. Assign the Line style to the paragraph return.

16. Select the text from DATE: through COMMENTS: except for (including cover). Choose bold. Change the text to Helv; the default size is 12 point.

17. Choose **File Save As fax2**. Choose **File Print**.

The 6-point space is used by most typesetters to add a small amount of line spacing. 12 points (the original spacing) would create too much space to separate the head from the address.

When you move the indent marker, a vertical guideline moves across the page, making it easy to line up the indent.

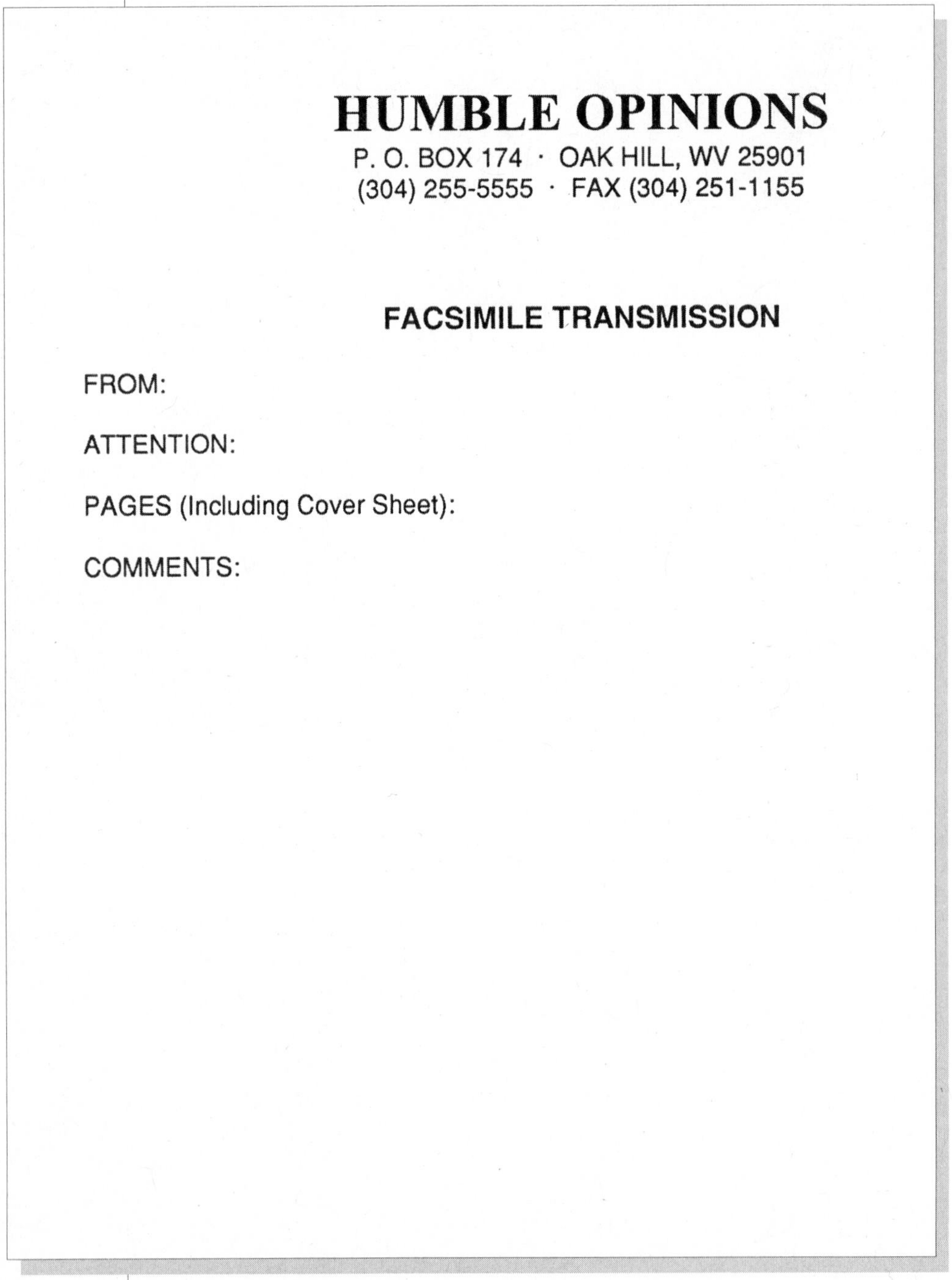

HUMBLE OPINIONS

P. O. BOX 174 · OAK HILL, WV 25901
(304) 255-5555 · FAX (304) 251-1155

FACSIMILE TRANSMISSION

FROM:

ATTENTION:

PAGES (Including Cover Sheet):

COMMENTS:

Fig. 11.1   A basic fax cover sheet.

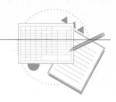

HUMBLE OPINIONS CORPORATION

P. O. BOX 174   (304) 255-5555
OAK HILL, WV 25901   FAX (304) 251-1155

DATE:

ATTENTION:

FROM:

PAGES (including cover):

COMMENTS:

Fig. 11.2   Graphic lines and indented text to add organization and interest.

Designing a Traditional Fax Cover Sheet

When balancing text and graphics on a page, the text and graphics are considered "gray," heavy graphics such as solid boxes or thick lines are "black" and areas with no text or graphics are "white" space. Try to create an equal amount of gray and white space in your designs.

Gutter Size defines the space before and after the line of text within the table.

When you turn on Automatic, pressing Enter within a table increases the height of the row. If Automatic is off, pressing Enter has no effect. To move from cell to cell, press the directional arrows or the Tab key.

As demonstrated in previous chapters, Ami Pro's Table feature is an excellent way to divide information. It's easy to use, enables you to add screens and rules, and is versatile. You can adapt a table to many uses. This fax cover sheet is completely within a table.

Figure 11.3 illustrates the one-column, five-row table design. The wide margins provide white space to contrast the graphic rules and gray of the text. The Humble Opinions name, address, and phone numbers form a head in the first row; the banner lines each have a row to themselves. The last row is larger to provide extra room for the message. The design is traditionally divided by graphic rules.

To produce the fax cover sheet shown in figure 11.3, follow these steps:

1. Choose File New. In the New dialog box, choose the default style sheet. Choose OK or press Enter.

2. Choose Page Modify Page Layout.

3. In the Modify dialog box, choose Type. In Margins, change the Left, Right, and Bottom margins to 1.8"; change the Top to 1.5". Choose OK or press Enter.

4. Choose Tools Tables. The Create Table dialog box appears.

5. In Number of Columns, type 1. Use the default 5 in Number of Rows. Choose Layout; the Layout dialog box appears.

6. In Default Columns, for Width type 4.5. The measurements are in inches.

7. In Default Rows, turn on Automatic by clicking the selection dialog box, or by pressing A. In Gutter Size, type .16.

8. In Options, choose Center Table on Page. Choose OK or press Enter. Ami Pro returns to the Create Table dialog box. Choose OK or press Enter again.

9. The cursor is in the first row; press Enter and type the following:

   FACSIMILE TRANSMISSION FROM:(Enter twice)
   HUMBLE OPINIONS CORPORATION(Enter)
   POST OFFICE BOX 174(3 spaces)**OAK HILL, WEST VIRGINIA 25901**(Enter)
   (304) 255-5555(3 spaces)**(304) 251-1155**(Enter twice)

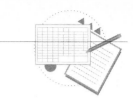

10. Place the cursor in the second row, type the following:

    DATE:(Tab)
    TO:(Tab)
    FROM:(Tab)
    MESSAGE:(Enter 21 times)

11. Select FACSIMILE TRANSMISSION FROM:. Choose Text Font. Choose Helv, 10 point. Choose OK or press Enter.

12. Place the cursor on the next (blank) line. Choose Text Font. Change the Size to 6 point to create a space.

13. Select, center, and bold HUMBLE OPINIONS CORPORATION. Choose Text Font. Choose Tms Rmn, 18 point. Choose OK or press Enter.

14. Select and center the text from POST OFFICE BOX 174 through (304) 251-1155. Choose Text Font. Choose Helv, 10 point. Choose OK or press Enter.

15. Select the text from DATE: through MESSAGE:. Choose Text Font. Choose Helv, 10 point. Choose OK or press Enter.

16. Select the table. Choose the Table Lines/Shades. In Position, choose All sides. In Line Style, choose the third pattern. Choose OK or press Enter.

17. Choose File Save As **fax3**. Choose File **P**rint.

Designing an Innovative Fax Cover Sheet

Producing an innovative fax cover sheet is one way to nearly guarantee that the receiver reads your fax. If your fax attracts attention—if your design is good—it is more likely to be noticed. There are many ways to attract attention with the cover, and figure 11.4 illustrates one option. The design is not a complicated one, but it's interesting. The word FACTS is a play on the word *fax*. The vertical placement of the word also draws attention. The banner lines are also placed vertically, and a rule along the left margin of the design adds to the vertical emphasis; the top rule confines the design.

If you enter a message on the computer, notice that the font is Times Roman, which adds emphasis to the message.

To add your company name, address, and phone number, move the banner lines down and place company information above the banner lines.

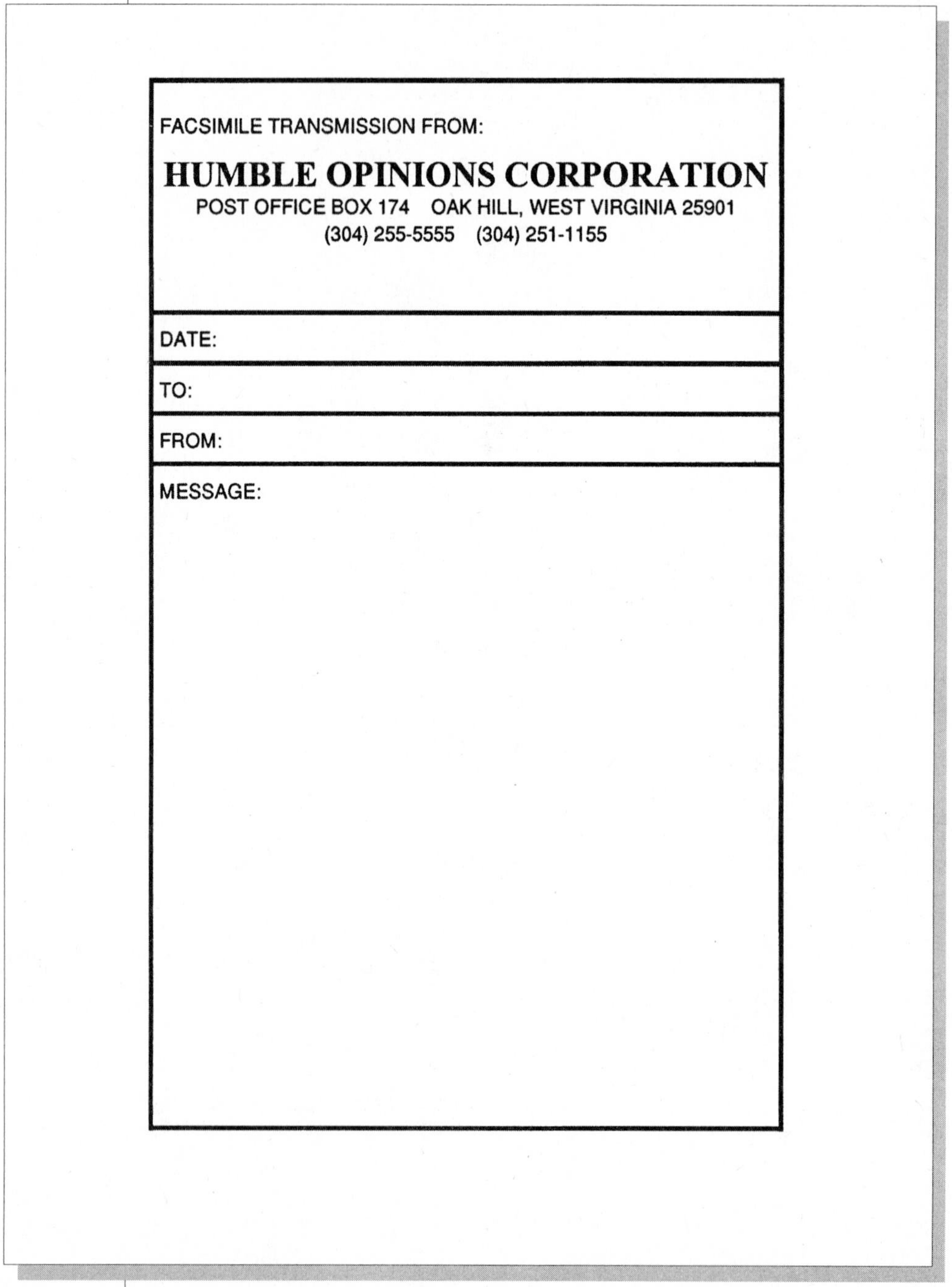

FACSIMILE TRANSMISSION FROM:

HUMBLE OPINIONS CORPORATION
POST OFFICE BOX 174   OAK HILL, WEST VIRGINIA 25901
(304) 255-5555   (304) 251-1155

DATE:

TO:

FROM:

MESSAGE:

Fig. 11.3 A traditional fax cover sheet design produced with a table.

FACTS

FROM

TO

Fig. 11.4 An innovative fax cover sheet that attracts attention.

The square corner of the frame mirrors the square appearance of the typeface used for the word FACTS.

If your printer is not capable of 125-point type, choose the largest type size you can print. You may want to create your type for this design in a draw or paint program and import it.

Normal Ami Pro spacing for 125-point type is 140 points (1.94"). To tighten up the leading, making the type more readable, change the line spacing to 108 points (1.50"). Note that the measurement in inches is not the same as the measurement in points.

To create the innovative design shown in figure 11.4, follow these steps:

1. Choose File New. In the New dialog box, choose the default style sheet. Choose OK or press Enter.

2. Choose Page Modify Page Layout.

3. In Margins, change all to .5". Choose OK or press Enter.

4. Draw a frame the width and height of the margins. Choose Frame Modify Frame Layout.

5. In Frame, choose Type. In Display, choose Square Corners.

6. In Frame, choose Size & Position. In Margins, change the Top margin to .30.

7. In Frame, choose Lines & Shadows. Choose the Top and Left lines. In Style, choose the fourth line pattern (a 4-point rule). In Shadow, choose None. Choose OK or press Enter.

8. Type the following:

   (Tab)**F**(Enter)
   (Tab)**A**(Enter)
   (Tab)**C**(Enter)
   (Tab)**T**(Enter)
   (Tab)**S**(Enter)

9. Choose Style Create Style. In the New text box, type **Facts**. Choose Modify or press Enter.

10. In Style, Choose Facts.

11. In Modify, choose Font. Choose Frank Gothic Cd, 125 point. (Frank Gothic Cd is an ATM font. If you do not have the ATM installed, choose Helvetica.)

12. In Modify, choose Alignment. In Tabs, set a center tab at .5" on the ruler. Choose Use Style Tabs.

13. In Modify, choose Spacing. In Line Spacing, change the measurement from inches to points. Type **108**. Choose OK or press Enter.

14. Choose Style Select a Style. Select Facts. In the Styles box, assign the Facts style to the text.

15. Draw another frame inside the first to hold the banner lines. Choose Frame Modify Frame Layout.

16. In Frame, choose Size & Position. In Size, for **Width** type **6.30**; for **Height**, type **9.30**. The default No Wrap Around should be selected.

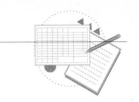

17. In Position, for **Down** from Top, type **1.08**. For **In** from Left, type **1.68**. The measurements are in inches.

18. In Margins, choose **Clear Margins**.

19. In Frame, choose **Lines & Shadows**. In Lines, deselect **All**. In Shadow, choose **None**. Choose OK or press Enter.

20. Place the cursor in the second frame and type the following:

    (Tab)**F**(Enter)
    (Tab)**R**(Enter)
    (Tab)**O**(Enter)
    (Tab)**M**(Enter twice)
    (Tab)**T**(Enter)
    (Tab)**O**(Enter)

21. Choose **Style Create Style**. In the New text box, type **TO, FROM**. Choose Modify or press Enter.

22. In Modify, choose **Font**. Choose Tms Rmn, 12 point.

23. In Modify, choose **Alignment**. In Tabs, set a center tab at .35" on the ruler. Choose **Use Style Tabs**.

24. In Modify, choose **Spacing**. In Line Spacing, change the measurement from inches to points. Type **12**. Choose OK or press Enter.

25. Select FROM TO. In the Styles box, assign the To, From style to the text.

26. Choose File Save **As fax4**. Choose File **Print**.

Looking at Design

You can make your fax cover sheet stand out from many other designs. Experiment with Ami Pro—it offers a lot of possibilities. Create many layouts with graphics: you can vary the width of a line, vary the width and height of graphic boxes, or vary the placement on the page. You can add shadows or screens as well. Be aware, though, that text with screens does not fax well. Never use even a 5% screen over text.

You can experiment, too, with typefaces. Designing a fax cover is a good way to have fun with type! Try extremely large type or a different typeface. Bookman, Palatino, or Avant Garde looks good in very large point sizes. If you have a paint or draw program, experiment with display type. Use outlined, shadowed, or rotated type. A logo is usually a good addition to a fax cover sheet as well. Be sure that the logo meets

S creens that are dark (60% or more) fax as fillers for graphics images that use no type.

C onsider using an ATM font such as CaslonOpenFace or Times New Roman. See Appendix D for samples of ATM fonts packaged with Ami Pro.

the guidelines for elements that are "faxable." You don't want to send your logo in a fax that doesn't look good.

The following designs are suggestions for your own cover sheets. Figure 11.5 uses three frames, all with the same double-ruled borders to create an eye-catching design. The word FAX is in Arial (an ATM font), and the banner lines are placed on tabs to provide more room for the comments.

If you want more of a letterhead design for your fax cover sheet, try one like the design in figure 11.6. The word FAX was produced by reversing the type in a frame with a black background. Ami Pro does not allow the letters to go to the edge of the frame, even with the frame margins turned off. To get the effect shown in figure 11.6, you must draw two extra frames; they must be opaque, with Lines & Shadows turned off. Place one frame above and slightly overlapping the FAX frame, the other below and slightly overlapping.

In the figure 11.6 cover sheet, the frame with the company name and other information is simply placed beside the FAX frame, with the FAX frame slightly overlapping. If you have problems overlapping, choose the Frame menu and choose Send to Front, or Send to Back.

Once again, Ami Pro's clip art provides a wealth of opportunity for ideas. The design in figure 11.7 uses CHECKMRK.SDW in a frame with the company name. Humble Opinions is in CaslonOpenFace, another ATM font. You can easily add any banner lines to this design.

Another clip-art file, BANNRPUL.SDW, provides the noticeable heading in figure 11.8. FAX is in BrushScript placed in a frame that overlaps the clip art. This design is somewhat light-hearted and fun—it may not fit every circumstance.

Figure 11.9 illustrates another innovative fax cover sheet. Three frames overlap on the page; each provides an area for information. The first contains the company name, address, and so on. The second frame lists the date, to and from, and the number of pages. The final frame leaves room for a message. For an interesting effect, these frames use a Deep Shadow that emphasizes the perspective.

B rushScript is a script typeface. Because it's not as decorative as most scripts, it does fax well.

F or longer messages, you can lengthen the message frame.

FAX

DATE: ATTENTION:

FROM: PAGES:

COMMENTS:

Fig. 11.5   A fax cover sheet design with double rules dividing the information.

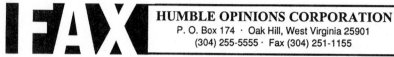

HUMBLE OPINIONS CORPORATION
P. O. Box 174 · Oak Hill, West Virginia 25901
(304) 255-5555 · Fax (304) 251-1155

Date:

Attention:

From:

Pages:

Fig. 11.6 Creative use of reversed type in a fax cover sheet.

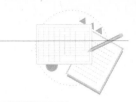

FAX FROM:

HUMBLE OPINIONS

Fig. 11.7 Clip art combined with the company name for a fax cover sheet design.

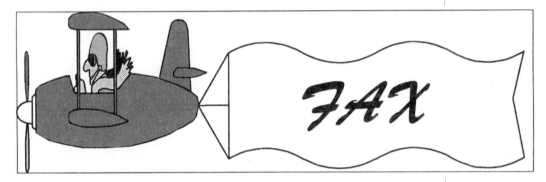

Fig. 11.8 A fun fax cover sheet design.

As an example of a logo in a fax cover sheet, figure 11.10 presents a logo created in CorelDRAW! This type of logo faxes well because it's bold and clear. Avoid small logos or logos with screens, small type, and detailed drawings.

A final idea for a fax cover sheet is to use a paint or draw program to produce display type. Use display type for the word *fax* as in these examples, or for a logo or company name. Figure 11.11 illustrates three ideas for display type, all created in CorelDRAW! The top example is a PostScript fill pattern called crosshatch that faxes well because it's a line pattern. The second example is outline type. The third example is expanded, or stretched, type. You can use almost any display type in a fax cover sheet to attract attention; however, be careful to use the type for only one or two words. Using too much variety creates chaos instead of emphasis.

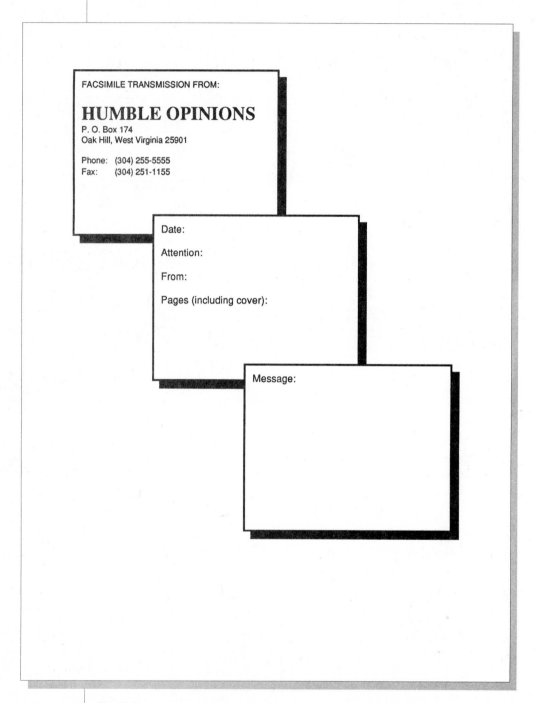

FACSIMILE TRANSMISSION FROM:

HUMBLE OPINIONS

P. O. Box 174
Oak Hill, West Virginia 25901

Phone: (304) 255-5555
Fax: (304) 251-1155

Date:

Attention:

From:

Pages (including cover):

Message:

Fig. 11.9   An innovative use of frames for a fax cover sheet.

 **humble opinions**
P. O. Box 174
Oak Hill, WV 25901
Fax (304) 251-1155

Date:

Attention:

From:

Message:

Fig. 11.10 A fax cover sheet with a logo that transmits well.

Fig. 11.11   Three examples of display type for a fax cover sheet.

Recapping

In this chapter, you learned to create several traditional and innovative fax cover sheets. The techniques used here, such as reversed type, overlapping frames, and modifying table text may also be used in other company documents.

Producing a Purchase Order

The business world could not operate without forms. Forms for purchases, sales, invoices, expenses, refunds—the list is endless. Paperwork takes an inordinate amount of time and effort every business day. Well-designed forms help to alleviate some of the labor involved.

For detailed information on how to create a form like this see page 284.

A form should organize the information so that it can be completed quickly and effortlessly. The form also should make the information easy to understand and summarize. To successfully accomplish these tasks, you can customize most forms to fit a particular purpose. That's where you and Ami Pro enter the picture.

Ami Pro provides many features that make it easier for you to create the forms you need in your business. Tables, frames, write protection, screens, rules, and tabs enable you to customize any form to suit your purpose. This chapter and the following two chapters detail techniques that can help you create your business forms. Before concentrating on the specific kinds of forms described in each chapter, however, you need some general tips for producing well-designed forms in Ami Pro.

The following sections describe some helpful information for creating forms. This chapter introduces many new Ami Pro features, such as using a right leader tab for a fill-in line, setting up 2-on for printing, using frame columns, and using inter-column rules.

Understanding the Contents of a Form

Forms should always contain certain information, such as the company name, address, phone number, and the name of the form itself (Purchase Order, Invoice, Expense Report). Additionally, a form could include other business information like fax numbers, 800 numbers, or logos.

Forms always ask for certain required facts, such as dates, names, addresses, phone numbers, prices, and descriptions. This relatively constant data is the *label text* of the form. On the other hand, the data that is added to complete the form is the *variable text*. Each time a form is filled out, the majority of the variable text changes. A date may remain the same, for instance, but the name and address of the person who completes the form may change.

Planning the Construction of the Form

Different kinds of forms require different types of labels and text. The purpose of the form is to organize this information in a way that's easy

U se Ami Pro's write protection feature to "lock" the document so that no one can tamper with your form.

A dditional label text may include terms of payment or delivery, and disclaimers.

for the reader to use. Ami Pro offers several ways to help you organize your forms. The following brief overview introduces the methods that are covered in detail in the forms chapters.

- *Tables* provide an excellent framework for your forms. Columns and rows can naturally divide text, both label and variable. Ami Pro's Table feature makes customizing simple. You can set column width and row height, vary rule thicknesses, add screens, connect cells, turn off certain borders, format text within a frame, and even add pictures and charts to a table. Entering your label text into a table is just as easy as formatting it.

- *Frames* are another alternative for structuring your forms. You can use several frames together and overlap frames. You can add borders, rules, columns, and tables to frames.

Each organizational method has its advantages and disadvantages. Sometimes it is best to combine the two methods to create a form. As you produce the forms in this part of the book, you learn more about each method and can better plan which to use on your own forms.

Planning a Form

If you're not sure of the label and variable text you need in your form, do some research by talking to the people who use the form. What information do they need? In what order do they need the text to make their jobs easier? Tailoring the form to the people who use it is important. The following sections give you ideas for adapting the designs of your forms to certain purposes, such as for use with a typewriter or as a preprinted form.

Once you produce a form, use it for a while to determine whether there are any changes you can make to facilitate its use. Because you will always identify necessary revisions, don't print too many copies of a form until you have experimented with it for at least a month or two. Any time you invest in this research is worthwhile.

Designing a Form

The design guidelines you should follow when producing your forms include line spacing—probably the most important consideration. To decide which line spacing to use, first determine how the form will be completed: handwritten, typewritten, or on a computer?

S tudy many forms before designing your own; you may find some alternatives to your own ideas.

A three-inch signature line is the standard length used in business forms.

Squeezing out a point here and there to get more on the page is not a possibility in forms produced for typewriters.

Because numbering forms in Ami Pro is a difficult process after number 999, the better plan is to contract with the print shop to add the numbers. Ask that details about numbering be included in your quote from the print shop.

Handwritten forms should allow enough space for the writer. At the very least, 1/4-inch line spacing is necessary, 3/8 inch is preferable, and 1/2 inch is not unheard of. Also, consider line length when producing a form to be completed by hand. Give the writer more than an inch or two to write his or her name. The width of your columns or information boxes should each increase by 1/2 to 1 inch when you produce a form for handwriting.

Typewritten forms must be produced with typewriter spacing. Ami Pro offers the choice of single, one-and-a-half, and double-line spacing, all of which are suitable for a typewriter. In typesetting terms, these options translate to 12 point, 18 point, and 24 point, respectively. If your form is for use with a typewriter, be sure to plan for the top margin, the company name, address, and other information with the same spacing.

If your form is designed for double spacing when you create a five-line margin, for example, you must add an extra line of space to start the next line on the typewriter. Similarly, if your company name, logo, and address take up seven lines, you must add another line of space to keep the even double spacing. The safest way to ensure proper spacing for a typewritten form is to test it in a typewriter, then adjust the spacing if necessary.

You may want to design your forms so that the variable text can be entered in Ami Pro. If this is the case, you simply save the framework of the form and any label text as a style sheet. Each time you need the form, begin a new document based on that form style sheet. If you find a form in the following chapters that suits your purposes, enter your own information and save it as a style sheet instead of as a document.

If your forms must be numbered consecutively, as with invoices, purchase orders, and so on, you must plan for the numbering in the design. You must leave space for the number, usually 1-inch wide by 1/4-inch tall.

If you plan to have your forms printed or copied, confer with the print shop as to the spacing and position of numbers produced by their numbering machine. Check, too, to determine whether the numbering machine includes the symbol for the number (NO., #, or Number). If so, do not add the symbol to your form when formatting.

Planning and Printing Preprinted Forms

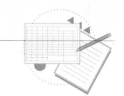

Preprinted computer forms are popular in many businesses. Many of these forms can be printed, just like blank computer paper, on a dot-matrix or other pin printer. You can easily create a copy of a preprinted computer form in Ami Pro, then hide the rules and label text so that you can print the variable text onto the preprinted forms.

To produce the form in Ami Pro, measure everything carefully. Measure from the top, sides, and bottom, as well as measuring column widths, and row heights. If you measure correctly, you should have no trouble producing the exact form after you're familiar with Ami Pro's form features. Reproduce all rules, boxes, and label text so that the form is easy to fill out on the computer. Ami Pro offers a means for hiding these components when you print the form.

To hide lines and label text when printing on a preprinted form, choose On Preprinted Form in the Print Options dialog box.

When you're ready to print on the preprinted form, you must perform two steps so that Ami Pro knows what to print on the preprinted form. First, mark the label text in your table as *protected text*. You protect text for two reasons: to print on the form without printing the label text and to protect the text from being accessed in Layout view so that others cannot easily edit or delete your work.

To mark text as protected text, using the following procedure:

1. Select the cells that contain label text.

2. Choose Table Protect. Ami Pro returns to the document.

3. Choose Table Modify Table Layout.

4. In Options, choose Honor Protect. Choose OK or press Enter.

The second step to printing on a preprinted form in Ami Pro is just as easy. Follow these steps:

1. Choose File Print.

2. In Options, choose On Preprinted Form. Choose OK twice or press Enter twice to return to the Print dialog box.

    This option tells Ami Pro not to print lines or screens associated with either frames or tables in this document.

Using Rules, Boxes, and Screens

Whether you use the Table feature or the Frame feature of Ami Pro to produce your forms, you probably want to use rules, boxes, or screens to help organize and divide the information. Both methods of producing forms make it easy to add graphics, but you should remember the following guidelines when doing so:

- Rules or boxes should be from 1 point to 4 points thick.

- The 1/2-point rule may suit some purposes, but generally, it is too thin to reproduce well (either by copying or offset printing).

- Rules thicker than 4 points may work in certain circumstances, such as screened rules.

A major problem in Ami Pro 2.0 and 3.0 concerns rules for tables. Sometimes, the rules you assign to a table are not the rules you get. For example, you may assign the second line pattern (a 2-point rule) to the entire table. When printed, some rules come out 2 point, but others come out 1 point. This problem seems centered around the 1/2-, 1-, and 2-point rules only. The Ami Pro technical staff is aware of the problem and is working on it for the next version. However, these deviations can make your design look inconsistent and somewhat unprofessional. You can see the rule-width problem both in your own work and in the examples presented in this book.

The use of screens is the major concern with graphics used in forms. Be careful to use screens that allow the text to show through. Follow these guidelines:

- Use light screens, 5% to 30%, with black text.

- Use dark screens, 60% to 90%, and solid black with white text.

Ami Pro enables you to reverse type, as you see in the following designs. Take advantage of this feature and the screen choices you have. Your primary test is to be sure that your reader can comfortably read the text.

Offset Printing or Copying Forms

You can, of course, print your forms—especially preprinted forms—on your own printer. Many of the forms you use, however, require two, three, or more copies. Consider having multiple-copy forms printed or copied at a print shop.

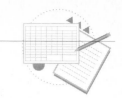

If your forms require duplicates, you can either use carbon paper or have them printed on carbonless paper. Carbon paper is messy and can be expensive to have a print shop insert for you. Carbonless paper is much less expensive; it is neat, clean, and comes in 2, 3, 4, and even 5 parts. Many copy shops carry carbonless paper and can produce forms that look professional. See Chapter 4, "Planning and Purchasing Printing," for information about paper, quotes, and choosing a print shop.

Many quick print shops can duplicate carbonless forms by coping instead of offset printing; copying is the less expensive process.

Designing a Purchase Order for Use with a Typewriter

The first form you produce can be used with a typewriter. It allows enough space for handwriting, or you can use this form with your computer. The line spacing, at one-and-a-half, makes this form useful for a typewriter. You produce this form by using a table. When you need rows of equally spaced lines, Ami Pro's Table feature is the recommended feature. In addition, the form uses a right leader tab to produce the fill-in lines in the first section (see fig. 12.1), a shortcut from the days of pressing the Shift and the underline keys that saves you much time.

To produce the purchase order form, follow these steps:

1. Choose File New. The New dialog box appears.

2. Choose the default style sheet. Choose OK or press Enter.

3. Choose Page Modify Page Layout.

4. In Modify, choose Margins & Columns. Change the Right, Left, and Bottom margins to .35. Change the Top margin to .25. The measurement is in inches. Choose OK or press Enter.

5. Type the following:

    HUMBLE OPINIONS CORPORATION(Enter)
    (Tab)P. O. Box 174(Tab)Fax (304) 251-1155(Enter)
    (Tab)Oak Hill, WV 25901(Tab)(304) 255-5555(Enter twice)
    PURCHASE ORDER(Enter twice)
    Date:(space, Tab twice)PO Number:(space, Tab, Enter)
    Purchased From:(space, Tab twice)Purchased By:(space, Tab, Enter)
    Attn.:(space, Tab twice)Dept.:(space, Tab, Enter)
    Address:(space, Tab twice)Approved By:(space, Tab, Enter)
    (Tab, Enter three times)

If your printer does not print to within 1/4 inch of the margin, adjust the top margin to .50"; then add one less row to the table in figure 12.1.

6. Format this text before continuing. Select HUMBLE OPINIONS CORPORATION. Choose center and bold.

HUMBLE OPINIONS CORPORATION

P. O. Box 174   Fax (304) 251-1155
Oak Hill, WV 25901   (304) 255-5555

PURCHASE ORDER

Date: _____   PO Number: _____

Purchased From: _____   Purchased By: _____

Attn.: _____   Dept.: _____

Address: _____   Approved By: _____

_____

QTY.	NUMBER	DESCRIPTION	UNIT PRICE	TOTAL

AUTHORIZED BY:

Fig. 12.1   A purchase order produced with right leader tabs and a table.

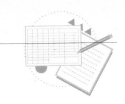

7. Choose Text Font. Choose Tms Rmn, 24 point. Choose OK or press Enter.

8. Select the address and phone numbers. Choose **Style Modify Style**.

9. In Modify, choose **Font**. Choose Helv, 12 point.

10. In Modify, choose **Alignment**. In Tabs, set a left tab at 1" and a right tab at 7.12" on the ruler. Choose **Use Style Tabs**. Choose OK or press Enter.

11. Select PURCHASE ORDER. Choose center and bold. Choose **Text Font**. Choose Helv, 14 point. Choose OK or press Enter.

12. Select the text from Date: through the tab under Address:. Choose **Style Create Style**. In the New Style text box, type **Info Tabs**. Choose Modify or press Enter.

13. In Modify, choose **Font**. Choose Helv, 10 point.

14. In Modify, choose **Alignment**. In Tabs, choose the Leader icon until the line appears. Set a right leader tab at 3.5" on the ruler (see fig. 12.2).

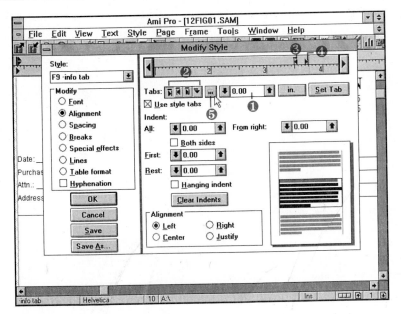

Fig. 12.2 Modify Style dialog box.

❶ Position text box

❷ Line leaders

❸ Right tab with line leader

❹ Left tab

❺ Select leader

15. In Tabs, select the Leader icon again until no leader appears. Set a left tab at 3.75" on the ruler.

16. In Tabs, select the Leader icon until the line leader appears. Set a right tab at 7.5" on the ruler.

Y ou can type the tab position in the Tab Position text box as an alternative to placing tabs on the ruler.

17. In Modify, choose **S**pacing. In Line Spacing, choose **1 1/2**. Choose OK or press Enter.

18. Choose **S**tyle **S**elect a Style. Choose Info Tabs to apply to the text from `Date:` through the tab below `Address`.

19. Place the cursor on the last paragraph return. Press Enter and move the cursor up one line. Choose Too**l**s Ta**b**les. The Create Table dialog box appears.

20. In Number of Columns, type **5**. In Number of **R**ows, type **21**. Choose Layout (see fig. 12.3).

21. In the Layout dialog box, under Default Rows turn off **A**utomatic by selecting it or clicking in the dialog box beside it.

22. In Height, type .24 (in.).

23. In Options, choose Center Table on Page. Choose OK or press Enter. Choose OK or press Enter again.

24. Choose **V**iew **F**ull Page.

25. Select the first column of the table. If you use a mouse, click and drag the mouse cursor from the top left corner of the column to the bottom of the column. If you use the keyboard, select the column by pressing Shift+Ctrl+down arrow until the column is selected.

26. Choose **T**able Column/Row Size. In **C**olumns, for **W**idth type .75 (in.). Choose OK or press Enter.

27. Repeat steps 25 and 26 for the rest of the columns. The widths are as follows: 2nd column is 1", 3rd column is 3.25", and the 4th and 5th are 1.15" each.

28. Select the entire table. Choose **T**able Lines/Shades.

29. In Position, choose **A**ll Sides. In Line Style, choose the second pattern. Choose OK or press Enter.

30. Choose **V**iew **W**orking or **S**tandard.

I f the table gridlines do not appear, turn them on by choosing View View Preferences Table Gridlines.

A mi Pro does not accept the width of column 3 if the table is wider than the margins. If necessary, adjust the other columns first and adjust column 3 last.

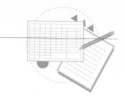

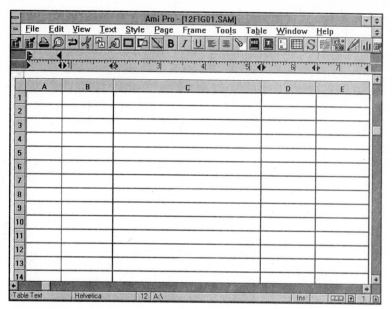

Fig. 12.3 The table with headings to identify columns (A, B, C) and rows (1, 2, 3).

31. In cell A-1 type the following:

(Tab) **QTY.**(Tab)**NUMBER**(Tab)**DESCRIPTION**(Tab)**UNIT PRICE**(Tab)**TOTAL**

32. Select, center, and bold the text. Choose **Text Font.** Choose Helv, 9 point. If your printer does not support 9 point, choose 8 point. Choose OK or press Enter.

33. Place the cursor on the last paragraph return (after the table). Press Enter and type the following:

(Tab twice, Enter)
(Tab)**AUTHORIZED BY:**

34. Select the first line (the two tabs). Activate the ruler.

35. On the ruler, set a left tab at 4". Set a right leader tab (line leader) at 8". This ruler looks similar to the one in figure 12.2.

36. Select AUTHORIZED BY:. Choose Helv, 10 point. Activate the ruler and set a left tab at 4".

37. Choose File Save **As poform1.** Choose File Print.

Designing a Purchase Order for Commercial Reproduction

You can have any of the documents in this book commercially reproduced. Because you do the typesetting and layout, your costs are reduced considerably. The next design illustrates a method that can further reduce your costs at a print shop.

Figure 12.4 shows two small purchase orders set up 2-on. A printer uses the term *2-on* to refer to printing two forms on the same press run. Because 8 1/2 by 11 inches is a common run size on a press, having two forms set up on that size sheet of paper is perfect for you and the print shop. If you take one 5 1/2-by-8 1/2-inch form to a shop, the print shop staff would shoot it with a camera and paste it up 2-on. If you originally set it up 2-on, you're not only saving them a step, but saving yourself money.

The 5 1/2-by-8 1/2-inch purchase orders are ready for the printer. Once printed, they are cut in half. You could print them on your printer and cut them yourself as well. Notice the column gutter (.80") is twice the width of either the left or right margin (.40") so that once the forms are cut apart, their individual left and right margins are even.

Again, the information at the top of the form uses right leader tabs, a small table provides the ordering space, and the entire form copies to the right column when completed. Notice, too, that there is room enough for numbering in the upper right corner, and that the rules in this figure are uneven due to the problem in Ami Pro.

To produce the short purchase orders, follow these steps:

1. Choose **File New**. The New dialog box appears.

2. Select the default style sheet. Choose OK or press Enter.

3. Choose **Page Modify Page Layout**.

4. In Modify, choose **Page Settings**. In Orientation, choose **Landscape**.

5. In Modify, choose **Margins & Columns**. Set all margins at **.40** (in.).

6. In Number of Columns, type **2**. In Gutter Width, type **.80** (in.). Choose OK or press Enter.

7. Enter your own information, or type the following:

    HUMBLE OPINIONS(Enter)
    P. O. Box 174(2 spaces, Alt+0183, 2 spaces)**Oak Hill, WV 25901**(Enter)

S maller forms can be set up 4-on.

A lways add a space between the label text and a right leader tab to create a less crowded and more professional looking form.

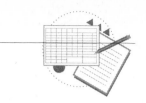

(304) 255-5555(Enter)
(Tab)**PURCHASE ORDER**(Enter)
Date(space, Tab, Enter twice)
Purchased From:(space, Tab, Enter)
(Tab, Enter)
(Tab, Enter)
(Tab, Enter)
Ship To:(space, Tab, Enter)
Attn:(space, Tab, Enter)
(Tab, Enter)
(Tab, Enter twice)

8. Format this text first, then insert the table. Select HUMBLE OPIN-
IONS. Choose bold. Choose Text Font. Choose Tms Rmn, 14 point.
Choose OK or press Enter.

9. Select and bold PURCHASE ORDER. The default is Tms Rms, 12
point. Activate the ruler. Set a left tab at 3.5" on the ruler. You
must delete the default tabs on the ruler first.

10. Select Date. Activate the ruler and clear the tabs. Set a right line
leader tab at 2.75".

11. Select the text from Purchased From: through the two tabs after
Attn:. Activate the ruler and clear the tabs. Set a right line leader
tab at 5" on the ruler.

12. Choose **Text Spacing.** Choose **Custom** and type **.25** (in.). Choose
OK or press Enter.

13. Place the cursor on the last paragraph return. Press Enter and move
up one line.

14. Choose **Tools Tables.** In **Number of Columns,** type **5**; in **Number of
Rows,** type **12.** Choose **Layout.**

15. In the Default Column dialog box, for **Width,** type **.5.**

16. In Default Rows, turn off **Automatic.** In **Height,** type **.24.** In
Options, choose **Center Table on Page.** Choose OK or press Enter.

17. Choose **View Full Page.** Select the first column of the table.

18. Using the mouse you can adjust the columns manually. Using the
keyboard, select **Table Column/Row Size.**

19. In Columns, for **Width in inches,** type **.5** for the first column; **.5** for
the second; **2** for the third; **.5** for the fourth, and **.75** for the fifth.

20. Select the table. Choose **Table Lines/Shades.** In Position, choose **All
Sides.** In **Line Style,** choose the second pattern. Choose OK or press
Enter.

Because Helvetica is a typeface with larger letters than most serif type, you can use 8- or 9-point type in a form.

21. Choose View Working in Version 2.0 or **Custom** in Version 3.0, or Standard. Place the cursor in A-1 and type the following:

    QTY.(Tab)**NO.**(Tab)**DESCRIPTION**(Tab)**EACH**(Tab)**TOTAL**

22. Select the text; choose center and bold. Choose **Text Font.** Choose Helv, 9 point. If you don't have 9 point, choose 8 point. Choose OK or press Enter.

23. Place the cursor on the last return in the column. Press Enter, Tab, Enter, and type the following:

    (Tab)**AUTHORIZED BY**(Enter)

24. Select the first tab, activate the ruler, and clear the default tabs. Set a right leader line tab at 5" on the ruler.

25. Select the second line, AUTHORIZED BY. Activate the ruler, clear the tabs, and set a right tab at 5".

26. Change the type to 9 point, or 8 if you don't have 9.

27. Choose View Full Page. Select the text from HUMBLE to the second line under Attn:. Choose **Edit Copy.** Place the cursor at the bottom of the first column. Press Enter to place the cursor at the top of the second column. Choose **Edit Paste.** Press the right-arrow key, then press Enter.

In Ami Pro, you can not copy text and a table at the same time. You must copy the table separately (table text moves with the table).

28. Select the table in the first column; **C**opy and **P**aste the table to the second column. Repeat with the signature line and AUTHORIZED BY.

29. Adjust the spacing above the AUTHORIZED line, if necessary, by adding a paragraph return.

30. Choose File Save As **poform2**. Choose File **P**rint.

Designing a Traditional Purchase Order

Often, you need more label text than the previous forms use. Depending on your business, you may need to know separate shipping and billing information, confirming or shipping dates, terms, and so on. Those items are in the next example, placed within a one-column table (see fig. 12.5). A second table contains information needed for ordering. A screen is added to the section for the totals and tax. This form can be commercially reproduced, copied, or printed from your printer. Again, there are major problems with the rules in this figure due to the problem with the Ami Pro program.

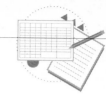

HUMBLE OPINIONS
P. O. Box 174 · Oak Hill, WV 25901
(304) 255-5555

PURCHASE ORDER

Date _____

Purchased From: _____
_____

Ship To: _____
Attn: _____

QTY.	NO.	DESCRIPTION	EACH	TOTAL

AUTHORIZED BY _____

HUMBLE OPINIONS
P. O. Box 174 · Oak Hill, WV 25901
(304) 255-5555

PURCHASE ORDER

Date _____

Purchased From: _____
_____

Ship To: _____
Attn: _____

QTY.	NO.	DESCRIPTION	EACH	TOTAL

AUTHORIZED BY _____

Fig. 12.4 Small purchase orders set up 2-on for printing.

HUMBLE OPINIONS

P. O. BOX 174 · OAK HILL, WV 25901 · (304) 255-5555

PURCHASE ORDER

DATE:	PO NUMBER:
PURCHASED FROM:	
SHIP ATTENTION TO:	
BILL ATTENTION TO:	
CONFIRMING ORDER REQUESTED BY:	SHIP BY:
TERMS:	

QTY	ITEM NUMBER	DESCRIPTION	UNIT PRICE	TOTAL PRICE
			SUBTOTAL	
			STATE TAX	
			TOTAL	

Fig. 12.5   A purchase order form created with two tables.

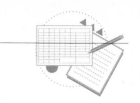

To produce the purchase order form in figure 12.5, follow these steps:

1. Choose File New. The New dialog box appears.

2. Select the default style sheet. Choose OK or press Enter.

3. Choose Page Modify Page Layout.

4. In Modify, choose Margins & Columns. Set all columns to .35 (in.).

5. In Modify, choose Lines. In Around Page, choose Top. In Line Style, choose the second rule. Choose OK or press Enter.

6. Enter your own information or type the following:

    (Enter)**HUMBLE OPINIONS**(Enter)
    P. O. BOX 174(2 spaces, Alt+0183, 2 spaces)**OAK HILL, WV 25901**(2 spaces, Alt+0183, 2 spaces)**(304) 255-5555** (Enter three times)
    PURCHASE ORDER(Enter three times)

7. Select and center the text from HUMBLE through PURCHASE ORDER.

8. Select and bold HUMBLE OPINIONS. Choose Text Font. Choose Times, 24 point. Choose OK or press Enter.

9. Select PURCHASE ORDER. Choose bold, Helv, 14 point.

10. Place the cursor on the next to the last return on the page. Choose Tools Tables. The Create Table dialog box appears.

11. In Number of Columns, type **1**. In Number of Rows, type **9**. Choose Layout.

12. In the Default Columns dialog box, for Width type **7.5** (in.). In Gutter Size, type **.11**.

13. In Default Rows, turn off Automatic. For Height, type **.25**. In Options, choose Center Table on Page. Choose OK or press Enter. Ami Pro returns to the Create Table dialog box. Choose OK or press Enter again.

14. Select the table. Choose Table Lines/Shades. In Position, choose All Sides. In Line Style, choose the second pattern. Choose OK or press Enter.

15. Choose Style Modify Style. In Style, choose Table Text.

16. In Modify, choose Font. Choose Helv, 9 point (10 point if you don't have 9).

17. In Modify, choose Alignment. In Tabs, set a left tab at 4" on the ruler. Choose Use Style Tabs.

Gutter size, in a table, forms a margin between the cell and the line between cells.

18. In Indent, Choose **All** and type **.10**.

19. In Modify, choose **Spacing**. In Paragraph Spacing, change the measurement to points in the measurement selection box.

20. In Above, type **3**. Choose Add in **Always**. Choose OK or press Enter.

21. The cursor is in the table. Type the following:

DATE:(Ctrl+Shift+Tab)**PO NUMBER:**(Tab)
PURCHASED FROM:(Tab twice)
SHIP ATTENTION TO:(Tab twice)
BILL ATTENTION TO:(Tab twice)
CONFIRMING ORDER REQUESTED BY:(Ctrl+Shift+Tab)**SHIP BY:**(Tab)**TERMS:**

22. Place the cursor on the last paragraph return. Press Enter. Choose **Tools Tables**. The Create Table dialog box appears.

23. In Number of Columns, type **5**; in Number of Rows, type **18**. Choose **Layout**.

24. In Default Columns, for **Width** type **.75**.

25. In Default Rows, turn off **Automatic**. In **Height**, type **.24**. In Options, choose **Center Table on Page**. Choose OK or press Enter. Choose OK or press Enter again.

26. Choose **View Full Page**.

27. Select the first column. If you use a mouse you can adjust the column widths manually. If you use the keyboard, select **Table Column/Row Size**. Change the **Width** of the columns as follows: the first column is .75"; second column is 1.25"; third column is 3.3"; fourth and fifth columns are each 1".

28. Select the table. Choose **Table Lines/Shades**.

29. In Position, choose **All sides**. In Line Style, choose the second pattern. Choose OK or press Enter.

30. Choose **View Working**.

31. Place the cursor in cell A-1. Type the following:

QTY(Tab)**ITEM NUMBER**(Tab)**DESCRIPTION**(Tab)**UNIT PRICE** (Tab)**TOTAL PRICE**

32. Select, center, and bold the text. In the Style dialog box (if it's not on-screen, choose **Style Select a Style**), choose **Body Text**. Choose **Text Font**. Choose Helv, 9 or 10 point. Choose OK or press Enter.

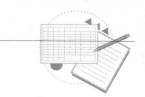

33. At the bottom of the second table, in cell D-16 type **SUBTOTAL**. In cell D-17, type **STATE TAX**. In cell D-18, type **TOTAL**.

34. Select, bold, and center the text. (The indented style is OK on this text, because it places the labels closer to the cells where the totals are entered.)

35. Select cells E-16, E-17, and E-18. Choose the Table Lines/Shades. Select the color bar and choose the gray screen third down and second from the right. Choose OK or press Enter.

36. Choose File Save **As poform3**. Choose File **P**rint.

It's simple and easy to add screens to tables, and depending on your form, you may wish to add screens in several places. Figure 12.6 illustrates the same form you just completed, but with added screens in the first table and the total column.

Designing an Innovative Purchase Order

Ami Pro offers you two methods of producing forms. You create the next purchase order using frames. You create three frames: one for the reversed text, one for filling out the ordering information, and one to contain the totals and tax. The largest frame, for the ordering information, is divided into five columns through Modify Frame Layout. This design contains no horizontal rules because the frame columns create difficulty in adding the rules. Figure 12.7 illustrates the final form.

Although you can fill this form in on the computer, the more efficient method is by hand or by using the typewriter, because of the way frame columns work. On the computer, you type everything in the first column, then the second, and so on. This design has limitations and advantages; one advantage, for example, is that you may need to enter information that cannot be confined by horizontal lines, like longer descriptions.

To create the purchase order form in figure 12.7, follow these steps:

1. Choose File **N**ew. The New dialog box appears.

2. Select the default style sheet. Choose OK or press Enter.

3. Choose **P**age **M**odify Page Layout.

4. In Modify, choose **M**argins & Columns. Change the **L**eft, **R**ight, and **B**ottom margins to **.35**. Change the **T**op to **.30**. Choose OK or press Enter.

The form in figure 12.7 allows sufficient room for handwriting or typewriting.

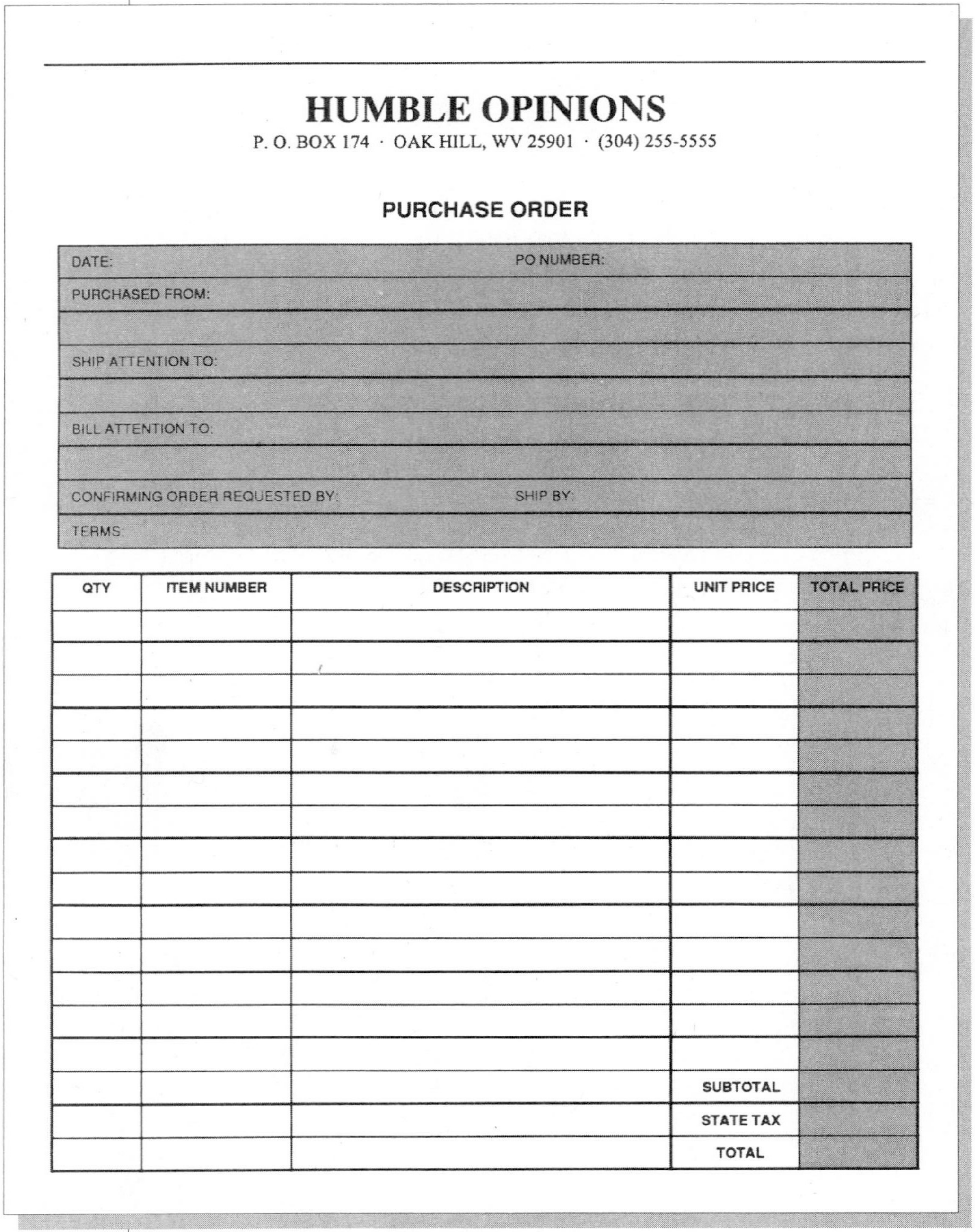

HUMBLE OPINIONS

P. O. BOX 174 · OAK HILL, WV 25901 · (304) 255-5555

PURCHASE ORDER

DATE: PO NUMBER:

PURCHASED FROM:

SHIP ATTENTION TO:

BILL ATTENTION TO:

CONFIRMING ORDER REQUESTED BY: SHIP BY:

TERMS:

QTY	ITEM NUMBER	DESCRIPTION	UNIT PRICE	TOTAL PRICE
			SUBTOTAL	
			STATE TAX	
			TOTAL	

Fig. 12.6   The form in figure 12.5 with screens added.

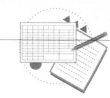

Humble Opinions Corporation

P. O. Box 174 · Oak Hill, WV 25901

(800) 251-1515

PURCHASE ORDER

Date: _____ Purchase Order Number: _____

Purchased By: _____ Ship To: _____

_____ _____

_____ _____

Ship By: _____ Terms: _____

QTY.	NUMBER	DESCRIPTION	UNIT	TOTAL

SUBTOTAL _____

STATE TAX _____

TOTAL _____

Fig. 12.7 Purchase order produced by drawing three frames and right line leader tabs.

5. Enter your own information, or type the following:

Humble Opinions Corporation(Enter)
P. O. Box 174(2 spaces, Alt+0183, 2 spaces)**Oak Hill, WV 25901**(Tab)**(800) 251-1515**(Enter twice)
PURCHASE ORDER(Enter twice)
Date:(space, Tab twice)**Purchase Order Number:**(space, Tab, Enter)
Purchased By:(space, Tab twice)**Ship To:**(space, Tab, Enter)
(Tab three times, Enter)
(Tab three times, Enter)
Ship By:(space, Tab twice)**Terms:**(space, Tab, Enter)

6. Select `Humble Opinions Corporation`. Choose Frank Gothic Cd (Helvetica if you don't have ATM installed), 24 point, and bold.

7. Select `P. O. Box 174` through `Oak Hill, WV 25901`. Choose Helv, 12 point.

8. Activate the ruler and clear the tabs. Set a left tab at 6" on the ruler.

9. Select the 800 number. Choose bold, Helv, 18 point.

10. Select `PURCHASE ORDER`. Choose bold, center, Helv, 12 point.

11. Select the text from `Date:` through the tab after `Terms:`. Choose Helv, 10 point.

12. Choose Text S**p**acing. In Line Spacing, choose 1 1/2. Choose OK or press Enter.

13. Activate the ruler and clear the tabs. Set a right tab with line leader at 4" on the ruler. Set a left tab at 4.25"; and set another right tab with line leader at 8".

Figure 12.8 illustrates the screen with the text selected, the ruler activated, and the first right tab and the left tab set. Notice that when you use the cursor to activate the tab, a vertical guide extends down the page. Notice, too, that the measurement you selected appears on the lower part of the ruler.

14. Choose View F**u**ll Page and draw a frame (the first frame contains columns). Begin drawing it under the line `Ship By:`. You size the frame in the next steps.

15. Choose F**r**ame Modify Frame Layout.

16. In Frame, choose **T**ype. In Display, choose **S**quare Corners.

17. In Frame, choose **S**ize & Position. In Size, for **W**idth type **7.80**; for Height, type **6.90**.

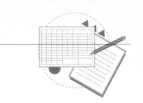

18. In Frame, choose **Lines & Shadows**. In Shadows choose **None**.

19. In Frame, choose **Columns & Tabs**. In Number of Columns, choose **5**. Choose **Line Between Columns**. In Style, choose the second pattern. Choose OK or press Enter.

20. Place the cursor in the frame. Activate the ruler. Position the column guidelines as follows: column 1 ends at .75" on the ruler; column 2 ends at 1.75"; column 3 at 5.75", and column 4 at 6.75". With the mouse, move the column guideline in the lower half of the ruler. With the keyboard, use the arrow keys to move the guideline.

21. Choose **View Full Page**. Draw the second frame at the top of the first one (this is the frame containing reversed text).

22. Choose **Frame Modify Frame Layout**.

23. In Frame, choose **Type**. In Display, choose **Square Corners**.

24. In Frame, choose **Size & Position**. In Size, for **Width**, type **7.75**; for Height, type **.45**.

25. In Margins, choose **Clear Margins**.

26. In Frame, choose **Lines & Shadows**. Deselect All Lines. In Shadow, choose **None**. In Background, choose black. Choose OK or press Enter.

27. Choose **View Enlarged**. Adjust this frame on the left and right to fit even with the first frame. Choose **View Standard**.

28. Choose **Text Font**. Choose **Helv**, 12 point; in the color dialog boxes, choose white. Choose OK or press Enter. Choose bold.

29. Place the cursor in the black frame, press Enter, and type the following:

    QTY. NUMBER DESCRIPTION UNIT TOTAL

30. Place the cursor on the paragraph mark. Choose 6 point.

31. Select the text. Activate the ruler and set center tabs at the following positions: .31", 1.20", 3.62", 6.20", and 7.20". (You can see the exact measurement of your tabs on the ruler; see figure 12.8 for the measurement location.)

32. Place the cursor in the space preceding `QTY.` and press Tab; repeat in front of `NUMBER`, `DESCRIPTION`, `UNIT`, and `TOTAL`.

33. Draw a frame in the lower right corner of the page, below the first frame.

34. Choose Frame Modify Frame Layout.

35. In Frame, choose Size & Position. In Size, set the **Width** at 3", the Height at .70". Choose Clear Margins.

36. In Frame, choose Lines & Shadows. In Lines, deselect All; in Shadows, choose None. Choose OK or press Enter.

37. In the frame, type the following:

SUBTOTAL(space, Tab, Enter)
STATE TAX(space, Tab, Enter)
TOTAL(space, Tab)

38. Select the text and choose Helv, 10 point, bold.

39. Choose Text Spacing. In Line Spacing, choose Custom and type .25. Choose OK or press Enter.

40. Activate the ruler. Set a right line leader tab at 2.83" on the ruler.

41. Choose File Save As **poform4**. Choose File Print.

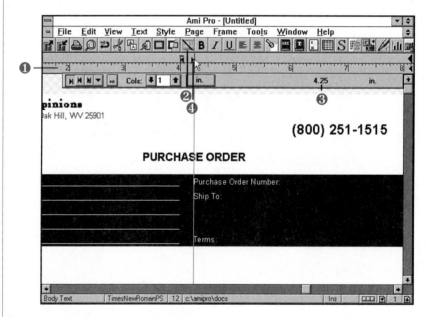

❶ Active ruler

❷ Right tab with line leader

❸ Ruler measurement

❹ Left tab

Fig. 12.8   The activated ruler with two tabs set for the text.

U se white text on a solid black frame and 60% to 90% screens. Use black text on screens that are 5% to 30%. For readability, do not use any text with 40% to 50% screens.

As a variation on the above form, you can use Ami Pro's screen features. Figure 12.9 illustrates an interesting change to the form; the form is just as useful, and now is more decorative. The same percentage of screen (60%) is used in all three frames. Note, too, that the type is reversed to white. Black type on a 60% screen would not be readable.

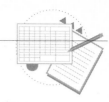

Humble Opinions Corporation

P. O. Box 174 · Oak Hill, WV 25901 **(800) 251-1515**

PURCHASE ORDER

Date: _____   Purchase Order Number: _____

Purchased By: _____   Ship To: _____

_____   _____

_____   _____

Ship By: _____   Terms: _____

QTY.	NUMBER	DESCRIPTION	UNIT	TOTAL

SUBTOTAL _____

STATE TAX _____

TOTAL _____

Fig. 12.9   The form in figure 12.8 with screens instead of solid white or black.

You may want to save your form as **poform5** before beginning the following example so that you don't lose the original. To make the changes in your form, follow these steps:

1. Place the cursor in the first, largest frame. Choose Frame Modify Frame Layout.

2. In Frame, choose Columns & Tabs. Line Between Columns is selected. In Style, choose the fifth line pattern (a 6-point rule). In the row of colors, select the gray screen that is second from the top, and in the first column on the right. Choose OK or press Enter.

3. Choose the frame containing SUBTOTAL. Choose the Frame Modify Frame Layout.

4. In Frame, choose Lines & Shades. In Background, choose the gray screen that is second from the top, in the first column on the right. Choose OK or press Enter.

5. Select the text in the frame. Choose Text Font. In the color bar, choose white. Choose OK or press Enter.

6. Select the frame containing QTY. through TOTAL. Choose the Frame Modify Frame Layout.

7. In Frame, choose Lines & Shades. In Background, choose the gray screen that is second from the top, and in the first column on the right. Choose OK or press Enter.

8. Choose File Save. Choose File Print.

Looking at Design

You can choose from many design possibilities when creating business forms. You can add logos, use columns or tabs to organize, connect cells in a table, and so on. In the following two chapters, you learn more advanced techniques for producing forms. This section provides you with some extra designs, illustrated in figures 12.10, 12.11, and 12.12, you may want to try.

Figure 12.10 illustrates the use of an ATM font (CaslonOpenFace) and a logo. The logo is an AmiDraw file altered with Ami Pro's Drawing feature. The table is similar to previous forms, with two differences. First, the rules are only 1-point rules to reflect the light feeling of the head. The second difference is at the bottom of the frame. Notice that the left cells have no border, leaving the two TOTAL cells hanging on the end. Chapter 14, "Producing an Order Form," explains deselecting borders and connecting cells in detail.

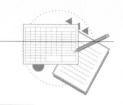

HUMBLE OPINIONS

POST OFFICE BOX 174
OAK HILL, WEST VIRGINIA 25901

(304) 255-5555   (800) 251-1515

PURCHASE ORDER

QTY.	ITEM #	DESCRIPTION	UNIT PRICE	TOTAL PRICE
			TOTAL	

Fig. 12.10   A purchase order design with a logo.

Humble Opinions Corporation

P. O. Box 174 · Oak Hill, WV 25901
(304) 255-5555

PURCHASE ORDER

P.O. NUMBER   DATE

QTY.	ITEM #	DESCRIPTION	PRICE	TOTAL

SUBTOTAL	
SALES TAX	
TOTAL	

Fig. 12.11   A form set up on tabs for easy data entry on the computer.

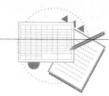

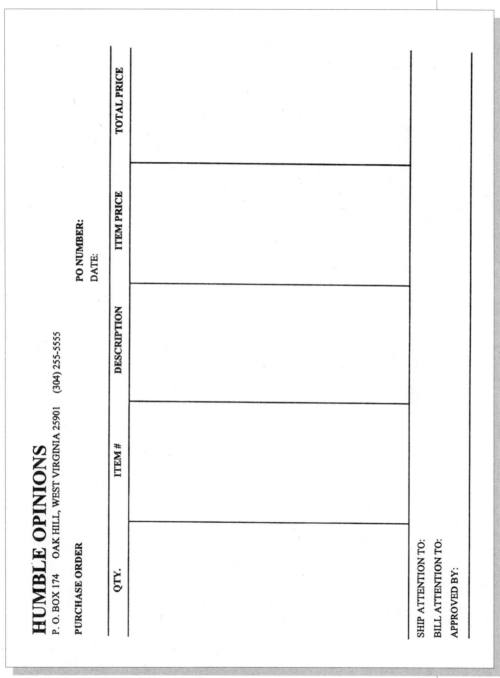

Fig. 12.12 A landscape-oriented form.

Figure 12.11 illustrates a table set up with tabs. Completing this form on the computer is very easy. The rules are created in the paragraph style. After you set your tabs, entering information is fast and simple.

Finally, figure 12.12 shows a purchase order set up in landscape orientation. This form design works especially well if you need more or wider columns than would fit in portrait orientation. These equally wide columns are set up in a frame. They could easily be adjusted to different widths.

Recapping

In this chapter, you learned to plan the contents, construction, and design of a form by using both the table feature and frames feature in Ami Pro. In addition, you learned to customize forms by using tabs, columns, screens and rules.

13

Producing an Expense or Travel Report

Expense reports and travel logs are examples of in-house forms. An in-house form, such as a work order, requisition, cash in/cash out form, and reimbursement request, is one that the employees, staff, and supervisors use within the company. These forms pass between departments to inform, request, or account for cash flow, job flow, and so on.

TRAVEL LOG	
NAME	WEEK OF
STARTING MILEAGE	ENDING MILEAGE

OUT	IN
DATE/TIME	DATE/TIME
MILEAGE	MILEAGE
DATE/TIME	DATE/TIME
MILEAGE	MILEAGE
DATE/TIME	DATE/TIME
MILEAGE	MILEAGE
DATE/TIME	DATE/TIME
MILEAGE	MILEAGE
DATE/TIME	DATE/TIME
MILEAGE	MILEAGE
DATE/TIME	DATE/TIME
MILEAGE	MILEAGE
DATE/TIME	DATE/TIME
MILEAGE	MILEAGE
DATE/TIME	DATE/TIME
MILEAGE	MILEAGE
DATE/TIME	DATE/TIME
MILEAGE	MILEAGE
SIGNATURE	TOTAL MILES

For detailed information on how to create a form like this see page 292.

You may want to re-search specific uses for forms before you design them; ask the people who use the forms for suggestions.

Salespersons, technicians, or anyone in the company who travels during the workday must account for business trips by using a travel log, mileage report, and expense report. Most companies pay for mileage if employees use their own cars, or they require mileage records when employees use a company car. Other expenses that may be reimbursed as part of a business trip are meals, hotels, supplies, postage, and tolls. Forms are the perfect way to record these business expenses. The form organizes the information and keeps all entries consistent for easy classification.

Because these are in-house forms, they do not require the company name and address. They do require some label text, however, to identify the variables. Names, dates, dollar amounts, and mileage records are the most common label text used in these forms. This chapter illustrates ways to organize and produce reports with both the common label text and some additional labels you may need.

Some Ami Pro features applied in this chapter include connecting table cells, using reversed rules in frames, and varying rules within a table. Because you are more familiar with many of Ami Pro's features now, many of those you have used in the preceding chapters are not explained in detail in this and the following chapters. You can find explanations by checking the Index or Appendix A. Only features being used for the first time are explained at length in this chapter.

Ami Pro offers one expense form style sheet that you may want to use: ~EXPENSE.STY (in Version 2.0) or _EXPENSE.STY (in Version 3.0). You can use this detailed expense form as-is or modify to meet your needs. To use the style sheet in a document, select File New. In the New dialog box, select the expense style sheet and then select With Contents. Select OK or press Enter. After you complete this chapter and Chapter 14, "Producing an Order Form," you easily will be able to modify Ami Pro's expense style sheet to suit your own purposes.

Designing a Travel Report

A travel report contains details such as dates, times, and mileage. How you arrange the information depends on your company's requirements. Some companies need the time in and out, others don't ask for the time at all. Most, however, do require the recorded mileage at the start and at the end of the trip.

The form in figure 13.1 organizes all these components into a travel report. The form is landscape oriented to allow more room for the information. The label text at the beginning of the document requests,

besides the name and date, the position of the user, a summary of miles traveled for the week, and the beginning and ending mileage recorded for the week. The table allows room for more detail.

To produce the travel report, follow these steps:

1. Choose **File New.** Choose the default style sheet. Choose **OK** or press **Enter.**

2. Choose **Page Modify Page Layout.**

3. In **Modify Page Settings,** choose **Landscape.**

4. In **Margins & Columns,** set all margins to **.35.**

5. In **Tabs,** clear the ruler. Set a right line leader tab at 5.25" on the ruler, a left tab at 5.5", and another right line leader tab at 10.5".

6. Type the following:

   TRAVEL REPORT(Enter twice)
   NAME:(space, Tab twice)**POSITION:**(space, Tab, Enter)
   WEEK OF:(space, Tab twice)**BEGINNING MILEAGE:**(space, Tab, Enter)
   TOTAL MILES:(space, Tab twice)**ENDING MILEAGE:**(space, Tab, Enter twice)

7. Select `TRAVEL REPORT`. Choose bold, center, Helv, 18 point.

8. Select the text from `NAME:` to include both Enter marks after `ENDING MILEAGE:`. Choose Helv, 10 point. Deselect only the last two Enter marks.

9. Choose **Text Spacing.** Choose **Double.** Choose **OK** or press **Enter.**

10. Place the cursor on the last paragraph return. Choose **Tools Tables.**

11. In **Number of Columns,** type **7;** in **Number of Rows,** type **15.** Choose **Layout.**

12. In **Default Rows,** turn off **Automatic.** In **Height,** type **.33.**

13. In **Options,** choose **Center Table on Page.** Choose **OK** twice or press **Enter** twice.

14. In the table, type the following:

    DATE(Tab)**TIME OUT**(Tab)**MILEAGE OUT**(Tab)**DESTINATION**(Tab)**TIME IN**(Tab)**MILEAGE IN**(Tab)**TOTAL**

15. Choose **View Full Page.** Select the line of text you just entered and choose bold, center, Helv, 10 point.

I n Ami Pro, choosing .33 is the same as double line spacing.

L eave the 1" measurement—the width of six of the seven columns in this example—in the Default Column Width to save time later.

16. Select the DESTINATION column. In Table Column/Row Size, change the column to 3.36" wide. Choose OK or press Enter.

17. Select the first row of the table. Choose Style Modify Style. Table Text appears in the Styles box.

18. In Modify, choose Spacing. In Paragraph Spacing, choose Above and type .04 (in.) In Add In, choose Always. Choose OK or press Enter.

19. Select the table. Choose Table Lines/Shades.

20. In Position, choose All Sides. In Line Style, choose the second pattern. Choose OK or press Enter.

21. Select the first row of the table. Choose Table Lines/Shades. In Position, select Top and Bottom by clicking them twice or by pressing T twice then B twice. In Line Style, choose the third pattern. Choose OK or press Enter.

The grayed boxes in Position indicate that they are chosen for a particular rule (the first you assigned was All Sides). By selecting the Top and Bottom again, you turn them off. Select them again, and you can choose a different line width.

22. Repeat step 21, selecting and changing the thickness of each of the following rules:

First column, Left position to third Line Style pattern.

Last row, Bottom position to third Line Style pattern.

Seventh (last) column, Right position to third Line Style pattern.

23. Choose File Save As. Choose File Print.

Designing a Travel Log

A travel log is similar to a travel report; it documents dates and mileage. Many companies require the time and mileage both at departure and upon arrival. This weekly travel log divides those requirements into two columns: out and in (see fig. 13.2). Because travel logs are usually filled in by hand, the rows are double-spaced for more writing room. The outline rules are thicker, as is the middle rule separating the out and in columns. The bottom of the form provides a place for the total miles as well.

M odify the paragraph spacing as in step 18 to center the line of text from top to bottom in the row.

A mi Pro has a glitch that varies the line widths when you choose any of the first three line styles. Even the glitch is not consistent.

TRAVEL REPORT

NAME: _____
WEEK OF: _____
TOTAL MILES: _____

POSITION: _____
BEGINNING MILEAGE: _____
ENDING MILEAGE: _____

DATE	TIME OUT	MILEAGE OUT	DESTINATION	TIME IN	MILEAGE IN	TOTAL

Fig. 13.1 A basic travel report that includes dates, times, and recorded mileage.

TRAVEL LOG

NAME: _____   WEEK OF: _____

STARTING MILEAGE: _____   ENDING MILEAGE: _____

OUT		IN	
DATE/TIME		DATE/TIME	
MILEAGE		MILEAGE	
DATE/TIME		DATE/TIME	
MILEAGE		MILEAGE	
DATE/TIME		DATE/TIME	
MILEAGE		MILEAGE	
DATE/TIME		DATE/TIME	
MILEAGE		MILEAGE	
DATE/TIME		DATE/TIME	
MILEAGE		MILEAGE	
DATE/TIME		DATE/TIME	
MILEAGE		MILEAGE	
DATE/TIME		DATE/TIME	
MILEAGE		MILEAGE	
DATE/TIME		DATE/TIME	
MILEAGE		MILEAGE	
DATE/TIME		DATE/TIME	
MILEAGE		MILEAGE	
DATE/TIME		DATE/TIME	
MILEAGE		MILEAGE	

SIGNATURE: _____   TOTAL MILES: _____

Fig. 13.2   An alternative travel log design.

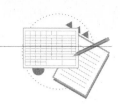

To produce the travel log shown in figure 13.2, follow these steps:

1. Choose File New. Choose the default style sheet. Choose OK or press Enter.

2. Choose Page Modify Page Layout.

3. In Margins & Columns, set all margins to .35.

4. In Tabs, clear the ruler. Set a right line leader tab at 4" on the ruler, a left tab at 4.25", and another right line leader tab at 8".

5. Type the following:

   TRAVEL LOG(Enter twice)
   NAME:(space, Tab twice)**WEEK OF:**(space, Tab, Enter)
   STARTING MILEAGE:(space, Tab twice)**ENDING MILEAGE:**
   (space, Tab, Enter three times)
   SIGNATURE:(space, Tab twice)**TOTAL MILES:**(space, Tab)

6. Select `TRAVEL LOG`. Choose bold, center, Helv, 18 point.

7. Select the text from `NAME:` through `TOTAL MILES:`. Choose Helv, 10 point.

8. Choose Text Spacing. Choose Double line spacing. Choose OK or press Enter.

9. Place the cursor on the second paragraph return after the line beginning `STARTING MILEAGE:`. Choose Tools Table.

10. In Number of Columns, type **4**; in Number of Rows, type **21**. Choose Layout.

11. The Default Column Width is 1". In Default Rows, turn off Automatic. In Height, type **.33**. In Options, choose Center Table on Page. Choose OK or press Enter. Choose OK or press Enter again.

12. Choose View Full Page. Select the second column of the table. Using the mouse, or by choosing Table Column/Row Size, change the second column to 2.75". Select and change the width of the fourth column to 2.75".

13. Select the table. Choose Table Lines/Shades. In Position, choose All Sides. In Line Style, choose the second line pattern. Choose OK or press Enter.

14. Select the first row. Choose Table Lines/Shades. In Position, choose Top and Bottom by selecting each one twice. In Line Style, choose the third line pattern. Choose OK or press Enter.

Thicker lines make the heading stand out from the rest of the table.

15. Select and change the following columns and rows by using the method in step 14:

    First column, **L**eft position to the third Line **S**tyle pattern

    Last row, **B**ottom position to the third Line **S**tyle pattern

    Third column, **L**eft position to the third Line **S**tyle pattern

    Fourth column, **R**ight position to the third Line **S**tyle pattern

16. Select cells A-1 and B-1. Choose Ta**b**le **C**onnect. Repeat for cells C-1 and D-1.

17. Place the cursor in cell A-1 and type the following:

    OUT(Tab)**IN**

18. Select the text you just entered and choose bold, center, Helv, 14 point.

19. Choose **S**tyle **M**odify Style.

20. In Modify, choose S**p**acing. In Paragraph Spacing, choose Above and type **.04** (in.). In Add In, choose Always. Choose OK or press Enter.

21. Place the cursor in cell A-2. Type the following:

    DATE/TIME(down arrow)
    MILEAGE(down arrow)

22. Select DATE/TIME and MILEAGE. Choose Helv, 10 point. Choose OK or press Enter.

23. Choose Text **I**ndention. Choose All and type **.05**. Choose OK or press Enter.

24. Copy and **P**aste the two lines of text to the rest of the OUT column of the form. Select the entire A column, Copy and **P**aste it to the IN column.

25. Choose File Save As. Choose File Print.

Designing a Daily Expense Report

Because many business expenses include more than mileage, an expense report may be necessary to document a business trip. The following example provides space for writing the specific details of the expenses.

B y indenting .05 in step 23 you keep the text from running into the line to the left.

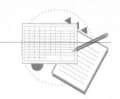

Hotel, meals, and mileage included, the form allows for a description of the expenditure and the amount. In addition, the bottom of the form provides a place for an account of the success of the trip.

This form uses frames to enclose the label and variable text (see fig. 13.3). All frames but the first one are divided into three columns; no rows are provided. The reversed text of the three headings makes the form easy to find and identify. This type of form is much less structured than the others in this chapter. This form may not be appropriate for all businesses; on the other hand, it may be just the form you need.

To produce the daily expense report, follow these steps:

1. Choose File New. Choose the default style sheet. Choose OK or press Enter.

2. Choose Page Modify Page Layout.

3. In Margins & Columns, set all margins to .35. Select OK or press Enter.

4. Draw a frame at the top of the page (you size the frame in the next steps).

5. Choose Frame Modify Frame Layout.

6. In Frame, choose Type. In Display, choose Square Corners.

7. In Text Wrap Around, choose No Wrap Beside.

8. In Frame, choose Size & Position. In Size, set the Width at 7.80". In Height, type .56. In Margins, clear all margins but the Top, set at .10.

9. In Modify, choose Lines & Shadows. In Shadows, choose None. In Background, choose black. Choose OK or press Enter.

10. Copy and Paste the frame. To reposition the second frame, choose Frame Modify Frame Layout.

11. In Frame, choose Size & Position. In Position on Page, for Down from the Top type 2.60. Choose OK or press Enter.

12. Place the cursor in the first frame. Choose Text Font. Choose Tms Rmn, 18 point, and white. Choose OK or press Enter. Type the following:

    DAILY EXPENSE REPORT

13. Select the text. Choose center, bold.

Modify the margins for the document in figure 13.3, if your printer does not print at .35 inch.

Save unnecessary steps by copying frames that you use again.

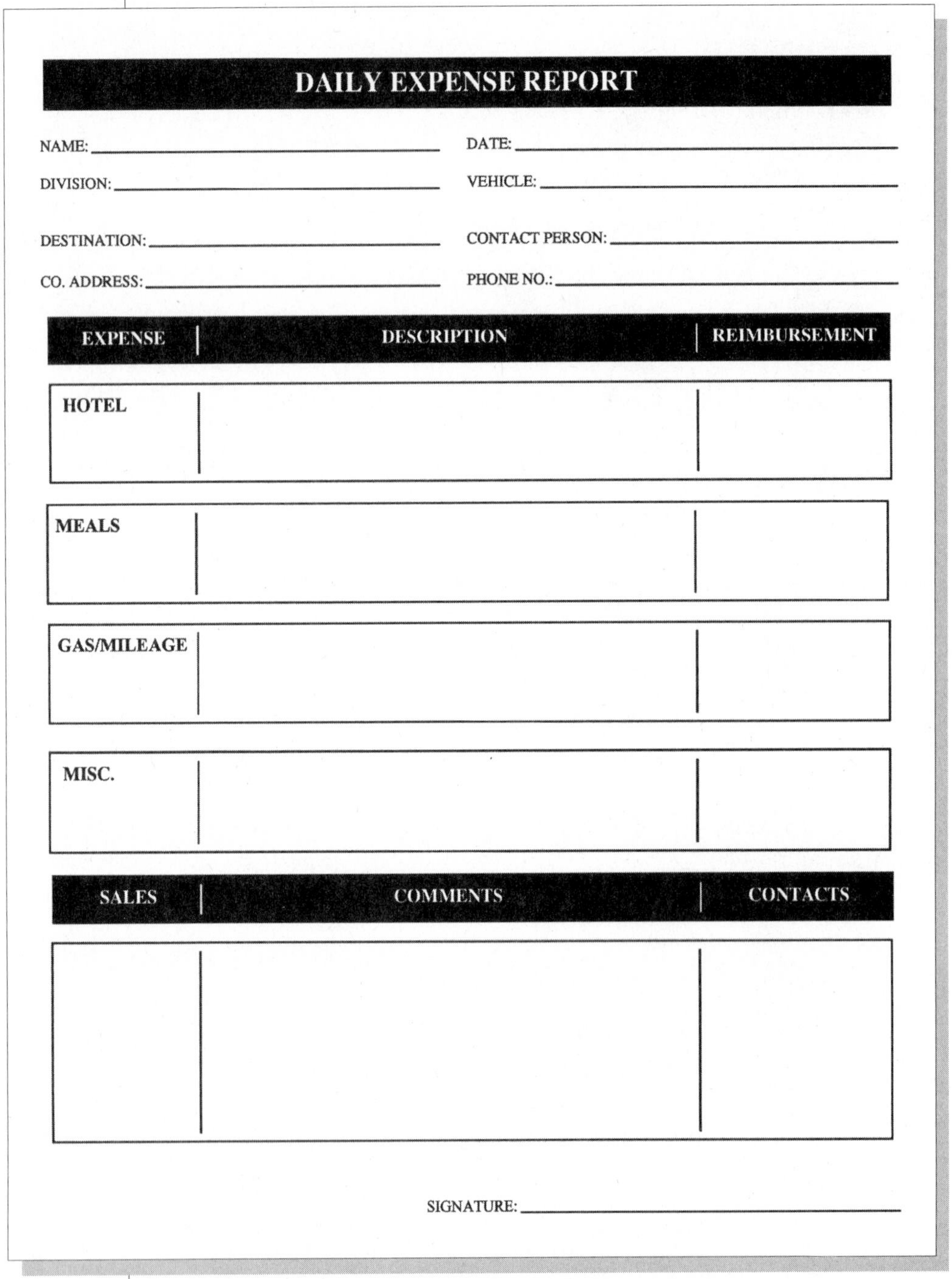

DAILY EXPENSE REPORT

NAME: _____   DATE: _____

DIVISION: _____   VEHICLE: _____

DESTINATION: _____   CONTACT PERSON: _____

CO. ADDRESS: _____   PHONE NO.: _____

EXPENSE	DESCRIPTION	REIMBURSEMENT
HOTEL		
MEALS		
GAS/MILEAGE		
MISC.		

SALES	COMMENTS	CONTACTS

SIGNATURE: _____

Fig. 13.3   A daily expense report produced with frames.

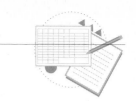

14. Place the cursor beneath the frame and type the following:

NAME:(space, Tab twice)**DATE:**(space, Tab, Enter)
DIVISION:(space, Tab twice)**VEHICLE:**(space, Tab, Enter twice)
DESTINATION:(space, Tab twice)**CONTACT PERSON:**(space, Tab, Enter)
CO. ADDRESS:(space, Tab twice)**PHONE NO.:**(space, Tab, Enter)

15. Select the text from NAME: to PHONE NO.:. Choose Tms Rmn, 10 point.

16. Activate the ruler. Clear the tabs. Set a right line leader tab at 4" on the ruler, a left tab at 4.25", and a right line leader at 8".

17. Choose **T**ext **S**pacing. Choose **D**ouble. Choose **O**K or press Enter.

18. Place the cursor on the paragraph return between DIVISION: and DESTINATION:. Choose **T**ext **S**pacing. Choose **S**ingle. Choose **O**K or press Enter.

19. Select the second black frame. Choose **F**rame **M**odify Frame Layout.

20. In Frame, choose **S**ize & Position. In Margins, make all margins .15.

21. In Frame, choose **C**olumns & Tabs. In Number of Columns, choose **3**. Choose **L**ine Between Columns. In Line **S**tyle, choose the second pattern. In the color bar, choose white. Choose **O**K or press Enter.

22. Set the columns of the frame to the following: first column is 1.35" wide, the second is 4.5", the third is 1.75".

23. Copy and **P**aste the frame. Move the second frame to 7.5" on the page. Place the cursor in the second black frame.

24. Choose **T**ext **F**ont. Choose Tms Rmn, 12 point, and the white square in the color bar. Choose **O**K or press Enter.

25. In the second black frame, type the following:

EXPENSE(Enter)
DESCRIPTION(Enter)
REIMBURSEMENT

Select the text. Choose center, bold.

26. Repeat steps 24 and 25 in the third black frame, typing the text:

SALES(Enter)
COMMENTS(Enter)
CONTACTS

27. To create the frames for the fill-in expense area, draw a frame beneath the second black frame.

U se a right line leader tab rather than the Shift+underline keys for even fill-in lines.

T yping in a black frame is easier if you change your type to white before you begin typing.

Margins within a frame help to vertically center the text in that frame.

28. Choose Frame Modify Frame Layout.

29. In Frame, choose Type. In Display, choose **Square Corners.** Choose No Wrap Beside.

30. In Frame, choose Size & Position. For **Height,** type **1.00** (in.). In Margins, type **.15** for all.

31. In Frame, choose Lines & Shadows. For Line, choose All Sides. For Line Style, choose the second line pattern. For Shadows, choose None.

32. In Frame, choose Columns & Tabs. In Number of Columns, choose 3. Choose Line Between Columns. Choose the second Line Style. Choose OK or press Enter.

33. Set the columns of the frame to the following: first column is 1.35" wide, the second is 4.5", the third is 1.75".

34. Copy and **P**aste the frame so that you have a total of five frames. Place the frames similarly to those in figure 13.3.

35. Place the cursor in the first white frame and type **HOTEL**. Select the text and choose bold. Repeat with the next three frames, typing **MEALS, GAS/MILEAGE,** and **MISC.**

36. Place the cursor on the last return on the page. Press Enter and type the following:

(Tab)**SIGNATURE:**(Tab)

37. Select the text and choose Tms Rmn, 10 point. Clear all tabs on the ruler. Set a left tab on the ruler at 3.75"; set a right line leader tab at 8".

38. Choose File Save **A**s. Choose File Print.

Designing an Expense/ Reimbursement Form

After cutting the forms, you may want the print shop to pad them for easier handling (see Chapter 4 for information).

Many times, a smaller reimbursement form serves a purpose in a business. The occasional purchase by an employee, for example, may not require a full form. Figure 13.4 illustrates an expense/reimbursement form that may suffice in these cases. Four forms are set up on the page (*4-up* in printing terms). These forms can be cut apart at a print shop, or you can cut them yourself.

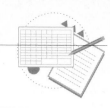

EXPENSE/REIMBURSEMENT

NAME: _____

DATE: _____

NATURE OF TRIP: _____

DATE	DESCRIPTION	TOTAL

TOTAL REIMBURSEMENT: _____

SIGNATURE: _____

EXPENSE/REIMBURSEMENT

NAME: _____

DATE: _____

NATURE OF TRIP: _____

DATE	DESCRIPTION	TOTAL

TOTAL REIMBURSEMENT: _____

SIGNATURE: _____

EXPENSE/REIMBURSEMENT

NAME: _____

DATE: _____

NATURE OF TRIP: _____

DATE	DESCRIPTION	TOTAL

TOTAL REIMBURSEMENT: _____

SIGNATURE: _____

EXPENSE/REIMBURSEMENT

NAME: _____

DATE: _____

NATURE OF TRIP: _____

DATE	DESCRIPTION	TOTAL

TOTAL REIMBURSEMENT: _____

SIGNATURE: _____

Fig. 13.4 Small reimbursement forms set up 4-on.

The final form measures 4 1/4 by 5 1/2 inches. The column gutter is wide enough to allow margins for both forms. In addition, the two forms in each column have space enough between them for margins. A simple table divides the information. After you create the first form, you copy and paste the text and table to make the other three forms.

To produce the small reimbursement forms, follow these steps:

1. Choose File New. Choose the default style sheet. Choose OK or press Enter.

2. Choose **Page Modify Page Layout**.

3. In **Margins & Columns**, set all margins to **.35**.

4. In **Number of Columns**, choose **2**. In **Gutter Width**, type **.75**.

5. In **Tabs**, set a right line leader tab at 3.75". Clear all tabs. Choose OK or press Enter.

6. Type the following:

   EXPENSE/REIMBURSEMENT(Enter twice)
   NAME:(space, Tab, Enter)
   DATE:(space, Tab, Enter)
   NATURE OF TRIP:(space, Tab, Enter twice)

7. Select EXPENSE/REIMBURSEMENT. Choose Tms Rmn, 14 point, bold, and center.

8. Place the cursor on the next paragraph return. Choose Text Font. Choose 6 point.

9. Select the text from NAME: through NATURE OF TRIP:. Choose Tms Rmn, 10 point.

10. Choose Text Spacing. In Line Spacing, choose 1 1/2. Choose OK or press Enter.

11. Place the cursor on the paragraph return after NATURE OF TRIP:. Choose Text Font. Choose 6 point.

12. Place the cursor on the next-to-the-last paragraph return. Choose Tools Table. In Number of Columns, type **3**; in Number of Rows, type **9**. Choose Layout.

13. In the Default Column box, for Width type **.75**.

14. In Default Rows, turn off **Automatic**. In Height, type **.25**. In Options, choose Center Table on Page. Choose OK or press Enter twice.

15. Select the center column of the table. Choose Table Column/Row Size.

16. In Column Width, type **1.75**. Choose OK or press Enter.

17. Select the table. Choose Table Lines/Shades. In Position, choose All Sides. In Line Style, choose the second pattern. Choose OK or press Enter.

18. Place the cursor in cell A-1. Type the following:

DATE(Tab)**DESCRIPTION**(Tab)**TOTAL**

19. Select the text you entered in step 18. Choose bold, center, Tms Rmn, 10 point.

20. Select the top row of the table. Choose Table Lines/Shades. In Position, choose Top and Bottom. Click twice, once to deselect gray, then to select with an X. Choose the third pattern in Line Style. Repeat, using the following values:

First column, **Left** Position to the third line pattern

Third column, **Right** Position to the third line pattern

Bottom row, **Bottom** Position to the third line pattern

21. Place the cursor in the last cell of the table. Press Enter and type the following:

TOTAL REIMBURSEMENT:(space, Tab, Enter)
SIGNATURE:(space, Tab, Enter)

22. Select the paragraph return after the table and choose 6 point.

23. Select TOTAL REIMBURSEMENT: and SIGNATURE:. Choose Tms Rmn, 10 point. Change the Text Spacing to 1 1/2.

24. Place the cursor at the end of the SIGNATURE: line and press Enter three times.

25. Select the three paragraph marks. Choose Text Spacing, and change to Single. Choose OK or press Enter.

26. Copy the text from EXPENSE/REIMBURSEMENT through NATURE OF TRIP:. Paste the copied text onto the last paragraph return in the column.

27. Copy the table and paste below the text. Copy TOTAL REIMBURSE-MENT: and SIGNATURE:. Paste below the second table. Press Enter to move the cursor to the second column.

28. Repeat the copying and pasting in the second column.

B e sure that the heads of the columns are even; if not, adjust the spacing.

29. To be sure that all forms are even with each other, select EXPENSE/ REIMBURSEMENT in each form. Change the Text Spacing to Single.

30. Choose File Save As. Choose File Print.

Looking at Design

Many ways to set up a travel or expense report are available to you; how you do it depends on your company's needs. Tables and frames help you organize and divide your information, and right line leader tabs make it simple to format the label text. If you experiment with some of the techniques you have learned, you easily can custom-design your own forms.

As one more example of an expense report, figure 13.5 illustrates a calendar-type form. The table's row height is .75" and all the columns but the first 1" are 1.25". The days of the week are listed along the top, and some expenses are listed on the side. An employee can fill in details in the spaces provided.

DAILY EXPENSE REPORT

NAME: _____

DESTINATION: _____

ADDRESS: _____

DATE: _____

CONTACT PERSON: _____

SALES: _____

COMMENTS: _____

EXPENSE	MONDAY	TUESDAY	WEDNESDAY	THURSDAY	FRIDAY	WEEKEND	TOTALS
TRAVEL							
MEALS							
SUPPLIES							
OTHER							
MILEAGE							
TOTALS							

SIGNATURE: _____

Fig. 13.5   A daily expense report in calendar form.

Recapping

In this chapter, you learned to create expense forms by using Ami Pro features such as tables, frames, and columns. In addition, you learned to apply varying line thicknesses to tables and to use reversed type on a black background.

Producing an Order Form

You can find as many designs for order forms as there are things to order. Some forms list products, and some forms let you list the products. Many order forms include specific areas for stock numbers, sizes, descriptions, and prices. Most order forms have a place for credit card information, shipping, handling, and tax. Other additions may be sections for purchase order numbers, bid numbers, terms of payment, or a place for gift orders. All order forms ask for the name, address, and phone number of the person placing the order.

For detailed information on how to create a form like this see page 325.

To add to your ideas for creating forms, look at forms from magazines, catalogs, and other businesses.

Organizing all this information so that it is easy for the customer to complete and easy for the company to fill is an enormous job. To begin this extensive project, you first must decide the format your form must take. Order forms can be cards, flyers, booklets, or inserts. The size can be 5 1/2 by 3 1/2 inches or 11 by 17 inches. The size, shape, and format you choose depends on the needs of the company. Ask the people who fill the orders what they need. What do the billing and shipping departments need? The layout of the order form must expedite the filling, shipping, and billing of the order.

You can structure an order form in several ways. Ami Pro offers many organizational techniques that can help you. As in preceding form chapters, you use tables and frames to produce the forms in this chapter. In addition, other features and techniques introduced in this chapter apply to many other kinds of forms.

Naturally, guidelines can help you organize the information on the form; many of these guidelines are discussed in Chapter 12, "Producing a Purchase Order." This chapter concerns using advanced techniques to produce forms, because you now know the basic guidelines. These techniques guide you in designing forms that are both efficient and pleasing to the eye. Some of the Ami Pro features and techniques included in the instructions are rotating an image, producing check boxes for information, and using screened words.

Designing a Basic Order Form

Alternatively, Ami Pro users can choose a box bullet by choosing Edit Insert Bullet.

The first order form is a traditional one. The label text is set up on right line leader tabs, and a table provides room to write the order. This table has two interesting additions that you haven't used thus far. First is the formation of the logo design (see fig. 14.1). To create this logo, you import an AmiDraw file into a frame, then alter it. Ami Pro's Drawing feature offers some powerful tools for working with any imported picture. The second addition is the check boxes. By using the Wingding font (Adobe Type Manager), you can add a professional touch to your forms. For other Wingding choices, refer to Appendix D.

To create the first order form, do the following:

1. Choose **File New**. Choose the default style sheet. Choose OK or press Enter.

2. Choose **Page Modify Page Layout**. Change all margins to **.35**. Choose OK or press Enter.

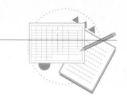

3. Draw a frame in the top left corner of the page. You size and position this frame in the next steps.

4. Choose Frame Modify Frame Layout.

5. In Frame, choose Type. In Text Wrap Around, choose Wrap Around.

6. In Display, choose Rounded Corners and type 55.

7. In Frame, choose Size & Position. In Size, make the frame 1" by 1". In Margins, choose Clear Margins.

8. In Frame, choose Lines & Shadows. Select the second line in Style. In Shadow, choose Deep. Click the bottom left arrow to move the shadow to the left.

9. In the Shadow color bar, choose the third screen down in the right column.

10. In the Line color bar, choose the fifth screen down in the right column. Choose OK or press Enter.

11. Choose File Import Picture. Choose STAR3D.SDW. Choose OK or press Enter.

If you use a mouse, you can alter the picture by using Ami Pro's Drawing feature. If you do not use a mouse, skip this part of the instructions and resume after figure 14.3.

To alter the AmiDraw file, do the following:

1. Choose Tools Drawing. You should enlarge your frame to about three inches square.

2. Click the star to choose it (small black handles appear in a frame around the star). Copy and paste the star.

   Note that the star's shadow is to the right. Because your frame's shadow is to the left, the star's shadow should match it. You can rotate the star to adjust the shadow in any direction you want.

3. Double-click the star. The handles should become small, double-headed arrows. Figure 14.2 shows the cursor pointing to one of the arrows.

4. Drag the arrow to the left; this action rotates the figure. You can release the mouse button, look at the figure, and rotate it more if necessary.

5. Rotate both stars until they look like the stars in figure 14.3. Reduce the frame to one inch square. Click outside the frame to exit the Drawing feature.

Remove the margins in a frame into which you import a drawing; the margins hide the edges of the image.

If you do not know how to use the Drawing feature, refer to your Ami Pro Reference Manual.

Starlight Productions

P. O. Box 174 · Oak Hill, West Virginia 25901
(304) 215 -5555   Fax (304) 215-1144

ORDER FORM
1-800-251-1155

ORDERED FROM: **SHIP TO:**

NAME _____   NAME _____
ADDRESS _____   ADDRESS _____
CITY _____   CITY _____
STATE (ZIP) _____   STATE (ZIP) _____
TELEPHONE _____   TELEPHONE _____

PAYMENT BY   ☐ CHECK OR MONEY ORDER   AMOUNT ENCLOSED _____

☐ CREDIT CARD: ☐ VISA   ☐ MASTERCARD   ☐ AM EXP   ☐ DISCOVER

CARD NUMBER _____   EXPIRES _____

SIGNATURE _____

QTY.	ITEM NUMBER	DESCRIPTION	PRICE EACH	TOTAL

SUBTOTAL _____

WV RES. ADD 6% TAX _____

SHIPPING ADD $3.95 _____

TOTAL _____

Fig. 14.1   A basic order form that uses check boxes for some of the
information.

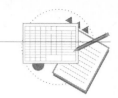

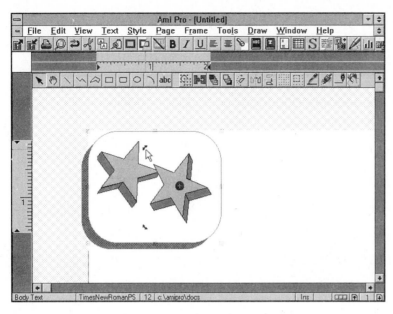

Fig. 14.2 The left star has been rotated; the right star illustrates the double-headed arrow.

Fig. 14.3 The original stars (left) and the completed, rotated stars (right).

To continue formatting the order form, follow these steps:

1. Place the cursor to the right of the frame and type the following:

(Tab)**Starlight Productions**(Enter)
(Tab)**P. O. Box 174**(2 spaces, Alt+0183, 2 spaces)**Oak Hill, West Virginia 25901**(Tab)**ORDER FORM**(Enter)
(Tab)**(304) 215-5555**(Tab)**Fax (304) 215-1144**(Tab)**1-800-251-1155**(Enter three times)
ORDERED FROM:(Tab)**SHIP TO:**(Enter)
NAME(space, Tab twice)**NAME**(space, Tab, Enter)
ADDRESS(space, Tab twice)**ADDRESS**(space, Tab, Enter)
CITY(space, Tab twice)**CITY**(space, Tab, Enter)
STATE (ZIP)(space, Tab twice)**STATE (ZIP)**(space, Tab, Enter)
TELEPHONE(space, Tab twice)**TELEPHONE**(space, Tab, Enter twice)

PAYMENT BY(Tab)**CHECK OR MONEY ORDER**(Tab)**AMOUNT ENCLOSED** (Shift+underline to create a line for the amount, Enter) (Tab)**CREDIT CARD:**(Tab)**VISA**(Tab)**MASTERCARD**(Tab)**AM EXP**(Tab)**DISCOVER**(Enter)
(Tab)**CARD NUMBER**(space, Tab twice)**EXPIRES**(space, Tab, Enter) (Tab)**SIGNATURE**(space, Tab, Enter twice)

2. Select `Starlight Productions`. Choose bold, DomCasual (Helv if ATM is not installed), 36 point.

3. Select from `Starlight Productions` through `1-800-251-1155`. Activate the ruler and clear default tabs. Set a left tab at 1.62" on the ruler; set another left tab 3.5", and a center tab at 7".

4. Select `P. O. Box 174` through `Fax (304) 215-1144`. Choose 10 point. The default font is Tms Rmn.

5. Select `ORDER FORM`. Choose bold, 14 point. The default font is Tms Rmn.

6. Select the 800 number and choose bold. The default font is Tms Rmn, 10 point.

7. Select the text from `ORDERED FROM` through `SIGNATURE`. Choose Helv, 10 point.

8. Select `ORDERED FROM` and `SHIP TO`. Choose bold.

9. Activate the ruler and set a left tab at 4.25" on the ruler.

10. Select the text from `NAME` through the second `TELEPHONE`. Activate the ruler.

11. Set a right line leader tab at 4", a left tab at 4.25", and a right line leader tab at 8" on the ruler.

12. With text still selected, choose Text Spacing. Choose 1 1/2. Choose OK or press Enter.

13. Select the text from `PAYMENT BY` through `SIGNATURE`. Activate the ruler and clear the default tabs. Set a left tab at 1.5" on the ruler.

    Version 2.0 users: The reason you select all four lines to set one tab is to save time. Each time you activate a new ruler, you must clear the tabs. If you clear them all at once for these four lines and set the first tab, your job is easier for each individual line.

14. Select the text `PAYMENT BY` through `AMOUNT ENCLOSED`. Activate the ruler and set a left tab at 4.25" on the ruler.

15. Select the second line, from `CREDIT CARD` through `DISCOVER`. Activate the ruler and, leaving the 1.5" tab, set additional left tabs as follows: 3", 4", 5.5", and 6.75".

C hanging ORDER FORM to 14 point adds a small space between the name and the address.

16. Place the cursor in front of CHECK OR MONEY ORDER. Type **p** and a space. Select the p. Choose **T**ext Font. In **F**ace, choose Wingding. Choose OK or press Enter.

17. Select the check box (❑) and the space. Copy and paste the box in front of CREDIT CARD, VISA, MASTERCARD, AM EXP, and DISCOVER.

18. Select the line of text beginning with CARD NUMBER. Activate the ruler. Set a right line leader tab at 4.5", a left tab at 4.75", and another right line leader tab at 8".

19. Select SIGNATURE. Activate the ruler and set a right line leader tab at 8" on the ruler.

20. Place the cursor on the last paragraph return on the page. Press Enter twice and move up one line. Choose **T**ools **T**ables.

21. In Number of Columns, type **5**; in Number of **R**ows, type **12**. Choose **L**ayout.

22. In Default **R**ows, turn off **A**utomatic. In **H**eight, type **.25**. In **O**ptions, choose **C**enter Table on Page. Choose OK or press Enter twice.

23. Choose View **F**ull Page. Select the first column and adjust the width by choosing Ta**b**le Column/Row Size. Using the mouse, you can adjust the width manually. The first column is .75" wide.

24. Repeat step 23 to adjust the following: the second column to 1.5", the third column to 3", the fourth and fifth columns to 1" each.

25. Select the table. Choose Ta**b**le Lin**e**s/Shades. In Position, choose **A**ll Sides. In Line **S**tyles, choose the second pattern.

26. Select the first row of the table. Choose Ta**b**le Lin**e**s/Shades. In Position, choose the **T**op and **B**ottom sides. In Line **S**tyles, choose the third pattern. Repeat with the following:

First column: **L**eft position to the third pattern

Bottom row: **B**ottom position to the third pattern

Last column: **R**ight position to the third pattern

27. Place the cursor in cell A-1 and type the following:

QTY.(Tab)**ITEM NUMBER**(Tab)**DESCRIPTION**(Tab)**PRICE EACH**(Tab)**TOTAL**

28. Select the line of type. Choose Helv, 10 point, bold, center.

29. Place the cursor on the last paragraph return on the page. Type the following:

Wingding is an ATM symbol font that comes packaged with Ami Pro. See Appendix D.

If you do not have ATM installed, type an underline (Shift+ underline key) in place of each box.

(Tab)**SUBTOTAL**(space, Tab, Enter)
(Tab)**WV RES. ADD 6% TAX**(space, Tab, Enter)
(Tab)**SHIPPING ADD $3.95**(space, Tab, Enter)
(Tab)**TOTAL**

30. Select the four lines of text. Choose Helv, 10 point.

31. Activate the ruler. Set a right tab at 6", a left tab at 6.25", and a right line leader tab at 8" on the ruler.

32. Choose Text Spacing Double. Choose OK or press Enter.

33. Bold TOTAL.

34. Save and print the document.

35. If you plan to go on to the next form, select the framed logo and copy it to the Clipboard.

Designing a Business-to-Business Order Form

Many companies do business with other companies. They may buy products or services from each other, and in doing so, they need order forms with different information. The customer's billing and shipping addresses may be different, a purchase order or bid number may be needed, or confirming or shipping dates may be required. The next order form includes these label texts in a three-column, screened table (see fig. 14.4).

Y ou can apply screened type to any messages, such as NOW DUE, on an invoice.

Another table, similar to the last design, contains the product information. The tax and totals are isolated at the bottom of the table by hiding rules. Another addition is the screened type phrase Thank You! This design gives the form a professional look and is a nice message to the customer.

To produce the second order form, do the following:

1. Choose File New. Choose the default style sheet. Choose OK or press Enter.

2. Choose Page Modify Page Layout. Change all margins to .35. Choose OK or press Enter.

A lternatively, create your own logo to import.

3. Choose Edit Paste to retrieve the logo from the Clipboard. (If you didn't copy the logo, you can open the preceding document and copy the logo now).

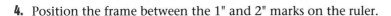
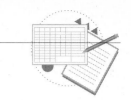

4. Position the frame between the 1" and 2" marks on the ruler.

5. Choose Frame Modify Frame Layout. In Frame Type, choose No Wrap Around. Choose OK or press Enter.

6. Place the cursor to the right of the frame and type the following:

(Tab)**Starlight Productions**(Enter)
(Tab)**Post Office Box 174**(Enter)
(Tab)**Oak Hill, West Virginia 25901**(Enter)
(Tab)**(304) 255-5555**(Enter three times)
ORDER FORM(Enter twice)
BILL TO:(Tab)**SHIP TO:**(Enter)
(Tab three times, Enter)
(Tab three times, Enter)
(Tab three times, Enter)
(Tab three times, Enter)

7. Select `Starlight Productions`. Choose Tms Rmn, 36 point, bold.

8. Activate the ruler and set a center tab at 4.75" on the ruler.

9. Select the text from `Post Office` through `(304) 255-5555`. Activate the ruler and set a center tab at 4.75" on the ruler.

10. Choose Helv, 12 point.

11. Select `ORDER FORM`. Choose center, bold, Helv, 14 point.

12. Select `BILL TO` and `SHIP TO`. Choose Helv, 10 point, bold.

13. Activate the ruler and set a left tab at 4.25" on the ruler.

14. Select the next four lines (the tabs). Activate the ruler and set a right line leader tab at 4", a left tab at 4.25", and a right line leader at 8".

15. Choose Text Spacing. Choose 1 1/2 line spacing. Choose OK or press Enter.

16. Place the cursor on the last return. Choose Tools Tables.

17. In Create Table, type **3** for Number of Columns and **3** for Number of Rows. Choose Layout.

18. In Default Columns, for Width type **2.5**.

19. In Default Rows, turn off Automatic. In Height, type **.25**. In Options, choose Center Table on Page. Choose OK or press Enter twice.

Starlight Productions

Post Office Box 174
Oak Hill, West Virginia 25901
(304) 255-5555

ORDER FORM

BILL TO:

SHIP TO:

PO NUMBER	CONFIRM?	DATE:
CASH?	BID NO.:	SHIP VIA:
CHARGE?	C.O.D.?	SHIP WHEN?

QTY.	PRODUCT #	DESCRIPTION	PRICE EACH	TOTAL PRICE
		Thank You!		

If you are tax exempt or use a Direct Pay Permit, please enclose a copy.

TERMS: NET; DUE ON RECEIPT

SUBTOTAL	
STATE TAX	
TOTAL	

Fig. 14.4 An order form produced by using two tables.

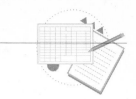

20. Select the table. Choose **Ta**ble **Li**nes/Shades.

21. In Position, choose **A**ll sides. In Line **S**tyle, choose the second line pattern. In Fill **C**olor, choose the second column from the right (the third screened box down). Choose OK or press Enter.

22. Place the cursor in cell A-1 and type the following:

    (space)**PO NUMBER**(Tab)**CONFIRM?**(Tab)**DATE:**(Tab)
    (space)**CASH?**(Tab)**BID NO.:**(Tab)**SHIP VIA:**(Tab)
    (space)**CHARGE?**(Tab)**C.O.D.?**(Tab)**SHIP WHEN?**

23. Select the text and choose Helv, 8 point, bold. Choose **S**tyle **M**odify Style.

24. In Modify, choose **S**pacing.

25. In Paragraph Spacing, choose **A**bove. Type **.04**. In Add In, choose **A**lways. Choose OK or press Enter.

26. Choose **S**tyle **D**efine Style. Ami Pro asks, `Change Table Text to have attributes of the selected paragraph's text. Are you sure?` Choose **Y**es.

27. Place the cursor on the last return on the page. Press Enter. Choose **T**ools Ta**b**le.

28. In Create Table, type **5** for Number of Columns and type **17** for Number of **R**ows. Choose **L**ayout.

29. In Default Rows, turn off Automatic. In **H**eight, type **.25**. In Options, choose Center Table on Page. Choose OK twice or press Enter twice.

30. Select the first column and change it to **.60**" (Ta**b**le **C**olumn/**R**ow Size). Repeat with the third column at **3.5**" and the fourth and fifth columns at **1.15**" each. (The second column is OK at the default **1**".)

31. Choose **V**iew **F**ull Page.

32. Select all the table but the last three rows (rows 15, 16, and 17). Choose **Ta**ble **Li**nes/Shades. Figure 14.5 shows the screen with cells identified.

33. In Position, choose **A**ll sides. In Line **S**tyle, choose the second line pattern. Choose OK or press Enter.

34. Select the first row of the table. Choose **Ta**ble **Li**nes/Shades.

35. In Position, choose the **T**op and **B**ottom sides. In Line **S**tyle, choose the third line pattern. Choose OK or press Enter.

The Define Style feature in Ami Pro enables you to completely format a style and then define it as a style, which is an alternative to choosing Style Modify Style.

It's easier to select a table in Full Page view.

36. Repeat steps 32 and 33 with the following settings:

Column and row	Position and pattern
A-1 through A-14	Left position with the third line pattern
A-14 through C-14	Bottom position with the third line pattern
D-14 through E-17	All position with the third line pattern
D-15 through D17	Left position with the third line pattern
D-17 and E-17	Bottom position with the third line pattern
E-1 through E-17	Right position with the third line pattern.

37. Place the cursor in cell A-1 and type the following:

QTY.(Tab)**PRODUCT #**(Tab)**DESCRIPTION**(Tab)**PRICE EACH**(Tab)**TOTAL PRICE**

38. Select the text. Choose center, bold.

39. Place the cursor in cell D-15 and type the following:

SUBTOTAL(down arrow)
STATE TAX(down arrow)
TOTAL

40. Select the text and choose 10 point. Choose Text Alignment. Align the text Right.

41. Select cells A-15 through C-15. Choose Table Connect. Repeat with cells A-16 through C-16.

42. Place the cursor in cell A-15 and type the following:

If you are tax exempt or use a Direct Pay Permit, please enclose a copy.

43. Place the cursor in cell A-16 and type the following:

TERMS: NET; DUE ON RECEIPT

44. Select the two lines of text and choose 10 point, center. Make the second line bold, beginning with TERMS.

A ll Table Text keeps the same formatting throughout the document.

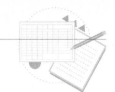

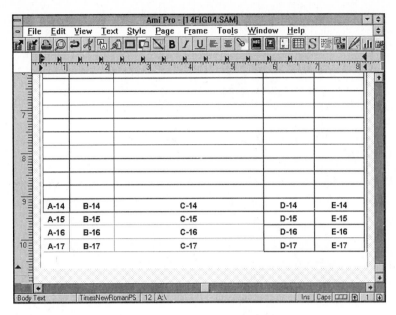

Fig. 14.5 The lower half of the second table with cells identified.

To create the screened Thank You box, do the following:

1. Draw a frame anywhere in the margin of the page. Choose Frame Modify Frame Layout.

2. In Frame, choose Type. In Display, choose Transparent.

3. In Frame, choose Size & Position. The Width is **3.33**; the Height is **.84**.

4. In Position, on Page Down from Top, type **7**. For In from Left, type **2.23**.

5. In Frame, choose Lines & Shadows. In Position, deselect All sides. In Shadow, choose None. Choose OK or press Enter.

6. Place the cursor in the frame and type the following:

   Thank You!

7. Change the type to centered. Choose Text Font. Change the Face to ShelleyAllegroScript, 36 point. (Helv if ATM isn't installed). In the color bar, choose the second column from the right, eighth screen down. Choose OK or press Enter.

8. Save and print the order form.

If you use a mouse, you have another option in creating the Thank You box. Figure 14.6 illustrates the rotated Thank You. You need a mouse to

If you use a mouse, copy the frame to the Clipboard for use in later steps.

rotate text because the rotation is done in the Drawing feature. You first must delete the frame containing the Thank You that you produced in the preceding instructions. You have to create a new frame to use for a drawing. After you type a frame, you cannot select it in the Drawing mode. Use the frame you copied in step 5.

To create the rotated Thank You!, do the following:

1. Choose Tools Drawing. In the SmartIcons, choose ABC (the text icon).

2. In the Text menu, choose Font. Choose ShelleyAllegroScript (or Helv) 36 point. In the color bar, choose the second column from the right, eighth screen from the top. Choose OK or press Enter.

3. Choose the ABC icon again. Place the cursor in the frame and type the following:

Thank You!

4. Select the text by double-clicking the words. Small black handles appear around the type. Click again to show the double-headed arrows. Drag one of the corner arrows to rotate the text.

A lternatively, choose Draw Rotate. The text in figure 14.6 is rotated to 333 degrees.

Designing an Order Form for Commercial Reproduction

The next order form is laid out 2-up for commercial reproduction. (Remember, 2-up refers to printing two forms to a sheet.) Of course, you can commercially reproduce any of the forms in this chapter. You also can print this order form on your printer and cut it apart yourself. An 8 1/2-by-11-inch sheet contains two forms for quicker, easier, and cheaper printing.

The landscape orientation is divided into two columns to make two 5 1/2-by-8 1/2-inch forms (see fig. 14.7). The structure of this design is different from any of the others you have created. This form uses tabs to divide the information. Note that the description and individual prices already are listed for the customer. All the customer fills in are the quantity, size, and total price columns. Once again, you produce the form in the left column, then copy and paste it to the right column.

Starlight Productions

Post Office Box 174
Oak Hill, West Virginia 25901
(304) 255-5555

ORDER FORM

BILL TO:

_____

_____

_____

_____

SHIP TO:

_____

_____

_____

_____

PO NUMBER	CONFIRM?	DATE:
CASH?	BID NO.:	SHIP VIA:
CHARGE?	C.O.D.?	SHIP WHEN?

QTY.	PRODUCT #	DESCRIPTION	PRICE EACH	TOTAL PRICE
		Thank You!		

If you are tax exempt or use a Direct Pay Permit, please enclose a copy.

TERMS: NET; DUE ON RECEIPT

SUBTOTAL	
STATE TAX	
TOTAL	

Fig. 14.6 The same form, with the Thank You! rotated.

Humble Opinions

P. O. Box 174
Oak Hill, WV 25901
(304) 251-5555

ORDER FORM
ORDER TOLL FREE
1-800-551-1155

NAME: _____

ADDRESS: _____

PHONE: _____

QTY.	SIZE	DESCRIPTION	PRICE EA.	TOTAL
		T-SHIRT	$10.00	
		KID'S T-SHIRT	7.00	
		SWEATSHIRT	15.00	
		KID'S SWEAT	12.00	
		HAT #234	6.00	
		KID'S HAT #234	4.00	
		HAT #235	9.00	
		KID'S HAT #235	7.00	
		RAIN POSTER	1.00	

SUBTOTAL
WV Res. add
6% STATE TAX
TOTAL

PLEASE ENCLOSE CHECK OR MONEY ORDER WITH ORDER

SIZES:	SHIRTS	S, M, L, XL
	KID'S SHIRTS	S, M, L
	HATS	7, 8
	KID'S HATS	5, 6

THANKS FOR YOUR ORDER!

Humble Opinions

P. O. Box 174
Oak Hill, WV 25901
(304) 251-5555

ORDER FORM
ORDER TOLL FREE
1-800-551-1155

NAME: _____

ADDRESS: _____

PHONE: _____

QTY.	SIZE	DESCRIPTION	PRICE EA.	TOTAL
		T-SHIRT	$10.00	
		KID'S T-SHIRT	7.00	
		SWEATSHIRT	15.00	
		KID'S SWEAT	12.00	
		HAT #234	6.00	
		KID'S HAT #234	4.00	
		HAT #235	9.00	
		KID'S HAT #235	7.00	
		RAIN POSTER	1.00	

SUBTOTAL
WV Res. add
6% STATE TAX
TOTAL

PLEASE ENCLOSE CHECK OR MONEY ORDER WITH ORDER

SIZES:	SHIRTS	S, M, L, XL
	KID'S SHIRTS	S, M, L
	HATS	7, 8
	KID'S HATS	5, 6

THANKS FOR YOUR ORDER!

Fig. 14.7   Order forms structured with tabs instead of tables.

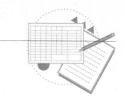

To create the 2-up order forms, do the following:

1. Choose File, then New. Choose the default style sheet. Choose OK or press Enter.

2. Choose Page Modify Page Layout.

3. In Modify, choose **Margins & Columns**. Change all margins to **.35**. In Number of Columns, choose **2**. In Gutter, type **.75**.

4. In Modify, choose **Page Settings**. In Orientation, choose **Landscape**. Choose OK or press Enter.

5. In the first column, type the following:

   Humble Opinions(Enter)
   P. O. Box 174(Tab)**ORDER FORM**(Enter)
   Oak Hill, WV 25901(Tab)**ORDER TOLL FREE**(Enter)
   (304) 251-5555(Tab)**1-800-551-1155**(Enter twice)
   NAME:(space, Tab, Enter)
   ADDRESS:(space, Tab, Enter)
   (Tab, Enter)
   PHONE:(space, Tab, Enter twice)

6. Select Humble Opinions. Choose Tms Rmn, 18 point, bold.

7. Select the next three lines of text, from P. O. Box 174 through 1-800-551-1155. Activate the ruler. Set a center tab at 3.75" on the ruler.

8. Select and bold ORDER FORM, ORDER TOLL FREE, and 1-800-551-1155. Change ORDER FORM to 14 point. The default font is Tms Rmn.

9. Select the text from NAME through PHONE. Choose Helv, 10 point with 1 1/2 line spacing.

10. Activate the ruler and set a right line leader tab at 5".

11. Place the cursor on the last paragraph return and type the following:

    QTY.(Tab)**SIZE**(Tab)**DESCRIPTION**(Tab)**PRICE EA.**(Tab)**TOTAL** (Enter)
    (Tab)**T-SHIRT**(Tab)**$10.00**(Enter)
    (Tab)**KID'S T-SHIRT**(Tab)**7.00**(Enter)
    (Tab)**SWEATSHIRT**(Tab)**15.00**(Enter)
    (Tab)**KID'S SWEAT**(Tab)**12.00**(Enter)
    (Tab)**HAT #234**(Tab)**6.00**(Enter)
    (Tab)**KID'S HAT #234**(Tab)**4.00**(Enter)
    (Tab)**HAT #235**(Tab)**9.00**(Enter)

The gutter, in this case, represents the right margin of the first form, and the left margin of the second form.

(Tab)**KID'S HAT #235**(Tab)**7.00**(Enter)
(Tab)**RAIN POSTER**(Tab)**1.00**(Enter twice)
(Tab)**SUBTOTAL**(Enter)
(Tab)**WV Res. add**(Enter)
(Tab)**6% STATE TAX**(Enter)
(Tab)**TOTAL**(Enter twice)

12. Select QTY. through TOTAL. Choose **Style** Create Style. Name the style **Line** Choose Modify.

13. In Font, change the type to Helv, 8 point, bold.

14. In Modify, choose **Lines**. Choose Line A**b**ove. In Spacing, type **.04** and choose the second line pattern. Choose Line **B**elow. In Spacing, type **.04** and choose the second line pattern. Choose OK or press Enter.

15. Choose **Style** Select a Style. In the Styles box, choose Line and apply it to the text QTY. through SIZE.

16. Select QTY. through SIZE. Activate the ruler and set the following center tabs: .56", 1.06", 2.44", 4", and 4.75".

17. Select the text from T-SHIRT to POSTER 1.00. Choose Helv, 10 point. Change the line spacing to **1 1/2**.

18. Activate the ruler and set a left tab at 2" and a right decimal tab at 4.06".

19. Select the paragraph return above SUBTOTAL. Choose **Style** Create Style.

20. In New style, type **Line 2**. Choose Modify.

21. In Font, choose 8 point.

22. In Modify, choose S**p**acing. In Paragraph Spacing, choose **B**elow. Type **.05**.

23. In Modify, choose **Line**. Choose Below and the second line pattern. Choose OK or press Enter.

24. Assign the Line 2 style to the paragraph return above SUBTOTAL.

25. Select the text from SUBTOTAL through TOTAL. Choose Helv, 10 point, bold.

26. Activate the ruler. On the ruler, set a right tab at 4.25".

A decimal tab ensures that your figures are organized for easy reading.

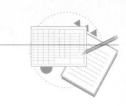

27. Place the cursor on the paragraph return below TOTAL. Assign the Line 2 style.

28. Place the cursor on the last paragraph return on the page and type the following:

PLEASE ENCLOSE CHECK OR MONEY ORDER WITH ORDER(Enter twice)
(Tab)**SIZES:**(Tab)**SHIRTS**(Tab)**S, M, L, XL**(Enter)
(Tab twice)**KID'S SHIRTS**(Tab)**S, M, L**(Enter)
(Tab twice)**HATS**(Tab)**7, 8**(Enter)
(Tab twice)**KID'S HATS**(Tab)**5, 6**(Enter twice)
THANKS FOR YOUR ORDER!(Enter)

29. Select the text from PLEASE ENCLOSE CHECK through KID'S HATS 5, 6. Choose Helv, 10 point.

30. Select and center the first line, PLEASE ENCLOSE CHECK OR MONEY ORDER WITH ORDER.

31. Select the text from SIZES through KID'S HATS 5, 6. Activate the ruler and set a left tab at 1", another left tab at 1.75", and a final left tab at 3".

32. Select the last line, THANKS FOR YOUR ORDER! Choose center and italic.

33. Select the entire first column of text. Copy it. Place the cursor in the second column and paste.

34. Save and print your order form.

Designing an Innovative Order Form

Ami Pro offers many features that enable you to produce complex forms. You have used most of these features in previous forms; however, in the next one, you bring all those features together. Figure 14.8 illustrates an order form used to divide orders for different delivery addresses. You use one table, one frame, the Wingding font, and line leaders to create this form. The table is a combination of ruled rows and columns, and nonruled, connected rows and columns. This technique organizes and divides the table to produce areas for addresses and gift orders.

You can use these features to customize your own forms.

24 HOURS A DAY!! CALL TOLL FREE 1-800-251-1212

SOLD TO:	SHIP TO: (if different from SOLD TO)
NAME: _____	NAME: _____
ADDRESS: _____	ADDRESS: _____
_____	_____
PHONE: _____	PHONE: _____

Please make checks payable to:

Method of Payment:
- ☐ Check/MO
- ☐ Credit Card: _____
- Acct. No.: _____

STARLIGHT PRODUCTIONS
P. O. BOX 174 · OAK HILL, WEST VIRGINIA 25901

Signature: _____

Expires: _____

SHIP THIS ORDER TO THE ABOVE ADDRESS:

QTY	NUMBER	DESCRIPTION	PRICE EACH	TOTAL

FOR OFFICE USE ONLY		SUBTOTAL	
ORDER NUMBER:		SALES TAX	
		SHIPPING	

GIFT ORDER #1:

NAME: _____   SUBTOTAL

ADDRESS: _____   SALES TAX

CITY: _____ ST: ____ ZIP: _____   SHIPPING

GIFT ORDER #2:   TOTAL #1

NAME: _____   SUBTOTAL

ADDRESS: _____   SALES TAX

CITY: _____ ST: ____ ZIP: _____   SHIPPING

TOTAL #2

DELIVERY: ADD $7.00 PER ADDRESS   DELIVERY

EXPRESS 2-DAY DELIVERY: ADD $6.00 PER ADDRESS

SHIPPING AND HANDLING: ADD $10.50 PER ADDRESS   TOTAL

Fig. 14.8   One table divided to provide space for information.

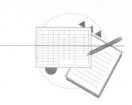

To create this innovative order form, do the following:

1. Choose **F**ile **N**ew. Choose the default style sheet. Choose OK or press Enter.

2. Choose **P**age **M**odify Page Layout. Change all margins to **.35**. Choose OK or press Enter.

3. Type the following:

    24 HOURS A DAY!! CALL TOLL FREE 1-800-251-1212 (Enter twice)

4. Select the text. Choose Frank Goth Cd (or Helv), 14 point, center, bold.

5. Draw a frame. You size and position it in the next steps.

6. Choose **F**rame **M**odify Frame Layout.

7. In Frame, choose **T**ype. Choose **N**o Wrap **B**eside. In Display, choose **S**quare Corners.

8. In Frame, choose **S**ize & Position. In Size, change the **W**idth to **7.90**, and the **H**eight to **1.48**. In Position on Page, change **D**own from Top to **.75**, change **I**n from Left to **.35**.

9. In Margins, change all to **.15**.

10. In Frame, choose **L**ines & Shadows. In Position, choose All sides. In Line Style, choose the second pattern. In Shadow, choose **N**one.

11. In Frame, choose **C**olumns & Tabs. Set a right line leader at 3.5", a left tab at 3.75", and another right line leader tab at 7.5". Choose OK or press Enter.

12. Place the cursor in the frame and type the following:

    SOLD TO:(Tab)**SHIP TO: (if different from SOLD TO)**(Enter)
    NAME:(space, Tab twice)**NAME:**(space, Tab, Enter)
    ADDRESS:(space, Tab twice)**ADDRESS:**(space, Tab, Enter)
    (Tab three times, Enter)
    PHONE:(space, Tab twice)**PHONE:**(space, Tab)

13. Select the `SOLD TO` and `SHIP TO` line. Choose bold. Set a left tab on the ruler at 3.75".

14. Choose **T**ext **S**pacing. Change the spacing to **.24**". Choose OK or press Enter.

15. Place the cursor on the paragraph return after the frame. Type the following:

Set the special tab in step 13 so that you don't have line leaders between the subheads.

Please make checks payable to:(Tab)**STARLIGHT PRODUCTIONS**(Enter)
Method of Payment:(Tab)**P. O. BOX 174**(2 spaces, Alt+0183, 2 spaces)**OAK HILL, WEST VIRGINIA 25901**(Enter)
(Tab)**Check/MO**(Enter)
(Tab)**Credit Card:**(space, Tab twice)**Signature:**(space, Tab, Enter)
(Tab)**Acct. No.:**(space, Tab twice)**Expires:**(space, Tab, Enter twice)
SHIP THIS ORDER TO THE ABOVE ADDRESS:

16. Select the first two lines of text, from `Please make checks payable` through `OAK HILL, WEST VIRGINIA 25901`. Activate the ruler and set a center tab at 5.75".

17. Select `STARLIGHT PRODUCTIONS`. Choose 18 point, bold. The default font is Tms Rmn.

18. Select the text from `Check/MO` through `Expires`. Activate the ruler and set a left tab at 1", a right line leader at 4", a left tab at 4.25", and another right line leader at 8".

19. Place the cursor in front of `Check/MO`. Type **q** and a space. Select the q. Choose **Text Font**. Choose Wingding.

20. Copy the box and the space. Paste it in front of `Credit Card`.

21. Select `SHIP THIS ORDER TO THE ABOVE ADDRESS`. Choose 10 point, bold. The default font is Tms Rmn.

To produce the table, do the following:

1. Place the cursor on the next paragraph return. Choose **Tools Tables**.

2. In the Create Table dialog box, type **5** for Numbers of Columns; type **22** for Number of Rows. Choose **Layout**.

3. In Default Columns, be sure that the **Width** is 1".

4. In Default Rows, turn off **Automatic**. In **Height**, type **.25**. In Options, choose **Center Table on Page**. Choose OK or press Enter twice.

5. Select the first column. Choose **Table Column/Row Size**. Change the first column to **.5"**. Change the third row to **3.90"**; the second, fourth, and fifth rows remain 1" each.

6. Choose **View View Preferences**. Choose **Table Row/Column Headings**. Choose OK or press Enter.

---

*A*lternatively, you can use an ATM font for the company name.

*A*mi Pro 3.0 users can use a bullet checkbox in place of the Wingding font character.

Your screen should look like the one in figure 14.9. The row and column headings you now see are nonprinting guides. You use these guides in the following instructions to help you locate the cells you need to create the form.

Ami Pro - [Untitled:2]				
File Edit View Text Style Page Frame Tools Table Window Help				
A	B	C	D	E
1				
2				
3				
4				
5				
6				
7				
8				
9				
10				
11				
12				
13				
14				
15				
16				
17				

Table Text   Times New Roman   12   c:\amipro\docs   Ins

Fig. 14.9 An example of how the screen looks when you turn on Table Row/ Column Headings.

7. Select cells A-1 through E-4. Choose Table Lines/Shades. In Position, choose All sides. In Line Style, choose the second line pattern. Choose OK or press Enter.

8. Select cells A-1 through E-1. In Table Lines/Shades, change the Position to Top and Bottom and the Line Style to the third line pattern. Choose OK or press Enter.

9. Select A-9 through E-10. In Table Lines/Shades, choose Position All sides. Change the Line Style to the second line pattern. Repeat with A-15 through E-16 (Position All sides; Line Style to the second line pattern).

10. Choose View Full Page. Select E-1 through E-22. In Table Lines/ Shades, choose All sides, second line pattern. In Fill Color, choose the second column from the right, the third screened box. Choose OK or press Enter.

11. By selecting first the row or column, then Table Lines/Shades, change the following settings:

A-1 through A-4	Left Position to third line pattern
A-4 through D-4	Bottom Position to third line pattern
E-5 through E-8	Left Position to third line pattern
A-9 through D-9	Top Position to third line pattern
A-9 through A-10	Left Position to third line pattern
A-10 through D-10	Bottom Position to third line pattern
E-11 though E-14	Left Position to third line pattern
A-15 through D-15	Top Position to third line pattern
A-15 through A-16	Left Position to third line pattern
A 16 through D-16	Bottom Position to third line pattern
E-17 through E-22	Left Position to third line pattern
E-22	Bottom Position to third line pattern
E-1 through E-22	Right Position to third line pattern

12. Place the cursor in cell A-1 and type the following:

QTY.(Tab)**NUMBER**(Tab)**DESCRIPTION**(Tab)**PRICE EACH**(Tab)**TOTAL**

13. Select the text. Choose bold, center.

14. Choose **S**tyle **M**odify Style.

15. In Modify, choose **F**ont. Choose 10 point. The default font is Tms Rmn.

16. In Modify, choose **S**pacing. In Paragraph Spacing, choose **A**bove. Type **.04**. In Add In, choose **A**lways. Choose OK or press Enter.

17. Select cells A-5 through C-6. Choose Ta**b**le Connect. Choose Table Lines/Shades. In Fill Color, choose the second column from the right and the third box down. Choose OK or press Enter.

18. Place the cursor in the shaded area and type the following:

FOR OFFICE USE ONLY(Enter)
(space)**ORDER NUMBER:**

19. Select, center and bold. FOR OFFICE USE ONLY.

20. Select cells A-8 and B-8. Choose Table Connect.

21. Place the cursor in the cell and type the following:

B ecause you selected text in a table, the Table Text style appears as the default.

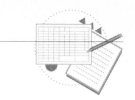

GIFT ORDER #1

22. Select and bold the text.

23. Repeat steps 20 through 22 in cells A-14 and B-14 (type **GIFT ORDER #2**).

24. Place the cursor in cell D-5 and type the following:

SUBTOTAL(space, down arrow)
SALES TAX(space, down arrow)
SHIPPING(space, down arrow)
TOTAL(space)

25. Select the text and choose bold, right-aligned.

26. Copy the four lines, from SUBTOTAL through TOTAL. Place the cursor in cell D-11 and paste. Place the cursor in cell D-17 and paste.

27. In cell D-14, change the type to **TOTAL #1**. In cell D-20, change the type to **TOTAL #2**.

28. Place the cursor in cell D-21 and type the following:

DELIVERY(space, down arrow)
TOTAL(space)

Right align and bold the text you just typed.

29. Select cells A-11 through C-14. Choose Ta**b**le **C**onnect.

30. Choose **S**tyle **M**odify Style. In the **S**tyle selection box, choose Table Table Text

31. In Modify, choose Ali**g**nment. In Tabs, set a right line leader tab at 5". Choose **U**se Style Tabs. Choose OK or press Enter.

32. Place the cursor in cell A-11 and type the following:

NAME:(space, Ctrl+Shift+Tab, Enter)
ADDRESS:(space, Ctrl+Shift+Tab, Enter)
CITY:(space, Ctrl+Shift+Tab, space)**ST:**(space, Shift+underline key five times, space)**ZIP:**(space, Shift+underline key ten times)

33. Select the text. Choose **T**ext **S**pacing. Change the Line spacing to 1 1/2. Choose OK or press Enter.

34. Select cells A-17 through C-22. Choose Ta**b**le **C**onnect.

35. Place the cursor in cell A-17 and type the following:

NAME:(space, Ctrl+Shift+Tab, Enter)
ADDRESS:(space, Ctrl+Shift+Tab, Enter)

The space after TOTAL keeps the text from running up against the line bordering the cell.

CITY:(space, Ctrl+Shift+Tab, space)**ST:**(space, Shift+underline key five times, space)**ZIP:**(space, Shift+underline key ten times, Enter twice)
DELIVERY: ADD $7.00 PER ADDRESS(Enter)
EXPRESS 2-DAY DELIVERY: ADD $6.00 PER ADDRESS(Enter)
SHIPPING AND HANDLING: ADD $10.50 PER ADDRESS(Enter)

36. Select and center the text from NAME through ZIP. Choose **T**ext **S**pacing. Change the Line spacing to **1 1/2**. Choose OK or press Enter.

37. Select and center the last three lines of text, and bold the words DELIVERY:, EXPRESS 2-DAY DELIVERY:, and SHIPPING AND HANDLING:.

38. Choose **T**ext **S**pacing. Change the spacing on the last three lines of text to Single. Choose OK or press Enter.

39. Save and print the order form.

Looking at Design

You can organize and divide the information in forms in many ways, such as using tables, frames, or tabs. By using the special features of each method, your forms look professional and better serve their purposes. You now have a solid basis for creating your own forms. The following are a few more ideas for you to consider.

Figure 14.10 illustrates a form that is a variation of a previous form. Note that the same logo and heading are used. Right line leader tabs form name and address lines. The table is a simple one. Cells A-11 through C-16 were connected and screened to form a box for the shipping and handling information. Cells D-11 and E-11, D-12 and E-12, and so on were connected so that a longer line of type could be added.

As already mentioned in this chapter, forms can be any size. Remember to keep the size convenient to use. A very large form (12 by 20 inches, for example) or a very small one (4 by 7 inches) may not be easy for you or the customer to use. Many sizes, however, are advantageous. Thus far, you have created forms that are 8 1/2 by 11, 5 1/2 by 8 1/2, and 4 1/4 by 5 1/2. These sizes are commonly used for forms. Another common size is 3 1/2 by 5 1/2, as in a postcard.

Postcard order forms are usually enclosed with magazines or mailings. They have a return postage or business reply panel on one side, and the form is on the other side. Remember to abide by postal regulations and guidelines on the mailing panel side.

Y ou can add screens to any section of the form.

R efer to Chapters 4 and 7 for details on paper, permits, text and spacing guidelines.

STARLIGHT PRODUCTIONS

P. O. BOX 174 · OAK HILL, WV 25901
(304) 215-5555   FAX (304) 215-1155

ORDER TOLL FREE
1-800-251-1155

ORDER FORM

ORDERED BY:

SHIP TO: (if different from ORDERED BY)

Name: _____

Name: _____

Address: _____

Address: _____

_____

_____

QTY.	ITEM NO.	DESCRIPTION	SIZE	PRICE	TOTAL

SHIPPING AND HANDLING CHARGES		
UNDER $25.00	$3.95	Total Merchandise
$25.01 TO $65.00	$5.25	Add $3 for Catalog
$65.01 TO $95.00	$6.95	Subtotal
OVER $95.00	FREE	WV Res. add 6% Tax

METHOD OF PAYMENT
Check or Money Order Preferred
Credit Card Only with our Pre-Approved Form

Shipping & Handling

TOTAL

Fig. 14.10   A variation of an order form.

Instead of using the line around the post-card, use crop marks when printing at a print shop.

The next two form designs are specifically for the form side of a post-card. The first, shown in figure 14.11, illustrates a simple design with a small amount of information on it. The Wingding font is used for the check boxes, and right line leader tabs form the name and address lines. The size of the post card is 5 1/2 by 3 1/2 inches. The rule around the postcard in the figure is only to show you the edges—the postcard cannot print with this rule. If you were laying out a post card this size for commercial reproduction, you would set it up as 4-up (landscape orientation). The paste-up size would be 11 by 6 1/2 inches.

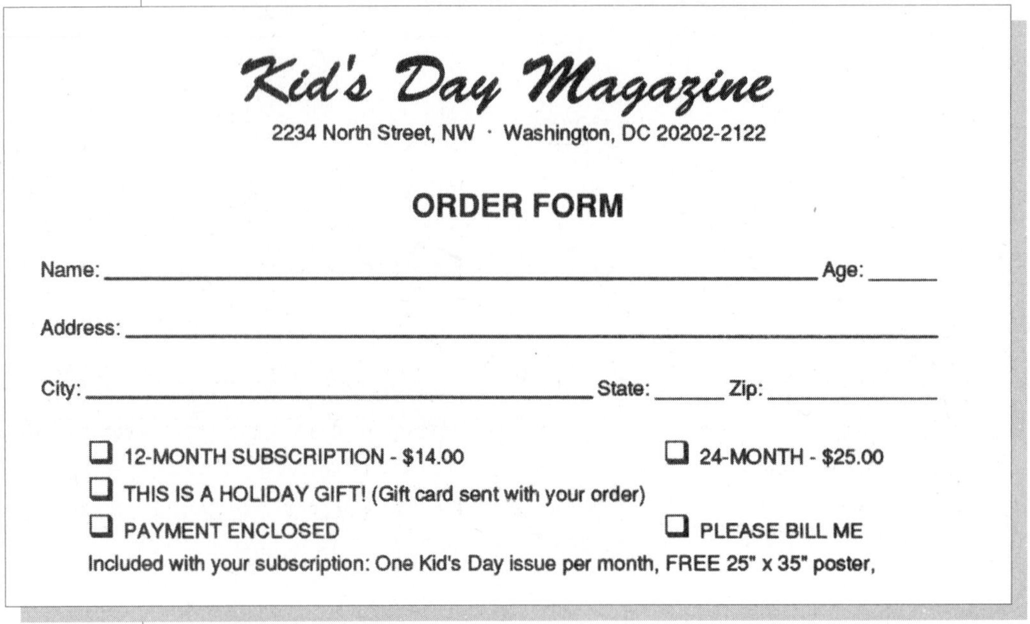

Kid's Day Magazine
2234 North Street, NW · Washington, DC 20202-2122

ORDER FORM

Name: _____ Age: _____

Address: _____

City: _____ State: _____ Zip: _____

❑ 12-MONTH SUBSCRIPTION - $14.00   ❑ 24-MONTH - $25.00
❑ THIS IS A HOLIDAY GIFT! (Gift card sent with your order)
❑ PAYMENT ENCLOSED   ❑ PLEASE BILL ME
Included with your subscription: One Kid's Day issue per month, FREE 25" x 35" poster,

Fig. 14.11 An order form for a postcard.

A postcard has limited space. If you use the card format, you can do the following three things to fit in the information:

- Make the card larger than 5 1/2 by 3 1/2 inches, which means that you pay more for postage and printing.

- Edit your information to fit.

- Squeeze more into the smaller space. If you choose this method, make sure that the information is readable.

Figure 14.12 illustrates a postcard with a lot of information in a small amount of space. The size is the same as the preceding postcard, but the margins are narrower. A frame placed beside the name and address information shows the postage and handling charges. A table allows four

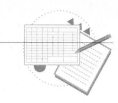

rows for ordering tapes or albums. The type is small (7 to 9 point), but it's Helvetica, so it's easy to read. The only problem with this design is that customers must write in small letters—and you must hope that their writing is legible.

GAN ANIN RECORDS AND TAPES
4147 N. ALVIS STREET, CHARLESTON, WEST VIRGINIA 25055

NAME: _____

ADDRESS: _____

CITY: _____

STATE & ZIP: _____

PHONE: _____

POSTAGE & HANDLING
(per tape or record)

Up to 5	$2
5 to 10	$3
11 to 20	$4
Over 21	Free

QTY.	LABEL	NUMBER	TITLE/ARTIST	PRICE	TOTAL

❑ BILL ME   ❑ PAYMENT ENCLOSED (WV Res. add 6% sales tax)   **TOTAL** _____

Fig. 14.12   A postcard with a great deal of label text.

Recapping

In this chapter, you learned to design a variety of forms by using methods such as rotating text and graphics, combining table cells, applying lines to specific areas of a table, and adding check boxes to your document. Many of these techniques also apply to other documents, as you learn in following chapters.

Creating Sales Documents

IV

15

Producing an Advertisement

Advertisements come in many forms. Newspaper ads, maga-zine ads, circulars, mailings, flyers, and brochures are only a few publications used for advertising. Newspapers and maga-zines provide limited space for advertising, whereas circulars and brochures supply more room to describe your product or service. This section of the book presents information on various methods of advertising, as well as on ways to design your ad to get the most for your money.

COMPUTER TRAINING

➢ Word Processing
➢ Desktop Publishing
➢ Spreadsheets
➢ Databases
➢ Accounting Programs
➢ Draw and Paint Programs

HUMBLE OPINIONS
Your Computer Training Specialists

1127 E. Main Street
Beckley, WV 25801
(304) 251-5151

For detailed information on how to create a form like this see page 344.

Choosing a Publication for Advertising

The publication in which you advertise depends on your product or service, your prospective customers, and the amount of money you want to spend. The following sections describe some advantages and disadvantages of advertising in various publications. Consider all the alternatives before deciding on one. You may want to try several options to see which is most profitable for your business.

Advertising in a Newspaper

Newspaper ads are an efficient way to advertise. You can choose from national, metropolitan, and local newspapers; and most cities have shopper-oriented, campus, business, or ethnic newspapers. With so many choices, you should be able to find the newspaper that reaches your public. If you own a health food store, for example, place your ad in the campus and shopper-oriented newspapers. If you sell business computers, place your ad in a business newspaper. You want your ad to reach your audience.

On certain days, a newspaper ad may attract the right customer. Food-oriented ads work best on Wednesday, when grocery stores advertise. Sunday's paper is good for any ad because most people read the paper from cover to cover on Sunday.

For quick recognition by your audience, request that your ad be placed in or near the same spot each time it's in the newspaper.

In addition, ask the newspaper to place your ad in a specific section of the newspaper. Reach business people in the business section, athletes in the sports section, homemakers in the food section, and so on. Ask that your ad be placed near the front of the newspaper, on a right-hand page, and above the fold. This is considered the prime placement for an ad in the newspaper because it is the location most often read.

Several factors determine the size of your ad. The first is probably the amount of money you can spend. Be sure to check with the newspaper for prices of display ads and choose a size before you design the ad. To stand out, an ad does not necessarily have to be the largest one on the page. Many of the ads in this chapter are small, yet distinctive.

The second factor that determines the size of your ad is the amount of copy, including text, photographs, illustrations, logos, and so on. When writing a newspaper ad, keep the copy short and to the point. Use adjectives, brief descriptions, and facts. Be sure that any graphic images

contribute to the message. When you have limited space for an ad, as in a newspaper, you want to attract attention with your ad copy.

You also can attract attention with the design of the ad. Remember that your ad must stand out among the competitors' ads. Take a moment to look at the newspaper in which you plan to advertise. Decide what you can do differently to make your ad noticeable. For one thing, most newspaper ads force too much information into a small space. If yours is a small space, limit your information and design your ad to support that information. Another factor is white space. No matter what size your newspaper ad is, white space makes it distinctive. Other design elements you can use to attract attention are type, images, and borders.

Be sure that you use clear, readable type. Try not to use type that's smaller than the newspaper's body type (normally 9, 10, or 11 point). If you must use small type, make it a typeface different from the one the newspaper uses. The newspaper usually sets the type for ads in the same type it uses for body and heads. Most newspapers use Times Roman as the body type and a variety of typefaces for headlines. If your text is a different typeface, it stands out among the other ads. Try typefaces such as the ATM fonts, or try PostScript fonts such as Bookman, Palatino, Friz Quadrata, or Avant Garde. These fonts attract attention by contrast.

The typefaces used in the following ads are Times Roman and Helvetica, plus some ATM fonts. These typefaces are used because they are common to most printers and you can judge your results with the figures for accuracy. The ATM fonts come with Ami Pro, and they need no special handling to use. If they are not installed on your system, consider installing them now. They are excellent for use in ads.

Display type is another useful addition to your ad. Using display type for one or two words emphasizes the purpose of your ad and attracts attention. Use words like *Sale*, *Free*, and *One day only* for display type. Ami Pro offers several typefaces you can use for display type, such as CaslonOpenFace, Frank Goth Cd, Brush Script, and DomCasual. If you can print Times or Helvetica very large (60 or 72 points), you can use them as display type as well, although an unusual typeface is better. You also can use a draw or paint program to design the type, then import it into Ami Pro.

The most important design element, especially in a newspaper ad, is white space. Most ads are so dark, crowded, or full that the ads with white space are the ones that stand out. Add white space around the outside edge of the border and the inside edge. Add white space between lines of text and around graphic images. The ads in this chapter illustrate the ways to use white space.

The majority of newspaper ads do not include sufficient white space; yours will stand out in that crowd if you make good use of white space.

Remember the two-font rule and limit display type, as described in Chapter 3.

Alternatively, a graphic artist can design display type that you can scan and import into Ami Pro.

See Chapters 3 and 5 for logo ideas.

Photographs, illustrations, logos—any graphic images—attract attention. A well-placed image emphasizes the product or service and also can pull in someone who's just briefly scanning the page. Don't use too many images, however; you can overcrowd the ad. One or two graphic images to a quarter of a newspaper page is sufficient. If possible, it's much better to use one large image than to use several small ones. Similarly, if your company has a logo, try to include it in your ad. The customer becomes familiar with a logo that's used over and over again.

Other possible additions to your ad include rules or borders, screens, and color. Contrast your ad to others with borders and screens. Extremely thick or extremely thin borders stand out. Reversed type in a dark or solid screen stands out. Graduated screens stand out as well. Adding one or two colors to your ad may be just the boost it needs. A color ad does attract attention, but it is more expensive. Also, remember that color registration in newspapers is often off on three and four colors. An ad that's poorly registered is not one that's often read. Chapter 4, "Planning and Purchasing Printing," explains registration.

Finally, if applicable to your situation, think about running the same ad several times. First, it's cheaper to run the same ad than to run a new one because the newspaper has completed the camera and prep work already. Second, when customers get used to seeing the same ad week after week, they are more likely to pay attention to it.

Advertising in a Magazine

A magazine may be another place for your ad. Magazine advertising gives your company more credibility. You also can target the ads for a magazine that goes to people who are interested in your product. If, for example, you sell musical instruments, advertise in a musician's magazine. If you sell software packages, advertise in a computer magazine.

Request ad prices from several magazines before deciding which magazine to use. Ask about the magazine's circulation and the geographic areas covered.

You may think it's expensive to advertise in a magazine, but the cost may not be all that high. Many magazines sell regional advertising, which means that they place your ad only in your area and the cost is less than advertising nationally in the magazine.

Design guidelines for a magazine ad are nearly the same as for a newspaper ad. Use a great deal of white space, an unusual typeface, interesting graphic images, and so on. A factor that is more important for a magazine ad, however, is color. You have more color choices in a magazine than in a newspaper. Most of the other ads are likely to be in color, so yours should be, too.

Advertising Circulars

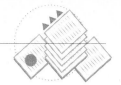

Circulars have two basic uses. One is as a newspaper insert; the other is for mailing. A circular can be any size, although 8 1/2 by 11 inches is probably the most preferred size. Smaller circulars may get lost or overlooked, and larger ones are more expensive and harder to handle. The basic design for either an insert or a mailed piece is the same; it's how you distribute them that is different.

A newspaper circular is inserted into the paper after printing. You can have either a commercial print shop or the newspaper print your ad. Having the newspaper print your circular is usually cheaper, but the final quality is not always good. A print shop offers better quality, and you have more control over the final piece.

A circular that is mailed can be folded, fastened, and mailed as is, or it can be placed in an envelope. When mailing a circular, consider the size and weight of the paper so that it doesn't cost too much to mail. See Chapter 4 for more information on paper.

Circulars are similar to display ads as far as design is concerned. Because newspapers contain many circulars, yours must be unique to be noticed. If you follow this chapter's guidelines for design in the newspaper ad section, your circular should attract attention.

The use of color, as with magazines, is one significant difference between designing a circular and designing a newspaper ad. All the inserts printed by the newspaper use the same paper, and all use similar colors. If you print your circular at a print shop, however, you can choose uncommon colors that make your ad stand out. Try using ivory paper, for example, or pastel or fluorescent colors; for ink, consider maroon, gray, forest green, or navy blue—all far from the standard newspaper colors. These colors also work well for mailed circulars.

One final Ami Pro point before you begin. When you work with Ami Pro's frame feature, the measurements of the frame are always about 1/8-inch smaller than you tell Ami Pro to make them. This disparity arises because Ami Pro includes a small margin around the outer edge of each frame. The borders do not form a box the same size as the frame. When you design an ad on your own, draw the frame and size it in the Size & Position dialog box, and then print it out before formatting your type. Measure it and adjust the size, then continue to format your ad.

B efore deciding whether to have the newspaper print your circular, ask for samples so that you can judge the newspaper's printing quality.

Designing a Newspaper Display Ad

The first ad is a traditional, text-only ad. Most newspapers place rules around each ad. If yours is borderless, it can stand out (see fig. 15.1). Because this display ad is for computer training, it should be placed in the business section. Its size is 3 by 5 inches. The width of the ad fills two columns of a daily newspaper. This ad would also work well in a magazine.

COMPUTER TRAINING

➢ Word Processing

➢ Desktop Publishing

➢ Spreadsheets

➢ Databases

➢ Accounting Programs

➢ Draw and Paint Programs

HUMBLE OPINIONS
Your Computer Training Specialists

1127 E. Main Street
Beckley, WV 25801
(304) 251-5151

Fig. 15.1   A newspaper ad with no rules or borders.

The heading of the ad is 36-point Frank Goth Cd (an ATM font), used here as display type because it is large and bold. Another addition is the unusual bullet character, which attracts attention because it's unique. The company's name is in Times Roman; the rest of the ad is Helvetica. Most ads do include rules. If you do not want your ad to have rules, be sure to tell the newspaper. If you don't use rules, use plenty of white space in the ad. The white space sets the ad apart from surrounding ads.

Finally, notice the addition of crop marks. Because the ad has no border, you should define the size of the ad for the newspaper. Ami Pro does not allow you to create a 3-by-5-inch page; therefore, you cannot print with crop marks. Instead, you add the crop marks with small frames. In figure 15.1, the two crop marks on the left show how they look coming out of the printer. The two on the right are how they should look when completed. To "cut off" the crop marks like those on the right, use a piece of white masking tape (available at art supply stores) to hide half of the frame.

To produce the first ad design with crop marks, follow these steps:

1. Choose File New. Choose the default style sheet. Choose OK or press Enter.

2. Choose Page Modify Page Layout. In Margins, change the Left and Right margins to **2.75"**. Change the Top and Bottom margins to 3". Choose OK or press Enter.

3. Choose Style Modify Style. Body Text is the default style.

4. In Modify, choose Alignment. In Indent, choose All and type **.20**. Choose From Right and type **.20**.

5. In Modify, choose Font. Choose Helv, 12 point. Choose OK or press Enter.

6. Press Enter and type the following:

   COMPUTER TRAINING(Enter twice)
   Word Processing(Enter)
   Desktop Publishing(Enter)
   Spreadsheets(Enter)
   Databases(Enter)
   Accounting Programs(Enter)
   Draw and Paint Programs(Enter twice)
   HUMBLE OPINIONS(Enter)
   Your Computer Training Specialists(Enter twice)
   1127 E. Main Street(Enter)
   Beckley, WV 25801(Enter)
   (304) 251-5151

The default style sheet contains two bullet styles, but neither one fits the style of the ad in figure 15.1.

7. Select COMPUTER TRAINING. Choose center, bold, Frank Goth Cd (use Helv if ATM is not installed), 36 point.

8. Select the text from Word Processing through Draw and Paint Programs.

9. Choose Style Create a Style. In the New text box, type **Bullet 3.** Choose Modify or press Enter.

10. In Modify, choose Alignment. In Indent, choose All. Type **.45.**

11. In Modify, choose Spacing. Choose Custom and type **.28.**

12. In Modify, choose Special Effects (Version 2.0) or Bullets and Number (Version 3.0). Choose Bullet. Choose the last bullet style in the list.

13. In Space For, type **.25.** (This setting defines the space between the bullet and the first letter of the text.) Choose OK or press Enter.

14. Choose Style Select a Style. Assign the Bullet 3 style to the list of software you have selected.

15. Select and center the rest of the text, from HUMBLE OPINIONS through the phone number.

16. Place the cursor on the paragraph return before HUMBLE OPINIONS. Change the type size to 18 point.

17. Select HUMBLE OPINIONS. Choose bold, Tms Rmn, 17 point.

18. Select Your Computer Training Specialists. Choose 10 point, italic. The default font is Tms Rmn.

19. Place the cursor on the blank paragraph return under Your Computer Training Specialists. Choose 6 point.

20. Select the phone number. Choose bold, 14 point.

21. Save and print the ad.

If you have questions about crop marks, refer to Chapter 4. You can add crop marks by drawing them yourself after printing the ad. Drawing them on the computer, however, is easy. To add the crop marks, do the following:

1. Draw a frame in the margin. The size should be approximately 1/4 by 1/4 inch. Position the frame so that its lower right corner touches the upper left corner of the margins of the ad.

2. Choose Frame Modify Frame Layout.

3. In Frame Display, choose **S**quare Corners.

4. In Frame, choose Lines & Shadows. In Line S**t**yle, choose the second pattern. In Shadow, choose None. Choose OK or press Enter.

5. Copy the frame three times. Position each frame outside a corner of the ad.

Designing a Text and Graphic Advertisement

This one-column display ad works for either a newspaper or a magazine. The design of this ad makes it unusual because most ads contain type that is left-aligned, justified, or center-aligned. Right-aligned type demands attention (see fig. 15.2).

MARIE'S
CRAFT SHOP

POTTERY
WEAVINGS
JEWELRY
CANDLES
PAINTINGS

Handmade Gifts
Open Daily 10 to 5

**MARIE'S
CRAFT SHOP**
3041 Elks Circle
Huntington, WV
(304) 311-5505

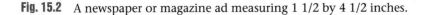

Fig. 15.2   A newspaper or magazine ad measuring 1 1/2 by 4 1/2 inches.

S elect each frame and display the proper line positions (such as **R**ight and **B**ottom for the top left frame), or use white tape to trim the crop marks.

See Chapter 3 for more information on using right-aligned text correctly.

The width of the ad is 1 1/2 inches; the height is 4 1/2 inches. Its size and shape are not at all uncommon; however, the placement of the type is unusual; it's right-aligned. Also included in the ad is a right-aligned logo. The logo draws attention, as do the two 4-point rules at the top and bottom of the ad. The copy is written with few words on each line, contributing to interesting white space.

To produce the one-column ad, follow these steps:

1. Choose File New. Choose the default style sheet. Choose OK or press Enter.

2. Draw a frame; you size it in the next steps.

3. Choose Frame Modify Frame Layout.

4. In Display, choose Square Corners.

5. In Frame, choose Size & Position. For Width, type 1.5; for Height, type 4.5. Choose Clear Margins.

6. In Frame, choose Lines & Shadows. In Position, choose Top and Bottom. In Line Style, choose the fourth pattern. In Shadow, choose None. Choose OK or press Enter.

7. Draw another, smaller frame for the logo. Position it inside the first frame, near the top.

8. Choose Frame Modify Frame Layout.

9. In Frame, choose Size & Position. Choose Clear Margins.

10. In Frame, choose Lines & Shadows. Deselect All lines; choose None for Shadow. Choose OK or press Enter.

11. Choose File Import Picture. In AmiDraw files, choose ARTTOOLS.SDW. Choose OK or press Enter.

If you do not use a mouse, skip the following instructions—continue with entering and formatting the type. If you have a mouse, you can stretch the art by performing the following steps:

1. With frame selected, choose Tools Drawing.

2. Click the picture. Small black handles appear.

3. Move the picture to the left, nearly out of the frame. The image enlarges and stretches. Repeat 2 or 3 times until the art work is stretched similarly to figure 15.2.

4. Use the Grabber Hand to position the image. Right-align it to the frame.

You must use the Grabber Hand to reposition the image; the Pointer Tool changes the size.

To enter and format the text, follow these steps:

1. Place the cursor below the logo. Choose **Text Alignment**. In the secondary command list, choose **Right**.

2. Type the following:

   MARIE'S(Enter)
   CRAFT SHOP(Enter twice)
   POTTERY(Enter)
   WEAVINGS(Enter)
   JEWELRY(Enter)
   CANDLES(Enter)
   PAINTINGS(Enter twice)
   Handmade Gifts(Enter)
   Open Daily 10 to 5(Enter twice)
   MARIE'S(Enter)
   CRAFT SHOP(Enter)
   3041 Elks Circle(Enter)
   Huntington, WV(Enter)
   (304) 311-5505

3. Place the cursor in front of the first `MARIE'S`. Choose **Tools Macros**. Choose **Playback**.

4. In the Macros list, choose SMARTYPE.SMM. Choose OK or press Enter. The macro changes the apostrophes to typographical apostrophes.

5. Select `MARIE'S`. Choose Tms Rmn, 24 point.

6. Select `CRAFT SHOP`. Choose Tms Rmn, 14 point.

7. Select the text from `POTTERY` through `PAINTINGS`. Choose Helv, 14 point.

8. Select `Handmade Gifts` and `Open Daily 10 to 5`. Choose 10-point, Tms Rmn.

9. Place the cursor on the paragraph return after `Open Daily 10 to 5`. Change the type size to 6 point.

10. Select and bold the second `MARIE'S CRAFT SHOP`.

11. Select the address and phone number and change it to 10 point. The default font is Tms Rmn.

12. Save and print the ad.

For ease in formatting documents, save this 6-point space to your default style sheet.

Designing a Two-Column Advertisement

The next ad is a simple one that includes a shadow box, a logo, and bullets. Notice the white space surrounding the text in the frame.

The barest minimum of text is used, and the ad still gets the message across (see fig. 15.3).

ROGHAN JOSH GOURMET FOODS

SPICE SALE
1/3 OFF

- CUMIN
- CORIANDER
- TUMERIC
- SAFFRON
- BLACK MUSTARD

ROGHAN JOSH
2436 N. 24TH STREET
HUNTINGTON, WV
(304) 871-9701

Fig. 15.3 A two-column newspaper ad that includes unusual bullets and a shadow box.

The shadow box and different bullets add interest to the advertisement and attract attention. This ad includes the name of the company twice in one small space. At the top, the company name is in small caps and uses a logo. At the bottom, the name is smaller and is followed by the address and phone number. If possible, repeat the company name somewhere in your ad. It never hurts for the customer to see the name

over and over. The ad measures 3 by 4 1/2 inches, to fit into two newspaper columns.

To produce the ad, follow these stpes:

1. You can create this design in the same document as the preceding ad, or choose File New. Choose the default style sheet. Choose OK or press Enter.

2. Draw a frame. Choose Frame Modify Frame Layout.

3. In Frame, choose Type. In Display, choose Square Corners.

4. In Frame, choose Size & Position. The Width is **3"**; the Height is **4.5"**. In Margins, make all margins **.25"**.

5. In Frame, choose Lines & Shadows. In Line Style, choose the third pattern. In Shadow, choose Deep. Choose OK or press Enter.

6. Draw another frame in the upper left corner of the first frame. Use this frame to hold the logo. Choose Frame Modify Frame Layout.

7. In Frame, choose Type. In Display, choose Square Corners.

8. In Frame, choose Size & Position. The Width is **.60"**; the Height is **.60"**. In Margins, choose Clear Margins.

9. In Frame, choose Lines & Shadows. In Lines, deselect All. In Shadow, choose None. Choose OK or press Enter.

10. Choose File Import Picture. Choose FLOWERS.SDW. Choose OK or press Enter.

11. Place the cursor to the right of the logo, in the original frame, and type the following:

    Roghan Josh(Enter)
    Gourmet Foods(Enter twice)
    SPICE SALE(Enter)
    1/3 OFF(Enter twice)
    CUMIN(Enter)
    CORIANDER(Enter)
    TUMERIC(Enter)
    SAFFRON(Enter)
    BLACK MUSTARD(Enter twice)
    ROGHAN JOSH(Enter)
    2436 N. 24TH STREET(Enter)
    HUNTINGTON, WV(Enter)
    (304) 871-9701

U se default Text Wrap Around option for the ad in figure 15.3.

12. Select Roghan Josh Gourmet Foods. Choose Tms Rmn, 18 point, bold. Select oghan. Choose Text Caps Small Caps. Repeat with osh, ourmet, and oods.

13. Place the cursor on the paragraph return above SPICE SALE. Choose 6 point. Repeat with the return under 1/3 OFF.

14. Select SPICE SALE. Choose Helv, 24 point, center, and bold.

15. Select 1/3 OFF. Choose Helv, 36 point, center, and bold.

16. Select the type from CUMIN to BLACK MUSTARD. Choose Style Select a Style.

17. In the Styles, choose Bullet 1.

18. Choose Style Modify Style.

19. In Modify, choose Font. Choose Tms Rmn, 12 point.

20. In Modify, choose Alignment. In Indent, choose All. Type .50. Choose OK or press Enter.

21. Select the second ROGHAN JOSH. Choose Tms Rmn, 14 point, center, and bold.

22. Select the two address lines and choose Helv, 10 point, center.

23. Select the phone number. Choose Helv, 10 point, center, and bold.

24. Save and print the ad.

Designing an Innovative Ad

The customer can easily locate the bold phone number.

Reversed type is an excellent way to attract attention in a newspaper ad, especially if the white type is large (24 to 36 point). In the next ad, Computer Training is reversed at the top in 24-point type (see fig. 15.4). The large reversed type distinguishes this ad from others, and the words Computer Training attract anyone interested in computers. A list of classes below the head provides a further focal point. The 2-point rule ties together the head and the rest of the ad. Another interesting aspect of this ad is that it measures 2 1/8 by 3 7/8 inches. The width of two columns in a daily newspaper is 3 inches. The white space on the sides provides a contrast to the black background of the top frame. You also can add extra space at the top and bottom by purchasing a 4 3/4-inch space.

COMPUTER TRAINING

WORD PROCESSING
DESKTOP PUBLISHING
SPREADSHEETS
DATABASES
ACCOUNTING
DRAW & PAINT

Call or stop by for information:
HUMBLE OPINIONS
1127 E. Main Street
Beckley, WV 25801
(304) 251-5151

Fig. 15.4 An innovative ad, using reversed type and plenty of white space.

To create the innovative ad, follow these steps:

1. Choose File New. Choose the default style sheet. Choose OK or press Enter.

2. Draw a frame. You size it in the next steps.

3. Choose Frame Modify Frame Layout.

4. In Frame, choose Type. In Display, choose Square Corners.

5. In Frame, choose Size & Position. The Width is **2.25"**; the Height is **1.15"**.

6. In Frame, choose Lines & Shadows. In Position, deselect All. In Shadow, choose None. In Background, choose black. Choose OK or press Enter.

7. Place the cursor in the frame. Choose Text Font. Choose Tms Rmn, 24 point, white. Choose OK or press Enter.

8. Type the following:

   COMPUTER(Enter)
   TRAINING(Enter)

9. Select, center, and bold the text.

10. Draw another frame below the first.

11. Choose Frame Modify Frame Layout.

12. In Frame, choose Type. In Display, choose Square Corners.

13. In Frame, choose Size & Position. The Width is **2.19"**; the Height is **2.95"**. In Margins, change the top to **.20**.

14. In Frame, choose Lines & Shadows. In Position, choose Left, **R**ight, and **B**ottom. In Line **S**tyle, choose the third pattern. In Shadow, choose None. Choose OK or press Enter.

15. Choose View Enlarged. Line the left and right rules of the second frame evenly with the edges of the first frame.

16. Place the cursor in the frame and type the following:

    WORD PROCESSING(Enter)
    DESKTOP PUBLISHING(Enter)
    SPREADSHEETS(Enter)
    DATABASES(Enter)
    ACCOUNTING(Enter)
    DRAW & PAINT(Enter twice)
    Call or stop by for information:(Enter)
    HUMBLE OPINIONS(Enter)
    1127 E. Main Street(Enter)
    Beckley, WV 25801(Enter)
    (304) 251-5151

17. Select all the text and center it.

18. Select the text from WORD PROCESSING through DRAW & PAINT. Choose Helv, 12 point.

19. Select Call or stop by for information:. Choose Tms Rmn, 10 point, italic.

20. Select HUMBLE OPINIONS. Choose Tms Rmn, 14 point, bold.

21. Select the two address lines and choose Helv, 10 point.

22. Select and bold the phone number. The default is Tms Rmn, 10 point.

23. Save and print the ad.

Aligning two frames exactly is easier in an enlarged view.

The balance of the two typefaces—both the amount and placement—adds to the ad's attractiveness.

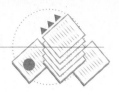

Designing a Five-Column Ad or Circular

You can use this next ad as a newspaper ad or as a circular. As a display ad, the size of the ad in figure 15.5 would be 6 1/4 by 8 3/4 inches. The width of five columns in a daily newspaper is 7 1/4 inches. This ad provides an extra 1/2 inch of white space on either side, thus separating it from all the rest of the ads on that page. An extra 1/2 inch also should be added at the top and bottom of the ad by purchasing a 9 3/4-inch space and informing the paper of your intentions. As a circular, this design easily can be printed on an 8 1/2-by-11-inch sheet of paper. You can insert it into the newspaper or mail it.

This design is unique because of the graphic image. The jet plane is an AmiDraw file that was rotated to break up the space. You stop and look at it for several reasons. First, the image is large. Second, the jet creates interesting white space in the frame around it. Third, the majority of the ad is light and airy; the heaviness of the jet throws the balance to the bottom of the ad and onto the name, address, and phone numbers of the company.

Ami Pro's powerful frame feature shines in this design. You can use many frames within a design; you can place text or graphics in them, add rules, create wrap arounds—the possibilities are endless.

If you do not use a mouse, you must draw an extra frame in which to place the jet, then in step 9 move the frame instead of the image. You can access the Drawing feature in Ami Pro only if you use a mouse. To achieve the same effect as in step 9, before you import the jet, have a second frame ready for it. The second frame should have no margins, no lines, and no shadows.

To produce the five-column ad, follow these steps:

1. Choose **File New**. Choose the default style sheet. Choose OK or press Enter.

2. Draw a frame. You size it in the following steps.

3. Choose **Frame Modify Frame Layout**.

4. In Frame, choose **Type**. In Display, choose **Square Corners** and **Transparent**.

Inform the newspaper of unusual requirements, such as leaving one-half inch of white space around your ad. Otherwise, they will crowd the ad.

JET AWAY TOURS

NEW SPRING TOURS

New York City Theater Tour   April 28 - May 2, 1993

Washington Cherry Blossom Festival May 7 - May 11, 1993

Bahamas Scuba Diving Adventure May 14 - May 18, 1993

Las Vegas Night Life Extravaganza May 23 - May 27, 1993

ALL TOURS INCLUDE:
Round Trip Air Fare
Hotel Accommodations
Two Special Dinners
Welcoming Cocktail Reception

JET AWAY TOURS

1322 Airport Complex
Beckley, WV 25802

(304) 256-1232 **(800) 250-1232**

Fig. 15.5 A five-column newspaper ad or a circular.

5. In Frame, choose **S**ize & Position. The **W**idth is **6.5"**; the **H**eight is **9"**. In Margins, choose **.35** for all.

6. In Frame, choose **L**ines & Shadows. In **P**osition, choose All. In Line Style, choose the second pattern. In Shadow, choose **C**ustom and type **.10.** Choose the lower left arrow for the shadow direction. Choose OK or press Enter.

7. Choose **F**ile **I**mport Picture. Choose CORPJET.SDW. Choose OK or press Enter.

8. Choose **F**rame **G**raphic Scaling. In **R**otate, type **25** (degrees). Choose OK or press Enter.

9. If you use a mouse, choose **T**ools **D**rawing. Use the Grabber Hand to move the jet to the bottom of the frame so that it's positioned like the one in the figure.

10. Draw another frame to hold the text at the top of the ad.

11. Choose **F**rame **M**odify Frame Layout.

12. In Frame, choose **T**ype. In **D**isplay, choose Transparent.

13. In Frame, choose **S**ize & Position. The **W**idth is **6"**; the **H**eight is **3"**. In Margins, choose Clear Margins.

14. In Frame, choose **L**ines & Shadows. In **P**osition, deselect All. In Shadow, choose **N**one. Choose OK or press Enter.

15. Copy and paste this frame twice. Move both copied frames out of the way for now. Place the cursor in the frame you drew in step 10 and type the following:

JET AWAY TOURS(Enter twice)
NEW SPRING TOURS(Enter twice)
New York City Theater Tour(Tab)**April 28 – May 2, 1993**(Enter)
Washington Cherry Blossom Festival(Tab)**May 7 – May 11, 1993**(Enter)
Bahamas Scuba Diving Adventure(Tab)**May 14 – May 18, 1993**(Enter)
Las Vegas Night Life Extravaganza(Tab)**May 23 – May 27, 1993**

16. Select JET AWAY TOURS. Choose Tms Rmn, 36 point, center, and bold.

17. Select NEW SPRING TOURS. Choose Helv, 18 point, center.

18. Select the text from New York City Theater Tour through Las Vegas Night Life Extravaganza May 23 – May 27, 1993. Choose Tms Rmn, 14 point.

You may want to experiment with the rotation of the image and the placement of the text frames.

By copying the frame now, you don't have to draw and set lines and margins for new frames later.

19. Activate the ruler. Set a left tab at 4".

20. Choose Text Spacing. Set the Line spacing to **1 1/2**. Choose OK or press Enter.

21. Select one of the empty, copied frames and position it below the cities and dates you just typed. Center the frame.

22. Choose Frame Modify Frame Layout.

23. In Frame, choose Size & Position. The Width is **3.15"**; the Height is **1.39"**. Choose OK or press Enter.

24. Place the cursor in the frame and type the following:

ALL TOURS INCLUDE:(Enter)
Round Trip Air Fare(Enter)
Hotel Accommodations(Enter)
Two Special Dinners(Enter)
Welcoming Cocktail Reception(Enter)

25. Select ALL TOURS INCLUDE:. Choose Helv, 12 point, bold.

26. Select the next four lines of text. Choose Helv. The default size is 10 point. Choose Text Indention. For All, type **.45**. Choose OK or press Enter.

27. Choose Text Spacing. Choose Custom and type **.23**. Choose OK or press Enter.

28. Select the second copied frame. Position it in the lower right corner, below the jet.

29. Place the cursor in the frame and type the following:

JET AWAY TOURS(Enter)
1322 Airport Complex(Enter)
Beckley, WV 25802(Enter)
(304) 256-1232(six spaces)**(800) 250-1232**

30. Select all four lines of text and center them.

31. Select JET AWAY TOURS. Choose Tms Rmn, 18 point, bold.

32. Select the two address lines and choose Helv. The default size is 10 point.

33. Select the phone numbers. Choose Tms Rmn, 18 point.

34. Choose Text Spacing. Choose Custom and type .35.

35. Save and print the ad.

Looking at Design

You can add many variations to your designs to make them unusual and, therefore, noticeable. Experiment with Ami Pro's Frame and Drawing features as well as with the ATM fonts. If you have another draw or paint program, try combining it with Ami Pro to produce effective, creative designs. This section contains a few ads and circulars that may give you additional ideas.

Figure 15.6 is another design for a five-column ad or a circular. The focal point is the computer in the center. The computer is dark and heavy, whereas the rest of the ad is light and airy. The image was rotated in the drawing feature. The shadow box surrounding the computer is actually two rectangles, one with a black background, the other with a white, opaque background. They also were drawn and rotated in Ami Pro's Draw feature. The rotated image in the center makes you stop and look at it.

You also can rotate text in the Drawing feature, as in figure 15.7. In Version 2.0 of Ami Pro, text rotation is more difficult. Each line of text is in a block by itself and must be rotated separately. This requirement makes rotating a great amount of text extremely time-consuming.

Version 3.0 allows you to group text blocks. Grouped objects then can be rotated as one object. The text in figure 15.7 is ShelleyAllegroScript, 36 point. The rest of the type is Times Roman. The triple-line border balances the shop name and address, especially because the script is so light. This ad is a 5-column ad, or a circular, with a wealth of white space on all sides.

An ad need not span three, four, or five columns to attract attention. Figure 15.8 illustrates a one-column ad that stands out in the crowd. The treble clef is from AmiDraw and tempts any music lover to read the ad. The copy for the ad is short, to the point, and offers the reader a free catalog.

Figure 15.9 illustrates a horizontal emphasis in an ad. The copy is basic, simple, and around tax time would attract anyone's attention. The type for the head is CaslonOpenFace, a nearly weightless type. The rest of the ad mirrors that feeling with a thin, 1-point rule and a good deal of white space.

To get ideas, you may want to look at other ads in magazines, newspapers, and mailings.

For rotation purposes and to create a deeper shadow than the Frame feature can produce, the design in figure 15.6 uses two rectangles.

Use Ami Pro's Drawing feature to change screens and line styles in any AmiDraw clip art.

COMPUTER TRAINING

Word Processing
Desktop Publishing
Spreadsheets

Databases
Accounting
Draw and Paint

HUMBLE OPINIONS
Your Computer Training Specialists

1127 E. Main Street
(304) 251-5151

Beckley, WV 25801
(800) 250-2369

Fig. 15.6 A circular ad design with a rotated graphic image.

Pottery   Weavings   Jewelry   Quilts

MARIE'S CRAFT SHOP

3041 Elks Circle · Huntington
(304) 211-5505

OPEN DAILY FROM 10:00 A.M. TO 5:00 P.M.

Fig. 15.7 An example of rotated text in an ad.

Using a familiar word in an ad, such as *sale, free, one day only*, and so on, involves the reader. Using several of these words promotes the feeling of urgency within the ad. Figure 15.10 illustrates one such example. The ad not only repeats the word SALE, it accentuates the word with screens. Each screened frame is a little lighter (85% at the top, 70% in the middle, and 55% at the bottom). The white type within the screen invites readers to look at the ad. The rest of the ad uses ONE DAY ONLY and 1/2 PRICE to further entice the reader to visit the store. The 1-point rule around the ad ties it all together. This ad is a five-column ad, again using white space around the outside of the frame.

Remember that a newspaper ad should use brief, descriptive words and phrases to get the point across quickly.

Fig. 15.8 An enticing one-column ad.

ARE YOUR RETURNS TAXING YOU?

Lucre Income Tax Preparation Service   1-800-888-9988

Fig. 15.9   A simple but eye-catching ad.

ONE DAY ONLY
JANUARY 21

EVERYTHING IN STORE
1/2 PRICE

TINKERS DEPARTMENT STORE
110 E. Main Street
Open 9 to 5

Fig. 15.10   Using the word SALE reversed in three screened boxes to attract attention.

Another idea for an eye-catching ad is to vary the border. Ami Pro offers various rule thicknesses for borders; you can even screen a rule. Figure 15.11 illustrates the use of two thicknesses of rules to form a border. In addition, the border formed is different from the norm. Two frames were used, both transparent, so that the rules would show through. The typefaces are Frank Gothic Cd and Times Roman. The Frank Gothic Cd commands attention; the Times Roman offers a bit of variety.

OFFICE SUPPLIES

1/3 OFF

**DESKS
CHAIRS
CABINETS
CALCULATORS
FAX MACHINES**

BOSWELL OFFICE SUPPLIES
567 N. Central Street
832-3256

Fig. 15.11 An unusual and appealing border to attract attention to an ad.

Recapping

In this chapter, you learned to create interesting and attractive advertisements by applying rules of white space, typefaces and sizes, and graphic images and elements. In addition, you learned to apply special Ami Pro features, such as image rotation, reversed text, text rotation, and the Drawing feature.

Producing
a Flyer

A flyer is a tool to support and encourage sales. A flyer advertises products, services, or specials. It also provides information like prices, dates, lists, or descriptions. A flyer can inform or announce; but mostly, a flyer sells. Flyers are very similar to circulars, but they're more descriptive. They usually offer useful information or detailed descriptions. A take-out menu, discount coupons, or a schedule of classes are good examples of subjects for a flyer. Because the primary purpose of a flyer is to sell, be sure that your information conforms to that goal.

For detailed information on how to create a form like this see page 371.

You can distribute flyers in many ways. Like circulars, flyers can be inserted into a newspaper. You also can mail a flyer. For instance, include a sale flyer with an advertising letter, or mail it alone. You can hand out flyers at seminars, classes, trade shows, concerts, or art exhibits. Give every customer who walks into your business a flyer describing new products or discounts. Leave flyers on the counter or near the door so that customers can pick them up. The choices for distribution of flyers are endless.

Planning the Content

All flyers should contain certain information. Your company name, address, and phone number should appear somewhere on the flyer. In addition, choose a point of emphasis. If the purpose of the flyer is to announce a sale, the word *sale* should stand out the most. If the purpose of the flyer is to offer classes, then *training* or *classes* should appear in large, bold, or display type. Let the customer know who you are and what you are selling. Other information included in a flyer should support the emphasized point. Add graphics images, descriptive phrases, a list of prices, dates, and so on to sway the customer your way.

The design of the flyer also must help to convince your customer to buy what you're selling. Several guidelines can help you accomplish this task. The main element is to attract attention. Depending on your business, you may be extremely creative or greatly reserved in your design. Either way, you can still attract the attention of your customers. This chapter illustrates several design alternatives for flyers.

Planning the Size

The size of a flyer is flexible. It can be 5 1/2 by 8 1/2 inches, 8 1/2 by 11 inches, or even 11 by 17 inches. Keep convenience in mind. Some flyers are throwaways, some are keepers. It's most convenient to keep and store a flyer that's 8 1/2 by 11 inches. If your flyer is convenient to keep, your customer will keep it.

Choosing Paper

Whether your flyer is a keeper or a throwaway, you must consider the paper you print it on. If your flyer is printed on one side only, 20# bond

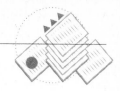

paper is a good choice. A two-sided flyer needs a heavier paper, like 60# offset, so the text or images won't bleed through. If your flyer is one that people may keep, such as a take-out menu, you may want to use 60# offset even if it is one sided so that it will last longer.

Another consideration is the color of the paper. Choose something that represents your company well, in addition to making your flyer attractive. Fluorescent colors of paper, for instance, may be fine for a sale flyer, but they may not work for a business seminar. Pastel colors may look nice for a class list, but are not bright enough for a sale flyer. Try to match your color choices to your audience, your business, and your message. You can buy the paper to print your own flyers on your printer or copy them on a photocopy machine, or you can have a print shop do them. Always ask for samples of paper so that you can decide which is best for your job.

New Ami Pro features introduced in this chapter include combining frames and columns, attracting attention with Wingdings, using dot and dash leader tabs, using hanging indents, and horizontally flipping an image.

See Chapter 4 for more information about paper choices and ink colors.

Designing a Price List

The first flyer contains a common subject, a price list. This one is in the form of a take-out menu. The typeface for the name of the restaurant is Times Roman. Notice, too, that the name is mentioned twice, as is the phone number (see fig. 16.1). The menu items are in Helvetica for easier reading. A dot leader guides the eye from the dish to the price. Two columns provide adequate space for the menu. This flyer prints on one side only, but use a heavier paper because you want your customer to keep the flyer.

To create the take-out menu, follow these steps.

1. Choose File New. Choose the default style sheet. Choose OK or press Enter.

2. Choose Page Modify Page Layout.

3. In Modify, choose Margins & Columns. In Margins, change all to .35.

4. In Number of Columns, choose 2. For Gutter Width, type .35.

5. In Tabs, select the leader icon until the third (dot) leader appears (see fig. 16.2) Set a right leader tab at 4". Choose OK or press Enter.

Horizontal rules divide information; they separate the one-column frames from the two-column price list in figure 16.1.

ROGHAN JOSH RESTAURANT
TAKE-OUT MENU
871-9701

APPETIZERS

Pakoras	$3.00
Samosas	$3.00
Chiura	$3.00
Bhelpuris	$4.00
Ekuri	$4.00

MAIN DISHES

FISH

Jhinga Kabab	$8.00
Jhinga Kari	$8.00
Tali Machli	$7.00
Machli aur Tabatar	$8.50

CHICKEN

Tandoori Murg	$9.00
Murg do Pyaza	$9.00
Tikka Murg	$8.00
Tithar	$8.00

LAMB

Kheema do Pyaza	$10.00
Badami Gosht	$10.00
Dhansak	$12.00
Kofta	$14.50
Husaini Kabab	$13.00
Raan	$13.00
Korma	$14.00

MAIN DISHES

PORK

Sorpotel	$11.00
Suvar Mas Ka Vindalu	$16.00

BEEF

Kofta Kari	$15.00
Masaledar Raan	$15.00
Kari Aviyal	$14.00

VEGETABLES

Simla Mirch	$10.00
Aviyal	$10.00
Mattar Pannir	$12.00
Khumbi Bhaji	$14.50
Sag	$13.00

BREADS

Paratha	$3.00
Alu Paratha	$3.00
Chippatis	$2.00
Puris	$3.00

SALADS

Alu Ka Rayta	$5.00
Pudine ka Rayta	$4.00
Rajma-Chana Salat	$5.00
Sag Rayta	$3.00

ROGHAN JOSH RESTAURANT
OPEN DAILY FROM 11 A.M. TO 9 P.M.

2436 N. 24TH STREET
871-9701

Fig. 16.1 A take-out menu as a flyer.

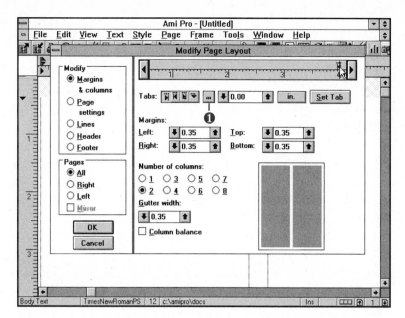

Fig. 16.2 The Modify Margins & Columns dialog box with margins, columns, gutter, and a leader tab selected; cursor pointing to the dot leader tab.

6. Choose View Full Page. Draw a frame along the top margin. You size and position it in the next steps.

7. Choose Frame Modify Frame Layout.

8. In Frame, choose Type. Choose No Wrap Beside. In Display, choose Square Corners.

9. In Frame, choose Size & Position. In Size, for Width type **8**; for Height, type **1.85**.

10. In Position, Down from Top, type **.24**. For In from Left, type **.25**. In Margins, change all to **.25**.

11. In Frame, choose Lines & Shadows. Choose the Top and Bottom Positions. In the Styles box, choose the third pattern. For Shadows, choose None. Choose OK or press Enter.

12. Copy the frame and paste it. Reposition the second frame along the bottom margin.

13. Place the cursor in the first frame, select the center icon or press Ctrl+C (2.0), Ctrl+E (3.0), and type the following:

ROGHAN JOSH RESTAURANT(Enter)
TAKE-OUT MENU(Enter)
871-9701

Formatting lines and margins before copying the frame saves you time later.

14. Select ROGHAN JOSH RESTAURANT. Choose Tms Rmn, 36 point, bold.

15. Select TAKE-OUT MENU and 871-9701. Choose Tms Rmn, 24 point, bold.

16. Place the cursor in the second frame, choose center, and type the following:

ROGHAN JOSH RESTAURANT(Enter)
OPEN DAILY FROM 11 A.M. TO 9 P.M.(Enter twice)
2436 N. 24TH STREET(Enter)
871-9701(Enter)

17. Select ROGHAN JOSH RESTAURANT. Choose Tms Rmn, 24 point, bold.

18. Select OPEN DAILY FROM 11 A.M. TO 9 P.M.. Choose 14 point, Tms Rmn.

19. Select 2436 N. 24TH STREET. Choose Tms Rmn, 18 point, bold.

20. Select the phone number and choose Tms Rmn, 24 point, bold.

21. Choose Style Modify Style. In the Styles box, choose Body Text.

22. In Modify, choose Font. Choose Helv, 12 point. Choose OK or press Enter.

23. Type the following:

APPETIZERS(Enter)
Pakoras(Tab, space)**$3.00**(Enter)
Samosas(Tab, space)**$3.00**(Enter)
Chiura(Tab, space)**$3.00**(Enter)
Bhelpuris(Tab, space)**$4.00**(Enter)
Ekuri(Tab, space)**$4.00**(Enter twice)
MAIN DISHES(Enter)
FISH(Enter)
Jhinga Kabab(Tab, space)**$8.00**(Enter)
Jhinga Kari(Tab, space)**$8.00**(Enter)
Tali Machli(Tab, space)**$7.00**(Enter)
Machli aur Tabatar(Tab, space)**$8.50**(Enter twice)

24. Choose Style Create Style. In the New text box, type **Centered Head**. Choose Modify or press Enter.

25. In Modify Font, choose Helv, 14 point, bold, center. Choose OK or press Enter.

Using Helvetica for the small type makes it easier to read and adds emphasis to the name, address, and phone number of the restaurant, by contrast.

26. Choose **S**tyle **S**elect a Style. Assign Centered Head style to both APPETIZERS and MAIN DISHES.

27. Select and bold FISH.

28. Place the cursor in the line of text, Pakoras $3.00. Choose **S**tyle Create Style. In the **N**ew text box, type **Body Two**. Choose Modify.

29. The **S**tyle is Body Text. In Modify, choose **S**pacing. In Line Spacing, choose **C**ustom. Type **.24**. Choose OK or press Enter.

30. Select all dishes on the price list and assign the style Body Two to the text.

31. At this point, you can either type the rest of the text from figure 16.1, or copy the text you typed and paste it until the first column is filled. Then, copy the entire first column, and paste it into the second column.

32. Save and print.

Designing a Coupon Flyer

Coupons always attract customers. By offering coupons, you can entice customers to visit your store. Once the customers arrive, they usually buy more than the discounted items. A flyer that contains coupons is a valuable advertising piece.

Figure 16.3 illustrates a flyer containing nine coupons. You completely format one coupon, then copy it and make minor text changes for the rest. The name of the store is listed twice on the flyer and on each coupon. The amount of the discount is in the center of each coupon in large (24-point) type; it attracts the most attention. In addition, it's a good idea to include an expiration date and other disclaimers on all coupons, as shown in the figure.

You can set up this flyer several ways. One way is similar to the last method. You can change the page to three columns and use frames for the top and bottom heads. Another method is to set up the page in one column, position the first three frames with the help of Size & Position, then paste them down the page. In the following design, you use the second way so that you learn an alternate method for use in your own documents.

Y ou create a new styles or the body because applying the .24" spacing to Body Text changes the spacing in the frame text; all other formatting remains the same.

A lways put your company name on all coupons, so that if one is separated from the flyer, the customer knows where to redeem it.

ROGHAN JOSH GOURMET FOODS
2436 N. 24th Street

VALUABLE COUPONS

ASAFETIDA 1/2 oz. jar **$1.00 OFF** ROGHAN JOSH Expires 3/29/93 Limit one per customer	**JAGGERY** 5 lb. bag **$2.00 OFF** ROGHAN JOSH Expires 3/29/93 Limit one per customer	**PHAO RICE** 1 lb. bag **$1.00 OFF** ROGHAN JOSH Expires 3/29/93 Limit one per customer
CARDAMOM 1/2 oz. jar **$1.00 OFF** ROGHAN JOSH Expires 3/29/93 Limit one per customer	**FENUGREEK SEED** 1/4 oz. jar **$.50 OFF** ROGHAN JOSH Expires 3/29/93 Limit one per customer	**ROSE WATER** 16 oz. jar **$1.00 OFF** ROGHAN JOSH Expires 3/29/93 Limit one per customer
RAJMA DAL 1 lb. bag **$1.00 OFF** ROGHAN JOSH Expires 3/29/93 Limit one per customer	**BASUMATI RICE** 1 lb. bag **$.50 OFF** ROGHAN JOSH Expires 3/29/93 Limit one per customer	**SAFFRON** 1/4 oz. jar **$1.00 OFF** ROGHAN JOSH Expires 3/29/93 Limit one per customer

ROGHAN JOSH SPICES
We offer spices from around the world!

2436 N. 24th Street   871-9701

Fig. 16.3   A flyer containing nine coupons with discounts in large type to attract the customer's attention.

To produce the coupon flyer, follow these steps:

1. Choose **File New**. Choose the default style sheet. Choose **OK** or press **Enter**.

2. Choose **Page Modify Page Layout**.

3. In **Modify**, choose **Margins & Columns**. In **Margins**, change all to **.75**. Choose **OK** or press **Enter**.

4. Place the cursor and type the following:

   ROGHAN JOSH GOURMET FOODS(Enter)
   2436 N. 24th Street(Enter twice)
   VALUABLE COUPONS(Enter five times)

5. Select all three lines and center them.

6. Select `ROGHAN JOSH GOURMET FOODS`. Choose **Tms Rmn**, 24 point, bold.

7. Select `2436 N. 24th Street`. Choose **Tms Rmn**, 18 point.

8. Select `VALUABLE COUPONS`. Choose **Helv**, 24 point, bold.

9. Draw a frame. You size and position it in the next steps.

10. Choose **Frame Modify Frame Layout**.

11. In **Frame**, choose **Type**. Choose **No Wrap Beside**. In **Display**, choose **Square Corners**.

12. In **Frame**, choose **Size & Position**. In **Size**, for **Width** type **2.10**; for **Height**, type **2**.

13. In **Position**, **Down from Top**, type **2.27**. For **In from Left**, type **.73**. In **Margins**, change the **Top** and **Bottom** to **.15**. Change the **Left** and **Right** to **0**.

14. In **Frame**, choose **Lines & Shadows**. Choose **All Position**. In the **Styles** box, choose the first double rule pattern. For **Shadows**, choose **None**. Choose **OK** or press **Enter**.

15. Place the cursor in the frame, select the center icon or press Ctrl+C (2.0) or Ctrl+E (3.0), and type the following:

    ASAFETIDA(Enter)
    1/2 oz. jar(Enter twice)
    $1.00 OFF(Enter twice)
    ROGHAN JOSH(Enter)
    Expires 3/29/93(Enter)
    Limit one per customer

U sing Helvetica in only one line of text makes that line attract attention.

Format the text in the first frame, and then copy that frame to speed up the production of the remaining eight coupons in figure 16.3.

16. Select ASAFETIDA. Choose 14 point, bold. The default font is Tms Rmn.

17. Place the cursor on the paragraph return after 1/2 oz. jar. Change it to 6 point. Repeat with the return after $1.00 OFF.

18. Select $1.00 OFF. Choose Tms Rmn, 24 point, bold.

19. Select and bold ROGHAN JOSH.

20. Copy the frame and paste it. Reposition the second frame to the right of the first. Choose **F**rame Modify.

21. In Size & Position, for **D**own from Top type **2.27**. For **I**n from Left, type **3.22**. Choose OK or press Enter.

22. Choose **E**dit **P**aste to copy and paste the first frame again. Choose the copied frame and position it to the right of the second frame. Choose **F**rame Modify.

23. In Size & Position, for **D**own from Top type **2.27**. For **I**n from Left, type **5.62**. Choose OK or press Enter.

24. Select all three frames by choosing the first frame and holding the Shift key. Choose the second frame, then the third. Release the Shift key.

25. Choose **E**dit Copy. Choose **E**dit **P**aste. In Version 2.0, you have to reposition the three frames separately. To do that, select each frame and then choose **F**rame Modify Size & Position. In Version 3.0, you can group the frames by choosing **D**raw **G**roup. Then move the three frames as one unit. For **D**own from Top, the second row is **4.63**, the third row is **7.06**.

26. After pasting and positioning the frames, you can place the cursor in each frame and change the text according to the figure.

27. Place the cursor on the last paragraph return on the page, and press Ctrl+C (2.0), or Ctrl+E (3.0). Type the following:

ROGHAN JOSH SPICES(Enter)
We offer spices from around the world!(Enter twice)
2436 N. 24th Street(Tab)**871-9701**

28. Select ROGHAN JOSH SPICES. Choose Tms Rmn, 18 point, bold.

29. Select We offer spices from around the world! Choose italic.

30. Select the next paragraph return and change it to a 6-point space.

31. Select the address and phone number. Choose Tms Rmn, 14 point, left aligned.

32. Activate the ruler and set an indent of .5"; set a right tab at 7.25" on the ruler.

33. Save and print.

As a variation on the coupons flyer, you also can add screens to any or all of the coupon frames. Figure 16.4 illustrates the flyer with some screens added. Be sure that your screens are not so dark that the type cannot be read. If you want to use a dark screen, you can select the text within that frame and change it to white without affecting size, positioning, or typeface. Any of these options creates an interesting, eye-catching effect.

Designing an Innovative Flyer

You can attract attention with your flyer in many ways. One way is with graphics. Graphics include images, rules, borders, and screens. The images can be photographs, clip art, illustrations, even Wingdings. The next design uses a combination of borders, screens, clip art, and Wingdings. Figure 16.5 shows the completed flyer. Although it sounds like a lot of graphics to add to one sheet, the final design doesn't look at all crowded or busy.

The heavy outside page border is the key to the entire design. Because the double rule surrounds all elements, it ties them together. Within the border are three design blocks. The first is the art and the name of the company. The second is the actual schedule of classes, and the third is the screened coupon. Each block has distinctive formatting.

The first block contains two clip-art files, the company and flyer names, and two lines of information. The centered text reflects the text arrangement of the coupon frame, which helps to unify the piece as well. In addition, all but one line of text in the flyer is Times Roman, which also helps create unity. The arrangement allows for plenty of white space.

The second block is divided into two columns, to accommodate more copy. Left-aligned text repeats the vertical rules of the page border, and right-aligned tabs do the same. The gutter space and extra spacing between class heads add enough white space to make the block comfortable to read.

If you choose to reverse the text in the coupons, choose only three or fewer to present in this style; more than three frames of reversed text would be overwhelming to the reader.

Use a different type face to announce the coupon and make it stand out.

ROGHAN JOSH GOURMET FOODS
2436 N. 24th Street

VALUABLE COUPONS

ASAFETIDA 1/2 oz. jar **$1.00 OFF** **ROGHAN JOSH** Expires 3/29/93 Limit one per customer	**JAGGERY** 5 lb. bag **$2.00 OFF** **ROGHAN JOSH** Expires 3/29/93 Limit one per customer	**PHAO RICE** 1 lb. bag **$1.00 OFF** **ROGHAN JOSH** Expires 3/29/93 Limit one per customer
CARDAMOM 1/2 oz. jar **$1.00 OFF** **ROGHAN JOSH** Expires 3/29/93 Limit one per customer	**FENUGREEK SEED** 1/4 oz. jar **$.50 OFF** **ROGHAN JOSH** Expires 3/29/93 Limit one per customer	**ROSE WATER** 16 oz. jar **$1.00 OFF** **ROGHAN JOSH** Expires 3/29/93 Limit one per customer
RAJMA DAL 1 lb. bag **$1.00 OFF** **ROGHAN JOSH** Expires 3/29/93 Limit one per customer	**BASUMATI RICE** 1 lb. bag **$.50 OFF** **ROGHAN JOSH** Expires 3/29/93 Limit one per customer	**SAFFRON** 1/4 oz. jar **$1.00 OFF** **ROGHAN JOSH** Expires 3/29/93 Limit one per customer

ROGHAN JOSH SPICES
We offer spices from around the world!

2436 N. 24th Street   871-9701

Fig. 16.4   The same coupon flyer with screens added.

 HUMBLE OPINIONS
COMPUTER
TRAINING CENTER

SCHEDULE OF CLASSES   **SPRING 1993**
All classes last from 8:00 a.m. to 4:00 p.m. with a one hour lunch.

WORD PROCESSING

		WORD PROCESSING		
Introductory	---------------- April 12	Introductory	------------------ May 5
Intermediate	---------------- April 13	Intermediate	------------------ May 6
Advanced	------------------ April 14	Advanced	-------------------- May 9

SPREADSHEETS   **SPREADSHEETS**

Introductory	---------------- April 15	Introductory	---------------- May 10
Intermediate	---------------- April 16	Intermediate	---------------- May 11
Advanced	------------------ April 19	Advanced	------------------ May 12

DATABASES   **DATABASES**

Introductory	---------------- April 20	Introductory	---------------- May 15
Intermediate	---------------- April 21	Intermediate	---------------- May 16
Advanced	------------------ April 22	Advanced	------------------ May 17

DESKTOP PUBLISHING   **DESKTOP PUBLISHING**

Introductory	---------------- April 23	Introductory	---------------- May 19
Intermediate	---------------- April 26	Intermediate	---------------- May 20
Advanced	------------------ April 27	Advanced	------------------ May 21

ACCOUNTING   **ACCOUNTING**

Introductory	---------------- April 28	Introductory	---------------- May 20
Intermediate	---------------- April 29	Intermediate	---------------- May 21
Advanced	------------------ April 30	Advanced	------------------ May 22

 # 10% DISCOUNT COUPON

Bring this coupon when registering for classes, and receive a 10% DISCOUNT.
Offer expires May 15, 1993. Good only for classes listed above.

HUMBLE OPINIONS COMPUTER TRAINING CENTER
1127 E. MAIN STREET   BECKLEY, WV   (304) 251-5151

Fig. 16.5 A flyer containing borders, a screen, a Wingding, and a clip-art file.

The left-aligned heads add extra white space to the design.

The rule around the coupon repeats the rule around the page to provide unity and consistency.

The third block in the design consists of a discount coupon. The block is lightly screened (10%) and surrounded by a thin rule that's the same width (1 point) as the outside rule of the page border. For a point of emphasis, the coupon contains a Wingding hand pointing to the line of text, 10% DISCOUNT COUPON. This line of text is Frank Goth Cd, which makes it stand out even more.

Repeated elements—such as the rules, centered text, and vertical lines—help to hold a design together. Emphasis is provided through the use of the Wingding and a different typeface. When you design your own documents, keep these techniques in mind to ensure consistency and interest.

To produce the innovative flyer, do the following:

1. Choose File New. Choose the default style sheet. Choose OK or press Enter.

2. Choose Page Modify Page Layout.

3. In Modify, choose Margins & Columns. In Margins, the default of 1" is fine.

4. In Number of Columns, choose 2. For Gutter Width, type .5.

5. In Modify, choose Lines. Choose All and choose the last style in the Styles box (an uneven double rule). For Position, choose Close to Inside. Choose OK or press Enter.

6. Choose View Full Page. Draw a frame along the top margin. You size and position it in the next steps.

7. Choose Frame Modify Frame Layout.

8. In Frame, choose Type. Choose No Wrap Beside.

9. In Frame, choose Size & Position. In Size, for Width type 6.5; for Height, type 2.5.

10. In Position, Down from Top, type 1. For In from Left, type 1. In Margins, change all to .20.

11. In Frame, choose Lines & Shadows. Deselect All Positions. For Shadows, choose None. Choose OK or press Enter.

Copying and resizing a frame is quicker and easier than drawing a new frame and formatting it from scratch.

12. Copy the frame and paste it. Make the second frame about 1" by 1" to hold the clip art. Position it in the top corner of the first frame. Choose Frame Modify Frame Layout.

13. In Frame, choose Type. Choose Wrap Around. Choose OK or press Enter.

14. Choose File Import Picture. Choose the 35FLOPPY.SDW, or any clip art you like. Choose OK or press Enter.

15. Copy the frame and place the copy on the right edge of the margin, as in the figure.

16. Place the cursor to the right of the first clip art, and type the following:

HUMBLE OPINIONS(Enter)
COMPUTER(Enter)
TRAINING CENTER(Enter twice)
SCHEDULE OF CLASSES(Tab)**SPRING 1993**(Enter)
All classes last from 8:00 a.m. to 4:00 p.m. with a one hour lunch.

17. Select HUMBLE OPINIONS. Choose Tms Rmn, 18 point, bold, center.

18. Select COMPUTER TRAINING CENTER. Choose Tms Rmn, 28 point, (24 point if your printer does not support 28), bold, center.

19. Select SCHEDULE OF CLASSES SPRING 1993. Choose Tms Rmn, 14 point, bold. Activate the ruler and set a right tab at 6 1/8" on the ruler.

20. Select and center All classes last from 8:00 a.m. to 4:00 p.m. with a one hour lunch.

21. Place the cursor in the first column, below the frame, and type the following:

WORD PROCESSING(Enter)
Introductory(Tab, space)**April 12**(Enter)
Intermediate(Tab, space)**April 13**(Enter)
Advanced(Tab, space)**April 14**(Enter twice)
SPREADSHEETS(Enter)
Introductory(Tab, space)**April 15**(Enter)
Intermediate(Tab, space)**April 16**(Enter)
Advanced(Tab, space)**April 19**(Enter twice)

22. Select the classes and activate the ruler to set the tab. Choose the dashed leader; set a right tab at 3.82" on the ruler.

23. Select and bold WORD PROCESSING and SPREADSHEETS.

24. At this point you may type the rest of the classes according to the figure; or you could copy the text from WORD PROCESSING to Advanced April 19 (under SPREADSHEETS). Copy and paste the text until the first column is full.

Y ou can type beside the frame because you chose the Text Wrap Around in step 13.

25. Draw a frame near the bottom of the page. It may force some text from column one to column two. You size and position the frame in the next steps.

26. Choose Frame Modify Frame Layout.

27. In Frame, choose Type. Choose No Wrap Beside. In Display, choose Square Corners.

28. In Frame, choose Size & Position. In Size, for Width type **6.60**; for Height, type **1.75**.

29. In Position, **Down** from Top, type **8.25**. For **In** from Left, type **1**. In Margins, change the Top to **.20**.

30. In Frame, choose Lines & Shadows. Choose All Positions, and the first line Style. For Shadows, select None. For Background, choose the second column from the right, the second screened box from the top. Choose OK or press Enter.

31. Place the cursor in the frame and type the following:

(Tab)**F**(Tab)**10% DISCOUNT COUPON**(Enter)
Bring this coupon when registering for classes, and receive a 10% DISCOUNT.(Enter)
Offer expires May 15, 1993. Good only for classes listed above.(Enter twice)
HUMBLE OPINIONS COMPUTER TRAINING CENTER(Enter)
1127 E. MAIN STREET(eight spaces)**BECKLEY, WV**(eight spaces)**(304) 251-5151**

32. Select the first line of type, the F 10% DISCOUNT COUPON. Activate the ruler and set a left tab at 1", and a center tab at 3.25" on the ruler.

33. Select the F. Choose Wingding, 36 point.

34. Select 10% DISCOUNT COUPON. Choose Frank Goth Cd, 24 point, bold.

35. Select and center the next two lines of text, from Bring this coupon through Good only for classes listed above.

36. Place the cursor on the paragraph return after Good only for classes listed above. Change the size to 6 point.

37. Select the line beginning with HUMBLE OPINIONS. Choose Tms Rmn, 14 point, center, bold.

38. Select the address and phone number. Choose Tms Rmn, 12 point, center, bold.

39. At this point, either type the class list from the figure into the second column, or copy the first column and paste it in the second to see what the finished flyer looks like.

40. Save and print.

Designing a Double-Sided Flyer

Most flyers are one side only. However, if you have a great deal of information, you may need to print it on both sides. Generally speaking, the second side of the flyer should be formatted the same as the first. Be sure always to add the company name on both sides, in case the customer doesn't turn the flyer over. The design elements, such as rules, borders, typefaces and sizes, and so on, should be repeated on the second side as well.

When you print on both sides of a flyer, you can use one side as an attention grabber, as in figure 16.6. There's no real information on this side of the flyer, but the design attracts attention. The extremely large computer is a clip-art file, with reversed text added in a frame over the monitor. The word *HELP* is a familiar one to computer users because most programs contain on-line help at the touch of a key. In this flyer, the word *HELP* on the computer screen graphic, combined with the phrase *Your Key to Help*, refers your reader directly to computer training. This is a good example of attracting attention with your copy.

The first side of the flyer is tied to the second side by repetition of the typeface and by the double rules along the top and bottom margins. These rules are page rules, which means you set them up on the first page of the document and they repeat on every page of the document. This method ensures that the rules are exactly the same on every page.

Figure 16.7 illustrates side two of the flyer, with the top and bottom border rules repeated. The information on this page refers directly to training. The name of the company repeats from the front, as does the name of the flyer. Also repeated are the phone numbers, making it easy for the reader to call for information.

The body type on side two is formatted as hanging indents. The topic, or subhead, hangs in the margin, while the description of the class indents. Specific topics are easier to find, and this page is organized in an attractive way.

W ide margins, interparagraph spacing and hanging indents create a wealth of white space.

HUMBLE OPINIONS
COMPUTER TRAINING
Your Key to Help

Fig. 16.6   One side of a flyer designed to invite the customer to pick the flyer up and turn it over.

HUMBLE OPINIONS
COMPUTER TRAINING CENTER

1127 E. Main Street
(304) 251-5151

Beckley, WV 25801
800-250-2369

INTRODUCTORY

Basic Computers   Learn about memory, DOS, files, directories, and popular software programs. Explore printers, modems, and hard and floppy drives. Discover new and innovative uses for the PC in your business!

Word Processing   Learn basic editing, function keys, margin and tab settings, and editing codes. Use retrieve, save and print, block operations for moving text, and spell checking.

Database   Learn database concepts, create and edit a form, add and edit data, modify file structures, create reports, and add and delete records. Also learn to sort data in a variety of ways.

Spreadsheets   Create, save, retrieve, and print a spreadsheet. Learn to use formulas, and copy rows and columns. Format ranges, change column widths, and use absolute cell addresses.

Desktop Publishing   Become familiar with documents, mouse and keyboard functions, basic formatting of page such as typeface, type size and style, columns and margins, tabs, tables, frames, graphics, importing and exporting, bullets, and indents.

INTERMEDIATE CLASSES

Word Processing   Learn about macros, tables, formatting columns, setting font types and sizes, and mail merge. Print envelopes, large and small paper sizes; learn the finer points of page make-up on the word processor.

Spreadsheets   Become more efficient with spreadsheets by freezing titles, and using named ranges and windows. Perform logical evaluation, use cell protection, and control recalculation.

Desktop Publishing   Learn to use desktop publishing to produce fliers, resumes, forms, newsletters, brochures, and any document you need for your business. Bring in your own word processing to format any document you want.

(304) 251-5151   CALL TODAY   800-250-2369

Fig. 16.7   Side two of the flyer; when printed or copied, the rules should line up on both sides of the flyer.

If you have these flyers printed or copied at a print shop, be sure that the rules are lined up; if not, insist that the shop redo the job at no cost to you.

When printing this two-sided flyer on your printer, be sure to feed the paper so that it prints head to head. Also, the top rules of the first side should be lined up with the top rules of the second side—resulting in a pleasing design. Anytime you use rules like this, the piece looks more professional if they line up. To see if the rules are lined up, place the completed piece on a light table, or hold it up to the light. Ami Pro's page borders are spaced exactly the same. If your rules are not lined up, then adjust your paper feed. To produce the first side of the double-sided flyer, do the following:

1. Choose File New. Choose the default style sheet. Choose OK or press Enter.

2. Choose Page Modify Page Layout.

3. In Modify, choose Margins & Columns. In Margins, change all to .5.

4. In Modify, choose Lines. Choose Top and Bottom. Choose the second double rule in the Styles box. Choose OK or press Enter.

5. Choose View Full Page. Draw a frame. You size and position it in the next steps.

6. Choose Frame Modify Frame Layout.

7. In Frame, choose Type. Choose No Wrap Beside.

8. In Frame, choose Size & Position. In Size, for Width type 5.5; for Height, type 5.

9. In Position, Down from Top, type 1.93. For In from Left, type 1.40. In Margins, choose Clear Margins.

10. In Frame, choose Lines & Shadows. Deselect All Positions. For Shadows, choose None. Choose OK or press Enter.

The second frame will hold the word HELP.

11. Copy and paste the frame. Reduce the size of the second frame to approximately 2 1/2 by 1 1/2 inches. Move the frame out of the way for now.

12. Select the first, large frame. Choose File Import Picture. Choose the COMPUTER.SDW file. Choose OK or press Enter.

13. Select the smaller frame and position it on the monitor of the computer (in the figure, where HELP is located). Choose Frame Modify Frame Layout.

14. In Frame, choose Type. In Display, choose Transparent. Choose OK or press Enter.

15. Choose Text Font. Choose Tms Rmn, 60 point (or as close to that as your printer allows), and white. Choose OK or press Enter.

16. Place the cursor in the frame. Choose bold and center, and type **HELP**.

17. Reposition the frame so that HELP is centered within the monitor.

18. Place the cursor on the page. Press Enter 10 times, choose center, and type the following:

> **HUMBLE OPINIONS**(Enter)
> **COMPUTER TRAINING**(Enter)
> **Your Key to Help** (Enter seven times)

19. Return to page one. Select HUMBLE OPINIONS COMPUTER TRAINING. Choose Tms Rmn, 48 point, bold.

20. Select Your Key to Help. Choose Tms Rmn, 36 point, bold.

To format page two of the flyer, do the following:

1. Move to page two by choosing the Page icon in the Status bar or pressing the PgDn key.

2. Press Enter twice and type the following:

> **HUMBLE OPINIONS**(Enter)
> **COMPUTER TRAINING CENTER**(Enter twice)
> **1127 E. Main Street**(Tab)**Beckley, WV 25801**(Enter)
> **(304) 251-5151**(Tab)**800-250-2369**(Enter four times)
> **INTRODUCTORY CLASSES**(Enter twice)
> **Basic Computers**(Tab)**Learn about memory, DOS, files, directories, and popular software programs. Explore printers, modems, and hard and floppy drives. Discover new and innovative uses for the PC in your business!**(Enter twice)
> **Word Processing**(Tab)**Learn basic editing, function keys, margin and tab settings, and editing codes. Use retrieve, save and print, block operations for moving text, and spell checking.**(Enter twice)
> **Database**(Tab twice)**Learn database concepts, create and edit a form, add and edit data, modify file structures, create reports, and add and delete records. Also learn to sort data in a variety of ways.**(Enter twice)

3. At this point, you can either continue typing the information in figure 16.7; or you can copy and paste the information you have already typed to fill the page. Select and bold each class name (Basic Computers, Word Processing, and so on). At the end of the body text, press Enter three times and type the following:

   (304) 251-5151(seven spaces)**CALL TODAY**(seven spaces)
   800-250-2369

4. Select HUMBLE OPINIONS COMPUTER TRAINING CENTER. Choose 24 point, bold, center. The default type is Tms Rmn.

5. Select the text from 1127 E. Main Street through 800-250-2369. Change the type to 14 point. The default font is Tms Rmn. Activate the ruler.

6. On the ruler, set a right tab at 7.75" on the ruler.

7. Select INTRODUCTORY CLASSES. Choose bold, 14 point. The default font is Tms Rmn.

8. Place the cursor in the line Basic Computers. Choose **Style** Create Style.

9. In the New style text box, type **Outdent**. Choose Modify or press Enter.

10. In Modify, choose Ali**g**nment. In Indent, for **R**est type **1.50**. For Version 3.0, select **H**anging Indent.

11. In Tabs, set a left tab at 2" on the ruler. Choose **U**se Style Tabs. Choose OK or press Enter.

12. Choose **S**tyle **S**elect a Style. Select the type from Basic Computers through the last line Also learn to sort data in a variety of ways. In the Styles box, assign the Outdent style to the selected text.

13. Select (304) 251-5151 CALL TODAY 800-250-2369. Choose 24 point, bold, center.

14. Save and print.

Designing a Sales Flyer

Sales flyers are probably the most popular flyers used. One problem in designing a sales flyer is the tendency to squeeze in too much information. If there's too much material, or it's poorly organized, the flyer may not be read. To guarantee that your flyer is read, design it with plenty of white space, one or two points of emphasis only, and don't crowd too much information into the flyer.

Figure 16.8 illustrates a sales flyer that's easy to read and understand. The sale at Marie's Craft Shop applies to pottery and craft supplies. It gives the address of the shop and two disclaimers. The flyer incorporates large type, display type, and white space to catch the eye.

T he "sale" arrows attract attention immediately.

Fig. 16.8   A sales flyer that is well-organized and easy to read.

On the other hand, figure 16.9 illustrates a sales flyer that is unorganized and too busy. Not only are pottery and craft supplies listed, but weaving, candles, batik, and other categories are listed as well. The flyer isn't clear whether these supplies are on sale, too, or are merely other supplies that Marie carries. This ad is confusing and hard to read. In your sales flyers, try to limit the amount of information you include and organize the flyers so that they are easy to understand.

Fig. 16.9 A sales flyer that is too crowded, too busy, and unorganized.

The flyer in figure 16.8 is made up of several frames. The arrows are from one AmiDraw file. The bottom arrow was flipped horizontally in Ami Pro's drawing feature. Even if you don't have a mouse, you can still flip the image; Ami Pro flips the arrow, but does not flip the text within it. The arrows make the flyer more noticeable. In addition, the flyer contains two typefaces, Times Roman and Frank Goth Cd. The sans serif contrasts the serif type to make the flyer interesting as well.

To produce the flyer in figure 16.8, do the following:

1. Choose File New. Choose the default style sheet. Choose OK or press Enter.

2. Choose Page Modify Page Layout.

3. In Modify, choose Margins & Columns. In Margins, change all to .5.

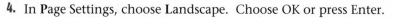

4. In Page Settings, choose Landscape. Choose OK or press Enter.

5. Draw a frame to fit the margins of the page. Choose Frame Modify Frame Layout.

6. In Modify, select Lines & Shadows. Choose All. In Line Style, choose the third pattern.

7. In Shadow, select Custom and type .09. Choose the bottom left corner to move the shadow to the left.

8. In Modify, choose Size & Position. In Margins, change all to .15. Choose OK or press Enter.

9. Draw a small frame inside the first.

10. Choose Frame Modify Frame Layout.

11. In Frame, choose Size & Position. In Size, for Width type 5.25; for Height, type 2.5.

12. In Position, Down from Top, type 2.28. For In from Left, type .67. In Margins, choose Clear Margins.

13. In Frame, choose Lines & Shadows. Deselect All. For Shadows, choose None. Choose OK or press Enter.

14. Copy the frame and paste it twice. Reposition the copied frames so that one is located where POTTERY SUPPLIES is in the figure, and the other frame is located where CRAFT SUPPLIES is on the figure.

15. Select the first frame, and choose File Import Picture.

16. Select the AmiDraw file, RTARROW.SDW. Choose OK or press Enter.

17. Choose Tools Drawing (or double click the frame containing the arrow). Choose ABC from the icons, and choose Text Font.

18. Choose Frank Goth Cd (Helvetica, if ATM isn't installed), 24 point, white. Choose OK or press Enter.

19. Place the cursor in the arrow to the left, and type SALE.

20. Select the frame containing the arrow. Copy and paste it. Reposition the second arrow as in the figure. Choose Draw Flip. Choose Horizontal (keyboard selects Horizontal by pressing Enter). The arrow flips, but the text doesn't.

21. Reposition the text in the second arrow.

C lip art must be placed in a frame of its own.

F ormat the clip art and enter the text before you copy the first frame.

Y ou can reposition the word by selecting the text block and moving it as a frame within the arrow.

Version 3.0 includes a Smart-Icon for the Smartype macro.

22. Place the cursor at the top of the page and type the following:

   MARIE'S CRAFT SHOP(Enter)
   3041 ELKS CIRCLE(Tab)**HUNTINGTON, WV**

23. Select `MARIE'S CRAFT SHOP`. Choose Tms Rmn, 60 point (or as close as possible), bold, center.

24. To change the apostrophe in `MARIE'S`, choose **Tools Macro**. In the secondary command menu, choose **Playback**. Choose SMARTYPE.SMM. Choose OK or press Enter.

25. Select the address. Choose 24 point, bold. On the ruler, set a left indent at .5"; set a right tab at 9.56".

26. Place the cursor in the frame to the right of the first sale arrow. Type the following:

   POTTERY SUPPLIES(Enter)
   10% OFF

27. Select `POTTERY SUPPLIES`. Choose Frank Goth Cd (or Helvetica), 36 point, bold, center.

28. Select `10% OFF`. Choose Frank Goth Cd (or Helvetica), 48 point, bold, center.

29. Place the cursor in the frame to the left of the second sale arrow. Type the following:

   CRAFT SUPPLIES(Enter)
   20% OFF

30. Format by following steps 27 and 28.

31. Draw one last small frame at the bottom of the page to contain the line of type beginning `SUPPLIES ARE LIMITED`.

32. Choose **Frame Modify Frame Layout**.

33. In Frame, choose **Lines & Shadows**. Deselect All. For Shadows, choose None. Choose OK or press Enter.

34. Place the cursor in the frame and type the following:

   SUPPLIES ARE LIMITED(nine spaces)**SALE ENDS MARCH 12, 1993**

Use frames to provide more control over where the text is placed.

35. Select the text and choose 18 point, bold, center.

36. Save and print.

Looking at Design

Experiment with Ami Pro to see what you can create. By using the graphic images, rules, borders, screens, Wingdings, and various typefaces and sizes, you can produce an attractive and eye-catching flyer design. Following are two additional flyer designs you may want to try. One contains a small amount of information, the other contains a great deal of information.

Figure 16.10 shows a design solution for a flyer with very little information. The type is larger than normal, making this flyer a good one to hang up, as well as to hand out. The typefaces used, Palatino and Avant Garde, give a different look to the piece. Palatino (serif) is an interesting typeface when used in all caps. It creates a horizontal movement because of the serifs, but it's also dark and somewhat heavy. On the other hand, the Avant Garde (sans serif) is light, open, and rounded. The bullet character is a Wingding, the lower case *v*. For more Wingding characters, refer to Appendix D.

In contrast to the last design, figure 16.11 illustrates a flyer containing a great deal of information. The type is much smaller: The typeface is New Century Schoolbook, which is perfect for small type sizes. Ami Pro's drawing feature was used to create the artwork at the top; it's balanced by the heavy rule at the bottom of the page. The distribution of text on the page creates white space for the eyes to rest upon.

Interesting bullets are used within a list to create an unusual effect in figure 16.11.

DESKTOP PUBLISHING TRADE SHOW

- ❖ Personal Computers
- ❖ Output/Imaging Devices
- ❖ Monitors
- ❖ Compact Disk Drives
- ❖ Data Compression Utilities
- ❖ Networking
- ❖ Scanners
- ❖ Color Printers

NEW HAVEN ARMORY
APRIL 21 - 25, 1993
HOURS 10 A.M. TO 6 P.M.

Fig. 16.10   Palatino and Avant Garde typefaces used to create a flyer.

MODERN ART - WHAT DOES IT MEAN?

A tutorial by C. L. Evans

○ Discover the use of color and texture as focal points.
○ Explore the feeling of detachment and distance in Modern art.
○ What role does the environment play?
○ Realize the architectural significance of large-scale painting.
○ Why is the technique of flattening space popular?

ARTISTS INCLUDED:

Andy Warhol	Wayne Thiebaud	Roy Lichtenstein
Robert Raushenburg	George Grosz	Jim Dine
Edward Kienholz	Gerald Oster	Robert Indiana
	Kurt Schwitters	Bridget Riley
	Victor De Vassarely	

Modern Art - What Does it Mean? by C. L. Evans is available from Treatise Publications, at $59.95 plus tax. For more information, or to purchase *Modern Art - What Does it Mean?* write Treatise Publications, 12881 North Davis Avenue, Suite 2309, Philadelphia, PA 23990.

Fig. 16.11 A flyer containing a lot of information, yet with enough white space to make reading easy.

Recapping

In this chapter you learned to create flyers for a variety of uses: price lists, coupons, class descriptions, and sales. Ami Pro techniques you learned, such as using dot and dash leaders, hanging indents, and flipping images, can be used in other business documents as well.

Producing a Brochure

A brochure is one of the most effective forms of advertising. It explains and details information about a company's products or services. A brochure is soft-sell, meaning it invites the customer to read at his or her leisure and refer back to it often. When designing a brochure, include information that is stable. Facts such as sale dates, price lists, and other temporary material should seldom go into a brochure because these facts are not stable. Instead, describe unchanging information such as descriptions of the product or service, maps, addresses, and phone numbers. Organize this stable information in a way that guides the customer through the brochure.

For detailed information on how to create a form like this see page 419.

Planning the Layout

Use Ami Pro's outline feature to help organize your information before you format the brochure.

Lead the eye in a methodical way. Tell the customer who you are and what you offer. Explain, in detail, how this benefits him or her. Finally, tell the customer where to purchase the product or service, and if you have room, briefly describe the main benefits again. Strengthen the effect of your organized copy with the design of your brochure.

The cover design invites the reader to open the brochure; attract the customer's attention with what you offer. The next panel the customer sees may list general services, a summary of benefits to the customer, special attractions of the product or service, and so on—this panel must persuade someone to read further. The following brochure panels (or pages) must depend on the copy, the design, and perhaps graphic images to maintain interest; these panels explain the details. Final panels either contain mailing information or repeat valuable information such as the company name, phone number, benefits, and so on.

Planning the Contents

Giving your customers useful information makes you an authority, someone they can come to for answers or solutions.

When producing your brochure, concentrate on what your company can offer the customer. Brochures that only describe a company, its history, staff, and qualities, hold little interest for readers; customers want to know what you can do for them. Add something pertinent to the brochure that makes customers depend on it, something they may want or need later. A paper company, for example, may add a list of paper weights and types used in printing letterheads. A computer training business can list keyboard shortcuts for a popular software program. Recipes, maps, important phone numbers, and coupons with varying expiration dates are all good ideas to include in your brochure.

Adding useful information helps ensure the customer will keep your brochure.

Brochures are special company advertising pieces. They are normally kept by the customer as reference pieces. Some may be kept for weeks, months, even years. For this reason, be careful to check all of your copy for consistency and accuracy; your spelling and grammar should be perfect. And be sure that the design of the brochure is useful and attractive.

The following document examples concentrate on the design elements you should include when creating a brochure, and on the ways Ami Pro can expedite production. You base the final design decisions about your brochure on your company, its products, its other advertising pieces, and the amount and type of copy.

Choosing a Format

You have many design choices to make. The size, shape, and number of panels and folds are the first considerations. You can consider the following configurations:

- 11 by 8 1/2 inches (landscape orientation) with two parallel folds that create three panels on the front and three on the back.

- 14 by 8 1/2 inches with three parallel folds that create four panels on the front and four on the back.

- 11 by 8 1/2 inches folded only once to create a 5 1/2-by-8 1/2-inch finished piece.

- 8 1/2 by 11 inches (portrait orientation).

- 8 1/2 by 14 inches (portrait orientation).

- 11 by 17 inches, folded to 8 1/2 by 11 inches.

Another design decision is whether to add rules, borders, graphic images, spreadsheets, and tables. Any graphics you add draw attention and make your brochure more attractive. In addition, Ami Pro's DDE (Dynamic Data Exchange) and OLE (Object Linking and Embedding) capabilities enable you to update the information in tables, charts, and spreadsheets that you add to your brochure. The following document examples offer you many ideas and variations on adding graphics to your brochures. For more information about DDE and OLE, refer to Appendix B.

Choosing Paper and Ink

An element relating to your brochure design is the paper you print it on. Because a brochure is a reference piece, it prints on higher quality paper than flyers or letters. Use a 60# or 70# book paper, either coated or uncoated; smooth, linen, or enamel finishes are all good choices. Choose a white, ivory, or pastel color for the brochure, so that the eyes won't tire easily. Furthermore, if you use colored ink, be sure that it combines with the paper choice for easy reading.

Black, blue, green, and red are the best choices for ink color. Within any of these colors, you have even more choices (navy blue, wedgewood, process blue, reflex blue, and so on). You may choose from one to four colors of ink to make your brochure more noticeable. By printing in black and one other color, you can attract a lot of attention. If you have good color photographs of your product, consider printing in full color (four-color process). The choice you make is limited only by your budget.

Refer to Chapter 4 for more information on paper and ink choices.

Some new Ami Pro features introduced in this chapter include easier modifying of style sheets, using column breaks, creating and using styles based on other styles, and using the Status bar to change typefaces and type sizes. Because you are now familiar with many of the basic formatting techniques used in Ami Pro, only the new techniques used in this chapter are fully described. In addition, you may want to use your own information to fill the designs instead of typing from the examples.

In the following document instructions, you may want to use the Status bar to change typefaces if you use a mouse. Click the Typeface button in the Status bar to display a list of available typefaces. You can also click on the type size and the styles. For more information, refer to Appendix A.

Designing a Basic Brochure

The first brochure design is basic and simple to produce. The size is 11 by 8 1/2 inches in a landscape orientation. You print the second page on the back of the first, then you fold the brochure in half to create four pages. This is a traditional brochure design that is informal and uncomplicated.

The basic brochure design is also good for adding more pages; two 11 x 8 1/2 sheets create an 8-page brochure; three produce a 12-page brochure, and so on.

When designing this type of brochure in Ami Pro, it's easiest to start with the back panel because you divide the page in columns; when typing into columns, you naturally fill in the information from left to right. Figure 17.1 illustrates the front (right) and back (left) panels of the brochure.

Notice the first thing the customer sees is *Whitewater*, thus attracting anyone interested in rafting or kayaking. Additionally, the art on the front cover reinforces the message. Because the first thing most people do when picking up a brochure is to turn it over to see the back (in the left column), this one offers general information about the two rivers discussed inside the brochure. The back panel mirrors the rules used on the front to help unify the piece. Because there's a lot of information on the back, the text is justified with first line indents.

If the prospective customer finds the information interesting, he or she will open the brochure. The inside panels (see fig. 17.2) repeat the rules to tie the piece together. The body text is formatted the same as on the back panel; and the inside also includes a bulleted list that helps attract the reader to that section.

WHITEWATER

in Wild, Wonderful West Virginia

WHITEWATER TRIPS · OAK HILL, WV
114 MAIN STREET ·

1-800-250-0009

ABOUT THE NEW RIVER

The New River, located in the New River Gorge National Park, is the oldest river in North America. Some say it's the second oldest river in the world! Winding through the Appalachian mountains, the New River provides exciting, and surprising, whitewater rafting. The beautiful scenery, monumental mountains, and calming pools of the New will beckon you to return.

Major rapids, ranging from Class II to Class V, are approximately 75 to 100 feet apart. This gives you just enough time to recover from the last one! The three most popular rapids, all Class V, are the Middle Keeney, the Lower Keeney, and the Double Z. They're full of huge rocks, colossal holes, and at level three and above, monster waves. We recommend an experience level of intermediate to advanced to run the New River.

ABOUT THE GAULEY RIVER

The Gauley River is the "Run of the East". Cutting a deep canyon through beautiful mountains, it sounds like a dream! Depending on the level, the weather, and your ability, it can be a nightmare! The boulders are deeply undercut, and the sandstone formations create dangerous mazes. If you can handle it, you're in for the run of your life.

The Gauley contains 100 rapids in 26 miles; and they come fast and furious!!! Ten of these rapids are in the Class IV to Class V+ category. You absolutely must have prior rafting experience; we recommend an experience level of advanced to expert. Since swimming in the Gauley is strictly forbidden, that should give you an idea of its dangers. Some of the Class V to V+ rapids you encounter on the Gauley are the Lost Paddle, Pillow Rock, Koontz Flume, and Sweet's Falls. You'll thrill to the exuberant pace of the Gauley River!

Since the Gauley's level of water depends on releases from the Summersville Dam, September is the primary season for the Gauley. The water ranges from three to five feet; the weather is cool and dry. The Gauley River supplies excitement, thrills, and the run of your life!

Fig. 17.1 The front and back covers of a basic brochure design.

NEW RIVER — ONE-DAY TRIP

We meet at our headquarters, ready to go by 8:00 a.m. The bus ride takes about 45 minutes; the safety lecture takes 10 minutes. Gear up and we're ready to go. We put in upstream from the bridge at Thurmond at 9:00 a.m. (or as sharp as possible) and begin our trip on the New.

Around noon we stop just after the Keeneys for lunch. Lunch is provided by Hurst Caterers and consists of luncheon meats, homemade bread, vegie pitas, fruit, and homemade cookies for dessert. Lunch takes about an hour; we put in again.

Several hours later, we take out at Fayette Station. After your bus trip to headquarters, we provide you with free refreshments. Our restaurant stays open until 9:00 p.m. if you want some dinner.

NEW RIVER — TWO-DAY TRIP

This is a leisurely trip that covers both the Upper and Lower New River. The Upper New is known for it's long stretches of pools and great fishing! Our dingy rides with us throughout the trip to supply us with fishing equipment, tents, food, and extra clothes. When you sign up for this trip, we send you a list of things you need to bring.

We meet at headquarters by 9:00 a.m. and catch the bus to the river. At 10:00 a.m. we put in. Around 11:30 a.m, we stop for lunch at a spot famous for its great fishing. We'll spend 3 hours at this spot, and then put in again. At about 5:00 p.m., we reach Surprise, which is the first rapid in the Lower New River. After this rapid, we take out and have a gourmet meal, provided by Hurst Caterers. At this point, we spend the night. We provide tents, campfires, marshmallows, and songs. You provide anything else you need.

On day two, we're up and going by 7:00 a.m. Put in by 8:00 a.m. and we're ready for a day of exciting whitewater! Lunch is around noon and lasts for an hour. Several hours well-spent in the afternoon, and we take out at Fayette Station. Two relaxing, fun-filled days on the New River.

THE GAULEY TRIP

The Gauley trip begins at 7:00 a.m. at our headquarter. The bus ride takes approximately one-and-a-half hours; but that's OK, because that's how long the safety lecture takes! We put in just below the Summersville Dam at around 8:30 a.m. From there its a frenzied, devil-may-care trip.

We do stop around noon for those who are willing and able to eat; most of you, however, will probably meditate on the meaning of life. We put in again around 1:00 p.m. and continue on our way. Take out is at Koontz Bend. A short walk through the railroad tunnel, and we catch the bus back to headquarters. We'll serve refreshments, and medical care is available for anyone who feels faint.

OTHER AREA ATTRACTIONS

Included at our headquarters are:

* Camping and Picnic Facilities
* Horseback Riding
* Mountain Hiking and Biking

Other Area Attractions include:

* New River Gorge Bridge
* New River Gorge National Park
* New River Gorge Visitors' Center
* Grandview State Park
* Grandview Outdoor Theater
* Babcock State Park
* Hawks Nest State Park
* Hawks Nest Tram

Fig. 17.2   The two inside panels of the brochure.

To create the front and back covers of the brochure, follow these steps:

1. Choose **File New**. Choose the default style sheet and choose OK or press Enter.

2. Choose **Page Modify Page Layout**.

3. In Modify, choose **Margins & Columns**. Change all margins to **.35**. Select 2 columns. Set a Gutter Width of **.75**.

4. In Modify, choose **Page Settings**. Change the orientation to Landscape. Choose OK or press Enter.

5. Choose **Style Create Style**. To name the New Style, type **Line Head**. Choose Modify or press Enter.

6. In Modify, choose **Font**. Choose Times, 14 point, bold, italic.

7. In Modify, choose **Spacing**. In Paragraph Spacing change Below to **.15**, Above to **.10**. Choose Always.

8. In Modify, choose **Lines**. Choose Line **Above** and the next to the last line style (a 3-point rule and a 1-point rule). In Spacing, type **.05**. The Length should be Margins. Choose OK or press Enter.

9. Choose **Style Modify Style**. In the Styles box, choose Body Text.

10. In Modify, choose **Font**. Choose Tms Rmn, 12 point.

11. In Modify, choose **Alignment**. Choose Justified. In Indent, choose the First at .30.

12. In Modify, turn on **Hyphenation**. Choose OK or press Enter.

13. Choose **Style Create Style**. To name the New Style, type **Line Below**. Choose Modify or press Enter.

14. In Modify, choose **Font**. Change the type to 10 point. The default is Tms Rmn.

15. In Modify, choose **Spacing**. Line Spacing should be Single. In Paragraph Spacing change Below to 0, Above to 0, and choose Always.

16. In Modify, choose **Lines**. Choose Line **Below** and the next to the last line style (a 3-point rule and a 1-point rule). In Spacing, type **.05**. The Length should be Margins. Choose OK or press Enter.

17. Place the cursor in the left column and type the following:

    ABOUT THE RIVER(Enter)

Y ou may need to set your margins to .40" and the gutter to .80" if your printer limits the printing edge.

You can assign styles by using the function keys listed beside them in the Styles box.

18. Continue to type your own information, or the text as it appears in figure 17.1, pressing Enter after each paragraph and three Enters before the second head, ABOUT THE GAULEY.

19. Select the two heads and change them to the style Line Head (use either the Styles box, or the Status bar).

20. Place the cursor on the last line in the column and change it to the style Line Below.

21. Place the cursor at the top of the second column and press Enter. Change the style of the first paragraph return to the Line Head style. Use the arrow key to move down one line.

22. Press Enter and type the following:

    WHITEWATER(Enter)
    in Wild, Wonderful(Enter)
    West Virginia(Enter eight times)
    WHITEWATER TRIPS(Enter)
    114 MAIN STREET(2 spaces, Alt+0183, 2 spaces)**OAK HILL, WV** (Enter twice)
    1-800-250-0009(Enter twice)

23. Change WHITEWATER to DomCasual, 68 point (or as close as your printer allows), bold, and center aligned. Choose Text Indention. For First Line Indent, type **0**. Choose OK or press Enter.

24. Change in Wild, Wonderful West Virginia to Times, 24 point, bold, center with no indent on first line.

25. Change WHITEWATER TRIPS and 114 MAIN STREET to WV to Times 18 point, bold, and center with no indent.

26. Change the 800 number to Times, 36 point, bold, center with no indent.

27. Add a clip-art or other graphic image to the space above the address. (The one in the figure is a pen and ink drawing that was manually pasted-up.)

To create the second page of the brochure, follow these steps:

1. Enter your own information, or type from figure 17.2 pressing Enter after each paragraph. Press three Enters before the second head in the first column, and four Enters before the second head in the second column. Type all text first; then assign heads and bullet text.

2. Select each head and assign it the Line Head style.

3. Select the last paragraph return in the first column and assign it the Line Below style.

4. The two subheads in the section, OTHER AREA ATTRACTIONS, are Body Text. Select and bold each one, then remove the indention.

5. To create the bullets, type the text, select it, and assign it the Bullet 1 style in the Styles box or in the Status bar.

6. Choose Style Modify Style. In the Styles box, choose Bullet 1.

7. In Modify, choose Spacing. In Paragraph Spacing, change Above to .05. Choose OK or press Enter.

8. Press Ctrl+Home to go to the beginning of the document. Choose Tools Spell Check. Choose OK or press Enter and answer any questions from the spell checker.

9. Choose Tools Macros. In the secondary command list, choose Playback. From the Macro list, choose SMARTYPE.SMM. Choose OK or press Enter.

10. Save your brochure.

11. To print the brochure, print page one. Turn it so that page two prints head to head and place it in your printer's paper tray. Print page two.

Designing a Text and Graphic Brochure

A more traditional format for a brochure is an 11-by-8 1/2-inch sheet divided into three panels on either side and folded twice. This size and shape of brochure provides six sections for information and is the perfect size for mailing (either in an envelope, or by itself). The following brochure is in this traditional format.

Figure 17.3 illustrates the first side of the brochure. The front cover (the third panel) announces the advertiser (Marie's), the address, phone number, and operating hours. Notice the design is similar to that of Marie's newspaper ad produced in Chapter 15, "Producing an Advertisement." The text is right aligned, the typeface is Times Roman, and the brochure uses the same clip-art logo as in Marie's ad.

You could leave the white space on the cover for emphasis, or add a photograph, perhaps in full color.

To produce a typographical or em dash, type two hyphens; the Smartype macro converts double hyphens to em dashes.

The top and bottom rules should line up from front to back. If they do not, first check that the paper is feeding straight; then, if necessary, adjust your document.

MARIE'S

CRAFT SHOP
ART GALLERY
SCULPTURE GARDEN

OPEN DAILY
10:00 A.M. TO 5:00 P.M.

**3041 ELKS CIRCLE
HUNTINGTON**
(304) 211-5505

ABOUT MARIE'S CRAFT SHOP

Marie's Craft Shop stocks the area's largest selection of arts and crafts. With more than 2,500 square feet of property, there is not only a craft shop, but also an art gallery and sculpture garden.

The Craft Shop separates into two specialized areas. One is completely stocked with the materials you need to create hundreds of crafts. Materials such as wax and wick, clay and glazes, gold, pewter and silver, looms and fibers; any and all of your craft needs. The other area of the store is filled with completed, original, hand-made crafts. Pottery, hand-blown glass, weavings, quilts, candles, jewelry, and much, much more, gathered locally!

Marie's Craft Shop also includes two rooms set apart as an art gallery. Paintings and photographs from the area are displayed for your enjoyment. All art works are for sale.

Finally, Marie's Craft Shop has an outside sculpture garden. Beautiful trees, flowers, and sculpted bushes encompass the area's finest bronze, wooden, and steel sculptures. Some works are as tall as 50 feet, other smaller ones hide and peek from the flora.

Visit Marie's Craft Shop, Art Gallery and Sculpture Garden. Open daily from 10:00 a.m. to 5:00 p.m. Special tours are available.

COMMON RECIPES FOR CLAY BODIES

Specific mixtures for clay bodies vary according to their use. Following are some common formulas for Earthenware and Stoneware, and their firing temperatures. Use these formulas only as a guide for mixing your clays (hand-built or thrown). The formulas are in parts per hundred. All clays, grog, feldspar, and so on, are available at Marie's Craft Shop.

EARTHENWARE BODIES	FORMULAS
Fires to a reddish color, matures between cones 08 and 1	60 red clay 22 red fire clay 8 ball clay 10 grog
Fires white, matures between cones 08 and 1	50 fire clay 25 ball clay 7 flint 9 soda feldspar 8 talc

STONEWARE BODIES	FORMULAS
Fires brown (when oxidized), matures between cone 6 and cone 9	42 fire clay 26 stoneware clay 25 red clay 7 soda feldspar
Fires orange-brown (reduction), matures at cone 9	30 stoneware 40 fire clay 8 red clay 12 flint 10 grog

More recipes available at Marie's!

Fig. 17.3   A brochure designed for Marie's Craft Shop.

The front cover of the brochure folds over the back cover (far left). When opened, the customer sees a description of the three shops and a summary of the inventory. The right-aligned heads and top and bottom rules create consistency throughout the brochure.

There is also a large amount of white space used in the design. The heads create unusual white space that is emphasized by the first line indent of the body text. Notice, too, the line spacing of the body text. A few points added to the line spacing make the information easier to read and add extra white space to the overall design.

The center panel serves as a reference piece to help make the brochure a keeper. Any potter who notices the clay recipes on the back of the brochure (the second place you look), grabs it up. The right-aligned heads and rules repeat; furthermore, the rules of the table mirror the column rules. Once again, Marie's Craft Shop is mentioned several times in the text to remind the customer where the brochure came from.

The inside of the brochure (see fig. 17.4) remains consistent in design with the outside of the brochure. The top and bottom column rules line up, the first head in each column lines up with the others, and the white space is similar to that of the outside of the brochure.

Two interesting and useful Ami Pro features used in this design are in the Modify Style dialog box. First, a Next Style is assigned to several styles of text. For example, the 18-point head has Body Text assigned as the Next Style. This means after you type the head, you press Enter, and the style automatically changes to Body Text. This type of assigning styles is useful in many circumstances. Because this brochure uses rules in the columns, you must format each panel as you type it so that the rules line up. Assigning Next Styles speeds up typing and formatting.

The second new feature you use in this design is applying column breaks to help anchor the rules at the top and bottom of each column. Anchoring, plus the Next Style feature, makes the rules easier to do.

To format the outside of the brochure, follow these steps:

1. Choose **File New**. Choose the default style sheet and choose OK or press Enter.

2. Choose **Page Modify Page Layout**.

3. In Modify, choose **Margins & Columns**. Change all margins to **.35**. Select 3 columns with a **Gutter Width** of **.35**.

4. In Modify, choose **Page Settings**. Change the orientation to Landscape. Choose OK or press Enter.

Sufficient gutter space (.30 inches or more) allows room for the justified text to breathe.

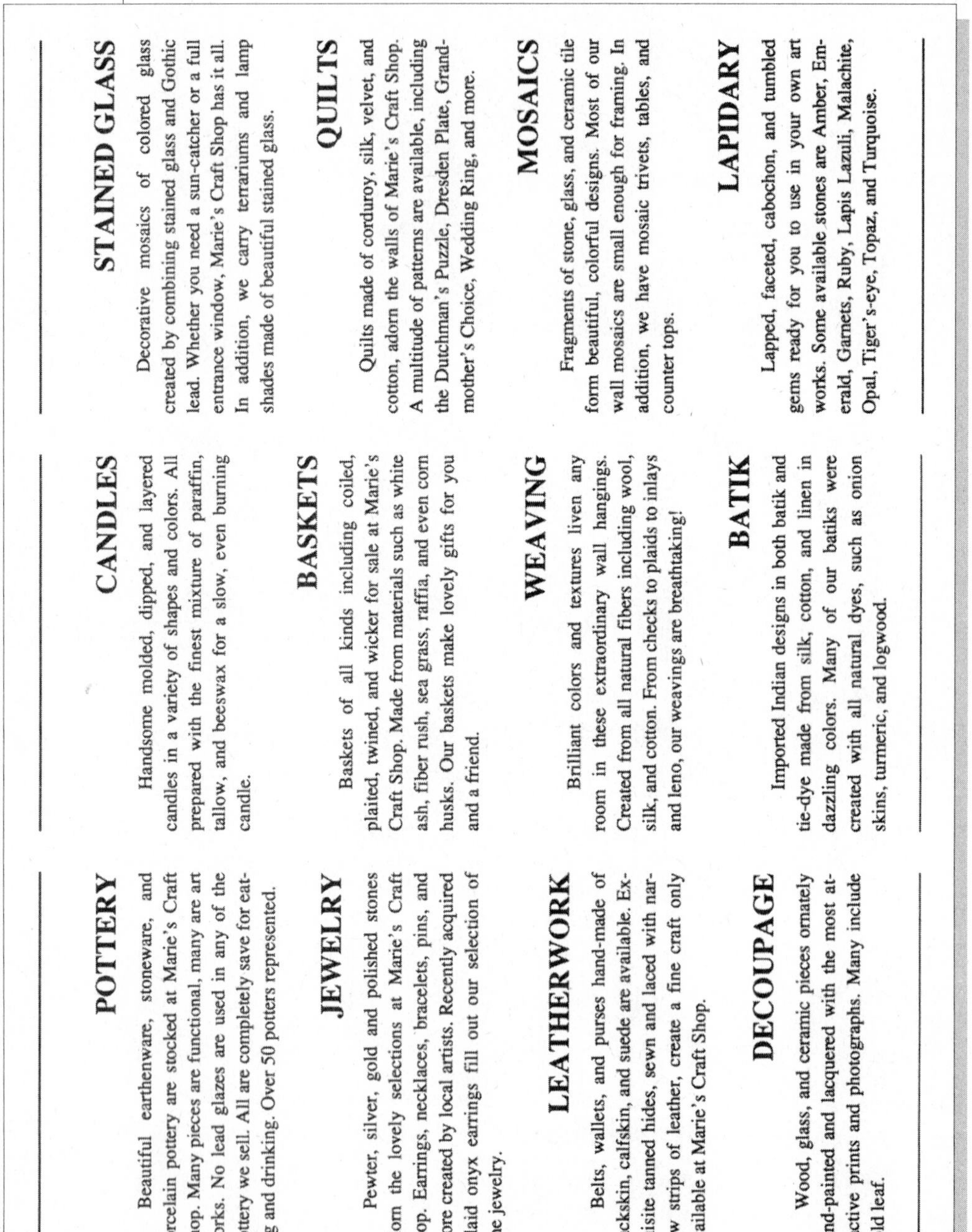

POTTERY

Beautiful earthenware, stoneware, and porcelain pottery are stocked at Marie's Craft Shop. Many pieces are functional, many are art works. No lead glazes are used in any of the pottery we sell. All are completely save for eating and drinking. Over 50 potters represented.

JEWELRY

Pewter, silver, gold and polished stones adorn the lovely selections at Marie's Craft shop. Earrings, necklaces, bracelets, pins, and more created by local artists. Recently acquired inlaid onyx earrings fill out our selection of fine jewelry.

LEATHERWORK

Belts, wallets, and purses hand-made of buckskin, calfskin, and suede are available. Exquisite tanned hides, sewn and laced with narrow strips of leather, create a fine craft only available at Marie's Craft Shop.

DECOUPAGE

Wood, glass, and ceramic pieces ornately hand-painted and lacquered with the most attractive prints and photographs. Many include gold leaf.

CANDLES

Handsome molded, dipped, and layered candles in a variety of shapes and colors. All prepared with the finest mixture of paraffin, tallow, and beeswax for a slow, even burning candle.

BASKETS

Baskets of all kinds including coiled, plaited, twined, and wicker for sale at Marie's Craft Shop. Made from materials such as white ash, fiber rush, sea grass, raffia, and even corn husks. Our baskets make lovely gifts for you and a friend.

WEAVING

Brilliant colors and textures liven any room in these extraordinary wall hangings. Created from all natural fibers including wool, silk, and cotton. From checks to plaids to inlays and leno, our weavings are breathtaking!

BATIK

Imported Indian designs in both batik and tie-dye made from silk, cotton, and linen in dazzling colors. Many of our batiks were created with all natural dyes, such as onion skins, turmeric, and logwood.

STAINED GLASS

Decorative mosaics of colored glass created by combining stained glass and Gothic lead. Whether you need a sun-catcher or a full entrance window, Marie's Craft Shop has it all. In addition, we carry terrariums and lamp shades made of beautiful stained glass.

QUILTS

Quilts made of corduroy, silk, velvet, and cotton, adorn the walls of Marie's Craft Shop. A multitude of patterns are available, including the Dutchman's Puzzle, Dresden Plate, Grandmother's Choice, Wedding Ring, and more.

MOSAICS

Fragments of stone, glass, and ceramic tile form beautiful, colorful designs. Most of our wall mosaics are small enough for framing. In addition, we have mosaic trivets, tables, and counter tops.

LAPIDARY

Lapped, faceted, cabochon, and tumbled gems ready for you to use in your own art works. Some available stones are Amber, Emerald, Garnets, Ruby, Lapis Lazuli, Malachite, Opal, Tiger's-eye, Topaz, and Turquoise.

Fig. 17.4 The inside of Marie's brochure.

5. Choose Style **M**odify Style. In the Styles box, choose Body Text.

6. In Modify, choose **F**ont. Change the type to Tms Rmn, 12 point.

7. In Modify, choose **A**lignment. Change the type to Justified. In Indent, choose the First at **.35**.

8. In Modify, choose S**p**acing. Choose Custom and type **.22**.

9. In Modify, turn on **H**yphenation. Choose OK or press Enter.

10. Choose Style **C**reate Style. To name the New Style, type **18 Point** and choose Modify or press Enter.

11. In Modify, choose **F**ont. Change the type to 18 point bold. Tms Rmn is the default font.

12. In Modify, choose Ali**g**nment. Choose **R**ight, change all indents to **0**.

13. In Modify, choose **B**reaks. Choose Next Style, choose Body Text. Choose OK or press Enter.

14. Choose Style **C**reate Style. To name the New Style, type **Line Above** and choose Modify or press Enter.

15. In Modify, choose **F**ont. Change the type to 10 point. The default font is Tms Rmn.

16. In Modify, choose Ali**g**nment. Change all indents to **0**.

17. In Modify, choose **L**ines. Choose Line **A**bove and the second line style. In Spacing, type **.15**. The Length should be **M**argins.

18. In Modify, choose **B**reaks. Choose Column Break Before Paragraph. For Next S**t**yle, choose 18 Point. Choose OK or press Enter.

19. Choose Style **C**reate Style. In **B**ased On, choose Line Above. To name the New Style, type **Line Below**. Choose Modify or press Enter.

20. In Modify, choose **L**ines. Deselect Line A**b**ove, and choose Line Below. In S**p**acing, type **.10**. Select the second line style.

21. In Modify, choose **B**reaks. Choose Column Break After Paragraph. For Next S**t**yle, choose Line Above. Choose OK or press Enter.

22. The cursor is in position in the first column. From the Status bar, choose the Style button. Choose Line Above to apply to the first paragraph return.

23. Press Enter (the style changes to 18 Point) and type the following:

    ABOUT MARIE'S CRAFT SHOP(Enter twice)

I n the Create Style dialog box, the default for New Style to be **B**ased on is Body Text.

T he descriptive style name Line Above is easy to identify in the Styles box. Transfer this paragraph style to other style sheets if you use it often.

U sing the Next Style feature saves you time and allows to format a document as you type it.

Divide the head after you type it so that the head won't change to Body Text after the first line.

When row height is on Automatic, the row enlarges as the text wraps. If you press Enter in a row, the row enlarges by one line.

24. Place the cursor after MARIE'S and press Enter. Place the cursor on the last paragraph return; it is the Body Text style.

25. Enter your own information, or type the material in figure 17.3 to the bottom of the first column. Press Enter after each paragraph and twice after the last paragraph in the column.

26. Place the cursor on the last paragraph return in column 1. Change the style to Line Below.

27. Press Enter. The cursor appears at the top of column 2, and its style automatically changes to Line Above. Press Enter and type the following:

COMMON RECIPES FOR CLAY BODIES(Enter twice)

28. Place the cursor after COMMON RECIPES FOR and press Enter.

29. Enter your own text, or type from figure 17.3, pressing Enter twice after the first paragraph.

30. To form the table, Choose Tools Tables. Choose 2 for Number of Columns, and 6 for Number of Rows. Choose Layout.

31. In Default Rows, be sure that Automatic is turned on. Choose OK or press Enter, twice.

32. Select the first column and change its width to 2".

33. Place the cursor in the first cell and type the following:

EARTHENWARE BODIES(Tab)**FORMULAS**(Tab)
Fires to a reddish color, matures between cones 08 and 1(Tab)**60 red clay**(Enter)
22 red fire clay(Enter)
8 ball clay(Enter)
10 grog(Tab)
Fires white, matures between cones 08 and 1(Tab)**50 fire clay**(Enter)
25 ball clay(Enter)
7 flint(Enter)
9 soda feldspar(Enter)
8 talc(Tab)
STONEWARE BODIES(Tab)**FORMULAS**(Tab)
Fires brown (when oxidized), matures between cone 6 and cone 9(Tab)**42 fire clay**(Enter)
26 stoneware clay(Enter)

25 **red clay**(Enter)
7 **soda feldspar**(Tab)
Fires orange-brown (reduction), matures at cone 9(Tab)30
stoneware(Enter)
40 **fire clay**(Enter)
8 **red clay**(Enter)
12 **flint**(Enter)
10 **grog**

34. Change EARTHENWARE BODIES FORMULAS and STONEWARE BODIES FORMULAS to Helv, 10 point, bold, center.

35. Choose **S**tyle **M**odify Style. In the Styles box, choose Table Text.

36. In Modify, choose **F**ont. Choose Helv, 10 point.

37. In Modify, choose **A**lignment. Left Align the text.

38. In Modify, choose **S**pacing. Choose **S**ingle. Choose OK or press Enter.

39. Select the table. Choose Ta**b**le Lines/Shades.

40. Choose **T**op and **B**ottom, and the first Line Style. Choose OK or press Enter.

41. Select EARTHENWARE FORMULAS. Following step 39, change the Top and **B**ottom lines to the second line style. Repeat with STONEWARE FORMULAS.

42. Place the cursor below the table and press Enter. Type the following:

More recipes available at Marie's!(Enter twice)

43. Select the text, and choose bold and center aligned with no indents.

44. Select the last return on the page, change its style to Line Below. Press Enter.

45. At the top of column three, press Enter and type the following:

MARIE'S(Enter)
CRAFT SHOP(Enter)
ART GALLERY(Enter)
SCULPTURE GARDEN(Enter)

46. Select CRAFT SHOP, ART GALLERY, and SCULPTURE GARDEN. Change the style to the 18 Point head, changing the spacing to single.

U sing thinner rules (.75 point) within the table divides the information.

47. Select MARIE'S. Choose 36 point. The default is Tms Rmn.

48. Draw a frame above MARIE'S. Choose Frame Modify Frame.

49. In Type, choose No Wrap Beside. In Size & Position, choose Width 2.5 and Height .5. Choose Clear Margins. In Lines & Shadows, deselect All, then select Shadow None. Choose OK or press Enter.

50. Choose File Import Picture. From AmiDraw, choose ARTTOOLS.SDW, or any clip art you want. Choose OK or press Enter.

51. If you use a mouse, you can double-click on the art and go to the Drawing feature. If you like, you can enlarge the art or stretch it. Reposition the art so that it is right aligned.

52. Place the cursor after the last return in the column. Press Enter until you reach the 6.5" mark on the vertical ruler, or Line 22 in the Status bar.

53. Choose Text Alignment Right. Type the following:

    OPEN DAILY(Enter)
    10:00 A.M. TO 5:00 P.M.(Enter twice)
    3041 ELKS CIRCLE(Enter)
    HUNTINGTON(Enter)
    (304) 211-5505(Enter)

54. Select the address, city, and phone number and choose 14 point, bold. The default font is Tms Rmn.

55. Select the paragraph return before the address, and change the type to 6 point.

56. Select the last paragraph return and change the style to Line Below.

To continue to the next page, press Enter. The cursor appears on page two, column one, in the style of Line Above. To format the second page, enter your own information or type from figure 17.4. Format the heads and lines as you did in the first page. Save your document. To print, place the printed page one in the paper tray so that it prints head to head with page two.

Designing an Innovative Brochure

A brochure that has an unusual design is more likely to attract attention than one that's like all the others. Unusual designs include a different

---

Alternatively, create your own logo in Ami Pro's drawing feature.

size, shape, or a surprising fold. The next design is a twist on the normal use of an 8 1/2-by-14-inch format. Generally, this size brochure is in landscape orientation and is folded three times. The following design is in portrait orientation and folds only twice. The orientation, combined with the stepped fold, makes the brochure design most unusual.

Figure 17.5 illustrates page one of the innovative brochure. At the top is a mailing panel, followed by the company name and two classes offered. The section about the company describes how the company can benefit the customer. Finally, two more classes are listed. The primary typeface used is Times Roman, and the extra paragraph spacing provides white space. The heads are in Helvetica for variety and emphasis.

The second page of the brochure (see fig. 17.6) again lists the company's name and adds the address and phone numbers. The rest of the page describes the classes in detail and ends with the phone numbers repeated. Note the body text is indented to provide the correct line length for the type size. Left-aligned body and heads and extra paragraph spacing add to the white space, which makes reading easier.

When printing this format, you print the head of page two to the foot of page one to get the final fold. Figure 17.7 illustrates the final, folded brochure. The class names and phone numbers stand out on each step of the piece, helping to reinforce the company name. To mail this brochure, you must fasten the steps. You can staple once in the center or on each side; or you can use small adhesive circles or colored tape to fasten the middle of the steps.

The mailing panel is on the opposite side of the final, folded brochure. Figure 17.8 illustrates the mailing panel.

When customers open the first fold of the brochure, they see the information about the company and the benefits it offers (see fig 17.9). Two classes now show, along with the phone numbers. When customers open the final fold, they see the full page of class descriptions (figure 17.6).

To fold the brochure, begin with page two facing you. Fold the top over at 6 1/2 inches so that the phone numbers are still showing at the bottom of page two. The second fold is at 2 3/4 inches, completing the three steps to the brochure. The fold is the hardest part of the design.

The Helvetica heads (class names) fall on the folds to produce a mini table of contents.

The inside of this brochure could also be used for a flyer or a newspaper ad.

HUMBLE OPINIONS
COMPUTER TRAINING
1127 E. Main Street
Beckley, WV 25801

HUMBLE OPINIONS
COMPUTER TRAINING

WORD PROCESSING   DESKTOP PUBLISHING

ABOUT HUMBLE OPINIONS

Humble Opinions offers training in more than 30 popular software programs. Please call for a list of brand names. Introductory, Intermediate, and Advanced classes are scheduled weekly. No matter what level you are, we have a class to suit your needs. In business for more than 10 years, and serving the business community in the tri-state area, Humble Opinions is here to serve you!

Each class instructor is a professional. Two months of intensive training at our headquarters in West Virginia gives these instructors knowledge and experience with their particular software program. Each instructor trains in only two programs, and is therefore an expert in the software. With no more than five students per class, every student receives quality training. We feel it's important for the student to spend time with the instructors in a hands-on situation.

Classes are taught in our spacious classroom containing 15 personal computers and 12 printers. The personal computers are of various capacities and memories. The printers represented include dot matrix, inkjet, and laser, so you work with a printer you are used to. Classes are scheduled to fit your individual needs. You can spend eight hours in one day, or break it up into smaller increments, as long as your return visit schedules with the same class.

SPREADSHEET   DATABASE

Fig. 17.5   The first page of the innovative brochure.

HUMBLE OPINIONS COMPUTER TRAINING

1127 E. Main Street
(304) 251-5151

Beckley, WV 25801
800-250-2369

Your Computer Training Specialists

INTRODUCTORY

BASIC COMPUTERS

If you're not familiar with computers but would like to know more, then this class is for you. Learn about operating systems such as DOS, Windows, and OS/2. Discover the connections between directories, sub-directories, and files. Explore various printers and popular software programs.

WORD PROCESSING

We teach classes in more than 30 popular word processing programs. Learn basic editing, function keys, and margin and tab settings. Learn to use retrieve, save, and print. Use the merge and customizing features.

DATABASE

Organize your mailing list, customer files, invoices, and any data you deal with daily. Learn basic concepts, create and edit a form, add and edit data, create reports, and add or delete records.

SPREADSHEETS

Regulate your accounting system with a spreadsheet program. Learn to create, save, retrieve, and print. Use formulas, copy rows and columns, format ranges, and use absolute cell addresses.

DESKTOP PUBLISHING

Produce professional-looking documents. Learn basic page formatting like changing typeface, size and style, columns and margins, tabs and tables, frames, and graphics.

INTERMEDIATE

WORD PROCESSING

Learn about macros, tables, formatting columns, and mail merge. Print envelopes and odd page sizes. Learn the finer points of page make-up on your word processor.

SPREADSHEETS

Become more efficient with spreadsheets by freezing titles, and using named ranges and windows. Perform logical evaluation, use cell protection, and control recalculation.

DESKTOP PUBLISHING

Learn to use desktop publishing to produce fliers, resumes, forms, newsletters, and long documents such as catalogs, books, and business reports. Bring your own word processing to format the documents you need for your business.

ADVANCED CLASSES

Advanced classes are offered in any of the above categories. Prerequisites are the Introductory and Intermediate classes. Advanced training covers tips and tricks of the programs, ways to improve speed and output, compatibility with other programs, and so on.

We also offer introductory and intermediate classes in paint and draw programs, accounting packages, and image scanning and processing. For a complete list of software packages, call or stop by today!

(304) 251-5151   CALL TODAY   800-250-2369

Fig. 17.6   Page two of the brochure.

HUMBLE OPINIONS COMPUTER TRAINING

WORD PROCESSING   **DESKTOP PUBLISHING**

SPREADSHEET   **DATABASE**

(304) 251-5151   **CALL TODAY**   **800-250-2369**

Fig. 17.7 The final, folded brochure.

**HUMBLE OPINIONS
COMPUTER TRAINING**
1127 E. Main Street
Beckley, WV 25801

Fig. 17.8 The mailing panel of the brochure.

ABOUT HUMBLE OPINIONS

Humble Opinions offers training in more than 30 popular software programs. Please call for a list of brand names. Introductory, Intermediate, and Advanced classes are scheduled weekly. No matter what level you are, we have a class to suit your needs. In business for more than 10 years, and serving the business community in the tri-state area, Humble Opinions is here to serve you!

Each class instructor is a professional. Two months of intensive training at our headquarters in West Virginia gives these instructors knowledge and experience with their particular software program. Each instructor trains in only two programs, and is therefore an expert in the software. With no more than five students per class, every student receives quality training. We feel it's important for the student to spend time with the instructors in a hands-on situation.

Classes are taught in our spacious classroom containing 15 personal computers and 12 printers. The personal computers are of various capacities and memories. The printers represented include dot matrix, inkjet, and laser, so you work with a printer you are used to. Classes are scheduled to fit your individual needs. You can spend eight hours in one day, or break it up into smaller increments, as long as your return visit schedules with the same class.

SPREADSHEET   DATABASE

(304) 251-5151   CALL TODAY   800-250-2369

Fig. 17.9   The second step of the brochure.

To create page one of the innovative brochure, follow these steps:

1. Choose **File New**. Choose the default style sheet. Choose **OK** or press Enter.

2. Choose **Page Modify Page Layout**.

3. In Modify, choose **Margins & Columns**. Change the **Top** margin to **.50**, and the **Bottom** margin to **.35**.

4. In Modify, choose **Page Settings**. Change the Page Size to **Legal**. Choose **OK** or press Enter.

5. Choose **Style Modify Style**. In the **Styles** box, choose **Body Text**.

6. In Modify, choose **Font**. Choose Tms Rmn, 12 point.

7. In Modify, choose **Alignment**. Change the Indent All to **.35**. Choose From Right and change it to **.35**.

8. In Modify, choose **Spacing**. In Paragraph Spacing, change **Below** to **.25** and choose Always. Choose **Save**.

9. In the **Styles** box, choose **Body Single**. The default font is Tms Rmn, 12 point.

10. In Modify, choose **Alignment**. In Indent, choose **All** and **.35**; change From Right to **.35**. Choose **Save**.

11. Still in the **Style Modify Style** dialog box, in **Style** choose Title.

12. In Modify, choose **Font**. Choose Helv, 18 point, bold.

13. In Modify, choose **Alignment**. Choose **Center**. Change all indents to **0**.

14. In Modify, choose **Spacing**. In Paragraph Spacing choose **0** for both Above and **Below**.

15. In Modify, choose **Breaks**. In Keep With, deselect **Next Paragraph**. Choose **Save**.

16. In the **Styles** box, choose **Subhead**.

17. In Modify, choose **Font**. Choose Helv, 14 point, bold. Deselect italic. Choose **OK** or press Enter.

18. Type the following:

    HUMBLE OPINIONS(Enter)
    COMPUTER TRAINING(Enter)
    1127 E. Main Street(Enter)
    Beckley, WV 25801(Enter)

U sing a narrower bottom margin will balance the text when you fold the brochure.

A mi Pro makes it easy to modify all the styles at once.

D eselecting Next Paragraph allows you to follow the Body Single style with other styles, such as Title or Body Text.

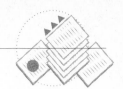

19. Select the first two lines and bold them. Select all four lines and change the style to Body Single.

20. Turn on the vertical ruler by selecting **View View Preferences Vertical Ruler.**

21. Press Enter until the cursor is positioned at 5" on the vertical ruler (or Line 24 on the Status bar).

22. Type the following:

    HUMBLE OPINIONS(Enter)
    COMPUTER TRAINING(Enter)

23. Apply the Title style. Choose Tms Rmn, 40 point (36 if your printer doesn't support 40).

24. Place cursor on the Past Enter; press Enter until the cursor is at 7" on the vertical ruler (Line 30 on the Status bar).

25. Type the following:

    WORD PROCESSING(2 spaces)**DESKTOP PUBLISHING**(Enter)

26. Apply the Title style. Place the cursor between PROCESSING and DESKTOP. Enter enough spaces to force the words as close to the side margins as possible.

27. Place the cursor on the last paragraph return; press Enter until the cursor is at 8" on the ruler (Line 34) and type the following:

    ABOUT HUMBLE OPINIONS(Enter)

28. Apply the Title style.

29. Place the cursor on the last return, press Enter twice. Either enter your own information, or type the text from figure 17.5, pressing Enter once after each paragraph.

30. At the end of the last paragraph, press Enter twice. Move the cursor up one line and type the following:

    SPREADSHEET DATABASE(Enter)

31. Apply Title style, and add enough spaces between the two words to force them to the right and left margins.

32. Place cursor on last paragraph return. Choose **Page Breaks Insert Page Break.**

To format page two of the brochure, follow these steps:

1. Move to page two by choosing the Page icon on the Status bar, or by pressing the Page Down key.

Change the Style to Title to save formatting time; the Title style is already bold and centered with no indent.

2. Type the following:

   HUMBLE OPINIONS COMPUTER TRAINING(Enter twice)
   1127 E. Main Street(Tab)**Beckley, WV 25801**(Enter)
   (304) 251-5151(Tab)**800-250-2369**(Enter)
   Your Computer Training Specialists(Enter)

3. Select HUMBLE OPINIONS COMPUTER TRAINING. Choose the Title style. Choose 20 point if your printer allows.

4. Select the text from the paragraph return before 1127 E. Main Street to the paragraph return in Your Computer Training Specialists. Change the text to the Body Single style.

5. Change the paragraph return before the address to 6 point.

6. Select the address and phone numbers. Activate the ruler.

7. Set an indent on the left to 1.62" on the ruler; set a right tab at 6.80" on the ruler.

8. Select Your Computer Training Specialist. Choose center and italic. In **Text Indention**, remove all indents.

9. Place the cursor on the last paragraph return, press Enter three times, and type the following:

   INTRODUCTORY(Enter)
   BASIC COMPUTERS(Enter)

10. Change INTRODUCTORY to the Subhead style.

11. Change BASIC COMPUTERS to the Body Single style and choose bold.

12. Enter your own information, or type the text from figure 17.6. Format the Subheads and class names the same as in steps 10 and 11.

13. At the bottom of the page, press Enter and type the following:

    (304) 251-5151 CALL TODAY 800-250-2369

14. Apply the Title style and add an equal amount of spaces between the phone numbers and CALL TODAY to force the phone numbers to the left and right margins.

15. Spell check the document, and perform the SMARTYPE.SMM macro.

16. Save your document.

An indent on Body Single text that is center-aligned would throw the text off-center by .35".

To print the brochure, you must change the printer setup in Ami Pro to accept 8 1/2-by-14-inch paper. To change the printer setup, follow these steps:

1. Choose File Printer Setup. Choose Setup.

2. In Paper Size, choose Legal 8.5 x 14 in. Choose OK or press Enter twice.

3. Print the brochure, head to toe.

Looking at Design

You can easily alter any brochure design to fit your company's needs. The size and shape are up to you. The formats presented in this chapter are, however, ones that have proven to be efficient and effective. There are two more traditional formats for brochures that you may want to use. Following are examples of each.

The first alternative format is an 8 1/2-by-11-inch portrait-oriented sheet. You can print on one side or both, and this format allows for as many pages as you need to do the job.

Figure 17.10 illustrates the cover of the 8 1/2-by-11-inch brochure. Wide margins are defined on the top and bottom by horizontal rules and provide plenty of white space. The company name is extremely large to attract attention. Also included on the front cover are a list of the types of music offered, the address, and toll-free phone number.

The company name, Gan Anin, was imported with the use of OLE (Object Linking and Embedding) from a Word Art program. Using OLE enables you to edit the art simply by double-clicking on the frame. Ami Pro then opens the Word Art program while you're in your document. When you're done editing, you simply close the application, and OLE updates your art. For more information on OLE, see Appendix B.

Figure 17.11 illustrates page two of the same brochure. Each following page would conform to this layout. The rules repeat for consistency, and the company name and address appear at the top of each page. In addition, the toll-free phone number appears at the bottom of each page. The ruled frames contain the various descriptions of music.

The frame containing the company name on page one was copied and added to page two. Furthermore, the frame was copied a second time and added to the first text block. The only frame modification in this instance was in Placement. You choose Flow With Text. Therefore, if you edit the copy containing the frame, the frame moves as if it were normal text.

Be sure to change your printer setup back to 8 1/2-by-11-inch paper after you complete this task.

If you print both sides of a brochure, be sure to use 60# or 70# book paper so that you can't see through the paper.

It's important to include the company name and phone number on each page of a brochure, in case one page gets separated from the rest.

Editing is easy when you copy a frame containing an OLE object because the copied frame can be edited in the same way as the original.

GAN ANIN
RECORDS AND TAPES

Music For The World!

IRISH	BLUES
ENGLISH	EARLY JAZZ
WELSH	CLASSIC FOLK
SCOTTISH	COUNTRY
AFRICAN	FOLK ROCK
REGGAE	CALYPSO
SALSA	SOCA
CUBAN	GOSPEL
CHINESE	APPALACHIAN

4714 N. Alvis Street, Charleston, WV 25303
CALL TODAY TOLL FREE
1-800-011-2345

Fig. 17.10   Another traditional format for a brochure.

GAN ANIN RECORDS AND TAPES

4714 Alvis Street, Charleston, West Virginia 25303

CELTIC MUSIC

Offering the world's largest selection of Celtic music, **GAN ANIN** stocks more than 8,000 titles. Our largest inventory is Irish music, both from the Republic of Ireland and Northern Ireland. Fiddle, banjo, bouzouki, tin whistle, accordion (button and piano), mandolin, and bodhran instrumentals, both in compilations and individual artists.

Including the dance music and songs of Ireland, our collection of Irish music totals 3,000 titles. The biggest names in Irish music today, and in years past, stocked in our warehouses.

WHOLE EARTH MUSIC

We stock a selection of 1,000 titles of world music including Greek, African, Chinese, and Mexican. Our African alternatives include African Pop, Funk, Pop Fusion, Zairean, and Ethiopian Pop. Our newest Chinese selections are blends of traditional and classical styles. Flute, keyboard, and percussion combine for expert arrangements and dynamic motion.

New to this publication are Cuban, Salsa, Reggae, Pakistani, Columbian, and Soca titles. Our new catalog describes them all. We also offer each selection on cassettes and CDs. Call or send the postage-paid reply card for our catalog today!

CALL TODAY TOLL FREE
1-800-011-2345

Fig. 17.11 Page two of the 8 1/2-by-11-inch brochure.

This addition takes only a minute or two, and you can copy the small frame now to add anywhere in the brochure. It offers quite an unusual effect throughout the text; and it forces the customer to notice the company name.

Another traditional format is the landscape-oriented 14-by-8 1/2-inch brochure. A brochure of this design has four panels on each side, and folds twice. The first fold is in half, the second in half again. For other ways to fold a brochure of this size, refer to Chapter 4.

Figure 17.12 illustrates a brochure formatted in the traditional manner; however, there are interesting variations in this design. One is the use of bordered frames to define the panels. Instead of containing four separate panels, this design combines two panels (the left two) to create an unusual effect. The design is interesting, and it provides more comfortable reading.

Notice, too, the clip art in the cover panel. By choosing the Drawing feature, you can copy and paste the art to create a field of flowers to dress up the front.

Another variation is the mailing panel. There are two ways to produce the mailing panel. One is to type the address normally, then cut and paste it after you print the brochure on your printer as was done here. This is by far the easiest method if you use Ami Pro Version 2.0. The reason it's easier to paste up the return address is because of Ami Pro 2.0's Drawing feature.

Notice that the name of the restaurant appears throughout the brochure.

Figure 17.13 illustrates the second page of the same brochure. Bordered frames define the combined panels (on the right), and the second panel. When the brochure is printed, the combined panels back each other. The first panel contains coupons to entice the customer to visit the store. When printed, the coupons back the front panel, and are easy to remove so that the customer can keep the other information offered.

Ami Pro 2.0's Drawing feature does offer you the option of rotating text; however, there are several problems associated with rotating text. First, when typing text directly in the drawing mode, a paragraph return signifies a new text block. Thus, each line of text must be rotated separately. This makes it hard to line up the text after it's rotated.

A second problem is getting each line straight; often the rotation is off by a degree or two that is noticeable on the final product. Finally, selecting the type once it's rotated is difficult because Ami Pro 2.0 retains the original text block instead of rotating it with the type. To illustrate these points, see figure 17.14.

ROGHAN JOSH

GOURMET FOODS
SPICES
RESTAURANT

2436 N. 24th Street
Washington, DC

871-9701

Open Daily From
11:00 a.m. to 9:00 p.m.

Roghan Josh
2436 N. 24th Street
Washington, DC 30003

ROGHAN JOSH GOURMET FOOD

Roghan Josh stocks the area's largest selection of gourmet foods. Our isles represent the food of 12 countries. Spices, rice, beans and lentils, meats, canned and fresh vegetables, breads, and desserts are all represented here. Although our largest inventory is Indian food, we also stock spices and staples from:

India	Nepal	Thailand
China	Korea	Malaysia
Pakistan	Laos	Vietnam
Turkey	Borneo	Sumatra

ROGHAN JOSH SPICES

Within our spacious Gourmet store, you will find a special section dedicated to the spices of various countries. Taking in more than half the Gourmet shop, Roghan Josh Spices stocks the finest, freshest herbs and spices found anywhere. We specialize in Indian Spices, with a stockpile of over 200. If you cannot find it here, we will order it for you and we will pay the shipping and handling charges.

ROGHAN JOSH RESTAURANT

Roghan Josh Restaurant, open from 11:00 a.m. to 9:00 p.m. daily, specializes in the food of India and Pakistan. Delicious meals prepared fresh daily at reasonable prices. Our menu includes appetizers, meat and vegetarian dishes, salads, breads, and desserts, all to delight your taste buds. Reservations are not necessary; our restaurant seats 200 people. Visit our lounge for live, Indian music nightly from 7:00 p.m. to 9:00 p.m.

Fig. 17.12 Page one of a 14-by-8 1/2-inch brochure.

COUPONS

GHEE
(5 lb. bucket)
10% OFF
ROGHAN JOSH - 2436 N. 24th Street
Offer not valid with any other discount.
Offer expires 2/12/93.

GARAM MASALA
(1/4 lb. bag)
10% OFF
ROGHAN JOSH - 2436 N. 24th Street
Offer not valid with any other discount.
Offer expires 2/12/93.

TAMARIND
(16 oz. jar)
10% OFF
ROGHAN JOSH - 2436 N. 24th Street
Offer not valid with any other discount.
Offer expires 2/12/93.

TIPS ON
INDIAN COOKING

Avoid substituting spices within a recipe; the entire flavor of the dish could change. Your meal will be the best when you use exactly the spices called for in the recipe. Also use hole spices whenever possible. Whole spices, such as peppercorns, mustard seeds, cumin, and coriander, retain their fresh, delicious flavor longer than those that are crushed. If you must use ground spices, use the same amount you would if using whole, then adjust the flavoring to taste when the cooking is done.

Hot chili peppers are essential to most Indian foods. Whether just enough is added for flavor, or a lot for the extremely hot, hot taste, use the reddest, freshest chili peppers available. Red does not signify hot as much as it means freshness. Tip: clean hot chili peppers under running water to prevent eyes and hands from burning.

A SPICE GUIDE

ASAFETIDA is a garlic-flavored gum resin used mainly with vegetable dishes. the taste is definitely an acquired one, as it is very strong and often bitter.

CARDAMOM is a dried fruit in the ginger family. We carry both the pod and seed of cardamom. The flavor is somewhat lemony and makes an excellent addition to duck and chicken dishes.

CORIANDER is an herb related to the parsley family. Its seeds and leaves are used in beef, lamb, and vegetable dishes. Coriander is especially good for adding to rayta.

CUMIN is a basic ingredient of all Indian cooking. A member of the parsley family, its seed is extraordinarily aromatic.

MUSTARD SEEDS (black) are a member of the mustard family with far less strong flavor than the yellow mustard seeds.

SAFFRON are dried stigmas of a flower in the crocus family. Mainly used for coloring, it has a mildly bitter flavor. Use to flavor and color chicken dishes, rice, and vegetables.

TURMERIC is a member of the ginger family with a pungent flavor. It's used to color food to a deep yellow-gold. Use Turmeric in cauliflower and potato dishes.

These spices and more are available at ROGHAN JOSH!

Fig. 17.13 Rotating text with Ami Pro 2.0's drawing feature.

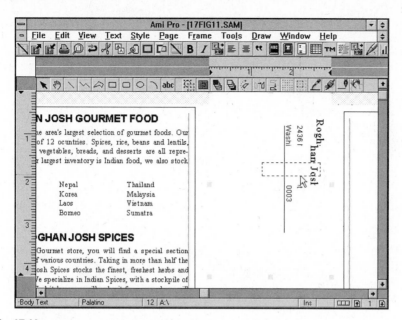

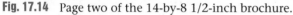

Fig. 17.14   Page two of the 14-by-8 1/2-inch brochure.

As you can see in the figure, the mouse cursor is pointing to the text block that belongs to Roghan Josh. The text block is horizontal, even though the text is vertical. Note, too, that as the text block moves, only a portion of the text moves. It's extremely difficult to move your text under these circumstances. The vertical rule you see was added to help insure the rotated type would be straight.

If you use Ami Pro 3.0, you'll have no problems with rotating text. Version 3.0 offers a Group option in the Drawing menu. If you group your text objects first, you can rotate them as one object.

Recapping

In this chapter you learned to design various brochures to suit your company's needs. You learned to apply the Status bar buttons to format type and styles, to apply column page breaks, and to base new styles on already formatted styles for making style sheets more quickly.

Creating Newsletters

TAITHNEAMH

COUNTY KERRY

May 1993   Travel Ireland   Vol. 1, No. 6

KILLARNEY

Welcome to the fourth issue of Taithneamh. This month we visit County Kerry in the West of Ireland. If you plan a trip to Ireland soon, you won't want to miss this lovely area. In the heart of Kerry is Killarney town. With its hustle and bustle of merchants, business, and tourist centers, Killarney is a town you will never forget.

Through the center of town is Main Street, the business and market center. Connecting to Main are High and New Streets, two very popular day and night tourist spots. High Street is lined with rows of lights overhead; souvenir shops and cafes line the sides of the narrow, always populated street. The pubs on High are well known for the dance music in the late evenings. The fiddle, banjo, and whistle ring out in merriment and revelry.

An offshoot of High Street is New. New Street has many guesthouses and it is home for the Post Office of Killarney. The guest houses welcome visitors with open doors, the smell of tea and scones, and of course, a nice, warm peat fire! What more could you want on a cold and rainy day? And the gardens, the

The fiddle, banjo, and whistle ring out in merriment and revelry.

wonderful, colorful gardens! New Street is the pride of the women's club in town, and so it should be! They plant every spring with new bulbs and seeds, making the street a virtual festival of dyestuff.

RING OF KERRY

During the day, if you base yourself in Killarney, there are a myriad of sights and attractions in the area. The Slieve Miskish Mountains, Ring of Kerry, and the Dingle Peninsula are jaunts that take no more than a day. Scenic beauty of the lakes, the heather, and good roads make County Kerry a wonderful place to visit. The Ring of Kerry is a trip you must not miss!

Stretching 110 miles, the Ring of Kerry offers excitement at every turn. It is a mountainous road

circling the Slieve Mish Mountains, through the Dingle Peninsula, and running parallel to the ocean during most of its length. Beginning in Killarney, the first leg of the Ring tenders a distant view of Macgillycuddy's Reeks, a glorious mountain range in the southwest of Ireland. Travelling further, you come to Killorglin, the scene of the famous Puck Fair. If, by chance, you visit in mid-August, do not miss the Puck Fair. Music, song, feasting, and brotherhood envelop the city for three lively, fun-filled days.

As you travel further on the Ring, you come across Caragh Lake, one of Kerry's finest fishing spots. You may wish to take a boat trip to the Blasket Islands, or Skellig Rock. Skellig Michael is a massive rock, jutting 700 feet high out of the Atlantic; what a sight to behold! Or perhaps you will take a side trip to Puffin Island, Kerry's own bird sanctuary where over 10,000 puffins gather each year to breed.

Whether you travel south or west on the ring, to the Islands or the Burrin, you will never forget the beauty and solitude of the landscape, and the love of life from the people. It is a memory to cherish your whole life through.

Includes

18

Producing a Basic Newsletter

Newsletters inform, announce, remind, advise, instruct, adver-tise, and communicate. Newsletters can be targeted toward employees, customers, prospective customers, executives, and the general public. Newsletters are so flexible that you can design them to fit any purpose.

For detailed information on how to create a form like this see page 455.

Y ou can advertise your products or services, for example, or urge attendance at sales, introduce a new manager, reveal new sales techniques, or recommend better health and safety practices. Newsletters can inspire your customers or employees. The opportunities are endless; however, you need some guidelines for writing and designing your newsletter that will improve your results.

Planning the Contents

Newsletters must contain information that is applicable to the audience. You can target your material to a specific group by including articles that interest the group's members. In addition to your newsletter's main message—selling your purpose, product, or service—add short, related articles that appeal to your audience. General interest stories, human interest, graphic images, and even cartoons can attract readers. After you have their attention, you can concentrate on your purpose.

If your goal is to sell customers a new product line, for example, describe that line in the main article, listing major selling points and benefits. Add a photo of the products and, perhaps, an illustration of someone using the products who appears to be like your customers in terms of age, sex, and occupation. In a short article, list a few quotes from satisfied customers. Another article may introduce the new equipment that produced that product line or highlight an employee who uses the products. Finally, you can add a comparison of your product lines to those of a competitor.

If you're writing an employee newsletter to inform employees of new safety regulations, make those new regulations your main article. Add shorter stories about employees who have good safety records, new equipment that promotes safety, and perhaps a cartoon illustrating what happens to someone who isn't careful.

You have many options for the content of your newsletter. Choose your goal, and then support that goal with interesting, useful information.

Planning the Design

In addition to valuable information, a newsletter also must be well-designed to make it easier to read. The design can be informal and unadorned, or complex and formal. The design should conform to your company's concepts and goals and should match the style of the company's other newsletters, brochures, or letterhead.

Consistency is a significant factor in all newsletter design. Your design must be consistent within each issue and among issues. Consistency within the issue makes reading comfortable; a newsletter that's easy to read is more likely to be read. Consistency among issues familiarizes the reader with the style and makes each issue of your newsletter more recognizable. Ami Pro has several features to help you maintain consistency, including style sheets, paragraph styles, and page setups.

You also want to include points of emphasis in your newsletter, for added interest. Bullets, jumplines, callouts, art work, graphic rules, boxes, and screens are all options for creating emphasis.

Planning the Format

When designing your newsletter, you should decide how often you want to publish it; then decide how much copy you want to gather. From this information, choose a format (size and shape) for your newsletter and stick with it. Also consider the size of your newsletter in relation to the method of distribution. A newsletter that you mail should not be too large; one that you hand out can be any size. For common newsletter sizes, see Chapters 2 and 4. The most common size is 8 1/2 by 11 inches, which is the size used in the following examples. Basing your design on this size enables you to enlarge the format either by adding more pages (2, 4, 8, or 16 pages) or by combining pages for a larger finished size (11-by-17-inch sheets folded to 8 1/2 by 11, or 25 1/2-by-11-inch sheets folded to 8 1/2 by 11).

In relation to the size of your newsletter, consider its weight. Its weight depends on the number of pages and the type of paper you use. A newsletter can have 1 to 16 pages. More than 16 pages is considered a magazine. When choosing the paper, remember that the type, color, and weight you choose creates an image for your company. Use at least 60# or 70# book paper. It can have a smooth, linen, or enamel finish, and you can choose any color as long as the type can be read easily. Refer to Chapter 4 for more information about paper and ink.

In creating the following examples, the document instructions direct you to save each design as a document; if you want, however, you can save designs as style sheets for later use. In addition, you only type the information for the newsletter once and then copy it for use with other designs. You may want to enter your own information, rather than the example, to create your own company newsletter.

Throughout this chapter, you will draw a lot of frames. Using Ami Pro's SmartIcon can help you format your frames more quickly. You can

Color is another excellent way to add emphasis: photographs, illustrations, headlines, and graphic elements.

If you print on the front and back of your newsletter, be sure that you use a heavy, opaque paper (60# linen, for example).

customize your SmartIcons to include the one described as Add Frame Using Previous Settings. Using this feature, when you click the icon, Ami Pro creates a frame by using the formatting from the previous frame. This method works only if you first use the Frame menu and the Create Frame command. If you use the Create Frame SmartIcon, the Add Frame Using Previous Settings command adds a frame that uses the settings in the Create Frame dialog box. To add the icon to your list and to customize SmartIcons, see Appendix A, "Understanding the Screen."

Creating a Nameplate

The nameplate can be printed in one or more colors to attract additional attention.

A nameplate is an identifier for your newsletter. Located at the top of the front page, the nameplate distinguishes your newsletter from all others. The nameplate consists of the name of the newsletter, or the company's name or abbreviation and a catchy phrase, and it may include a graphic image. Any text in the nameplate is usually in a different typeface from the body text and heads; you can create the nameplate in Ami Pro in a draw or paint program, or have an artist hand draw it. The text can be displayed, stretched, condensed, slanted, vertical, in an arc, or changed in any way that makes it stand out.

This chapter contains several nameplate designs that you can use as ideas to create your own nameplates.

The first example of a nameplate is a stylish, sophisticated design. Figure 18.1 illustrates a nameplate that uses CaslonOpenFace as the typeface. Interest is added by making the first and last letters larger than the others and by using a round-cornered frame and a screen, rather than solid black, to create a shadow to the left. Your use of type in Ami Pro is limited only by your printer's capabilities.

Fig. 18.1 A formal newsletter nameplate.

If you use this nameplate in a newsletter, you can tie its design elements to others in several ways. You can use a round-cornered, screen-shadowed frame for one or two stories, for example. You also can use the CaslonOpenFace elsewhere in the newsletter, perhaps as the smaller

head of a special article. Don't overuse it though. The nameplate's typeface should be special; it becomes common and doesn't stand out if you use it for every head.

Figure 18.2 shows another nameplate suitable for accountants, attorneys, physicians, and other professionals. The typeface is Palatino, set in initial caps and small caps. Two frames with black backgrounds and reversed type combine to form this nameplate. A word of caution is necessary, however, if you plan to have this nameplate offset printed: be sure that the print shop gets an even coverage of ink on the solid areas. If the ink is splotchy or thin, the nameplate will not look good.

BUSINESS EXCHANGE

The Computer Report   **May 1993**

Fig. 18.2   Reversed type in two black frames for an interesting nameplate.

To tie in this nameplate with the rest of the newsletter, create a style for the heads that uses reversed type. Use a sans serif typeface to contrast with the nameplate's Palatino typeface. Also, repeat the square-corner box as a black rule around special articles.

The next nameplate design uses ShelleyAllegroScript to create an informal, graceful look (see fig. 18.3). The clip art of Ireland was cropped from AmiDraw's EUROPE.SDW. This nameplate also includes a sample dateline. Note that the rules of the dateline match those of the nameplate.

U se the Draw feature to crop and change the screen fill of the clip art.

May 1993   Vol. 1, No. 1

Fig. 18.3   An open, light nameplate.

The rules in this design offer one way to match the nameplate to the newsletter. Repeat the rules throughout by using them with heads or at the top and bottom of each page. Another element to repeat here is the white space, which creates a light, airy feeling.

Remember to match the newsletter nameplate design to your company's image. As an example, figure 18.4 shows a unique nameplate for a childcare center. The letters look as if they're falling and the vertical layout emphasizes that feeling. In addition, the typeface, DomCasual, is extremely informal. The design fits the business.

You can rotate letters or art in Ami Pro's drawing feature. One obvious way to match the design of the Days Care nameplate to the newsletter is to add small graphic images beside each head and rotate them like the letters shown here. You can use Wingdings, clip art, or scanned art. Also, repeat the vertical emphasis throughout the piece by adding more vertical rules and using two columns of text instead of one.

Figure 18.5 combines a catchy name, Legal Tender, with a chart illustrating profits on the rise. The chart was created in Ami Pro's charting feature and illustrates another graphic image you can add to your nameplate. The type is Arial, set in 60-point and 36-point sizes.

Use double-ruled frames to encompass stories throughout the newsletter. You can use charts to unify the document. If your main article is about stock prices, for example, create a chart illustrating their progress. Using a chart is one of the best ways to ensure that your message is understood.

N ote that the lines around the smaller frames containing clip art are thinner than the line around the larger frame in figure 18.6. Remember proportion.

Another Ami Pro feature, clip art, is added to the nameplate in figure 18.6. Four different clip-art files illustrate travel, which is the business of Alacrity. Grouping the images in a box of four is more interesting than if they were spread out, and the arrangement of the boxes creates an orderly appearance.

All boxes in the nameplate and the newsletter have round corners, thus creating unity. The clip-art images also can be used throughout the newsletter to emphasize particular cruises, car or bus tours, flights, and other trips.

Finally, you can use display type from a paint or draw program for your nameplate. Figure 18.7 illustrates type that was created and stretched in CorelDRAW!. The typeface is unusually dark and heavy, so the rules are light to create contrast. Also, this nameplate includes a simple dateline.

Fig. 18.4 An appropriate nameplate for a childcare center.

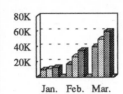 LEGAL TENDER

Fig. 18.5 A clever nameplate for a newsletter that deals with money.

Fig. 18.6 A nameplate that uses Ami Pro's clip art.

Taithneamh

May 1993

Fig. 18.7 A nameplate created in a drawing program.

To tie this nameplate to the rest of the newsletter, repeat the horizontal rules only. Don't use the typeface again; because it's so unusual, it attracts attention. If that typeface is repeated throughout the newsletter, it becomes less interesting and eye-catching.

Designing a Text-Only Newsletter

Most newsletters today use graphics. Rules, borders, boxes, screens, and images are used in nearly every newsletter you see. Graphics do attract attention, but they are not necessary for an eye-catching newsletter.

Text in itself can create an interesting design. Figure 18.8 illustrates page one of a two-page newsletter. The nameplate is extremely unusual and it attracts attention without the use of graphics. The nameplate was created in two frames. One frame contains the screened text; the other contains the solid text. And the wealth of white space surrounding the nameplate increases its appeal.

This two-page newsletter design is a traditional, two-column layout. The typeface of the screened part of the nameplate is repeated as solid heads throughout the newsletter. The white space is also repeated in the gutter and interparagraph spacing.

Page two of the design uses the same design as the first page to create consistency (see fig. 18.9). The nameplate is repeated on the second page to attract attention and because there isn't enough copy to fill the space.

Page two contains a mailing panel. By folding the piece twice, you can attach postage and mailing labels, thus sending a single sheet in the mail. Distributing a newsletter this way is more convenient and inexpensive than using envelopes.

The steps to produce the text for a newsletter that you can use throughout this chapter are as follows:

1. Choose File New. Use the default style sheet to begin your newsletter.

2. Choose Page Modify Page Layout.

3. Change the margins to .5".

4. Enter your own information or refer to the figure and type the text from KILLARNEY to the end of the story about THE PEOPLE (disregarding the nameplate and the section LEARNING IRISH). Press Enter after each head and after each paragraph.

5. Check the spelling of your document.

6. Run the Smartype macro on the document to change apostrophes to typographical characters.

7. Save the document as **Newsbase**.

8. Save again as **Newslet1**.

The nameplate in figure 18.8 gains additional white space with the added space typed between the letters.

In months when you have more copy, you can eliminate the second nameplate.

TAITHNEAMH
ENJOY IRELAND'S MAGIC

May 1992   *Vol. 1, No. 6*

KILLARNEY

Welcome to the fourth issue of Taithneamh. This month we visit County Kerry in the west of Ireland. If you plan a trip to Ireland soon, you won't want to miss this lovely area. In the heart of Kerry is Killarney town. With its hustle and bustle of merchants, business, and tourist centers, Killarney is a town you will never forget.

Through the center of town is Main Street, the business and market center. Connecting to Main are High and New Streets, two very popular day and night tourist spots. High Street is lined with rows of lights overhead; souvenir shops and cafes line the sides of the narrow, always populated street. The pubs on High are well known for the dance music in the late evenings. The fiddle, banjo, and whistle ring out in merriment and revelry.

An offshoot of High Street is New. New Street has many guesthouses and it is home for the Post Office of Killarney. The guest houses welcome visitors with open doors, the smell of tea and scones, and of course, a nice, warm peat fire! What more could you want on a cold and rainy day? And the gardens, the wonderful, colorful gardens! New Street is the pride of the women's club in town, and so it should be! They plant every spring with new bulbs and seeds, making the street a virtual festival of dyestuff.

LEARNING IRISH

Taithneamh	Enjoyment, pleasure
Le fada an la	For many a day
Bail o Dhia ort	God bless you
A lainm	Beaurtiful, lovely

RING OF KERRY

During the day, if you base yourself in Killarney, there are a myriad of sights and attractions in the area. The Slieve Miskish Mountains, Ring of Kerry, and the Dingle Peninsula are jaunts that take no more than a day. Scenic beauty of the lakes, the heather, and good roads make County Kerry a wonderful place to visit. The Ring of Kerry is a trip you must not miss!

Stretching 110 miles, the Ring of Kerry offers excitement at every turn. It is a mountainous road circling the Slieve Mish Mountains, through the Dingle Peninsula, and running parallel to the ocean during most of its length. Beginning in Killarney, the first leg of the Ring tenders a distant view of Macgillycuddy's Reeks, a glorious mountain range in the southwest of Ireland. Travelling further, you come to Killorglin, the scene of the famous Puck Fair. If, by chance, you visit in mid-August, do not miss the Puck Fair. Music, song, feasting, and brotherhood envelop the city for three lively, fun-filled days.

As you travel further on the Ring, you come across Caragh Lake, one of Kerry's finest fishing spots. You may wish to take a boat trip to the Blasket Islands, or Skellig Rock. Skellig Michael is a massive rock, jutting 700 feet high out of the Atlantic; what a sight to behold! Or perhaps you will take a side trip to Puffin Island, Kerry's own bird sanctuary where over 10,000 puffins gather each year to breed.

Whether you travel south or west on the ring, to the Islands or the Burrin, you will never forget the beauty and solitude of the landscape, and the love of life from the people. It is a memory to cherish your whole life through.

Fig. 18.8   A text-only newsletter with an exciting nameplate.

TAITHNEAMH

ENJOY IRELAND'S MAGIC

MUCKROSS ESTATE

Also located near Killarney, County Kerry, is a tremendous National Park called Muckross Estate. Over 10,000 acres of mountains, lakes, and green, green flora preserved by the Republic for your enjoyment. Cars are not allowed on the estate; there are, however, alternatives. You may rent or bring your own bicycle. Or take a jaunting car. Jaunting cars line the entrance to the park (as well as line the streets of Killarney), ready to transport you to this scene of serenity and beauty. The horse-drawn carriages are driven by gents who spin tales and weave stories of old Ireland, Killarney, Muckross, and the fairies.

Your first stop on the Estate is Muckross Abbey. A Francisian Abbey built in the 15th century, it is one of the best kept and restored abbeys in all of Kerry. Your next stop is Muckross House. A monumental 19th century home donated, along with the land, to the people of Ireland by its former owners. The house is filled with intricately hand-carved furniture, home-made crafts, tapestries, and original art works. The basement contains a stable, and fully stocked print shop, pub, blacksmith shop, kitchen, and weavers shop; all have presenters working as you tour, answering any and all questions.

THE LAKES

Contained within the National Park are three very famous, and pulchritudinous, lakes. The first you come to by jaunting car is the Lower Lake, also called Lough Leane. The second, or Middle Lake, is also called Muckross Lake. The third is simply known as the Upper Lake. In addition, don't miss Torc Mountain and its stupendous waterfall. Water from the Devil's Punch Bowl rushes over Torc's 60' waterfall, gushing and glorious, it is a sight you will not want to miss.

THE PEOPLE

Of course, as we have said before, the people of Ireland are its main tourist attraction. Their warm, friendly smiles await your visit. Their music greets you; their song welcomes you. Men resting along the side of the road from working in the peat bogs. Their worn, shiny suits a symbol of days gone by. The women, with their rosy red cheeks, shopping for fresh bread and potatoes; chatting with their friends. The children, smiling and lighthearted, running and playing along the roadside. These are the people of Ireland; they welcome you to their country, their county, their homes, their hearts.

**TAITHNEAMH
TRAVEL IRELAND**
23 Killoglen Road
Killorglin, County Kerry
Ireland

Fig. 18.9 Page two of the newsletter.

The steps to produce page one of the newsletter are as follows:

1. Choose **Page** Modify **Page Layout**.

2. In **Number of Columns**, choose **2**. In **Gutter Width**, choose **.5**". Choose OK or press Enter.

3. Draw a frame along the top margin. Choose **Frame** Modify **Frame**.

4. In **Frame**, choose **Type**. Choose No Wrap **Beside**.

5. In **Frame**, choose **Size & Position**. **Clear Margins**.

6. In **Size**, change the **Width** to **7.5**", and the **Height** to **1.6**".

7. In **Frame**, choose **Lines & Shadows**. In **Lines**, deselect **All**. In **Shadows**, choose **None**. Choose OK or press Enter.

8. Place the cursor in the frame and type the following:

   T(space)A(space)I(space)T(space)H(space)N(space)E(space)A(space)M(space)H(Enter, Enter)
   May 1993(Tab)**Vol. 1, No. 6**

9. Select, bold, and center the text.

10. Choose **Text** Font. Choose Frank Goth Cd, 60 point, and the color bar. Select the second column from the right on the last screen. Choose OK or press Enter.

11. Select the dateline. Choose italic and activate the ruler. Set a right tab at 7.25".

12. Draw another frame.

13. Choose **Frame** Modify **Frame**.

14. In **Frame**, choose **Type**. Choose No Wrap **Around**. Choose **Transparent**.

15. In **Frame**, choose **Size & Position**.

16. In **Size**, change the **Width** to **7.3**" and the **Height** to **.70**". In **Position**, set **Down From Top** at **.78**"; set **In From Left** at **.64**".

17. In **Frame**, choose **Lines & Shadows**. In **Lines**, deselect **All**. In **Shadows**, choose **None**. Choose OK or press Enter.

18. Place the cursor in the second frame and type the following:

   Enjoy Ireland's Magic

19. Select the text and choose Tms Rmn, 18 point, bold, center. Run the Smartype macro in this frame.

U se Full Page View to draw a frame that fills the page.

C hoose No Wrap Around so that you can place the text directly on top of the original frame.

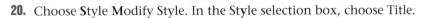

20. Choose **St**yle **M**odify Style. In the Style selection box, choose Title.

21. In Modify, choose **F**ont. Choose Frank Goth Cd, 18 point, bold, center.

22. In Modify, choose **S**pacing. In Paragraph Spacing, choose **B**elow at **.10**". Choose **S**ave.

23. In the Style selection box, choose Body Text.

24. In Modify, choose **F**ont. Choose Tms Rmn, 12 point.

25. In Modify, choose **A**lignment. Choose **J**ustified. In Modify, choose Hyphenation to turn it on.

26. In Modify, choose **S**pacing. In Paragraph Spacing, change **A**bove to .10" and **B**elow to .10". Choose OK or press Enter.

27. Select KILLARNEY, RING OF KERRY, MUCKROSS ESTATE, THE LAKES, and THE PEOPLE. Change each to the style Title.

28. Draw a frame at the bottom of the first column to force RING OF KERRY to the top of the second column.

29. Choose **F**rame **M**odify Frame Layout.

30. In Frame, choose **T**ype. Choose No Wrap **B**eside.

31. In Frame, choose **S**ize & Position. Clear Margins.

32. In Frame, choose **L**ines & Shadows. In **L**ines, deselect **A**ll. In shadows, choose **N**one. Choose OK or press Enter.

33. Place the cursor in the frame. Enter your own information or type the section LEARNING IRISH from figure 18.8.

34. Select all five lines of text in the frame. Change them to the style Body Single.

35. Select LEARNING IRISH. Choose Tms Rmn, 18 point, bold, center.

36. Select the next four lines of text, activate the ruler, and set the left tab at 1.75".

37. Choose **T**ext Spacing. Choose **C**ustom and type **.22**. Choose OK or press Enter.

The steps to group and copy the nameplate frames to the second page are as follows:

1. Press Ctrl+Home to go to the beginning of the document.

2. Choose one of the frames. Press and hold the Shift key and choose the other frame. Choose **F**rame Menu **G**roup.

If you need to move, resize, select, or type into just one frame, choose Frame Group to turn off Group.

After you format the frame, copying it over and over for use throughout the newsletters speeds up formatting.

3. Choose Edit Copy. Go to page two. Choose Edit Paste. The two frames appear at the top of page two.

4. Turn off Group and place the cursor in the largest frame. Delete the dateline. Resize the largest frame to **1.25"** in Height.

The steps to complete the formatting on page two are the following:

1. Draw a frame at the bottom of the page that forces THE LAKES to the top of column two.

2. Choose Frame Modify Frame Layout.

3. In Frame, choose Type. Choose No Wrap Beside.

4. In Frame, choose Size & Position. Clear Margins. In Size, change Width to **7.5"**, and Height to **2.6"**.

5. For Position On Page, set Down From Top at **7.9"**; set In From Left at **.5"**.

6. In Frame, choose Lines & Shadows. In Lines, deselect All. In Shadows, choose None. Choose OK or press Enter.

7. Place the cursor in the frame and type the following:

TAITHNEAMH(Enter)
TRAVEL IRELAND(Enter)
23 Killoglen Road(Enter)
Killorglin, County Kerry(Enter)
Ireland

8. Select the five lines of type and change the style to Body Single.

9. Select the first two lines. Choose 14 point, bold.

10. Save your document.

11. To print, print page one first. Turn it over and insert it into the paper feeder so that page two prints head to head (so that the top of each page is at the same end of the sheet of paper) on the back.

12. To mail, fold the newsletter into thirds with two parallel folds, like a letter or a brochure, leaving space for the mailing label up.

Designing a Text and Graphics Newsletter

Graphics not only attract attention in a newsletter, but help to organize information. Figure 18.10 shows a newsletter that uses clip art in the nameplate and graphic rules to separate stories. You can create this newsletter with a series of frames divided into one and two columns.

The nameplate on page one uses the ShelleyAllegroScript typeface and a cropped portion of clip art from AmiDraw. Notice that the almost weightless feel of the nameplate is balanced by the white space in the body of the newsletter. White space is created by left-aligned body text, wide gutter width, and interparagraph spacing. In addition, space is added to the right of the heads to enhance the light, open look of the nameplate. The horizontal rules divide the stories in an interesting manner and, by repetition, create unity and consistency. Most newsletters have a vertical emphasis; this one stands out because it has a horizontal emphasis.

Page two of the newsletter follows the same style, with one exception. A reservation confirmation at the bottom of the page is formatted into one column, so readers have more room to fill in the form (see fig. 18.11).

Page four of the newsletter includes a calendar produced with Ami Pro's table feature, and a mailing panel (see fig. 18.12).

This design is for a four-page newsletter. To duplicate it, use the information you typed at the beginning of the chapter, formatting only pages one, two, and four. Page three is the same style as pages one and two.

You can use the calendar in many other documents or by itself.

The steps to produce page one of the newsletter are as follows:

1. Choose File Open. Choose NEWSBASE.SAM. Choose OK or press Enter.

2. Choose File Save As. Save the newsletter base as **Newslet2**. Choose OK or press Enter.

3. Choose Page Modify Page Layout.

4. In Margins & Columns, change the Top and Bottom margins to .35". Choose OK or press Enter.

5. Draw a frame along the top margin. Choose Frame Modify Frame.

6. In Frame, choose Type. Choose No Wrap Beside.

7. In Frame, choose Size & Position. In Margins, change the Top margin to .20" and the Bottom margin to .10".

8. In Size, change the Width to 7.5" and the Height to 1.6".

9. In Frame, choose Lines & Shadows. In Lines, change to Top and Bottom, select the third Line Style. In Shadows, choose None. Choose OK or press Enter.

Taithneamh

May 1993

KILLARNEY

Welcome to the fourth issue of Taithneamh. This month we visit County Kerry in the West of Ireland. If you plan a trip to Ireland soon, you won't want to miss this lovely area. In the heart of Kerry is Killarney town. With its hustle and bustle of merchants, business, and tourist centers, Killarney is a town you will never forget.

Through the center of town is Main Street, the business and market center. Connecting to Main are High and New Streets, two very popular day and night tourist spots. High Street is lined with rows of lights overhead; souvenir shops and cafes line the sides of the narrow, always populated street. The

pubs on High are well known for the dance music in the late evenings. The fiddle, banjo, and whistle ring out in merriment and revelry.

An offshoot of High Street is New. New Street has many guesthouses and it is home for the Post Office of Killarney. The guest houses welcome visitors with open doors, the smell of tea and scones, and of course, a nice, warm peat fire! What more could you want on a cold and rainy day? And the gardens, the wonderful, colorful gardens! New Street is the pride of the women's club in town, and so it should be! They plant every spring with new bulbs and seeds, making the street a virtual festival of dyestuff.

RING OF KERRY

During the day, if you base yourself in Killarney, there are a myriad of sights and attractions in the area. The Slieve Miskish Mountains, Ring of Kerry, and the Dingle Peninsula are jaunts that take no more than a day. Scenic beauty of the lakes, the heather, and good roads make County Kerry a wonderful place to visit. The Ring of Kerry is a trip you must not miss!

Stretching 110 miles, the Ring of Kerry offers excitement at every turn. It is a mountainous road circling the Slieve Mish Mountains, through the Dingle Peninsula, and running parallel to the ocean during most of its length. Beginning in Killarney, the first leg of the Ring tenders a distant view of Macgillycuddy's Reeks, a glorious mountain range in the southwest of Ireland. Travelling further, you come to Killorglin, the scene of the famous Puck Fair. If, by chance, you visit in mid-August, do not

miss the Puck Fair. Music, song, feasting, and brotherhood envelop the city for three lively, fun-filled days.

As you travel further on the Ring, you come across Caragh Lake, one of Kerry's finest fishing spots. You may wish to take a boat trip to the Blasket Islands, or Skellig Rock. Skellig Michael is a massive rock, jutting 700 feet high out of the Atlantic; what a sight to behold! Or perhaps you will take a side trip to Puffin Island, Kerry's own bird sanctuary where over 10,000 puffins gather each year to breed.

Whether you travel south or west on the ring, to the Islands or the Burrin, you will never forget the beauty and solitude of the landscape, and the love of life from the people. It is a memory to cherish your whole life through.

Fig. 18.10   Page one of a text and graphics newsletter.

MUCKROSS ESTATE

Also located near Killarney, County Kerry, is a tremendous National Park called Muckross Estate. Over 10,000 acres of mountains, lakes, and green, green flora preserved by the Republic for your enjoyment. Cars are not allowed on the estate; there are, however, alternatives. You may rent or bring your own bicycle. Or take a jaunting car. Jaunting cars line the entrance to the park (as well as line the streets of Killarney), ready to transport you to this scene of serenity and beauty. The horse-drawn carriages are driven by gents who spin tales and weave stories of old Ireland, Killarney, Muckross, and the fairies.

Your first stop on the Estate is Muckross Abbey. A Francisian Abbey built in the 15th century, it is one of the best kept and restored abbeys in all of Kerry. Your next stop is Muckross House. A monumental 19th century home donated, along with the land, to the people of Ireland by its former owners. The house is filled with intricately hand-carved furniture, home-made crafts, tapestries, and original art works. The basement contains a stable, and fully stocked print shop, pub, blacksmith shop, kitchen, and weavers shop; all have presenters working as you tour, answering any and all questions.

THE LAKES

Contained within the National Park are three very famous, and pulchritudinous, lakes. The first you come to by jaunting car is the Lower Lake, also called Lough Leane. The second, or Middle Lake, is also called Muckross Lake. The third is simply known as the Upper Lake. In addition, don't miss Torc Mountain and its stupendous waterfall. Water from the Devil's Punch Bowl rushes over Torc's 60' waterfall, gushing and glorious, it is a sight you will not want to miss.

THE PEOPLE

Of course, as we have said before, the people of Ireland are its main tourist attraction. Their warm, friendly smiles await your visit. Their music greets you; their song welcomes you. Men resting along the side of the road from working in the peat bogs. Their worn, shiny suits a symbol of days gone by. The women, with their rosy red cheeks, shopping for fresh bread and potatoes; chatting with their friends. The children, smiling and lighthearted, running and playing along the roadside. These are the people of Ireland; they welcome you to their country, their county, their homes, their hearts.

RESERVATION CONFIRMATION

Your trip is scheduled to leave June 1, 1993. You must send this confirmation prior to May 16 with your first payment of $642. Be sure you have your passport in order.

Name _____

Address _____

Phone _____

     Check or money order enclosed for $ _____

Fig. 18.11   Page two of the newsletter.

JUNE 1993

SUNDAY	MONDAY	TUESDAY	WEDNESDAY	THURSDAY	FRIDAY	SATURDAY
		1 Trip leaves New York for Shannon Airport	**2**	**3** Tea on New Street from 10 to 11 a.m.	**4**	**5** Open House Lahinch Guest House - 9 a.m.
6	**7** Boat Trip to Blaskets 9 a.m.	**8**	**9** Muckross House Tour 9 a.m.	**10**	**11** Jaunting Car leaves at 2 p.m.	**12**
13	**14**	**15** Muckross Abbey Tour 11 a.m.	**16**	**17** Weaving Workshop 3 p.m.	**18**	**19**
20 Torc Waterfall Tour 2 p.m.	**21**	**22**	**23** Lecture at Gardens of Muckross 2 p.m.	**24**	**25** Alpine Tour 4 p.m.	**26**
27	**28**	**29** Ring of Kerry Tour 8 a.m.	**30**			

**TAITHNEAMH
TRAVEL IRELAND**
23 Killoglen Road
Killorglin
County Kerry, Ireland

Fig. 18.12 The fourth page of the newsletter contains a calendar of events and the mailing panel.

10. Copy this frame and paste it. Reposition the second frame below the first. Place the cursor in the first frame.

11. Type the following:

    (Tab)**Taithneamh**(Enter)
    (Tab)**May 1993**

12. Select both lines and set a left tab on the ruler at .25".

13. Select Taithneamh and choose ShelleyAllegroScript, 60 point.

14. Choose Text Spacing. In Custom, type **.67**.

15. Select May 1993. Choose Helv, 14 point.

16. Draw a second frame within the first to hold the clip art.

17. Choose Frame Modify Frame.

18. In Frame, choose Type. Choose No Wrap Around.

19. In Frame, choose Size & Position. In Margins, choose Clear Margins.

20. In Size, change the Width to **2.5"** and the Height to **1.10"**.

21. In Frame, choose Lines & Shadows. In Lines, deselect All. In Shadows, choose None. Choose OK or press Enter.

22. Choose File Import Picture. In the list of AmiDraw files, choose EUROPE.SDW. If you use a mouse, crop the clip art to include Ireland and part of England.

    To crop, go to the drawing feature. Use the selection arrow to move the art diagonally to the upper left corner. Moving the art up and to the left enlarges it. Use the grabber hand to reposition the art by dragging it to the lower right corner. The selection arrow resizes the art; the grabber hand repositions the art. Continue this procedure until your art looks like that in figure 18.10.

23. Choose Style Modify Style. In the Style selection box choose Title.

24. In Modify, choose Font. The default is Helv. Choose 18 point, bold.

25. In Modify, choose Spacing. In Paragraph Spacing, choose Below at **.15"**. Choose Save.

26. In the Style selection box, choose Body Text.

27. In Modify, choose Font. Choose Tms Rmn, 10 point.

28. In Modify, choose **S**pacing. In Paragraph Spacing, change **B**elow to .25. Choose OK or press Enter.

29. Choose the third frame on the page. Choose **F**rame **M**odify Frame Layout.

30. In Frame, choose Lines & Shadows. Deselect the **T**op position.

31. In Frame, choose Columns & Tabs. Choose **2** columns. For **G**utter Width, type **.50**. Choose OK or press Enter.

32. Copy the frame. Paste the frame and reposition it toward the bottom of the page.

33. Select the text from `KILLARNEY` through `...making the street a virtual festival of dyestuff`. Cut the text by choosing Edit Cut, or by pressing Shift+Del (for Version 2.0) or Ctrl+X (for Version 3.0).

34. Place the cursor in the top empty frame and paste the text.

35. Change `KILLARNEY`, `RING OF KERRY`, `MUCKROSS ESTATE`, `THE LAKES`, and `THE PEOPLE` to the Title style.

36. Place the cursor in the second column in front of `...pubs on High are well known...`. Press Shift+Enter twice to even the two columns of body text and to create white space after the title.

37. Select and copy the last frame on the page; paste it to page two. Select and copy the text under `RING OF KERR` and paste it into the last frame on page one. Press Shift+Enter to even the lines of body text.

The steps to format page two are as follows:

1. Copy and paste the frame and text for `MUCKROSS ESTATE`, `THE LAKES`, and `THE PEOPLE` as you did in step 37.

2. Select the last frame on the page. Choose **F**rame **M**odify Frame Layout.

3. In Frame Margins & Columns, change Number of Columns to **1**. Place the cursor and type the following:

   RESERVATION CONFIRMATION(Enter)
   Your trip is scheduled to leave June 1, 1993. You must send this confirmation prior to May 16 with your first payment of $642. Be sure you have your passport in order.(Enter)
   Name(space, Tab, Enter)
   Address(space, Tab, Enter)
   Phone(space, Tab, Enter)
   Check or money order enclosed for $(space, Tab)

S hift+Enter is a line break; use it to move down in the document without creating a new paragraph.

4. Select RESERVATION CONFIRMATION. Apply the Title style and choose center.

5. Select the text from Name through Check or money order enclosed for $. Activate the ruler and set a right line leader tab at 7".

6. Select Check or money order enclosed for $. Activate the ruler and set a 1" indent on the left.

The steps to produce page four, the calendar, are as follows:

1. Move to page four and press Enter three times. Move up to the first paragraph return and type the following:

   JUNE 1993

2. Select the text and assign the Title style. Choose 36 point, center.

3. Place the cursor on the second paragraph return. Choose Tools Tables.

4. Create a table with seven columns and six rows. Choose Layout.

5. In Default Rows, deselect Automatic. In Height of Row, type **1**". In Options, choose Center Table On Page. Choose OK or press Enter twice.

6. Select the cells from A-2 to the end. Choose Table Column/Row Size. Change the Row Height to **1** inch. Choose OK or press Enter.

7. Select the entire table. Choose Table Lines/Shades.

8. In Position, choose All sides. Use the second Line Style. Choose OK or press Enter.

9. Place the cursor in cell A-1 and type the following:

   SUNDAY(Tab)**MONDAY**(Tab)**TUESDAY**(Tab)**WEDNESDAY**(Tab)**THURSDAY**(Tab)**FRIDAY**(Tab)**SATURDAY**(Tab three times)**1**(space, Tab)**2**(space, Tab)...

   Continue to type the numbers to 30, the end of the month, separating them with spaces and tabs.

10. Select and bold all the numbers. The default type is Tms Rmn; change the type size to 9 point.

11. To type in any calendar, place the cursor after the number and space in the box and press Enter. Choose center. Type the text. To begin a new line within a cell, press Enter.

The default column width is 1".

12. Place the cursor on the last paragraph return on the page and type the address (see fig. 18.12). Change the five lines of text to Body Single and make the first two lines bold.

13. Save and print the document.

Designing a Traditional Newsletter

Traditional newsletters consist of three columns per page. This design incorporates left-aligned heads and body text with intercolumn rules to help separate the text (see fig. 18.13). This design is for a four-page newsletter, but in this series of steps you will produce only two pages, because pages three and four are formatted similarly.

The nameplate of this newsletter uses CaslonOpenFace. The white space around the text and the lightness of the typeface create an open look for the page. The design applies even more white space in the left-aligned heads, body text, and interparagraph spacing to mirror the openness of the nameplate. The callout in the middle column also is surrounded by plenty of white space and uses a large, italic type to attract attention.

Double 2-point rules define the page and confine the nameplate, adding some solidity to the design. In contrast, the rules in the gutter space and bordering the callout are 1-point rules, which reinforce the page's light look.

Page two of the newsletter opens up the page even more (see fig. 18.14). Two frames are added for graphics to break up the monotony of the text. The top frame contains a drawn illustration that was pasted-up. The bottom frame consists of an ad. Notice, too, how the placement of the frames balance the page. The frames are somewhat large, but their placement doesn't interrupt the text flow.

The steps to create page one of the newsletter are as follows:

1. Choose File Open. Choose NEWSBASE.SAM. Choose OK or press Enter.

2. Choose File Save As. Save the newsletter base as **Newslet3**. Choose OK or press Enter.

3. Choose Page Modify Page Layout.

4. In Modify, choose **Margins & Columns**. Choose **3** for Number of Columns. For **Gutter Width**, choose **.35"**.

5. In Modify, choose **Lines**. Choose the Top and Bottom lines and choose the second double-line pattern. In Position, choose Close to Inside. Choose Line Between Columns and the first line pattern. Choose OK or press Enter.

6. Draw a frame along the top margin. Choose **Frame Modify Frame**.

7. In Frame, choose **Type**. Choose No Wrap Beside.

8. In Frame, choose **Size & Position**. In Margins, choose Clear Margins.

9. In Size, change the **Width** to **7.8"** and the **Height** to **1.65"**.

This frame is wider than the actual margins of the page so that the double rules you add to the bottom of the frame match the width of the page rules.

10. In Frame, choose **Lines & Shadows**. In Lines, change to Bottom, choose the second double Line Style. In Shadows, choose None. Choose OK or press Enter.

Between the top frame and the top of the page, the two vertical rules appear if your frame is not butted up against the margin. The same is true for the second frame in step 16. If the frame is not butted up against the first frame, the column rules will show.

11. Copy this frame and paste it. Reposition the second frame below the first. Place the cursor in the first frame and type the following:

(Enter)**TAITHNEAMH**(Enter)
COUNTY KERRY

12. Place the cursor on the first paragraph return. Change it to 6 point and change the line spacing to **.08"**.

13. Select COUNTY KERRY and choose CaslonOpenFace, 56 point, bold, center.

14. Choose Text Spacing. In Custom, type **.78**.

15. Select TAITHNEAMH. Choose CaslonOpenFace, 24 point, bold.

16. Position the second frame against the first and type the following:

May 1993(Tab)**Travel Ireland**(Tab)**Vol. 1, No. 6**

17. Select the text and choose Helv, 12 point.

Ami Pro's page rules extend past the margins.

When positioning the frames in this design, you must be careful to hide the vertical rules from the gutters.

TAITHNEAMH
COUNTY KERRY

May 1993   Travel Ireland   Vol. 1, No. 6

KILLARNEY

Welcome to the fourth issue of Taithneamh. This month we visit County Kerry in the West of Ireland. If you plan a trip to Ireland soon, you won't want to miss this lovely area. In the heart of Kerry is Killarney town. With its hustle and bustle of merchants, business, and tourist centers, Killarney is a town you will never forget.

Through the center of town is Main Street, the business and market center. Connecting to Main are High and New Streets, two very popular day and night tourist spots. High Street is lined with rows of lights overhead; souvenir shops and cafes line the sides of the narrow, always populated street. The pubs on High are well known for the dance music in the late evenings. The fiddle, banjo, and whistle ring out in merriment and revelry.

An offshoot of High Street is New. New Street has many guesthouses and it is home for the Post Office of Killarney. The guest houses welcome visitors with open doors, the smell of tea and scones, and of course, a nice, warm peat fire! What more could you want on a cold and rainy day? And the gardens, the

The fiddle, banjo, and whistle ring out in merriment and revelry.

wonderful, colorful gardens! New Street is the pride of the women's club in town, and so it should be! They plant every spring with new bulbs and seeds, making the street a virtual festival of dyestuff.

RING OF KERRY

During the day, if you base yourself in Killarney, there are a myriad of sights and attractions in the area. The Slieve Miskish Mountains, Ring of Kerry, and the Dingle Peninsula are jaunts that take no more than a day. Scenic beauty of the lakes, the heather, and good roads make County Kerry a wonderful place to visit. The Ring of Kerry is a trip you must not miss!

Stretching 110 miles, the Ring of Kerry offers excitement at every turn. It is a mountainous road

circling the Slieve Mish Mountains, through the Dingle Peninsula, and running parallel to the ocean during most of its length. Beginning in Killarney, the first leg of the Ring tenders a distant view of Macgillycuddy's Reeks, a glorious mountain range in the southwest of Ireland. Travelling further, you come to Killorglin, the scene of the famous Puck Fair. If, by chance, you visit in mid-August, do not miss the Puck Fair. Music, song, feasting, and brotherhood envelop the city for three lively, fun-filled days.

As you travel further on the Ring, you come across Caragh Lake, one of Kerry's finest fishing spots. You may wish to take a boat trip to the Blasket Islands, or Skellig Rock. Skellig Michael is a massive rock, jutting 700 feet high out of the Atlantic; what a sight to behold! Or perhaps you will take a side trip to Puffin Island, Kerry's own bird sanctuary where over 10,000 puffins gather each year to breed.

Whether you travel south or west on the ring, to the Islands or the Burrin, you will never forget the beauty and solitude of the landscape, and the love of life from the people. It is a memory to cherish your whole life through.

Fig. 18.13   Page one of a three-column newsletter.

MUCKROSS ESTATE

Also located near Killarney, County Kerry, is a tremendous National Park called Muckross Estate. Over 10,000 acres of mountains, lakes, and green, green flora preserved by the Republic for your enjoyment. Cars are not allowed on the estate; there are, however, alternatives. You may rent or bring your own bicycle. Or take a jaunting car. Jaunting cars line the entrance to the park (as well as line the streets of Killarney), ready to transport you to this scene of serenity and beauty. The horse-drawn carriages are driven by gents who spin tales and weave stories of old Ireland, Killarney, Muckross, and the fairies.

Your first stop on the Estate is Muckross Abbey. A Francisian Abbey built in the 15th century, it is one of the best kept and restored abbeys in all of Kerry. Your next stop is Muckross House. A monumental 19th century home donated, along with the land, to the people of Ireland by its former owners. The house is filled with intricately hand-carved furniture, home-made crafts, tapestries, and original art works. The basement contains a stable, and fully stocked print shop, pub, blacksmith shop, kitchen, and weavers shop; all have presenters working as you tour, answering any and all questions.

THE LAKES

Contained within the National Park are three very famous, and pulchritudinous, lakes. The first you come to by jaunting car is the Lower Lake, also called Lough Leane. The second, or Middle Lake, is also called Muckross Lake. The third is simply known as the Upper Lake. In addition, don't miss Torc Mountain and its stupendous waterfall. Water from the Devil's Punch Bowl rushes over Torc's 60' waterfall, gushing and glorious, it is a sight you will not want to miss.

THE PEOPLE

Of course, as we have said before, the people of Ireland are its main tourist attraction. Their warm, friendly smiles await your visit. Their music greets you; their song welcomes you. Men resting along the side of the road from working in the peat bogs. Their worn, shiny suits a symbol of days gone by. The women, with their rosy red cheeks, shopping for fresh bread and potatoes; chatting with their friends. The children, smiling and lighthearted, running and playing along the roadside. These are the people of Ireland; they welcome you to their country, their county, their homes, their hearts.

Fig. 18.14   Page two of the three-column newsletter.

18. Choose Text Spacing. Set the Custom line spacing to **.44"**. Choose OK or press Enter.

19. Activate the ruler. Set the center tab at 3.75" on the ruler and the right tab at 7.5".

20. Select the frame containing the dateline. Choose Frame Modify Frame.

21. In Frame, choose **S**ize & Position. In Size, change the **H**eight to **.60"**.

22. In Frame, choose **L**ines & Shadows. In Lines, deselect All. Choose OK or press Enter.

23. Choose Style Modify Style. In the Style selection box, choose Title.

24. In Modify, choose **F**ont. Choose Helv, 18 point, bold.

25. In Modify, choose **A**lignment. Change the alignment to **L**eft.

26. In Modify, choose **S**pacing. In Paragraph Spacing, choose **B**elow at **.10"** and Above at **0"**. Choose **S**ave.

27. In the Style selection box, choose Body Text.

28. In Modify, choose **F**ont. Choose Tms Rmn, 12 point.

29. In Modify, choose **S**pacing. In Paragraph Spacing, change **B**elow to .20. Turn on **H**yphenation. Choose OK or press Enter.

30. Select KILLARNEY and change it to the Title style. Repeat with RING OF KERRY, MUCKROSS ESTATE, THE LAKES, and THE PEOPLE.

31. Draw a frame at the top of column two to hold the callout. Choose Frame Modify Frame Layout.

32. In Frame, choose **S**ize & Position. In Margins, change the **T**op to **.20"**. Change the **H**eight to **2.46"**.

33. In Frame, choose **L**ines & Shadows. Choose the Top and Bottom positions and change the Line Style to the second line pattern. In Shadows, choose None. Choose OK or press Enter.

34. Copy the frame. Paste it onto page two. Return to page one. Place the cursor in the callout frame and type the following:

    The fiddle, banjo,(Enter)
    and whistle(Enter)

ring out in(Enter)
merriment(Enter)
and revelry.

35. Select the text and choose Helv, 16 point, center, italic.

36. Choose Text Spacing. Choose Custom and type **.20**". Choose OK or press Enter.

Format page two as follows:

1. Select the copied frame and choose Frame Modify Frame.

2. In Frame, choose Size & Position. Change the Width to **4.90**" and the Height to **2.75**". Choose OK or press Enter.

3. Copy the frame. Position it at the top left corner of the page; position the second frame at the bottom right corner of the page.

4. You can place clip art, illustrations, a map, or an ad in the frames.

5. Save and print your document.

Designing an Innovative Newsletter

Newsletters are extremely versatile. You can add so many different design elements that you must be careful to not to use too many. Producing an innovative newsletter is easy; keeping it consistent and somewhat reserved is the hard part.

The next design illustrates an innovative newsletter that has an exciting design without becoming busy or inconsistent (see fig. 18.15). The first page contains the nameplate, set with a simple, bold display type. The airplane graphic offsets the vertical emphasis of the display type, as do the italics. The heads and subheads are all caps, repeating the format of the display head, set in italics for contrast. The screened story stands out because of the screen and the subheads. The rules of the nameplate repeat at the top and bottom of the screened frame.

Page two of the newsletter mirrors the column layout. The screened frame is on the right side of the page, which makes facing pages more interesting (see fig. 18.16). Subheads appear in the screened frame and as a head for the continuing story from page one. The rules repeat.

Draw your own illustration or use a halftone (see Chapter 4).

Note that the text in the screened frame does not extend to the margins, which creates a more professional look.

TAITHNEAMH

Presented by Travel Airlines

KILLARNEY

WELCOME

Welcome to the fourth issue of Taithneamh. This month we visit County Kerry in the West of Ireland. If you plan a trip to Ireland soon, you won't want to miss this lovely area. In the heart of Kerry is Killarney town. With its hustle and bustle of merchants, business, and tourist centers, Killarney is a town you will never forget.

HIGH STREET

Through the center of town is Main Street, the business and market center. Connecting to Main are High and New Streets, two very popular day and night tourist spots. High Street is lined with rows of lights overhead; souvenir shops and cafes line the sides of the narrow, always populated street. The pubs on High are well known for the dance music in the late evenings. The fiddle, banjo, and whistle ring out in merriment and revelry.

NEW STREET

An offshoot of High Street is New. New Street has many guesthouses and it is home for the Post Office of Killarney. The guest houses welcome visitors with open doors, the smell of tea and scones, and of course, a nice, warm peat fire! What more could you want on a cold and rainy day? And the gardens, the wonderful, colorful gardens!

New Street is the pride of the women's club in town, and so it should be! They plant every spring with new bulbs and seeds, making the street a virtual festival of dyestuff.

RING OF KERRY

During the day, if you base yourself in Killarney, there are a myriad of sights and attractions in the area. The Slieve Miskish Mountains, Ring of Kerry, and the Dingle Peninsula are jaunts that take no more than a day. Scenic beauty of the lakes, the heather, and good roads make County Kerry a wonderful place to visit. The Ring of Kerry is a trip you must not miss!

Stretching 110 miles, the Ring of Kerry offers excitement at every turn. It is a mountainous road circling the Slieve Mish Mountains, through the Dingle Peninsula, and running parallel to the ocean during most of its length. Beginning in Killarney, the first leg of the Ring tenders a distant view of Macgillycuddy's Reeks, a glorious mountain range in the southwest of Ireland. Travelling further, you come to Killorglin, the scene of the famous Puck Fair. If, by chance, you visit in mid-August, do not miss the Puck Fair. Music, song, feasting, and brotherhood envelop the city for three lively, fun-filled days.

Fig. 18.15 Page one of the innovative newsletter.

RING OF KERRY
(continued)

As you travel further on the Ring, you come across Caragh Lake, one of Kerry's finest fishing spots. You may wish to take a boat trip to the Blasket Islands, or Skellig Rock. Skellig Michael is a massive rock, jutting 700 feet high out of the Atlantic; what a sight to behold! Or perhaps you will take a side trip to Puffin Island, Kerry's own bird sanctuary where over 10,000 puffins gather each year to breed.

Whether you travel south or west on the ring, to the Islands or the Burrin, you will never forget the beauty and solitude of the landscape, and the love of life from the people. It is a memory to cherish your whole life through.

THE LAKES

Contained within the National Park are three very famous, and pulchritudinous, lakes. The first you come to by jaunting car is the Lower Lake, also called Lough Leane. The second, or Middle Lake, is also called Muckross Lake. The third is simply known as the Upper Lake. In addition, don't miss Torc Mountain and its stupendous waterfall. Water from the Devil's Punch Bowl rushes over Torc's 60' waterfall, gushing and glorious, it is a sight you will not want to miss.

MUCKROSS ESTATE

JAUNTING CARS

Also located near Killarney, County Kerry, is a tremendous National Park called Muckross Estate. Over 10,000 acres of mountains, lakes, and green, green flora preserved by the Republic for your enjoyment. Cars are not allowed on the estate; there are, however, alternatives. You may rent or bring your own bicycle. Or take a jaunting car. Jaunting cars line the entrance to the park (as well as line the streets of Killarney), ready to transport you to this scene of serenity and beauty. The horse-drawn carriages are driven by gents who spin tales and weave stories of old Ireland, Killarney, Muckross, and the fairies.

MUCKROSS ABBEY

Your first stop on the Estate is Muckross Abbey. A Francisian Abbey built in the 15th century, it is one of the best kept and restored abbeys in all of Kerry. Your next stop is Muckross House. A monumental 19th century home donated, along with the land, to the people of Ireland by its former owners. The house is filled with intricately hand-carved furniture, home-made crafts, tapestries, and original art works. The basement contains a stable, and fully stocked print shop, pub, blacksmith shop, kitchen, and weavers shop; all have presenters working as you tour, answering any and all questions.

THE PEOPLE

Of course, as we have said before, the people of Ireland are its main tourist attraction. Their warm, friendly smiles await your visit. Their music greets you; their song welcomes you. Men resting along the side of the road from working in the peat bogs. Their worn, shiny suits a symbol of days gone by. The women, with their rosy red cheeks, shopping for fresh bread and potatoes; chatting with their friends. The children, smiling and lighthearted, running and playing along the roadside. These are the people of Ireland; they welcome you to their country, their county, their homes, their hearts.

Fig. 18.16   Page two of the newsletter mirrors the column balance.

The steps to create page one of the innovative newsletter are as follows:

1. Choose File Open. Choose NEWSBASE.SAM. Choose OK or press Enter.

2. Choose File Save As. Save the newsletter base as **Newslet4**. Choose OK or press Enter.

3. Choose Page Modify Page Layout.

4. In Margins & Columns, change the Top margin to .75" and the Left, Right, and Bottom margins to .60".

5. In Number of Columns, choose 3; in Gutter Width, type .32.

6. Choose Style Modify Style. In the Style selection box, choose Title.

7. In Modify, choose Font. Choose Tms Rmn, 24 point bold, italic.

8. In Modify, choose Spacing. In Paragraph Spacing, choose **B**elow at .10" and Above at .15".

9. In the Style selection box, choose Subhead.

10. In Modify, choose Font. Choose Tms Rmn, 14 point, bold, italic.

11. In Modify, choose Spacing. In Paragraph Spacing, choose **B**elow at .10" and Above at .10".

12. In the Style selection box, choose Body Text.

13. In Modify, choose Font. Choose Tms Rmn, 12 point.

14. In Modify, choose Alignment Justified. Turn on Hyphenation.

15. In Indent, choose First and type .25.

16. In Modify, choose Spacing. In Line Spacing, choose Custom and type .21. Choose OK or press Enter.

17. Draw a frame along the top margin. Choose Frame Modify Frame.

18. In Frame, choose Type. Choose Square Corners.

19. In Frame, choose Size & Position. In Margins, set all at .15".

20. In Size, change the Width to 7.25" and the Height to 1.62".

21. In Frame, choose Lines & Shadows. In Lines, change to Top and Bottom and then choose the fourth Line Style. In Shadows, choose None. Choose OK or press Enter.

22. Copy this frame and paste it. Reposition the second frame below the first. Place the cursor in the first frame. Type the following:

(Tab)**TAITHNEAMH**(Enter)
(Tab)**Presented by Travel Airlines**

23. Select both lines. Choose the **T**ext **S**pacing. Choose **S**ingle. Choose OK or press Enter.

24. Choose Text In**d**ention. Remove the **F**irst line indent. Choose OK or press Enter.

25. Select TAITHNEAMH and choose Frank Goth Cd, 60 point, bold, left-aligned. Set a left tab at **.15** on the ruler.

26. Select Presented by Travel Airlines. Choose Tms Rmn, 14 point, italic, left-aligned. Set a left tab at **.15** on the ruler.

27. Draw a second frame within the first to hold the clip art.

28. Choose F**r**ame **M**odify Frame. Choose Wrap Text Around.

29. In Frame, choose **S**ize & Position. In Margins, choose Clear Margins.

30. In Frame, choose **L**ines & Shadows. In Lines, deselect All. In Shadows, choose **N**one. Choose OK or press Enter.

31. Choose File **I**mport Picture. In the list of AmiDraw files, choose CORPJET.SDW.

32. Select the third frame on the page and enlarge it to cover the first and second columns. Choose F**r**ame **M**odify Frame Layout.

33. In Frame, choose **S**ize & Position. Change all Margins to .30".

34. In F**r**ame, choose **L**ines & Shadows. In **B**ackground, choose the second column from the right, the third screen down. Choose OK or press Enter.

35. Copy the frame. Paste it onto page two. Return to page one.

36. Select the text in the third column, and then cut and paste it into the screened frame. Cut the rest of the text, up to and including ...making the street a virtual festival of dyestuff. Paste it after the text in the screened frame.

37. Change KILLARNEY, RING OF KERRY, MUCKROSS ESTATE, THE LAKES, and THE PEOPLE to the Title style.

38. Place the cursor in front of Welcome to the fourth issue of Taithneamh... Press Enter and move up one line. Type the following:

WELCOME

The screen in figure 18.16 is equivalent to a 15 percent screen; you can read the type easily through the light screen.

Change the text to Subhead.

39. Using the figure for a reference, repeat these steps with the other subheads on page one.

The steps to format page two of the newsletter are as follows:

1. Position the pasted frame over the second and third columns.

2. Place the cursor in front of `As you travel...` in the first column and press Enter. Type the following:

   RING OF KERRY(Enter)
   (continued)

3. Select the two lines of type. Choose Text Indention. Remove the First Line indent.

4. Select the first line of text, `RING OF KERRY`. Choose Tms Rmn, 14 point, bold, left-aligned, italic (the Subhead style).

5. Choose `(continued)`. Choose italic, left-aligned.

6. Cut the text from `MUCKROSS ESTATE` through `...answering any and all questions`. Paste this text into the screened frame.

7. Cut the from `THE PEOPLE` through `... their country, their county, their homes, their hearts`. Paste this text into the screened frame below the story about Muckross Estate.

8. Referring to the figure, add the Subheads under `Muckross Estate`.

9. Position the story `THE LAKES` in the first column, as shown in the figure.

10. Save and print your newsletter.

Looking at Design

You can emphasize certain articles or stories in a newsletter in many ways (see figs. 18.17 and 18.18). Surrounding an article with a bordered frame is one popular way. Adding a screen to the frame is a variation. Figure 18.17 shows an article with a screened frame. The newsletter is a simple one: left-aligned text and heads, a simple nameplate and dateline, the use of Helvetica for the heads, and Times Roman for the body text. The article about the people of Ireland, however, draws attention.

Consistency is created through interparagraph spacing, left-aligned heads and body text, and repetition of the rules on the page.

TAITHNEAMH

May 1993   *Travel Ireland*   *Issue No. 12*

KILLARNEY

Welcome to the fourth issue of Taithneamh. This month we visit County Kerry in the West of Ireland. If you plan a trip to Ireland soon, you won't want to miss this lovely area. In the heart of Kerry is Killarney town. With its hustle and bustle of merchants, business, and tourist centers, Killarney is a town you will never forget.

Through the center of town is Main Street, the business and market center. Connecting to Main are High and New Streets, two very popular tourist spots. High Street is lined with rows of lights; souvenir shops and cafes along the narrow, always populated street. The pubs on High are well known for the dance music in the evenings. You'll enjoy the musicians and the dancers.

An offshoot of High Street is New. New Street has many guesthouses and it is home for the Post Office of Killarney. The guest houses welcome visitors with open doors, the smell of tea and scones, and of course, a nice, warm peat fire! What more could you want on a cold and rainy day? And the gardens, the wonderful, colorful gardens!

RING OF KERRY

During the day, if you base yourself in Killarney, there are a myriad of sights and attractions in the area. The Slieve Miskish Mountains, Ring of Kerry, and the Dingle Peninsula are jaunts that take no more than a day. Scenic beauty of the lakes, the heather, and good roads make County Kerry a wonderful place to visit. The Ring of Kerry is a trip you must not miss!

Stretching 110 miles, the Ring of Kerry offers excitement at every turn. It is a mountainous road circling the Slieve Mish Mountains, through the Dingle Peninsula, and running parallel to the ocean during most of its length. Beginning in Killarney, the first leg of the Ring tenders a distant view of Macgillycuddy's Reeks, a glorious mountain range in the southwest of Ireland. Travelling further, you come to Killorglin, the scene of the famous Puck Fair. If, by chance, you visit in mid-August, do not miss the Puck Fair. Music, song, feasting, and brotherhood envelop the city for three lively, fun-filled days. The featival is free to all, and you will not soon forget it!

THE PEOPLE

Of course, as we have said before, the people of Ireland are its main tourist attraction. Their warm, friendly smiles await your visit. They love visitors, especially from America, where everyone has a cousin, an aunt, a brother, sister, or friend. "Oh, you're from New York? Do you know my cousin Kara Whelan? She's lived there for two years now. Surely, you must know her!"

The Irish are so happy you have come to visit; they want you to feel at home. They offer you tea, scones, a warm peat fire, or their company as you sit and watch the rain.

Men resting along the side of the road from working in the peat bogs. Their worn, shiny suits a symbol of days gone by. The women, with their rosy red cheeks, shopping for fresh bread and potatoes; chatting with their friends. The children running and playing along the roadside. These are the people of Ireland; they welcome you to their country, their county, their homes, their hearts.

Fig. 18.17 A screened frame draws attention to the article.

WHEN YOU VISIT. . .

Following are a few tips on things you will need to know when you visit County Kerry.

BED AND BREAKFASTS

There are two excellent guest houses in town. Both are fairly inexpensive; both offer tidy rooms, and full service breakfasts.

The first, Mrs. Meaney's Bed and Breakfast, is a lovely white, three-story, four-room house. Mrs. Meaney will be happy to help you arrange for a jaunting car, bikes, boats, and so on. Rates are about $18 per person, with a half rate for children.

The second bed and breakfast is called Doheny's Guest House. It's on the eastern side of town, just minutes from the railroad station. A comfortable, clean, and brightly painted home, you will be amazed at the antiques in the parlor. Rates are about $21 per person with a 25% discount for children.

BUDGET MEALS

Curran Pub and Fish
Nesbitt Coffee Shop
The Spellissy
Considine's Restaurant
McCarrigg House

MUCKROSS ESTATE

Also located near Killarney, County Kerry, is a tremendous National Park called Muckross Estate. Over 10,000 acres of mountains, lakes, and green, green flora preserved by the Republic for your enjoyment. Cars are not allowed on the estate; there are, however, alternatives. You may rent or bring your own bicycle. Or take a jaunting car. Jaunting cars line the entrance to the park (as well as line the streets of Killarney), ready to transport you to this scene of serenity and beauty. The horse-drawn carriages are driven by gents who spin tales and weave stories of old Ireland, Killarney, Muckross, and the fairies.

Your first stop on the Estate is Muckross Abbey. A Francisian Abbey built in the 15th century, it is one of the best kept and restored abbeys in all of Kerry. Your next stop is Muckross House. A monumental 19th century home donated, along with the land, to the people of Ireland by its former owners. The house is filled with intricately hand-carved furniture, home-made crafts, tapestries, and original art works. The basement contains a stable, and fully stocked print shop, pub, blacksmith shop, kitchen, and weavers shop. Each room of the estate has a presenter available to anwer any and all questions you may have about the furniture, the arts and crafts, and the people of Ireland.

THE LAKES

UPPER, LOWER, MIDDLE, AND CARAGH

Contained within the National Park are three very famous, and pulchritudinous, lakes. The first you come to by jaunting car is the Lower Lake, also called Lough Leane. Lough Leane is the largest of the three lakes.

The second, or Middle Lake, is also called Muckross Lake. Muckross is indeed a smaller lake; however, there are none that are fairer.

The third is simply known as the Upper Lake. In addition, don't miss Torc Mountain and its stupendous waterfall. Water from the Devil's Punch Bowl rushes over Torc's 60' waterfall, gushing and glorious, it is a sight you will not want to miss.

In addition to the above lakes, you will notice that as you travel on the Ring of Kerry, you come across Caragh Lake. One of Kerry's finest fishing spots, Caragh Lake is a fine place for a picnic, a swim, or a hike. There are benches located around the perimeter for resting and enjoying the view.

All the lakes of Muckross offer beautiful scenery. The greenest trees, the bluest water, and the loveliest flowers you will see anywhere. Ireland's scenery is a memory to cherish your whole life through.

Fig. 18.18 Page two of the newsletter uses a plain box for emphasis.

Similarly, a plain frame can attract the reader to an important article. Page two of the newsletter illustrates this point (see fig. 18.18). Both screened and plain frames can be used within the same newsletter; but be sure to use the same width rules for both types of boxes.

Recapping

In this chapter, you learned how to plan the contents and design of your newsletter and a nameplate. You also learned to add callouts, jumplines, datelines, graphic images and elements, and advertisements to your newsletters.

S ubheads add emphasis to page two.

Producing a
Complex
Newsletter

Ami Pro features help you create complex layouts by using the frame and drawing options, headers and footers, automatic page numbering, and other features. Adding any of these components to a newsletter helps organize the information, attracts attention, and makes it easier to read and understand. As your newsletters become more complicated, you will depend more on Ami Pro's help.

19

For detailed information on how to create a form like this see page 486.

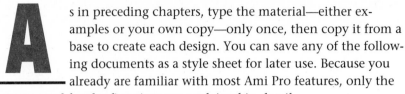

Refer to Chapter 18 for more information about planning the content and design of a newsletter.

If you choose to justify the body text of this design, you should leave the callout text and heads left-aligned for consistency and easier reading.

As in preceding chapters, type the material—either examples or your own copy—only once, then copy it from a base to create each design. You can save any of the following documents as a style sheet for later use. Because you already are familiar with most Ami Pro features, only the features used for the first time are explained in detail.

Designing a Newsletter with a Page Border

The first complex newsletter design has a page border. These rules work as ornaments as well as information organizers. Figure 19.1 shows both of these uses in a newsletter. The one-point rule that forms the border ornaments the page and ties the information together. The horizontal and vertical rules divide information.

The nameplate is simple, using CaslonOpenFace initial and small caps to form the name. The description of the newsletter is set in Helvetica. A horizontal rule separates the nameplate from the three-column text. The first column of text is similar to a callout. This column uses a type size and type attribute different from the body text to make it stand out. Unlike a callout, however, the text is not quoted from the body of the newsletter. Instead, this text provides additional information. The text in the first column is left-aligned, as are the heads and body text. This alignment, as well as interparagraph spacing, creates white space for easier reading. The vertical rule between the first and second columns divides this section from the body text.

Page two of the newsletter is formatted exactly the same way (see fig. 19.2). The callout style text is in the left column, with body text in the center and right columns. One variation is to mirror the left and right page designs. You can place the column containing the callout style text in the first column on left pages (pages 2, 4, 6, and so on), for example, and in the third column on right pages (pages 1, 3, 5, and so on). This design is not mirrored because the callout style text is left-aligned, which naturally leads the eye into the page. If the callout were in the right column, the left-aligned text would lead the eye off the page.

MOUNTAIN SORREL

A Quarterly Newsletter of Herbal Curatives and Preventatives

The North American Indians used many herbs and plants to promote health and vitality, to heal the afflicted, to strengthen the weak . . . Using common weeds and plants from the meadows, forests, and river's edge, the Indians created magnificent curative concoctions. Now, you can learn the Indian's secrets . . . the power of natural healing.

THE HEALING POWER OF LAVENDER

Everyone knows of the delicious fragrance of lavender, especially English lavender, but few know of its medicinal qualities. Any of the three species of lavender make potions.

A terrific calmative, lavender has the power to soothe headaches and nervous tension. Simply steep lavender in hot water for 15 to 20 minutes, and sip a cupful of the tea two or three times during the day.

A stronger tea of lavender is good as a gargle for sore throats; it also relieves stomach aches. We stock dried English and French lavenders in bunches and one pound bags, at a reasonable price. We also sell lavender oil extract for use as a medicinal oil.

ROSEMARY, MORE THAN A COOKING HERB

Both the leaves and flowers of rosemary have been used to alleviate depression and insomnia. A simple rosemary tea, with a bit of ginger added, also comforts a nervous or up-set stomach. Rosemary oil is widely known for its antibacterial properties, as well. Lastly, if you have dark hair, try a strong rosemary tea for a rinse after washing. It not only makes your hair shiny and soft, but it clears up your dandruff, too.

We stock a full supply of rosemary leaves, flowers, oil and our special home-made rosemary shampoo and rinses.

CATNIP, NOT JUST FOR CATS

A member of the mint family, catnip contains many properties other mints do. As a pleasant tasting tea, catnip is an antispasmodic and a calmative. Treat stomach ailments, colic and intestinal complaints. Catnip calms nervousness and anxiety.

Having a sleepless night? Try some catnip tea. If you have a cat, though, watch out, he'll try to drink your tea, too!

We stock catnip in one-half and one pound cans, as well as seeds to start your own plants in your garden. Your family, and your cat, will love you for it.

Fig. 19.1 Page one of a newsletter with a page border.

Joe-Pye Weed was named after a New England Indian, Joe Pye, who used it to treat typhus. North American Indians also used Queen of the Meadow as a diuretic, to treate kidney and bladder stones. The flowers, which bloom from August to September, range from white to deep purple in color. Use both the flowers and the rootstock of this magnificent herb as a tonic, diuretic, and as an astringent.

IT'S NOT JUST A WEED, JOE-PYE WEED

Often seen growing along the railroad tracks or roadsides, in fields and meadows, Joe-Pye Weed is also known as Queen of the Meadow. The root is traditionally used to ease lower back pain and rheumatism. Leaves are sometimes used to break a fever by bringing on intense sweating. Use the root or leaves in teas and tinctures; but do be careful, too much, too often, can be toxic.

We not only keep Joe-Pye Weed roots in four and eight ounce containers, but in one-pound bags, as well. Our Joe-Pye is collected fresh each Saturday morning during the spring, and fall. From the moist forests and meadows within the area, only the most perfect roots and flowers are gathered. We then dry the herb by hanging it upside down in a cool, dark place, to guarantee you receive only the best.

MULLEIN, EVERY PART BENEFICIAL

The flowers, leaves and roots of this plant are all valuable medicines. Perfect as an anti-spasmodic, emollient and sedative, mullein is also an astringent. Prepare an infusion of one half cup mullein leaves and flowers to two pints water for most complaints; be sure to strain well. Mullein oil is very useful as a sedative. Simply place a few drops in your tea

and sweet dreams. The root is very strong, leaves and flowers less so. Remember to never use the seed of mullein, except to plant. The seeds are very noxious.

We stock all parts of the mullein plant, roots, leaves, flowers, and oil.

POULTICES, NATURAL HEALING

Poultices are used to treat the outer body. Skin ailments, muscle pain, cuts, burns, even colds and flu. Many herbs can make a natural poultice. The ever popular Mustard Plaster has been used for centuries to treat weakness and fatigue. Burdock is great for gout; cayenne is perfect for a cold or the flu.

Of course, you're familiar with the properties of the Aloe plant for burns, but did you know borage, comfrey and plantain are excellent treatments as well? Plantain, by the way, is the best thing for a bee sting, especially when you're caught out in the garden, or the woods. Just chew the leaf for a moment or two and place it on the sting. It draws out the poison and reduces swelling.

WILD EDIBLE PLANTS

If you like to gather your own plants and roots for cooking, we suggest the following for some of the most exciting dishes ever! Cookbooks of all

Page 2

Fig. 19.2   Page two of the newsletter; the same layout with an added page number.

Many variations of page number placement are possible. Here, the page numbers are centered. Another option places left page numbers on the left, and right page numbers on the right. This option looks better, however, when the page design is not mirrored. Notice that no page number is on the first page. A tradition in typesetting is to leave the first and last pages of newsletters and magazines unnumbered.

The layout for page three is the same as for page two (see fig. 19.3). The callout style text is on the left, separated from the body text by a vertical rule. By using an Ami Pro numbering feature, the page number automatically changes.

Page four of the newsletter is designed somewhat differently from pages one through three (see fig. 19.4). The page border repeats, continuing to tie the document design together, but page four contains a masthead, a variation of the three-column formatting, and a mailing panel. The masthead contains publishing information such as volume and issue numbers, editors, circulation, subscription information, and disclaimers. Notice that a ruled box contains the masthead and that type is 9-point Helvetica.

In addition, an ad for spring specials is formatted into three columns, but it looks different from the rest of the newsletter because it's a list. Two horizontal, one-point rules separate the ad from the rest of the text. This ad breaks up the space of the back page and attracts attention. A mailing panel completes the page. Also, no page number is on the last page. If this newsletter contained 8 or 16 pages, this page still would be the last page because of its layout. The additional inside pages would be formatted like pages two and three.

The following directions are for only two pages of this design. After you set up the design, you easily can continue to format the rest of the newsletter from the figures. Lay out page two so that you can work with Ami Pro's automatic page-numbering feature.

The steps to set up the newsletter base for all designs in this chapter—using your own information if you want—are as follows:

1. Choose File New. Use the default style sheet. Choose OK or press Enter.

2. Enter your own material or type the text from the figure, beginning with the callout, `The North American Indians used many herbs...` Continue to type the text through `WILD EDIBLE PLANTS` on page two, pressing Enter after each paragraph and at the end of each head.

3. Check the spelling of the document. Use the Smartype macro to convert quotes and apostrophes.

4. Choose File Save As. Name the document **Newbase2**. Choose OK or press Enter.

5. Choose File Save As, and this time name the document **News1**. Choose OK or press Enter.

In figure 19.2 the callout in the first column is centered vertically to create even white space at the top and bottom of the column.

In figure 19.2 the masthead type is justified to set it further apart from the body text and to fit more copy into a smaller area.

Wild plants can give you one of the best meals you've ever eaten. Just spend a little time spent in the woods, gathering nuts, berries, roots, and leaves. You'll be surprised when you're cooking your meal; the aroma of wild plants cooking will attract everyone on the block. And when you're ready to eat, you'll think you're in a gourmet restaurant. We have many recipe books for cooking the wild plants you gather; plus specialty books on baking breads, making desserts, and making salads with wild plants.

kinds are available at our store to give you hints and tips on cooking your favorite wild, edible plants.

Fresh young flower buds of the cattail are great when boiled and served with lots of butter. The thick yellow pollen is just like flour when mixed 1/2 and 1/2 with white or wheat flour and used for baking. Peel the young stems to eat raw or cooked like vegetables. Fall roots, boiled like potatoes, taste great, too!

Arrowhead tubers bake, boil, cream or scallop just like potatoes. They are also good boiled then sliced up in salads.

Burdock, found in any meadow, is tasty when simmered and served with butter. Be sure to use two waters to simmer them in. Burdock leaves, when boiled in two waters, taste like greens. Add a little vinegar and bacon bits before serving. Use the inside of the flower stalks like a vegetable, too. Just boil, again in two waters, and serve with butter. The flower stalk piths, of the burdock plant, boiled with an equal amount of sugar, and a little orange juice make a delicious candy.

For recipes for these and many, many more edible wild plants, see our large selection of cookbooks. We also forage plants weekly for the freshest leaves, flowers, and roots. Stop by our store, or send for a catalog today!

SALVES FOR YOUR SKIN

Salves made from olive oil, beeswax and concentrated amounts of roots, leaves and flowers are the best medicines for skin irritations. All natural and pure, no preservatives or chemicals, our salves are the best around! Listed here are only a few of the salves we stock.

Chickweed - skin rashes, soothe itching

Calendula - insect bites, rashes

Comfrey - bee stings, burns

Plantain - bee stings, itches

Green Elder - cuts, bruises

Sage - sore muscles

Beech - blisters, swelling

Aloe - any skin problem

Mint Mixture - soothing and cooling

HERBAL TERM

Infusion
An infusion is much like a tea, however, you actually boil the plant first, then steep it. Use 1 oz. or so of the herb (flower or leaves) to a pint of water. Bring the water and plant to a boil, then remove from heat and steep for at least 10 minutes. You may add honey or sugar while hot. Then cool to lukewarm before drinking.

Page 3

Fig. 19.3   Page three of the newsletter.

MOUNTAIN SORREL
Published Quarterly
Volume 9, Issue No. 2

Editor .... L. J. Hummel
Circulation Ed. ... D. E. Dunn
Advertising Ed. ... D. M. Hawk

MOUNTAIN SORREL is the official publication of Silver Bark's Herbal Remedies and Book Store. Subscriptions to customers are free with purchase of yearly catalog at $7.95.

Orders for any product in this newsletter are welcomed by mail, phone, or in person. We do not guarantee our products, recipes or any advice in this newsletter as a medication or cure. We take no responsibility for misuse of any product we sell.

TERRY MILFORT-HALE HERBALIST VISITS OUR STORE

Terry Milfort-Hale, an expert herbalist who's studied in Wyoming, Texas, West Virginia, North Carolina, and many other states visits our store on Friday, June 12, 1993. From 2:00 p.m. to 4:00 p.m., Terry will lecture on herbs and plants found in our area of the state.

Terry, who lives in Houston, lectures around the country about edible wild plants and herbs. She's world-famous for her tinctures, salves, oils and other herbal concoctions.

Both Terry, and her husband John, play music as well as study herbs. Perhaps we can convince them to favor us with a fiddle and bagpipe tune during their visit.

We're honored to have both Terry and John at our store for one day only. Don't miss your chance to discuss your herb garden!!! We'll also be selling Terry's latest best seller, *John and Terry's Garden*, as well as her other three books, and some of her favorite concoctions.

OUR SPRING SPECIALS

SILVER BARK BRAND:
Chamomile Wash
Peppermint After-Shave
Mugwort Bath Mixture
Sage Shampoo
Fennel and Mint Toothpaste
Natural Insect Repellent

TINCTURES:
Spearmint
Lemon Balm
Cherry Bark
White Pine
Thyme
Anise

EQUIPMENT:
Drying Racks
Suribachis
Beeswax
Pint Jars
Dehydrators
2 oz. jars

SILVER BARK'S HERBAL REMEDIES AND BOOK STORE
13259 Main Street
Beckley, WV 25801

Fig. 19.4 Page four with a masthead and a mailing panel.

The steps to produce page one of the newsletter are as follows:

You need a larger bottom margin in a document that uses page numbers.

1. Choose **Page Modify Page Layout**.

2. In Modify, choose **Margins & Columns**. Change the Top, Left, and Right margins to .75". Change the Bottom margin to 1".

3. In Number of Columns, choose **3**. Set the Gutter Width to **.35"**.

4. In Modify, choose **Lines**. In Around Page, choose **All**. For the Line Style, choose the second rule. In Position, choose **Close to inside**. Choose OK or press Enter.

5. Choose **View Layout Mode**. Go to page two. Place the cursor in the bottom margin and press Ctrl+C (for Version 2.0) or Ctrl+E (for Version 3.0).

6. Choose **Page Page Numbering**. In Start On **Page**, type **2**; in Start With Number, type **2**. In Leading Text, type the following:

   Page(space)

   Choose OK or press Enter. The page number appears on this and following pages.

7. Return to page one and draw a frame along the top margin.

8. Choose **Frame Modify Frame Layout**.

9. In Frame, choose Type **S**quare Corners.

10. In Frame, choose **Size & Position**. In Size, choose **Width** and type **7"**; in Height type **1.5"**. Clear Margins.

11. In Frame, choose **Lines & Shadows**. In Lines, choose **Bottom**. In Line **S**tyle, choose the second pattern. In Shadows, choose **None**.

Choose Make Default to format all subsequent drawn frames the same way until you change the default again. If you use one type of frame often in a document, changing the default saves time; you easily can change the default back to the original setting when you finish.

12. Choose **Make Default**. Choose OK or press Enter.

13. Place the cursor in the frame and type the following:

    MOUNTAIN SORREL(Enter)
    A Quarterly Newsletter of Herbal Curatives and Preventatives

14. Select MOUNTAIN SORREL. Choose CaslonOpenFace, 36 point, bold, center. Select the M and change it to 60 point (or as close as your printer allows). Repeat with the S.

15. Select A Quarterly Newsletter... Choose Helv, 12 point, center.

16. Choose **Style Modify Style**. In the **S**tyle selection box, choose Title.

17. In Modify, choose **F**ont. Choose Tms Rmn, 14 point, bold.

18. In Modify, choose **A**lignment. Choose **L**eft.

19. In Modify, choose **S**pacing. In Paragraph Spacing, select **0**" for Ab**o**ve and **.10**" for **B**elow. Choose **S**ave.

20. In the Style selection box, choose Body Text.

21. In Modify, choose **F**ont. Choose Tms Rmn, 12 point.

22. In Modify, choose S**p**acing. In Paragraph Spacing, choose **.15**" for **B**elow.

23. In Modify, turn on **H**yphenation. Choose OK or press Enter.

24. Place the cursor in front of THE HEALING POWER OF LAVENDER and press Enter once. Move up one line and change the paragraph return to the style Body Single and its size to 8 point. Repeat at the top of the third column.

25. Change THE HEALING POWER OF LAVENDER to the style Title. Repeat with the other heads as shown in the figures.

26. Place the cursor in front of The North American Indians... Press Enter twice.

27. Choose **S**tyle Create Style. In the New Style dialog box, type **Callout** as the name of the style. Choose Modify or press Enter.

28. In Modify, choose **F**ont. Choose Tms Rmn, 14 point, italic.

29. In Modify, choose S**p**acing. In Line Spacing, change to 1 1/2". In Paragraph Spacing, change **B**elow to **0**".

30. In Modify, turn **H**yphenation off. Choose OK or press Enter.

31. Select the text from The North American Indians... through ...the power of natural healing. Change this text to the style Callout.

32. Referring to the figure, press Enter after any long lines in the callout so that the text spreads out over the column.

Ami Pro does not allow you to turn on only one column rule; you therefore must create a narrow frame for the vertical rule dividing the callout from the body text. After you create the frame, copy it to the remaining pages.

Y ou should not hyphenate any text in the callouts; doing so is distracting to the reader.

The steps to create this frame are as follows:

1. Draw a long, narrow frame in the gutter between columns 1 and 2. Choose Frame Modify Frame.

2. In Frame, choose **Size & Position**. In Size, set the **Width** at **.15"** and the **Height** at **7.6"**. In Position On Page, set **Down** From the Top at **2.2"** and **In** From the Left at **2.9"**. The Margins should be cleared if you saved them as a default setting in the preceding directions.

3. In Frame, choose Lines & Shadows. Choose **Left** and the first Line Style. Choose OK or press Enter.

4. Select the frame and copy it. Go to page two.

Format page two as follows:

1. Paste the frame from page one. Lengthen the frame to stretch from the top to the bottom margin.

2. Place the cursor in front of `Joe-Pye Weed was named after...` Press Enter twice.

3. Select the text from `Joe-Pye Weed was named after...` through `...and as an astringent."` Change this type to Callout.

4. Select and change the heads as shown in the figure.

5. Save and print your document.

Designing a Newsletter with Headers

You can add page numbers in a newsletter in many simple ways by using Ami Pro's automatic numbering. Another way to add page numbers is to combine Ami Pro's automatic numbering feature with the headers and footers feature, beginning on page two.

Page one of the newsletter uses a different combination of body text and heads (see fig. 19.5). The body text is justified and uses interparagraph spacing, and the heads are centered. This design employs an interesting use of white space because the gutters and margins are well-defined, but the space around the heads is free-form.

You can select the page number at the bottom of the page and change its formatting to italic or a smaller type if you want.

Mountain Sorrel

A Quarterly Newsletter of Herbal Curatives and Preventatives

The Healing Power of Lavender

Everyone knows of the delicious fragrance of lavender, especially English lavender, but few know of its medicinal qualities. Any of the three species of lavender make potions.

A terrific calmative, lavender has the power to soothe headaches and nervous tension. Simply steep lavender flowers in hot water for 15 to 20 minutes, and sip a cupful of the tea two or three times during the day.

A stronger tea of lavender is good as a gargle for sore throats; it also relieves stomach aches and colic. We stock dried English and French lavenders in bunches and one pound bags, at a reasonable price. We also sell lavender oil extract for use as a medicinal oil.

...the power to soothe headaches and nervous tension...

Rosemary, More Than a Cooking Herb

Both the leaves and flowers of rosemary have been used to alleviate depression and insomnia. A simple rosemary tea, with a bit of ginger added, also comforts a nervous or upset stomach. Rosemary oil is widely known for its antibacterial properties, as well. Lastly, if you have dark hair, try a strong rosemary tea for a rinse after washing. It not only makes your hair shiny and soft, but it clears up your dandruff, too.

We stock a full supply of rosemary leaves, flowers, oil and our special home-made rosemary shampoo and rinses.

Catnip, Not Just For Cats

A member of the mint family, catnip contains many properties other mints do. As a pleasant tasting tea, catnip is an anti-spasmodic and a calmative. Treat stomach ailments, colic and intestinal complaints. Catnip calms nervousness and anxiety.

Having a sleepless night? Try some catnip tea. If you have a cat, though, watch out, he'll try to drink your tea, too!

We stock catnip in one-half and one pound cans, as well as seeds to start your own plants in your garden.

It's Not Just a Weed, Joe-Pye Weed

Often seen growing along the railroad tracks or roadsides, in fields and meadows, Joe-Pye Weed is also known as Queen of the Meadow. The root is traditionally used to ease lower back pain and rheumatism. Leaves are sometimes used to break a fever by bringing on intense sweating. Use the root or leaves in teas and tinctures; but do be careful, too much, too often, can be toxic.

We not only keep Joe-Pye Weed roots in four and eight ounce containers, but in 1 pound bags, as well. Our Joe-Pye is collected fresh each Saturday morning during the spring, and fall. From the moist forests and meadows within the

Fig. 19.5 Page one of the newsletter design; justified body text with no indent and interparagraph spacing.

The nameplate contains a combination of right-aligned text and clip art. The Brush Script and the shadow around the nameplate create a dark, heavy nameplate. This combination contrasts well with the white space in the body of the newsletter. Finally, a callout that uses heavy rules helps balance the heavy nameplate. The rules bordering the callout are the same ones used in the nameplate.

On page two, the same rules border the screened masthead (see fig. 19.6). The rest of the formatting is the same as on page one, with the exception of the header. Because page two is a left page, the page number appears on the left of the header. On the right is the name of the newsletter. The type is Helvetica 10-point bold. The entire header is separated from the text by a one-point rule. Neither page one nor the last page contains a header.

Figure 19.7 shows page three of the newsletter so you can see the right page header. The page is a right page with the number on the right. Ami Pro's automatic numbering fills in the proper page numbers after the initial left and right pages. The rest of the page is similar to page two. Subheads are used to break the article Herbal Terms into manageable sections. In addition, an ad at the bottom announces a sale. Note that the bordering rules are the same as those of the nameplate, with a screen and a three-column width for increased emphasis.

The steps to set up the page and headers of the newsletter are the following:

1. Choose File. **O**pen NEWBASE2. Save **As News2**.

2. Choose **P**age **M**odify Page Layout.

3. In Modify, choose **M**argins & Columns. Change the **L**eft and **R**ight margins to **.70"**. Change the **B**ottom margin to **.60"** and the **T**op to **1"**.

4. In Number of Columns, choose **3**. Set the **G**utter Width to **.35"**.

5. To set margins for the header, in Modify, choose **H**eader. In Pages, choose **L**eft. In the Header margins, change the **L**eft and **R**ight margins to **.70"**. Choose **B**egin on Second Page.

6. In the Header ruler, move the tab from 7" to 7.75".

7. In Pages, choose **R**ight. In the Header margins, change the **L**eft and **R**ight margins to **.70"**. Change the tab to 7.75" on the Header ruler. Choose OK or press Enter.

8. Go to page two. Place the cursor in the top margin. Type the following:

Page(space, Tab)**Mountain Sorrel**

9. Place the cursor after the space, choose **Page Page** Numbering. In Start on **Page**, type **2**; in Start with Number, type **2**. Choose OK or press Enter. The page number appears in the header.

10. Choose **Style Create** Style. Name the new style **Header**. Choose Modify or press Enter.

11. In Modify, choose **Font**. Choose Helv, 10 point, bold.

12. In Modify, choose **Lines**. Choose the Line **B**elow and the second Line Style. In **S**pacing, type **.05**. Choose OK or press Enter.

13. Select the type in the header and assign the style Header.

14. Go to page three. Place the cursor in the top margin. Type the following:

    Mountain Sorrel(Tab)**Page 3**

    From here, the automatic numbering takes over.

15. Select the text and assign the style Header.

The steps to format page one of the newsletter are as follows:

1. Press Ctrl+Home to go to page one.

2. Draw a frame along the top margin.

3. Choose **F**rame **M**odify Frame Layout.

   If you changed the default in the last instructions you need not make many of these changes. All changes, however, are listed here in case you didn't modify Ami Pro's default frame formatting.

4. In Frame, choose **T**ype. Choose **S**quare Corners.

5. In Frame, choose **S**ize & Position. In Size, choose **W**idth and type **7.18"**; in **H**eight, type **1.64"**. Set the **L**eft, **T**op, and **B**ottom margins to **.15"**; set the **R**ight margin to **.25"**.

6. In Frame, choose **L**ines & Shadows. In Lines, choose All. In Line Style, choose the last pattern in the box. In Shadows, choose Normal and choose the bottom left arrow to move the shadow. Choose OK or press Enter.

7. Choose **Style Create** Style. Name the style **Nameplate**. Choose Modify or press Enter.

8. Choose Brush Script, 56 point (or as close as your printer allows), bold, right-aligned. Choose OK or press Enter.

9. Choose **Style Create** Style. Name the new style **Nameplate 2**. Choose Modify or press Enter.

C reate a new style for the nameplate text so that changes in spacing to other styles do not affect the nameplate.

Page 2   Mountain Sorrel

MOUNTAIN SORREL

Published Quarterly
Volume 9, Issue No. 2
Editor
L. J. Hummel
Circulation Editor
G. E. Durham
Advertising Editor
D. M. Hawk

MOUNTAIN SORREL is the official publication of Silver Bark's Herbal Remedies and Book Store. Subscriptions to customers are free with purchase of yearly catalog at $7.95.

Orders for any product in this newsletter are welcomed by mail, phone, or in person. We do not guarantee our products, recipes or any advice in this newsletter as a medication or cure. We take no responsibility for misuse of any product we sell.

area, only the most perfect roots and flowers are gathered. We then dry the herb by hanging it upside down in a cool, dark place, to guarantee you receive only the best.

Mullein, Every Part Beneficial

The flowers, leaves and roots of this plant are all valuable medicines. Perfect as an anti-spasmodic, emollient and sedative, mullein is also an astringent. Prepare an infusion of one half cup mullein leaves and flowers to two pints water for most complaints; be sure to strain well. Mullein oil is very useful as a sedative. Simply place a few drops in your tea

and sweet dreams. The root is very strong, leaves and flowers less so. Remember to never use the seed of mullein, except to plant. The seeds are very noxious.

We stock all parts of the mullein plant, roots, leaves, flowers, and oil.

Poultices, Natural Healing

Poultices are used to treat the outer body. Skin ailments, muscle pain, cuts, burns, even colds and flu. Many herbs can make a natural poultice. The ever popular Mustard Plaster has been used for

centuries to treat weakness and fatigue. Burdock is great for gout; cayenne is perfect for a cold or the flu. Of course, you're familiar with the properties of the Aloe plant for burns, but did you know borage, comfrey and plantain are excellent treatments as well? Plantain, by the way, is the best thing for a bee sting, especially when you're caught out in the garden, or the woods. Just chew the leaf for a moment or two and place it on the sting. It draws out the poison and reduces swelling.

Wild Edible Plants

If you like to gather your own plants and roots for cooking, we suggest the following for some of the most exciting dishes ever! Cookbooks of all kinds

are available at our store to give you hints and tips on cooking your favorite wild, edible plants.

Fresh young flower buds of the cattail are great when boiled and served with lots of butter. The thick yellow pollen is just like flour when mixed 1/2 and 1/2 with white or wheat flour and used for baking. Peel the young stems to eat raw or cooked like vegetables. Fall roots, boiled like potatoes, taste great, too!

Arrowhead tubers bake, boil, cream or scallop just like potatoes. They are also good boiled then sliced up in salads.

Burdock, found in any meadow, is tasty when simmered and served with butter. Be sure to use two waters to simmer them in and each cooking should be for at least 20 minutes. Burdock leaves, when boiled in two waters, taste like greens. Add a little vinegar and bacon bits before serving. Use the inside of the flower stalks like a vegetable, too. Just boil, again in two waters, and serve with butter. The flower stalk piths, of the burdock plant, boiled with an equal amount of sugar, and a little orange juice make a delicious candy.

For recipes for these and many, many more edible wild plants, see our large selection of cookbooks. We also forage plants weekly for the freshest leaves, flowers, and roots.

Fig. 19.6   Page two of the newsletter with a masthead and a header.

Herbal Terms

Infusion

An infusion is much like a tea, however, you actually boil the plant first, then steep it. Use 1 oz. or so of the herb (flower or leaves) to a pint of water. Bring the water and plant to a boil, then remove from heat and steep for at least 10 minutes. You may add honey or sugar while hot. Then cool to luke-warm before drinking.

Decoction

Similar to an infusion, decoction is used with the roots of the plant. Since they are hard, you must boil them for at least 10 minutes, then steep for 10 minutes more. Use 1 cup root to 1 pint water.

Arthritis

Many plants are suited for the pains of arthritis. Try infusions or decoctions of horseradish, black elder, chickweed, comfrey, drop wart and shave grass. Make an arthritis liniment of yerba santa and wintergreen. Or try a poultice of cayenne, lobelia, mullein and slippery elm bark.

We have recipes for all of the above.

Terry Milfort-Hale Visits Our Store

Terry Milfort-Hale, an expert herbalist who's studied in Wyoming, Texas, West Virginia, North Carolina, and many other states visits our store on Friday, June 12, 1992. From 2:00 p.m. to 4:00 p.m., Terry will lecture on herbs and plants found in our area of the state.

Terry, who lives in Houston, lectures around the country about edible wild plants and herbs. She's world-famous for her tinctures, salves, oils and other herbal concoctions. Terry and her husband, John, have traveled throughout the US; she in search of unusual herbs; he in search of music.

While both Terry and John play music, John is the more entranced of the two. Perhaps we can convince him to favor us with a bagpipe tune during their visit. We're honored to have both Terry and John at our store for one day only. Don't miss your chance to discuss your herb garden and adventures with Terry!!! We'll also be selling Terry's latest best seller, John and Terry's Garden, as well as her other three books, and some of her favorite concoctions.

Our Spring Specials

Visit our store between April 1st and June 1st to receive tremendous savings. During our Spring Special, the following items are discounted 10%. If you bring this newsletter with you, you'll receive another 10% off. In addition, if you purchase $100 or more of anything in our store, you'll receive another 10% off. You can't afford to miss our Spring Special!

Silver Bark Brand:

   Chamomile Wash

   Peppermint After-Shave

   Mugwort Bath Mixture

   Sage Shampoo

   Fennel Toothpaste

Tinctures:

   Spearmint

   Lemon balm

   Cherry Bark

   White Pine

   Thyme

Equipment:

   Drying Racks

   Suribachis

   Beeswax

   Pint Jars

   Dehydrators

BAY AND EUCALYPTUS MASSAGE OIL

ON SALE DURING THE MONTH OF JUNE — 40% OFF

Fig. 19.7   Page three of the newsletter; a right page with the header information switched.

10. Choose Helv, 12 point, right-aligned. Choose OK or press Enter.

11. Position the cursor in the frame. Type the following:

    MOUNTAIN SORREL(Enter)
    A **Quarterly Newsletter of Herbal Curatives and Preventatives**

12. Select MOUNTAIN SORREL. Apply the Nameplate styles.

13. Select A Quarterly Newsletter... Choose the Nameplate 2 style.

14. Draw a frame below the first frame to create even spacing between the nameplate and the text. Choose F**rame** M**odify** Frame Layout.

15. In Frame, choose Size & Position. In Size, choose **Width** and type **7.18"**; in **Height** type **.30"**.

16. In Frame, choose Lines & Shadows. In Lines, deselect A**ll**. In Shadows, choose N**one**. Choose OK or press Enter.

17. Copy and paste this frame. Resize the copied frame to hold the clip art in the nameplate and reposition it in the first frame to the left. Text Wrap should be set to Wrap Text Around on the frame that holds the clip art.

18. Choose File Import Picture. In AmiDraw files, choose FLOWERS.SDW. Choose OK or press Enter.

19. Choose Style Modify Style. In the Style selection box, choose Title.

20. In Modify, choose Font. Choose Helv, 18 point, bold.

21. In Modify, choose Alignment. Choose Center.

22. In Modify, choose S**pacing**. In Paragraph Spacing, select **0** for Above and Below. In Line Spacing, choose Custom and type **.29"**. Choose S**ave**.

23. In the Style selection box, choose Body Text.

24. In Modify, choose Font. Choose Tms Rmn, 12 point.

25. In Modify, choose Alignment. Choose J**ustify**.

26. In Modify, turn on H**yphenation**.

27. In Modify, choose S**pacing**. In Paragraph Spacing, set **Below** and **Above** at **.10"**. Choose S**ave**.

28. In the *Style* selection box, choose Subhead.

29. In Modify, choose **F**ont. Choose Helv, 14 point, bold, italic.

30. In Modify, choose **A**lignment. Choose **C**enter.

31. In Modify, choose S**p**acing. In Paragraph Spacing, set **B**elow at 0" and **A**bove at .05". Choose OK or press Enter.

32. Draw another frame for the callout in column one. Choose F**r**ame Modify Frame Layout.

33. In Frame, choose **T**ype. Choose **S**quare corners.

34. In Frame, choose **S**ize & Position. In Margins, set the **L**eft, **R**ight, and **B**ottom margins to .05". Set the Top margin at **.25"**.

35. In Frame, choose Lines & Shadows. In Lines, choose Top and **B**ottom and the last style in the Line Style box. In Shadows, choose None. Choose OK or press Enter.

36. Copy this frame. Go to page two and paste the frame. Return to page one.

37. Position the cursor in the frame. Type the following:

> **...the power to soothe**(Enter)
> **headaches and**(Enter)
> **nervous tension...**

38. Choose **S**tyle **C**reate Style. Name the style Callout. Choose Modify or press Enter.

39. In Modify, choose **F**ont. Choose Helv, 14 point, italic.

40. In Modify, choose A**l**ignment. Choose **C**enter.

41. In Modify, choose S**p**acing. In Line Spacing, choose **C**ustom and type .30". In Paragraph Spacing, change **A**bove and **B**elow to 0".

42. In Modify, turn off **H**yphenation. Choose OK or press Enter.

43. Select the type in the frame and assign the Callout style.

The steps to format page two of the newsletter are as follows:

1. Choose **S**tyle **C**reate Style. Name the style **Masthead**. Choose Modify or press Enter.

2. In Modify, choose **F**ont. Choose Tms Rmn, 10 point.

3. In Modify, choose A**l**ignment. In Indents, choose First and type **.20"**.

*C*opying the formatted frame ensures consistency in your newsletter.

4. In Modify, choose **S**pacing. In Paragraph Spacing, change A**b**ove and **B**elow to 0". Choose OK or press Enter.

5. Position the frame you copied onto page two in the first column, as shown in the figure, and enlarge it. You can add a light screen to it if you want.

6. Position the cursor in the frame. Choose the style Masthead. Type the following:

MOUNTAIN SORREL(Enter, Enter)
Published Quarterly(Enter)
Volume 9, Issue No. 2(Enter)
Editor(Enter)
L. J. Hummel(Enter)
Circulation Editor(Enter)
G. E. Durham(Enter)
Advertising Editor(Enter)
D. M. Hawk(Enter, Enter)

7. Select the text you just typed. Choose Text In**d**entions. Change the First line indent to 0". Choose OK or press Enter.

8. Select MOUNTAIN SORREL and choose 12 point, bold.

9. Enter your own text or refer to the figure. Type the rest of the text in the masthead.

10. Save and print your document.

Designing a Newsletter with Tables

Using Ami Pro's column and frame features is an excellent way to produce newsletters. The table feature offers another way to create columns with a different look. You can use one or two tables per page, divide each table into two columns, and use automatic row height to create the layout shown in figure 19.8.

One of the reasons to create columns this way is that your screens and borders look different from those added with columns or frames. Working with tables, however, can be somewhat difficult until you get used to it. Sometimes the tables jump to the next page or extend onto two or more pages. This situation is easy to rectify, but can be disconcerting to a new user.

A Quarterly Newsletter of Herbal Curatives and Preventatives

The Healing Power of Lavender

Everyone knows of the delicious fragrance of lavender, especially English lavender, but few know of its medicinal qualities. Any of the three species of lavender make potions.

A terrific calmative, lavender has the power to soothe headaches and nervous tension.

A stronger tea of lavender is good as a gargle for sore throats; it also relieves stomach aches and colic. We stock dried English and French lavenders in bunches and one pound bags, at a reasonable price. We also sell lavender oil extract for use as a medicinal oil.

Rosemary, More Than a Cooking Herb

Both the leaves and flowers of rosemary have been used to alleviate depression and insomnia. A simple rosemary tea, with a bit of ginger added, also comforts a nervous or upset stomach. Rosemary oil is widely known for its antibacterial properties, as well. Lastly, if you have dark hair, try a strong rosemary tea for a rinse after washing. It not only makes your hair shiny and soft, but it clears up your dandruff, too.

We stock a full supply of rosemary leaves, flowers, oil and our special home-made rosemary shampoo and rinses. Stop by and see our selection today!

Catnip, Not Just For Cats

A member of the mint family, catnip contains many properties other mints do. As a pleasant tasting tea, catnip is an antispasmodic and a calmative. Treat stomach ailments, colic and intestinal complaints. Catnip calms nervousness and anxiety.

Having a sleepless night? Try some catnip tea. If you have a cat, though, watch out, he'll try to drink your tea, too! We stock catnip in one-half and one pound cans, as well as seeds to start your own plants in your garden.

It's Not Just a Weed, Joe-Pye Weed

Often seen growing along the railroad tracks or roadsides, in fields and meadows, Joe-Pye Weed is also known as Queen of the Meadow. The root is traditionally used to ease lower back pain and rheumatism. Leaves are sometimes used to break a fever by bringing on intense sweating. Be very careful, however, Joe-Pye Weed can be toxic.

Fig. 19.8   A newsletter created with tables.

Because the tables contain lines, the body text is justified to repeat the vertical emphasis. The design in figure 19.9 does create a grayer page, however.

Because the type styles of this newsletter are the same as those of the last newsletter, directions for formatting body text and heads are not included here.

Page two is shown so that you can see how the design works (see fig. 19.9). The header is the same as in the last design and the table is formatted the same as on the first page of this newsletter. No screen was added to the right column of this table. Again, you can mirror the column designs and headers for a nice effect.

Because you must use the Draw feature to create the nameplate in figure 19.8, you have to use a mouse. If you do not use a mouse, you can substitute another nameplate for the one shown in figure 19.8.

The steps to create the nameplate are as follows:

1. Draw a frame with any border and shadow you want to use along the top margin of the page, similar to that in the figure.

2. Choose Tools Drawing. Using the curve, or any tool, draw the background designs. These lines were drawn with the curve tool; many were copied, resized, and repositioned.

3. You also can change the line widths by choosing the line or curve and choosing the **Draw Line Style**.

4. Exit the Draw feature.

5. Draw another frame on top of the first, choosing **F**rame **M**odify Frame Layout.

6. In Frame, choose Type. Choose Transparent.

7. In Frame, choose Size & Position. In Size, set the **Width** at **7.37"** and the **Height** at **2.31"**. In Position, set **Down From the Top** at **.93"** and **In From the Left** at **.51"**. In Margins, set all margins at **.15"**.

8. In Frame, choose Lines & Shadows. In Lines, deselect All. In Shadows, choose None. Choose OK or press Enter.

9. Position the cursor in the frame. Type the following:

   MOUNTAIN SORREL(Press Enter three times)
   A Quarterly Newsletter of Herbal Curatives and Preventatives

10. You must create new styles for the nameplate type because when you add interparagraph spacing to the Body Text, it also affects this text. Mountain Sorrel is Brush Script, 60 point, bold, center. A Quarterly Newsletter... is Tms Rmn, 12 point, italic, center.

Mullein, Every Part Beneficial

The flowers, leaves and roots of this plant are all valuable medicines. Perfect as an antispasmodic, emollient and sedative, mullein is also an astringent. Prepare an infusion of one half cup mullein leaves and flowers to two pints water for most complaints; be sure to strain well. Mullein oil is very useful as a sedae you receive only the best.tive. Simply place a few drops in your tea and sweet dreams. The root is very strong, leaves and flowers less so. Remember to never use the seed of mullein, except to plant. The seeds are very noxious. We stock all parts of the mullein plant, roots, leaves, flowers, and oil.

Poultices, Natural Healing

Poultices are used to treat the outer body. Skin ailments, muscle pain, cuts, burns, even colds and flu. Many herbs can make a natural poultice. The ever popular Mustard Plaster has been used for centuries to treat weakness and fatigue. Burdock is great for gout; cayenne is perfect for a cold or the flu. Of course, you're familiar with the properties of the Aloe plant for burns, but did you know borage, comfrey and plantain are excellent treatments as well? Plantain, by the way, is the best thing for a bee sting, especially when you're caught out in the garden, or the woods. Just chew the leaf for a moment or two and place it on the sting. It draws out the poison and reduces swelling.

Terry Milfort-Hale, Herbalist Visits Our Store

Terry Milfort-Hale, an expert herbalist who's studied in Wyoming, Texas, West Virginia, North Carolina, and many other states visits our store on Friday, June 12, 1992. From 2:00 p.m. to 4:00 p.m., Terry will lecture on herbs and plants found in our area of the state.

Terry, who lives in Houston, lectures around the country about edible wild plants and herbs. She's world-famous for her tinctures, salves, oils and other herbal concoctions. Terry has traveled throughout the US in search of unusual herbs. Don't miss her exciting lecture.

Wild Edible Plants

If you like to gather your own plants and roots for cooking, we suggest the following for some of the most exciting dishes ever! Cookbooks of all kinds are available at our store to give you hints and tips on cooking your favorite wild, edible plants.Fresh young flower buds of the cattail are great when boiled and served with lots of butter. The thick yellow pollen is just like flour when mixed 1/2 and 1/2 with white or wheat flour and used for baking. Peel the young stems to eat raw or cooked like vegetables. Fall roots, boiled like potatoes, taste great, too!

Arrowhead tubers bake, boil, cream or scallop just like potatoes. They are also good boiled then sliced up in salads. Burdock, found in any meadow, is tasty when simmered and served with butter. Be sure to use two waters to simmer them in and each cooking should be for at least 20 minutes. Burdock leaves, when boiled in two waters, taste like greens. Add a little vinegar and bacon bits before serving. Use the inside of the flower stalks like a vegetable, too. Just boil, again in two waters, and serve with butter. The flower stalk piths, of the burdock plant, boiled with an equal amount of sugar, and a little orange juice make a delicious candy.

For recipes for these and many, many more edible wild plants, see our large selection of cookbooks.

Fig. 19.9 Page two of the newsletter created with tables.

The steps to create the table for the body text are as follows:

1. Choose Tools Tables. In Number of Columns, choose **2**; in Number of Rows, choose **1**. Choose Layout.

2. In Default Columns, the Width is **4.12"** and the Gutter is **.25"**.

3. In Default Rows, be sure that Automatic is turned on. In Options, choose Center Table On Page. Choose OK or press Enter.

Now that you have created the table, you can add a border or screens and then copy that table to other pages before you place text into it.

If you plan to mirror table columns on the second page, copy the table and then adjust the column widths.

To add text to the table, select the text to fit in the first column. The exact amount of text for the column may be hard to determine. After you format the body and heads, work with a small amount of text at a time until text fills the first column.

Make sure that the tables don't jump around on you. If you add too much text, the table may move to the second page. If you choose Automatic in the Default **R**ows dialog box, the table enlarges automatically to accommodate the text.

With each section of the text that you highlight, cut the text, place the cursor in the first column, and paste the text. When Ami Pro prompts, `Paste all of the data in current cell?`, choose **Yes**. Repeat the procedure with the second column.

Looking at Design

Because you are familiar with many formatting techniques, the following designs offer suggestions for adding variety to your newsletter. Brief instructions are added to any technique not yet covered in this book. The best way to discover Ami Pro's capabilities is to experiment with the program and then choose the designs that work best for your document.

Avant Garde is an open, extremely rounded typeface that gives a light feeling to the page. Because it's a difficult typeface to read, never use it as body text.

Figure 19.10 shows the first page of an innovative newsletter. Two frames make up the nameplate. The first contains the four rules created in Ami Pro's Draw feature. The second frame contains the right-aligned text. The nameplate's typeface and heads are set in Avant Garde.

The heads are right-aligned to mirror the alignment of the nameplate and are not set in bold type like most heads, thus creating a lighter, more open look for the page. The body text is Times Roman, justified with interparagraph spacing. Notice that the first letter of each story is set with larger (18 point) bold type. Variations on the large first character include changing the typeface (in this case, Avant Garde would look good), placing the large first character in a box, or creating a drop cap (moving the baseline of the first character down so that its top is even with the rest of the paragraph).

MOUNTAIN SORREL

A Quarterly Newsletter of Herbal Curatives and Preventatives

The Healing Power of Lavender

Everyone knows of the delicious fragrance of lavender, especially English lavender, but few know of its medicinal qualities. Any of the three species of lavender make potions. A terrific calmative, lavender has the power to soothe headaches and nervous tension. Simply steep lavender flowers in hot water for 15 to 20 minutes, and sip a cupful of the tea two or three times during the day.

A stronger tea of lavender is good as a gargle for sore throats; it also relieves stomach aches and colic. We stock dried English and French lavenders in bunches and one pound bags, at a reasonable price. We also sell lavender oil extract for use as a medicinal oil.

Rosemary, More Than a Cooking Herb

Both the leaves and flowers of rosemary have been used to alleviate depression and insomnia. A

simple rosemary tea, with a bit of ginger added, also comforts a nervous or upset stomach. Rosemary oil is widely known for its antibacterial properties, as well. Lastly, if you have dark hair, try a strong rosemary tea for a rinse after washing. It not only makes your hair shiny and soft, but it clears up your dandruff, too.

We stock a full supply of rosemary leaves, flowers, oil and our special home-made rosemary shampoo and rinses. Our supplies are limited, and believe us, they go fast! All natural, no preservatives, so order yours today, don't dare delay! Call, stop by, or mail your order today!

Catnip, Not Just For Cats

A member of the mint family, catnip contains many properties other mints do. As a pleasant tasting tea, catnip is an antispasmodic and a calmative. Treat stomach ailments, colic and intestinal complaints. Catnip calms nervousness and anxiety.

Having a sleepless night? Try some catnip tea. If you have a cat, though, watch out, he'll try to drink your tea, too!

We stock catnip in one-half and one pound cans, as well as seeds to start your own plants in your garden.

It's Not Just a Weed, Joe-Pye Weed

Often seen growing along the railroad tracks or roadsides, in fields and meadows, Joe-Pye Weed is also known as Queen of the Meadow. The root is traditionally used to ease lower back pain and rheumatism. Leaves are sometimes used to break a fever by bringing on intense sweating. Use the root or leaves in teas and tinctures; but do be careful, too much, too often, can be toxic. We not only keep Joe-Pye Weed roots in four and eight ounce containers, but in 1 pound bags, as well.

INSIDE:

Fig. 19.10 An innovative newsletter.

This design also includes a table of contents set off with rules that have the same thickness as those in the nameplate. You generally use a table of contents in a newsletter with more than four pages, although you can use one in a four-page newsletter to attract attention to interesting articles on the inside.

Figure 19.11 shows an inside page of a newsletter. The screened line above each head creates an attractive variation from the norm. When formatting the Title style, choose Lines, and choose one of the rules (this one is 9 point) to attach to the style. Then choose a screen from the color bar to apply to that rule.

If you use a thick rule, make sure that the rule doesn't overpower the heads.

Figure 19.12 shows an interesting head, `The Healing Herbs...` This head is not a nameplate. You can create this head by first drawing a frame that contains only a screen. Then draw another frame to hold the type. The second frame must be transparent and must be in front of the first frame. The typeface uses both Brush Script and Avant Garde.

Use the type of head in figure 19.12 as a title for a page of related articles.

You can create major heads for newsletters by using display type, graphics, and other elements to attract attention to sections or to specific stories, as shown in the preceding figure. You can create a variation on the major head by using a table. Select certain cells of the table and add a border or screen for an interesting effect. Figure 19.13 shows the table guidelines and the added borders on the screen.

The next step is either to connect the cells or, for more control over your type, to draw transparent frames with no lines or shadows in which to place the type. Figure 19.14 illustrates the finished major head. The type is DomCasual 48 point bold.

Photographs add appeal to any newsletter. It's important to consider the images you plan to add when designing your newsletter and to allow space for both the image and the caption. The image should be as wide as the columns. Also, you must place the image so that the page remains balanced and complements, rather than detracts from, the articles. Refer to Chapter 2 for more information about planning and designing a document with photographs and other graphic images.

Contrast the sans serif body text with serif heads.

Figure 19.15 shows a scanned image added to the newsletter. Notice that the image has plenty of breathing room and that a caption was added to identify the image. The caption is set in Helvetica, 9 point, bold, centered. Sufficient white space remains between the caption and the body text to separate the two. In this design, the body typeface is Arial, an ATM sans serif font, which adds a crisp look to the newsletter.

The Healing Power of Lavender

Everyone knows of the delicious fragrance of lavender, especially English lavender, but few know of its medicinal qualities. Any of the three species of lavender make potions.

A terrific calmative, lavender has the power to soothe headaches and nervous tension. Simply steep lavender flowers in hot water for 15 to 20 minutes, and sip a cupful of the tea two or three times during the day.

A stronger tea of lavender is good as a gargle for sore throats; it also relieves stomach aches and colic. We stock dried English and French lavenders in bunches and one pound bags, at a reasonable price. We also sell lavender oil extract for use as a medicinal oil.

Rosemary, More Than a Cooking Herb

Both the leaves and flowers of rosemary have been used to alleviate depression and insomnia. A simple rosemary tea, with a bit of ginger added, also comforts a nervous or upset stomach. Rosemary oil is widely known for its antibacterial properties, as well. Lastly, if you have dark hair, try a strong rosemary tea for a rinse after washing. It makes your hair shiny.

Catnip, Not Just For Cats

A member of the mint family, catnip contains many properties other mints do. As a pleasant tasting tea, catnip is an antispasmodic and a calmative. Treat stomach ailments, colic and intestinal complaints. Catnip calms nervousness and anxiety. Having a sleepless night? Try some catnip tea. If you have a cat, though, watch out, he'll try to drink your tea, too! We stock catnip in one-half and one pound cans, as well as seeds to start your own plants in your garden.

It's Not Just a Weed, Joe-Pye Weed

Often seen growing along the railroad tracks or roadsides, in fields and meadows, Joe-Pye Weed is also known as Queen of the Meadow. The root is traditionally used to ease lower back pain and rheumatism. Leaves are sometimes used to break a fever by bringing on intense sweating. Use the root or leaves in teas and tinctures; but do be careful, too much, too often, can be toxic.

Mullein, Every Part Beneficial

The flowers, leaves and roots of this plant are all valuable medicines. Perfect as an antispasmodic, emollient and sedative, mullein is also an astringent. Prepare an infusion of one half cup mullein leaves and flowers to two pints water for most complaints; be sure to strain well. Mullein oil is very useful as a sedative. Simply place a few drops in your tea and sweet dreams.

Poultices, Natural Healing

Poultices are used to treat the outer body. Skin ailments, muscle pain, cuts, burns, even colds and flu. Many herbs can make a natural poultice. The ever popular Mustard Plaster has been used for centuries to treat weakness and fatigue. Burdock is great for gout; cayenne is perfect for a cold or the flu. Of course, you're familiar with the properties of the Aloe plant for burns, but did you know borage, comfrey and plantain are excellent treatments as well? They all work especially well on bee stings. Next time you're out in the woods, search for the plantain first. You just may need it!

Fig. 19.11   Screened rules added to the head style.

The Healing Herbs All Natural

The Healing Power of Lavender

Everyone knows of the delicious fragrance of lavender, especially English lavender, but few know of its medicinal qualities. Any of the three species of lavender make potions.

A terrific calmative, lavender has the power to soothe headaches and nervous tension. Simply steep lavender flowers in hot water for 15 to 20 minutes, and sip a cupful of the tea two or three times during the day.

A stronger tea of lavender is good as a gargle for sore throats; it also relieves stomach aches and colic. We stock dried English and French lavenders in bunches and one pound bags, at a reasonable price. We also sell lavender oil extract for use as a medicinal oil.

Rosemary, More Than a Cooking Herb

Both the leaves and flowers of rosemary have been used to alleviate depression and insomnia. A simple rosemary tea, with a bit of ginger added, also comforts a nervous or upset stomach. Rosemary oil is widely known for its antibacterial properties.

Catnip, Not Just For Cats

A member of the mint family, catnip contains many properties other mints do. As a pleasant tasting tea, catnip is an antispasmodic and a calmative. Treat stomach ailments, colic and intestinal complaints. Catnip calms nervousness and anxiety.

Having a sleepless night? Try some catnip tea. If you have a cat, though, watch out, he'll try to drink your tea, too!

We stock catnip in one-half and one pound cans, as well as seeds to start your own plants in your garden.

It's Not Just a Weed, Joe-Pye Weed

Often seen growing along the railroad tracks or roadsides, in fields and meadows, Joe-Pye Weed is also known as Queen of the Meadow. The root is traditionally used to ease lower back pain and rheumatism. Leaves are sometimes used to break a fever by bringing on intense sweating. Use the root or leaves in teas and tinctures; but do be careful, too much, too often, can be toxic.

We not only keep Joe-Pye Weed roots in four and eight ounce containers, but in 1 pound bags, as well. Our Joe-Pye is collected fresh each Saturday morning during the spring, and fall. From the moist forests and meadows within the area, only the most perfect roots and flowers are gathered. We then dry the herb by hanging it upside down in a cool, dark place, to guarantee you receive only the best.

Mullein, Every Part Beneficial

The flowers, leaves and roots of this plant are all valuable medicines. Perfect as an antispasmodic, emollient and sedative, mullein is also an astringent. Prepare an infusion of one half cup mullein leaves and flowers to two pints water for most complaints; be sure to strain well. Mullein oil is very useful as a sedative.

Poultices, Natural Healing

Poultices are used to treat the outer body. Skin ailments, muscle pain, cuts, burns, even colds and flu. Many herbs can make a natural poultice. The ever popular Mustard Plaster has been used for centuries to treat weakness and fatigue. Burdock is great for gout; cayenne is perfect for a cold or

Fig. 19.12   An interesting major head created with two frames.

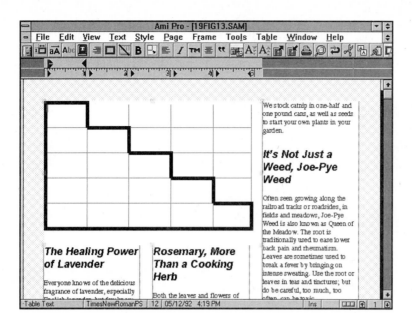

Fig. 19.13 Selecting various cells with an added border to create an interesting shape for a major heading.

You can add a photograph in two ways. One way is by using a scanned image. The other way is by pasting up a halftone. If you plan to use a scanned image in a document, be sure that you size the photograph before you scan it. Resizing the photograph after you bring it into Ami Pro creates a pattern of stripes that resembles plaid. Depending on how much you resize the image, the stripes can be extremely large or small.

After you import the scanned image, you can crop it to any size in Ami Pro. In addition, Ami Pro offers you image-processing options to change the image. You can lighten, darken, and adjust the brightness of an image to make it more attractive, and you can adjust the contrast, darkness, lightness, and so on, to help it print more clearly. An image processed in Ami Pro, however, takes much, much longer to print than one processed in the scanning program. Experiment with both alternatives to determine which works best for you.

The other way to add a photograph to your newsletter is to paste up a halftone. A halftone is a specially screened photograph that print shops produce and use. You should use this method only when you take the final output to a print shop for printing. Chapter 4 explains halftones and their use in detail.

Mullein, Every Part Beneficial

The flowers, leaves and roots of this plant are all valuable medicines. Perfect as an antispasmodic, emollient and sedative, mullein is also an astringent. Prepare an infusion of one half cup mullein leaves and flowers to two pints water for most complaints; be sure to strain well. Mullein oil is very useful as a sedative.

The Healing Power of Lavender

Everyone knows of the delicious fragrance of lavender, especially English lavender, but few know of its medicinal qualities. Any of the three species of lavender make potions.

A terrific calmative, lavender has the power to soothe headaches and nervous tension. Simply steep lavender flowers in hot water for 15 to 20 minutes, and sip a cupful of the tea two or three times during the day.

Rosemary, More Than a Cooking Herb

Both the leaves and flowers of rosemary have been used to alleviate depression and insomnia. A simple rosemary tea, with a bit of ginger added, also comforts a nervous or upset stomach. Rosemary oil is widely known for its antibacterial properties.

Catnip, Not Just For Cats

A member of the mint family, catnip contains many properties other mints do. As a pleasant tasting tea, catnip is an antispasmodic and a calmative. Treat stomach ailments, colic and intestinal complaints. Catnip calms nervousness and anxiety.

It's Not Just a Weed, Joe-Pye Weed

Often seen growing along the railroad tracks or roadsides, in fields and meadows, Joe-Pye Weed is also known as Queen of the Meadow. The root is traditionally used to ease lower back pain and rheumatism. Leaves are sometimes used to break a fever by bringing on intense sweating. Use the root or leaves in teas and tinctures; but do be careful, too much, too often, can be toxic.

Poultices, Natural Healing

Poultices are used to treat the outer body. Skin ailments, muscle pain, cuts, burns, even colds and flu. Many herbs can make a natural poultice. The ever popular Mustard Plaster has been used for centuries to treat weakness and fatigue. Burdock is great for gout; cayenne is perfect for a cold or the flu. Of course, you're familiar with the properties of the Aloe plant for burns, but did you know borage, comfrey and plantain are excellent treatments as well?

Wild Edible Plants

If you like to gather your own plants and roots for cooking, we suggest the following for some of the most exciting dishes ever! Cookbooks of all kinds are available at our store to give you hints and tips on cooking your favorite wild, edible plants.

Fresh young flower buds of the cattail are great when boiled and served with lots of butter. The

Fig. 19.14 The completed major head, Ten Steps to Good Health, formed in a table.

The Healing Power of Lavender

Everyone knows of the delicious fragrance of lavender, especially English lavender, but few know of its medicinal qualities. Any of the three species of lavender make potions.

A terrific calmative, lavender has the power to soothe headaches and nervous tension. Simply steep lavender flowers in hot water for 15 to 20 minutes, and sip a cupful of the tea two or three times during the day.

A stronger tea of lavender is good as a gargle for sore throats; it also relieves stomach aches and colic. We stock dried English and French lavenders in bunches and one pound bags, at a reasonable price. We also sell lavender oil extract for use as a medicinal oil.

Rosemary, More Than a Cooking Herb

Both the leaves and flowers of rosemary have been used to alleviate depression and insomnia. A simple rosemary tea, with a bit of ginger added, also comforts a nervous or upset stomach. Rosemary oil is widely known for its antibacterial properties, as well. Lastly, if you have dark hair,

One view from our gardens.

try a strong rosemary tea for a rinse after washing. It not only makes your hair shiny and soft, but it clears up your dandruff, too.

Catnip, Not Just For Cats

A member of the mint family, catnip contains many properties other mints do. As a pleasant tasting tea, catnip is an antispasmodic and a calmative. Treat stomach ailments, colic and intestinal complaints. Catnip calms nervousness and anxiety.

Having a sleepless night? Try some catnip tea. If you have a cat, though, watch out, he'll try to drink your tea, too!

We stock catnip in one-half and one pound cans, as well as seeds to start your own plants in your garden.

It's Not Just a Weed, Joe-Pye Weed

Often seen growing along the railroad tracks or roadsides, in fields and meadows, Joe-Pye Weed is also known as Queen of the Meadow. The root is traditionally used to ease lower back pain and rheumatism. Leaves are sometimes used to break a fever by bringing on intense sweating. Use the root or leaves in teas and tinctures; but do be careful, too much, too often, can be toxic.

We not only keep Joe-Pye Weed roots in four and eight ounce containers, but in 1 pound bags, as well. Our Joe-Pye is collected fresh each Saturday morning during the spring, and fall. From the moist forests and meadows within the area, only the most perfect roots and flowers are gathered. We then dry the herb by hanging it upside down in a cool, dark place, to guarantee you receive only the best.

Mullein, Every Part Beneficial

The flowers, leaves and roots of this plant are all valuable medicines. Perfect as an antispasmodic, emollient and sedative, mullein is also an astringent. Prepare an infusion of one half cup mullein leaves and flowers to two pints water for most com-

Fig. 19.15 A newsletter with a scanned image and caption added.

Recapping

In this chapter, you learned to use advanced Ami Pro techniques to create a complex newsletter. You learned to create a page border, a header with page numbers, a masthead, and a newsletter design that uses tables.

Creating Long Documents

VI

MARKETING SUMMARY FOR HUMBLE OPINIONS

BY PEAR ASSOCIATES, LTD.
JUNE 4, 1992

Includes

Producing a Business Report

Business reports inform and explain, and they usually focus on one specific project or one aspect of a project. Progress reports, annual reports, sales reports, inventory summaries, and marketing plans are only a few subjects for a business report. Almost all reports contain specific information regarding progress, profits, and expenditures. Finally, business reports incorporate figures, charts or graphs, spreadsheets, and text to explain these elements.

This chapter walks you through formatting several pages of a traditional business report and shows you other innovative report designs. The chapter also contains information about cover pages, tables of contents, footers, logos, imported spreadsheets, graphs, and more.

For detailed information on how to create a form like this see page 517.

Because you know about formatting procedures—such as setting fonts, style sheets, tabs, tables, indents, and adding borders—the instructions in this and the following chapter are less detailed than preceding chapters. Keystrokes for new procedures, however, are explained in detail. Some of the Ami Pro features included in this chapter are adding a table of contents, using the charting feature, and creating two types of charts.

Planning the Design Elements

Some reports may include photographs. You also can add artwork or illustrations. Predominant, however, are spreadsheets or other figures that represent the budget, profit, or losses in easy-to-understand terms. If you use a spreadsheet program or a graphing program, you easily can import your figures into Ami Pro. Microsoft Excel and Lotus 1-2-3 are two examples of spreadsheet program files you can import. Lotus Freelance for graphs and charts is another good program; Ami Pro even contains a charting feature that you can use to create your own charts and graphs. For specific information about saving and importing files into Ami Pro, refer to Appendix B, "Using Other Programs with Ami Pro." The instructions in this chapter refer to a spreadsheet and a chart and explain how to insert these elements into Ami Pro.

Choosing the Layout

The layout of a business report usually is not complicated. A standard design includes one or two columns printed on one side of an 8 1/2-by-11-inch page. The report may include headers or footers (or both), logos, footnotes, cross-references, page numbers, a table of contents (TOC), an index, and a bibliography. The contents are up to you; you may want to include all components that make the report easy to read and understand. If a report is short—8 to 10 pages, for example—you may decide not to use page numbers or a table of contents. If a report contains many figures and frequently refers to each figure, an index or a table of figures may be appropriate.

Proposals are similar to a business report in layout and design. Although proposals suggest a plan for the future, the subjects can be financial prospects, new business possibilities, marketing, and so on. You also may include graphs, charts, illustrations, and photographs. If you're planning a business proposal, apply the design and layout elements of this chapter to the proposal.

Business reports can be any length that is appropriate for the material you are presenting.

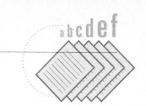

Determining the Size

Business reports and proposals usually are printed on one side of an 8 1/2-by-11-inch sheet of paper. Some reports, however, such as annual reports, are printed on both sides of 11-by-17-inch sheets, folded and saddle stitched to an 8 1/2-by-11-inch final size. Most businesses invest a great deal of time, money, and effort in annual reports. Photographs, full color, perfect typesetting, and high-quality printing are common for annual reports. Proposals are also often elaborate. Other business reports may be less refined, depending on the business, the report, and to whom the report is targeted.

Selecting the Paper and Binding

A good paper color choice for a business report is white or ivory, which enables the recipient to read the report comfortably. Customarily, the paper is 60# to 70#, the finish is generally smooth, vellum, linen, or enamel. The cover should match the paper in color and finish; use cover paper of 65# or 80#. (65# paper runs through most laser printers with no problems; 80# paper does not.)

Reports usually are bound by stapling or by spiral binding. If you side stitch the report, be sure that you leave the extra margin on the binding edge. If the report is printed on both sides, consider the design of the facing pages.

Designing a Traditional Business Report

A traditional business report consists of a cover and text, as well as tables, spreadsheets, charts, or any combination of graphic elements. The design you work with in this chapter contains all these elements and also includes footers and a table of contents.

This particular report is a marketing summary, and it includes text that explains the advertising techniques, the results of these techniques, a spreadsheet, and a chart.

A *binding margin* on the left allows room for side stitching or spiral binding. As part of the design, the left margin is much larger than is necessary for a binding margin, so the line length is comfortably readable.

O ften the cover is die cut, a rectangle or oval cut out in the cover so that you can read the title on the first page of the report.

S ee Chapter 4 for more information on finishing techniques.

S ee Chapter 2 for more information on binding margins.

If you place a graphic image on the cover, be sure that you left-align the image so that it mirrors the alignment of the text.

The table of contents is the last page you produce in a report.

The default style sheet includes a paragraph style for the numbered list.

With Ami Pro, you can use the information from any table to create a chart with the charting feature.

For information about data exchange, see Appendix B.

The simple cover page consists of left-aligned heads and double rules that border both the top and bottom margins (see fig. 20.1). You can place a photograph in the center of the page for emphasis, or you can let the white space speak for itself. The style of the cover matches the design of the inside pages.

If the report contains more than 8 or 10 pages, a table of contents is important. Figure 20.2 shows the table of contents for the report. Ami Pro makes compiling a table of contents easy when you use styles such as Title, Subhead, and so on. Notice that the header and the footer repeat the double rule.

The first page of the body of the report, page three, repeats the cover design with double rules and left-aligned heads. The left-aligned type and interparagraph spacing make the text of a long report easier to read. Because all pages are right-hand pages, all the page numbers in the footer are located on the right (see fig. 20.3). The header simply repeats *MARKETING SUMMARY*.

Page four continues the design, incorporating the default style sheet's numbered list. Notice that the new head begins at the top of a page (see fig. 20.4) and that extra white space is left at the bottom of the preceding page.

Figure 20.5 shows page five, which contains two subheads. These heads are in bold italic type and indented, along with their text, to set them apart from the rest of the body.

A table adds variation to the page (see fig. 20.6). Tables, charts, spreadsheets, graphs, and so on help the reader understand the text. You can use many illustrations in a business report to increase clarity, comprehension, and appeal.

Figures 20.7 and 20.8 contain further descriptions of the marketing techniques. Pages seven and eight leave white space at the bottom of the page rather than crowd all the text onto one page.

Figure 20.9 shows a pie chart that represents the information in the text. You can import charts from many programs into Ami Pro (see Appendix B), or you can create a chart with Ami Pro. The chart in figure 20.9 was produced with Ami Pro.

Figure 20.10 includes a spreadsheet to summarize the data in the report. Two fields are available in Ami Pro that help you update information from other applications. If you use other Windows applications that support DDE (Dynamic Data Exchange) and OLE (Object Linking and Embedding), you can import a spreadsheet and then update it automatically when the figures change. Most figures in a business report must be accurate up to the minute.

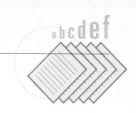

MARKETING SUMMARY FOR HUMBLE OPINIONS

BY PEAR ASSOCIATES, LTD.
JUNE 4, 1993

Fig. 20.1   Traditional cover design for a business report.

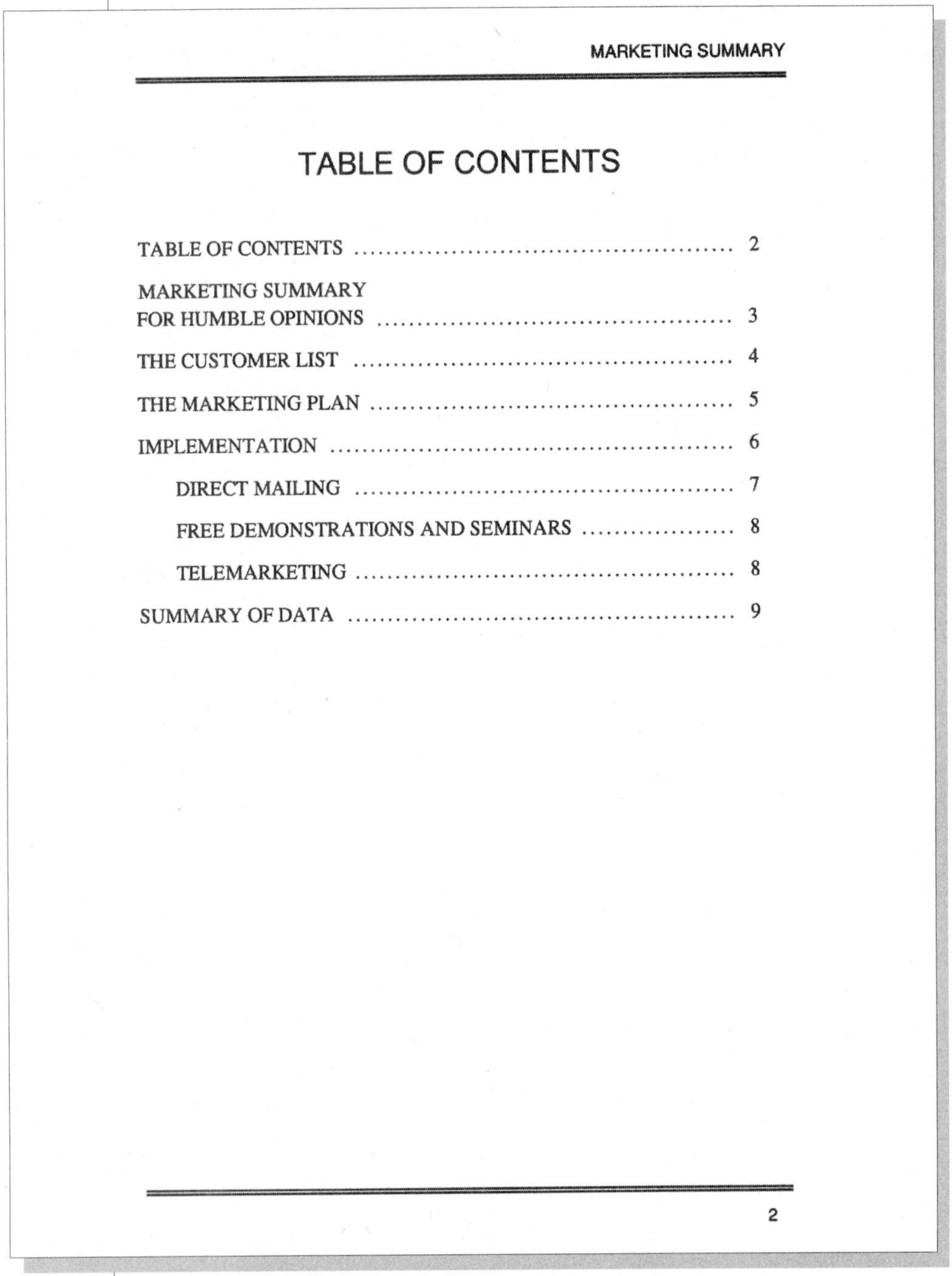
MARKETING SUMMARY

TABLE OF CONTENTS

2

Fig. 20.2 Table of contents generated by Ami Pro.

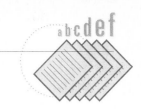

MARKETING SUMMARY
FOR HUMBLE OPINIONS

JUNE 4, 1993

Humble Opinions, a corporation dedicated to quality computer software training, initiated the Marketing Plan on June 4, 1992. Involved in this plan were
many strategies for client expansion and increased financial gain. This summary analyzes the success of the Marketing Plan in terms of customer base increase and profit from services offered.

Current economic trends in our area greatly affect the figures of the past three
months; however, earlier reports reveal that the basic premise of the Marketing
Plan is working. Should future trends prove to follow the same path as the past
three months, a new Marketing Plan will then be developed. We do suggest this
plan be followed for an additional period of six months before any long-term
decision is made.

Despite this recent decline in profits and sales, the Marketing Plan proved to be
both beneficial and profitable to Humble Opinions in the first nine months of
execution. The first three months, from June 1992 to August 1992, were considered the initiation period. Although contact with clients increased considerably, profits increased only slightly. During the second three months of the
Marketing Plan, from September 1992 to November 1992, profits showed incredible growth. This is attributed to initial planning and advertising to build
the customer base. The three-month period from December 1992 to February
1993 proved to support the objectives of the Plan through substantial client referrals and increased profits for the company.

We estimate the Marketing Plan, with minimum modifications, can and will
benefit the company in countless ways over the next six months. Customer lists
will continue to expand; profits will continue to rise at a reliable and constant
rate.

3

Fig. 20.3 The design elements repeated on page three; page numbers automatically changed.

THE CUSTOMER LIST

Humble Opinions is a business based solely on the customer; software instruction aimed specifically at people who buy and use personal computers in their business. The first requirement of the Marketing Plan was to accumulate a comprehensive list of clients who need software instruction. Many methods were implemented to accomplish this task.

As the list was compiled, pertinent information about each client was entered into a database for use in mailings, telemarketing and careful examination. Common data such as client name, address, and phone number as well as the company name, and key contact personnel and their phone numbers comprised the list. As time went on, we added specific information to each file, such as interest areas of the client, software products owned by their company, types of documents used by the company, and so on. In addition, comments were added to the files by the client about seminars, classes and demonstrations given by Humble Opinions that they attended. We then used these files as a basis for composing mailings and telemarketing scripts.

Following is a list of sources used for building the customer lists:

1. Customer records
2. Invoices from the last two years
3. Professional organizations' membership lists
4. Sign-up sheets from seminars, trade-shows, give-a-ways
5. Mailing lists purchased - specific to personal computer users
6. Salesman's cold calls

As part of the client listing process, we initiated a program to update customer files every six months. Executed by office staff members, telephone calls made regularly to the customer base serves to verify phone numbers, addresses, and key personnel. In addition, the telemarketing script includes questions directed to personal knowledge of new software instruction and training offered by the company.

4

Fig. 20.4 Page four of the report, showing a major head at the top of the page.

THE MARKETING PLAN

Using the client list as a foundation, our people created advertising that addressed the specific needs and concerns of the customers. Each project was dedicated to individual software programs, and the particular features that applied to a targeted group of clients.

By approaching the Plan in this way, more attention was devoted to the details of the software training that applied to individual customers. Thus, each customer perceived himself as distinctive, unique.

We used two methods of marketing for this project, Direct Marketing and Parallel Marketing. More time and effort were aimed at Direct Marketing. Considerable advantages were realized from this effort. In addition, the Parallel Marketing concentrated on one specific program and proved to be extremely profitable.

DIRECT MARKETING

Among the Direct Marketing techniques utilized in the Plan were free demonstrations and seminars, direct mailing of fliers and letters, and telemarketing. Each approach was carefully researched and executed to enable us to measure results. Coupons for discounts identified clients who received the direct mailings. Different coupons distinguished seminar and demonstration attendants. Those customers accepting training through telemarketing efforts referred to a key word for a discount. Naturally, this summary is based solely on those clients whose proven response corresponds with each marketing technique. Any who did not reply with the coupon or key word could not feasibly be included in this report.

PARALLEL MARKETING

Parallel Marketing targeted customers of one computer store in the area. Customers of that store were given such advertising items as mouse pads, shortcut key cards, and fliers with class descriptions. All of these items displayed a special phone number that identified them with this particular marketing approach.

5

Fig. 20.5   Indented text setting topics apart from the rest of the text.

IMPLEMENTATION

Before analyzing the comprehensive outcome of the Marketing Plan, let us first look at the four stages divided into three-month periods. We first concentrate on Direct Marketing; the second half of the summary is devoted to Parallel Marketing. The following calendar of events the implementation of the Marketing Plan by use of Direct Marketing.

	1st period Jun. - Aug.	2nd period Sept. - Nov.	3rd period Dec. - Feb.	4th period Mar. - May
Direct Mail	2 mailings 10,000	1 mailing 7,500	2 mailings 10,000	1 mailing 7,500
Seminars	4 seminars 2 demos.	2 seminars 4 demos.	4 seminars 2 demos.	2 seminars 4 demos.
Telemarketing	2,500 calls	1,500 calls	1,500 calls	2,500 calls

To further demonstrate the expenses versus profits of the Marketing Plan, let us now examine a sampling of each Direct Marketing technique as shown on the calendar. Each of these examples directly quotes expenditures and revenues as they apply to Humble Opinions.

Fig. 20.6   Page six of the report including a calendar of events in a table.

DIRECT MAILING

Our Direct Mailing campaign consisted of advertising letters and/or flyers dispatched to customers in the compiled database. The first mailing of 5,000 letters is typical in costs of subsequent ones, so following is an analysis of the expenses and proceeds from that mailing.

Primary costs include printing and postage. Humble Opinions personnel performed typesetting and composition of the letter. The printing company charged for paper and envelopes; camera, press, folding and inserting the letters; and printing and attaching the mailing labels. The total printing costs were $645.

Postage was $1,000. A coupon attached to the letter identified it as the first mailing so response could be accurately measured. Out of 5,000 letters mailed, 1,287 responded for more information. Out of those 1,287, 490 took classes at $145 each. The total cost of classes per person is $100, including the cost of printing and mailing, instructor, supplies, and overhead. At this rate, total profit resulting from this one mailing is $12,050.

Fig. 20.7 Page seven of the report.

FREE DEMONSTRATIONS AND SEMINARS

Free seminars and demonstrations were advertised in the above mailings and by the use of fliers displayed in the company's office and classroom. Each seminar or demonstration concentrated on one particular software program and lasted about one hour. To add to the customer list, a sign-up list for a door prize was presented at each seminar. Refreshments served allowed the attendants to remain in the classroom for questions and discussion when the activity ended. A different coupon was utilized to measure response to the advertising.

Costs for each seminar or demonstration, including refreshments, door prize, lecturer, technicians, and overhead amounted to $300 per seminar. Attendance was 120 people at the first activity, 42 of which signed up for classes. At a cost of $100 per person per class, the total profit realized from the seminar was $1,890.

TELEMARKETING

The telemarketing consisted of follow-up calls to seminars, demonstrations and mailings. Each call went strictly by a script; offered in the call was a key word the client could use for a discount when he signed up for class. Out of the first 2,500 calls made, 75 people registered for classes. Total cost of the phone calls, including time and overhead, was $ .50 per call. Total cost per person per class is $100; therefore, total profit was $3,375.

8

Fig. 20.8 Page eight continuing the style and layout of the report.

SUMMARY OF DATA

The pie chart in figure 1 illustrates a comparison between profits from the three marketing techniques. The actual figures are represented in the following spreadsheet.

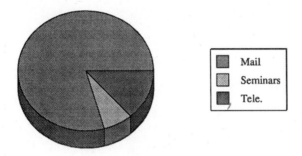

Mail
Seminars
Tele.

Figure 1. Clearly the profit from the direct mail far exceeds the other techniques.

9

Fig. 20.9   Charts added to interpret results or to illustrate text in a report.

Following is a spreadsheet of the previous data so you can compare expenditures and profits as they applied to these three specific activities. Clearly, the direct mailing has demonstrated the highest return for the invested monies with 84.6% of total income from the three marketing methods. Telemarketing has an 8.8% share; the free seminars and demonstrations only 6.6%.

	DIRECT MAIL	SEMINARS	TELEMARKETING
No. of Contacts	5,000	120	2,500
No. of Sales	490	42	75
Gross Income	$71,050.00	$6,090.00	$10,875.00
Cost of Marketing	$1,645.00	$300.00	$1,250.00
Cost of Class	$49,000.00	$4,200.00	$7,500.00
Gross Profit	$20,405.00	$1,590.00	$2,125.00
Market. Cost/Contact	$0.33	$2.50	$0.50
Total Cost/Sale	$103.36	$107.14	$116.67
Marketing Cost/Sale	$3.36	$7.14	$16.67
Profit/Sale	$41.64	$37.86	$28.33

The next section of this Marketing Summary details information about the Parallel Marketing plan. As we compare its great success to the results of the Direct Marketing plan, we believe you will see a need to continue the Plan for at least one year. With conservative changes in the basic approach, that is eliminating the free demonstrations and seminars, we believe the Marketing Plan will continue to succeed and benefit the company.

10

Fig. 20.10   Page 10 of the report including an imported spreadsheet.

To create the page setup and style modifications for the traditional business report, follow these steps:

1. Begin a new document, using the default style sheet. Choose **Page** Modify Page Layout.

2. In Margins & Columns, set the **Left** margin to **2"**; set the **Right** margin to **1.15"**; and set the **Top** and **Bottom** margins to **1.25"**.

3. In Modify, choose **Header**. Choose **All Pages**.

4. In the Header margins, set the **Left** at **2"**; set the **Right** at **1.15"**; set the **Top** at **.75"**; and set the **Bottom** at **.05"**. Choose **Begin** on Second Page.

5. Set the Header tab as right at **7.12"**.

6. In Modify, choose **Footer**. Choose **All** pages.

7. In the Footer margins, set the **Left** to **2"**; set the **Right** to **1.15"**; set the **Top** to **.15"**; and set the **Bottom** to **.75"**. Choose **Begin** on Second Page.

8. Set the Footer tab as right at **7.12"**. Choose OK or press Enter.

9. Move to page two and place the cursor in the top margin. Type the following:

    (Tab)**MARKETING SUMMARY**

10. Choose **Style** Create Style. Name the new style **Header**. Choose **Modify** or press Enter.

11. In Modify, choose Font. Choose Helv, 10 point.

12. In Modify, choose Lines. Choose Line **Below** and the first double rule in Line Style. In **Spacing**, choose .10. Choose OK or press Enter.

13. Place the cursor in the header, MARKETING SUMMARY, on page two, and assign it the style Header. Ami Pro automatically assigns the style to the rest of the headers.

14. On page two, place the cursor in the bottom margin. Press Tab. Choose **Page** Page Numbering.

15. In the Page Numbering dialog box, choose Start on **Page** 2 and Start with Number 2. Choose OK or press Enter.

16. Choose **Style** Create Style. Name the new style **Footer**. Choose **Modify** or press Enter.

17. In Modify, choose Font. Choose Helv, 10 point.

Because all pages of the report are right pages, you choose **All** when setting the Header.

The ruler does not accept the tab marker at 7.25"; you should set the tab as close as possible to 7.25", which is approximately 7.12".

See Appendix D for information and examples about ATM fonts.

By formatting most of your styles before entering text, you not only save time later, but your styles remain consistent.

18. In Modify, choose Lines. Choose Line Above and the first double rule in Style. In Spacing, choose .10. Choose OK or press Enter.

19. Select the page number in the footer and assign it the style Footer. All the following footers are formatted the same way.

20. Choose Style Modify Style. In the Styles box, choose Title.

21. In Modify, choose Font. Choose Arial (Helvetica if ATM is not installed), 18 point, bold.

22. In Modify, choose Alignment. Choose Left.

23. In Modify, choose Spacing. In Paragraph Spacing, choose 0 for both Above and Below. Choose Save.

24. In the Styles box, choose Subhead.

25. In Modify, choose Font. Choose Tms Rmn, 14 point, bold, and italic.

26. In Modify, choose Spacing. In Paragraph Spacing, choose 0 for Above and .05 for Below. Choose Save.

27. In the Styles box, choose Body Text.

28. In Modify, choose Font. Choose Tms Rmn, 12 point.

29. In Modify, choose Hyphenation.

30. In Modify, choose Spacing. In Paragraph Spacing, choose 0 for Above and .20 for Below. Choose OK or press Enter.

31. Choose Style Create Style. Name the new style Page 1 Head. Choose Modify or press Enter.

32. In Modify, choose Font. Choose Tms Rmn, 36 point, bold.

33. In Modify, choose Spacing. In Paragraph Spacing, choose 0 for Above and 0 for Below. In Line Spacing, choose Custom, .64. Choose OK or press Enter.

34. Choose Style Create Style. Name the new style Space. Choose Modify or press Enter.

35. In Modify, choose Font. Change the type to 6 point.

36. In Modify, choose Spacing. In Paragraph Spacing, choose 0 for Above and 0 for Below. Choose OK or press Enter.

37. Choose Style Create Style. Name the new style Pear Associates. Choose Based on Style SUBHEAD. Choose Create.

In step 37, you create a style that looks just like the Subhead style. To keep the name `Pear Associates` consistent with the text, you keep it in the same style as the Subhead style. Use this style for the dates on the first and second pages also. Ami Pro generates a table of contents from styles you assign, such as Title and Subhead. You don't want Ami Pro to add *Pear Associates* and the dates to the table of contents.

At this point, type the text (you can create your own information or use the text in the figures.) You know how to format the majority of the document. The detailed instructions resume with the pie chart. Following are a few pointers for the beginning pages of the report:

- On page one, create a frame with double rules at the top and bottom. Position the top rules exactly at 1" on the vertical ruler; the bottom rules are at 10". This format ensures consistency with the headers and footers. The symbol above `Pear Associates` is a Wingding, 48-point.

- Always compile the table of contents last so that the page numbers are correct. For instructions on compiling the table of contents, refer to the end of this section.

- On page three, use the style Pear Associates for the date (June 4, 1993) as you did on page one. Use a page break after the last paragraph of body text. Use the Space style after all heads. Use the Title style for the heading `Market Summary`.

- On page four, use the style Numbered List for the list of sources. The numbers and tabs are included in the style, but you should add .05" below in paragraph spacing. Use a page break after the last paragraph of body text.

- For page five, indent the text from `DIRECT MARKETING` up to and including the text below `PARALLEL MARKETING` to .5". Use a page break at the end of the text.

- On page six, create the calendar in a table or with tabs. Contain the calendar within a frame to create the rule above and below, or create a text style with a line above. Use a page break at the end of the text.

- Pages seven and eight are formatted the same as the preceding pages.

- Page nine is explained in the following section.

- Page ten contains a spreadsheet. You can import a spreadsheet from another Windows application and even update it with DDE or OLE. Refer to Appendix B, "Using Other Programs with Ami Pro," for more information.

Creating a Chart

Ami Pro's Charting feature contains many types of charts (for details, see Appendix A, "Getting To Know Ami Pro 2.0 and 3.0"). The chart you use depends on the type of information you want to compare. This chapter shows a pie chart that compares gross profits and a bar chart that shows profit per sale.

Ami Pro enables you to create a chart in two ways. The following steps illustrate the first method. The second technique is to select a table of figures or a spreadsheet you want to compare in a chart. Copy those figures to the Clipboard, draw your frame, and choose Charting. You may want to try this method next by using either the table on page 6 or the spreadsheet on page 10.

To create the data and the pie chart on page 9 (again see fig. 20.9), you first must draw a frame. You can format the frame any way you like. To add the chart and data, follow these steps:

1. Select the frame, and then choose Tools Charting.

    Ami Pro displays the following message:

    ```
    The clipboard contains no data text. Do you wish to
    enter the data now?
    ```

2. Choose OK or press Enter. The Charting Data dialog box appears.

3. Type the following data in the dialog box:

    Mail(2 spaces)**50645**(down arrow)
    Seminars(2 spaces)**4500**(down arrow)
    Tele.(2 spaces)**8750**

4. Choose OK or press Enter.

5. In the Charting dialog box, choose the first pie chart. In Options, choose Legend and then select 3D.

6. In the Color Set selection box, choose the first column, second color from the bottom.

7. Choose OK or press Enter. The chart appears in the frame. To edit the chart or the data, double-click in the frame. If you use the keyboard, select the frame and then choose Tools Charting.

When you type in the Data dialog box, do no use the Tab or Enter keys. To separate numbers into columns, use two spaces, to move to the next line, press the down arrow.

You can import your own spreadsheet to use in place of the example in figure 20.10.

Using some of the figures in the spreadsheet on page 10 of the report, you can create various other types of charts. Figure 20.11 illustrates the Charting Data dialog box with some of these figures entered.

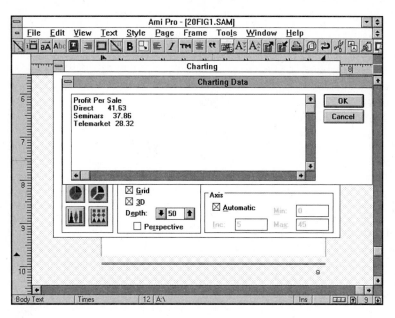

Fig. 20.11 Charting data for a bar chart.

Figure 20.12 illustrates the chart that results from the data entered in figure 20.11. Note that the Legend, Grid, and 3D features are turned on to create a more professional-looking chart.

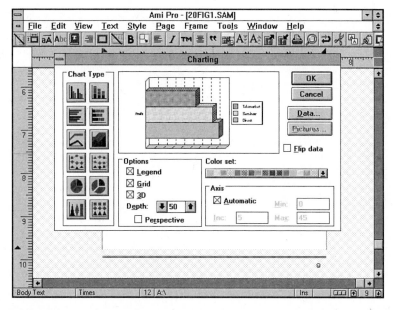

Fig. 20.12 The Charting dialog box with a bar chart created from the Profit Per Sales data.

Creating a Table of Contents

The table of contents is compiled from the Title and Subhead styles you assigned to your document; your completed table of contents may not look like the one in figure 20.2.

You create a table of contents (TOC) in Ami Pro by using assigned styles such as Title and Subhead. You also can create your own styles to use for the TOC. Ami Pro limits you to three different styles. You can assign, for example, a Chapter Head style, a Main Head style, and a Subhead style to your text. You then use those three styles to compile a table of contents. In the following example, you use two of Ami Pro's style names, Title and Subhead, for the table of contents.

Elsewhere in this chapter, you created a new style for Pear Associates and the dates. Pear Associates, therefore, does not appear in the table of contents. Likewise, don't assign styles used for the table of contents to blank lines, because Ami Pro will add those blank lines to the TOC.

When compiling the table of contents, you can direct it either to the beginning of your document or to another file. If you insert the TOC at the beginning of a document, the text assumes the style it represents. In this report, for example, THE MARKETING PLAN would appear in the Title style and DIRECT MARKETING would appear in the Subhead style . In addition, Ami Pro automatically creates style names for the contents and page numbers, including indents, leaders, and right-aligned tabs. This technique is demonstrated in Chapter 21, "Producing a Book."

If you assign your TOC to a document by itself, Ami Pro inserts it into a table in the TOC style sheet. The following steps provide an example of the second technique. To create the table of contents, follow these steps:

1. Open the original document, the business report.

2. Choose Tools TOC Index.

3. In Generate, choose Table of Contents.

4. In TOC Output File, type **Marketoc**. Assign the file to the proper drive and directory (preferably the same one that contains your report).

5. Choose TOC Options.

6. In Level 1, place the cursor in the Style selection box. In the Styles list, choose Title. Then choose Page number.

7. In Level 2, place the cursor in the Style selection box. In the Styles list, choose Subhead. Choose Page Number. Choose OK or press Enter twice.

Ami Pro generates the table of contents and creates the document on-screen. A table contains the text. You can leave the TOC formatted as it is, or format it in its own document and print it. You also can select the text, copy it, switch to the original document, and paste the text. Format the text in a style that is consistent with the report.

Looking at Design

Experiment with Ami Pro and use some of the techniques you have learned to produce creative reports for your company. Following are two alternative designs for a business report. The first presents two pages of a report, including a cover page. The second presents one page of the design.

Figure 20.13 illustrates the cover page of a marketing summary. The screened frame to the left produces an interesting effect. The type used in this report is Bookman, a bold, serif type that gives a completely different look to the piece than Times Roman would.

Figure 20.14 shows page two of the marketing summary. The screen to the left contains the heads for the body text. These heads are Avant Garde 18 point; subheads are Avant Garde 14 point italic. The body text is Bookman 12 point. Notice that Bookman is a larger typeface than Times Roman. For that reason, the style contains more interline spacing.

Figure 20.15 illustrates a different approach to the report design: the page is formatted in two columns. The body text is justified with interparagraph spacing, and the margins and gutter allow for enough white space to provide relaxed reading. The head is large, bold, and contained between two horizontal rules, eliminating the need for a cover page. Finally, the horizontal rule repeats at the bottom of the page. The footer includes the Humble Opinions logo, which means that the logo repeats on each page of the report.

Any pages you add to either example report should follow the same formatting as the sample pages.

Adjust the interline spacing in figure 20.14 in Modify Style Spacing Line Spacing.

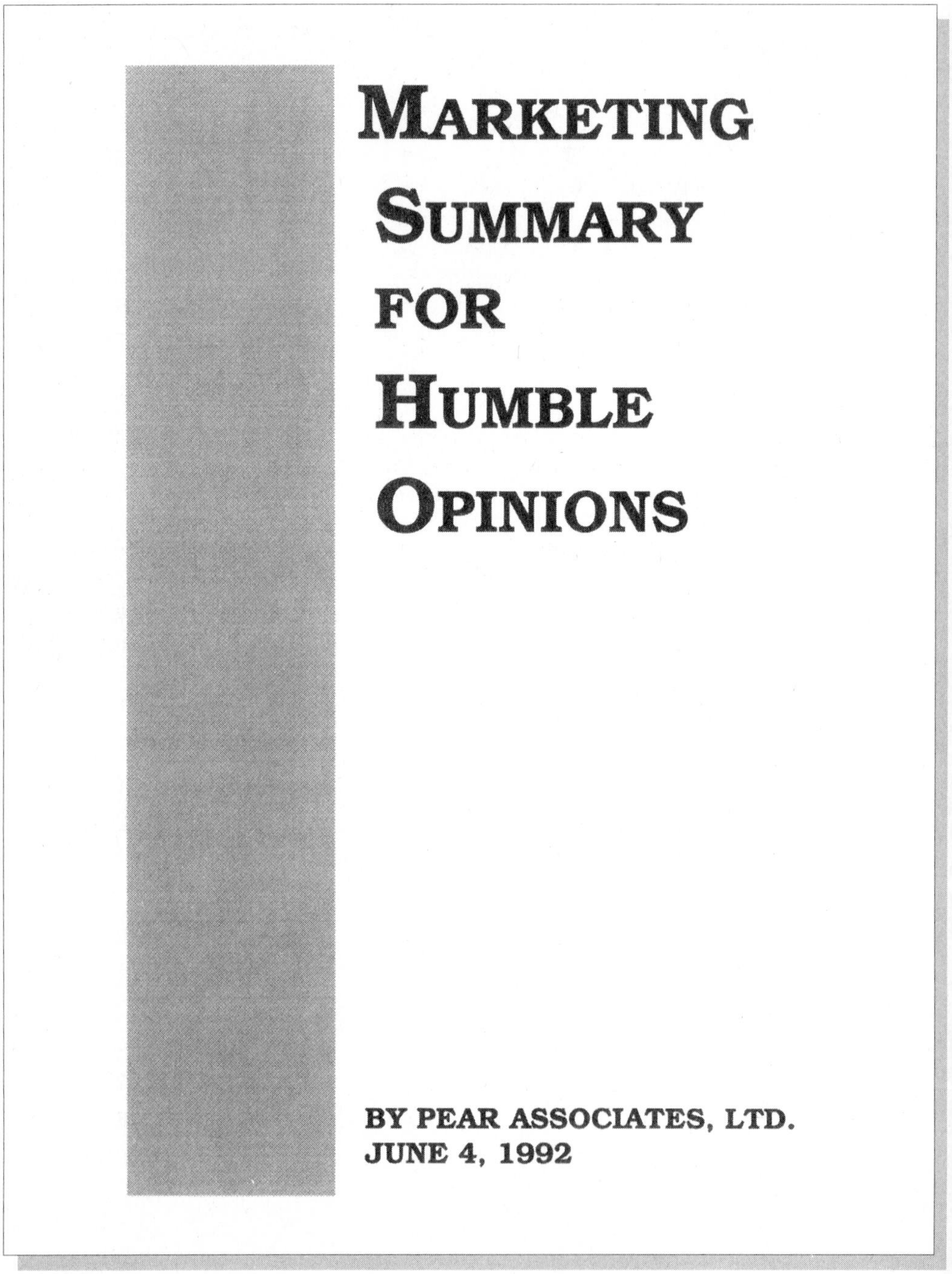

MARKETING SUMMARY FOR HUMBLE OPINIONS

BY PEAR ASSOCIATES, LTD.
JUNE 4, 1992

Fig. 20.13 Cover page for a business report.

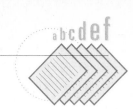

THE MARKETING PLAN

Using the client list as a foundation, our people created advertising that addressed the specific needs and concerns of the customers. Each project was dedicated to individual software programs, and the particular features that applied to a targeted group of clients.

By approaching the Plan in this way, more attention was devoted to the details of the software training that applied to individual customers. Thus, each customer perceived himself as distinctive, unique.

We used two methods of marketing for this project, Direct Marketing and Parallel Marketing. More time and effort were aimed at Direct Marketing. Considerable advantages were realized from this effort. In addition, the Parallel Marketing concentrated on one specific program and proved to be extremely profitable.

DIRECT MARKETING

Among the Direct Marketing techniques utilized in the Plan were free demonstrations and seminars, direct mailing of fliers and letters, and telemarketing. Each approach was carefully researched and executed to enable us to measure results. Coupons for discounts identified clients who received the direct mailings. Different coupons distinguished seminar and demonstration attendants. Those customers accepting training through telemarketing efforts referred to a key word for a discount. Naturally, this summary is based solely on those clients whose proven response corresponds with each marketing technique. Any who did not reply with the coupon or key word could not feasibly be included in this report.

PARALLEL MARKETING

Parallel Marketing targeted customers of one computer store in the area. Customers of that store were given such advertising items as mouse pads, shortcut key cards, and fliers with class descriptions. All of these items displayed a special phone number that identified them with this particular marketing approach.

Fig. 20.14 Page two of the report with the screened frame containing the heads and subheads.

MARKETING SUMMARY FOR HUMBLE OPINIONS

JUNE 4, 1992
BY PEAR ASSOCIATES, LTD.

Humble Opinions, a corporation dedicated to quality computer software training, initiated the Marketing Plan on June 4, 1991. Involved in this plan were many strategies for client expansion and increased financial gain. This summary analyzes the success of the Marketing Plan in terms of customer base increase and profit from services offered. Additional spreadsheets, charts, files, and records are available at any time through our office. Copies are also available for department heads, staff members, or any empolyee you deem necessary.

Current economic trends in our area greatly effect the figures of the past three months; however, earlier reports reveal that the basic premise of the Marketing Plan is working. Should future trends prove to follow the same path as the past three months, a new Marketing Plan will then be developed. We do suggest this plan be followed for an additional period of six months before any long-term decision is made.

Despite this recent decline in profits and sales, the Marketing Plan proved to be both beneficial and profitable to Humble Opinions in the first nine months of execution. The first three months, from June 1991 to August 1991, were considered the initiation period. Although contact with clients increased considerably, profits increased only slightly. During the second three months of the Marketing Plan, from September 1991 to November 1991, profits showed incredible growth. This is attributed to initial planning and advertising to build the customer base. The three-month period from December 1991 to February 1992 proved to support the objectives of the Plan through substantial client referrals and increased profits for the company.

We estimate the Marketing Plan, with minimum modifications, can and will benefit the company in countless ways over the next six months. Customer lists will continue to expand; profits will continue to rise at a reliable and constant rate.

Fig. 20.15   A two-column layout for a business report.

Recapping

In this chapter, you learned how to design a business report in both traditional and innovative styles. You also learned how to create two types of charts and a variation of a table of contents.

Producing a Book

Ami Pro makes producing a book quick and easy. The program's many features, such as outlining, style sheets, Doc Info, table of contents, master pages, indexing, and headers and footers, contribute to the ease of formatting a book or other long document.

**Chapter 1
Finding a Print Shop**

What do you look for in a printer? What are your priorities? A quick turn-a-round? A superior print job? An inexpensive printing bill? Someone who treats you fairly and honestly? These are all attributes desired in a printer, but, unfortunately, you may not be able to find one who fills all of the above requirements.

Before you choose a printer, you should talk to and visit many shops. Ask questions, ask to tour their shop, meet the people with whom you will be working. If you are having a job typeset, meet the proofreader or head of that department. If you need artwork done, talk to the artist. If you need high-resolution output, talk to someone who has knowledge of the computer and desktop publishing programs. People who work in print shops are specialists in their fields. Rarely does one person know about all departments. Never depend on just one person in a print shop.

In addition, ask your friends and business associates who they use as a printer. Find out if they have had dealings with local shops, and what they think. If possible, find out who to talk to when you visit the shop, and who to stay away from. All print shops have at least one person who knows printing and is good at helping customers. A production manager, the head of composition.

For detailed information on how to create a form like this see page 530.

You may want to type the information from the sample chapter, and then copy it for the second chapter. Alternatively, you can use your own information in place of the examples.

This chapter describes elements necessary for planning the book, such as organizing files and directories; planning the body, front and end matter, size, and layout; and using a style sheet. In addition, the exercises lead you through creating two chapters to a sample book, including formatting the page with margins, headers or footers, page numbers, and so on.

After you complete the layout of the sample chapters, you create a *master document* that contains the two chapters. Ami Pro uses a master document to work collectively with different documents. You can compile the index and table of contents, consecutively number pages, and even print the entire book from a master document.

The exercises also introduce you to other Ami Pro features, including the outline feature, printing crop marks, and formatting running heads.

Working with Disks, Files, and Directories

Always back up every document, large or small. When you experience a power failure or a glitch in the program (and sooner or later, you will), you will be grateful for your backup copy. Also, remember to save your files frequently.

Prior to formatting the pages of your book, you should plan how you may use all the files involved. If you use a hard disk, create a directory for the book; then create subdirectories for each chapter. You can even break each subdirectory into two separate directories: one for text and one for figures, illustrations, and graphics. If you plan to use floppy disks, use one disk for each chapter's text, and one for each chapter's illustrations.

If possible, work from the hard disk rather than from floppy disks. Most computers work faster and more efficiently, with tasks such as creating indexes and tables of contents, when long documents are on a hard drive. If you divide a book into chapter files on a hard disk, you can gather all these files together to create indexes or tables of contents, figures, and so on. If you keep the files on floppy disks, you need to transfer the files to the hard disk to accomplish these tasks. Floppy disks are excellent, however, for saving backups of important files.

Ami Pro efficiently handles 20 to 30 pages in each file. Because 20 pages is the optimum number for a working file, split chapters that contain more than 30 pages into two or more documents.

Planning the Book

After you set up the directories or floppy disks for your book, you should develop a plan for the book. Included in this plan should be the body of the book and any graphic images you want to include, front and end matter, the book and page sizes, and the layout of the pages. Both the author and the typesetter of the book can benefit from the following planning guidelines.

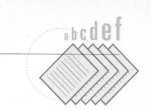

Planning the Body

The body of the book is the most important element. The text should be well-written and organized in such a way that the reader understands it and is comfortable reading it. In addition, you may incorporate graphic elements such as illustrations, photographs, and line art to support the text of the book.

Whether you are the author or the typesetter of the book, using Ami Pro's outline feature can help to organize the book and rearrange sections, if necessary. If you are the author of the book, you can write it directly in Ami Pro. Begin by using the outline feature to organize the chapter heads and then the main topics. Using up to nine outline levels, you add subheads and text under each main topic; add notes, key words, and so on as you create the outline. As you write the body of the book, you can easily refer to the entire outline, or any portion of it in Ami Pro's outline mode.

If you are the typesetter of the book, you may want to consult with the author to create an outline of the chapter heads, main topics, and subheads. Using Ami Pro's outline feature, you can easily move heads (and the text attached to them) to any position and any level of the outline. The section, "Using Ami Pro's Outline Feature" gives you step-by-step instructions to efficient use of this feature.

Planning Front and End Matter

Besides planning the body of the book, outline the front and end matter. Plan the length of the book, and include the *front matter*—the dedication, copyright, title pages, table of contents, list of illustrations, preface, forward or introduction, and acknowledgments—in the plan. *End matter* includes the appendix, glossary, index, notes, and bibliography. Naturally, many of these items are optional, depending on the book and the needs of its readers. This chapter includes instructions on how to use the Ami Pro features to plan and format front and end matter effortlessly.

Planning the Size

Three traditional page sizes for books are 5 1/2 inches by 8 1/4 inches, 6 1/8 inches by 9 1/4 inches, and 7 3/8 inches by 9 1/2 inches. Common sizes for printing at a commercial print shop are 8 1/2 inches by 11 inches, 5 1/2 inches by 8 1/2 inches and 6 inches by 8 inches.

Use Ami Pro's spell checker, thesaurus, and grammar checker when writing or editing the body of the book.

Because front matter pages are usually numbered as lowercase Roman numerals, in Ami Pro you can either place these pages in a separate document and number them with headers or footers, or insert a new page layout. This chapter includes an example to assist you in planning for this numbering scheme.

If you submit the book to a publisher, the publisher probably will specify the page size you use.

When you plan the size of the book, you plan the size of the pages. You must consider several elements when planning size. Foremost is the purpose of the book. The material may suggest a particular size or shape. For example, this book was designed for 8 inches by 10 inches so that the documents are larger, and clearer, to the reader. On the other hand, an abridged reference dictionary may require a smaller size because the information is often limited. In addition, consider where the book is most used or stored to help you determine the size. Some books may be designed to fit on a shelf, on the coffee table, or in a pocket.

If you have the book printed at a commercial print shop, you can save money by considering the page size of the book in relation to the sheet size stocked by the print shop. See Chapter 4, "Planning and Purchasing Printing," for more information.

Be sure that the paper you choose is heavy enough to prevent type showing through from the other side.

If possible, choose the paper type and finish when planning the size of the book. Book papers come in various finishes, weights, and colors. The best choice is 60# or 70# weight; 60# is optimum. Smooth or vellum finish is best for a book with a great deal of text; enamel finish is best for a book with photos. Usually, white paper is used in a book, although ivory is another popular possibility.

Planning the Layout

As important as planning the book size, the text, and the files and directories, is planning the page layout of the book. The size of your book directly relates to the page size, and the page size determines page formatting choices for facing pages, headers, footers, column, even paper choices.

Photographs, like art, may be used on the first page of a chapter to make it stand out.

Chapters always begin on a right page, even if the preceding page is blank. The first page of the chapter should not contain a header or footer. To make the first page of the chapter stand out visually, add a wider top margin or right align the chapter number and head. You can use a large first character or drop cap for the first letter of the first paragraph of the chapter to let the reader know where a new chapter starts.

When you format the book, remember that a book usually is made up of facing pages. Consistency in design (both across facing pages and throughout the book) and special attention to page numbers as well as headers or footers (or both) is important. Furthermore, try to balance any page that contains illustrations or graphics with the facing page.

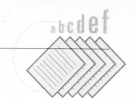

Facing pages usually include running heads. A *running head* identifies the book title, author, chapter or section, and the page number. Left and right pages also may differ; the left page header, for example, may include the chapter name and the page number, and the right page may contain the book title and page number.

You can plan the body of the book for a one- or two-column layout. Consider the type of book and how it will be read. A reference book is not read from cover to cover like a novel. Many reference books—such as dictionaries and encyclopedias—use two columns to conserve space; many novels use only one column for easier, more comfortable reading. A reader who is comfortable with the page layout (number of columns, margin space, line length, and so on), is more likely to read the page.

You must also consider margins in your planning. Traditionally, the margins are equal on the left and right. The top margin may be 1/4 inch to 1/2 inch larger than the side margins; and the bottom margin may be 1/4 inch to 1/2 inch larger than the top margins. If the left and right margins are 1/2 inch, for example, the top margin may be 3/4 inch and the bottom margin 1 inch. The sizes of your margins and columns depend on the page size, the amount of material and how you lay it out, and the size of type you use for the body text.

Book text is usually 10-point type, although you may use 12 point if the text is aimed at an older group of people. Choose a serif type font, such as Times Roman, Bookman, or Trump, that is easier to read than a sans serif font.

In addition, you should choose to left align or justify the body text. Be sure that you hyphenate all text that you justify—rivers of white space running through the paragraphs due to nonhyphenated justified type are distracting to the reader. Remember, the goal is to provide for comfortable reading for your readers.

Another matter important in book production is avoiding awkward page breaks, such as widows and orphans. A *widow* occurs when the last line of the paragraph ends on the top of a page and the rest of the paragraph is on the preceding page. An *orphan* occurs when the first line of the paragraph appears at the bottom of the page, with the rest of the paragraph on the following page. You can plan to avoid this layout problem by using Ami Pro's default setting to control widows and orphans. If necessary, you can change the option in Tools, **U**ser Setup, **O**ptions.

When you plan to produce a book, create a style sheet in Ami Pro after you choose the format; then use the style sheet to begin each new chapter. This procedure saves you time and ensures consistency throughout the book. As you have worked through this book, you've learned to

The first page of a chapter contains no running head, no header or footer, and no page number.

The smaller the type size, the narrower the line length should be. See Chapter 3, "Defining and Explaining Typography," for more information about line length and column width.

If you like one of the following book designs, after you complete the design, save it as a style sheet; then delete the text. See Chapter 5, "Producing a Letterhead," for detailed instructions on saving as a style sheet.

create style sheets and customize them for your own purposes. The exercises that follow in this chapter offer formatting you can save as a style sheet.

Using Ami Pro's Outline Feature

Ami Pro's outline mode can help you organize every stage of writing and editing a book. While in the Outline mode, you can assign levels to chapter titles, heads, subheads, and so on; then use the levels to organize the document. You can show only level one or all levels, and you can promote or demote any level. By simply choosing an icon, you can display the body text that goes with any head or subhead; you can even move a head, and the body text moves with it. You will find that Ami Pro's outline feature is an excellent organizational tool for producing a book.

To acquaint you with this feature, figure 21.1 illustrates the screen as it appears in Outline mode. Notice that the second row of SmartIcons contains commands that you can use in creating your document.

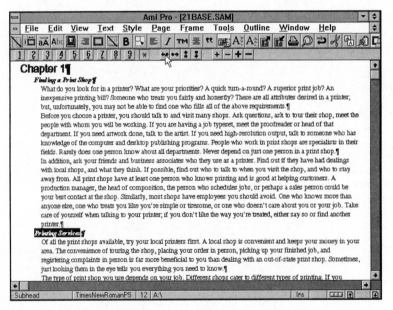

Fig. 21.1 Ami Pro's Outline mode.

You can reassign levels to any head, as well as rearrange the heads, in outline mode.

The title, Chapter 1, has been promoted to level one. Ami Pro uses default type styles for each level; you can modify them any way you want. The subhead, Finding a Print Shop, is level two, and Printing Services, which is selected, is also a level two subhead.

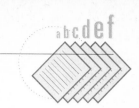

Notice that the mouse cursor is placed on the SmartIcon for the left-arrow button. This button promotes an outline level. The right-arrow button demotes levels. The up and down arrows move the head (and its text) up and down on the list.

After you select the outline levels of your text, you can use some outline features to organize the document. Figure 21.2 illustrates the Outline mode with levels one, two and three heads displayed. (Ami Pro calls this display "level three heads showing.") Note that the text below the level three head, `Special Purpose Printer`, is displayed, and the mouse cursor is pointing to the plus icon. With the head selected, or the cursor placed within the head, click on this icon to display the text belonging to that head; click on the minus icon to hide the text.

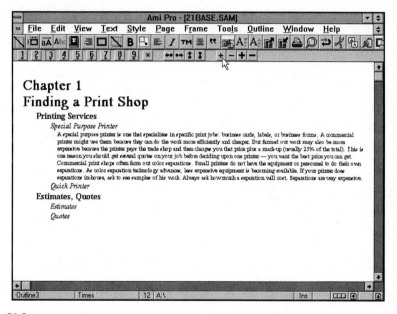

Fig. 21.2   A level three head with selected text.

You can only use the SmartIcons if you use a mouse. With the keyboard, however, you can choose **S**tyle **O**utline Styles. In the dialog box that appears (see fig. 21.3), you can assign outline levels to styles in your document.

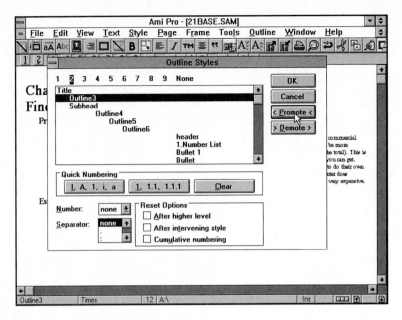

Fig. 21.3   The Outline Styles dialog box.

Producing a Traditional Book Design

The first book design in this chapter is a basic layout that uses running headers, left-aligned heads, and justified body text with interparagraph spacing. The page size is 7 1/4 by 9 1/2 inches and uses no binding margin. Figure 21.4 illustrates the first page of the book.

The first page of the chapter must stand out so that readers can find it easily. The chapter number and title are right-aligned and positioned nearly three inches from the top of the page. The body text is indented from the left margin so that the line length is correct for the type size. In addition, page one is a right-facing page and has no header or page number. The crop marks were added in Ami Pro just before printing.

Page two of the chapter, figure 21.5, follows the type and page design. In this layout, the heads extend to the left margin so that they stand out from the body text. The subheads are indented with the body text; but their type size and style are different so that they, too, stand out.

The crop marks will only print if your page size is smaller than the paper size you're printing.

The wide left margin, the inter-paragraph spacing, and the wide bottom margin creates white space that makes reading more comfortable.

Chapter 1
Finding a Print Shop

What do you look for in a printer? What are your priorities? A quick turn-a-round? A superior print job? An inexpensive printing bill? Someone who treats you fairly and honestly? These are all attributes desired in a printer; but, unfortunately, you may not be able to find one who fills all of the above re-quirements.

Before you choose a printer, you should talk to and visit many shops. Ask questions, ask to tour their shop, meet the people with whom you will be working. If you are having a job typeset, meet the proofreader or head of that department. If you need artwork done, talk to the artist. If you need high-resolution output, talk to someone who has knowledge of the computer and desktop publishing programs. People who work in print shops are specialists in their fields. Rarely does one person know about all departments. Never de-pend on just one person in a print shop.

In addition, ask your friends and business associates who they use as a printer. Find out if they have had dealings with local shops, and what they think. If possible, find out who to talk to when you visit the shop, and who to stay away from. All print shops have at least one person who knows printing and is good at helping customers. A production manager, the head of composition,

Fig. 21.4   Page one of a traditional book design.

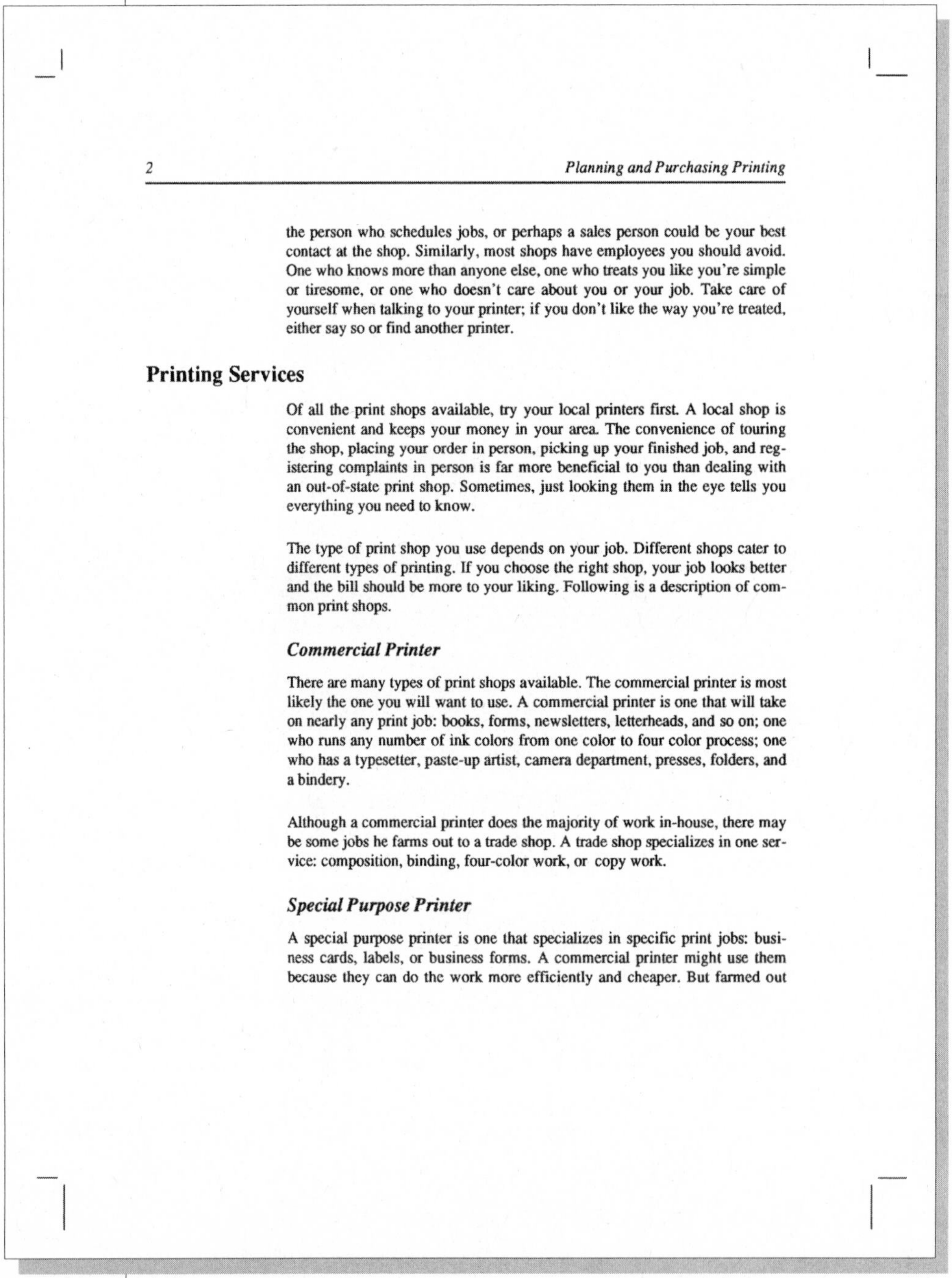

the person who schedules jobs, or perhaps a sales person could be your best contact at the shop. Similarly, most shops have employees you should avoid. One who knows more than anyone else, one who treats you like you're simple or tiresome, or one who doesn't care about you or your job. Take care of yourself when talking to your printer; if you don't like the way you're treated, either say so or find another printer.

Printing Services

Of all the print shops available, try your local printers first. A local shop is convenient and keeps your money in your area. The convenience of touring the shop, placing your order in person, picking up your finished job, and registering complaints in person is far more beneficial to you than dealing with an out-of-state print shop. Sometimes, just looking them in the eye tells you everything you need to know.

The type of print shop you use depends on your job. Different shops cater to different types of printing. If you choose the right shop, your job looks better and the bill should be more to your liking. Following is a description of common print shops.

Commercial Printer

There are many types of print shops available. The commercial printer is most likely the one you will want to use. A commercial printer is one that will take on nearly any print job: books, forms, newsletters, letterheads, and so on; one who runs any number of ink colors from one color to four color process; one who has a typesetter, paste-up artist, camera department, presses, folders, and a bindery.

Although a commercial printer does the majority of work in-house, there may be some jobs he farms out to a trade shop. A trade shop specializes in one service: composition, binding, four-color work, or copy work.

Special Purpose Printer

A special purpose printer is one that specializes in specific print jobs: business cards, labels, or business forms. A commercial printer might use them because they can do the work more efficiently and cheaper. But farmed out

Fig. 21.5   The second page of the book illustrating the left page header.

The header on page two illustrates a *running head*. Because page two is a left page, the page number appears on the left. The text on the right, `Planning and Purchasing Printing`, is the name of the book. With the help of a line below the text, this header runs into the header on page three.

Figure 21.6 illustrates page three of the layout. The header includes the author's name on the left and the page number on the right. The rest of the page is formatted in the same style as page two.

Finally, page four of the book completes the chapter (see fig. 21.7). Left- and right-page designs are consistent throughout the book. If, by chance, this chapter ended on page five, page six would be blank and chapter two would begin on page seven.

To format this layout, create your own text or type the text from the figures. Save the text under two different names, such as **Chapter1**, and **Chapter2**. After you have finished formatting both chapters, you will use them to create a master document. The master document enables you to compile a table of contents and an index, as you would if you were producing a book.

Because you know how to modify styles for body text, subheads, and so on, the following instructions do not include that part of creating the style sheet. To set up the page for the traditional book design, follow these steps:

1. Choose **Page Modify Page Layout**.

2. In **Modify**, choose **Page settings**. In Size, type **7.19 x 9.5**.

3. In **Modify**, choose **Margins & Columns**. Change the **Left** and **Right** columns to **.75**, the **Top** to **1.25**, and the **Bottom** to **1.5**.

4. In **Modify**, choose **Header**. In Pages, choose **Left**.

5. Change **Left** and **Right** Header margins to **.75** and **Top** to **.70**. Repeat for the **Right** page.

6. Choose **Begin on second page**. Choose **OK** or press Enter.

7. Move to page two of the document. Place the cursor in the top margin.

8. Choose **Page Page Numbering**. Choose **OK** or press Enter.

   You can, at this point, choose page numbers to insert into the document. If you plan to create a master document later, however, do not set page numbers now. Instead, tell Ami Pro where the number will go by positioning the cursor (step 7); the master document that you create later in this chapter will number the pages consecutively throughout the chapters.

T he line of the header, and the left- and right-aligned header text help define the margins of the page.

A lways begin a chapter on a right page. Even if the result is more space at the bottom of some pages, try to begin new topics, heads, or subheads at the top of a new page.

A mi Pro fills in the number 2 for you, and automatically numbers all following pages.

9. On page two, (the cursor is located in the top margin from step 7) in the header, press Tab and type the following:

   Planning and Purchasing Printing

10. Choose Style Create Style. Name the new style, **Header**. Choose Modify or press Enter.

11. In Modify, choose **Font**. Choose Tms Rmn, 10 point, italic.

12. In Modify, choose **Alignment**. Remove all indents.

13. In Modify, choose **Lines**. Choose Line **Below** and select the second line style. In **Spacing**, choose **.05**. Choose OK or press Enter. Assign the Header style to the text in the margin.

14. On page three, place the cursor in the top margin. Then type the following:

    S. Plumley(Tab)

15. Choose **Page** Page Numbering. Choose OK or press Enter.

16. Assign the Header style to the type.

To print the document, with crop marks, follow these steps:

1. Choose File **Print**. Choose **Options**.

2. In Print Options, choose Crop **marks**. Choose OK or press Enter, in response to both dialog boxes.

Ami Pro enables you to print crop marks with most printers. If, however, you use Windows 3.1 and a PostScript printer (including Hewlett-Packard III SI, and Hewlett-Packard III with PostScript cartridge), you may have a problem. The PostScript printer driver in Windows 3.1 does not work the same as in Windows 3.0; therefore, crop marks may not appear when you print. Microsoft Windows offers a driver library for Version 3.1, which includes a PostScript driver that works with Ami Pro 3.0 and 2.0.

If you have a problem with printing crop marks, two other options are available. You can draw your own crop marks; for more information, refer to Chapter 2, "Using Elements of Design." The better option is to draw a frame outside each of the four corners of the page, turn on the proper borders, and copy the four frames to each page. This technique is described in Chapter 15, "Producing an Advertisement."

work may also be more expensive because the printer pays the trade shop and then charges you that price plus a mark-up (usually 25% of the total). This is one reason you should get several quotes on your job before deciding upon one printer — you want the best price you can get.

Commercial print shops often farm out color separations. Small printers do not have the equipment or personnel to do their own separations. As color separation technology advances, less expensive equipment is becoming available. If your printer does separations in-house, ask to see samples of his work. Always ask how much a separation will cost. Separations are very expensive.

Quick Printer

A quick printer is one who does mostly photocopying by using a xerographic process that allows the copying of short-run quantities. The quality is usually low to medium; however some quick print shops do produce quality work. The standard page sizes for photocopying are 8-1/2" x 11" and 11" x 17". Quick print shops may also have a small press or two, and do some offset printing. They may farm out work such as binding large jobs, typesetting, some camera work, and so on. A quick print shop is good to use for certain jobs: fliers, invitations, inserts, or jobs that don't require precision in width of margins, registration, and so forth.

The type of shop you choose depends upon your job. If you need high-quality printing within a reasonable amount of time, you may choose a commercial printer. If you need 500 fliers yesterday, then choose a quick print shop.

It is important to patronize several shops. Don't just get quote after quote. Actually take them some business once in a while. This way, when you are in need of something special or something fast, and one printer cannot do it — you have the option of taking your job to another printer.

Estimates, Quotes

It's important to find out how much your job will cost before you have it printed. If you don't ask ahead of time, the printer could increase the price to whatever he wishes. Many print shop's are principled; many are not. There are two ways to find out the cost of your job, by an estimate or by a quote.

Fig. 21.6   Page three, a right page, with a right page header.

Estimates

Some printers will give estimates on the cost of your job. You must give complete details on your job, as you would with a quote, to get a reasonable estimate. Estimates, however, are not what the printer guarantees the price to be. An estimate is just that — an estimate. If the printer finds extra costs in running the job, he will raise the price accordingly. For this reason, it is important you get a quote instead of an estimate, if at all possible.

Quotes

It is important to get quotes on all of your jobs before you print them. A quote is the printer's stated price for the cost of your specific job. You should consider getting quotes from several printers, because prices can vary greatly from shop to shop. Also, be sure your quote is in writing; and keep your copy in case there is a question later. Most quotes are good for 30 days, so you'll have time to check out other printers. A quote should be honored by your printer as the price he will charge you — as long as you don't make any alterations after the piece is in process.

A quote from the printer includes the cost of materials and labor for your job: composition, paste-up, camera, stripping, plate-making, paper, ink, press, and bindery. Not only that, but the quote also adds in a fee for overhead items such as electricity, cost of water, equipment, office help, and insurance for employees and the building.

The more information you give printers, the better they will be able to quote your job. Describe your piece in a term the printer will recognize: newsletter, brochure, flier. This will give the printer an immediate basic understanding of your piece before the quote. If possible, include a mock-up of your job.

Make sure you provide all the information about your job to the person who quotes the job. If you omit details, expect the printer to alter the quote accordingly. Omitted details may also affect scheduling and delivery time. The printer has only the information you provide him when he quotes, plans, and schedules your job.

Fig. 21.7   The final page of the chapter, page four.

Producing an Alternative Traditional Book Design

This book design is also traditional. The body text is still justified, but it is indented rather than spaced between paragraphs. The heads are left-aligned. The page size is 6 by 8 inches, and the design uses both headers and footers.

Page one of the second book design illustrates the first page of the chapter (see fig. 21.8). Again, a larger top margin distinguishes the first page; furthermore, the chapter number attracts attention. The 2 is 82-point Chancery typeface. CaslonOpenFace or ShelleyAllegroScript would look attractive, as well.

Page two of the chapter shows the page with a header and a footer (see fig. 21.9). The header, separated from the body with a double rule, announces the title of the book. The footer, formatted in a similar style, contains the page number. Notice that the page number is 6; the master document you produce in the next section numbers the pages automatically.

The third page of the chapter shows a right page header and footer (see fig. 21.10). The header announces the chapter title; the footer contains the page number. The body text, titles, and subheads, carry the same formatting as page one of this design.

Finally, page four completes the chapter (see fig. 21.11). The styles are the same as the other pages in the chapter, as are the left header and footer.

Be sure that you use the same style names—Title, Subheads, Heads, and so on—for this chapter as you did for the last chapter, because the table of contents is compiled from the style names. In a real book design you also must use the same formatting for consistency. For this example, however, you don't format the text the same as the first chapter.

Notice that the left and right margins in this page design are equal.

This style of formatting (justified body text, indented, with minimum paragraph spacing), condenses the information to fewer pages.

2

Finding a Print Shop

Printing Services

What do you look for in a printer? What are your priorities? A quick turn-a-round? A superior print job? An inexpensive printing bill? Someone who treats you fairly and honestly? These are all attributes desired in a printer; but, unfortunately, you may not be able to find one who fills all of the above requirements.

Before you choose a printer, you should talk to and visit many shops. Ask questions, ask to tour their shop, meet the people with whom you will be working. If you are having a job typeset, meet the proofreader or head of that department. If you need artwork done, talk to the artist. If you need high-resolution output, talk to someone who has knowledge of the computer and desktop publishing programs. People who work in print shops are specialists in their fields. Rarely does one person know about all departments. Never depend on just one person in a print shop.

In addition, ask your friends and business associates who they use as a printer. Find out if they have had dealings with local shops, and what they

Fig. 21.8   Page one of an alternative design.

think. If possible, find out who to talk to when you visit the shop, and who to stay away from. All print shops have at least one person who knows printing and is good at helping customers. A production manager, the head of composition, the person who schedules jobs, or perhaps a sales person could be your best contact at the shop. Similarly, most shops have employees you should avoid. One who knows more than anyone else, one who treats you like you're simple or tiresome, or one who doesn't care about you or your job. Take care of yourself when talking to your printer; if you don't like the way you're treated, either say so or find another printer.

Of all the print shops available, try your local printers first. A local shop is convenient and keeps your money in your area. The convenience of touring the shop, placing your order in person, picking up your finished job, and registering complaints in person is far more beneficial to you than dealing with an out-of-state print shop. Sometimes, just looking them in the eye tells you everything you need to know.

The type of print shop you use depends on your job. Different shops cater to different types of printing. If you choose the right shop, your job looks better and the bill should be more to your liking. Following is a description of common print shops.

Commercial Printer

There are many types of print shops available. The commercial printer is most likely the one you will want to use. A commercial printer is one that will take on nearly any print job: books, forms, newsletters, letterheads, and so on; one who runs any number of ink colors from one color to four color process; one who has a typesetter, paste-up artist, camera department, presses, folders, and a bindery.

Special Purpose Printer

A special purpose printer is one that specializes in specific print jobs: business cards, labels, or business forms. A commercial printer might use them because they can do the work more efficiently and cheaper. But farmed out work may also be more expensive because the printer pays the trade shop and then

6

Fig. 21.9   Page two of a traditional book design.

charges you that price plus a mark-up (usually 25% of the total). This is one reason you should get several quotes on your job before deciding upon one printer — you want the best price you can get.

Commercial print shops often farm out color separations. Small printers do not have the equipment or personnel to do their own separations. As color separation technology advances, less expensive equipment is becoming available. If your printer does separations in-house, ask to see samples of his work. Always ask how much a separation will cost. Separations are very expensive.

Quick Printer

A quick printer is one who does mostly photocopying by using a xerographic process that allows the copying of short-run quantities. The quality is usually low to medium; however some quick print shops do produce quality work. The standard page sizes for photocopying are 8-1/2" x 11" and 11" x 17". Quick print shops may also have a small press or two, and do some offset printing. They may farm out work such as binding large jobs, typesetting, some camera work, and so on. A quick print shop is good to use for certain jobs: fliers, invitations, inserts, or jobs that don't require precision in width of margins, registration, and so forth.

The type of shop you choose depends upon your job. If you need high-quality printing within a reasonable amount of time, you may choose a commercial printer. If you need 500 fliers yesterday, then choose a quick print shop.

It is important to patronize several shops. Don't just get quote after quote. Actually take them some business once in a while. This way, when you are in need of something special or something fast, and one printer cannot do it — you have the option of taking your job to another printer.

Estimates, Quotes

It's important to find out how much your job will cost before you have it printed. If you don't ask ahead of time, the printer could increase the price to whatever he wishes. Many print shop's are principled; many are not. There are two ways to find out the cost of your job, by an estimate or by a quote.

7

Fig. 21.10   Page seven of the book; page three of the chapter.

Estimates

Some printers will give estimates on the cost of your job. You must give complete details on your job, as you would with a quote, to get a reasonable estimate. Estimates, however, are not what the printer guarantees the price to be. An estimate is just that — an estimate. If the printer finds extra costs in running the job, he will raise the price accordingly. For this reason, it is important you get a quote instead of an estimate, if at all possible.

Quotes

It is important to get quotes on all of your jobs before you print them. A quote is the printer's stated price for the cost of your specific job. You should consider getting quotes from several printers, because prices can vary greatly from shop to shop. Also, be sure your quote is in writing; and keep your copy in case there is a question later. Most quotes are good for 30 days, so you'll have time to check out other printers. A quote should be honored by your printer as the price he will charge you — as long as you don't make any alterations after the piece is in process.

A quote from the printer includes the cost of materials and labor for your job: composition, paste-up, camera, stripping, plate-making, paper, ink, press, and bindery. Not only that, but the quote also adds in a fee for overhead items such as electricity, cost of water, equipment, office help, and insurance for employees and the building.

The more information you give printers, the better they will be able to quote your job. Describe your piece in a term the printer will recognize: newsletter, brochure, flier. This will give the printer an immediate basic understanding of your piece before the quote. If possible, include a mock-up of your job.

Make sure you provide all the information about your job to the person who quotes the job. If you omit details, expect the printer to alter the quote accordingly. Omitted details may also affect scheduling and delivery time. The printer has only the information you provide him when he quotes, plans, and schedules your job.

8

Fig. 21.11   Page eight of the book; page four of the chapter.

To set the page for the second design, follow these steps:

1. Choose **Page** Modify Page Layout.

2. In **Modify**, choose **Page** settings. In Size, type **6 x 8**.

3. In **Modify**, choose **Margins & Columns**. Change the Left and Right columns to **.75**; the Top and Bottom to **1**.

4. In **Modify**, choose **Header**. In Pages, choose Left.

5. Change the Left and Right header margins to **.75**; change the Top header margin to **.60**.

6. Repeat step 5 for the **Right** page. Choose OK or press Enter.

7. Move to page two of the document. Place the cursor in the top margin.

8. In the header, type the following:

   Planning and Purchasing Printing

9. Choose **Style** Create Style. Name the new style **Header**. Choose Modify or press Enter.

10. In **Modify**, choose **Font**. Choose Helv, 9 point, Normal.

11. In **Modify**, choose **Alignment**. Remove all Indents. Set a right tab at 4 1/2".

12. In **Modify**, choose **Lines**. Select Line below using the first double rule pattern. In **Spacing**, choose **.05**. Choose OK or press Enter. Assign the Header style to the text in the margin.

13. On page three, place the cursor in the top margin, and type the following:

    (Tab)**Looking for a Printer**

14. Assign the Header style to the text.

15. Choose **Page** Modify Page Layout.

16. Choose **Footer**. In Pages, choose Left.

17. Set the Left and Right margins to **.75**. Choose **Begin** on second page.

18. Repeat step 17 for the **Right** page. Choose OK or press Enter.

19. Choose **Style** Create Style. Name the new style **Footer**. In Based on, choose Header. Choose Modify, or press Enter.

In this example, you can format the footers after step 6, as well.

20. In Modify, choose Alignment. Set a right tab at 4 1/2".

21. In Modify, choose Lines. Choose Line above using the first double rule pattern. In Spacing, choose .05. Choose OK or press Enter.

22. On page two, place the cursor in the bottom margin. Choose Page Page numbering. Choose OK or press Enter. (You don't want to insert a page number if you intend to produce a master document in the next section.)

23. Assign the Footer style to the cursor insertion point in the margin. Repeat with the right page (except press Tab first before assigning the Page numbering).

Creating a Master Document

A *master document* enables you to compile an index and a table of contents for multiple documents. Using the master document, you can also number pages and footnotes consecutively between multiple documents and print them easily and efficiently. Ami Pro recognizes the master document, and its contents, as one large document. As an example, you can collect the separate chapters of your book in a master document, and then perform tasks, such as numbering pages, indexing, printing, and so on.

You must perform several steps to create the master document and its contents. First, you must complete all the individual documents (each in its own file) that you will combine in the master document. All editing should be finished prior to creating the master document; editing one part after you compile the master document means repeating many steps when you finish editing.

When you're ready to create a master document, choose the individual files that will comprise the master document and assign them to a source document (usually the first chapter). Next, select TOC and Index options. You can then generate a table of contents and an index, number pages, print, and so on.

The following instructions guide you to create a master document with the two chapters you just completed. If possible, store both chapters on your hard drive so that your work will be quicker and easier.

When you have no text, assign the style to the cursor insertion point. When you insert page numbers in the master document, the numbers will be in the correct style.

The master document does not alter any original file. If you assign page numbers to run consecutively in all files, only the page numbers change.

Working with the Source File

To create the master document, follow these steps:

1. Open the first book chapter you produced. This is your *source document*.

2. Choose File Master Document.

3. In the list of Files, choose the first chapter. Choose Include. The file moves to the Master doc files list.

4. Repeat with the second chapter. Choose OK or press Enter.

5. Choose File Save.

To modify the master document at any time, open the source file, choose File Master Document, and add or remove any files. Be sure that you save the source file when you're finished.

To delete a Master Document, choose File, Master Document, and then remove all files from the Master doc files list.

Before you can generate a table of contents or an index, you must first specify Master Document Options. To specify the options, follow these steps:

1. Open your source file (the first book chapter).

2. Choose File Master Document. Choose Options.

3. In Table of Contents choose Generate TOC. In Output file, type a name for the TOC document. Ami Pro automatically creates the file and adds an SAM extension. Choose the appropriate directory and/or drive.

4. In Index, choose Generate Index, and then choose Include alphabetical separators.

5. In Output file, type a name for your index document (you cannot use the same name as for the table of contents). Choose the appropriate directory and/or drive.

6. Choose TOC Options. A dialog box appears.

7. In Level 1, place the cursor in the Styles box. From the list of Styles, choose Title. The word title automatically copies to the Styles list box.

A ny chapter you open becomes the source document; chapter one is a logical choice because it's easy to remember, and it's the first file.

B y following step 3, you instruct Ami Pro to include chapter one (even though it is open) in all further master document procedures, such as compiling an index, table of contents, and printing.

A mi Pro places the table of contents in its own document file that you name; Ami Pro uses the TOC.STY sheet.

8. In the Separator text box, type a period (representing a dot leader). Choose **P**age number, and then choose **R**ight align page number to turn these options on.

9. In Level 2, place the cursor in the **S**tyles box. From the list of Styles, choose Subhead.

10. In the Separator text box, type a period (representing a dot leader). Choose **P**age number, and **R**ight align page number.

11. Repeat steps 9 and 10 with your third level style. Choose OK three times or press Enter three times.

Creating a Table of Contents

Now that you have completed the preliminaries, you can create a table of contents. Figure 21.12 illustrates the completed TOC for the two book chapters. This page is formatted to match the style of the second book chapter you created. The header and footer match the right page style in the text, and double rules separate them from the page.

Note that the header reads Table of Contents, and the footer uses the Roman number i for the page number. These elements are the reasons you placed the TOC in a document by itself. If the TOC were in the same document as chapter one, chapter one's headers and footers would apply to the TOC, as well.

To create the table of contents, follow these steps:

1. Place the cursor anywhere on the first page of the source document.

2. Choose **T**ools TOC, **I**ndex.

3. In the dialog box, under Generate, choose Table of contents. Choose OK or press Enter.

    Notice that the same options are available in this dialog box as are available in the dialog box used in step 2 of the master document directions.

Ami Pro compiles the table of contents for the two chapters, using the styles you assigned. When Ami Pro is finished compiling, the table of contents appears in the window.

You should now make two adjustments to the table of contents. Place the cursor in front of the second Finding a Print Shop. Type **Chapter 2,**. (This heading did not appear in the TOC because it was not in the original document.) Note that the index and its page number have been added. You can now format the text in the style of your document.

Use Ami Pro's preformatted styles or modify the styles to suit your own purposes for consistency in design.

When creating a table of contents for one document, you can use the options in Tools TOC, Index. When creating a table of contents for a master document, use File Master Document.

Table of Contents

Table Of Contents

i

Fig. 21.12 The Table of Contents for the two book chapters or master document.

Creating an Index

You can create an index two different ways. The first method pertains to a large document; the second pertains to a small one. Using either method takes time and patience. You must mark the index entries within the text of your document before you can compile the index. This step, in itself, requires planning. You must decide which references are primary, secondary, and so on. You must also decide whether to mark each occurrence of a word or only the first occurrence. You may want to look at several indexes before deciding on a style for yours.

You use the first method when you are compiling the entries in several documents (chapters) into a single index. You create the entries in a separate document, insert them into each individual document, and mark your index references and entries. This method is long and complicated, and you can learn more about it in the Ami Pro reference manual.

So that you will become familiar with marking text and compiling an index, with the example in this chapter, you use the second method. This method works best with shorter documents, such as the two chapters in your master document. Figure 21.13 illustrates the index. Although the index is not complete, it does enable you to see how an index compiled with Ami Pro will appear. Ami Pro compiles the index and creates a new document based on the INDEX.STY style sheet. In this example, formatting of the INDEX.STY was altered slightly by changing the columns from three to two in **Page M**odify Page Layout. This change was made because some secondary entries are extremely long; for them to remain on one line, the column width must be wider than the three-column layout allowed. The formatting is Ami Pro's choice, with one exception: it contains only two columns instead of three. You may want to reformat the type styles, the columns, and so on.

To create an index, follow these steps:

1. Open your source document.

2. On page one, in the second paragraph, select the word `proofreader`.

3. Choose Edit Mark text. In the secondary command list, choose **I**ndex Entry. A dialog box appears.

4. The word `proofreader` appears in the Primary text box. Select the word and press Shift+Del. Place the cursor in the Secondary text box and press Shift+Ins.

5. Place the cursor in the Primary text box, and type the following:

   Personnel

The first method of marking index entries takes extensive planning before you begin marking.

Ami Pro creates the index, alphabetizes the primary and secondary entries, and adds the page numbers.

Use **N**ext Mark or **P**rev Mark to find the first occurrence of marked index entries you want to edit.

Use Next Same or Prev Same to move the insertion point to the next or previous reference for the index entry referenced in the Primary text box.

6. Choose Mark, and then choose OK or press Enter.

7. On page one, in the third paragraph, select the words production manager.

8. Choose Edit Mark text. In the secondary command list, choose Index Entry. A dialog box appears.

9. The words production manager appear in the Primary text box. Select the words and press Shift+Del. Place the cursor in the Secondary text box and press Shift+Ins.

10. Choose the arrow to the right of the Primary text box. In the drop-down list, select Personnel.

11. Choose Mark, and then choose OK or press Enter.

12. Continue to mark the index entries in chapters one and two in this manner. Use figure 21.13 to guide you in primary and secondary references.

13. Save the document.

To generate the index, follow these steps:

1. Place the cursor anywhere on page one of the source document.

2. Choose Tools TOC, Index.

3. In the Generate box, choose Index, and then choose Include alphabetical separators. Choose OK or press Enter.

   Ami Pro compiles the index and places it in the document you specified. After the index document appears on-screen, you can format the page and the text.

Ami Pro uses the INDEX.STY style sheet with Primary and Secondary paragraph styles already formatted for your use.

Ami Pro picks up the capitalization from the text. To apply initial capitalization to words that are not capitalized when they come into the index choose Style Modify Style; in Modify, choose Font; in Attributes, choose Initial caps. Then continue to format the index.

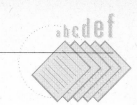

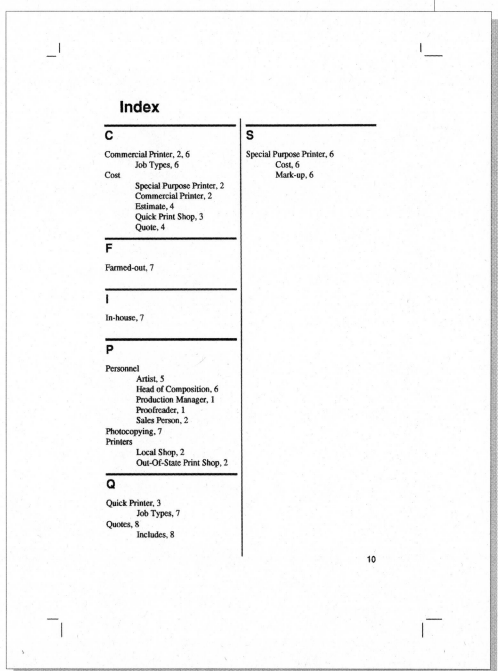

Index

C

Commercial Printer, 2, 6
    Job Types, 6
Cost
    Special Purpose Printer, 2
    Commercial Printer, 2
    Estimate, 4
    Quick Print Shop, 3
    Quote, 4

F

Farmed-out, 7

I

In-house, 7

P

Personnel
    Artist, 5
    Head of Composition, 6
    Production Manager, 1
    Proofreader, 1
    Sales Person, 2
Photocopying, 7
Printers
    Local Shop, 2
    Out-Of-State Print Shop, 2

Q

Quick Printer, 3
    Job Types, 7
Quotes, 8
    Includes, 8

S

Special Purpose Printer, 6
    Cost, 6
    Mark-up, 6

10

Fig. 21.13 The index, page 10 of the book.

Looking at Design

The chapter number in figure 21.14 is in CaslonOpenFace, to attract attention on the first page.

The best way to decide which format you will use for your book is to look at other book designs and experiment with Ami Pro. The rest of this section explains two design alternatives.

The first design is a layout for an 8 1/2-by-11-inch page (see fig. 21.14). The left margin is extremely wide for two reasons: to provide the correct line length for the 10-point type and to list the heads in the left margin. The reader can use the heads in the margin to reference any subject quickly and effortlessly.

Page two of the same layout follows a similar style (see fig. 21.15). In this case, all heads are the same size and are left-aligned in the margin. The body text is justified with interparagraph spacing, which creates plenty of white space for comfortable reading. The header of this design presents the page number on the left (a left page) and the chapter number and name on the right. A screened rule separates the header from the body, which gives the page a lighter look.

When using justified text, be sure to allow extra gutter space between columns.

Consistency is maintained by repeating the size, shape, and line thickness of the graphic.

The second design is completely different from others in this chapter. Figure 21.16 illustrates the first page of the chapter. The page size is 11 by 8 1/2 inches—landscape orientation. The text is set in two columns, justified body text defines the margins and gutter, and left-aligned heads are all caps.

Page two of the design continues the two-column layout, with the addition of a page number at the bottom (see fig. 21.17). The uppercase, italicized subheads attract attention, and the body remains justified with a 1/4-inch indent. This page is especially interesting because of the added graphic. You could fill the frame with a photograph, an illustration, or line art. This example uses AmiDraw's laser printer clip art to show you how a graphic looks on the page. The one-point rule around the graphic helps define the column width, and it allows plenty of white space, as well.

Finally, page three of the same design adds another image (AmiDraw's dot-matrix printer) (see fig. 21.18). Notice that the graphic mirrors the layout on its facing page—page two. The page number appears in the lower right corner of this right page.

1

Finding a Print Shop

What do you look for in a printer? What are your priorities? A quick turn-a-round? A superior print job? An inexpensive printing bill? Someone who treats you fairly and honestly? These are all attributes desired in a printer; but, unfortunately, you may not be able to find one who fills all of the above requirements.

Before you choose a printer, you should talk to and visit many shops. Ask questions, ask to tour their shop, meet the people with whom you will be working. If you are having a job typeset, meet the proofreader or head of that department. If you need artwork done, talk to the artist. If you need high-resolution output, talk to someone who has knowledge of the computer and desktop publishing programs. People who work in print shops are specialists in their fields. Rarely does one person know about all departments. Never depend on just one person in a print shop.

In addition, ask your friends and business associates who they use as a printer. Find out if they have had dealings with local shops, and what they think. If possible, find out who to talk to when you visit the shop, and who to stay away from. All print shops have at least one person who knows printing and is good at helping customers. A production manager, the head of composition, the person who schedules jobs, or perhaps a sales person could be your best contact at the shop. Similarly, most shops have employees you should avoid. One who knows more than anyone else, one who treats you like you're simple or tiresome, or one who doesn't care about you or your job. Take care of yourself when talking to your printer; if you don't like the way you're treated, either say so or find another printer.

Services

Of all the print shops available, try your local printers first. A local shop is convenient and keeps your money in your area. The convenience of touring the shop, placing your order in person, picking up your finished job, and registering complaints in person is far more beneficial to you than dealing with an out-

Fig. 21.14 An 8 1/2-by-11-inch layout for a book design.

of-state print shop. Sometimes, just looking them in the eye tells you everything you need to know.

The type of print shop you use depends on your job. Different shops cater to different types of printing. If you choose the right shop, your job looks better and the bill should be more to your liking. Following is a description of common print shops.

Commercial

There are many types of print shops available. The commercial printer is most likely the one you will want to use. A commercial printer is one that will take on nearly any print job: books, forms, newsletters, letterheads, and so on; one who runs any number of ink colors from one color to four color process; one who has a typesetter, paste-up artist, camera department, presses, folders, and a bindery.

Although a commercial printer does the majority of work in-house, there may be some jobs he farms out to a trade shop. A trade shop specializes in one service: composition, binding, four-color work, or copy work.

Special Purpose

A special purpose printer is one that specializes in specific print jobs: business cards, labels, or business forms. A commercial printer might use them because they can do the work more efficiently and cheaper. But farmed out work may also be more expensive because the printer pays the trade shop and then charges you that price plus a mark-up (usually 25% of the total). This is one reason you should get several quotes on your job before deciding upon one printer — you want the best price you can get.

Commercial print shops often farm out color separations. Small printers do not have the equipment or personnel to do their own separations. As color separation technology advances, less expensive equipment is becoming available. If your printer does separations in-house, ask to see samples of his work. Always ask how much a separation will cost. Separations are very expensive.

Quick Printer

A quick printer is one who does mostly photocopying by using a xerographic process that allows the copying of short-run quantities. The quality is usually low to medium; however some quick print shops do produce quality work. The standard page sizes for photocopying are 8-1/2" x 11" and 11" x 17". Quick print shops may also have a small press or two, and do some offset printing. They may farm out work such as binding large jobs, typesetting, some camera work, and so on. A quick print shop is good to use for certain jobs: fliers, invitations, inserts, or jobs that don't require precision in width of margins, registration, and so forth.

The type of shop you choose depends upon your job. If you need high-quality printing within a reasonable amount of time, you may choose a commercial printer. If you need 500 fliers yesterday, then choose a quick print shop.

It is important to patronize several shops. Don't just get quote after quote. Actually take them some business once in a while. This way, when you are in need of something special or something fast, and one printer cannot do it — you have the option of taking your job to another printer.

Fig. 21.15   Page two, with a left page header.

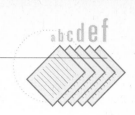

CHAPTER 1
FINDING A PRINT SHOP

What do you look for in a printer? What are your priorities? A quick turn-a-round? A superior print job? An inexpensive printing bill? Someone who treats you fairly and honestly? These are all attributes desired in a printer; but, unfortunately, you may not be able to find one who fills all of the above requirements.

Before you choose a printer, you should talk to and visit many shops. Ask questions, ask to tour their shop, meet the people with whom you will be working. If you are having a job typeset, meet the proofreader or head of that department. If you need artwork done, talk to the artist. If you need high-resolution output, talk to someone who has knowledge of the computer and desktop publishing programs. People who work in print shops are specialists in their fields. Rarely does one person know about all departments. Never depend on just one person in a print shop.

In addition, ask your friends and business associates who they use as a printer. Find out if they have had dealings with local shops, and what they think. If possible, find out who to talk to when you visit the shop, and who to stay away from. All print shops have at least one person who knows printing and is good at helping customers. A production manager, the head of com-

position, the person who schedules jobs, or perhaps a sales person could be your best contact at the shop. Similarly, most shops have employees you should avoid. One who knows more than anyone else, one who treats you like you're simple or tiresome, or one who doesn't care about you or your job. Take care of yourself when talking to your printer; if you don't like the way you're treated, either say so or find another printer.

PRINTING SERVICES

Of all the print shops available, try your local printers first. A local shop is convenient and keeps your money in your area. The convenience of touring the shop, placing your order in person, picking up your finished job, and registering complaints in person is far more beneficial to you than dealing with an out-of-state print shop. Sometimes, just looking them in the eye tells you everything you need to know.

The type of print shop you use depends on your job. Different shops cater to different types of printing. If you choose the right shop, your job looks better.

Fig. 21.16 A landscape-oriented book design.

charges you that price plus a mark-up (usually 25% of the total). This is one reason you should get several quotes on your job before deciding upon one printer — you want the best price you can get.

Commercial print shops often farm out color separations. Small printers do not have the equipment or personnel to do their own separations. As color separation technology advances, less expensive equipment is becoming available. If your printer does separations in-house, ask to see samples of his work. Always ask how much a separation will cost. Separations are very expensive.

QUICK PRINTER

A quick printer is one who does mostly photocopying by using a xerographic process that allows the copying of short-run quantities. The quality is usually low to medium; however some quick print shops do produce quality work. The standard page sizes for photocopying are 8-1/2" x 11" and 11" x 17". Quick print shops may also have a small press or two, and do some offset printing. They may farm out work such as binding large jobs, typesetting, some camera work, and so on. A quick print shop is good to use for certain jobs: fliers, invitations, inserts, or jobs that don't require precision in width of margins, registration, and so forth.

The type of shop you choose depends upon your job. If you need high-quality printing within a reasonable amount of time, you may choose a commercial printer. If you need 500 fliers yesterday, then choose a quick print shop.

It is important to patronize several shops. Don't just get quote after quote. Actually take them some business once in a while. This way, when you are in need of something special or something fast, and one printer cannot do it — you have the option of taking your job to another printer.

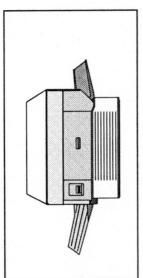

COMMERCIAL PRINTER

There are many types of print shops available. The commercial printer is most likely the one you will want to use. A commercial printer is one that will take on nearly any print job: books, forms, newsletters, letterheads, and so on; one who runs any number of ink colors from one color to four color process; one who has a typesetter, paste-up artist, camera department, presses, folders, and a bindery.

Although a commercial printer does the majority of work in-house, there may be some jobs he farms out to a trade shop. A trade shop specializes in one service: composition, binding, four-color work, or copy work.

SPECIAL PURPOSE PRINTER

A special purpose printer is one that specializes in specific print jobs: business cards, labels, or business forms. A commercial printer might use them because they can do the work more efficiently and cheaper. But farmed out work may also be more expensive because the printer pays the trade shop and then

2

Fig. 21.17 Page two of the design adds a graphic and a footer.

ESTIMATES, QUOTES

It's important to find out how much your job will cost before you have it printed. If you don't ask ahead of time, the printer could increase the price to whatever he wishes. Many print shop's are principled; many are not. There are two ways to find out the cost of your job, by an estimate or by a quote.

ESTIMATES

Some printers will give estimates on the cost of your job. You must give complete details on your job, as you would with a quote, to get a reasonable estimate. Estimates, however, are not what the printer guarantees the price to be. An estimate is just that — an estimate. If the printer finds extra costs in running the job, he will raise the price accordingly. For this reason, it is important you get a quote instead of an estimate, if at all possible.

QUOTES

It is important to get quotes on all of your jobs before you print them. A quote is the printer's stated price for the cost of your specific job. You should consider getting quotes from several printers, because prices can vary greatly from shop to shop. Also, be sure your quote is in writing; and keep your copy in case there is a question later. Most quotes are good for 30 days, so you'll have time to check out other printers. A quote should be honored by your printer as the price he will charge you — as long as you don't make any alterations after the piece is in process.

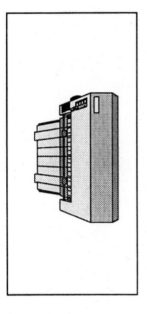

A quote from the printer includes the cost of materials and labor for your job: composition, paste-up, camera, stripping, plate-making, paper, ink, press, and bindery. Not only that, but the quote also adds in a fee for overhead items such as electricity, cost of water, equipment, office help, and insurance for employees and the building.

The more information you give printers, the better they will be able to quote your job. Describe your piece in a term the printer will recognize: newsletter, brochure, flier. This will give the printer an immediate basic understanding of your piece before the quote. If possible, include a mock-up of your job.

Make sure you provide all the information about your job to the person who quotes the job. If you omit details, expect the printer to alter the quote accordingly. Omitted details may also affect scheduling and delivery time. The printer has only the information you provide him when he quotes, plans, and schedules your job.

3

Fig. 21.18 Page three, the facing page to page two.

Recapping

In this chapter you learned to change the page size of a document, to print crop marks, add headers, footers, running heads, and page numbers. Furthermore, you used the outline mode and the master document, indexing, and table of contents features.

A

Getting To Know Ami Pro 2.0 and 3.0

The document chapters in this book assume that you know Ami Pro for Windows. If you are not familiar with Ami Pro, however, you can read this appendix for a general survey of the basic operations and features of Ami Pro, Versions 2.0 and 3.0. This appendix includes detailed material about the screen, menus, commands, dialog boxes, mouse, and keyboard features. If you are not familiar with any of these features, you may want to refer to the information presented here before you work through the document chapters. If you have further questions about any feature, read the Ami Pro reference manual or consult Ami Pro's on-screen help.

ost of the features of Ami Pro 2.0 and 3.0 are the same; Ami Pro 3.0, however, contains new shortcuts and some innovative characteristics. The following descriptions refer to both versions unless otherwise indicated.

Understanding Ami Pro's Screen

Ami Pro uses the style of Microsoft Windows for its menus. If you're familiar with Windows, you should feel comfortable with Ami Pro. Ami Pro uses Windows characteristics for items such as menus, commands, dialog boxes, command buttons, and so on. The Title and Menu bars work the same as in other Windows applications. The Control, Minimize, and Maximize boxes are located in the same place, for example, and they perform the same functions they perform in other Windows programs. In addition, activating a menu or choosing a command is the same in Ami Pro as it is in other Windows applications.

Figure A.1 illustrates the Ami Pro screen. Each part of the screen performs a specific function in operating the program. Menus allow you to choose commands that save files; edit text; create drawings, frames, and charts; format the page and the text; and so on. Scroll bars enable you to move around the page. The Status Bar defines the location of the cursor, gives the number of pages, and identifies certain functions.

❶ Title bar
❷ Menu
❸ SmartIcons
❹ Horizontal ruler
❺ Vertical ruler
❻ Vertical scroll bar
❼ Horizontal scroll bar
❽ Status bar

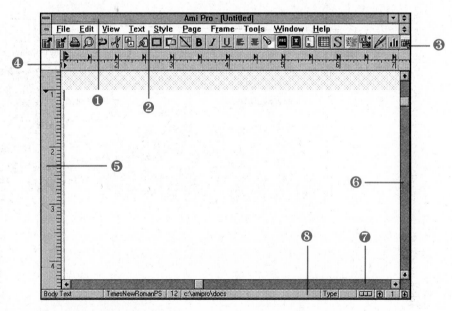

Fig. A.1   The Ami Pro screen.

The following sections describe each part of the screen in detail.

Title Bar

The Title Bar contains the Control Menu control box (on the far left), which allows you to Restore, Move, Size, Minimize, Maximize, and Close the current program window. You also can use the Control Menu to switch to another Windows application, or to run the Clipboard or Control Panel. To run the Clipboard, you must have something copied or pasted to it. The name of the program (Ami Pro) and the name of the current document also appear on the Title Bar. To the far right of the Title Bar are the Minimize and Maximize boxes. The first control box switches you to other open programs or to the Program Manager. The second control box changes the size of the current window.

Menu Bar

Menus control most features you use to format a document in Ami Pro. You choose a menu by clicking it with the mouse or, if you're using the keyboard, by pressing and holding the Alt key while pressing the under-lined letter of the menu name and then letting up on the Alt key. To access the File menu with the keyboard, for example, press Alt+F. Letters underlined in any Ami Pro menu or dialog box are in bold in this book. See the sections "Understanding the Mouse" and "Getting Accustomed to the Keyboard" if you aren't sure how to use the mouse and keyboard.

Some menus contain secondary command lists. These secondary com-mands are listed in this appendix, and their uses are explained in detail in the next section. Some commands, such as Tables, Drawing, and Charts, create new menus. These new menus also are listed in this section.

The following sections list the available menus in Ami Pro and give a brief description of commands in each menu.

File Menu

The File menu contains commands for controlling and accessing docu-ments. Included are New, Open, Close, Save, Save As, and Revert to Saved. From this menu, you also can access Import Picture, Doc Info, File Management, Master Document, Merge, Print, Printer Setup, and Exit Ami Pro. Version 3.0 adds the command Print Envelope to the File menu.

You use Save As when you first save a document. The Save As command allows you to name your document and to assign it to a specific drive. You use the Save command only to save the most recent changes after naming the document. If you Save before Saving As, Ami Pro prompts you to name the document. If you Save As just to add recent changes, Ami Pro asks you to name the document again.

Edit Menu

The Edit menu offers commands that deal directly with the current document, such as Undo, Cut, Copy, Paste, Paste Link, Paste Special, and Link Options. You also can Find & Replace, add Bookmarks, and Go To a specific point in the document. The next three commands offer secondary command lists. The Insert command presents options for what you want to insert, such as Date/Time, Note, Merge Field, Doc Info Field, Glossary Record, or New Object. Ami Pro 3.0 also enables you to insert Bullets. The Power Fields command includes a secondary command list that includes Insert, Update, Update All, Next Field, and Previous Field. Finally, Mark Text offers Index Entry, Glossary, Revision Insertion, Protected Text, and No Hyphenation. In addition, Version 3.0 includes TOC in Mark Text.

View Menu

The View menu lets you choose how the screen looks while you're working. You can view the Full Page, Facing Pages, a Working (Version 2.0) or Custom (Version 3.0), Standard, or Enlarged view. Also available are Layout, Outline, or Draft modes. Layout mode shows you exactly how the printed page looks; Draft mode contains no formatting, for quicker data entry; and Outline mode shows you headings and subheadings in your outline. In View, you can turn on or off the following options: Ruler, Styles Box, and Power Fields. Version 3.0 adds Smart-Icons and Clean Screen. If you use the Clean Screen feature (which removes all but the scroll bars for a larger view area), be sure that you first turn on the Return icon in the Clean Screen Options under View Preferences. View Preferences offers more options, such as table gridlines, the vertical ruler, and so on.

Text Menu

Use the Text menu to format small amounts of selected text, such as a heading or unusual paragraph settings. You can change the Font, Alignment (the secondary command list offers Left, Center, Right, and

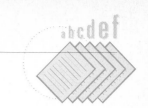

Justify), Indention, and Spacing. You also can apply various attributes to selected text by selecting Bold, Italic, Underline, Word Underline, Caps (Upper Case, Lower Case, Initial Caps, or Small Caps) or by adding Special Effects (such as bullets or numbered lists). Finally, you can change any text with an applied attribute back to Normal. Version 3.0 also offers Fast Format, a shortcut for assigning text attributes and paragraph styles.

Style Menu

The Style menu applies to the style sheet for use over and over again. Use it to format fonts, type sizes, alignment, tabs, indents, lines, and so on. Commands include Create, Modify, Define, and Outline Styles; Use Another Style Sheet; Save as a Style Sheet; Style Management; and Select a Style.

Page Menu

The Page menu controls margins, columns, tabs, rules, borders, and so on as they relate to the page. Commands include Insert Page Layout (secondary commands: Insert, Remove, Revert); Modify Page Layout; Floating Header/Footer (Version 2.0) or Header/Footer (Version 3.0); Ruler (Insert or Remove); Page Numbering; Line Numbering; and Breaks.

Frame Menu

This menu controls the formatting related to the frame, such as margins, columns, tabs, size, and position. Commands include Create Frame, Modify Frame Layout, Graphics Scaling, Group, Bring to Front, and Send to Back.

Tools Menu

The Tools menu contains Spell Check, Thesaurus, Tables, Image Processing, Drawing, Charting, Equations, Footnotes, Revision Marking, Doc Compare, Sort, TOC, Index, SmartIcons, User Setup, and Macros (secondary command list: Quick Record, Quick Playback, Record, Playback, and Edit). Version 3.0 offers a Grammar Checker as well.

Some commands in the Tools menu activate new menus. When you add a table to your document, for example, a Table menu appears. The following sections contain summaries of the added menus.

Table Menu

The Table menu appears only when you are working in a table. The Table menu commands are Modify Table Layout, Lines/Shades (Version 2.0) or Lines/Color (Version 3.0), Insert or Delete Column/Row, Column/Row Size, Connect, Headings, Leaders (the secondary command list offers leader choices: dots, dashes, line, or none), Protect, Edit Formula, and Quick Add (Row, Column). Version 3.0 offers more options, such as Delete Entire Table and Select Column, Select Row, and Select Entire Table.

Image Menu

Use the Image menu for fine-tuning scanned or halftone art. Commands include Processing, Revert, Halftone (secondary commands: Fastest Printing, Best Picture Quality, Automatically Selected, and Posterize), and Leave Image.

Draw Menu

Ami Pro contains a drawing program. When activated, the Draw menu appears, which contains the following commands: Line Style, Fill Pattern, Extract Line & Fill, Apply Line & Fill, Rotate, Flip (Horizontal or Vertical), Snap To, Show Grid, Grid Settings, Select All, Group, Bring To Front, and Send To Back.

Equation Menu

Ami Pro's Equation menu contains these commands: Text Mode, Limits & Size Big, Greek Keyboard, Symbol Keyboard, Hide Matrix Lines, Hide Input Boxes, Preferences, and Insert. Insert includes the secondary commands Fraction, Radical, Superscript, Subscript, Operator, Brackets, Matrix, Function, Spaces, Label, Over/Under, and TeX Command.

Window Menu

The Window menu controls multiple document windows by using the commands New Window, Tile, and Cascade and by listing open document windows.

Help Menu

The Help feature in Ami Pro is an excellent on-screen reference. You should take time now to familiarize yourself with this feature. The command list includes Index (Version 2.0) or Contents (Version 3.0),

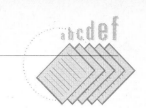

Using Help, Keyboard, How Do I?, Basics (Version 2.0), For Upgraders, Macro Doc, Enhancement Products, and About Ami Pro. If you have any questions about Ami Pro, use the Help Feature. Version 3.0 also offers a Quick Start Tutorial that includes information on frames, charts, styles, and so on.

Help includes context-sensitive help, point-and-shoot help, and indexed help. *Context-sensitive help* relates to the function you are using at the time you access Help. If you are in Edit Paste Special, for example, and you press F1 (the Help key), Ami Pro displays a dialog box that contains information specific to that dialog box and subject.

Point-and-shoot help works in a similar way. Point to a menu or a command and press Shift-F1. Choose the command in question, and Ami Pro displays Help relating to that command.

Indexed help is available by selecting the Help menu. Ami Pro offers you several forms of help. The Index (Contents in Version 3.0) is a list of Help topics. Using Help consists of information on how to use the help function. Keyboard lists shortcuts on the keyboard. How Do I? contains a list of common functions. For Upgraders describes new and improved features of Ami Pro for those already familiar with previous versions of the program.

Menu Commands

After accessing a menu, a command list appears (see fig. A.2). Commands perform functions relating to the menu. Some of the File menu commands, for example, are Save, Print, Merge, or Close the current document. These commands relate to managing the document. On the other hand, the Style menu contains commands such as Modify a Style, Create a Style, and Select a Style; all style commands relate to the styles within the document or style sheet.

Note in the figure that New is highlighted, which means that New is the selected command. If you click New with the mouse or press Enter, that command is executed. Also notice that the sixth command, Revert to Saved, is grayed. Grayed commands are not available to you for various reasons—in this case, the sixth command is not available at this time because the document has not been saved.

You access a command the same way you access a menu. The only difference between the menu and command list in figure A.2 (Version 2.0) and that of Version 3.0 is that the latter version adds the command Print Envelope.

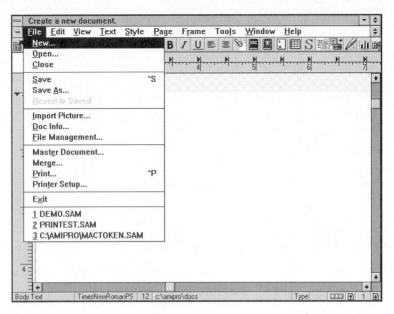

Fig. A.2 The command list for the File menu (Version 2.0 screen).

One of three things happens when you access a command. One possibility is that a check mark may appear beside the command. In figure A.3, Font and Alignment have check marks to their left. These check marks signify that you either have changed a characteristic of that command or have turned on the option. Font is checked because it was changed from Times Roman to Times New Roman. The default alignment had been Left, but it has been changed to justified—Justify also is checked. The check marks remain beside the commands unless you revert to the original style. In the command list shown here, check marks also would appear beside Normal, **B**old, **I**talic, **U**nderline, and **W**ord Underline if you selected them. In addition, notice that to the right of each of these text attributes is a shortcut. The shortcut for **B**old is Ctrl+B; the shortcut for **I**talic is Ctrl+I. Many shortcuts are included beside the commands; after you learn them, you can use the shortcuts instead of accessing the menu.

Some commands offer a secondary command list, as shown in figure A.3. After you choose Alignment, a secondary list appears, offering choices of Left, Center, **R**ight, or **J**ustify. Any command that offers a secondary command list has an arrow to the right of the command name, as does Caps in figure A.3 (the arrow beside Alignment is hidden by the secondary command list).

Three dots (an ellipsis) next to a command name signify that a dialog box appears when you choose that command. Following is a detailed description of how dialog boxes work.

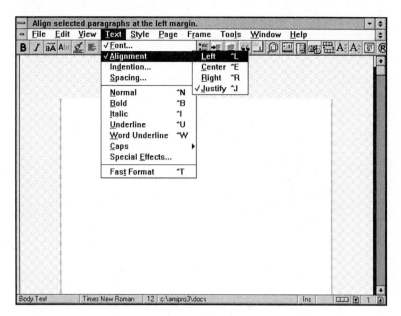

Fig. A.3 The Text menu commands (Version 3.0 screen).

Dialog Boxes

Dialog boxes in Ami Pro range from simple to complicated. A dialog box appears when you choose any menu command followed by an ellipsis, and the dialog box contains additional options and choices relating to that command. Figure A.4 illustrates a simple dialog box in Version 2.0. When you choose File New, the New dialog box appears. Within this box, you choose the style sheet on which you want to base the new document. Choose from the list of style sheets either by clicking the style sheet's name with the mouse or by pressing the down arrow and then Enter to select with the keyboard. You use the grayed command buttons, OK and Cancel, to indicate that you accept this choice or you want to cancel the operation. Choose OK with the mouse or press Enter. Choose Cancel with the mouse or press Esc.

Many dialog boxes in Ami Pro contain multiple choices and multiple dialog boxes. These dialog boxes are available when you choose Modify a Style, Page Layout, or Frame Layout. The following figures illustrate examples of multiple dialog boxes within the original. If you choose

Style Modify Style, a dialog box like that shown in figure A.5 appears. The following figures for the Modify Style dialog boxes are Version 2.0 screens. Many of the Version 3.0 screens are the same or only slightly different.

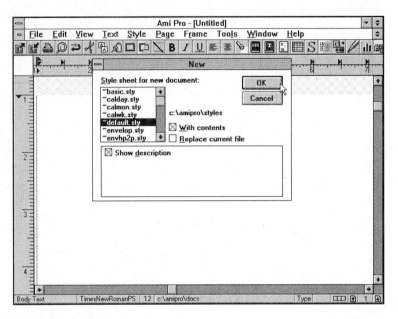

Fig. A.4   A simple dialog box.

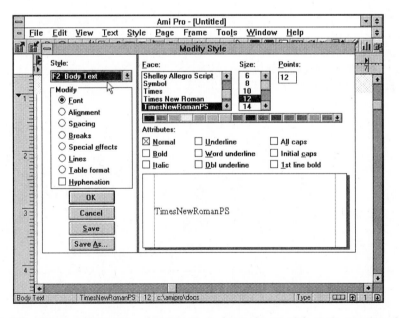

Fig. A.5   The first dialog box, Modify Font, from the Modify Style command.

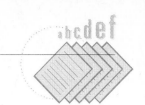

Notice that the Style you are modifying is Body Text (the cursor is pointing to the Style selection box).

Listed below the style are the various characteristics you can modify within this one dialog box, as well as gray command buttons (OK, Cancel, Save, and Save As). This modify list remains the same within the dialog box, as do the options. The only difference between Versions 2.0 and 3.0 in the Modify box is that Version 3.0 changes Special Effects to Bullets & Numbers.

To the right of the list is another dialog box, which changes depending on which characteristic you are modifying. In this figure, you choose Modify Font. You can change Face, Size, and attributes of the Body Text. The ruled box in the lower right area of the dialog box shows you what your changes look like. Ami Pro Version 3.0 contains the same Font dialog box as Version 2.0.

After you format the Font characteristics, you have several choices to make. You can choose OK to close the dialog box (accepting the changes you made) and return to the document. You also can choose Save or Save As to save the change to the style sheet. On the other hand, you can choose any of the other characteristics in the Modify dialog box and continue making changes to the Body Text.

Figure A.6 illustrates the resulting dialog box when you choose Modify Alignment. In this box, you change Tabs, Indents, and Alignment. You also see what the changes look like as you change them. Version 3.0 of Ami Pro allows you to Clear Tabs with one button and also lets you apply an indent to both sides by using a shortcut. Again, you can accept these changes, cancel, or change more characteristics.

Figure A.7 shows the Modify Spacing dialog box. You can choose to alter the Line Spacing of the selected style—in this case, Body Text. Also provided is an area for adjusting Paragraph Spacing and choices for Text Tightness (kerning). Again, Ami Pro shows the results so that you can adjust spacing before accepting the changes. Versions 3.0 and 2.0 are the same.

Defining Breaks is controlled in the next Modify choice. You can insert a break into a page or a column. In addition, you can place a break at the top or bottom of a particular paragraph. Figure A.8 illustrates the Break options and the results. Versions 3.0 and 2.0 are the same.

Special Effects includes bullets, numbered lists, and specific attributes pertaining to them. Figure A.9 shows this dialog box. You can choose the character for the bullet or the numbering pattern, or you can use your own text instead of a bullet or number. You can assign attribute changes such as bold, italic, and so on, as well as the space between the bullet and text. Again, the results of your changes appear in the bordered box. In Ami Pro 3.0, this Modify option is called Bullets & Numbers. All choices are the same as in Version 2.0 except an added option allows you to right-align numbers.

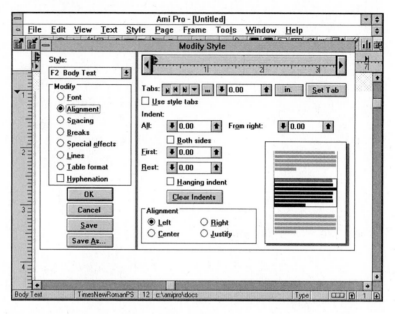

Fig. A.6 The dialog box for Modify Alignment.

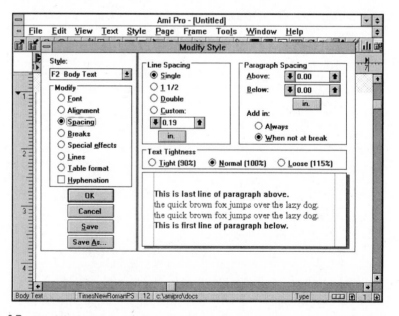

Fig. A.7 Modify Spacing, to change line and paragraph spacing and to kern text.

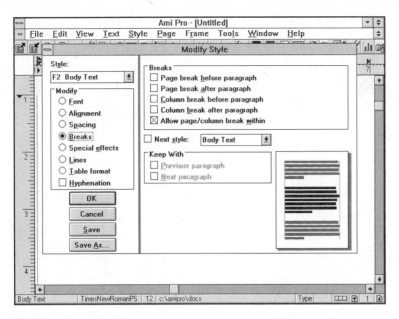

Fig. A.8 The Modify Style dialog box with Modify Breaks chosen.

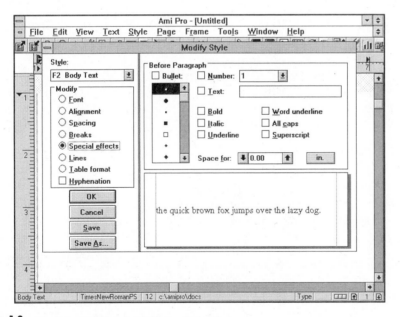

Fig. A.9 The Modify Special Effects dialog box.

Figure A.10 illustrates the Modify Lines dialog box. Using this box, you can choose to place a rule above (as shown in the figure) or below a line of text.

You also set the length, width, and spacing of the rule here. Versions 3.0 and 2.0 are the same.

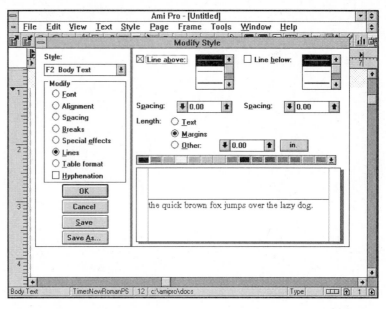

Fig. A.10 The Modify Line dialog box is used to add rules above or below text.

Figure A.11 illustrates the Table Format dialog box in the Modify choice. If you use Body Text within a table, these options format the cell, numeric, negative, and currency formats as they appear in the table. Versions 3.0 and 2.0 are the same.

Note that **Hyphenation** is preceded by a square box (in figure A.11) instead of a circle. Square boxes in Ami Pro mean that you turn on or off that option. If you choose **Hyphenation** (by clicking the box with the mouse or by pressing Alt+H on the keyboard), an X appears in the box. The X means that the option is turned on, and Ami Pro automatically hyphenates this style. If you choose the option again, the X disappears and the option is turned off. Versions 3.0 and 2.0 are the same.

Rules and Borders

In many dialog boxes, you may notice line style patterns from which you choose for borders, boxes, and rules. Ami Pro does not indicate the thickness of these rules. In designing page layout, you must know which thicknesses of rules you are using so that you can judge the balance, consistency, and quality of your design. Figure A.12 shows the Modify

Page Layout dialog box containing the rules and each rule's thickness in points. The Page Layout rules are the same thicknesses as frame rules, paragraph rules, drawing rules, and so on. Figure A.12 illustrates the first five rules in the Lines Style selection box. Versions 3.0 and 2.0 are the same.

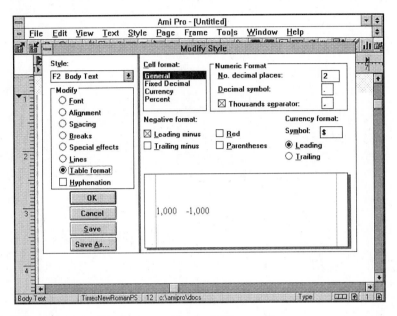

Fig. A.11   Modify Table format in the Body Text style.

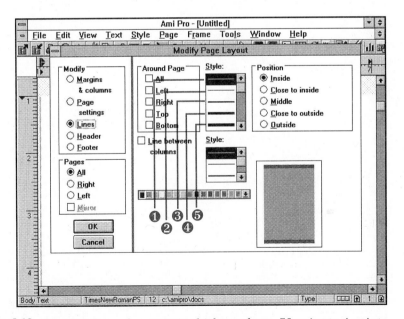

❶ .75
❷ 1.00
❸ 2.00
❹ 3.00
❺ 4.00

Fig. A.12   The first five rules range in thickness from .75 point to 4 points.

If you scroll to the next five line patterns in the same dialog box, you see the rules shown in figure A.13.

1 5.00

2 8.00

3 Two 1-pt. lines

4 Two 1 1/2-pt. lines

5 .75/1 pt./.75 pt. (three lines)

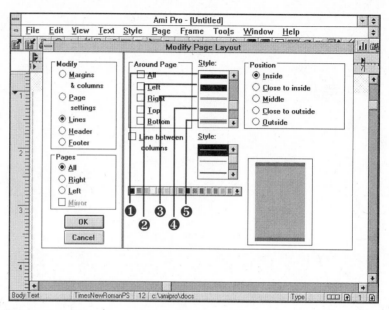

Fig. A.13   The next five line patterns.

Scrolling to the end of the line patterns, you see that the last two rules in the dialog box are double rules (see fig. A.14).

1 3 pt/1 pt

2 1 pt/3 pt

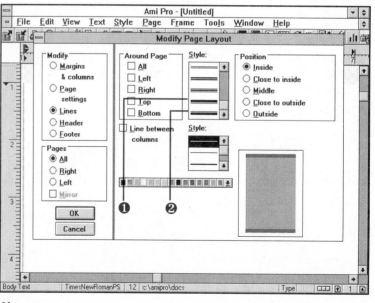

Fig. A.14   The last two line patterns each contain a 3- and a 1-point rule, in opposite order.

SmartIcon Bar

SmartIcons are shortcut buttons that quickly and effortlessly perform many of the commands in the menus. You must have a mouse to use SmartIcons. If you do not have a mouse, use the keyboard shortcuts later in this appendix. By using the Tools menu and choosing SmartIcons, you can move the icons to various positions on the screen. Turn the icons on or off by selecting icons (three small boxes) in the right corner of the Status Bar.

By choosing Tools SmartIcons, you also can assign new icons and change the old icons on your screen. You should assign icons representing the functions you use the most to the SmartIcons. If you import a lot of pictures, for example, you can add an icon to speed up the process; or if a particular macro is useful in your work, add the SmartIcon that represents it to your list.

Version 2.0 of Ami Pro divides the SmartIcons into Standard and Custom icons. The Standard icons represent menu commands such as Cut, Paste, Open File, Draw a Frame, Charting, and so on. The Custom icons depict macros. If you assign a macro to an icon, Ami Pro performs that macro when you click the icon. Ami Pro 2.0 gives you only one set of icons (about 25) at any one time. You also can change the position of the SmartIcons on the screen to top, bottom, left, right, or floating. Figure A.15 shows the Customize SmartIcons dialog box; notice that the mouse cursor is pointing to the description of the first icon.

Figure A.16 illustrates the SmartIcons dialog box in Version 3.0. The descriptions are easier to associate with the icons because they appear beside their respective icons. Notice that you have only two lists in the 3.0 box: Available Icons appear on the left; the current palette appears on the right. Icons that represent macros are included at the end of the Available Icons list. Notice, too, the sets from which you can choose: Proofing, Default, Editing, Graphics, and so on (see fig. A.17). Each set contains various SmartIcons to which you can switch while you're working. You can customize these sets, plus create and save your own.

In Version 3.0, you also can change the icon sizes to small, medium, or large and change the position of the SmartIcons on the screen to top, bottom, floating, and so on.

The default SmartIcons that appear when you install either version of Ami Pro represent the basic functions. The number of icons that show on your screen depends on the display adapter you use. Which SmartIcons you prefer to appear on your screen depends on the work you do.

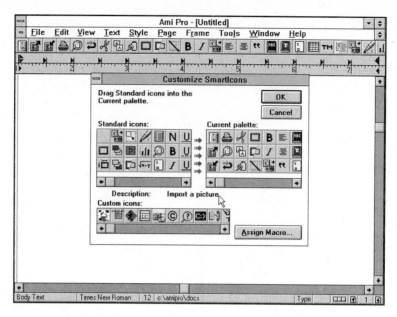

Fig. A.15 The Customize SmartIcons dialog box in Version 2.0.

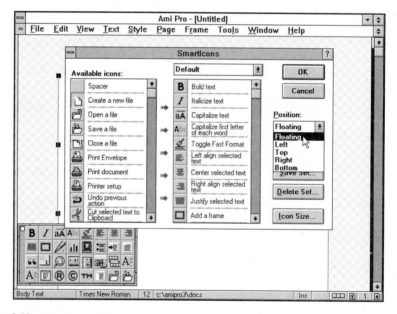

Fig. A.16 The SmartIcons dialog box in Version 3.0.

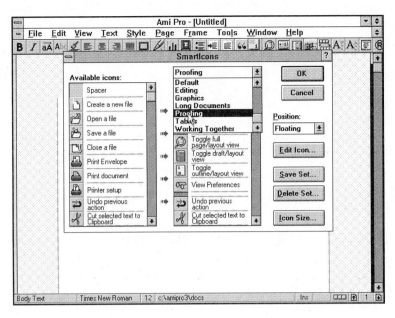

Fig. A.17   The mouse pointer points to the sets of SmartIcons from which you can choose.

To familiarize you with customizing the SmartIcons, follow these instructions for adding the Vertical Ruler icon. The Ruler icon is a *toggle view*, meaning you click it once to turn it on and click it again to turn it off.

For Ami Pro Version 2.0, follow these steps:

1. Turn icons on in the Status Bar.

2. Choose Tools SmartIcons. Choose Customize.

3. In the Customize dialog box, in Standard, click any icon. Notice that Description tells you what the icon stands for. Use the Scroll Bar to go as far right as possible.

4. In the top row, choose the third icon from the right, which is the Vertical Ruler icon. Click this icon and drag it to the first position in the Current Palette selection box. Choose OK, then choose OK again. The Vertical Ruler icon now appears on your screen in the first position of the SmartIcons.

For Ami Pro Version 3.0, follow these steps:

1. Choose Tools SmartIcons. The SmartIcons dialog box appears.

2. The Show/Hide Vertical ruler is about 1/4 of the way down on the list. Click the icon and drag it to the first position of the SmartIcons. Choose OK or press Enter.

You can place the icon at any position. When you add a new icon, the last one in the list of current icons disappears. If you don't use a particular icon, you can remove it from the Current Palette by clicking the icon and then dragging it to the Standard (or Available) Icon list.

Ami Pro 3.0 lists prewritten macros at the end of the Available Icons list. Choose any of these icons to add to the current list by dragging. Ami Pro Version 2.0 assigns macros in a different manner. Version 2.0 contains icons from which to choose, then you assign the macro you want to use. To assign a macro to an icon for Version 2.0 of Ami Pro, follow these steps:

1. Turn icons on.

2. Choose Tools SmartIcons. Choose Customize.

3. At the bottom of the dialog box, in Custom Icons, scroll to the end of the list. Choose the icon that looks like quote marks.

4. Choose Assign Macro. The Assign selection box appears.

5. In the Macro list, choose SMARTYPE.SMM.

   SMARTYPE.SMM is a macro that converts quotes and apostrophes to typographical quote marks and also converts two hyphens to em dashes. Other macros are listed in the Assign selection box.

6. Choose Save. Choose OK or press Enter. Choose OK again. The icon appears in your SmartIcons.

Horizontal Ruler

The Horizontal Ruler (also called the Current Ruler) helps you measure frames, text blocks, pictures, and so on. The primary purpose of the ruler is to set indents, columns, and tabs for selected text. The ruler referred to in these directions is the one on the screen; however, rulers in dialog boxes (such as Page, Modify Page Layout, and Style Modify Style) work the same as the screen ruler. The current ruler appears only in Layout mode.

You can set tabs or indents for selected text on the page, in a frame, or in a table. Anytime you set a measurement on the current ruler, that measurement overrides measurements set in a dialog box. Suppose that you set a left tab at 1 inch for Body Text in the Modify Style (Alignment) dialog box. You then select a paragraph of body text and activate the ruler. On the ruler, you set a left tab at 2 inches for the selected paragraph. The 2-inch tab overrides the 1-inch tab, unless you revert to the style.

When you use the Current Ruler to set tabs or indents, Ami Pro inserts a nonprinting ruler marker in your text to identify the ruler measurements for the selected text. If you copy text containing the ruler marker, the copied text remains formatted to the ruler. If you delete the ruler marker, the measurements revert to the page or style sheet.

The following are some basic instructions for using the Current Ruler:

- To turn on the ruler, choose **V**iew Show **R**uler.

- To turn off the ruler, choose View **H**ide Ruler.

- To view the ruler marker, choose **V**iew View **P**references; in the Preferences dialog box, choose Tabs & **R**eturns and then choose OK or press Enter.

Figure A.18 illustrates the activated Current Ruler. The mouse pointer is pointing to the Leader icon. Figure A.18 is a Version 2.0 screen, but Version 3.0 is the same except for one addition, a Clear Tabs button.

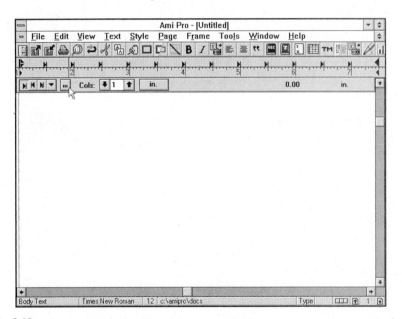

Fig. A.18   The activated ruler.

To activate the ruler by using a mouse, click the ruler.

To activate the ruler by using the keyboard, follow these steps:

1. Choose **E**dit **G**o To.

2. In the **N**ext Item selection box, choose Ruler.

3. Press Tab to choose `Go To ^H`. Ami Pro returns you to the document, with the ruler activated.

Figure A.19 illustrates an activated ruler with three tabs set. The first is a left tab at 2 1/2 inches; the second is a center tab with a line leader set at 4 inches; the third is a right tab with a dash leader set at 5 inches. You can identify the type of leader by the symbol over the tab marker. Also in this figure, note that the two indent arrows are being moved with the mouse. The solid line extending down the page indicates the indention.

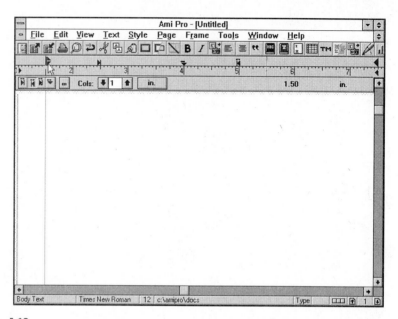

Fig. A.19   Activated ruler with tabs and indention set.

To set a tab in the current ruler by using the mouse, follow these steps:

1. Select the text. Activate the ruler. Clear any tabs that appear on the ruler. In Version 2.0, drag the tab marker up or down off the ruler. In Version 3.0, choose Clear Tabs.

2. Click the tab button (left, right, center, or decimal).

3. Click the desired measurement in the upper part of the ruler.

4. To move a tab on the ruler, drag the tab to the new position.

5. Click anywhere on the page to deselect the text.

To set a tab in the current ruler by using the keyboard, follow these steps:

1. Select the text. Activate the ruler. Clear default tabs. In Version 2.0, press Tab until the cursor reaches a tab and then press Delete. In Version 3.0, choose Clear Tabs.

2. Press Tab until the desired tab button is highlighted. Use the right-arrow key to select it.

3. Press Tab again to move the insertion point to the ruler. Press the arrow keys to move the solid line to the desired position. Press the space bar to add the tab.

4. To move a tab on the ruler, move to the tab marker you want to move, hold the space bar while pressing the left- or right-arrow key to move the tab to the desired position.

5. Press Esc to deselect the ruler.

In the left corner of the ruler are two arrows that control indents for the current ruler. To indent all lines of the selected text, you must move both arrows (they are represented by a solid rule, which you can move). To change only the first line indention of selected text, move the top arrow. To change the rest of the lines in a paragraph (a hanging indent, for example), move the second arrow.

To use the ruler to set indents with the mouse, follow these steps:

1. Select the text. Activate the ruler.

2. Place the cursor on the double arrows on the left side of the ruler and drag them to the desired measurement.

To use the ruler to set indents with the keyboard, follow these steps:

1. Select the text. Activate the ruler. Position the insertion point on the ruler.

2. Press the arrow keys to move the solid rule to the desired point. Press 3 to indent all the text; press 1 to indent the first line only; press 2 to indent the rest of the lines of a paragraph.

Vertical Ruler

The Vertical Ruler assists you in measuring frames, pictures, and text blocks. To turn on or off the Vertical Ruler, do the following:

1. Choose View View Preferences.

2. Choose Vertical Ruler. Choose OK or press Enter.

Vertical and Horizontal Scroll Bars

The scroll bars enable you to quickly move around the document. Move from the beginning of the document to the end by using the Vertical Scroll Bar. Move from the left side of a document to the right by using the Horizontal Scroll Bar. The arrows at the ends of the scroll bars move in small increments. To cover larger areas with the scroll bars and a mouse, place the cursor in the small gray box within a scroll bar and drag it in the direction you want to move.

Status Bar

The Status Bar provides information about your document. The buttons in the Status Bar provide you with shortcuts for choosing typing mode, typeface and size, and so on. You can access the Status Bar buttons only by using a mouse. The following paragraphs offer brief descriptions of each button on the Status Bar, beginning on the left:

- *Style Status.* The Style Status tells you the current style of text. If you place your cursor in body text, Body Text appears in the Style Status area. If you click your mouse cursor in the Style Status area, a list of currently available styles appears from which you can choose a style to assign to selected text. Figure A.20 illustrates the results of clicking the Style Status button.

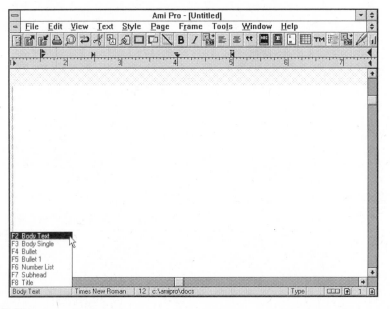

Fig. A.20 The Style Status list.

- *Face.* The Face button operates the same way the Style Status button works. Click the Face, and you can choose from a list of available typefaces.

- *Point Size.* This button also works the same way the Style Status button works; it governs the size of the type.

- *Document Path.* The information in this area toggles (by clicking it with your mouse) through the drive/path/document; the current date and time; and the line, column, and position of the insertion point.

- *Insert.* This button displays the typing mode you are in currently: Insert, Typeover, or Revision Marking. By clicking the Insert button, you can toggle between modes.

- *Caps Lock.* If Caps Lock is on, this button indicates it by displaying the word Caps. If Caps Lock is off, the button is blank.

- *SmartIcons.* Toggle the SmartIcons on and off by clicking this button with your mouse. In addition, Version 3.0 allows you to choose the set of SmartIcons (Default, Proofing, Editing, and so on) with this button.

- *Page Arrows.* The up arrow takes you to the preceding page; the down arrow takes you to the following page. Between the two pages is the number of the current page.

Understanding the Mouse

You should be familiar with several mouse movements when you use the mouse with the document chapters of this book. If you aren't comfortable with using a mouse, you should practice with it before beginning any document chapters. Unless otherwise stated, all clicks refer to the left mouse button.

- *Click* means to quickly press and release the mouse button. You must click on the page before you begin typing; you must click on a menu before the commands appear.

- *Double-click* means to quickly press and release the mouse button twice. Double-clicking is a shortcut in a dialog box. Instead of clicking on a file name and then clicking OK, for example, double-click on the file name.

- *Drag* means to press and hold the mouse button while moving the mouse pointer to another position. When you have the mouse pointer where you want it, release the mouse button. This technique enables you to select text and tables and to draw frames, among other things.

- *Place the cursor* means to place the cursor and click. You can place the cursor to type, select, or drag, but you must click the mouse button before you can perform those actions.

Notice that the mouse pointer changes shape depending on where it is and what it is doing. Table A.1 is a brief summary of the shapes the mouse pointer takes.

Table A.1   Mouse Pointer Shapes

Pointer Shape	Meaning
I-beam	Inserts typing, either in the text area or in a dialog box.
Arrow	Appears when you are pointing to menus, scroll bars, the Styles box, frames, and SmartIcons.
Double arrow	Indicates that you are positioned to size a window.
Grabber hand	Appears in the Drawing and Help features of Ami Pro. Use the grabber hand in the Drawing feature to crop or move the picture within the frame; use it in Help to access a cross-reference.
Frame	Appears for drawing a frame.
Four-sided arrow	Signifies that you are in a table and manually sizing a column or row guideline.
Hourglass	Lets you know that you must wait while Ami Pro is performing a function such as saving a document, opening a document, and so on.
Question mark	Indicates that you are using point-and-shoot help (Shift-F1).

Version 3.0 of Ami Pro adds a shortcut use for the right mouse button. Position the mouse cursor in the margin of your text area and click the right button; the Modify Page Layout dialog box appears. Place the cursor in text and click the right button, and the Modify Style dialog box appears. Finally, place the cursor in a frame and click the right mouse button, and the Modify Frame Layout dialog box appears.

Getting Accustomed to the Keyboard

Along with the normal typing characters on a keyboard, Ami Pro uses several other keys to perform shortcuts, menu functions, and command functions. Many keys have a dual purpose in Ami Pro; others are used in combination to execute special actions. If you use a mouse, you still can use many of the keys listed later in this section as shortcuts. If you do not use a mouse, you need to learn the basics of operating Ami Pro with the keyboard. In addition to the shortcut keys listed in the following sections, the document chapters guide keyboard users in working with frames, outlines, headers and footers, the ruler, tables, and so on.

Dual Purpose Keyboard Keys

The following keys have two or more functions in Ami Pro:

Key	Function
Enter	Ends a paragraph; inserts blank lines; signifies OK in a dialog box
Esc	Closes a dialog box by canceling any changes; exits activated current ruler
Tab	Inserts a tab; allows you to move through the choices within a dialog box
Arrow keys	Moves within the text area; moves within dialog boxes; moves within the activated ruler

Combination Keys

Combination keys are two or three keys used together to perform a function. Most commonly used with combination keys are Shift, Ctrl, and Alt. To use any two-key combination (such as Alt+F), you must press and hold the first key (Alt), press and release the second key, then release the first key. To use a three-key combination (such as Shift+Ctrl+End), press and hold the first key, press and hold the second key, press and release the third key, then release the second and first keys.

The Alt key is the most important key for the user without a mouse. To access the File menu, for example, press and hold the Alt key while you press the letter **F**. Release the F key and then the Alt key, and the File menu is accessed. Then, to access a command, press only the underlined (bold) letter. After the File menu appears, for example, press N to begin a New document. When written in instructions in this book, the letter *F* in File and the letter *N* in New are in bold type.

Many other combination keys give you access to menus, commands, functions, features, and so on. Many of these key combinations are listed at the end of this section. If you have further questions, check your reference manual or Ami Pro's on-screen help.

Function Keys

Function keys have special purposes in Ami Pro. Function keys, for example, are assigned to paragraph styles within a style selection box. To see how function keys work in this capacity, choose **S**tyle **S**elect a Style. The Style selection box appears.

To the left of each style (Body Text, Bullet, and so on) is a corresponding function key. These keys are used as shortcuts to assigning styles. In the default style sheet, for example, Body Text is F2. Select a paragraph of text and press F2; that paragraph is then formatted as Body Text.

The second use of function keys in Ami Pro is with macros. Macros are miniprograms that perform common functions automatically. You can use macros for tasks such as printing master documents, converting typographical quotes, formatting specific text, and so on. You can assign a shortcut key combination to any macro. You can create a macro to search for and replace a certain word in your document, for example, and assign Shift+F11 as a shortcut key (you can use any function key). Each time you need to search and replace, press the shortcut combination key.

Shortcut Keys

All shortcut keys refer to both versions of Ami Pro unless otherwise noted. The keys and combination keys shown in table A.2 are for use by either the mouse or the keyboard user.

Table A.2   Ami Pro Shortcut Keys

Key Combination	Function
Text	
Ctrl+B	Bold
Ctrl+C	Center Align (2.0)
Ctrl+E	Center Align (3.0)
Ctrl+I	Italic
Ctrl+J	Justify
Ctrl+L	Left Align
Ctrl+N	Normal
Ctrl+R	Right Align
Ctrl+T	Fast Format (3.0 only)
Ctrl+U	Underline
Ctrl+W	Word Underline
Styles	
Ctrl+A	Modify Style
Ctrl+Y	Access Styles Box
Ctrl+Z	Show/Hide Styles Box (2.0 only)
Edit	
Ctrl+F	Find and Replace
Ctrl+G	Go To
Ctrl+K	Glossary
Ctrl+V	Paste (3.0)
Shift+Ins	Paste (2.0)
Ctrl+X	Cut (3.0)
Shift+Del	Cut (2.0)
Ctrl+Z	Undo (3.0 only)
Alt+Backspace	Undo (2.0 and 3.0)
Ctrl+Backspace	Delete the preceding word
Ctrl+Del	Delete the next word
Ctrl+Ins	Copy

continues

Table A.2   Continued

Key Combination	Function
View	
Ctrl+D	Full Page/Current View (toggle—3.0)
Ctrl+M	Draft/Layout Mode (toggle)
Ctrl+Q	Show/Hide SmartIcons (toggle)
Ctrl+V	Full Page/Current View (toggle—2.0)
File	
Ctrl+O	Open (3.0 only)
Ctrl+P	Print
Ctrl+S	Save
Moving Around the Page	
Up/Down arrow	Move up/down one line
Ctrl+PgUp/ Ctrl+PgDn	Move up/down one page
PgUp/PgDn	Move up/down one screen
Left/Right arrow	Move left/right one character
Ctrl+Left arrow/ Ctrl+Right arrow	Move left/right one word
Home	Move to the beginning of a line
End	Move to the end of a line
Ctrl+(period)	Move to the beginning of the next sentence
Ctrl+(comma)	Move to the beginning of the preceding sentence
Ctrl+Up arrow/ Ctrl+Down arrow	Move to the beginning/end of the paragraph
Ctrl+End	Move to the end of the document
Ctrl+Home	Move to the beginning of the document
Up/Down Arrow	In a dialog box, move within a list or within check boxes
Tab	In a dialog box, move to the next group of options

Hold down the Shift key while using any of the combination keys for moving around the page, and Ami Pro selects that text. To select text to the end of the document, for example, press Shift+Ctrl+End; to select the text to the end of a line, press Shift+End.

Using Ami Pro's Special Features

Ami Pro provides you with built-in Drawing and Charting features. Either of these functions can enhance your business documents. The following sections contain brief descriptions of the icons used with the Drawing and Charting features, and include basic instructions for using each feature. For more detailed information, consult your reference manual or on-screen Help.

Using the Drawing Feature

Ami Pro's Drawing feature enables you to create your own drawings and add text or to import AmiDraw files, Windows Bitmap files, or Windows Metafiles. You can edit Lotus PIC, Freelance, or DrawPerfect files in the Drawing function as well (for more information about importing files, see Appendix B). When activated, the Drawing feature adds a new menu and a new set of SmartIcons. Figure A.21 illustrates the drawing screen. Notice that you must draw a frame before you can access the drawing mode. You must have a mouse to use Ami Pro's Drawing function.

The Drawing Screen

The set of SmartIcons provided in the drawing mode represents tools you use to create and edit pictures. Many of these icons represent shortcuts for the Draw menu. Table A.3 gives a description of each drawing mode icon, beginning on the left of the screen.

Table A.3 Drawing Feature SmartIcons

Icon	Description
Selection Arrow	Selects and sizes objects
Grabber Hand	Crops or moves the picture within the frame.

continues

Table A.3   Continued

Icon	Description
Line	Draws a straight line. Shift+drag to draw the line for a 45-degree angle
Polyline	Draws connecting lines
Polygon	Works similarly to the polyline for closed shapes
Square	Draws a rectangle. To draw a square, press Shift while dragging the mouse
Rounded Square	Draws a square; Shift+drag to draw a square
Circle	Draws a circle (Shift+drag) or an ellipse
Arc	Draws a parabolic arc
Text	Types in drawing mode
Select All	Selects all objects within a frame
Group/Ungroup	Selects two or more objects, then groups them for copying, cutting, moving, and so on
Bring to Front	Overlaps other objects
Send to Back	Overlaps the object
Rotate	Rotates an object or group by dragging a corner around a center spot
Flip Horizontally	Flips an object or group from left to right (does not flip text)
Flip Vertically	Flips an object or group from top to bottom (does not flip text)
Show/Hide Grid	Displays or hides a nonprinting grid for help in object placement
Snap To	Aligns objects to the grid
Extract Line & Fill	Changes the default line style and fill pattern to that of the selected object
Apply Line & Fill	Changes the line and fill of the selected object to the default
Line Style	Displays dialog box for the line style
Fill Pattern	Displays dialog box for the fill pattern

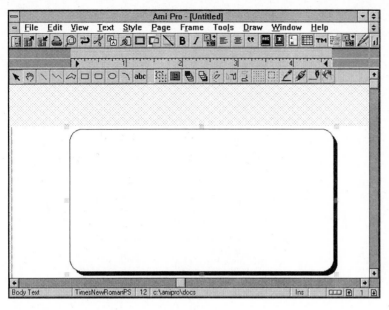

Fig. A.21   Ami Pro's Drawing feature screen.

The Drawing Function

The best way to learn the possibilities of the Drawing feature is to experiment with it. Ami Pro's Drawing feature offers a variety of options. Other techniques are explained in the document chapters.

You can activate the Drawing function two possible ways. First, you can draw a frame (you must create a new frame to draw in) and then choose **Tools Drawing**. Alternatively, you can draw a frame, import a picture, and double-click within the frame.

To add text to a drawing, click the Text icon and choose **Text Font**. Make your choices for type size, typeface, and color. Choose OK or press Enter. Place the cursor in the drawing and type.

While you are using the Drawing function, you can select objects in a number of ways. After you have selected objects, copying, cutting, and pasting objects is the same as with frames, text, and so on. Grouping objects makes it easier to perform editing functions on several objects at once. Grouping text objects allows easier rotation, moving, cutting, and so on. Both versions of Ami Pro let you group drawn and imported objects such as lines, rectangles, clip art, and TIFF files. Ami Pro Version 2.0 does not allow you to group text objects, but Version 3.0 does.

- *To select one object.* Select the Arrow icon and click the desired object.

- *To select an object behind another.* If the object is behind another, hold the Ctrl key and click the top object until the one behind is selected.

- *To select multiple objects.* To select multiple objects, hold the Shift key while clicking each object.

- *To select all objects in a frame.* To select all objects in a frame, use the Select All icon.

- *To select several close objects.* To select several objects that are close to each other, use the selection arrow. Drag the arrow from the top left corner to the bottom right corner of the objects as if you were drawing an imaginary frame around them (see fig. A.22).

- *To deselect an object.* Click the mouse anywhere in the frame except on the selected objects.

- *To move an object.* Select the object, click the selection arrow inside it, and drag the object anywhere within the frame.

- *To size an object.* Select the object, click a corner or side handle with the selection arrow, and drag the mouse until the size is changed.

- *To exit the Drawing function.* Press Esc or click outside the drawing frame.

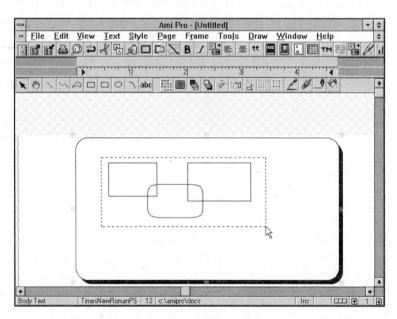

Fig. A.22 The selection arrow to draw a "frame" around several objects.

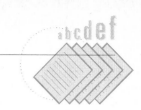

Using the Charting Feature

The Charting feature provides you with the means to add many charts to your documents, including bar, line, area, pie, and picture charts. You select the data and choose the type of chart, and Ami Pro creates your chart. You can customize your chart by adding a legend or text, changing colors or chart types, and so on. Again, if you take time to experiment with the charting feature now, you can be more comfortable with it—and be better able to apply it—when you need it in the future.

The Charting Screen

The Charting screen contains; icons to describe the chart types. Figure A.23 illustrates a simple column chart. Note the icons in the Chart Type dialog box; these icons represent chart types available.

Table A.4 is a brief explanation of the chart types, beginning at the top two icons (left, then right).

Table A.4   Chart Types Available in the Charting Feature

Chart Type	Explanation
Column Chart	The data you type first appears on the left of the chart, then works its way right.
Stacked Column Chart	The data you type first appears at the bottom of the chart and works its way up.
Bar Chart	The data you type first appears at the bottom of the chart and works its way up.
Stacked Bar	The data you type first appears on the left side of the chart and works its way right.
Line Chart or Area Chart	The data you type first appears on the left side of the chart and works its way right.
Line and Picture Chart	The data you type first appears on the left side of the chart and works its way right.
Pie or Expanded Pie Chart	These charts use only the data in the first column.
Picture Chart	The data you type first appears on the left side of the chart and works its way right.
Stacked Picture Chart	The data you type first appears on the bottom of the chart and works its way up.

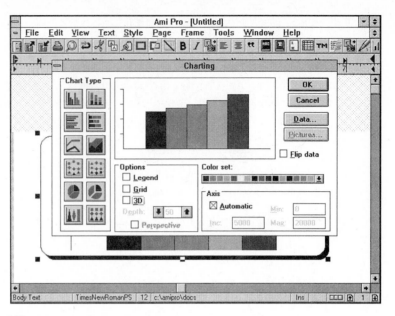

Fig. A.23 The Charting dialog box.

Under Options, you can add a legend or a grid, or make the chart three dimensional (3D). You can even adjust the depth and perspective of a 3D chart. You can choose colors, flip the data, and revise the data while working on the chart. Figure A.24 illustrates the chart in figure A.23, with the legend, grid, and 3D options selected.

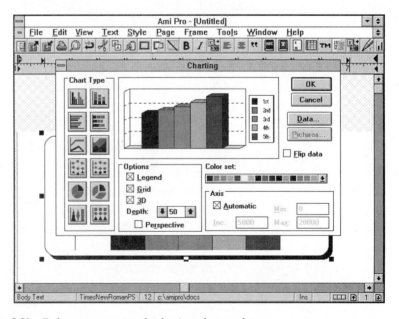

Fig. A.24 Enhancements to the basic column chart.

Basic Charting Instructions

To use the Charting function, you must provide the data Ami Pro uses to create the chart. You can enter the data in two ways. First, you can copy data either from another Ami Pro document or from another Windows application to the Clipboard. The other way to enter data is to type it directly into the Charting dialog box. Figure A.25 illustrates the data used for the column chart in figures A.23 and A.24.

Remember the following guidelines when creating data for a chart in Ami Pro:

- The data must be numeric and must be separated by spaces or tabs.

- Columns must be separated by one or more spaces or a tab.

- Commas and currency symbols are not used in charts even though Ami Pro accepts them.

- Formatted text is acceptable, but Ami Pro does not use the formatting in the chart.

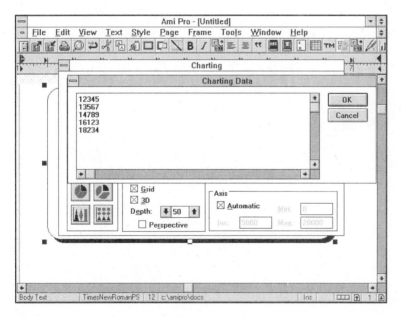

Fig. A.25 Data for the column chart typed directly into the Charting dialog box.

To enter data in a chart, cut or copy the data to the Clipboard and then draw a frame to contain the chart. Choose Tools Charting. Ami Pro displays the Charting dialog box.

To enter data in the Charting dialog box, draw a frame and then choose Tools Charting. Because Ami Pro finds no data in the Clipboard, it asks whether you want to create the data. Choose OK or press Enter, and the Charting Data dialog box appears. Type your information and then choose OK or press Enter.

To import a chart from another application, draw a frame and then choose File Import Picture. In File Type, choose the type of file you want to import. In the File list, choose the file name. Choose OK or press Enter.

B

Using Other Programs with Ami Pro

Ami Pro enables you to import graphics and convert text files to support your documents. Converting other word processing program files to Ami Pro files is easy, as is converting Ami Pro files to other file formats. In addition, Ami Pro makes importing graphics easy, whether they are draw and paint files, clip art, or scanned art.

Before importing or converting files, you must have the correct filters installed. If you installed the entire Ami Pro package, you should have no problem with your filters. If you performed a custom installation, however, you may need to add the filters you need for converting files. Without the proper filter, Ami Pro cannot import or convert files from other programs.

Converting Text Files

Ami Pro offers numerous text file filters and options for converting the various text files so that you easily can convert almost any file. This section describes the types of files you can convert, lists the style formatting options used in conversions, and gives instructions for converting other file formats.

Text File Filters

You can insert or convert any file format for which Ami Pro has a filter. Ami Pro 2.0 and 3.0 contain text file filters for the following file formats:

- Advance Write
- Ami Pro Macro
- ASCII
- dBASE III, III+, and IV
- DCA/FFT (Final Form Text)
- DCA/RFT (Revisable Form Text)
- DIF
- DisplayWrite 4 and 5
- E-Mail
- Enable Versions 1.5 through 2.5 (in Lotus 1-2-3 format)
- Excel Versions 3.0 and prior
- Executive MemoMaker
- Lotus 1-2-3 Releases 1, 1A, 2.0, 2.01, 3.0, and 3.1
- Lotus Manuscript Releases 2.0 and 2.1

- Lotus Symphony Releases 1.0, 1.01, and 1.1

- Microsoft Word Versions 4.0, 5.0, and 5.5

- MultiMate Version 3.3

- MultiMate Advantage II

- Navy DIF

- Paradox Versions up to 3.5

- PeachText Version 2.11 and prior

- RTF (Rich Text Format)

- Samna Word

- SmartWare Version 1

- SuperCalc Versions 3 and 4

- Windows Write

- Word for Windows 1.x

- WordPerfect Versions 4.1, 4.2, 5.0, and 5.1

- WordStar Versions 3.3, 3.4, 4.1, and 5.0

- WordStar 2000 Versions 1.0 and 3.0

The following text file is new with Ami Pro 3.0:

- Excel 4.0

Text File Conversion

You *open* Ami Pro files, but you must *convert* other file formats. Each word processing, spreadsheet, or database file has its own formatting codes. These codes are usually unrecognizable to other programs until you convert them. After being converted, the formatting may not be exactly the same as in the original file. Most styles and formatting, however, convert with no problem. Ami Pro maintains some formatting for all files (see the list in the following section). To further assist you in converting other files, Ami Pro offers you options concerning styles and style sheets.

Ami Pro always maintains some style formatting such as alignment, typeface, and line spacing. In addition, Ami Pro imports certain file types, such as style sheets, which maintains more formatting, such as typeface and size. The following section contains a brief listing of generally maintained style formatting, as well as formatting for some specific programs.

If you're working with word processing files, most conversion options concern the formatting styles. Ami Pro distinguishes between independently assigned styles and paragraph styles. A *paragraph style* is a style you assign to specific text within the entire document (to all body text or to all headlines, for example). An *independently assigned style* is one that applies only to selected text, such as changing the indent in one paragraph or italicizing a callout. The following sections cover these two formatting types.

When you convert databases or spreadsheets, the options are both for styles and for how much of the file you want to import. You need to know some important facts before importing database or spreadsheet data into Ami Pro. First, when you import databases into an Ami Pro document, fields are separated by tabs and each record begins a new paragraph. Second, if you import a spreadsheet into a frame in Ami Pro, the program creates a table that contains the correct number of rows and columns. Finally, when you import data into a table, Ami Pro uses the rows and columns in the current document but does not add new ones if needed. Headers, footers, and page numbers are not imported into Ami Pro.

General Formatting

When converting other file types, Ami Pro maintains the following formatting:

- Alignment (center, left, right, and justified)
- Capitalization (initial caps, lowercase, small caps, and uppercase)
- Dates (from date functions or macros)
- Font (typeface, point size, and color)
- Footnotes
- Text frames
- Headers and footers
- International characters
- Line spacing
- Page layout (margins, page breaks, rulers, and tabs)
- Page numbering
- Paragraph styles

- Special formatting (hard hyphens, nonbreaking spaces)

- Text attributes (bold, double underline, italics, overstrike, strikethrough, superscript, subscript, underline, and word underline)

Specific File Types

Ami Pro offers you style or import options when you convert certain file types. Following is a summary of those options for some of the more popular programs or file types. For information on other file types, see your reference manual.

ASCII Files

ASCII is one of the most popular file types because it's so common. When you choose ASCII as a file type, Ami Pro displays the ASCII Options dialog box. The options for converting an ASCII file are as follows:

- *CR/LF at Lines*. Formatted with a carriage return/line feed at the end of every line and two at the end of every paragraph. Ami Pro converts this file type to one paragraph return at the end of the paragraph.

- *CR/LF at Paragraph Ends Only*. Formatted with the carriage return/ line feed at the end of each paragraph only. Ami Pro converts the file with a paragraph return at the end of each line.

- *Keep Style Names*. For use if the ASCII document has paragraph style names that match those in the Ami Pro document and you want the format to be the same.

The ASCII file types are as follows:

- *7 bit ASCII*. This file type contains typewriter characters only (the first 128 characters of the IBM PC ASCII character set).

- *8 bit PC-ASCII*. This file type contains characters from the entire IBM PC ASCII character set (including Greek symbols, math symbols, and so on). Some of these characters are not available in Ami Pro.

- *8 bit ANSI*. This file type contains characters from the Windows ANSI character set, all of which are available in Ami Pro.

Microsoft Word, Word for Windows, or RTF (Rich Text Format)

Ami Pro displays the Import Options dialog box when you import one of these file types. The following is a brief summary of the options available to you:

- *Convert Styles*. Ami Pro creates paragraph styles and names in the current document that match all the attributes in the converted file.

- *Apply Styles*. Ami Pro applies only the text attributes assigned independently in the original document, but matches the paragraph style of the current document.

- *Keep Style Names*. If your converted files have style names that match names in the current Ami Pro document, this option assigns them to the formatting in Ami Pro.

- *Ignore Styles*. Ami Pro assigns only the character and paragraph attributes of the converted file. The paragraph style of the converted text matches that of the current Ami Pro document.

In addition to style options, if Ami Pro cannot find the printer file, it displays a Fonts dialog box that asks you where the printer file is located. You can type the path, choose to ignore fonts, or cancel. If you cancel, Ami Pro ignores the font information.

If Ami Pro cannot find the style sheet connected to the converted file, it displays a Styles dialog box that asks where the style sheet is located. You can type the path, ignore styles, or cancel.

WordPerfect 5.1

When converting WordPerfect 5.1 files, Ami Pro displays an Import Options dialog box. The following are the options from which you choose:

- *Apply Styles*. Ami Pro assigns all attributes of the WordPerfect 5.1 document as text enhancements. The paragraph style used is the one in the current Ami Pro document.

- *Ignore Styles*. Ami Pro applies only those attributes assigned independently in the WordPerfect document to the current Ami Pro document. The paragraph style used is the one in the current Ami Pro document.

- *Import Style Sheet*. Ami Pro creates paragraph styles to match those of the converted style sheet.

Microsoft Excel

Ami Pro offers two separate dialog boxes when you import an Excel file. The first, the Import Options dialog box, simply allows you to import an entire file or to specify the range of the file to import.

The second dialog box is another Import Options dialog box and is only offered if you import Excel Version 3.0 files. The following is a brief summary of those options:

- *Convert Styles*. Ami Pro creates styles in the current document to match those of the Excel file.

- *Apply Styles*. Ami Pro assigns all attributes (assigned and independent) as text enhancements in the current document. The paragraph style used is the one in the current document.

- *Keep Style Names*. If the style names in the Excel file match those in the current Ami Pro document, this option matches the styles.

- *Ignore Styles*. Ami Pro assigns only the independently assigned attributes of the Excel file as text enhancements. The paragraph style used is the one in the current document.

Lotus 1-2-3

Ami Pro offers only one dialog box when you import a Lotus 1-2-3 file, except for 1-2-3 Version 3.0 or 3.1 files (see the following section). The Import dialog box allows you to import an entire file or to specify the range of the file to import. In addition, Ami Pro uses the default settings from Window 1 and ignores dates prior to January 1, 1980. Finally, Ami Pro does not support the Numeric Display format TEXT.

Lotus 1-2-3 Version 3.0 or 3.1

Ami Pro offers two separate dialog boxes when you import a Lotus 3.0 or 3.1 file. The first, the Import dialog box, allows you to import an entire file, import the active worksheet, or specify the range of the file to import. Sometimes, you may have problems importing a file with extremely large or extremely small numbers. ERR appears in a cell that has a problem.

The second dialog box is an Import Options dialog box and is only offered if you import an FM3 file. The following is a brief summary of those options:

- *Convert Styles*. Ami Pro creates styles in the current document to match those of the Lotus file.

- *Apply Styles.* Ami Pro converts all attributes (assigned and independent) to text enhancements in the current document. The paragraph style used is the one in the current document.

- *Keep Style Names.* If the style names in the Lotus file match those in the current Ami Pro document, this option matches the styles.

- *Ignore Styles.* Ami Pro assigns only the independently assigned attributes of the Lotus file as text enhancements. The paragraph style used is the one in the current document.

dBASE

Ami Pro displays the Import dialog box when you import a dBASE file. The dialog box asks whether you want to import the entire file or selected fields.

Basic Instructions for Converting Text Files

Ami Pro provides two ways to manage a converted text file. You can import a text file into an untitled document in Ami Pro and save it as a new document, or you can combine a text file from another program with information in a current Ami Pro document. The method you choose depends on the type of document you're converting.

The first method is to convert the text file. Figure B.1 illustrates the dialog box with File Types chosen.

To convert a text file and save it as a new document, follow these steps:

1. Choose File Open.

2. Choose the correct file type by clicking the arrow beside the File Type selection box or by pressing Alt+T then the down arrow.

3. Choose Drive Directory.

4. From the Files list, choose the file you want to convert. Choose OK or press Enter.

5. Ami Pro may display a dialog box, depending on the file type. This dialog box refers to styles. Choose the correct response and choose OK or press Enter.

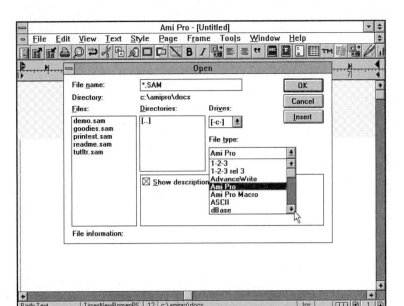

Fig. B.1   The File Open dialog box with File Types chosen.

Your file is now converted and displayed in the untitled Ami Pro document. To save as a new document, follow these steps:

1. Choose File Save As.

2. In the File Name text box, type the name of the new document.

3. Direct the file to the proper drive and directory. Choose OK or press Enter.

To combine another file type with an Ami Pro document, follow these steps:

1. Open the Ami Pro document and place the cursor at the point where you want the new file to be inserted (main text, frame, or table).

2. Choose File Open.

3. In File Type, choose the type of file to convert.

4. Choose the Drive and the Directory.

5. In the Files list, choose the file name to be inserted.

6. Choose Insert.

7. Ami Pro may display a dialog box that refers to styles. Answer the prompt and choose OK or press Enter.

8. Ami Pro inserts the text at the cursor's position.

Ami Pro offers a Quick Import option for certain file types. Using the Quick Import method, you don't have to specify a File Type in the File Open dialog box. This method is simply a shortcut for importing to help speed up your work. You can use Quick Import with the following file types:

- dBASE
- DCA/RFT
- DIF
- DisplayWrite
- Excel
- Lotus 1-2-3
- Manuscript
- Microsoft Word
- Rich Text Format (RTF)
- Samna Word
- SmartWare
- SuperCalc
- Windows Write
- Word for Windows
- WordPerfect 5.x
- WordStar 2000

To use Quick Import with one of the applicable file types, follow these steps:

1. Choose File Open.

2. Choose the proper drive and directory for your file.

3. In the File Name text box, type an asterisk, a period, and the extension of the file to import (***.doc** for a Word for Windows file; ***.wp5** for WordPerfect, and so on). Press Enter.

4. Choose your file from the list of Files. Choose OK, press Enter, or choose Insert.

You use an asterisk (*) as a wild card when working with files to choose all files. If you type ***.sam**, for example, you want to list all files that end with the extension SAM. Typing **chapter1.*** means to list all files that begin with chapter1. Using wild cards is convenient when you use the same name for different types of documents, such as CHAPTER1.TIF, CHAPTER1.SAM, and CHAPTER1.WK3. Finally, typing ***.*** chooses all files. Figure B.2 illustrates the File Open dialog box with the wild-card characters. Notice that the Files list box lists all files in the directory.

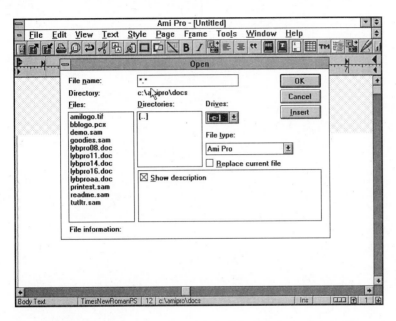

Fig. B.2 The mouse cursor pointing to the wild-card characters in the File Open dialog box.

Ami Pro Conversion to Another File Type

You just as easily can save an Ami Pro file in another file format. The following is a list of file formats to which you can convert your document with Ami Pro 2.0 and 3.0:

- Advance Write
- Ami Pro Macro
- ASCII

- DCA/FFT (Final Form Text)

- DCA/RFT (Revisable Form Text)

- DIF

- Display Write 4 and 5

- E-Mail

- Enable Versions 1.5 through 2.5

- Executive MemoMaker

- Microsoft Word Versions 4.0, 5.0, and 5.5

- MultiMate Version 3.3

- MultiMate Advantage II

- Navy DIF

- PeachText Version 2.11 and prior

- RTF (Rich Text Format)

- Samna Word

- Windows Write

- Word for Windows

- WordPerfect Versions 4.1, 4.2, 5.0, and 5.1

- WordStar Versions 3.3, 3.4, 4.1, and 5.0

- WordStar 2000 Versions 1.0 and 3.0

Ami Pro has added the following file formats with Ami Pro 3.0:

- Manuscript

- Office Writer

- Professional Write

- Symphony

- Symphony Document

- Word for Windows 2.0

Converting an Ami Pro file is as simple as saving it in another file format. Figure B.3 illustrates the File Save As dialog box, showing the File Types selected.

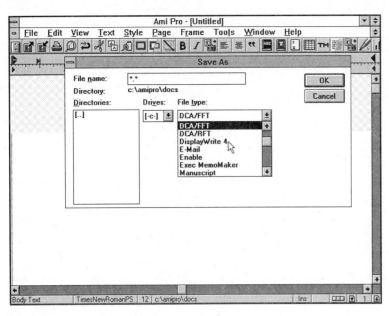

Fig. B.3 Saving as another file format.

To convert an Ami Pro file to another file type, follow these steps:

1. Choose File Save As.

2. Choose the drive and directory to which you want to save.

3. Choose the File Type.

4. In the File Name text box, type the name of your file. Choose OK or press Enter.

Importing Graphic Files

Ami Pro makes importing graphics effortless. Ami Pro can import graphics from draw programs, paint programs, clip-art programs, scanners, and so on. After you import a graphic, you can scale, crop, and add a border to it (for more information, see Appendix A). You must have the proper filters to import graphics, and you first must have a frame in which to place the graphic.

You can use two basic graphic formats: bit-mapped and object. *Bit-mapped graphics* tend to be rough around the edges, especially when enlarged. *Object graphics* are formed differently so that their edges are smooth; they reproduce well at any size.

Figures B.4 and B.5 illustrate the difference between a bit-mapped image and an object image. The figures are the same—a simple arrow reversed in a circle. Notice that in figure B.4, the bit-mapped image, the edges of the circle and the point on the arrow are extremely rough. The edges illustrate how the pixels are arranged in a bit-mapped object.

Fig. B.4   A simple bit-mapped image.

In contrast, figure B.5 shows that both the circle and the arrow have smooth and crisp edges. An object image is formed by outlining the image first, then filling it in.

Fig. B.5   A simple object image.

Bit-mapped graphics (also called *paint* graphics), images, and pixel-based graphics are stored as patterns of 0s and 1s in the computer. The digital pattern has a one-to-one correspondence to the pattern of dots in the image. The result is that the edges are noticeably ragged. If you must use

bit-mapped graphics, try scanning or drawing the object larger than you need it. When you reduce its size in your document, the edges appear less ragged.

Bit-mapped graphics are present in some scanners, some clip-art collections, PC Paintbrush, Windows Bitmap (see fig. B.6), and Tagged Image File Format (TIFF).

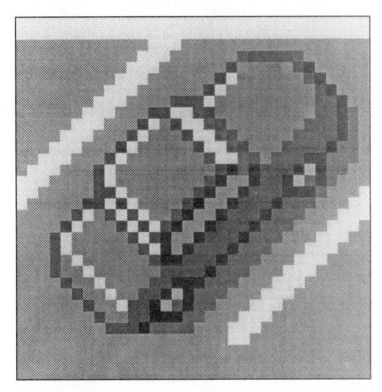

Fig. B.6   Windows Bitmap image of a parked car, illustrating the way pixels are formed in a bit-mapped graphic.

Object graphics, also called *vector* graphics, are made up of lines and geometric shapes. They are stored in the computer in the form of a compact mathematical description. The result is that object graphics have smooth, crisp, clean edges. They also use less memory than bit-mapped graphics, but they take longer to appear on your screen.

Some programs that produce object graphics include AmiDraw (see fig. B.7), Computer Graphic Metafiles, DrawPerfect, Freelance, Lotus 1-2-3, and Windows Metafiles.

Fig. B.7   An AmiDraw file that illustrates object, or vector, graphics.

Graphic File Filters

Ami Pro 2.0 and 3.0 can import the following graphic files if the filter is installed:

- AmiDraw (SDW)

- AmiEquation (TEX)

- Computer Graphic Metafiles (CGM)

- DrawPerfect (WPG)

- Encapsulated PostScript (EPS)

- Freelance (DRW)

- Hewlett-Packard Graphics Language (HPGL)

- Lotus 1-2-3 Graphics (PIC)

- PC Paintbrush (PCX)

- Scanners (TIF)

- Windows Bitmap (BMP)

- Windows Metafiles (WMF)

Basic Instructions for Transferring Graphic Files

Ami Pro accepts graphic files in three ways: by importing, by pasting from the Clipboard, and by *paste linking* from another application, if that application supports DDE or OLE (see the next section for information on DDE and OLE).

To paste a graphic by using the Clipboard, follow these steps:

1. Start the application in which the graphic was produced and open the graphic file.

2. Choose the graphic and copy it.

3. Start Ami Pro and open the document in which the graphic is to be pasted.

4. Create an empty frame. Select the frame.

5. Choose Edit Paste. The graphic is pasted into the frame; you can size or crop it.

To import a graphic file, follow these steps:

1. Open the document in Ami Pro and create the frame in which the graphic is to be placed.

2. Choose File Import Picture.

3. In File Type, choose the program in which you created the graphic.

4. Choose the drive and directory containing the file.

5. Choose the File Name. Choose Copy Image. Choose OK or press Enter.

By copying the image, you save the graphic file to the Ami Pro document. This fact is especially important if you copy the document to another disk to take to a print shop or elsewhere to be printed. Otherwise, you must copy the graphic through File Management in Ami Pro.

Before using the next method, you should read the information about DDE and OLE in the next section. To paste link a graphic file by using DDE or OLE, follow these steps:

1. Start Ami Pro and open your document. Start the other application and open the file you want to link.

2. Choose the graphic and choose Edit Copy.

3. Switch to Ami Pro and select an empty frame.

4. Choose Edit Paste Link. (Some other applications use Paste Special; refer to the documentation of the application you are using if you are in doubt.)

5. By double-clicking the OLE or DDE linked object, you can open the other application at any time from within the Ami Pro document.

Placing Charts Created in Other Applications

Ami Pro contains its own charting features to produce bar, column, line, and pie charts (plus many more), but you may want to import a chart that you created in another application. You can paste a chart from another application as you would a graphic file, or you can import a chart stored as a file. These imported charts can be linked if the other application supports DDE or OLE, and the charts also can be altered in the drawing feature of Ami Pro.

To paste a chart from another application, follow these steps:

1. Start the application in which the chart was produced and open the file.

2. Select the chart and copy it.

3. Start Ami Pro and open the document in which you want to paste the chart.

4. Create an empty frame. Select the frame.

5. Choose Edit Paste. The chart is pasted into the frame.

To import a chart, follow these steps:

1. Open the document in Ami Pro and create the frame in which you want to place the chart.

2. Choose File Import Picture.

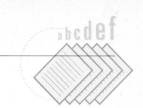

3. In File **T**ype, choose the program in which you created the chart.

4. Choose the drive and directory containing the file.

5. Choose the File **N**ame. Choose OK or press Enter.

To paste link a chart by using DDE or OLE, follow these steps:

1. Start Ami Pro and open your document. Start the other application and open the file you want to link.

2. Select the chart and choose Edit **C**opy.

3. Switch to Ami Pro and select an empty frame.

4. Choose Edit Paste **L**ink. (Some other applications use Paste **S**pecial; refer to the documentation of the application you are using if you are in doubt.)

5. By double-clicking the OLE or DDE linked object, you can open the other application at any time from within the Ami Pro document.

Using Data Exchange with Ami Pro

In addition to converting data and importing data into Ami Pro, other forms of data exchange are available. The data-exchange methods discussed in this section are Windows-oriented; therefore, you can use them in conjunction with other Windows applications that support these methods. Following is a brief description of each method; consult your reference manual for more information.

The two forms of linking with Ami Pro are DDE (Dynamic Data Exchange), and OLE (Object Linking and Embedding). Ami Pro supports both linking methods, although not all Windows applications do. *Linking* is a way of connecting two documents from different programs so that information can be shared by both and updated easily. If you have a question about another application, consult the reference manual for that program.

DDE (Dynamic Data Exchange)

Dynamic Data Exchange, or *DDE*, is a type of link that allows supporting applications to share information and update that information automatically. To use DDE with Ami Pro, you first must copy to the Clipboard the data you want to link from another application. You then paste the link into the Ami Pro document. The DDE link is an active one, meaning that the information is updated automatically. One problem with this method is that both applications must be running at the same time, which takes up a lot of memory.

To create a DDE link with an Ami Pro document, follow these steps:

1. Open the Ami Pro document, then open the application from which you are going to link (the application must support DDE).

2. Select the data you want to link. Choose **Edit Copy**. Switch to the Ami Pro document by pressing Ctrl+Esc and choosing your document.

3. Place the cursor in the area in which you want to paste the data.

4. Choose **Edit Paste Link**. (If Paste Link is grayed, the other application does not support DDE.) The data is inserted into the Ami Pro document.

OLE (Object Linking and Embedding)

With Object Linking and Embedding, or *OLE*, you can use several different Windows applications within your Ami Pro document. OLE is another form of linking that allows sharing of information between different programs; OLE also allows you to open the linked programs directly in your Ami Pro document. Although not all Windows applications support OLE, Ami Pro does. You can use OLE in Ami Pro in two ways: by linking an object to your document; or by embedding the object in your document.

Linking with OLE

Linking is similar to pasting a link by using DDE. You can link an object to the document text or to a frame in the Ami Pro document. To link an object with OLE, follow these steps:

1. Start Ami Pro and open your document. Start the other application and open the file you want to link.

2. Select the data and choose **Edit Copy**.

3. Switch to Ami Pro and place the cursor in the document text or in a table. Alternatively, select an empty frame.

4. Choose Edit Paste Link. (Some other applications use Paste Special; refer to the documentation of the application you are using if you are in doubt.)

5. By double-clicking the OLE linked object, you can open the other application at any time.

Embedding with OLE

When embedding with OLE, you must embed the object in a frame in the Ami Pro document. To embed an existing object with OLE, follow these steps:

1. Start Ami Pro and open your document. Create an empty frame.

2. Start the other application and open the file you want to embed. Select the entire object or a part of the object.

3. Choose Edit Copy.

4. Switch to Ami Pro. Choose Edit Paste.

To embed a new object with OLE, follow these steps:

1. Start Ami Pro and open your document. Create an empty frame.

2. Start the other application and open the file you want to embed.

3. Choose Edit Insert. A secondary command list appears.

4. Choose New Object. The Insert New Object dialog box appears.

5. In the Object Type list, choose the application. Choose OK or press Enter.

6. The application is now loaded into the frame, and it appears in the window.

7. Create the object.

8. Choose File Update to exit the other application and to update the Ami Pro document. Some other applications may not have Update in the File menu; if the application you are using doesn't, choose OK or press Enter. You can edit the object at any time by double-clicking inside the object frame.

Using Printers and Output

You should base your choice of printer on the type of documents you do, the amount of work you do, and the quality of the printout you require. If you want draft-quality printouts, or if you produce letters and other in-house documents, a dot-matrix printer may be sufficient. If you produce camera-ready masters, however, you need a laser printer.

Print quality is measured in terms of resolution. This appendix describes terms related to print quality, printer types, output resolution, and screen and printer fonts. The end of this appendix includes a description of the printer setup for Ami Pro.

Understanding Resolution

Resolution describes the quality of the type and graphics output. Ragged, rough-edged type, much like that of dot-matrix printers, is low resolution. Type that has smooth and refined edges, like that of a laser printer, is higher resolution.

Resolution is measured in *dots per inch* (dpi). The dpi rating describes how many dots, or *pixels*, make up a letter or graphic image. Most dot-matrix 24-pin printers print at 70 to 75 dpi. Most laser printers are rated at 300 dpi. Image typesetters, or imagesetters, have 1265, 2540, or more dots per inch. Because of their high price, you find imagesetters almost exclusively in print shops and service bureaus. For the average user, a 300-dpi laser printer is reasonably priced, and the quality is very good. A laser printer can produce camera-ready masters.

Using Page Description Languages

Another factor to consider when purchasing a printer is the *page description language* it uses. The Hewlett-Packard Printer Control Language and Adobe's PostScript are two common page description languages.

A laser printer with the Hewlett-Packard Printer Control Language (HPPCL), or compatible, can reproduce most of the formatting you do in Ami Pro. Adobe PostScript (PS) or a PostScript-compatible language is more sophisticated. The major difference between the HPPCL and PS languages is in the way they form characters. HPPCL forms text by using bit-mapped images; PostScript forms text by using outlines.

Working with the Hewlett-Packard Printer Control Language

Bit-mapped text and images are made up of patterns of dots on a very fine rectangular grid. The arrangement of dots that make up each

character is stored as a pattern of digital bits in the laser printer. Bit-mapped images that output at 300 dpi are fairly good quality, but not the highest.

A problem with the bit-mapped fonts is the amount of memory they require. Each typeface, type size, and style is stored separately in memory, using a significant amount of memory.

HPPCL offers limited font choices and graphic capabilities. You should compare the limitations and advantages with your needs before making your selection.

Working with the Adobe PostScript Page Description Language

PostScript stores fonts as mathematical descriptions of the character outlines. The outlines are formed and then filled in. For this reason, the edges are much smoother and more uniform than bit-mapped fonts. In addition, fonts formed by outline do not require storage in memory. The PS language can make any size font from just one outline. With PostScript, you have more font choices, and you can use features, such as type rotation, reversal, stretching, and filling with patterns.

Using Screen and Printer Fonts

Printer fonts are those fonts that are included with the printer, either bit-mapped or outlined. You cannot print a document unless you have the proper printer fonts installed. Some printer fonts are resident, some are stored in the program, others are downloaded. *Resident fonts* are those that remain in the printer, such as Courier, Helvetica, Times, and so on. *Downloaded fonts* are the special typefaces you use, such as Goudy, Friz Quadrata, and Helvetica Black. Downloaded fonts can come from software or from a cartridge that you insert into your printer.

Screen fonts are for the video display, or monitor, only. Screen fonts are important for matching the appearance of the printed page with the actual output, but you can print without screen fonts. If you don't see an accurate representation of the font on-screen, however, your formatting may not look the way you expect on the printed page.

Remember this exception to the preceding rule about printer and screen fonts: when you use Microsoft Windows, dot-matrix printers can print most Windows screen fonts, even without printer fonts. Using this option is not a wise choice, however, for two reasons. First, printing the

Windows screen fonts produces lower resolutions than the printer's capabilities; therefore, the print quality is much lower. Second, printing takes longer with only these screen fonts.

Using Adobe Type Manager

The Ami Pro package includes the Adobe Type Manager (ATM). ATM provides both screen and printer fonts that look like PostScript fonts—high-quality typefaces of any size or style. ATM uses the PostScript outline font technology that enables even inexpensive printers to output smooth-edged, professional-looking fonts. Examples of the ATM fonts provided with Ami Pro are included in Appendix D.

Adobe Type Manager works with Windows 3.0 or higher and is compatible with most Windows 3.0 applications. You can use these fonts with Ami Pro, spreadsheet applications, graphics programs, and so on. You must have an IBM PC AT, a PS/2, or 100%-compatible 286, 386, 386SX, or 486 computer to use ATM. ATM also works with any of the following printers:

- PostScript printers
- The Hewlett-Packard LaserJet family of laser printers
- IBM Laser Printer, LaserPrinter E
- IBM Proprinter, Epson, and other dot-matrix printers
- Most other Windows-supported printers

To install ATM, follow these steps:

1. Insert the ATM disk.

2. Start Windows and choose **File Run**.

3. In the Command line, type **a:\install**. Choose OK or press Enter.

4. Answer any questions asked by the Installer. After installation is completed, you must restart Windows.

You will find an ATM Control Panel included with your fonts. The purpose of the Control Panel is to add and remove fonts, remove ATM, and change the font cache size. Your Ami Pro package includes an Adobe Type Manager User Guide that explains more about ATM.

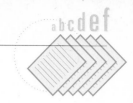

Choosing a Printer

Be sure to choose the printer that is right for you and the job you do. Consider all the options—resolution, price, speed, and compatibility—before you buy a printer. The following sections provide some basic information about each printer type.

Dot-Matrix Printers

A dot-matrix printer is perfect for many situations; also, it is inexpensive and provides many capabilities. The output is grainy and rough, however, even on a 24-pin printer. Dot-matrix printers are not suitable for camera-ready material, or even for professional-looking correspondence (see fig. C.1).

Dot Matrix
24 Pin Printer

Fig. C.1   Sample output from a 24-pin dot-matrix printer.

Inkjet Printers

Inkjet printers are very popular, quiet, and economical, with a better print quality than dot-matrix printers provide. Inkjet printers have wide carriages that can accommodate larger paper sizes, and their output is close to laser quality (see fig. C.2). Color inkjet printers are now available at a relatively low cost. Inkjet printers are best suited for business correspondence, not for camera-ready material.

Inkjet
Printer

Fig. C.2   Sample output from an inkjet printer.

Basic Laser Printers

The basic laser printer is much more suitable for producing high-quality output. The higher resolution of 300-600 dpi produces text and graphics that are camera-ready and of high quality (see fig. C.3). Usually employing the Hewlett-Packard Printer Control Language, the basic laser printer offers many font choices for less money than a PostScript printer.

HP-PCL
Laser Printer

Fig. C.3   Sample output from a laser printer with HP-PCL.

PostScript Laser Printers

A PostScript laser printer is a high-quality printer, offering many font choices and many type alternatives. The graphics are high quality, presenting you with many type and graphic options (see fig. C.4). A PostScript laser printer offers a resolution of 300-600 dpi. PostScript laser printers are more expensive than basic laser printers and require more memory.

PostScript
Laser Printer

Fig. C.4   Sample of PostScript laser printer output.

Imagesetters

Imagesetters are very expensive, very high-resolution printers used in service bureaus and print shops. If you create a document in Ami Pro and plan to have it printed, consider using an imagesetter's high-resolution output. The type and images are sharp, clear, and of very high quality (see fig. C.5).

High-resolution
Output

Fig. C.5   Sample output from an imagesetter.

Usually reserved for large quantities (5,000 or 10,000 printed pieces or more) or material requiring very high quality, high-resolution output is sometimes available for any kind of job. A print shop that deals with desktop publishing every day often runs text on an imagesetter for free, if the shop prints the job.

A *service bureau* is a specialty shop that only produces output; service bureaus do not do paste-up, layout, and printing, as a print shop does. Service bureaus specialize in high resolution, and usually charge a fairly reasonable (per page) fee for output.

If you take your job to a printer or service bureau for output, you should discuss several things with them before you commit to the job:

- Do they have a PC-compatible system?

- Do they have Ami Pro for Windows, and if so, which version?

- Do they use the same size disks you use?

- Do they have the fonts you used in your document?

Understanding Printer Installation Terminology

Before you format documents in Ami Pro, be sure that you have selected the correct printer in Printer Setup. Ami Pro offers font choices depending on your printer; if you change printers after formatting a document, the fonts you originally chose may no longer be available.

You can choose the printer driver and the printer port, and you can configure your printer in either Windows (Control Panel) or in Ami Pro (Printer Setup). For information and the steps for any of these procedures, consult your Windows reference manual.

Selecting Your Printer Driver

The *printer driver file* gives the program (Ami Pro) details about your printer features (descriptions and sizes of fonts, control sequences, and so on). Windows lists common printer drivers in its setup. If your printer is not listed, check your printer manual for compatibility and emulation mode. If neither of these options is available with your printer, consult the Windows manual for further alternatives.

If your printer driver is not installed, you can choose the generic printer driver—but it does not print most page and type formatting.

Choosing a Printer Port

The printer port choices are serial, parallel, or file. Windows automatically sets common communications settings for serial printers. If you need to change some of the settings or choose another port, consult your manual.

Configuring Your Printer

Configuring your printer consists of choosing the correct printer driver file, size and orientation of paper, paper source, amount of timeout, cartridges, and so on. These choices are all dependent on your printer. Some printers accommodate various paper sizes and font cartridges.

If you use a PostScript printer, you need to download the PostScript header, located in the Print Setup dialog box. When working with one program all day—Ami Pro, for example—you should download the header at the beginning of the day. After downloading it, tell Ami Pro, in the Printer Setup box, that the header is downloaded. Your documents output faster this way. If you use several different programs during the day, such as Ami Pro and CorelDRAW!, downloading the header with each job gives you the quickest output.

To change the download option in Ami Pro, follow these steps:

1. Choose File Printer Setup.

2. Choose the Setup button and then the Options button.

3. Choose the Send Header button. In the dialog box, choose Select Printer Send Now. Choose OK or press Enter three times.

Figure C.6 shows the layers of dialog boxes to the Send Header dialog box.

Setting Up Your Printer

The printer setup in Ami Pro is similar to the Windows printer setup. If you're familiar with the Windows setup, you should have no problem with Ami Pro.

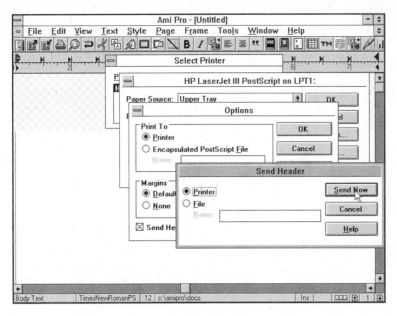

Fig. C.6 The Send Header dialog box for downloading the PostScript header.

To configure your printer in Ami Pro, follow these steps:

1. Choose File Printer Setup.

2. Your printer should appear in the Printer selection box. Choose the gray command button, Setup. The dialog box that appears displays information about your printer.

   If your printer does not appear in the selection box, you must Add a printer; see your Windows reference manual.

3. In the Printer dialog box, you can choose various printers that are installed in Windows and, therefore, in Ami Pro. The differences between Windows Versions 3.0 and 3.1 are indicated in the following by parentheses around the Version 3.1 variances.

   - *Paper Source.* Chooses the feed.

   - *Paper Size.* Has many options; however, your printer may not be able to print them all. Document orientation should be Portrait. To print Landscape, change the option in Ami Pro's Modify Page Layout dialog box. (Added in Windows 3.1 is an option for Margins; choose Default.)

   - *Copies.* Indicates how many copies you want to print. If you occasionally need extra copies, it's more convenient to set it in the Print dialog box (No Copies dialog box in Windows 3.1). Choose the number of copies in your program.

- *Scaling (Scaling in 3.1).* Reduces or enlarges a document by percentage.

  Many of these options are available, depending on the printer you selected. The gray command buttons in the Print dialog box open new dialog boxes that give you more choices for printer setup.

- *Options.* Prints to the **P**rinter or an **E**ncapsulated PostScript (EPS) file. You may want to print to an EPS file, for example, if you take your file to a service bureau that doesn't have Ami Pro for Windows. The bureau can run an EPS file directly to a high-resolution PostScript imagesetter without the use of Ami Pro.

- *Job Timeout.* Enables you to set the amount of time that Ami Pro, or Windows, tries to print before giving up. If you already have sent a job to the printer, the printer is busy. When you send the next job, Ami Pro waits the specified amount of time and tries again. If the printer is not available, the program cancels printing. You may want to set Timeout for 0 seconds because Windows can try to print all day. (Windows 3.1 does not include this option.)

- *Header.* Located in this dialog box if you have a PostScript printer.

- *Handshake.* Device used for data transfer between hardware or software. Refer to your Windows manual if you have a problem. (Not included in Windows 3.1.)

- *Add Printer.* A method of installing by inserting the disk with the printer driver.

- *Help.* This command button displays Windows **H**elp on your specific printer. About tells you the printer driver that's installed in your Windows program.

- *Advanced.* In Windows 3.1, enables you to substitute fonts, choose resolution, halftone frequency and angle, and so on.

For more information about these features, refer to your Windows reference manual.

D

Adobe Type Manager Fonts

Your Ami Pro package includes Adobe Type Manager (ATM), a program that provides sharp, clear type with Windows programs. The fonts in ATM simulate the PostScript outline font, which means that the resulting output is high quality and professional looking. ATM fonts are smooth and clear. Most of the fonts are appropriate for subheads, headlines, and display type. Some fonts are useful as symbols or interesting characters, and some of them will work for body text.

This appendix contains samples of the ATM fonts. Not only can you use them with Ami Pro, you can use ATM fonts with almost any Windows 3.x application. Your ATM user guide and Appendix C list system requirements, compatible printers, and installation instructions for the Adobe Type Manager.

Using Font Symbols

The following two ATM typefaces use letters or numbers to represent symbols or characters. One, the Symbol typeface, produces Greek and mathematical symbols. The other, Wingdings, creates useful characters such as file folders, pointing hands, and arrows. Symbol is not really an ATM font; however, it is available on most computers and in many programs.

To produce either the Symbol font or the Wingding font, follow these steps:

1. In tables D.1 and D.2, decide which symbol (on the right) you want. Type the corresponding letter (on the left). Select the letter you typed.

2. Choose Text Font.

3. In Face, choose Symbol or Wingding. Choose OK or press Enter.

The second type of character in tables D.1 and D.2 is represented by numbers. To duplicate these characters, follow these steps:

1. Place the cursor where you want the character, press and hold the Alt key, then press the numbers to the left of the character (Alt+128, for example). Be sure that you use the keypad (with Num Lock on) to type the numbers.

2. Select the character you just typed and change the font to Symbol or Wingding.

The Symbol Character Set

The Symbol font is available in most applications. Even if you haven't installed ATM, you probably have the Symbol font. It's made up of mathematical, Greek, scientific, and other useful symbols like the trademark, register mark, and copyright mark symbols (see table D.2).

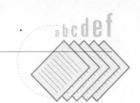

The Wingding Character Set

Adobe Type Manager added a special font called Wingding to its set. The Wingding font consists of bullets, hands, crosses, books, letters, arrows, clocks, and more. Wingdings are especially useful for dressing up a flier, coupon, or newsletter. Table D.2 illustrates the Wingding font.

Using Other ATM Typefaces

The remaining Adobe Type Manager fonts are useful for display type, headlines, and subheads; some of these fonts work as body text. Adding different fonts to your documents makes them unusual and eye-catching. To use any of the ATM fonts, you first must install the Adobe Type Manager. (See Appendix C and the ATM user guide that is packaged with Ami Pro, for details.) You then select your text or modify the style just as you would to change other typefaces.

In all the following examples except Times New Roman, the head is 48-point type, followed by four alphabets in 14 point, 18 point, 24-point bold, and 36-point bold, respectively. The letters in each alphabet are separated by one space; they are not letter spaced (or kerned).

Arial

Arial is an unadorned, sans serif type (see fig. D.1). The bold is not very bold at all, because the typeface is a very thin, even-stressed stroke. Arial does not work for display type, but is fine for body text, subheads, and heads. You can use Arial in forms instead of Helvetica.

Brush Script

Brush Script is an italic type—informal and comfortable (see fig. D.2). In the larger sizes, Brush makes an excellent display type, and it works equally well for headlines and subheads. Don't use Brush as body text or in all caps, however, because it is too difficult to read.

Table D.1   The Symbol Character Set

Code	Character	Code	Character	Code	Character
a	α	w	ω	128	∩
b	β	x	ξ	129	⌉
c	χ	y	ψ	130	⌈
d	δ	z	ζ	131	®
e	ε	C	Χ	132	™
f	φ	D	Δ	133	◊
g	γ	F	Φ	134	Σ
h	η	G	Γ	137	⌊
i	ι	J	ϑ	138	⎩
j	φ	L	Λ	140	⎰
k	κ	P	Π	141	⌠
l	λ	Q	Θ	142	⊗
m	μ	R	P	143	⊕
n	ν	S	Σ	144	⊃
o	ο	V	ς	145	⎛
p	π	W	Ω	146	∅
q	θ	X	Ξ	147	⎜
r	ρ	Y	Ψ	148	⎞
s	σ	$	∃	149	∫
t	τ	\	∴	150	⌋
u	υ	'	϶	151	⌉
v	ϖ	"	∀	153	√

Code	Character	Code	Character
154	⟸	0181	∝
155	'	0182	∂
156	≤	0183	●
157	∞	0184	÷
158	Π	0185	≠
160	⟨	0192	ℵ
161	⟨	0193	ℑ
162	∫	0194	ℜ
163	|	0195	℘
164	⟩	0203	⊄
165	∇	0205	⊆
166	♠	0206	∈
167	≡	0207	∉
168	↵	0208	∠
169	_	0209	∇
170	←	0211	©
173	ϒ	0217	∧
174	↔	0218	∨
180	ƒ	0219	⇔

Table D.2 The Wingding Character Set

Code	Character	Code	Character	Code	Character	Code	Character
a	♋	w	◆	S	⬥	%	🔔
b	♌	x	⊠	T	❄	^	♈
c	♍	y	⬔	U	✝	&	📖
d	♎	z	⌘	V	✚	*	✉
e	♏	A	✌	W	✛	(	☎
f	♐	B	👌	X	✠	)	☽
g	♑	C	👆	Y	✡	-	📫
h	♒	D	👎	Z	☾	_	♉
i	♓	E	☜	1	📁	=	💾
j	er	F	☞	2	📄	+	🖃
k	&	G	👆	3	📃	[	☯
l	●	H	☝	4	📑	]	✾
m	◯	I	✋	5	🗄	{	✽
n	■	J	☺	6	⌛	}	"
o	□	K	☻	7	⌨	\	ॐ
p	◻	L	☹	8	🖱	|	✤
q	◻	M	💣	9	🖲	;	🖳
r	◻	N	☠	0	📂	:	💻
s	◆	O	⚐	!	✏	'	🕯
t	◆	P	⚑	@	✑	"	✂
u	◆	Q	✈	#	✂	,	📬
v	❖	R	☼	$	ﻌ	.	📪

Code	Character	Code	Character	Code	Character
128		148		168	
129		149		169	
130		150		170	
131		151		171	
132		152		172	
133		153		173	
134		154		174	
135		155		175	
136		156		180	
137		157		0180	
138		158		0181	
139		159		0182	
140		160		0183	
141		161		0184	
142		162		0185	
143		163		0190	
144		164		0192	
145		165		0193	
146		166		0194	
147		167		0222	

CaslonOpenFace

Another exceptional display type is CaslonOpenFace. Note the head in figure D.3. The size, 48 points, complements the type design. CaslonOpenFace is sophisticated and classy, but you never use it as body text. The 14-point line is extremely hard to read, and 12 or 10 points would be unreadable. Another interesting point about Caslon is that it's an uncommonly light typeface. Even the bold (the 24- and 36-point type) is not that bold. Be careful when using this typeface—don't allow borders, rules, graphic images, or even heads and subheads to overrun it. Keep layouts and designs light and airy when using CaslonOpenFace.

Frank Goth Cd

The perfect display type is Frank Goth Cd—dark, heavy strokes that stand out in very large sizes (see fig. D.5). The bold is clearly bold. Use Frank Goth Cd for subheads, heads, and display type. Be sure that if you use it for a subhead, you also use it for the head; no other typeface in this font package is appropriate as a head to a Frank Goth Cd subhead.

Shelley Allegro Script

A beautiful, flowing typeface, Shelley Allegro Script is perfect for invitations, advertisements, and selective heads or subheads. Note, in figure D.6, that the letters in the head connect to simulate handwriting. Never use this script as body text in a letter, however. Too much script is difficult to read. Use Shelley Allegro Script sparingly, and never use it in all caps; as you can see from the alphabet in figure D.6, it would be too hard to read.

Times New Roman

Figure D.7 illustrates the Times New Roman typeface with a 48-point head, 12-point lightface, 12-point bold, and 12-point italic. Following the body text sizes are 14 point, 18 point, 24-point bold, and 36-point bold. Extremely similar to Times Roman, this font can be used as body text, subheads, heads, and display type. Times New Roman is a versatile font you can use in any document.

Arial

A B C D E F G H I J K L M N O P Q R S T U V W X Y Z a b c d e f g h i j k l m n o p q r s t u v w x y z 1 2 3 4 5 6 7 8 9 0

A B C D E F G H I J K L M N O P Q R S T U V W X Y Z a b c d e f g h i j k l m n o p q r s t u v w x y z 1 2 3 4 5 6 7 8 9 0

A B C D E F G H I J K L M N O P Q R S T U V W X Y Z a b c d e f g h i j k l m n o p q r s t u v w x y z 1 2 3 4 5 6 7 8 9 0

A B C D E F G H I J K L M N O P Q R S T U V W X Y Z a b c d e f g h i j k l m n o p q r s t u v w x y z 1 2 3 4 5 6 7 8 9 0

Fig. D.1 The Arial typeface.

Brush Script

ABCDEFGHIJKLMNOP2RSTUVWXYZ
abcdefghijklmnopqrstuvwxyz1234567890

ABCDEFGHIJKLMNOP2RSTUVV
XYZabcdefghijklmnopqrstuvwxyz12
34567890

ABCDEFGHIJKLMNOP2
RSTUVWXYZabcdefghijkl
mnopqrstuvwxyz1234567
90

ABCDEFGHIJKL
MNOP2RSTUVW
XYZabcdefghijkl
mnopqrstuvwxyz1
234567890

Fig. D.2 The Brush Script typeface.

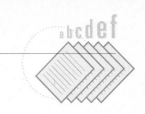

CaslonOpenFace

ABCDEFGHIJKLMNOPQRSTUVWXYZabcd
efghijklmnopqrstuvwxyz1234567890

ABCDEFGHIJKLMNOPQRSTUV
WXYZabcdefghijklmnopqrstuvwxyz1
234567890

ABCDEFGHIJKLMNOPQ
RSTUVWXYZabcdefghijk
lmnopqrstuvwxyz12345678
90

ABCDEFGHIJK
LMNOPQRSTUV
WXYZabcdefghijk
lmnopqrstuvwxyzl
234567890

Fig. D.3 The CaslonOpenFace typeface.

DomCasual

DomCasual is a relaxed, nonchalant typeface (see fig. D.4). Use it on fliers, advertisements, posters, and so on. Be sure to use as large a point size as you can for display type (72, 96, even 125 points, if possible). DomCasual also works for headlines and subheads, and even small amounts of body text. DomCasual is a smaller typeface than most; its height is normal, but it is a narrow type. Notice, too, that the bold is not very bold until the type is larger.

DomCasual

ABCDEFGHIJKLMNOPQRSTUVWXYZabcdefghijklmnop qrstuvwxyz1234567890

ABCDEFGHIJKLMNOPQRSTUVWXYZabcde fghijklmnopqrstuvwxyz1234567890

ABCDEFGHIJKLMNOPQRSTUV WXYZabcdefghijklmnopqrstuv wxyz1234567890

ABCDEFGHIJKLMNO PQRSTUVWXYZabcde fghijklmnopqrstuvw xyz1234567890

Fig. D.4 The DomCasual typeface.

Frank Goth Cd

ABCDEFGHIJKLMNOPQRSTUVWXYZabcdefghijkl
mnopqrstuvwxyz1234567890

ABCDEFGHIJKLMNOPQRSTUVWXYZabc
defghijklmnopqrstuvwxyz12345678
90

ABCDEFGHIJKLMNOPQRSTU
VWXYZabcdefghijklmnopqr
stuvwxyz1234567890

ABCDEFGHIJKLMN
OPQRSTUVWXYZab
cdefghijklmnopqr
stuvwxyz1234567
890

Fig. D.5   The Frank Goth Cd typeface.

Shelley Allegro Script

A B C D E F G H I J K L M N O P Q R S T U V W X Y Z a b c d e f g h i j k l m n o p q r s t u v w x y z 1 2 3 4 5 6 7 8 9 0

A B C D E F G H I J K L M N O P Q R S T U V W X Y Z a b c d e f g h i j k l m n o p q r s t u v w x y z 1 2 3 4 5 6 7 8 9 0

A B C D E F G H I J K L M N O P Q R S T U V W X Y Z a b c d e f g h i j k l m n o p q r s t u v w x y z 1 2 3 4 5 6 7 8 9 0

A B C D E F G H I J K L M N O P Q R S T U V W X Y Z a b c d e f g h i j k l m n o p q r s t u v w x y z 1 2 3 4 5 6 7 8 9 0

Fig. D.6   The Shelley Allegro Script typeface.

Times New Roman

ABCDEFGHIJKLMNOPQRSTUVWXYZabcdefghijklmnopq
rstuvwxyz1234567890

ABCDEFGHIJKLMNOPQRSTUVWXYZabcdefghijklmno
pqrstuvwxyz1234567890

*ABCDEFGHIJKLMNOPQRSTUVWXYZabcdefghijklmnopqrs
tuvwxyz1234567890*

ABCDEFGHIJKLMNOPQRSTUVWXYZabcdefghij
klmnopqrstuvwxyz1234567890

ABCDEFGHIJKLMNOPQRSTUVWXYZ
abcdefghijklmnopqrstuvwxyz1234567
890

ABCDEFGHIJKLMNOPQRS
TUVWXYZabcdefghijklmno
pqrstuvwxyz1234567890

ABCDEFGHIJKLM
NOPQRSTUVWXY
Zabcdefghijklmno
pqrstuvwxyz12345
67890

Fig. D.7 The Times New Roman typeface.

Glossary of Desktop Publishing Terms

E

alignment Definition of text edge: flush right, flush left, justified, or centered.

anchoring Placement of boxes at a specific location: on the page or in a paragraph.

ascender The portion of the lowercase letters b, d, f, h, k, l, and t that rises above the height of the letter x. The height of the ascender varies in different typefaces. See *descender*.

ASCII (American Standard Code for Information Interchange) A standard computer character set devised in 1968 to enable efficient data communication and achieve compatibility among different computer devices.

The standard ASCII code consists of 96 displayed upper- and lowercase letters, plus 32 nondisplayed control characters. An individual character code is composed of seven bits plus one parity bit for error checking. The code enables the expression of English-language textual data but is inadequate for many foreign languages and technical applications. Because ASCII code includes no graphics characters, most modern computers use an extended character set containing needed characters.

ASCII file   A file that contains only characters drawn from the ASCII character set.

attribute   A character emphasis, such as boldface or italic, and other characteristics of character formatting, such as typeface and type size. See *formatting sequence*.

automatic font downloading   The transmission of disk-based, downloadable printer fonts to the printer, done by an application program as the fonts are needed to complete a printing job.

banner   A newsletter title.

baseline   The lowest point characters reach (excluding descenders). For example, the baseline of a line of text is the lowermost point of letters like a and x, not the lowest points of p and q. See *descender*.

bit-mapped font   A screen or printer font in which each character is composed of a pattern of dots. Bit-mapped fonts represent characters with a matrix of dots. To display or print bit-mapped fonts, the computer or printer must keep a full representation of each character in memory.

Because the computer or printer memory must contain a complete set of characters for each font, bit-mapped fonts consume large amounts of disk and memory space. Outline fonts, however, are constructed from mathematical formulas and can be scaled up or down without distortion. Because outline fonts are considered technically superior, printers that can print outline fonts are more expensive.

bit-mapped graphic   A graphic image formed by a pattern of pixels (screen dots) and limited in resolution to the maximum screen resolution of the device being used. Bit-mapped graphics are produced by paint programs, such as PC Paintbrush, MacPaint, SuperPaint, GEM Paint, and some scanners.

bleed   A photograph, shaded box, bar, or other element that extends to the edge of the page. Laser-printed pages have a 0.3" margin and may not have bleeds.

blurb   A subtitle printed above or below a headline, usually set in a smaller type size than the headline.

body type   The font (normally 8 to 12 point) used to set paragraphs of text (distinguished from the typefaces used to set headings, subheadings, captions, and other typographical elements).

boldface   A character emphasis visibly darker and heavier in weight than normal type. **This sentence is set in boldface.**

bow   White space inside letters, such as a, b, o, p, and q.

brush style   A typeface design that simulates script drawn with a brush or broad-pointed pen.

byline   An author's name, often including the author's title.

callout   A quotation printed in large letters, 14-point italic, for example, to spark interest in an article. A callout is usually separated from the body of the article by a box, or bordering lines above and below.

caption   A descriptive phrase, separate from the text, that identifies a photograph, image, chart, or graph.

cartridge   A removable module that expands a printer's memory or font capabilities.

cartridge font   A printer font supplied in the form of a read-only memory (ROM) cartridge that plugs into a receptacle on Hewlett-Packard LaserJet printers and clones.

Hewlett-Packard LaserJet printers rely heavily on cartridge fonts that have some merits over their chief competition, downloadable fonts. Unlike downloadable fonts, the ROM-based cartridge font is immediately available to the printer and does not consume space in the printer's random-access memory (RAM), which can be used up quickly when printing documents loaded with graphics.

CGM (Computer Graphics Metafile)   An international graphics file format that stores object-oriented graphics in device-independent form so that users of different systems (and different programs) can exchange CGM files.

Personal computer programs that can read and write to CGM file formats include Harvard Graphics, Lotus Freelance Graphics, and Ventura Publisher.

character   Any letter, number, punctuation mark, or symbol that can be produced on-screen by pressing a key.

character set The fixed set of keyboard codes that a particular computer system uses. See *ASCII (American Standard Code for Information Interchange)*.

characters per inch (cpi) The number of characters that fit within a linear inch in a given font. Standard units drawn from typewriting are pica (10 cpi) and elite (12 cpi).

clip art A collection of graphics images, stored on disk and available for use in a spreadsheet, page layout, or presentation graphics program.

Clipboard A temporary storage area used by Microsoft Windows compatible programs to copy or move text or images from one area of a document, between documents, or between programs.

clustering A method of grouping small visual elements together on the page to create a single, larger illustration; for example, a series of small head-and-shoulder portrait photographs.

color separation Separate color negatives (magenta, cyan, black, and yellow) created by a printer to produce four-color printed images.

compose sequence A series of keystrokes that enables a user to enter a character not found on the computer's keyboard.

composite newsletter A newsletter created with desktop publishing and traditional graphic design techniques—for example, when the newsletter is produced by desktop publishing methods except for photographic halftones, which are pasted into black squares.

condensed type Type narrowed in width so that more characters will fit in a linear inch. In dot-matrix printers, condensed type usually is set to print 17 characters per inch (cpi). See *characters per inch (cpi)*.

constraining A method used by many desktop publishing and draw programs to maintain the original proportions of an image while reducing or enlarging its size.

contrast The range of light and dark tones in a text page, graphic image, line drawing, or photograph.

continuous-tone photograph A photographic print, which must be photographed through a halftone screen by the printer before it can be printed.

copyfitting The common practice of designing the space for an article, and then cutting or expanding the text to fit the allotted space.

counter   Concave space inside such letters as c, e, and s that opens onto the white space next to the letter.

Courier   A monospace typeface, commonly included as a built-in font in laser printers, that simulates the output of office typewriters.

crop marks   Marks on a page or photograph that tell the printer how to trim the page or position the photograph. Some desktop publishing programs can print crop marks on the page automatically.

cropping   Sizing a box to eliminate a portion of a photograph, image, chart, and so on.

default font   The font that the printer uses unless the user instructs otherwise.

descender   The portion of the lowercase letters g, j., p, q, and y that falls below the baseline. The height of the descender varies in different typefaces. See *ascender*.

desktop publishing (DTP)   The use of a personal computer as an inexpensive production system for generating typeset-quality text and graphics. Desktop publishers often merge text and graphics on the same page and print pages on a high-resolution laser printer or typesetting machine.

dingbats   Ornamental characters such as bullets, stars, and arrows used to decorate a page.

discretionary hyphen   A manually inserted hyphen that the program uses to break a word at the end of a line; useful for telling the software where to hyphenate unusual words, such as pneumococcus, Lebensraum, and Indianapolis.

display type   A typeface, usually 14 points or larger and differing in style from the body type, that is used for headings and subheadings. See *body type*.

dot leader   Pronounced "leeder;" a line of dots (periods) that leads the eye horizontally from one text element to another—for example, from a chapter title to a page number.

dot-matrix printer   An impact printer that forms text and graphics images by pressing the ends of pins against a ribbon. Dot-matrix printers are fast, but the output they produce is generally poor quality because the character is not fully formed. Some dot-matrix printers that use 24 pins rather than 9 pins have better-quality output. These printers also can be extremely noisy.

dot pitch The size of the smallest dot that a monitor can display on-screen. Dot pitch determines a monitor's maximum resolution.

downloadable font A printer font that must be transferred from the computer (or the printer) hard disk drive to the printer random-access memory before the font can be used.

drop cap A large initial capital letter used to guide the reader's eye to the beginning of body text.

drop out type White characters printed on a black background.

drop shadow A shadow placed behind an image, slightly offset horizontally and vertically, that creates the illusion that the topmost image has been lifted off the surface of the page.

elite A typeface that prints 12 characters per inch. See *pitch*.

ellipsis Three or four dots that represent omitted text.

em dash A long typographer's dash (—) used to separate phrases. The name indicates that the length of an em dash is the same as the width of the capital M in the current typeface.

em space A horizontal space equal to the width of a capital M in the current typeface.

en dash A typographer's hyphen equal in width to a capital N in the current typeface.

en space Half an em space.

extended character set A character set that includes extra characters, such as foreign language accent marks, in addition to the standard 256-character IBM character set.

eyebrow A word or phrase printed above an article heading that indicates a document department name; for example, *Lifestyles:* could be an eyebrow for an article titled *Boating on Snake River.*

feathering Making very small changes in line spacing to line up the bottoms of adjacent columns of text.

flag A newsletter title.

flush left The alignment of text along the left margin, leaving a ragged-right margin. Flush-left alignment is easier to read than right-justified text.

flush right The alignment of text along the right margin, leaving a ragged-left margin. Flush-right alignment is seldom used, except for decorative effects or epigrams.

folio   Printed next to a document title, the folio indicates issue date, volume, and issue number.

font   One complete collection of letters, punctuation marks, numbers, and special characters with a consistent and identifiable typeface, weight (Roman or boldface), posture (upright or italic), and font size.

Technically, font still refers to one complete set of characters in a given typeface, weight, and size, such as Helvetica italic 12. The term, however, often refers to typefaces or font families.

Two kinds of fonts exist: bit-mapped fonts and outline fonts. Each comes in two versions, screen fonts and printer fonts. See *bit-mapped font, font family, outline font, screen font, typeface, type size,* and *weight.*

font cartridge   Some printers accept plug-in font cartridges to add font variations to the printer's repertoire.

font editor   A software package that enables the user to alter letters; generally used to create custom logos.

font family   A set of fonts in several sizes and weights that share the same typeface.

The following list describes a font family in the Helvetica typeface:

Helvetica Roman 10
Helvetica bold 10
Helvetica italic10
Helvetica Roman 12
Helvetica bold 12
Helvetica italic12
Helvetica bold italic12

font metric   The width and height information for each character in a font. The font metric is stored in a width table.

footer   A short version of a document's title or other text positioned at the bottom of every page of the document. See *header.*

formatting   The process of changing the appearance of a page by setting margins, choosing fonts, changing line spacing, alignment, column width, headers and footers, and other printed elements.

fountain effect   Smooth blending of print density from a dark to a light area.

frame A box. Some desktop publishing and word processing programs use frames to hold various page elements, including body text, graphic images, charts, and headers and footers.

frame-grabber A combination of hardware and software that captures images from a video camera, still video camera, or videocassette.

full justification The alignment of multiple lines of text along the left and the right margins. See *justification*.

graphics mode In IBM and IBM-compatible computers, a mode of graphics display adapters in which the computer can display bit-mapped graphics.

graphics monitor A computer monitor that can display both text and graphic images.

gray scale A series of shades from white to black.

gray-scale monitor A monitor that can reproduce many shades of gray, typically 256 or more. Ordinary monitors can display only from 4 to 16 shades of gray.

greeking Displaying unreadably small text as solid lines or abstract symbols, called greeked text.

grid The underlying design that establishes a consistent pattern for the position and style of columns, headings, fonts, line spacing, photos, and other document elements.

gutter The vertical space between text columns. Some designers use gutter to refer to the empty space in the middle of a two-page spread, and alley to refer to the space between columns.

halftone A photo that has been copied through a printer's screen to create an image composed of dots or lines.

hanging indent Paragraph formatting in which the first line extends into the left margin.

hard hyphen A hyphen that prevents software from breaking a word; useful for preventing hyphenation of such words as *anti-inflammatory*.

hard space A space used to prevent two words from being separated by word wrap at the end of a line; for example, the name of a city, *Oak Hill*.

header Repeated text, such as a page number and a short version of a document's title, that appears at the top of each page in a document. See *footer*.

Helvetica   A sans serif typeface frequently used for display type applications and occasionally for body type. One of the most widely used fonts in the world, Helvetica is included as a built-in font with many laser printers. See *sans serif* and *font family*.

high-resolution output   Typesetting; generally refers to printing quality of 1200 dots per inch or better.

hyphenation   A program feature that automatically hyphenates words based on program rules (algorithmic hyphenation) or a list of hyphenated words (dictionary hyphenation).

image scanner   Hardware that converts photos, drawings, or line images into computer-readable graphic files.

indentation   The alignment of a paragraph to the right or left of the margins set for the entire document.

initial cap   A large letter that indicates the beginning of body text. An initial cap can be dropped (inset) into the text, raised above the first line of text, or printed to the left of the body text.

italic   A posture of a typeface that slants to the right and commonly is used for emphasis. *This sentence is set in italic.* See *oblique*.

jumpline   Text placed at the bottom of a column of text to guide the reader to the page where the article continues—for example, *Continued on page 5* and *Continued from page 1*.

justification   The alignment of multiple lines of text along the left margin, the right margin, or both margins. The term justification often is used to refer to full justification, or the alignment of text along both margins. See *full justification*, *left justification*, and *right justification*.

kerning   The reduction of space between certain pairs of characters in display type so that the characters print in an aesthetically pleasing manner.

landscape orientation   The rotation of a page design to print text and/or graphics horizontally across the longer axis of the page. See *portrait orientation*.

laser printer   A high-resolution printer that uses a version of the electrostatic reproduction technology of copying machines to fuse text and graphic images to the page.

Alternative technologies include light-emitting diode (LED) imaging printers, which use a dense array of LEDs rather than a laser to generate the light that exposes the drum and liquid crystal shutter

(LCS) printers, which use a lattice-like array of liquid crystal gateways to block or transmit light as necessary. See *resolution*.

layout   In desktop publishing, the process of arranging text and graphics on a page.

leading   (pronounced LED-ing) The space between lines of type, measured from baseline to baseline. Synonymous with *line spacing*.

The term originated from letterpress-printing technology, in which thin lead strips were inserted between lines of type to control the spacing between lines.

left justification   The alignment of text along only the left margin. Synonymous with *ragged-right alignment*.

letter-quality printer   An impact printer that simulates the fully formed text characters produced by a high-quality office typewriter.

ligature   Combinations of letters printed in formal typography as a single letter; for example, ff and $\iint$.

line spacing   See *leading*.

Linotronic   Brand name of the best known PostScript-compatible typesetting machines. The Linotronic typesetters print at 1270 or 2540 dots-per-inch resolution.

live area   The area of a page on which the printing hardware can print. Laser printers require a 0.3" margin around the live area on the page. Printing presses may require a nonprinting gripper area used to pull the sheet of paper through the press.

logo   An identifying name or symbol, often designed for an artistic effect.

masthead   An area that lists the staff, subscription information, ownership, and address of a newsletter or other publication, generally printed near the front of the issue.

mezzotint   A photograph printed through a line or dot screen that adds an interesting texture or pattern to the image; for example, a pattern of fine concentric circles.

moiré pattern   A distracting pattern that may result when the printer makes a halftone screen of an already halftoned photograph.

monospace   A typeface such as Courier in which the width of all characters is the same, producing output that looks like typed characters. `This sentence is set in a monospace typeface.` See *proportional spacing*.

nameplate   The title of a newspaper, newsletter, magazine, or other serial publication.

near-letter quality (NLQ)   A dot-matrix printing mode that prints typewriter-quality characters. As a result, printers using this mode print slower than other dot-matrix printers.

newspaper-style columns   Columns in which text *snakes* from the bottom of one column to the top of the next.

nonbreaking space   A space that prevents the software from breaking two letters, words, or phrases, such as *US Mail* or *Pac Bell*, at the end of a line.

oblique   The italic form of a sans-serif typeface. See *sans serif.*

OCR (Optical Character Recognition)   A hardware and software system that can scan printed text into the computer for editing.

open, closed quote   True typographer's opening and closing quotation marks that curve toward the enclosed text.

orientation   See *landscape orientation* and *portrait orientation.*

orphan   A layout flaw in which the first line of a paragraph appears alone at the bottom of a page.

Most word processing and page-layout programs suppress widows and orphans; the better programs enable the user to switch on and off widow/orphan control and to choose the number of lines for which the suppression feature is effective. See *widow.*

outline font   A printer or screen font in which a mathematical formula generates each character, producing a graceful and undistorted outline of the character; the printer then fills in the outline at maximum resolution.

Because mathematical formulas produce the characters, the user needs only one font in the printer's memory to use any type size from 2 to 127 points. With bit-mapped fonts, a complete set of characters for each font size must be downloaded into the printer's memory; the user cannot use a type size that has not been downloaded.

overstrike   The printing of a character that is not found in a printer's character set, by printing one character, moving the print head back one space, and printing a second character on top of the first.

page layout program   An application program that assembles text and graphics from various files with which the user can determine the precise placement, sizing, scaling, and cropping of material in accordance with the page design represented on-screen.

page orientation See *landscape orientation* and *portrait orientation*.

palette An on-screen display containing a set of color or pattern options.

pica A unit of measure equal to approximately 1/6 inch, or 12 points. In typewriting and letter-quality printing, a 12-point monospace font that prints at a pitch of 10 characters per inch (cpi).

Picas usually describe horizontal and vertical measurements on the page, with the exception of type sizes, which are expressed in points.

pitch A horizontal measurement of the number of characters per linear inch in a monospace font, such as those used with typewriters, dot-matrix printers, and daisywheel printers.

By convention, pica pitch (not to be confused with the printer's measurement of approximately 1/6 inch) equals 10 characters per inch, and elite pitch equals 12 characters per inch. See *monospace*, *pica*, and *point*.

pixel The smallest element (a picture element) that a device can display on-screen and out of which the displayed image is constructed. See *bit-mapped graphic*.

placeholder A tool provided with many desktop publishing programs to ensure consistent spacing of headlines, subheads, body text, photos and captions, and other document elements.

PMS (Pantone Matching System) The universal standard for creating colors by mixing red, blue, black, white, and green.

point The fundamental unit of measure in typography; 72 points equals an inch.

portrait orientation The default printing orientation for a page of text, with the longest measurement oriented vertically. See *landscape orientation*.

posterization High-contrast effect created by removing the gray midtones from a scanned image.

PostScript A sophisticated page description language for medium- to high-resolution printing devices.

PostScript, developed by Adobe Systems, Inc., is a programming language that describes how to print a page that blends text and graphics.

PostScript laser printer   A laser printer that includes the processing circuitry needed to decode and interpret printing instructions phrased in PostScript—a page description language (PDL) widely used in desktop publishing.

preprinting   Printing color elements on a page before printing page elements in black in a second pass; an inexpensive way to print nameplates, logos, and other document elements in color.

presentation graphics   Text charts, bar graphs, pie graphs, and other charts and graphs that the user enhances so that they are visually appealing and easily understood by the audience. See *presentation graphics program.*

presentation graphics program   An application program designed to create and enhance charts and graphs so that they are visually appealing and easily understood by an audience.

A full-featured presentation graphics package such as Harvard Graphics includes facilities for making text charts, bar graphs, pie graphs, high/low/close graphs, and organization charts.

The package also provides facilities for adding titles, legends, and explanatory text anywhere in the chart or graph. A presentation graphics program includes a library of clip art with which the user can enliven charts and graphs by adding a picture related to the subject matter (for example, an airplane for a chart of earnings in the aerospace industry). The user can print output, direct output to a film recorder, or display output on-screen in a computer slide show.

printer font   A font available for printing, unlike screen fonts available for displaying text on-screen.

process color   A standard color that does not require custom ink mixing.

proof   Preliminary draft, used to proofread and check layouts.

proportion scale   A graphic design tool used to size photos.

proportional spacing   The allocation of character widths proportional to the character shape so that a narrow character, such as i, receives less space than a wide character such as m. See *kerning* and *monospace.*

pull quote   A quotation printed in large letters to spark interest in an adjoining article.

ragged-left alignment   The alignment of each line of text so that the right margin is even, but the left remains ragged. Synonymous with *flush right*.

ragged-right alignment   The alignment of each line of text so that the left margin is even, but the right remains ragged. Synonymous with *flush left*.

raised cap   A large initial capital letter that extends above the first line of text. Raised and drop caps are used to guide the reader's eye to the beginning of body text.

registration mark   A printer's guide mark which ensures that color separations used in four-color printing will print in perfect alignment.

resident font   A font built into printer hardware. Most PostScript printers, for example, have 35 resident fonts.

resolution   A measurement—usually expressed in linear dots per inch (dpi), horizontally and vertically—of the sharpness of an image generated by an output device such as a monitor or printer.

In monitors, resolution is expressed as the number of pixels displayed on-screen. A CGA monitor, for example, displays fewer pixels than a VGA monitor; therefore, a CGA image appears more jagged than a VGA image.

Dot-matrix printers produce output with a lower resolution than laser printers.

reverse type   Type or graphic images printed in white on a dark background.

right justification   The alignment of text along the right margin and the left margin, producing a superficial resemblance to profession-ally printed text. The results may be poor, however, if the printer is incapable of proportional spacing; in such cases, right justification can be achieved only by inserting unsightly gaps of two or more spaces between words. For readability, most graphic artists advise computer users to leave the right margin ragged.

rotated type   In a graphics or desktop publishing program, text that has been rotated from its normal, horizontal position on the page. The best graphics programs, such as CorelDRAW!, enable the user to edit the text even after it has been rotated.

rule   A horizontal or vertical line used to separate text and images; often used to separate a newsletter nameplate from the body text area.

sans serif   A typeface that lacks serifs, the fine cross strokes across the ends of the main strokes of a character.

Sans serif typefaces, such as Helvetica, are preferred for display type but are harder to read than serif typefaces, such as Times Roman, when used for body type. See *body type, display type, serif,* and *typeface.*

scalable font   See *outline font.*

scalloped columns   An informal design grid in which columns are allowed to end before they reach the bottom of the page.

screen   A shade of gray added to a box. Screens darker than 10% interfere with readability of black text; and screens lighter than about 60% may interfere with the readability of reversed (white) text.

screen font   A bit-mapped font designed to mimic the appearance of printer fonts when displayed on medium-resolution monitors.

script   A typeface that resembles handwriting.

separations   A negative used in four-color printing. Each layer contains one of the colors used to produce the four-color image.

serif   The fine cross strokes across the ends of the main strokes of a character.

Serif fonts, such as Times Roman, are easier to read for body type, but most designers prefer to use sans serif typefaces for display type. (The body text in this book is serif text.) See *sans serif.*

service bureau   A business that provides phototypesetting of desktop published files.

shadow box   A box with a shadow that creates the illusion that the box is floating above the page.

sidebar   A short section of text accompanying a main article, usually set in a separate box.

sink   White space at the top of the pages of a document that remains the same on each page.

slide show   A predetermined list of on-screen presentation charts and graphs displayed one after the other.

Some programs can produce interesting effects, such as fading out one screen before displaying another and enabling the user to choose a path through the charts available for display. See *presentation graphics.*

soft font   See *downloadable font*.

spot color   Color applied selectively to rules, boxes, headline text, and so on.

spread   Two facing pages.

standing head   A headline that introduces a regular feature, such as a department, in a newspaper, newsletter, or magazine.

stroke   The thickness of the letters of a font. Typeface stroke variations may include boldface, narrow, and heavy.

subscript   A number or letter printed slightly below the typing line. See *superscript*.

superscript   A number or letter printed slightly above the typing line. See *subscript*.

template   A file containing the basic formatting commands for a certain type of document. A newsletter template, for example, may contain the nameplate, column formatting codes, headers and footers, and standard rule lines.

text file   A file consisting of nothing but standard ASCII characters (with no control characters or higher order characters).

thumbnail A small, hand-drawn or computer-generated sketch of one or more document pages. Some programs can print up to 16 thumbnails on an 8 1/2-by-11-inch page.

TIFF (Tagged Image File Format)   The file format used to store scanned images.

Times Roman   A serif typeface frequently used for body type applications and occasionally for display type. See *serif*.

tombstone headlines   Two headlines that accidentally align horizontally in adjacent columns, creating unwelcome ambiguity for the reader.

trim size   The final size of a document page after the pages have been physically trimmed to equal size by the printer.

typeface   The distinctive design of a set of type—distinguished from its weight and size.

Typefaces are grouped into two categories, serif and sans serif. Serif typefaces frequently are chosen for body type because they are more legible. Sans serif typefaces are preferred for display type. See *sans serif* and *serif*.

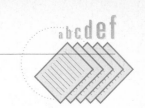

type size The size of a font, measured in points (approximately 1/72 inch) from the top of the tallest ascender to the bottom of the lowest descender. See *pitch*.

type style The weight (such as Roman or boldface) or posture (such as italic) of a font[md]distinguished from a font's typeface design and type size. See *attribute*.

vertical justification Aligning the bottoms of adjacent columns by selectively adding or subtracting small amounts of leading to text or adding extra space between paragraphs, between text and headings, between photos and text, and so on.

weight The overall lightness or darkness of a typeface design or the gradations of lightness to darkness within a font family.

A type style can be light or dark. Within a type style, the user can see several gradations of weight (extra light, light, semilight, regular, medium, semibold, bold, extrabold, and ultrabold). See *typeface*.

widow A layout flaw in which the last line of a paragraph appears alone at the top of a new column or page.

Most word processing and page layout programs suppress widows and orphans; better programs enable the user to switch widow/orphan control on and off and to choose the number of lines. See *orphan*.

word wrap A feature of word processing programs (and other programs that include text-editing features) that wraps words down to the beginning of the next line when they would extend beyond the right margin.

WYSIWYG (What-You-See-Is-What-You-Get) A design philosophy in which formatting commands directly affect the text displayed on-screen so that the screen shows the appearance of the printed text.

Index